A TREASURY OF SUPERSTITIONS

Claudia DeLys

GRAMERCY BOOKS
New York

To My Friends

Copyright © MCMXLVIII by Philosophical Library Inc.
All rights reserved under International and Pan-American
Copyright Conventions.

This 1997 edition is published by Gramercy Books,
a division of Random House Value Publishing, Inc.,
201 East 50th Street, New York, NY 10022
by arrangement with the Philosophical Library, Inc.

(originally published as *A Treasury of American Superstitions*)

Gramercy Books and colophon are trademarks of
Random House Value Publishing, Inc.

Random House
New York • Toronto • London • Sydney • Auckland
http: / / www.randomhouse.com/

Printed and bound in the United States of America

Library of Congress Catalog card number: 73-87440

ISBN: 0-517-18130-4

Library of Congress Cataloging-in-Publication Data

Lys, Claudia de.
    A treasury of American superstitions / by Claudia de Lys.
        p.   cm.
    Originally published : New York : Philosophical Library, 1948.
    Includes bibliographical references and index.
    ISBN 0-517-18130-4
    1. Superstition—United States.   2. Folklore—United States.
I. Title.
BF1775.L9   1996
398'.41'0973—dc21   96-47411
                                                                CIP

10 9 8 7 6 5 4 3 2 1

DEAR READER:

In *A Treasury of American Superstitions*, you will find an abbreviated survey of current beliefs and practices, which are traceable, for the most part, to primitive, and other symbolic origins and expressions. My sole aim is to clarify the approach to seemingly mystifying questions and clear the mind of any possible fear or prejudice. However, I do not claim to have the *last word* in any of the subjects presented. I stand ready to accept any future knowledge which may be unveiled, as the years go by, for further use and interpretation.

A Treasury of American Superstitions is an adventure in the form of a short journey into folklore, or symbolic lore, through the simplest route; that is, via the familiar by-paths and lanes of sayings, customs, beliefs and superstitions, in everyday use. Because of the vast territory to be covered, which covers a multitude of ideas and ideals, over a span of thousands of years, only a bird's-eye view may be indulged in at this time, so to speak. This mental flight into the past, with which to bridge the present will serve, I hope, to give the "lift" for which it is intended. The itinerary was planned for us to meet on the avenue where there is neither sect, class or race and the passport to frontiers we may have to cross is an open mind, so let us embark on the cosmic chariot of thought transmuted into the printed word, shall we? If it gives your exploring spirit half as much joy and understanding in reading it, as I have achieved already in being your anthropological guide, we will both have achieved our goal, that of sharing a cultural excursion on the road which leads to mutual knowledge and happiness.

CLAUDIA DE LYS

New York City

ACKNOWLEDGMENTS

THROUGHOUT *A Treasury of American Superstitions*, authorities in various fields and many nationalities, have been drawn upon extensively. It would be a physical impossibility to give due credit to each one individually. Therefore, my appreciation and gratitude are herewith expressed to all those whose knowledge and "brain-children" appear here and there, in this book.

However, I would like to mention a few, such as Waldemar Kaempffert, John J. O'Neill, Gobind Behari Lal, D. A. Laird, David Dietz, and many other Science editors, and Dr. Hamilton Montgomery of the Mayo Clinic. Dr. Alfred Edward Wiggam, E. V. Durling, Uncle Ray (Ramon Coffman), Lawrence Gould, and many other writers whose syndicated columns appear all over America and elsewhere; Robert R. Coles (astronomy); Bernard Chiego, Sc.D. (bio-chemistry); William J. Plews (Electrical engineer and inventor); Alan Devoe (widely known writer—Down to Earth, The American Mercury); Lucy Shepherd-Kilbourn (Metaramist—Color consultant); Freling Foster (Keep Up With the World, Collier's); A. Cressy Morrison, (Former president of the New York Academy of Sciences); Henry S. Evans, Orientalist (Science Illustrated); Eleanore J. Kendrick, loyal friend and adviser, and Dr. Dagobert D. Runes, editor of the Philosophical Library publications, whose valuable suggestions have made *A Treasury of American Superstitions* possible.

CLAUDIA DE LYS

Contents

CHAPTER III

CURSED AMONG WOMEN

CHAPTER IV

DENIZENS OF THE DEEP

Contents

CHAPTER V

THE ANIMAL KINGDOM

CHAPTER VI

THE HUMAN ANIMAL

CHAPTER VII

THY NAME IS WOMAN

Contents

CHAPTER VIII

THE CONSTANT FLAME

CHAPTER IX

WITH THIS RING

CHAPTER X

EVERYBODY LOVES A BABY

CHAPTER XI

GIVE US THIS DAY

Contents

CHAPTER XII

FASHION BY FOLKLORE

CHAPTER XIII

EYE OF THE GODS

CHAPTER XIV

PERCHANCE TO DREAM

Contents

CHAPTER XV

THAT FLESH IS HEIR TO

Contents

CHAPTER XVI

SOUNDS IN THE NIGHT

CHAPTER XVII

HOLIDAYS AND HOLY DAYS

CHAPTER XVIII

OF WORK AND PLAY

CHAPTER XIX

WATER, WATER, EVERYWHERE

CHAPTER XX

APOLLO'S CHARIOT

CHAPTER XXI

MOONBEAMS SHINING

Contents

CHAPTER XXII

TWINKLE, TWINKLE, LITTLE STAR

CHAPTER XXIII

THE WORSHIP OF THINGS

CHAPTER XXIV

TELL ME NOT IN MOURNFUL NUMBERS

The more you know the more luck you will have.

—CONFUCIUS

CHAPTER I

Our Feathered Friends

"A Little Bird Told Me"

THE EXPRESSION, "A little bird told me," is only one among hundreds of superstitious ideas in which human beings and birds are related to each other. One of these, that birds have a speech of their own and can bring information to persons, is very ancient. Even today, when we learn a secret that we do not intend to tell anyone, we reply, "A little bird told me," to the question, "Who told you?"

In the Bible, in the 20th verse of the 10th chapter of the Ecclesiastes, Solomon, the wise king of Israel, says: "Curse not the king, no, not in thy thoughts; and curse not the rich in thy bedchamber; a little bird of the air shall carry the voice, and that which hath wings shall tell the matter." In many legends about this all-knowing monarch of ancient times, we find the words: "All the birds had been summoned before Solomon."

"A little bird told me," or an equivalent expression, also appears in the Koran, the bible of the Mohammedans. Shakespeare used this same phrase in "Henry IV." In Wagner's "Twilight of the Gods" the forest bird warns Siegfried that Mine is plotting against his life, and tells him where he will find his beautiful bride, Brunhilde.

In folklore, birds not only symbolized the soul, sun, wind, storms, fecundity, growth and immortality, but were also the "fates." In many legends and myths, birds are chosen to be the guiding spirits of heroes, especially when they set out on a dangerous mission.

The flight and behavior of birds was a great mystery to very early peoples and the ancients. Aristotle was one of the first to study and to teach about bird migration. However, together with some facts, he included many superstitious ideas, which, coming from such an authority, persisted for years. One of his false conclusions was that certain birds hibernated during the cold seasons, as he had no other way of explaining their appearance and disappearance, year in and year out.

He did not have the facilities, in his day, to discover that birds travel back and forth, although to this day we do not know what it is that gives them the signal to migrate, or to return.

It was also believed in Aristotle's time that certain birds were capable of transmutation—changing themselves from one species into another, or even into other types of animals.

Birds are the best ventriloquists in the world. They sing from the lower end of their windpipe and can appear to be far or near, while singing within ten feet of a listener. Perhaps man learned this trick of the vocal chords from the winged creatures, and so developed ventriloquism. In ancient times, the few who mastered this difficult art seemed very mysterious. The ventriloquists of that day made the most of their gift to mystify others, pretending to report supernatural information, or divine messages to those whom they wished to control or impress. This led to the belief that wise men could understand and speak the languages of birds.

Ventriloquism was also the means by which oracles of old imparted so-called supernatural knowledge, as though it came out of the belly of the gods or goddesses upon whom they called for advice or the like, or out of the bowels of the earth, when the voice but not the body was revealed!

Bird Tapping at Window and Other "Bird" Superstitions

"Every bird that upward swings
Bears the Cross upon its wings."
(Attributed to John M. Neale, 1818–1866)

To THE superstitious-minded, if a bird flies into the house, or taps at a window, it is a bad omen; auguring death within the year to someone living in the house.

Since the bird was once believed to be the "spirit of spirit," it was assumed that when it taps on the window, or flies into the home, it is this bird-soul inviting another soul to join him; meaning death.

This dread of having a bird in the house is so strong, that even in modern times many persons will not have wall-paper with bird designs because they feel that good luck will fly away on the wings of even paper birds. Many interior decorators will testify to this.

Doubtless the belief that the sky was the abode of spirits was suggested by the birds themselves as they soared upward and faded into the distant heavens. Since they disappeared and reappeared after their flight into the upper regions, it must be that they had visited the celestial abode.

In direct line with this belief, birds were reputed to be the messengers of departed souls or spirits. The notion was then added that these spirits, always benevolent ones, wished those whom they had cared for in their lifetime to be brought to them by the birds.

Throughout the history of symbolism, the bird has represented the spirit of air, or the spirit of life. Among the Egyptians, the bird symbolized the soul of man. Their supreme deity was depicted as a circle or globe with the extended wings of a bird on either side. The bird was used in the same way by Babylonians and Assyrians. A bird in flight expressed a flying cross, or man's own symbol. In Christian art, the bird in flight was the symbol of the spirit—the dove or Holy Ghost of biblical days.

For ages and ages, a bird has expressed more in art than words ever could. For instance, a bird perched upon a pedestal or pillar signified life; the two in combination representing the union of matter and spirit.

The importance of birds in ancient times is well illustrated by the fact that the Romans did not trust human judgment as much as they believed in the wisdom of the birds. The official soothsayers of that time were empowered with sacerdotal orders, and their chief function was to interpret human affairs by means of signs and portents, including what the birds might foretell. These augurs, sedate old men, clothed in special robes and carrying long staffs, were supposed to spend long years studying the language and lore of birds, so as to be able to answer all questions asked by man.

In order to interpret favorably or unfavorably the messages brought by the feathered creatures of the sky, the augurs charted the horizon and marked it into sections, somewhat like the charts of gunners in modern warfare. A ceremony then followed in which the augur proceeded to the nearest elevation of ground, where he sacrificed a living creature, uttered a few prayers, and with his staff poised, awaited the appearance in the sky of the first bird. If the bird flew into a certain square, at a certain time, and behaved in a certain way, it was a good omen—provided another bird came along shortly afterwards and did the same things. If the second bird did not show up, the sign was unfavorable. Of course, there were many variations of this.

The observations made from the rectangular spaces charted in the sky were given meanings in words by the augurs, whose authority and wisdom were accepted without question.

A practice similar to this, that is, divination by means of birds, was followed in ancient Greece and was known as ornithomancy.

Many birds, such as the raven, swallow and the magpie, still play an important role in the superstitious minds of many, who, like the ancients, believe these feathered beings of the air have mysterious powers that enable them to foretell the future.

One striking example, among many, is the small green parrot, companion wage-earner of the hurdy-gurdy man in the streets of the most highly civilized cities in the world today, who, for a coin—usually ten cents—will select with its beak a small ticket-like card upon which the individual's *fortune* is told!

"Robin" Superstitions

> *If the Robin sings in the bush*
> *The weather will be coarse,*
> *If the Robin sings on the barn*
> *The weather will be warm.*
>   Traditional Saying

THE THRUSH, generally known in North America as the robin, is considered on the whole as a harbinger of good fortune. He is a bringer of good luck so long as he is not injured or driven away. To find a robin's nest with eggs in it is particularly fortunate, but great care must be taken not to disturb the nest. Dire consequences will fall on those who dare take a robin's egg.

Most of the superstitions attached to the true robin or redbreast of England and Europe have been imported into America and applied to the thrush-robin, which has orange and brown feathers instead of the red-breast of the Old World robin. The female thrush-robin is quite dull, often gray.

There is a familiar saying that when robins show signs of friendliness, a hard winter is ahead. If the first robin you see in the spring flies up, you will have good luck; but if it flies down, you have bad luck. Good luck follows if a robin builds its nest near your house. If you see a robin in the morning, someone will visit you that day. Make a wish if you see a robin and it will come true. It is unlucky to keep a robin that accidentally flies into the house.

The folklore about the robin's redbreast is given in a legend which relates that it was produced by the blood of Jesus. When he was on his way to Calvary, a robin plucked a thorn from his temple. A drop of blood, falling on its breast, turned its bosom red. Another legend is that the robin used to carry dew to refresh sinners parched in hell, and the scorching heat turned its feathers red:

> "He brings cool dew on his little bill,
>   And lets it fall on the souls of sin;
> You can see the mark on his redbreast still,
>   Of fires that scorch as he drops it in."
> > *The Robin*, John Greenleaf Whittier

Maybe the reason we are so fond of robins is that they are such companionable birds. They like lawns, even lawns with people and "Keep Off the Grass" signs. They seem to enjoy human company, or at least don't resent it. They will nest under the very porch eaves in an apple tree just outside the kitchen window. They sing at the top of their voices shortly after midnight.

"Swallow" Superstitions

> *"If a swallow doth build upon your thatch*
> *Then the hand of good is upon the latch!*
> *Plenty he will bring to house and field,*
> *Of the fruits of the garden an uncommon yield."*

Twittering, circling swallows with their mass arrival in spring and mass departure in the fall have aroused the interest and admiration of all peoples, at all times, and they have inspired the poets and nature-lovers of every land.

It was a common belief with the ancient Greeks that swallows did not fly away at all, but buried themselves in the mud at the bottom of ponds; hibernating there with the frogs and turtles. There have even been accounts by fishermen, who, during the winter, claimed to have brought up their nets filled with swallows as well as fish, as evidence that swallows had been hiberating in the mud. This theory was endorsed by naturalists for a long time, but of course it is not true.

The reason for this superstitious attitude is, no doubt, the fact that swallows are generally so quiet in their migration that it remained a mysterious phenomenon for a long time. Even with modern knowledge, there is still a great deal to be learned about the swallows' long seasonal flights.

Just as they do today, barn swallows of ancient times built their nests of mud, which led to the assumption that they hibernated in the mud. Superstitions relating to the place where a swallow builds its nest are many. If a swallow leaves its nest on a house, it is a sign that the house will soon burn down. If one has a nest under the eaves of a house, it means good luck for the whole family.

In folklore, nearly all birds have some special quality attributed to them to make them weather prophets. Sometimes there is a grain of prophecy in a bird's behavior, but not always. For example, when swallows go skimming along close to the ground to feed on insects which are flying low, it may or may not be a sign of rain. Atmospheric changes are rapid sometimes, and while both birds and insects fly low before the rain, rain does not follow inevitably when they do so. However, regardless of weather, swallows generally fly high for bugs over the woods, and sail low for mosquitoes and water bugs above the ponds.

Both good and evil superstitious beliefs have been woven around the homing instinct of swallows, which to this day has not been accurately explained by scientists. One of the most outstanding modern phenomena regarding their migration and return has been happening with the swallows of the Mission San Juan Capistrano, near San Diego, California. Here, as everywhere, we suppose, the birds fly by the oldest clock in the world, the sun, and they are guided with "Nature's compass," or what we choose to call, for lack of a better word, "instinct," of which man's nearest scientific equivalent is radar.

The so-called miracle of the famous swallows of San Juan Capistrano is that regardless of the weather, every year since the mission was built more than one hundred fifty years ago, swallows have appeared each spring on St. Joseph's Day, March 19. They take up their abode in the nests under the eaves of the old structure. They remain until fall, when they fly away on San Juan's Day, October 23. The arrival and departure of these swallows on two sacred days has been hailed and observed for years as an occasion for celebration with devotional and attendant festivities.

In the fall of 1940, however, the mission fathers strolled out through the mission grounds one morning only to find the swallows gone. They had flown away to their unknown winter quarters two months ahead of schedule, and thus broke the sacred tradition!

Superstitions connected with swallows are very ancient. The Egyptians thought that human beings might be reincarnated in the falcon, heron and swallow. Isis is said to have lamented that the death of Osiris took the form of a swallow.

Ancient classical, medieval and even modern tradition holds to the superstition that if young swallows are blinded, their eyes can grow again. Pliny tells us that the herb celandine is used by swallows for the purpose, and also that the swallow brought a stone home from the seashore which gave sight to its fledgling.

> "Seeking with eager eyes that wondrous stone
> which the swallow
> Brings from the shore of the sea,
> to restore the
> Sight of its fledgling."
> —Longfellow. *Evangeline*

In folklore swallows are considered lucky birds of passage. To kill a swallow is unlucky. If young swallows are found kissing each other, and are taken and dissolved in oil of roses and applied according to formula, they will win you the affections of the best girl in the parish. If a swallow forsakes its nest, it is a bad omen. When swallows are flying across the sea, they are said to carry bits of sticks with them which they place on the water from time to time to rest on. The first time you hear them in the spring, if you go to a stream or fountain and wash your eyes, at the same time making a silent prayer, the swallow will carry away all your eye troubles.

> "When the swallow's nest is high, summer is dry;
> When the swallow's nest is low, you can safely
> reap and sow."

The modern approach to the ancient superstition that swallows bring good luck, is in the form of brooches made to represent two or three swallows in flight. The birds generally have blue-tipped wings to symbolize the sky. These pins are very popular and are sold everywhere. Swallows are used in designing nearly every type of ornamental fabric or object, except wall-paper, because all birds are taboo, as so many think it means luck will fly out of the window.

"Chimney Swift" Superstitions

As FAR AS its migration and winter quarters were concerned, the chimney swift mystified people everywhere for ages. The sudden and complete disappearance of these birds was so puzzling to the ancient Greeks that they imagined that the birds dived into ponds and hibernated in the mud at the bottom. Many persons still believe this even in the United States.

However, the mystery of their migration has been checked off the unsolved list. In 1944 it was reported that chimney swifts wearing bands that had been put on their legs in the United States, had finally been discovered in Peru.

An old superstition persists that scares householders into thinking that whenever a chimney swift is nesting in the chimney, it brings bedbugs to the house. These birds have been blamed for the unexpected appearance of bedbugs where there had been none before. To prove how fallacious this is, in the first place, chimney swifts nest and sleep only in unused chimneys as the smoke and heat passing up a used chimney drives them out and suffocates their fledglings. In the second place, these harmless birds never carry bedbugs.

There is a legend about the swifts of San Juan Capistrano, California, just as there is about the swallows. Swifts, like most birds, are believed to have an uncanny ability of timing their departure as well as their return to a given spot. It is reported that on October 23, when the swallows leave San Juan Capistrano, thousands of swifts swoop down from the sky and immediately take possession of the empty nests.

How they know the date is a mystery. The swifts remain in the swallows' home all winter, and on the morning of March 19, when their original owners return, there is quite a battle royal between the swallows and the swifts for possession of the nests. The swallows are always victorious, and the swifts depart to return again on October 23.

Swifts keep flying all day long, rarely, if ever, taking a rest from dawn to dusk; and they fly with their mouths open. They are rightly named, as a speed far exceeding one hundred miles an hour has been recorded.

Many persons believe that if they are able to see a swift on the wing it is not only lucky; but if they can make a wish before it is out of sight, the wish will soon come true.

"Canary" Superstitions

BECAUSE CANARIES are known for their conjugal faithfulness, there is a superstition that prevails everywhere that their presence in a home brings joy and harmony to the occupants. This is one reason for the universal popularity of the birds.

There are many other superstitious beliefs about the canary. If a strange cat kills your canary, you will not have good luck for two years. If your canary sings after dark, it is a sign that it will not live much longer. To see a dead canary is a sign that you will shed blood that day. When young canaries are desired, a sage leaf should be placed with the eggs so that they will hatch safely. If a strange canary bird flies into your home, and flutters before the window pane, it is a sign of death in the family; even if all are apparently well at the time.

Although the domesticated canary is found all over the world today, its ancestors were wild canaries found only in the Canary and Madeira Islands in the South Atlantic, and in the Midway Islands in the Pacific. However, it is erroneous to think that wild canaries sing the way a good breed of domesticated birds do. Wild canaries can still be found in their natural habitat.

Raising canaries goes back at least to the 16th Century in Italy, where the birds had to be taught to sing. Although they are apt pupils, they are not all fine singers. Only the males are the really good singers, although the females can sing also.

There are those who are inclined to disbelieve the exploited characteristic of the male's fidelity toward its mate. This has come about because, under artificial conditions imposed by man for commercial purposes, forced bigamy not only made the male canary polygamous, but it disrupted the harmony between otherwise docile and loving couples. This frequently endangered the lives of the young canaries, through bird-like jealousy and frustration. One male and two females in the same cage is especially destructive of domestic bliss, but two males and one female, because of the love rivalry, spurs the vocal efforts of the contesting males. Less harm results from this arrangement and it also makes for better singing.

Whenever a canary remains silent for too long a period, the superstition is that there is evil in the air which prevents the bird from singing in its accustomed happy fashion. Therefore, this is supposed to prognosticate trouble of some kind. Canaries are moody, perhaps; but they are also extremely sensitive to foul air and unpleasant odors, which might cause them to be silent at times.

Because of their unusual sensitivity to odors, particularly noxious gases and opium, which cause them to become ill or even die, it was formerly interpreted to mean a similar catastrophe in the house where these birds lived. This was before we had knowledge of why they behaved that way. However, the Chinese who lived in the Western world discovered long ago that if they kept canaries in their opium dens, and the canaries became ill, it was a sign that the fumes were seeping out into the street and they might be discovered by the authorities. And so they always kept canaries to guide them.

During the war canaries played an important part in warning of gas attacks, and they are still used as poisonous gas detectors in deep mines threatened with unexpected gas seepage.

Although canaries and parrots are well-known examples of birds whose feathers change color with changes in diet, there is no known food to make canary feathers turn blue, as many people believe. The bluish cast of some canaries, which is really a shade of grey, is obtained by careful selective breeding.

There is an old superstition, and a happy one, that when canaries and gold fish are found in a house, harmony is there to stay. It is said that in America, dogs as pets come first, canaries second, and cats, third.

"Starling" Superstitions

ALTHOUGH ENEMIES, of necessity, in their natural habitat, starling and sparrow settle their differences and become fast friends in civilization, living side by side in the country and city, where they refuse to be dislodged, no matter how much superstitious persons resent their presence in the neighborhood.

Women, especially, dread the presence of starlings which carry off the combings of their hair and use them in fashioning their nests. By so doing, according to superstition, the mind of the one to whom the hair belonged is endangered, as her hair is now enmeshed in the bird's evil doings. Or else, the belief is, this theft may cause a cataract in her eyes.

On the whole, in folklore of olden days, starlings were generally lucky birds of passage. But nowadays, they are no longer birds of passage, but gather in groups of thousands at a time, and make their nests where they please and stay as long as they please. Another reason that superstitious persons fear their presence is that if these birds settle in a particular house or building it is taken as a prophecy of death for one of the occupants.

The Romans, who inherited the practice of bird divination from the Etruscans, foretold future events as being lucky, if a bird appeared on the right; and as unlucky if it appeared on the left of a given section of the heavens. And for certain things, the left was sometimes deemed a propitious side. Starlings were their favorite "birds of passage,"—literally, because of their passage through a loosely designated region of the sky. Starlings were the preferred creatures because flocks of them could be seen in the skies daily, which was of great assistance to the Augur, or diviner, in settling the questions of the day.

Starlings are birds of the Old World, as there were no true starlings in the New World until they were brought to America by white men. As a matter of fact, starlings are said to have been introduced into New York in 1894 by the scion of an old Dutch family who brought them from England, and freed them in the Hudson Valley near his home. Some believe that starlings may have been brought here a few years earlier.

One of the reasons the birds were brought to America was to fight insect pests. However, these quarrelsome birds, which annoy martins, bluebirds and other well-liked birds, have become disliked by the general American public. Starlings drive off the desirable birds, and that is another reason why they are regarded as birds of doom.

The starling is now primarily a city-dwelling pest and is a most unpopular bird for good reason. It is strong, stubborn and tough. Although somewhat smaller than the robin, when starlings take possession of a public building, it is almost impossible to get rid of them. Their refusal to move has suggested that starlings may have inspired the original sit-down strike.

These unwelcome city residents, or "gangsters with wings," as they are sometimes called, in addition to all their other evil attributes, eat ten times as much as similar species of native birds.

"Sparrow" Superstitions

> *"If a sparrow doth perch beneath your thrall (eaves)*
> *Then presage of woe, woe to all:*
> *Trouble he will bring to field and store*
> *Death and destruction will enter your door."*

BECAUSE SUPERSTITIONS about sparrows have travelled around the world, similar beliefs are found among peoples of different races and nationalities. The English sparrow, the most common name for this species of bird although it has a variety of others, was first brought to American shores in 1851 and 1852, and superstitions, popular abroad and elsewhere, came with it. These beliefs are still held by a large number of persons.

To catch a sparrow and keep it confined in a cage will bring death into the house where it is kept, striking either the father or mother. It is lucky, however, to see a white sparrow. If the hedge-sparrow is heard before the grapevine buds, it is a sign that a good crop is in store. When a sparrow builds its nest above your window, it is a sign that you will take a trip.

The Koreans have a delightful legend to explain why sparrows hop on both feet instead of putting one foot before the other. The same legend tells why flies rub their feet together when they alight. The sparrow had a quarrel with some flies and they decided to ask the governor of the Korean provinces to arbitrate the matter. He found them both guilty, and ordered them to be whipped. It made the sparrow jump up and down with pain, but the flies put their hands together and prayed to be forgiven. He forgave both, but as a sign of their misbehavior, he decreed that sparrows should always hop and that flies should rub their feet together when they alighted.

In the Tyrol, eating a sparrow is believed to cause St. Vitus Dance. To the Hindus, the sparrow is the symbol of passion. Hence, Kam, their god of Love, is represented as riding a sparrow; his bow of sugar cane strung with bees.

English sparrows are supposed to have more lives than the proverbial cat, because they survive as lustily in city grime as in clean suburbs and sylvan fields. They are immune to broiling heat and boreal cold, and are content with whatever food they can forage.

Sparrows multiply with incredible rapidity, having at least two broods a season, with three, and sometimes four or five fledglings. Despite every effort to get rid of sparrows which are very destructive and of a combative nature, many suburban localities have lost most of their song birds instead. For this reason superstitious beliefs and prejudices connected with the sparrow are likely to survive for some time to come.

"Pigeon" and "Dove" Superstitions

SUPERSTITIONS ABOUT doves and pigeons are quite similar because the birds belong to the same species. The word *pigeon* is a somewhat broader term, whereas *dove* designates more specifically the smaller members of the family such as the turtle-dove and mourning-dove.

Pigeons and doves have been featured in many historic incidents. Fables have been woven around them and they appear in pagan bird-lore as messengers, and as various symbols. Naturally, birds that have aroused such interest at all times wherever they were found occasioned many superstitions.

The cooing of a strange dove at the window is a sign of sad news. If turtle-doves live near a house, they are believed to banish rheumatism, which accounts for the presence of dove-cotes in many vicinities. When doves make more noise than usual, and pass in and out of their cotes a great deal, it is a sure sign of a change in the weather. It is unlucky to eat the eggs of a dove. For a dove to coo in the doorway foretells a death. A dead dove, placed on the chest of a person suffering from pneumonia, is supposed to insure prompt recovery. There are many more such superstitions.

The pigeon is supposed to be greedy, so pigeon-toed persons are branded as stingy. Feeding strange pigeons will bring new true friends. It is good luck to have a stray pigeon come to your door. Pigeons flying in a circle over a body of water indicate rain. If pigeons make their home on the roof of a house, it is a harbinger of good fortune and foretells a change for the better in the life of the occupants. It is believed that the wife in a home will die if the pigeon's house is pulled down. A dead pigeon, as it grows cold, placed on a sick child's chest will draw out the disease.

At first the dove was looked upon as a bird of good omen. In Babylonian mythology it was assigned to Ishtar or Ashtoreth, the earth goddess, because it was amorous and prolific, and therefore represented connubial bliss and productiveness. White doves were sold in Ishtar's temple to be offered to her in sacrifice in return for favors. Today, however, white birds terrify some persons who believe they are omens of trouble and even death, and a white dove is no exception. White has been the symbol of purity and peace as well as of death, which has made for many paradoxical superstitions.

In early Christian belief, the dove symbolized the Holy Ghost. It came as a messenger from on high, and the seven rays proceeding from it were the seven gifts it bore. It was the symbol of the soul and as such was often represented as coming out of the mouth of saints at death. The soul was supposed to fly to Heaven in the form of a dove, and this symbolism is commonly used today on monuments in cemeteries. The association of the white dove with the soul and death led to the morbid superstitions of the later period.

The dove was sacred to Venus; this dedication probably copied from an older superstition which symbolized the turtle-dove as representing conjugal fidelity and harmlessness. In the Biblical story of the Deluge, peace and a fresh new world to live in were suggested by the return of the dove, bearing an olive branch in its beak, to the Ark. This symbolism is still popularly used in art and peace is associated in the minds and hearts of millions with the image of the dove.

The truth is, however, that during the mating season, these seemingly gentle birds fight fierce and bloody battles with rival males; and as a matter of fact, they are anything but peace-loving creatures in general. They have, on the other hand, a very admirable virtue, since it is said that a dove mates only once, and if either the male or female dies, the remaining widow or widower never remates.

Birds of the pigeon species were unknown in Europe until they were brought there from the Near East and later from India, where they were looked upon as messengers of death. The pigeon came to Europe with rather a bad reputation, but this did not apply to the dove.

Because of their homing instinct, which was little understood in past days, pigeons for centuries have been the symbols of flight, and were messengers carrying the written word. History does not tell us when these remarkable birds were first used as mail-carriers, but it is certain that in the time of King Solomon they took part in races. Cyrus, King of the Medes and the Persians, used them five centuries before the Christian era to send messages to various parts of his empire. Before the advent of radio, pigeons were used exclusively to send news or other information to and from ships at sea during wartime. Homing pigeons handled the first authorized air-mail service.

In recent years various experiments have been made with homing or carrier pigeons to learn more about the so-called instinct by which they arrive at a given place and then return home. The opinion seems to be that these birds do not have a "sixth sense" or a special instinct with which to find their way back after they have been released on an errand. Tests were made with thousands of birds, and the conclusion seems to be that only those that had been carefully trained in specific areas returned to the starting point.

In other words, carrier pigeons that were sent out without training or with very little, with few exceptions, never returned. Those that had been trained in a group over the selected course did very well, most of them making the round trip within a reasonable time. The conclusions arrived at were that homing pigeons, through training, familiarize themselves with landmarks and use other means of identifying the terrain, and this is what they depend on in their flights. Whether a homing pigeon flies by instinct or not, this bird, nevertheless, performs a remarkable feat to achieve the results it does.

"Grouse" Superstitions

THERE ARE SEVERAL versions of the story of how the male ruffled grouse, popularly known in the United States as "pheasant" in the Central States and "partridge" in New England, makes the characteristic sound known as "drumming." One superstitious notion is that it is produced by the bird striking its wings together behind its back. Another idea is that the sound comes from beating its wings against a log, while a third theory is that the ruffled grouse beats its own sides with its wings.

The reason for the difficulty in ascertaining the truth is that this "drumming" sound is made only during the mating season, by the cock which is very shy and is rarely seen at close range, and for only a very short time. However, in the spring, the cock struts to impress the females; its drumming no doubt equivalent to a "courtship song" in fowl language.

By means of a cleverly contrived hide-away up a tree, motion pictures of the ruffled grouse have been made in the very act of "drumming," and so the mystery has been cleared. The cock grouse beats the air with its wings without touching its body or a log. The sound is produced by the vibration of the feathers close to the body, and it is quite an exhibitionistic performance for an otherwise shy bird.

For this achievement, the cock perches itself on a log, grips the log firmly with its feet, and begins to beat its wings, at first slowly, then increasing the tempo until the thumping, booming or "drumming" sound is produced.

The snipe, the woodcock, and the nighthawk produce sound in the same way. There are other members of the same family of game birds, such as the prairie chicken, that make a booming "courtship song" by deflating the air sacs in the neck.

Among several superstitions about the ruffled grouse is one that the gathering of grouse into large flocks indicates snow; and another, that when grouse do their "drumming" in winter and at night, a heavy snowstorm may be expected.

"Cuckoo" Superstitions

AMERICAN SUPERSTITIONS about the cuckoo-bird are for the most part importations from Europe and elsewhere. Although there are six different species of cuckoos in the New World, known as yellow-billed and black-billed birds, they differ in at least one respect from cuckoos in England, the European continent and Australia, in that the American species build their own nests and rear their own young. The American bird that is similar in parasitic habits to the foreign cuckoo is the cowbird, or black bird of the grackle family. Because of the Old World cuckoo's bad habits, many superstitions prevail pertaining to false love and affection. The term "cuckoo" applied to a person is an insult.

The cuckoo, like several other birds, has always been looked upon everywhere as a mysterious bird, and reputed to have a double sight, by which superstitious persons think they can look into the future. The interpretation is by means of the cuckoo's cries, the sound of which, incidentally, gave the name to the bird. For example, superstitious farmers have a sort of unwritten cuckoo code, by which, when they hear the bird's call on the first of May, they can prophesy what the season will be and other events in their lives. If the call comes from the north, it is an ominous sign and foretells tragedy. If they hear the bird from the south, it is a sign of a good harvest. From the west, it signifies good luck in general. And if the call is heard from the east, it means luck in love. If the bird is heard while one is standing on hard ground, bad luck; standing on soft ground, good luck; sitting on the ground, bad luck.

The old superstition of "wish and turn your money," or jingle your coins, when wishing on the moon, applies also when a person hears the cuckoo call the first time in spring. It means the wish will come true. If a superstitious young lady hears the cuckoo's notes in May, she kisses her hand to it and says:

> "Cuckoo, cuckoo,
>   Tell me true,
>   When shall I be married?"

By counting the number of times the bird cries "Cuckoo," she can tell the number of years that will elapse until her wedding day. She must count each cry as one year!

Another old superstition is that whatever you happen to be doing when you first hear the cuckoo in any season, you will be doing for the most part for the rest of the year. In the southern states of this country, where superstitions about the cuckoo are very popular, the plaintive "koo koo" is called "rain-crowing" or "raincrow" by country people and is supposed to predict rain or a storm, especially if the cuckoo is concealed in a wood or thicket when it calls.

An Old World superstitious holdover, observed in the south, is that to see a cuckoo implies the treachery of one woman to another. Still worse, it also means the victim of the treachery will be barren. This notion is probably based on the Old World cuckoo's refusal to build a nest of its own, and its habit of dispossessing other birds from their nests. These cuckoos wantonly devour all the eggs they find in the captured nest, and if the incursion is made late in the season, it is apt to mean no more offspring for that bird family.

"Whippoorwill" Superstitions

THE WHIPPOORWILL has been considered a bird of misfortune and doom, probably because it is nocturnal in habit, since superstitious people usually associate darkness and night with mysterious and ominous events. This bird, named for its call, is found in the eastern part of the United States and Canada. The whippoorwill is allied to the European nightjar, so that superstitions about the American species are a mixture of Old World and American Indian beliefs.

The whippoorwill is seldom seen, but its weird peculiar call is often heard at nightfall and just before dawn, two periods in the day to which the imagination is most susceptible. This may explain why most superstitions relating to this strange bird are connected with love, marriage and death. Country people feel that the whippoorwill can foretell and interpret events, which may, however, reflect an individual's own desires, but which, nevertheless, follow a traditional pattern, as the following superstitions indicate.

Unmarried women believe that if the whippoorwill's first call in the spring is not followed immediately by a second call, it means that they will have to wait another year for a husband. If several calls follow in succession, it indicates no husband at all. There are variations of this superstition. For instance, if a man or woman makes a wish upon hearing the first call of the bird in the spring, and keeps the wish a secret, it is bound to come true.

When the whippoorwill calls near a house, it is generally regarded as an omen of death. To avoid the tragedy, one should find where the whippoorwill is perched, and point a finger at it, as if killing it symbolically, at the same time making a sound with the mouth in imitation of a gun shot. This should be done even if it is very dark and the bird cannot be seen. Those who are superstitious feel that even if the bird calls are heard again, no evil happening can take place for the next twenty-four hours. On the other hand, there are some who believe that when a whippoorwill sings close to the house, it signifies only minor trouble or difficulty in respect to certain matters in which the ones who hear it are most interested.

Some superstitions that were learned from the American Indians include: when whippoorwills sing together at night making the sound "hohin, hohin," one should reply "No!" If the birds stop singing at once, it is a sign that the hearer will die soon; but if the birds continue their singing, it means a long life instead. Whenever two whippoorwills are seen flying side by side—a very rare occasion—it means a disappointment. Children must not destroy the eggs or the fledglings, even though the whippoorwill is a bird of ill portent, lest each egg or fledgling destroyed represent the future loss of a loved one.

Although the whippoorwill is not a happy bird to superstitious country folk, many a man with a continuous backache turns a somersault when a whippoorwill whistles at a certain time, to insure the cure of this ailment which all hard-working farmers dread. Those who do not have a backache perform the same operation as a means of prevention.

The principal reason that the whippoorwill is hard to locate at night is because it perches lengthwise on tree limbs, which is contrary to nearly all species of birds as they perch crosswise. This peculiarity adds another element of mystery to the bird. The whippoorwill is dull in color, and blends with the background, another reason it is hard to detect. These facts, together with its companionship with the nighthawk, another bird of mystery and one that also perches lengthwise, have emphasized the strange powers of the whippoorwill in the minds of superstitious persons.

There are two other birds around which there are almost identical superstitions. They are the poorwill, a bird found in the western part of the United States and Mexico. It is smaller than the eastern species and has a note of only two syllables. There is also the chuck-will's-widow, a bird of the United States that resembles the whippoorwill but is larger. It is so called because of the sound it makes.

"Gull" Superstitions

SUPERSTITIOUS SAILORS are not too fond of seagulls, because they believe that these birds are the spirits of their dead mates. Drowned men's souls are believed to relive in gulls so that those who believe this fantasy are very indignant if anyone tries to shoot the birds. Many sailors think it is lucky for their ship if they see gulls sitting on the water.

Gulls are believed to be weather prophets, and when they fly inland it is a sign of rain. There is some truth in this idea. The appearance of seagulls inland may indicate stormy weather at sea, and as fish disappear during storms, the gulls, deprived of their seafood, fly on shore to seek worms and grubs. It is generally considered a sign of bad luck if a gull perches on someone's home.

It is universally believed by the superstitious that if seagulls are killed, evil will follow; but it is in America that the greatest esteem for the seagulls has been demonstrated. The Sea Gull Monument at Salt Lake City, Utah, commemorates what is known as a Mormon "miracle," when the first crop planted by the pioneers of this sect was saved from a locust plague by swarming Pacific gulls.

These gulls are a variety of the Franklin gull which inhabit the interior of North America and breed in marshes and on islands in lakes and rivers.

If their first crop had failed, the Mormons would have been without provision for winter seed for another sowing. In May, 1848, vast clouds of black flying insects descended upon the fields and began to devour every leaf and blade. The people, overcome with despair and exhaustion, fell on their knees and prayed. Then a curious phenomenon took place. Myriads of gulls flocked everywhere, covering the fields in clouds of blessings on wing. The birds gorged themselves with the insects, and saved a good portion of the crop. This saved the pioneers from complete disaster and starvation.

Because of this so-called miraculous visitation of seagulls, they are protected in Utah by statutes. This is hardly necessary since the public at large holds a traditional respect for them even today.

In 1913 the Sea Gull Monument was unveiled. The column supports a ball upon which two gulls, done in bronze, and covered with gold leaf, are gently alighting. A tablet bears the inscription: "Sea Gull Monument, Erected in Grateful Remembrance of the Mercy of God to the Mormon Pioneers."

Nursery Lore and Facts About the Stork, Bringer of Babies

> *"Constancy is like unto the stork, who wheresoever*
> *she fly cometh into no nest but her own."*
>
> —(Euphues—185)

OLD-FASHIONED MOTHERS tell their children that the stork brought the new baby, carrying it in its beak. To explain further, she says that the bird bites the mother's foot purposely so that she may remain in bed for a while and take care of her infant.

"The stork came" is an every-day expression in North America and elsewhere to announce a new arrival in the family.

In his fairy tales, Hans Christian Andersen, the Danish writer, (1805–1875) immortalized the myth of north European countries, that the stork brings a baby sister or brother to a family, and drops it down the chimney. In this part of Europe storks commonly nest in chimneys.

The legend of the baby and the stork was inspired, no doubt, by parents who were at a loss to explain to their inquisitive children where the new baby came from. To support the fanciful explanation, however, are some facts in favor of the stork. For instance, the life span of this bird may reach seventy odd years, during which time it returns to nest to the same chimney year after year. Children noticed this regularity, as well as the parallel in the family life of the stork and of human beings. The stork then came to be regarded as the bird-guardian of the home and a friend of the entire household.

In northern Greece, at the time of Aristotle, (384–322 B.C.), it was a capital offense to kill a stork, and the bird has retained its sacred character to this day. It is never killed. Among superstitious reasons for not killing the stork is one that it is a lucky omen for the householder on whose roof it nests. The bird is supposed to protect the house against fire lightning, and other evils.

It is interesting to find the stork closely associated with marital fidelity, home-life and birth in many early fables and legends. These long-legged creatures are the enemies of free love, and the offender who dares to stray from the path of virtue is picked to death by the long spear-like beaks of his judge. Storks are the only monogamists in the true sense of the word. Once a stork loses its mate, it never remates.

In imitation of the stork, the old Romans enacted the "Stork's Law" or *Lex Ciconaria*, which compelled children to maintain their needy parents in old age. From time immemorial, especially in Chinese ethics, the stork was a symbol of filial piety which was defined by Confucius as "carrying on the aims of our fore-fathers." He recommended the stork's conduct as the perfect example of behavior toward mates and babies, as well as toward parents and the family in general.

"Ostrich" Superstitions

"I'll make thee eat iron like an ostrich, and swallow my sword."
—Shakespeare, *Henry IV*, Act iv, Sc. 10

THERE IS THE time-honored superstitious belief that when in danger, the ostrich promptly hides its head in the sand, earth or in a bush. Hence the ostrich has become the symbol of folly and is proverbial in literature for its stupidity.

The belief that ostriches bury their heads in the sand to escape their enemies is said to have been invented by Diodorus Siculus, a Greek naturalist who tried to outshine Aristotle (384–322 B.C.) in knowledge. Or Siculus may have offered it as a "tall" tale, telling Aristotle what we know today to be only a half truth.

When they crouch, ostriches sometimes stretch out their long necks flat and rest them on the ground. While in that position, their keen eyes are on the alert, and they crane their necks to look about for anything unusual and dangerous to their safety. When something appears strange or in the nature of an enemy, the ostrich takes to its long legs; and since it is an unusually fast runner, makes a quick getaway. No, these birds are not as stupid as one might think.

Even the African natives who hunt for ostriches admit that these birds are not only canny, but their legs, which can kick backwards, make their attack upon the hunter comparable to the swift kick of a mule.

The same superstition also implies lack of knowledge as to why the ostrich actually thrusts its head in the sand. It is not for hiding, but for the purpose of finding water, which is frequently under the sand of the desert. This posture probably led misguided observers, but not African hunters, to conclude that the bird actually buried its head in the sand.

The story of the ostrich burying its head in the sand to escape detection may be fabulous, but a similar phenomenon has been observed in the case of the moorhen of Europe. When surprised, it is reported that the moorhen sometimes hides its head in something, crouches, and remains perfectly still, while its body is fully exposed and outlined to the pursuer. It obviously feels perfectly safe by "playing dead."

Because the ostrich is attracted to anything shiny and eats it, Aristotle and others thought it could digest iron, stones, pebbles and the like which were fed them. Then the keepers wondered why they died in their zoos following this diet.

The superstitious notion that hard metals and minerals assisted the functions of the ostrich's gizzard is of course preposterous. When these things have been tried on ostriches in zoos, the birds died, victims of their own greed, and all the undigested articles were found in their stomachs.

Pliny the Elder, another ancient naturalist (23–79 A.D.) made the most of this myth in his writings: "The ostrich has the marvelous faculty of being able to digest every substance without distinction, but its stupidity is no less remarkable, for although the rest of its body is exposed it imagines that when it has thrust its head and neck into a bush, the whole body is concealed."

There is another ancient superstition that the ostrich does not hatch its own eggs, but leaves them in the sun to hatch. This is not true. In fact, it is known that the male ostrich sits on the eggs at night and the female takes over by day. The male first builds a nest for its mate, in which she lays 12 or 18 eggs, which weigh as much as 3½ to 4 pounds each, equalling the weight of about three dozen hen's eggs. The eggs are edible and their yolks are the largest cells known to exist. The nest is merely a depression in the sand.

In the Bible, the ostrich is used as a sign of cruelty and indifference. (Lamentations 4—verse 3, and Job 39—verse 13). This is contrary to the facts as they will protect their young at the risk of their lives. The Arabs think it is good luck to hang ostrich eggs in large numbers in mosques. They think, as do many others, that ostriches hatch their eggs simply by looking at them.

The old Egyptians believed that the ostrich plume was emblematic of truth, and their goddess of Truth was represented with an ostrich plume as headgear. They thought that the ostrich could tell by looking at one of its eggs whether it was bad, and then broke it so as not to bother hatching it. In keeping with the Egyptian belief that ostriches were lucky birds, rings made of the bone were considered charms and were worn in England not so very long ago.

The fashion of wearing ostrich plumes actually originated with the Egyptian suggestion that they were lucky to the wearer, and gave him insight to things. As height and speed were two wonderful assets from which human beings could benefit, on the theory of imitative magic, these attributes of the bird, by contact with man through the plumes, might be transferred.

In our enthusiasm for ostrich feathers, we have overlooked the chaste beauty of the ostrich eggs. The ancients had a more classic taste. The ruins of Kish, in Mesopotamia, include thousands of fragments of ostrich egg cups, five thousand years old at least. They had been used as drinking cups or goblets. The top was sliced off and the edges smoothed and covered with a pottery lid overlaid with bitumen. A normal ostrich egg will hold forty fluid ounces, and the egg will make an excellent omelet for eight persons. Ostrich eggshells were probably the first egg cups.

The credulous Spartans thought they had on exhibition the actual egg laid by Leda when she was in the form of a swan, after Zeus had visited her. Castor and Pollux were supposed to have been hatched from this egg, and there is no doubt that an ostrich egg did service for this magnificent myth.

Africa is the classic home of the ostrich, where it ranged from the Cape of Good Hope to the Mediterranean. It crossed into Asia, and is found in Arabia and east of Palestine and Damascus. It probably still runs the wastes of northwest Persia. There are pictures of ostriches on three thousand-year-old Assyrian seals, which seem to indicate that the bird was once used in sacrificial rites.

It was Chang K'ien, the same Chinese general who traditionally brought the grape from Persia to China in the second century B.C., who first reported the existence of "great birds with eggs the size of a pottery jar." "Great bird" is the early Greek term for the ostrich. Later writers both in Greece and China called it "camel sparrow."

Ostrich farming is a very recent development as compared with other animals which have been domesticated. Yet eleven centuries ago the Persians and the Chinese must have tamed ostriches to a considerable extent, or else how can one account for their transportation five thousand miles overland?

It was the Victorian passion for the ostrich feather hat which gave birth to the ostrich farm. In 1865 there were only eighty domesticated ostriches in South Africa, and most of the feathers exported came from wild birds. Commercial ostrich farming in California dates back to 1882, and while shifting fashion has made the business less profitable, there are still successful ostrich farms in several states.

"Swan" Superstitions

"Swans a little before their death sing sweetly."
Pliny, *Natural History*, x 23

MOST FAMOUS of many swan superstitions is the one that they always sing before they die. "A swan's song" is an expression often used for the last work of a poet or composer, originating in the old Greek legend that the soul of Apollo, the god of Music, passed into a swan. In the *Phaedo*, Plato quotes Socrates as saying that at their deaths swans sing "not out of sorrow or distress, but because they are inspired of Apollo, and they sing as foreknowing the good things their god hath in store for them."

Most species of swans, however, have anything but melodious voices. Some are known as whooping and whistling swans. The trumpeter swans in North America have voices which are said to be so deep-throated that their sonorous calls can be heard two miles distant.

The Dakota Indians thought the female swan was sacred and should never be killed. Since swans are always in pairs, a single swan seen on a lake or elsewhere was believed a precursor of death. The superstition was that its mate had died and the misfortune would be transferred to one who saw the swan or to someone dear to his heart.

In County Mayo, Ireland, it is believed that virgins after death become enshrined in the form of swans. In Persia and other countries, it is believed unlucky to show a dead swan to children, as they would catch some disease and die. When the swan builds its nest high, it foretells high waters; if it builds low, there will be no unusual rains. If swans fly toward the wind, it is certain indication of a hurricane within twenty-four hours.

The fact that swans on the water are very graceful probably inspired watercraft designs such as the gondola and the Vikings' ships, which are more or less a stylistic representation of the swan.

Like most water fowl, swans are symbolic of fertility. Primitive peoples noticed that water always preceded the instance of childbirth, hence the symbolic association. Both the swan and the goose are deified as mother-goddesses of mankind, and both were believed to be the offspring of the solar eye or egg, the seat of life itself, when sun-worship was at its peak.

Greek mythology contains many legends of gods and heroes transformed into animals, trees, and stones. According to tradition, Zeus took the form of a swan to seduce Leda, who gave birth to two eggs. From one came Castor and Clytemnestra; from the other, Pollux and Helen. The subject of Leda and the Swan has been a favorite with artists. Paul Veronese, Correggio, and Michelangelo have left paintings of it.

Swans are known to be strictly monogamous. They are also long-lived. From these two outstanding characteristics, many superstitious beliefs evolved.

Various accounts of singing swans have been reported. One from Iceland describes the wild swans singing like a violin during the long and dark night of winter. From Siberia it is reported that when wounded the dying swan pours forth its last breath in notes most beautifully clear and loud. Some years ago in a biological survey of the United States, it was reported that "on rare occasions wounded or dying swans do produce notes which are very different from the ordinary notes of the species and which give rise to the theory that the bird sings before dying." However, the myth could be based on the fact that a wounded or dying swan moans itself out of existence, not singing sweetly as the popular superstition goes.

It has been reported also that the wild swans of northern regions, when hastening away ahead of a storm or blizzard, beat a harp-like song with their wings. Only two notes are said to be alternately repeated. Perhaps they are signal notes of distress or direction. However it may be, with only flimsy evidence and heresay at hand, the belief that swans actually sing sweetly before dying is not fully substantiated, and for the present must be classified as a superstition.

"Goose" Superstitions

*"To hear the cackle of a goose
Betokens gifts of price and use."*

THE GOOSE is proverbially a wise fowl, around which has grown legends and superstitions among all peoples of the ancient world and which, for the most part, are still observed today. Scores of traditional beliefs about the goose have been imported to America where they are popularly indulged in by millions of persons.

The traditional jar of goose fat is kept in thousands of homes today, year in and year out, not only for choicer cooking, but for various home medicaments which represent a whole series of old wives' remedies. The most familiar of these is goose-grease and turpentine rubbed on chests for colds, coughs, wheezing ailments such as bronchitis and asthma, and on the head for baldness. Goose-grease is highly absorbable and disappears into the skin, a fact that was taken as a sign that it was rushing to the seat of the trouble.

There are dozens of formulas for the use of goose-grease in oleo-therapy to ease sore joints, rheumatism, earaches, and the like. The top vertebra of a goose has the virtue of curing cramps and easing childbirth pains, provided that it remains pure by not touching the ground. Goose-dung mixed with the middle bark of the elder tree and fried in May butter is not only believed a good salve to soothe burns, but if permanently kept from year to year—from May to May—it will protect the inmates from any serious injuries caused by fire.

The goose-bone figures largely in winter weather forecasting by rural weathermen. If the breast-bone of a goose in November is thick, preparation for a rigorous winter is suggested. This prediction appears as regularly as the return of the seasons. When the goose bones are red, usually cruel weather is forecast, while pink bones foretell of a mild one. If there is a generous tuft of down at the base of the feather, a severe winter is in store. The down probably suggested to the ancients in cold regions to make feather-beds, a practice which is still the custom today with many people and is the forerunner of today's eider-down bed-covering!

Because the goose and the gander have been associated with love and devotion in the past, many superstitions survive today which guide lovers to their fate. In ancient times the goose was sacred to Isis, the Egyptian goddess of love. For thousands of years the goose and gander set a noble example of fidelity. Some historians claim that this example of fidelity is one of the reasons that Egypt prospered and remained a leading nation longer than any other in all history. The Egyptians took their gods very seriously, greatly loved and feared them as well, and thus they had a stern pattern of behavior set before them which was faithfully observed.

In Greece, Eros, god of love, is depicted riding a goose. The goose, as the emblem of love, was sacrificed to Venus, and in Rome and Italy, to Priapus. In Germany and France, the goose was believed to be en-dowed with the power of forecasting events as well as weather. Among the Hindus the goose was the symbol of eloquence. The Greeks gave the goose to Peitho, goddess of "winning speech." For centuries the goose represented love and watchfulness. Called a "blessed fowl" by mystics, it was known as the fowl which never sleeps. The oath taken by Socrates and his disciples was "by the goose"! There are many other such examples in the folklore and history of many nations.

"The goose that laid the golden egg" is merely a saying today, symbolizing generosity of some sort. Originally in Egypt, however, this fowl was looked upon as the chaos goose which cackled loudly to the chaos gander when she laid the egg of the sun, the Golden Egg of the ancients. Ra then became the Solar Eye-God, symbolic in historic and classical lore as the Goose-Egg; Seb became the earth-god, or the gander. Later, Ra of Thebes combined the two deities, symbolic of fidelity and devotion, and the goose and gander became one. The name "goose" is generally used as a generic term, a duality expressed in the common saying today that "What is sauce for the goose is sauce for the gander," meaning that one cannot have anything without the other participating in it also, since the goose and the gander formed the perfect entity in antiquity!

In China, geese are looked upon as related to their main ancestors because they are believed to have taught them the art of domesticity. Sacred geese were kept in Rome, and their hissing and clamoring are said to have saved the Romans from a surprise attack by the Gauls in 390 B.C. The Hindus depict Brahma the Creator—the Breath of Life—riding on a goose. From the earliest days, perhaps because of its sibilant hiss, the goose became associated with the sound of the rushing wind, symbolically the breath of life! The goose, or "breath bird," was sacred to Juno and to the Greek Hera, and other deities.

There is an old saying that on Candlemas Day the good housewife's goose will lay an egg, meaning that if the geese are well kept and warm, they will lay by the 2nd of February. Candlemas Day is also Groundhog Day in America, a solar holiday when the goose, symbolic of the cosmic egg—the sun and birth or rebirth—lays its first egg of the season; when Venus becomes a morning star, and the sun charts its course toward spring and summer. Goose was the traditional fowl eaten on Christmas Day in olden times, and was symbolic of the sun's turn in the heavens and the return of longer days of sunlight.

Some of the American Indians believed that when the wild geese flew south in early August a severe winter was ahead. When they returned and flew high and in large droves it meant a long and wet spring. The old familiar expression, "Everything is love—or jake—and the goose hangs high," meaning the weather is good and everything prosperous, obtains from the observation that when the goose "honks high" clear weather is indicated, since bad weather descends upon us from the higher strata of the atmosphere and the geese flying high are the first to feel its approach. Hence there is some truth in the saying.

Despite its modern reputation for silliness, the goose is said by bird experts to be the most intelligent of feathered creatures. Not only can the goose be trusted, but it cannot be bribed and shows devotion to its owner. As a matter of fact, the ancient Greeks knew this quality and used geese as guardians and companions for their children. Geese sometimes live 30 or 40 years and have strong family ties. The much maligned gander is loyal to its mate and guards her jealously from all interlopers.

There is a type of "Mother Goose" fairy-tale in the traditions of most races and nations. Superstitious sayings related to this fowl are legion, the least of which is calling a woman "a silly goose," to which no woman raises much objection. Perhaps she senses the long and glorious history of this honorable female fowl, and accepts the remark philosophically as more a compliment than an offense!

"Turkey" Superstitions

ALTHOUGH THE turkey is an American wild fowl, and a comparatively recent addition to the barnyard, a great many superstitious beliefs have developed about it. For instance, if you go to a house and a turkey gobbles at you, you are welcome. When turkeys stretch their necks to stare upward from their roosts, it will rain before morning. However, wherever this fowl is raised, superstitious beliefs attributed to other barnyard birds have been transferred to interpret the turkey's behavior as a sign of good or evil, in relation to human beings or to weather.

The wild turkey, taken from North America by the Spaniards, was domesticated by them and returned to America from Spain to become an important source of food.

The turkey gobbler is only half as big as it looks. It fills an air sac on its breast and fluffs its feathers. Therefore, it has gained the reputation of being a bluffer. As superstitious signs are often interpreted in reverse, its unpleasant gobble of greeting is assumed to be a favorable reception.

Thanksgiving Day in the United States is a special day for turkey on the menu, but in Ecuador, South America, New Year's Day is Turkey Day. Since it is believed there that the turkey may gobble all sorts of maledictions upon its killer, and upon those who eat it, Ecuadorians have solved the problem with a strange but convenient custom to silence the bird before its end comes.

Just as in North America, the turkey is penned and fattened for some time in advance of the slaughter. On the appointed day, however, and early in the morning, the servants assigned to the task approach the turkey-pen with a bottle of Aguardiente, the Ecuador equivalent of "fire-water," and a cheap but powerful brew of rum. One of the servants holds the turkey while the other pours over and over again until the turkey is well on the way to being intoxicated. Then a rope, loose enough not to choke it, is placed around its neck and it is urged to walk in a circle. This is kept up even though the turkey falls and rises, until it falls to the ground in a stupor and can no longer get up.

This is an occasion for the family and servants to laugh and enjoy the antics of the staggering and inebriated turkey. The poor bird's throat is then cut with a knife or hatchet. After the turkey is eaten everyone makes a wish which is expected to come true during the coming year.

The turkey's wishbone carried the same superstition as the chicken's and whoever gets the long end gets his wish.

The behavior of the turkey, when it indulges in a favorite pastime of taking a bath of dust, provides superstitious persons with a means of divination from the way the turkey acts, the way the dust and the down fly, and the length of time the bath takes. Turkeys or other fowls may have suggested to man long ago the mud baths and mud packs which are indulged in to the present time, to alleviate the aches and pains of old age, such as rheumatism. Fowls, however, usually take their dry dust bath to rid themselves of parasites, an operation which superstitious ones frequently interpret to mean it's going to rain.

"Peacock" Superstitions

"When the peacock's distant voice you hear,
Are you in need of rain? Rejoice, 'tis here!"

SOME PEOPLE regard the peacock as a divine bird, while others consider it a bird of evil intent. Few fowls enjoy the varied reputation of the peacock, with its supernatural attributes, from favorable to unfavorable from a mosaic of customs, beliefs and superstitions, rarely excelled in bird-lore.

If a woman sees a peacock as she enters a park, she will marry a handsome man. A child will never be born in a house where peacock feathers are kept. When the peacock ruffles its feathers it warns of danger. The screech of a peacock is generally an ominous warning.

Live peacocks outdoors are not in themselves unlucky, but their feathers should never be taken indoors because of the ancient belief that the watchful eye on each feather may be harmful to the occupants.

"When the peacock loudly bawls, soon you'll have both rain and squalls."

The cry of a peacock immediately under a window, like the Banshee's call, bodes the death of someone within.

In Italy, and elsewhere in the western world, including America, the feather of the peacock is associated with bad luck and the Evil Eye. Those who are superstitious about peacock feathers believe they bring illness and death, especially when there are children in a home. In the home of a marriageable girl, peacock feathers are said to keep all eligible suitors away.

The East Indians, and North American Indians as well, are generally of the belief that feathers endow the wearer with the qualities, whether virtues or vices, of the birds from which they are taken. Since the peacock is vain, arrogant and greedy, its feathers are supposed to bring bad luck. In both England and America, and to a lesser degree in Italy, France, Spain, Germany, and Mohammedan countries, this superstition is observed.

On the other hand, it is lucky to own a peacock in India, because of the belief that by its behavior, it warns of evil. Hindus have a saying which they share with Mohammedans, that the peacock has an angel's feathers, a devil's voice and a thief's walk. For this reason it is looked upon as a bird of magic.

The Japanese and Chinese hold the bird in high esteem, and since earliest times, its feathers have been used in religious, imperial and artistic ceremonies. In China, in the 8th Century B.C., peacock feathers were bestowed upon military men and civilians alike as a reward for faithful services, or as a mark of rank.

Theatrical people in America have a horror of peacock feathers, and refuse to wear them on the silver screen or in the theatre, even when the rôle calls for them. However, in New York City in 1903, the bad luck tradition of peacocks was challenged by Richard Anderson, a believer in the good luck of the bird, who was assigned to decorate the New Amsterdam Theatre. He placed two peacocks in mosaic, in panels over two fountains which adorned the promenade, and sixteen peacocks to decorate the proscenium arch. The design was executed by Hertz and Talent. The theatre opened with a production in which Nat C. Goodwin played and was a success!

Not to be outdone in breaking the traditional taboo, Florenz Ziegfeld followed there with the presentation of his wife, Anna Held, in "Miss Innocence," a musical extravaganza in which a group of girls dressed as peacocks danced the "peacock strut." Miss Held made a spectacular entrance as a glorified white peacock.

"Peacock Alley" of the old Waldorf Astoria, although a fashionable meeting place of old New York society, served to diminish only to a small degree the fear of having peacock feathers in the home or anywhere about, as the superstition is still prevalent.

The peacock, as a living fowl, is not as tabooed as its feathers. It is claimed that the European superstitions about peacocks came from Saracen sources, probably during the Crusades. Others believe that the origin was the Greek fable of Argus which was borrowed from the Egyptian legend of the hundred-eyed minister of King Osiris. This legend eventually reached Roman mythology, where the peacock became Juno's bird with its innumerable eyes placed on its tail.

In the Greek legend, Argus, the one-hundred-eyed creature, was placed by Hera, the Olympian goddess of marriage, to watch over her rival, Io, of whom she was extremely jealous. Argus had the power of keeping some of his eyes open, ever watchful, even when he slept. Hermes, lover of both women, and master of all kinds of tricks, was not to be outwitted so easily, and charmed Argus into a sound sleep which closed all of his hundred eyes, so that he could woo Io. Hera, learning of this, in revenge promptly transformed Argus into a peacock with all his eyes in its tail. From then on the eyes were to remain always open, and to be harmful to whoever possessed them, even though but a single feather with a single eye was owned. The Greek legend further relates that Zeus changed his favorite, Io, into a cow to escape the vengeance of Hera.

The ancient superstition that associated the eyes of the peacock's tail with the Evil Eye was revived effectively in the 16th Century when garlands of peacock feathers were bestowed on liars and cheats, to signify a traitor.

It is not possible to ascertain definitely whether the peacock came from India, Persia or Phoenicia when it was brought to the Mediterranean region, but we know it is a native of peninsular India and

Ceylon. These birds add color to an estate or farm, as well as to the wooded hills of India and Ceylon to this day. Wild peacocks are common and live in small flocks. The sportsmen of India like to hunt them, but certain castes hold them sacred. One variety, the white peacock, is actually an object of worship; forming one of three animal deities,— the peacock, the cow, and the monkey.

There is a famous Peacock Throne that was formerly used by the kings of Delhi, India, but since 1739, when it was carried off by Nadir Shah, it has been held by the shahs of Persia. The throne is so called because it contains a fully expanded peacock's tail studded with gems.

There is another legend that relates that the peacock was brought into Palestine by King Solomon. It is also claimed that Alexander the Great, after his eastern conquests, came to think so much of the bird that he inflicted punishment on anyone who dared to harm it.

Because of the mythical belief that the peacock did not deteriorate, it was associated with immortality and resurrection, and in early Christian art, was a symbol of immortality. On Easter Day, in Rome, the eye-spots from peacock feathers are sewed on ostrich feathers to make the fan the Pope uses to wave over the heads of bowed worshippers, when he is borne in state into St. Peter's.

A Mohammedan tradition relates that the peacock was the traitor who opened the wicket of Paradise to admit the Devil, for which the peacock received a good share of the Devil's punishment. For that reason it is regarded as a bird never to be trusted.

In Europe during the Middle Ages, many looked on the peacock as a sacred bird. Among the customs of chivalry was one in which knights and squires took oath on the king's peacock. The peacock's flesh was esteemed a great delicacy. In various solemnities of the time, the peacock was stuffed and brought to the table. The Normans were very fond of the peacock's head as food which was served to the blare of trumpets and much ceremony.

Another source for the bad omen of peacock feathers was the ancient custom of using the plumes of the peacock in funeral ceremonies, as a symbol of immortality. It was a reverential gesture toward the departed to assist him in the hereafter. Because the feathers had been used in conjunction with death, the superstition evolved making the feathers unlucky, and the good implications became bad ones when transferred to the living. Peacock feathers are still taboo in decorative schemes in the home!

"Bat" Superstitions

THE BAT, creature of mystery and darkness, is, in the East, a creature of good omen. Five symbolic bats are worn as a talisman and denote five blessings—namely, happiness, wealth, peace, virtue and long life. We of the West, however, still believe that the bat is the harbinger of evil and around it cluster countless medieval and baseless superstitions.

In the Middle Ages the bat was believed to be in league with the devil as well as in partnership with witches. It is still called the "witches'" bird. The bat was credited with the power to transform itself into a human form or that of a wolf or other unrelated species. Both witches and bats worked at night and mysteriously disappeared at dawn. Hence the bad reputation was acquired by these harmless animals that were in reality only chasing and eating insects around the witches' fire.

To make matters worse, Cortez' true tales of blood-sucking vampire bats in South America (1485–1547) were brought to the Old World where no such vampire bats exist; and fantastic stories like that of the *Dracula*, for instance, strengthened the superstitious beliefs about the imaginary wrong-doings of the bat. The *Dracula*, for example, was a man who took the form of a blood-sucking vampire at will and made many beautiful girls his victims.

And, by the way, the bat is the only mammal capable of true flight. Contrary to popular notion, the bat is not blind; its eyes are small but keen, but of no use in guiding its flight. The bat is able to perform its "blind flying" in darkness or actually blind-folded with perfect precision, because it flies by ear. About 1941, scientists discovered, with a special device, that bats' ears guide them in their seemingly noiseless flight, through their ability to hear supersonic sounds. The clamor of shrill cries which accompanies the bats' flight are echoed from the wall. The bats hear them and know that they are in danger of collision and pattern their flight accordingly.

Hence, radar and a bat's ears have much in common.

The Eagle, Good and Bad Bird

WE CAN MENTION only a few of the eagle's glorious or evil associations among various peoples of the ancient world. In Egypt this creature, with the power to out-stare the sun, was worshipped as sacred to the solar god. No doubt this belief arose because of the fact that the eagle can look straight at a fiery sun, and it can do so simply because its eyes are protected by a third eyelid.

The eagle, which is actually long-lived, was nicknamed the Bird of Regeneration by the Egyptians. They, the Persians and others believed that an eagle's presence safeguarded against thunder and lightning, prolonged life, and foretold of an approaching death if it flew from the left of a person as it uttered its warning cry of impending doom. When it flew from the right of a person about to make a decision, it was deemed a good omen; especially for a man who was seeking public office. When the bird came from the left, however, no decisions were ever made.

Because an eagle drops at lightning speed, relying upon the shocking power of its drive to strike a vulnerable spot in its victim, the ancients thought that the eagle had some affinity with the fire and thunder of the heavens, and therefore was immune from its dangers. In turn, those in whose presence the eagle happened to be during a storm were protected from danger. It was therefore good luck to own an eagle.

In primitive mythology, the eagle was believed to have the power to procure fire from Heaven and bring it to man. In the later legends, Prometheus—a name given to the eagle to express its farsightedness and prophetic power—became the cunning Titan who surreptitiously stole fire from Heaven and gave it to mankind. Zeus, the all-powerful Greek god, objected, and punished the thief by chaining him to a rock while an eagle devoured his liver which was perpetually renewed.

Because the eagle was believed immune from the dangers of lightning, it served as a lightning conductor atop Greek temples!

It is well known that the ancients appropriated certain animals to certain gods, and the eagle, for instance, was sacred to Jupiter, the Roman god. When the soldiers of Rome tramped the roads of Gaul, mascots were popular. One of the legions of Vespasian boasted a mascot eagle caught in the Austrian Alps, which had been trained to ride on the standard of the Legion in place of the traditional golden eagle. The Roman legions carried the eagle symbol into all the Empire and it has been accepted as the emblem of many nations, such as old France, Germany, Russia and the United States.

Incidentally, the bald eagle is truly an American bird, native to this continent. Other nations take their emblems from the golden eagles.

The American bald eagle derives its name from its snow-white head which at a distance appears to be bald.

The Aztecs considered the eagle a holy bird, and in religious art, even today, the eagle is assigned to St. John the Divine. In some parts of Ireland a curious belief is that Adam and Eve still survive as eagles. Among some Indians, eagle feathers are worn to ward off evil as well as to single out the brave and worthy who wear this most honorable mark of distinction. Instances of this sort can be found throughout the history of many peoples, giving the eagle great prominence in the lore of birds in general.

We know that the harpy eagle of Central and South America attacks and kills animals of more than three times its own size and weight. It is quite possible that this powerful eagle, when hungry, might help himself to an unprotected child. Ornithologists, however, generally agree that the American eagle cannot carry off a lamb or a baby. Controversy on this subject persists even when all the stories, including "photographs" of eagles stealing babies, have been proved false! It is possible that the powerful blow of a swift eagle might well knock down a small animal, but, of course, that does not mean that the eagle could even then carry off its victim.

The Kirghiz Tartars of Central Asia and European Russia train eagles to hunt foxes, wolves and other animals with great success.

Legends and mythology have a way of being transformed, and the eagle, alternating between being a good and evil bird, executioner or victim, meets with varied and surprising contrasts all through its traditional journey.

The Owl, Bird of Wisdom and Bird of Doom!

PARADOXICAL superstitions surround the owl's reputation, and associate him with both wisdom and evil. Their attitudes seem odd, but there are fascinating facets which reflect primitive as well as ancient symbology and psychology, especially when we acquaint ourselves with various aspects of fables and facts which may have led to such beliefs in remote antiquity.

Many legends have been woven around the owl, the world over, since time immemorial. In ancient Greece we find the owl sacred to Athena, the goddess of wisdom and learning. Athena was preeminently a civic goddess, wise in the industries of peace and the arts of war. At the same time she presided over the whole intellectual side of human life.

Since the owl was an attribute of Athena, it was considered a very good omen by the Athenians to see an owl or hear its call. Hence the saying, "The owl is out!" which in our daily parlance corresponds to "Everything is fine!" Therefore, when speaking of its wisdom, we are reminded that the owl was associated with the archaic Greek worship at Athens.

Now the question of why the owl was chosen instead of some other bird arises. No one knows exactly, but one of the answers may be that near the temple dedicated to Athena was an olive grove thickly infested with owls that slept all day, their eyes fixed ahead, an attitude regarded as that of meditation or deep thought.

Gradually, both the olive and the owl became identified with Athena, and "Wise as an owl" is a saying retained to this day. However, the Athenian owl, the bird whose figure was represented on coins, sculpture, vases and other things, suggests that in some remote period the owl was a totem bird, a creature which probably preceded the cult of the goddess Athena.

As a matter of record, Homer (epic poet of Greece, about 900 B.C.), first applied the term, "keen-eyed" to Athena, which leads us to believe that the expression signified owl-faced. From Homer's observation, it is not unreasonable to suppose that the goddess may have been a combination of bird and woman, beginning with the worship of the owl, then of the goddess with a wise or owl-face, and later still, of the goddess alone, with the owl as attribute.

The Greeks eventually gave up the superstitious idea that the owl was a bird of wisdom, and in reverse mood, the owl was then looked upon as the very abomination of mankind, associated with crimes and dreadful deeds.

The Roman equivalent of Athena was Minerva, who retained the same attributes as the Greek goddess. However, the Romans always believed that the owl was capable of doing both good and evil service to man. We have a tale, handed down from the ancients, that tells of Ceres, goddess of growing vegetation, who transformed Ascalaphus, a minor deity, into an owl, for tale-bearing and mischief-making.

Among other Roman superstitions was one that if the heart of a horned-owl were applied to the left breast of a woman while she was asleep, it would make her reveal all her secrets!

Frequent allusions are made throughout history and literature to the fact that if an owl shrieked at noonday or at some other time, it heralded an impending defeat in battle, a plague, sickness or a death, as in the case of Julius Caesar. Today, even among the most learned of individuals, the hooting of an owl stirs a sense of disaster or impending tragedy, because of the age-old belief that the owl has the gift of presage.

Another legend about the owl presents a Christian fragment of mythology, again borrowed from the Greek and preserved in literature by Shakespeare. In the first place, the Greeks had a legend of feminine impiety in which it was explained that one of three disobedient sisters was transformed into an owl. The Christian version is that the owl was once a baker's daughter who behaved rudely to the Lord, and for punishment was changed into the bird that "looks not into the sun." And Shakespeare immortalized this legend by making Ophelia say, in Hamlet, (Act IV. Scene V), "The owl was a baker's daughter. Lord, we know what we are, but know not what we may be!"

The owl has played a large role in the folklore of practically every nation on earth. In India where the white or albino owl was and still is sacred to the goddess of prosperity, natives are pleased when it builds its nest in their homes. By way of contrast, it is interesting that in the Vedic mythology of the Hindus, Yama, the god of the dead, had as his messengers the owl and the pigeon. The Vedas, representing the most sacred literature of the Hindus, is conservatively dated from 1500 to 1000 B.C., which attests the antiquity of diametrically opposed superstitions regarding the owl.

It is not uncommon, even today, to find people in northern India who eat the eyeballs of an owl in the belief that it will enable them to see in the dark.

The American Indian believed that the owl was not a real bird, but the spirit of the dead, taking that form to give warning of approaching death. They also believed the dead sometimes communicated with the living by means of an owl's hooting. The bird itself was supposed to be the pulse or heartbeat of the dead person who came to tell news in the gloom of midnight.

In Florida, if a Seminole Indian hears an owl sing, "Who-Whoo," he whistles to it. If there is no answer to his whistle, he bows his head in resignation, in the full belief that he has received the summons of approaching death. If the owl answers his whistle by repeating its cry, the Indian goes on his way rejoicing, as this is a sign of good luck to him.

In keeping with its old title of a bird of wisdom, an owl is featured in the Alma Mater statue on the campus of Columbia University in New York City; and "lucky charms" in its likeness are still carried by students to bring them success in their examinations and studies. This statue was designed by Daniel Chester French, who based it on the design of the university seal which was adopted in 1754. The owl was not in the original design but was worked in later as the conventional symbol usually associated with the goddess Minerva. In fact, the owl used in this way is common on many college campuses in the United States.

It is quite impossible to trace the thread and process of savage ideas from their inception to the time when totem, or holy animals, of different tribes and nations became attributes or symbols of deities, as may have been the case in Greece and elsewhere. As an example of the belief in animism—a term employed to denote the most primitive and superstitious forms of religion—it is known that the early Germans were profoundly animistic. Every tree in their sacred forests had its genius, which took the form of an owl, a vulture or a wildcat.

Later on, during the evolutionary course of ideas and concepts, we find that the owl lost most of his reputation as a sage and soothsayer. Perhaps the change came about as deliberate fiction on the part of some ancient parent, to give an object lesson to an unruly child. The many so-called evil habits which the goggle-eyed owl has acquired, such as its night life and strange cries, seem to suggest the source for the owl's later reputation. No doubt, another opportunity for moralizing that the disciplining parent took advantage of was the fable that the owl had once talked too much and unwisely, and, as punishment, was left with only a few weird and ominous sounds with which to express himself.

In rural communities nowadays, the owl is still an evil omen and there are countermagic measures which are supposed to neutralize the bad luck or evil. Some of these are: tying a knot in the corner of a handkerchief or an apron string to stop the hooting of an owl; turning a pocket wrong side out, wearing an apron backwards, or wearing any garment wrong side out, for the same effect. There are those who believe that when the night owl cries by day, it is a sign of fire; and that to put salt, pepper and vinegar in the fire will give the owl a sore tongue and it will go away and hoot no more. Others put irons in the fire to avert the bad luck, and so on.

Geographically speaking, owls inhabit almost every country in the world, and their peculiar habits are very well known to ornithologists and others. However, it is quite understandable how the owl's lugubrious and sinister cries, together with its weird ways, created terror and foreboding in primitive man's mind. Its night-flying habit undoubtedly had a great deal to do with this bird's ill repute among savage tribes. "Late hours" has ever been an unforgivable sin since the dawn of civilization; needless to say, the precautionary warning against staying out late, "owl-style," was an essential measure for the preservation of the tribe and the safety of the family. Primitive man, at the approach of darkness, feared for the life of any member of the group who might be away from the camp during the night, and especially for that of a child who might have strayed. Early man's efforts to rid the forests of all owls is therefore excusable.

But to enlightened moderns, the owl's behavior is perfectly in keeping with its instincts, and indeed, this creature is most useful to man in ridding farms, fields, and forests of destructive pests such as rodents. Nevertheless, there is still much opposition, from superstitious minds, to programs for the conservation of this species, especially the barn-owl. In fact, owls are actually decimated, as well as being made taboo, by those who regard them as evil birds that come around only to prepare people to expect misfortune or death!

Of course, certain owls deserve a bad reputation, as in the case of the horned-owl, which sometimes satisfies its greed with young poultry; but there is nothing supernatural about this.

Many fallacies that have grown in connection with this strange and interesting bird should be explained. "Wise as an owl" is the commonest. To bird experts, however, the grotesque and ludicrous expression on the owl's face suggests anything but wisdom and erudition. As a matter of fact, the owl is not intelligent at all, as birds go. On the contrary, it is probably more stupid than average. This arouses in some anthropologists the suspicion that the ancient Greeks, who were by no means dull, chose the owl as a symbol of wisdom with tongue in cheek. The choice may have been made to denote that not uncommon type of person who says little, looks wise, and thereby gives the impression of mental superiority.

"Blind as an owl" is another fallacy. Owls are not blind in the daytime, merely far-sighted. The familiar barn owl acts bewildered in daylight as he is strictly a nocturnal bird. By day it is the prey of crows, but revenges itself at night by attacking the now helpless crow. On the other hand, the widely distributed barred owl sees equally well both night and day, but it prefers to roost by day.

Another popular, but mistaken, idea is that the owl sees *better* in complete darkness. No animal can! However, the owl, like the cat, has better sight when it is partly dark or at dusk, because its eyes are sensitive to the ultra-violet rays of the spectrum, and the pupils are capable of great expansion, thus admitting all the light available.

In connection with the owl's eyes, there is an expression among those who imbibe, which is not at all flattering to the feathered creature,—"Cockeyed as an owl." What is referred to as bleery or "cockeyed" in the appearance of the owl's orbs is not due to over-indulgence of any kind, but only to a need for sleep. What really takes place when the owl's eyes have this queer look is that a "third" eyelid drops over the eyes to shut out strong daylight. The expression, "Drunk as a boiled owl," is probably intelligible only to those who use it.

Another curious but false notion about the owl is that it can wring its own neck. Of course it cannot. As has been said, the owl's eyes are set in the head in such a way that they can only see straight ahead, not sideways. The eyes are fixed immovably in their sockets by strong cartilaginous cases. Perhaps to compensate for this handicap, the owl's neck is so jointed that it can readily turn its head very far to the left or right, almost in a complete circle. And so it is this unusual faculty that has given rise to the belief that if an owl's head is made to turn around and around, the poor bird will end its own life by wringing its own neck.

No wonder the owl, with its enormous eyes staring through feathered eyelashes, its weird and haunting calls, its rotating head and its other strange characteristics, has been an object of superstition and legend since man first took notice of this creature!

"Crow" Superstitions

> *Crow on the fence,*
> *Rain will go hence.*
> *Crow on the ground,*
> *Rain will come down.*

A CURRENT superstition, popular in rural communities, is that when a single crow begins cawing near a house it is announcing to the occupants an approaching calamity. Some country people take off their hats when they see one crow alone, or bow to it if they are bareheaded. This is the countercharm to forestall the evil that the sight of one crow signifies.

If the first single crow seen in the spring is in the act of flying, it means one will take a journey. The reason it is hard to shoot a crow is because it is supposed to be able to smell powder miles away, and so it keeps out of the path of the hunter. If a crow flies to the left, it is a sign of bad news; but flying on the right is a warning to be on guard that day.

If you see a crow flying through the air, make a wish. If it does not flap its wings before it is out of sight, the wish will come true. But if it does, you must look away, and if you do not see him again, your wish has a good chance of coming true. The list of crow superstitions is almost endless, having been built up through the centuries.

Although as a rule the crow is looked upon as a harbinger of misfortune, many persons discard this idea and keep the bird as a pet. It is thought to be intelligent and amusing, which it is, to a certain degree as birds go; and it is also regarded as a weather prophet and a protection against evil influences. However, not all pet crows are kept for superstitious reasons.

All through history we find the crow a bird of sinister omen, foretelling evil and death. It is said that on the day Cicero was murdered, several crows fluttered about his head and one even made its way into his bedchamber and pulled at the bedclothes.

A superstition with an interesting background is found in Greek mythology. Apollo was the god of prophecy, and the crow was his inseparable companion. In those days, the legend tells us, the crow was as white as a swan. When Apollo fell in love with a nymph named Coronis, the crow informed him of her unfaithfulness. In a rage, Apollo slew the nymph, and turned the crow black. However, in spite of its downfall, the crow could still talk, and it also retained its gift of prophecy. Hence, it became a prophet of evil tidings, a reputation that has stood the test of many centuries. For instance, when a crow is seen immediately before or after a wedding ceremony, the superstition, which many believe, is that the couple will be unhappy and the marriage will end in divorce.

"As the crow flies," meaning to express a straight line, or a short route, is a familiar phrase. However, except when migrating, the crow is said never to take the shortest route between two points.

It is still believed that if the tongue of a crow is split the operation will increase its ability to talk. This is a superstition, of course, and a very cruel practice, which in no way accomplishes what is intended. Crows, magpies and parrots may be taught to say certain words and phrases, but no surgery assists their ability.

Some crows seem to be ventriloquists, at times, as they have the ability to make their voices sound as though they came from the opposite direction from where they are cawing. Those who do not understand this characteristic become superstitious when these birds appear. They are called raincrows and are supposed to prophesy rain.

There is no basis for the many superstitions about the crow as a bird of evil. It is undeniable, however, that this noisy feathered creature is a mischievous bird with a passion for thievery, constantly snatching brightly-colored objects such as beads, buttons, and jewelry, and hiding them in strange and often inaccessible places. No doubt such behavior, together with its annoying and raucous cawing, damage to crops, destruction of smaller birds, and habit of pecking the eyes of farm animals, entitles the crow to its evil reputation.

The crow is still a bird of mystery and a puzzle. For instance, legends persist that these birds hold "crow trials," and the one on trial is condemned and put to death by fellow members of a flock. These trials are believed held with all the solemnity found in a real court. It is true that a crow is often found pecked to death, but to credit these birds with the faculty of human judgment, which condemns others for a breach of ethics, seems very far-fetched.

Some superstitious persons endow the crow with the human quality of sympathy toward a wounded companion in distress. It is said that crows form rescue squads to help other crows, and also post a sentinel to give warning of danger.

Experiments have demonstrated that wild crows, when tamed, can be taught to count to three or four, but no conclusion has been reached that this interesting bird has reasoning power, as many believe.

The Scarecrow or Man-Cross

As CROWS ARE regarded by ornithologists as birds of very high intelligence, compared to other feathered creatures, it is doubtful that they on the whole pay much attention to the scarecrow set up to frighten them. Most farmers agree that crows are not easily scared.

Since this is so, there must be some other reason for placing a scarecrow in gardens and fields. The custom was not always as pointless as it seems today.

A scarecrow, with its disreputable-looking trousers, ragged coat and hat, upon a wooden cross, is supposed to look like a man. However, originally it was the *cross-symbol*, in the guise of a man, that was placed outdoors as a protective power to keep away robber-birds and other intruders. The scarecrow is a ridiculous object today, but once, with its suggestion of a human cross, it was intended to keep at a distance all evil influences and to terrify without inflicting injury.

Dr. Ralph Bienfang, professor of pharmacy in the University of Oklahoma, an eminent authority on odors, attributes nothing of the supernatural to the fact that a scarecrow keeps the birds away, at least for a while: "In attempts to repel birds, one thinks first of a scarecrow. However, it has been observed that although a scarecrow will serve well for a while eventually the birds will come closer and closer to it, finally perching contentedly on its shoulders. Let us hazard a guess here as to the reason. As the scarecrow is assembled in the first place, well-worn articles of family clothing are carried from the house and hung upon the poles. These clothes carry with them the scent of people rather strongly, for even if they have not been worn for some time, they still carry some personal scent and a great deal of general house odor. Thus the scarecrow at first erected literally reeks of man. Sensitive wild birds scent the man in the scarecrow and stay away. As time passes, wind and rain gradually take away all vestiges of odor, removing at the same time the 'scare' from the scarecrow. A crow repellent is now on the market. Perhaps the scarecrow could occasionally be given an application of it for continued effectiveness against marauding birds."

Crows have a bad reputation, which, no doubt, most of them deserve. They destroy or damage young corn and other farm products, and their notes jar the ears. However, they are not entirely a nuisance, as they destroy cutworms, grubs and other larvae. Farmers may hope that the superstitious device of the scarecrow will drive away the bad crows, but it takes more than this kind of faith to keep birds and others from helping themselves to the hard-earned fruits of the labor of those who work.

"Hawk" Superstitions

THE BEHAVIOR of hawks of all species has aroused human curiosity from remotest times to the present day. Superstitions connected with this bird, however, that have survived, are the immediate concern of farmers and poultry raisers, and there are all kinds of signs and omens, both good and evil, with which they identify the hawk.

If a hawk is seen in the act of seizing its prey, it signifies a loss of some kind—other than a lost chicken—as the omen is particularly a loss of money. If a hawk is seen flying overhead, while someone is in the act of making a decision, or during a contest of some kind including a battle, it is symbolic of success or victory. This belief was held by the American Indians of old as well as by ancient Greeks and Romans.

Other superstitions are: if fish-hawks collect around a house, it is a sign of flood; when sea hawks are flying at sea, it signifies clear skies ahead; when they fly low, a sign of rain that will soon be followed by a rainbow. In general, when a hawk is seen at sea it means good weather. To keep hawks from catching chickens, put a horseshoe in the fire; a round rock in the fire will draw up a hawk's claws, which is another way to save the chickens.

Although it is generally assumed that all hawks prey upon barnyard fowls, it is said that nine-tenths of these birds seen hovering about the farm have no designs whatever on fowl as most of them are looking for mice. Hawks are therefore approaching extinction because of the superstitious belief that the only good hawk is a dead one. This is a pity as hawks are valuable mice killers. Another superstition that is helping to wipe them out is the belief that hawk skins are not only lucky, but afford the owner all kinds of protection, a profitable notion for hawk-hunters.

In mythology, the hawk, together with the eagle, has been a symbol of sovereignty, majesty and grace. Both birds were identified as solar birds, and therefore superstitions relating to each have been interchangeable. The Egyptians thought so much of this swift, powerful winged creature that they even fashioned their solar gods, Ra and Horus, for example, in the form of a hawk. The ancient Greeks also favored the hawk as an expression of supreme energy. Like others among the ancients, however, the Greeks believed that the cry of the hawk was ominous and could addle eggs, unless iron—a potent magic antidote in early days, one of its descendants being the horseshoe—or a clod which had stuck to the plough was placed under the laying hen. The cry of the hawk was always a signal of some kind, voicing a warning of evil to be prepared for with countermagic of some kind.

The hawk was Apollo's oracle and bird-messenger. When it appeared on the right it was a good omen. This particular superstition has changed with time, but many Americans still believe it in this form. When a hawk appears on the right on the eve of an important event it augurs well for many.

Hawks were trained in falconry early in Egyptian history. It is said that Genghis Khan owned about ten thousand falcons. Falconry has come into its own again in the United States and Canada. However, superstitious persons continue to give supernatural attributes to this mighty bird. For instance, hawk amulets are carried on board ships, both large and small, and on airplanes, for protection against disaster that might be caused by gales and storms.

CHAPTER 2

The Bees and the Flowers

"Bee" Superstitions

LIKE PRIMITIVE PEOPLES, the ancients were very observant of natural phenomena, but they had advanced greatly in knowledge. They saw that the bee was highly industrious, and its habits and sharp instincts led them to believe that the insect was endowed with human intelligence. In fact, they regarded the bee as endowed with senses much keener than those of man, so that a hive of bees was treated as part of the family circle.

Because bees were felt to be in sympathy with a family's activities, it was the custom, for thousands of years, to tell them the important events that were taking place in the home, such as betrothals, marriages, births and so on. This practice of talking to the bees opened the way for countless superstitions, many of which are still observed.

For example, if a bee flies into the window, it is a harbinger of good news. If you kill a bee on the first of May and keep it in your purse, you will always have money. Stick a knife in the lid of the beehive, when a new swarm is put in, and they will not go away. Many country people believe that if a swarm of bees settles near a home and is not claimed by the owner, there will be a death in the family within a year, or some other great calamity will follow. If a menstruating woman so much as places a finger on the beehive, all the bees will fly away and never return.

One of the most common superstitions is that if a bee or wasp stings a person, it can never sting again. Some bees do lose their stinging apparatus when they sting, but most of them do not. That dead bees burned to ashes, and sprinkled in the shoe, will cure flat feet is another superstition. If you ignore a bee it will not sting you, it is believed.

A widely believed superstition, and one that is rather dangerous, is that bees, wasps and other insects will not sting a person if he holds his breath, clenches his fists, or grips one wrist firmly with the other

46

hand. This formula is based on the assumption that a bee cannot ply its stinger through skin the pores of which have been closed by the tenseness that is supposed to result.

The fact that a bee will not sting at times under such a circumstance is probably because a person is apt to be more quiet and less disturbing to the bee. Any quick, nervous movement which indicates fear is readily detected by the bee, which no doubt in such a case stings in self-defense.

The fact, according to entomologists, that bees have an exceedingly sensitive sense of smell and can detect the slightest of body odors, some of which excite them and others which repel them, undoubtedly led to other superstitions about them. For example, beekeepers claim that bees know their masters, probably by this sense of smell, and therefore do not sting them. Some scientists disagree with this idea and think that the comparative immunity of the beekeeper is due to his familiarity with their habits, and consequently he knows how to handle them. Another explanation by entomologists is that the average life of the worker-bee during the honey season is about six weeks, of which not more than two are spent in the hive. It is therefore believed unlikely that such short-lived creatures would recognize their keeper, even if they distinguish between different human beings. The keeper is not around the bee enough for it to pay much attention to him. On the other hand, it is a fact that bees dislike the odor of alcohol to such an extent that an otherwise welcome master of the beehive, if he has indulged in it, will be exposed to bee stings.

A persistent superstition about bees, everywhere, including America, is the custom of "telling the bees." This consists of tying a bit of white ribbon on the hive, when there is a wedding in the family, or a bit of black crepe when a death has taken place. The strange thing about this superstition is that it has come down from ancient times when the occupation of apiarist was relegated to one man in each family. Because of the sacred character of the bee, this position was looked upon as a great honor at that time. It was believed that if the bees were not informed of the death of their master, they would die and dwindle out because they would be deprived of proper care and protection, or else swarm away.

In those days, after announcing to the bees that their master had died, the mourning and wailing began. As soon as a new bee master had been found, the bees were treated to sweet talk, serenading or soft soothing music. Some believed that if bees swarmed away following the death of their master, they were following the soul of their beloved keeper.

The old superstitious custom of beating pans, shouting, ringing cowbells or making other loud sounds to induce swarming bees to settle does not meet with scientific sanction. Some naturalists are not even sure whether bees can hear or not.

The ancient Egyptians symbolized their kings under the emblem of the bee. The honey indicated the reward they gave the meritorious, and the sting the punishment they inflicted on the unworthy.

The common expression, "To put the bee on him" derives from old laws that dealt with infidelity. For instance, a man's unfaithfulness was anciently punished by having bees sting him, so that when a man went about showing several bee stings, he was properly suspected. It is also a superstition, that by their acute sense of smell, bees can quickly detect an unchaste woman, and they strive to make her infamy known by stinging her at once. In a pastoral by Theocritus, the shepherd laughingly tells Venus to run to the bees! Pliny says that if a woman in her sickness contacts the hive, the bees will fly away and never return, if they do not die instantly. This superstition is still held by many.

The Greeks believed bees to be symbols of eloquence. It is said of Plato, the great Greek philosopher, that when he was in his cradle a swarm of bees lighted on his mouth. Hence he was called "the Bee of Athens" or the "Attic Bee." The same epithet was given to the Greek dramatist, Sophocles, on account of the sweetness and melody of his verse, and it was believed that a swarm of bees had settled on his lips in infancy too. Pindar, the chief lyric poet of Greece, was believed to have been nourished in his youth, like the god Jupiter, by bees with honey instead of with milk. There are many other such legends.

The endearing term of "honey," used particularly in the southern part of the United States, also derived from ancient times. Among many old poems and songs in which it is used, the Dalmatian wedding song is one of the loveliest:

> "The bride comes in a happy hour. . . .
> Peace and concord brings she with her,
> In her mouth the honey's sweetness. . . ."

Both as the nectar of the Greeks and as the metheglin or mead of Northern races, honey bestowed immortality. Wax, another bee product, had the same attribute. The product of the sacred bee was made into a drink when wine was unknown, and was believed to be a necessary aphrodisiac to be indulged in during the "honeymoon."

The Greeks consecrated the bees to the moon. The Romans considered a flight of bees as a bad omen, signifying a loss of some kind, especially a war.

There are many notions in folklore as to the origin of bees. One version is that they lived in Paradise, and because of man's sin, they came to live on earth. Wax derived much of its sacredness from its use for candles at funerals and other uses in churches and temples throughout the ages.

One of the reasons the honey bee became such a popular insect in folklore is because honey was man's only sweetening substance for thousands of years. Symbols of the bee are found in the art and religious rites of most peoples of the world. Countless Asiatics still believe that each bee contains the soul of a departed person, which explains its intelligence, its thrift and its other remarkable attributes.

Originally when a colony of bees left a hive, the owner of the land on which it settled would claim it as his own. In time, an unwritten law of all nations allowed the original owner of the bees to follow the swarm. As he invaded his neighbor's property, he was supposed to make a great deal of noise, so as to give warning that he was after his bees and that they were his. He was thus permitted to retain title to his own bees until such time as he could persuade them to return to his home. The noise was not only to warn his neighbors, but to keep the bees moving so that they would not settle down in his neighbor's place. However, this procedure is exactly contrary to the modern superstition of making a loud noise to cause the bees to settle down.

Reverend E. Cobham Brewer, in *A Dictionary of Phrase and Fable*, writes: "The name *bee* is given, particularly in America, to a social gathering for some useful work, the allusion being to the social and industrious character of bees. The name of the object of the gathering generally precedes the word, as a *spelling bee* (for a competition in spelling), *apple-bees*, *husking-bees*, and so forth. It is an old Devonshire custom, carried across the Atlantic in Stuart times, but the *name* appears to have originated in America.

"*To have your head full of bees*, or *to have a bee in your bonnet!* To be cranky; to have an idiosyncrasy; to be full of devices, crotchets, fancies, inventions, and dreamy theories. The connexion between bees and the soul was once generally maintained: hence Mahomet admits bees to Paradise. Porphyry says of fountains, 'they are adapted to the nymphs, or those souls which the ancients called bees.' "

"Firefly" Superstitions

IN THE LONG long ago Mother Nature fashioned the little beetle with the neon light which flits here and there to twinkle in the summer darkness. The purpose of its light is believed to be the mating signal. The female shows a much brighter glow than the male which may indicate that she is doing the courting.

To superstitious people, from primitives to moderns, the appearance of this luminous insect foretells certain signs which are not necessarily related to human courtship. Different countries have individual superstitions for interpreting the activities of the firefly. Americans, however, are apt to follow European beliefs, with variations. For instance, if a firefly appears in a house, where it does not belong, it is the sign that there will be a visitor, probably a stranger. Two fireflies in the house mean there will be a marriage, provided there is an unmarried young woman in the household. Otherwise it is just an omen of good luck to the married couple. A large number of fireflies in the house means the coming of cheerful company very soon.

There are others, however, who believe that a firefly, or "lightning bug," as it is sometimes called in the United States, spells death to one of the occupants, unless it is captured and placed under a glass until it dies. In this way, it symbolically takes the place of the doomed one.

There is a curious superstition that fireflies are earthworms in disguise. This false observation is due to the fact that the firefly goes through the larva or wormlike stage. During the entire process of its development, however, from egg to firefly, it is always luminous, and is a beetle, so that it could not be evolved from an earthworm.

"Praying Mantis" Superstitions

BECAUSE OF AN age-old superstition, many persons will not kill a praying mantis, (*mantis religiosa*), for the reason that it is holy and bad luck will befall the one who exterminates it. It is also believed that this insect bears a charm against evil.

In the South, particularly the Carolinas, the praying mantis is known as a "mule killer," based on the superstition that the brownish liquor it exudes from the mouth is fatal to mules. Actually, however, the praying mantises never injure man or large animals.

Praying mantises are especially valuable in America as they exterminate Japanese beetles. However, their helpfulness is cut short as they are apt to leave the country in September. At this time they may be seen in large cities flying at skyscraper windows. Superstitious ones believe that their sudden appearance is a sign of good luck for the person who chances to gaze on them. But no harm must come to the praying mantis, or the beholder's luck will fly away.

In ancient Greece, the praying mantis was called the Prophet, and a very ancient superstition obtains even today, that whenever a praying mantis appears, it is a good omen.

Numerous other superstitions are connected with this sanctimonious-looking insect. One is that if it assumes a kneeling position, it either sees an angel or hears the rustle of its wings. There are those who believe, like the French entomologist Fabre, that the praying mantis pretends to be a ghost, and anyone who kills it will meet with dire misfortune. This is another reason why it is never disturbed by superstitious persons.

A similar superstition obtains in the Deep South in the United States, where the praying mantis is called an agent of the devil. If it is disturbed, it will spit in your eye and blind you, so the superstitious say, and therefore they leave it severely alone.

Mohammedans consider the praying mantis sacred and it is a sacrilege to kill one. Among the ancient superstitious Greeks and Hindus, whenever a praying mantis was observed in its praying attitude, it was treated with reverential consideration. The insect often assisted soothsayers, by being regarded as one of them, and then it foretold who would be fortunate or unfortunate.

Some very old superstitions around this insect are still with us and include the belief that when it alights on your hand, you will make the acquaintance of a distinguished person. When it alights on your head, a great honor will be conferred on you shortly. If it injures you in any way—which it seldom does—you will lose a valued friend by calumny.

No doubt the ancients endowed the praying mantis with holiness because of its posture with its front legs in the position of hands clasped in prayer, an attitude of innocence that commands respect. In reality, it is a very deceitful bug, since its forelegs constitute one of the most efficient pairs of nutcrackers in nature.

The praying mantis is not the holy thing it seems. The female eats her husband—frequently a half a dozen or more in succession—while he is mating with her. The chances are that the praying mantises that are seen flying or wandering about belong to the deadlier sex.

The praying mantis is the only insect that can direct its gaze wherever it will, which is due to the fact that it is probably the only insect that can turn its head without turning its body at the same time. The praying mantis has a neck, and may be said to have almost a face.

"Ladybug" Superstitions

"Ladybug, ladybug, to your home you must turn,
Your house is on fire and your children may burn."

THERE ARE MANY superstitious sayings addressed to a ladybug when it lands on one's garment, and which warn it should never be killed. These are merely symbolic verbal formulas to send the insect back where it belongs—that is, to where it can devour insect pests. Ladybugs rid orchards and gardens of agricultural pests such as aphids, red spiders and potato beetle eggs and others.

The ladybug is known as the ladybird in Europe, where, as an insect —a beetle, in fact—it enjoyed the honor of being sacred to the Norse goddess of Love and Beauty, Freya. It was believed, once upon a time, that the ladybird, or ladybug, was carried to earth in flashes of lightning.

The ladybug was formerly considered a remedy for abdominal pains. Today when it lands on a person, the belief is that whatever ailment the person suffers from will fly away with the ladybug. If the spots on the wing-cover of the ladybug exceed seven, it is a sign of famine. If less than seven, it means a good harvest. The very sight of a ladybug is believed lucky; to kill one brings inevitable misfortune. When the insect is placed on the hand while making a wish, the direction in which it flies away indicates that from which the luck will come.

Because of the ancient relation to the goddess of Love, unmarried young women, when they catch a ladybug, let it crawl about the hand and repeat this formula: "She measures me for my wedding gloves." Then they watch it fly away to see from what direction the groom will come.

The children of the Abdah district in Asiatic Turkey have a superstition among themselves similar to the one in the United States and Europe. In America, a child places a ladybug on its finger and chants the well-known doggerel: "Ladybug, ladybug, fly away home, your house is on fire and your children will burn." The Arab child procures a black beetle, called a "bogharanga," and while holding it between forefinger and thumb, addresses it as follows: "Bogharanga, bogharanga, hear my speaking and tell me the truth!" Then he proceeds to ask it various questions regarding his child-like wishes. Sometimes the bogharanga will remain silent and obstinate, whereupon it is thrown away in disgust. Often, however, if pinched hard enough, it will respond with a peculiar clicking noise, nodding its head repeatedly. This, of course, is taken as an affirmative reply.

American children and those of other countries use not only ladybugs for divination purposes, but find that grasshoppers are also good. In the case of the grasshopper, its life is threatened unless it indicates its willingness to grant the wish asked, which it does by giving up some of its syrup which it leaves on the hand of the inquirer.

There are various ways of talking to the ladybug, and certain factors are involved, such as, the time, the place and whether it alights on the hand, shoulder, right or left side of the body and so on. They are interpreted differently according to local traditional beliefs. However, the landing of a ladybug on an individual is, of itself, a happy omen of good cheer and good news. For the superstitious farmer, it is always a lucky insect. An old saying goes: "Plenty of ladybugs, plenty of hops!"—or whatever the crop might be.

The ladybug destroys many injurious insects and is of great benefit to humanity. Few persons, except entomologists, recognize this beetle in the larval stage, in which it renders its greatest service. There are about two thousand species of ladybeetles that have been identified. Some are striped, some have spots and others are plain. The one around which so many superstitions exist, the *Novius Cardinalis*, was imported into the United States in 1889 from Australia to aid in the control of the scale insect, *Icerya Purchasi*, a pest of citrus fruit trees. It proved so effective in California that it has now been sent to all countries where scale is a pest.

One of the most unusual "bug houses" in the country is in the state of Washington where ladybugs are actually an industry. There are ladybug "prospectors" who hunt hidden ladybugs, and collect and ship hundreds of thousands of these beetles for use in the destruction of harmful insects.

Ladybeetles usually live not much more than a year, sometimes less. They hibernate under leaves, rocks, roofs and windowsills. Sometimes they hibernate in clusters, many of which may be found on mountain heights in the state of Colorado.

The intelligence of the ladybug is proverbial, and has been known from remotest times. It must have been noted that it protects itself by "playing possum," that is, dropping to the ground and remaining motionless on its back until all danger is past. Also, when frightened, it gives off a repulsive odor; and ancient superstition interpreted any offensive odor as a means of driving away evil influences.

A fact also significant in olden days is that this lucky insect is at least partly red in color, a warning coloration in nature, so that the ladybug has few enemies. The praying mantis, however, does not seem to mind the ladybug's "playing possum," or its red coloration, or its unpleasant odor, and devours the insect wherever it finds one. Other insect-eaters, including birds, find the ladybug distasteful, and avoid it in their diet. With nature's help, and with the happy superstition of not killing ladybugs, many parasitic insects have found their Waterloo wherever this ladybeetle makes its home. So that the superstition that it is a lucky bug is hardly a superstition, after all.

"Cricket" Superstitions

CRICKETS ARE generally considered symbols of good fortune, particularly in money matters. From time immemorial, crickets have been regarded as the personification of cheeriness and comfortable domesticity. Their chirp, which is strictly a male performance, produced by the friction of the wing-covers being rubbed together, has been mentioned in literature both for its soporific quality and its sprightliness.

Cricket amulets were raised high above the people in the temples of ancient Greece to protect everyone from the evil glances of wicked spirits lurking around when the bells were silent. Shakespeare alluded repeatedly to the fact that crickets in the house are a sign of mirth and plenty. There are those, here and abroad, who believe that if a cricket departs from a hearth that has long echoed with its chirp, it is an omen of misfortune, and it is regarded as a direct calamity by the family.

There are any number of cricket superstitions. A strange cricket chirping in the house is an unfailing sign of death. If the crickets sing louder than usual, expect rain. Crickets will eat holes in the clothes, especially stockings, of those who kill their mates. To kill a cricket on Sunday is especially unlucky. To see a white cricket denotes that an absent love will return.

There is an old superstition among Irish people that crickets are enchanted beings, hundreds of years old. They believe that if we could understand the cricket's talk, it would tell us the history of the world. This superstition has reached American shores, and is popular in Maryland and Virginia, where crickets are referred to as "old folks," and it is believed unlucky to destroy one. The superstition probably arose from the fact that the cricket loves the warmth, and is found on or near the hearth where old folks, in olden times, used to sit.

Superstitious country folks looked upon the cheerful cricket found in the house or around the chimney, as a bringer of good cheer to all occupants. It must never be killed, however, lest a member of the family meet the same fate soon after.

Musical insects, such as the grasshopper, locust, giant cicada, katydid and cricket make popular charms, or lucky pieces or amulets, especially for superstitious musicians and singers. They believe that to be near or in contact with a musical cricket, for instance, will inspire them in their own professional work, and by the same token, keep them cheerful and happy.

No doubt the fact that among crickets, the black cricket's notes are pitched in E natural, two octaves above the middle C, has aroused interest in such insects and their so-called musicianship. On the other hand, many house crickets are flat, and persistently so.

The cricket does not really sing. Its shrill noise is technically called stridulation. In the Orient, crickets instead of birds are placed in cages, but the "song" of the Chinese cricket is not considered cozy nor sweet, nor even "domestic." The Chinese hold cricket fights, matching one cricket against another, and betting on the outcome.

The Chinese and Japanese make "watchdogs" out of crickets. They keep them in cages in a room where they chirp loudly all night long. Directly a stranger enters the house, the insects, sensing his presence, stop chirping. Strange to say, it is the sudden *silence* that awakens the householder, and warns him that all is not as it should be!

Crickets can be used as thermometers sometimes, but it is the showy tree-cricket whose chirp varies with the temperature. It is said that if one counts the number of chirps a cricket makes in fifteen seconds, and the nadds forty, the sum will be within a few degrees of the correct temperature.

Southern Negroes, like African natives, carry cricket nests about them for good luck. Primitive peoples, as well as more civilized races of early times, believed that crickets were sent by the gods to teach mortals to be cheerful. Some crickets seem to be fiddling their lives away, when on a calm night, they may be heard half a mile away, as they draw their bows or wings to make music.

An ordinary cricket on the hearth may be considered as a sign of good fortune, but a cricket in the earth, the mole cricket, is a serious farm pest, and a sign of bad luck to the farmer; it uproots seedlings in its nocturnal ramblings and menaces the newly planted farm or garden.

"Spider" Superstitions

THERE IS NO DOUBT that the age-old and universal interest in spiders is due to the fact that it is one of nature's most gifted creatures. It is an architect, engineer, balloonist, and spinner, and has many other accomplishments. The spider is one of the most resourceful of creatures and taught early man many things.

Folk medicine is rich in old wives' formulas using spiders and spider webs in odd cures. Modern science, however, has found that a few of the old superstitions were basically sound, just as in many other instances, the gropings of the primitive mind arrived at scientific truths.

The collection of superstitions about spiders is unusually large. Among the old wives' cures we have: swallow a spider with syrup for a fever, as the spider will eat up the fever; or, to prevent fever of any kind, place a spider in a nut shell and wear it around the neck. A walnut shell is a special charm in which to house a spider to keep plagues away. This superstition came from the ancient belief that a dead or live spider around the neck was a watchful ally. Then superstitious peoples took to eating it for protection against certain diseases. After this the spider became a part of pharmacopoeia, lasting from ancient to modern times.

The germ-infested webs of spiders were used to staunch blood on minor cuts. Pulverized webs, the dustier the better, to cure infections produced more of the causes than the cures. Arachnidin, a substance in the web, was finally isolated and is now actually a drug in modern scientific medicine.

Other spider superstitions include:

> "If you see a spider in the morning
> It is a warning.
> If you see a spider at noon,
> It is bringing you good news.
> If you see a spider at night,
> It will bring you joy and delight."

If you see a spider on your dress, you may expect a new one. This belief associates the spider with spinning and clothes. The superstitious belief that a spider runs away from noise has led to the belief that to see one at night means peace. The fact that spiders spin their webs in cellars and attics where it is relatively quiet also contributed to this superstition.

If a spider crawls toward you, it is a sign of a quarrel. When you see a spider run down its web in the afternoon, it means that you are going to travel. There are some persons who hate all spiders and kill them whenever they can, in the belief they are slaying a potential enemy each time. Others think spiders are friends and never kill them. Some persons think all spiders are poisonous.

If you run into a spider web, you may expect to meet a friend. When a spider drops a single thread before you, and he returns upward, you will hear good news. If he continues downward, expect bad news instead. If you see a little red spider, called a "money spider" it indicates good fortune. To walk through a spider web is a sign you will receive a letter.

Carry a spider web in your pocket or in the hem of your skirt or trousers and you will never want for anything. To see a black spider, however, is generally interpreted as bad luck. It is lucky to carry a dead spider wrapped in brown paper in your shoe. There are hundreds of similar superstitions.

The superstition that all spiders are poisonous to man has been denied. It is claimed that all spider bites contain some poison, and those of large spiders, such as tarantulas, much, but the only spider bite that has been known to be fatal is that of the black widow, or hourglass spider.

The tarantula, known scientifically as the bird-spider, seldom bites under any circumstances. It is the largest of all spiders and looks worse than it is. The venom of the tarantula is comparatively weak, but its large jaws and big teeth can take out a large piece of flesh.

The origin of the tarantula superstition, or "leaping madness," goes back to the 16th Century. Spiders abounded near the town of Taranto, Italy, and the people became obsessed with an unreasoning fear of spiders. They dreaded especially the European tarantula, a medium sized "wolf-spider" with its hairy covering. Its bite was supposed to cause dizziness followed by depressing melancholy and eventually death. Popular superstition held that only the medical "choreographers" could save *taranti* or bitten persons. If only the right tune could be found, music and dance would make them well. Skipping and cavorting with great vigor, and with a variety of steps, made the patient perspire freely, and supposedly the deadly poison left the body with the perspiration. In the wild antics designed to shake off the dread *tarantism*, originated a charming dance, the tarantella.

Superstition and quackery gave way slowly before scientific experiments proved the European tarantula really quite harmless. In the meantime, white settlers in America had come in contact with some larger and more ferocious-looking spiders. The American spiders could kill little snakes, or toads or even birds. It was natural, therefore, that these fearsome creatures, though unrelated to the European tarantula, should be classified as such, and become the objects of the same fears and superstitions as those held abroad. This accounts for the prevalent notion in America that all spiders are poisonous. However, the bite of the largest so-called tarantula in America's southern and southwestern states is no worse than the sting of a bee.

There are many superstitions pertaining to daddy longlegs, known in different parts of the world as harvest spider, pseudo-spider and shepherd spider. It is not a spider at all, but a relative of scorpions and crabs. The commonest superstition about the daddy longlegs—and there are many—is that it means good luck and should not be killed.

The spider has played many rôles in mythology and historical legend. One of the most famous is the story of the Lydian maiden Arachne, the weaver, who depicted the metamorphoses of the gods and their amorous adventures in her work. She acquired such skill in the art of weaving that in her foolish conceit, she ventured to challenge Athena, the Roman goddess of Wisdom, who had taught her how to weave, although Arachne denied it.

When the nymphs themselves left their groves and fountains to gaze on the beauty of Arachne's work, this so antagonized Athena that she accepted the challenge, being unable to control herself any longer. The contest was to demonstrate to Athena the perfection of Arachne's weaving and embroidery. But Athena's skill proved to be far superior to that of her pupil, so that Arachne, overcome with shame, hanged herself. Athena, however, took pity on Arachne when she saw her hanging from a rope, and transformed her into a spider. From this myth comes the name of the spider or Arachnida. Many superstitious tales have been woven around this myth, many of which make the spider a participant in wicked deeds.

A historical legend in which the spider inspired confidence and respect, and from which many superstitious beliefs evolved, is the story of Robert Bruce, who was crowned king of Scotland in 1306. Bruce, after being routed by the English, was confined on the island of Rathlin, off the coast of Antrim in Ireland. To pass the time, Bruce watched a spider trying to fix its web to a beam on the ceiling. The spider failed six times. "Now shall this spider," said Bruce, "teach me what I am to do, for I also have failed six times." In the seventh attempt, the spider succeeded in fixing its web to the beam. Bruce took it as a sign, gathered a handful of followers and returned to Scotland. After a series of successful campaigns, he won the battle of Bannockburn in 1314, after which England acknowledged the complete independence of Scotland. To kill a spider in Scotland, or wherever the superstitious Scotch may be, is still supposed to bring the offender all kinds of bad luck.

Another famous spider tale is that related of Mahomet when he fled from Mecca and hid in a cave. The Koreishites who were on his heels failed to discover him because fate interfered. An acacia in full bloom sprang up at the mouth of the cave, and a spider's web, that had previously been built between the tree and the cave, completely closed the entrance. When the Koreishites reached the cave and saw the spider's web, they concluded that no one could have entered recently and they went on their way. And so, Mohammedans everywhere still have a great deal of respect for the spider and keep it alive, as it means good fortune to have it around.

The Pawnee Indians, formerly living along the Platte River in Nebraska and now settled on the Indian Reservation in Oklahoma, have a spider goddess, their Earth Mother of fertility. Like all primitive peoples, the American Indians made use of the webbed hoop, patterned after the spider's web. The Pawnees even used the webbed hoop for catching buffaloes. This netted spider-web hoop was adapted to many purposes, including simple games of dexterity such as cat's cradle of which there are many forms. The Zuni Indians of New Mexico say that the game was taught by their grandmother, the Spider, to her grandsons, the Twin War Gods. Another Indian derivation of the spider web is the lacrosse stick, used in a game played largely in Canada.

Scientists claim that spiders have inhabited the earth for about thirty million years. Although they are more abundant and diversified in the tropics, they are found everywhere, and include twenty to forty thousand different species. Small spiders have been found in the Himalaya Mountains in India at an altitude of more than 22,000 feet. These spiders live on rocks, surrounded by snow and nearly a mile above the last vegetable or animal life. How they subsist is unknown.

In America in 1920, it was officially reported in a test flight by Major Rudolph W. Shroeder, that spiders were encountered seven and a half miles above the earth. Millions of baby spiders swarmed in a temperature of 67 degrees below zero, proving their hardiness, to say the least!

There are sky-spiders, water spiders, bird spiders and others. Although the spider has eight eyes, it is near-sighted and its eyes are of no special use as far as catching its prey is concerned. A spider's eyes have a strange quality similar to that of cats, which causes them to shine in the dark. These eyes are beckoning beacons, as it were—Nature's subtle way of guiding insects into the spider's web, as suggested by the nursery rhyme: " 'Will you walk into my parlor,' said the spider to the fly."

"Mistletoe" Superstitions

KISSING UNDER the mistletoe is a very ancient custom. However, depending on the various rôles that this parasitic plant has played in the legends and mythologies of different peoples, it is both a golden bough and a villain.

The origin of kissing under the mistletoe is generally attributed to the ancient Scandinavians. One very popular legend associates the mistletoe with Baldur, god of the Sun and god of Justice. His mother, Frigga, after whom Friday was named, was the goddess of the Sky, and presided over love, marriage and domestic affairs. She undertook to get all living creatures as well as inanimate things to swear that they would not harm Baldur.

By some mistake, however, she overlooked the mistletoe, which took no such oath. Loki, god of Evil and Jealousy, after due conniving, found this out, and fashioned an arrow of mistletoe, which he ordered Hodur, the blind god of Darkness and reputedly Baldur's twin brother, to shoot at the sun-god. It pierced Baldur's heart and killed him.

Frigga wept bitter tears at the tragedy and when these tears turned into pearls as they fell on the mistletoe, Baldur came back to life. Frigga, in gratitude, then placed the mistletoe under her protection to prevent its ever again being employed as an instrument of evil.

In this legend, the kiss under the mistletoe symbolizes the assurance that the goddess of love and marriage will never permit lovers to be harmed.

In later legends, the mistletoe is said to have been created by the falling tears of Venus when she was accidentally wounded by one of Cupid's arrows.

Many superstitions about the mistletoe survive. An unmarried woman who is *not* kissed while she stands under it will not marry for another year; and any woman who refuses to be kissed under the mistletoe will die an old maid.

It was once believed that the first single man who walked under the mistletoe would marry the daughter of the house. Mistletoe was formerly considered effective against epilepsy and convulsions. Some persons still keep a few berries in a sachet, from Christmas to Christmas, to ward off diseases and all other misfortunes. If the sachet is worn around the neck, the mistletoe berries are supposed to serve as a specific against sterility, and as an antidote against poisons.

If a girl is kissed seven times under the mistletoe in one day, she will marry within the year—obviously! There was an old custom that as each young man kissed a girl, he would pluck a berry from the mistletoe, and when the last berry was gone, there could be no more kissing.

The Druids regarded the mistletoe as a sacred plant, and handled it with great reverence because of its mysterious birth. It held an important place in their ceremonies. When the first growth was discovered, especially on the oak tree, a tree sacred to them, it was gathered by white-robed priests, who cut it from the main bough with a golden sickle which was never used for any other purpose. The mistletoe was never allowed to touch the ground. Hence the reason for hanging it even today.

The Druids hung mistletoe over their doorways, believing that only happiness could enter a house so protected, and it was credited with curative powers in the homes where it was hung.

Pliny records that the Druidic name for mistletoe meant "heal all," or "all heal." He also said that it was considered good "*conceptum foeminarum adjuvare, si omnio secum habeant,*" (to aid conception on the part of women, if they have a little of it with them). It was kept in the home of a married couple.

Since the Druids were sun-worshippers, at their equivalent to our Christmas, or the return of the sun in the north, they observed the custom of greeting people under the mistletoe as a sign of good will and friendship. The mistletoe was a solar symbol to the Druids; its white berries representing radiance from heaven. They hung a spray of the plant generally in the center of the main room, and felt that no Evil Eye nor evil influences could enter the premises.

Mistletoe is now associated with the frivolous side of Christmas, but originally it was symbolic of serious and sacred matters.

Ancient Phoenician mythology is another source of mistletoe symbolism. There is the story that this early people compelled a married woman, if, after a reasonable time, she remained sterile and without child, to have relations with a stranger once in her lifetime. The meeting took place in the temple of the goddess of love and fertility, Mylitta —similar to Venus. The woman sat under a sprig of mistletoe, and the stranger who saw her there greeted her with a kiss and then invited her into an alcove. The fee for the service contributed to the upkeep of the temple of Mylitta, in gratitude for the respective favors received. For a long time one of the botanical names of the mistletoe in ancient times was Mylitta, reminiscent of the Phoenician goddess who bestowed fertility upon those who met under the mistletoe.

In the early Christian church it was customary, at Christmas time, to bestow the "kiss of peace," to spread good-will and friendship toward all. The act of kissing and the mistletoe plant have become interwoven symbols of romance, scarcely ever absent from Christmas festivities today.

"Ivy" Superstitions

SOME CLAIM that ivy is a lucky plant and others think the opposite. This same conflict in the superstitious interpretation of the plant was expressed in ancient times, which accounts for the modern attitude, as most superstitions were born in past ages.

Several current superstitions which show the ivy's dual role may be mentioned. Some persons think it is unlucky to have it in the house. A gift of an ivy plant will break friendship and implies misfortune to the one who receives it, if not something more ominous—a death in the family. Others like to have ivy growing indoors and believe that it is an auspicious plant and graciously receive it for a gift.

If ivy does not thrive on a grave it is believed to signify that the soul of the one buried is uneasy in the other world. If it grows profusely on the grave of a young woman who died prematurely, it means that a secret love-sickness took her away. Ivy is thought by many to be unlucky for the planter but lucky for the one over whose house or walls it creeps.

Once upon a time there were symbols with which to express the character of certain plants. Holly and ivy, for instance, were made male and female symbols respectively, and were displayed in the home at a special time of the year to welcome the return of the sun. This custom still obtains at our Christmas time. As both holly and ivy are evergreens, holly symbolized the master of the house, and ivy the mistress. Holly is a steadfast, sedate and holy plant, supposedly masculine qualities; whereas ivy is prolific and represented fertility, as well as unpredictableness, female attributes. Ivy, believed to be a riotous plant, was used with great caution and always under proper auspices. In Egypt, Greece and Rome, ivy was under the protection of tree-god spirits, or gods of vegetation, under various names according to the pagan beliefs of each country.

A wreath of ivy was the prize at the Isthmian Greek games at Corinth, until it was replaced by another evergreen garland. Ivy was dedicated to Bacchus, Roman god of Wine, and a drink made from the berries of this plant was believed to be an antidote for poison and able to check inebriety. A custom observed anciently and at the present time is to have a garland or bush of ivy in front of a tavern or inn to indicate that spirituous liquors are sold within.

Most of the favorable implications in regard to ivy, a plant once sacred to many peoples, were lost when it became the custom to plant it on graves and cemetery walls. The choice of this vine goes back to the superstitious association of an evergreen with immortality in the Middle Ages. However, because of the natural tendency among superstitious persons to relate "like with like," ivy in cemeteries meant contact with death, or gloom and doom, so that ivy acquired the unlucky side of superstition.

There are many old wives' cures for poison ivy, and one of them is to carry a wild cherry or elderberry in the pocket so that if one touched some poison ivy, it would have no effect, no matter how sensitive one might be.

Rubber Plants or Trees in the House, Unlucky!

RUBBER PLANTS or trees, growing indoors, are generally looked upon as unlucky for the occupants of the house. This attitude is especially noticeable in the colder areas of the northern part of North America. As a matter of fact, this species of plant often dies when kept in homes, and there are many reasons why this happens. The main cause, of course, is that the rubber plant or tree, originally the product of tropical and semi-tropical regions, does not thrive in changeable and colder climes, and is allergic to chill. They wither and die in steam-heated or artificially heated rooms where the temperature varies—not because they are unlucky plants!

There is also a superstition that a snake plant is unlucky. However, there are also those who feel that because the plant is hardy and needs little attention and yet thrives, it is lucky to have in the house.

Anything that withers and dies prematurely, especially if there is a convenient misfortune to couple with the event, has always been interpreted by primitive and civilized peoples alike to mean a catastrophe of some sort, and even death. And should the same ill fortune or tragedy be repeated, the belief becomes not only stronger, but from then on is looked upon as an absolute fact. Hence the superstition!

Acorn Superstitions

CARRYING AN ACORN for general good luck, or especially to keep off disease and insure a long life, may seem odd to some, but this fruit of the oak tree is a much sought after lucky charm by thousands of persons.

Today little acorns of gold, silver or other material, including plastics, are designed to be used as lucky pieces on bracelets, or for other ornamental purposes, by those who still believe that it holds magic properties in keeping with the traditional superstitions handed down through the ages.

In times long past, the acorn was under the protection of Cybele, the goddess of Nature, and sacred to her. This deity was worshipped by the people of Anatolia, in Asia Minor.

In ancient Scandinavia, it was seriously believed that the oak belonged to Thor, the Thunder god. This tree was therefore under the protection of this powerful super-god who controlled both thunder and lightning. As lightning was thought to strike or enter a house through the window, an acorn was placed there to protect the premises. It was believed that Thor, pleased with this expression of respect to him, would in return spare the house that displayed his own symbol.

The acorn, because of its shape, has been looked upon as a phallic symbol of the male generative organ, and was a powerful charm against all sorts of dangers. Wherever the acorn was displayed, it was expected that life would continue uninterruptedly, symbolic of the male keeping the family line alive through a chain of successive births.

Oddly enough, the little knobs or tassel-ends on window shades were once real dried acorns, over which practical but superstitious house-wives crocheted or knitted covers. They attached them to a cord to pull the shade up or down. In time, real acorns were replaced by wooden ones.

The circle has also been used as a tassel-end, and still is, for that matter. The twin symbols of the circle and acorn, representing male and female generative power, when used in the house, made the home safe from all possible dangers and assured an unbroken family line for all time.

"Hay" Superstitions

To SEE A LOAD OF HAY and make a wish immediately is still considered a lucky incident by superstitious country and city folk alike. If the hay is baled, the wish that has been made is not expected to come true until the bales have been broken.

There are other hay superstitions. When seeing a "hay wagon," count thirteen and make a wish, and then turn away so as not to see the load of hay again. If you accidentally see it, your wish will not be granted. If you fail to make a wish when you see some hay, it means that a serious sickness or even death will ensue. If you see a load of hay pass, and you make a wish, you must not say a word to anyone until someone asks you a question that you can answer with the word, "yes." This will surely make the wish come true.

To steal hay the night before Christmas, and give it to the cattle, will make them thrive better. As a matter of fact, bunches of hay are often put conveniently aside for neighbors to help themselves to, but no one mentions it.

Hay superstitions are probably as old as agriculture itself. In early times, there is no doubt that hay symbolized a good harvest, which provided for the welfare of the cattle as well as the cattle-keepers themselves.

Primitive psychology derived its peculiar logic from the principle of "wishful thinking." Therefore, the making of a wish while looking at or touching something identified with prosperity or other good fortune made early man expect the realization of the wish, as, according to sympathetic magic, like brings like.

Planting a Tree or Other Plant at Birth

MANY PERSONS still observe the superstitious custom of planting a tree or other plant at the birth of a child, mentally associating the little new life with the health and growth of the plant. Whether the plant flourishes or withers is supposed to foretell the infant's chances for or against health and long life.

This custom is purely sentimental and the result of thousands of years of legendary tales which have not yet died out. As there is no scientific relation between a human being's health span and the growth of a tree or plant, this superstition is rather dangerous because of the fears it may instil in the minds of the parents.

However, the planting of an evergreen at the birth of a child has been in favor since time immemorial because the evergreen character of the tree symbolized long life. An evergreen was believed to be a favorite of the gods, particularly spring gods who watched over mortals. Because of its pleasant aroma, the pine tree was especially revered. Its phallic-shaped cone added to its sanctity as symbolic of the life-generative force.

That the tree is related to human life and is the progenitor of the human race is a very old belief. We have the "Tree of Life" in the Bible, in the Eddas, in Iranian mythology, among Sioux Indian legends as well as among other ancient and primitive peoples. The classical idea was that human beings are the fruit of the tree.

Folklore and mythology contain many fascinating stories about trees in connection with birth. Rhea gave birth to Zeus beneath a poplar tree in Crete. Hera was born and brought up under a willow tree in Samos. Leta gave birth to Apollo and Artemis while clasping two trees on the island of Delos. Some authorities say these were an olive and a palm tree. Others, with the idea that Apollo must have been born at the foot of his own particular tree, declare these trees were laurels. Romulus and Remus were found under a fig tree near the Tiber.

In Hindu mythology, Vishnu was born in the shade of the banyan, and Buddha was born and died under a sâl-tree.

The term "family tree" is a modern application of the association of humans and trees.

Knocking on Wood Superstitions

PRACTICALLY EVERYONE subscribes to the primitive and still almost universal superstition of touching wood. The gesture is made to prevent ill fortune, or reverse action, following a boastful statement of one's accomplishments or good fortune, or after an expression of exultation of some kind. Knocking on wood just once is generally in order, but to be on the safe side of Lady Luck, superstitious persons believe that knocking three times increases the chances of avoiding the bad luck.

All wood comes from trees, and it is in the folklore of trees that we find the probable origin of this superstition. Some trees change with the seasons, while others are evergreens. Therefore trees which expressed the seasons were believed to possess a supernatural nature which affected these transformations—symbols of life, death and resurrection. The evergreens symbolized immortality.

All trees, however, were thought to be the abodes of gods, who brought on the seasonal changes in the trees, or kept them in an evergreen state. These supernatural beings were believed kindly, when properly approached, and well-disposed to protect those who contacted them. The tree, or wood, was touched when asking favors, and touched again in appreciation of favors received.

The ancient Egyptians thoroughly endorsed the belief that the evergreen was the symbol of everlasting life. They used small pillows of balsam needles to sleep on, as we do today, although we are not aware of the long history of the custom. It was believed that when the body ceased to function, meaning death, the spirit was liberated, and the symbolic protective evergreen balsam needles acted as sponsors to the land of everlasting bliss.

All through the centuries, wood has been touched for different reasons, and objects of wood, shaped to meet the belief of the superstitious, have assumed many forms. For instance, medieval Christians wore pendant wooden crosses, and touched them in reverent apology when they caught themselves boasting to remind themselves of a sense of humility, in keeping with the humble ways of Christ Who was crucified on a wooden cross.

Others, believing that unseen supernatural beings were always about, jealous of the happiness or success of mankind, knocked on wood so that these kill-joys could not hear any good news. These naive notions were regarded as reality in the not so very long ago.

Touching a chair or other article of wood that is close at hand has become so much a part of everyday life that it is done quite automatically, seemingly without thinking, by most persons. Fanatics on the subject usually look for plain wood, without paint or varnish on it, so that when they touch it, they will be in closer contact with the wood —or tree.

We still have evidence of the belief in the invulnerability of the tree, as handed down from primitive tree-worship, when we see children playing the old game of "tree-tag," or "wood-tag," in which, when the wood base is touched, the player is safe from capture.

There are other interpretations of the practice of knocking on wood. One version is coupled with the old proverb, "He that talks much of happiness, summons grief." That things work or happen in reverse is a deep-rooted notion in the mind of man, closely related to the birth of many of his ideas. Touching wood as a charm-gesture is founded on this presumption, so that it will prevent joy from turning into sorrow. This reminds us of a corresponding saying, also allied to the theory of things being equalled by the opposite: "There is always a silver lining to a dark cloud."

In the barren parts of Tibet, no wood to speak of can be found, and so, in the distant past, the natives evolved a primitive rosary made of wood gotten from afar, so that a bit of a tree might be touched although the woods were far away.

In the study of folklore and allegorical designs, woman is the Rose, in all secret symbology. Woman's fruit is the apple which grew on the Tree of Knowledge in the Garden of Eden. Botanically, the apple belongs to the rose family, the seed-pod of the rose being in reality a kind of apple. This explains the fact that the origin of the Rosary, used in prayer today by peoples of many races and creeds, stems from the belief that life flowed through the navel, the connecting link between woman and the life-line, or umbilical cord. Early man thought the navel a spiral *rose* of flesh, not a scar as we know it to be, and believed it to be the area for the extension of life's forces and spiritual enfoldment. The Rosary with its rose beads was carved out of wood from special trees, and was, and still is, touched when asking favors or when giving thanks for favors granted.

CHAPTER 3

Cursed Among Women

Traditional Superstitions of the Snake

THE TRADITION of the snake as the symbol of Evil is of such great antiquity that its origin is uncertain. We are all familiar with the story of the temptation of Eve in the Garden of Eden. However, the symbol of the snake also appears with other meanings. A snake ring is presumed to bring the wearer long life and good health. The symbol of medicine, the Caduceus, with two snakes entwining the rod of harmony, representing healing, was the emblem of the god, Mercury.

In ancient Egypt, the serpent was both worshipped and hated. Because of its longevity, it symbolized old age and wisdom. When depicted with its tail in its mouth, it formed the Circle, symbol of Eternity.

The ability of the snake to cast off its old skin, or molt, perhaps led to the belief in its immortality. This characteristic, plus the fear produced by the deadliness of many poisonous snakes in the country, led to the development of the snake cult and snake worship in India.

Even more widespread was the belief in transmigration, that is, that the souls of the dead appeared in snake form, and therefore it should not be killed. This belief was common in South Africa and in ancient Greece, as well as in India. There followed from this the belief in the supernatural powers of the snake. Many myths and legends exist in which a serpent has the power to confer upon certain men the ability to understand the language of animals. There is an active snake cult in America, even today.

In medieval legends, the snake is turned into a dragon, usually the guardian of some important treasure, and represents the forces of evil, which had to be overpowered and slain by the young knight representing courage and purity of soul.

The snake is a phallic symbol, denoting the male generative organ. Through the centuries, man's imagination has been inspired to glorify or villify this member of the animal kingdom with weird symbols, myths and powers.

Misconceptions as to the Actions of Snakes

THERE ARE many common superstitions connected with the behavior and habits of snakes. For instance, the popular belief that a snake jumps off the ground to strike its victim is a fallacy. The reason for thinking so is due to an optical illusion, which is produced when the snake's coils or S-curves straighten out to strike, but actually its body never leaves the ground completely. The distance attained in a stroke is never its full length, but generally about three-quarters of its length.

It is also erroneous to think that a snake must be coiled before it can strike. Observation has revealed that when irritated, most poisonous snakes can strike as well uncoiled from almost any position at not too great a distance. The diamond-back rattler of the western part of the United States, when excited, frequently raises its head, and makes an S-shaped loop ten or fifteen inches above the ground, from which position it strikes sideways and downward.

Most persons are under the false impression that a snake crawls, whereas it literally "walks" on the ends of its ribs. A snake's ribs are joined to the backbone, like other vertebrates, and as they extend around either side of the body, their ends articulate with the outside ventral plates. The ends of the ribs run in a series almost the full length of the snake's "belly" side, and have projecting edges at the rear margin. As the plates come in contact with rocks, and other uneven surfaces underneath the snake, its body is brought forward by muscular movement upon the supporting and movable ribs.

This method of locomotion is the reason why snakes cannot "run" on glass nor over a brussels carpet or other very flat surface. Glass is so smooth that the ventral plates are unable to take hold. After they have been thrown before the snake, it cannot carry itself along on them.

The ancient peoples who used snakes in their divinatory ceremonies and snake-cult rituals must have known exactly how snakes move, and at such times they employed smooth surfaces to keep serpents from getting away during the performance. This quiet attitude and forced attention of the snakes was explained to the ignorant participants in the rituals to mean that the snakes reverently remained on the spot because they understood that the activities were in their honor. It stands to reason that since they were rendered quite helpless by the smooth surface under them, these snakes were not able to strike either.

Another mistaken idea is that snakes, when crawling at a slow pace, travel in zigzag fashion; in reality they go in a perfectly straight line.

The Fear of Snakes

A SUPERSTITIOUS FEAR of snakes is felt by millions, especially in the western world. Before children have been told the story of the Garden of Eden and the serpent, or other early legends about the deadliness and viciousness of snakes, they are no more afraid of them than of animals in general. The common dread of snakes, therefore, is a good example of "emotional conditioning."

Evidence points to the fact that the fear of this species of reptile is not instinctive nor inherited, but due to misstatements about them, which usually leave disturbing and lasting impressions on children's minds, and are carried over into adulthood.

Although apes and monkeys seem to have an innate fear of serpents of all kinds, man should be free of it, as much of it is unwarranted. Snakes are nervous and easily frightened, and only bite in self-defense. They will fight only after bluffing, or wiggling, when their chances of escape have failed. Of the one hundred ten species of snakes in the United States, only four are poisonous: the cottonmouth moccasin, coral snake, copperhead and rattlesnake. In spite of claims to the contrary, snake venom is fatal to other snakes, and rattlesnakes can kill each other.

The fear of snakes has created such a repulsive impression in the minds of people that it has been almost impossible to popularize it as a food. Snakes are just as clean and edible as lobsters or oysters, if not more so. However, canned rattlesnake meat is gradually appealing to the palates of Americans who now consume quantities of it annually.

That "Glass" Snakes Break into Pieces

THE SUPERSTITION that "glass" snakes can be broken into pieces, and reassemble themselves again, is definitely untrue. Nor is it possible for each piece to grow into another snake, as is sometimes believed.

This myth probably arose from the fact that what is often taken for a snake is in reality a "legless lizard," found in various parts of America. This reptile has the ability, when caught, to wriggle itself out of the hand of its captor, and run away, parting with its tail in the act. It is not true that this so-called "glass" snake returns to recover its tail and replace it on its body. However, strange to say, when left alone, it can actually grow a new tail, although the second one is rarely as long as the first.

The "glass" snake or lizard belongs to the genus *Ophisaurus ventralis*. It is covered with hard, shingle-like plates, that give it a very shiny or glassy appearance. When struck with a stick, it often breaks into several pieces, but as a rule, it only breaks into two pieces, when the body and tail are separated. This is a common happening in the life of this type of lizard, and naturalists are quite familiar with it.

All snakes are descended from lizards, but now, only lizards have the protective measure to detach their tails when in trouble. Snakes themselves lost this privilege during their evolutionary process.

That the Age of a Rattlesnake Can Be Told by its Rattles

THE NUMBER OF RINGS on the rattle does not tell the age of a rattlesnake, as is generally believed. Normally, one ring is added each time the snake sheds its skin. Although it varies, a snake may shed its skin three times a year.

The reason it is not possible to tell the age of a rattler is because, after it has grown to a certain length, and reached its third or fourth year, the end rings are frequently broken off. From the button or initial stub, however, which sometimes remains, a fair estimate of the snake's age may be made by counting a year for every three rings.

More than twelve rings are rare because the frequent rapid vibrations of the button or rattle cause them either to wear out or break off. That is why the accurate age of a rattlesnake cannot be determined by the remaining rings, as there is no way of guessing how many might have been formed in all.

The young rattlesnake has no rattle, but it begins to add one horny ring to the button the first year, and each time it sheds its slough, a new ring is exposed. This ring is formed under the skin at the base of the rattle. The rattle, itself, is a horny appendage composed of loosely fitted rings. It does not contain "beads" as is commonly believed. The whole tail vibrates rapidly when the snake is agitated and is sounding a warning, and at the same time, the loosely fitted rings rattle shrilly to create the horrifying sound which tells that a rattlesnake is near.

That a Rattlesnake Always Gives Warning

THE COMMON NOTION that a rattlesnake always gives warning before it strikes is a very dangerous superstition. Zoologists, themselves, are not too sure that the sound of the rattle is intended as a warning.

The truth of the matter is that a rattlesnake, like all snakes, is subject to a nervous reaction to fear, and when frightened, it will shake its tail, and the rattles which are attached to it may then be heard. On the other hand, when a rattler is taken by surprise, and has not time to shake its tail, it will strike its victim instantly, without warning.

Darwin and other scientists, including herpetologists, who specialized in the study of reptiles to learn their structure, habits and classifications, have been inclined to conclude that the rattle on this type of snake are an appendage which is used in summoning a mate, as well as to let enemy snakes know that a rattlesnake is around.

Snakes Are Not Charmed by Music

DESPITE THE ADAGE, "Music hath charms to soothe the savage breast," experiments have proved that snakes do not respond to music. The famous snake "charmers" of India produce the swaying movement in their snakes, not by the music of their flutes, but by the motion of their hands and heads which the snakes follow, awaiting the moment to strike when the action has ceased.

Experiments have been conducted to study the effect of music on snakes, and the consensus of opinion is that music, as such, does not affect them. The ears of reptiles are crude organs, deeply embedded, and the chances are that snakes feel the vibrations of sound, through the surface of their sensitive scales, rather than that they hear with their ears. Nervous snakes, cobras in particular, seem to be quite susceptible to certain vibrations.

It is true that often a cobra can be enticed out of its hiding place, and captured by means of the musical notes played by these so-called "charmers," but this is usually part of a professional act. There is no doubt that these professional snake charmers do produce remarkable effects upon the cobra through certain vibrations from their strains of music.

In the case of the cobra, its response to music has been both endorsed and denied by men of science, who have seen these creatures rendered momentarily helpless by certain sounds. It must be assumed, however, that certain vibrations may be pitched so stridently, that they cause the reptile to sway slightly for a few minutes, and then fall forward as though knocked out.

The human being is greatly irritated by particular sounds, and these same sounds may make the snake groggy and then helpless. This reaction of the snake to an irritating musical sound remains a mystery, but there is no doubt that it is not "soothed" by it.

The Hindus have inherited the experience of centuries in handling snakes, a fact that is full of mystery to those elsewhere. Orientals learned about the habits of snakes through necessity, as a self-protective measure. Later they made use of their knowledge and keen observations in various ways, among them in the art of entertainment.

Hindu and Arab performers keep the secret of snake-charming to themselves, or within the family circle, so that the public believes them to be miracle workers. There is no doubt that these entertainers know how to produce the exact pitch to which a snake will sway, or give the illusion of dancing, but it is not the music itself to which the beast responds.

That Snakes "Hypnotize" Birds

THE SUPERSTITIOUS BELIEF that snakes possess the power to "charm" birds, small animals or even human beings, by means of their hypnotic gaze, probably arose from observing their habit of remaining motionless with lifted head and eyes fixed, trance-like, for long and short spaces of time.

There is no snake that can charm or hypnotize persons or birds. However, this legend is believed not only in Asia, where snakes are found in great numbers, but also by American Indians. It is still widely believed in both Europe and America today.

Whether snakes paralyze their victims with a hypnotic stare has been the subject for much experimentation over the years, with no evidence as yet to support the theory. No snake possesses the occult power of fascination with which superstitious persons have endowed it. What appears to be an act of "charming" a victim by an immobile snake is either its own natural reaction to fear, or just plain indifference. Far from being hypnotized, many birds attempt to decoy snakes from their nests by fluttering about, and what is more, they often succeed.

Even when birds are purposely put in cages with snakes at the zoo, neither the birds nor the snakes show any signs that it makes much difference to either of them that they are enclosed together in small quarters. No proof is yet at hand that, in such circumstances, snakes ever "charmed" their future victims—this part of their menu having been prepared by the keeper himself.

Snake Venom Facts and Superstitions

THE SNAKE CULT, also part of the modern scene in America, evolved from many superstitious beliefs. Among them is the notion that through some supernatural dispensation, one can be bitten by a poisonous snake, and at times thereafter be immune from the deadly venom.

There have been cases among primitive peoples where the bite of a venomous snake was not fatal. From observing these exceptional instances, the conclusion was probably reached that while most persons died from the bite of a poisonous snake, others survived, who, therefore, must possess magical powers of immunity. It was also noted, in the tribe, that repeated bites from venomous snakes lost their effect on the system, and sometimes resulted in complete immunity.

In time, inoculation with snake venom was employed as an antidote to snake bite, although at first it was not done with the scientific knowledge we have on the subject today.

In the long, long ago, as well as in recent times, Mexican Indians frequently inoculated themselves with rattlesnake poison for various reasons. Immunization ceremonies in which rattlesnake poison was injected into the bodies of young men, in small doses and at repeated intervals, were a common practice. The injections were given by the *shaman*, or medicine man or witch doctor. The purpose of this inoculation was to permit these young lads to become sufficiently immunized against blood-poisoning so that they could handle, without danger, all poisonous animals, including rattlesnakes.

The Mexican Indians believed that the bite of persons who had been treated in the immunization ceremonies, could infect others—a purely superstitious notion. These young men, naturally, were left severely alone. This belief remains prevalent in many places, although it has no basis in fact.

The custom of using snake venom is still in effect in both India and Africa. Methods vary, but the purpose is usually to build up immunity to poisonous bites.

Wherever venomous snakes are found among primitive tribes, the natives use snake venom as an antidote, and the snakes themselves are a part of ritual ceremonies. We are indebted to these simple-minded peoples for valuable clues that have led to important discoveries for mankind, such as the use of snake venom to save a life once doomed by snake bite.

That Snakes Roll into a Hoop, or Sting with Their Tails

A FAMILIAR SUPERSTITION of today, that snakes can put their tails in their mouths and roll away like a hoop, is a very ancient belief. However, it is incorrect to think that a "hoop" or horn snake can roll after persons, or roll away from its pursuer. The peculiarities of the vertebral column of snakes make this feat impossible. The snake's skeleton is marvelously flexible from side to side, but to bring the tail around to the mouth in a circle would fracture at least two or three vertebrae.

The belief in "hoop" snakes is a world-wide myth, and it is strange how many people still believe that this creature will imperil anyone in its path, as it lets go of its tail and drives the stinger into its victim, thereby causing death.

In America, especially, it is believed by a great many that the "hoop" snake has a venomous and deadly sting in its tail, that works like that of a wasp or scorpion, as it leaps angrily at its victim.

The little snake known as the "hoop" snake or horn snake is harmless. Still, there are those who believe that it inflates itself and becomes luminous at night, as a warning to those who fear it. Others think that it squirts a venomous fluid from its tail. All these myths have made the little "hoop" or horn snake very unpopular; its unearned bad reputation having been circulated from one generation to another.

There is, on the other hand, a dwarf boa snake which rolls itself into a ball, and one can play ball with it without making it unwind; but it does not have the ability to roll to and from places.

Another odd superstition in connection with snakes is that when a tree is seen to wither and die for no apparent reason, some persons will say that an infuriated snake must have struck it and injured the bark so badly that it died from the snake's tail-sting blow.

In America there is a mud snake which has the terminal scale of its tail enlarged to form a hard, sharp spine. Naturally, a careless or unknowing person who handles the mud snake may prick his skin. Even so, the injury does not poison or kill anyone, as this is a harmless species of snake.

Nearly all notions about "hoop" snakes stem from the old superstitious belief which associated coiled snakes of any species with the "magic circle," a sacred symbol of ancient times. From time immemorial, the similarity of the coil to the circle made snakes sacred also, an attitude largely responsible for the snake cults of antiquity. Also, the fact that snakes shed their skins symbolized regeneration or immortality to the ancients.

Apollo, the handsome Greek god, had a high regard for snake symbols. Among his many attributes, he was also the god of prophecy, and used the snake as a symbol of that power.

That Snakes Are Slimy

THOSE WHO HAVE an ingrained horror of snakes in general are upset at the very thought of them, and shudder to touch or handle them because they say they are "cold" and "slimy."

Others think that if they touch a snake it will poison them, or at least cause an irritation of the skin. Fear of snakes leads others to believe that if they come in close contact with these strange creatures, they will have nightmares with snakes in them.

Much of the aversion to touching a snake is purely psychological, so that seemingly shiny scales are assumed to be slimy.

Because a snake is cold-blooded, its body temperature is never much higher than that of the surrounding environment. Therefore, a snake is apt to feel cold or "clammy" to our touch, by contrast to our own body temperature. However, a snake is never slimy—it only seems so.

That a Snake Is Safe After Losing Its Fangs

A MOST DANGEROUS superstition for those who are not acquainted with the facts is to think that once the poison fangs of a snake have been removed, it is safe to handle it.

This misconception is due to not knowing that it is not the fangs alone that convey the poison. The fact is that no matter how many times the fangs are extracted, other fangs will soon grow in their place.

Nature has provided the rattlesnake with a magazine of fangs that is practically inexhaustible. Normally, rattlesnakes shed their fangs twice a year. These snakes are relatively harmless for only a very short time between the loss of the old fangs and the growth of the new ones, which are as deadly as the first set.

In order to render venomous snakes permanently harmless, it is necessary to remove not only the fangs, but also a portion of the bone to which they are attached, an operation which very few care to perform.

Whip or Coachwhip Snake Superstitions

A CURIOUS SUPERSTITION, very prevalent years ago among Indians and Negroes in America, and still believed by many white persons, relates to the whip snake or coachwhip snake and its supposed evil behavior. The belief is that they attack human beings with their long tapering tails, and whip or lash their victims to death. This species of snake is commonly found in the southern and southwestern parts of the United States.

As this is one of the few snakes that can outrun a man, the superstitious person thinks, therefore, that if a whip snake is after him he has little chance, as the reptile will first wrap itself around the leg or body of its victim and then proceed to lash him to death with its tail.

Actually, the whip snake is quite harmless to human beings. All evidence gathered so far merely shows that instead of running after, or attacking a person, it tries to get away from him as fast as it can.

The origin of this odd superstition may possibly have been that landowners spread the myth as a convenient form of warning to keep their superstitious slaves from straying from the plantation at night.

Superstitions About Snake Stings

> *"And when they from thy bosom pluck a flower*
> *Guard it, I pray thee, with a lurking adder*
> *Whose double tongue may with a mortal touch*
> *Throw death upon thy sovereign's enemies."*

THE SUPERSTITIOUS NOTION that a snake stings with its flickering, double or forked tongue, is a very ancient belief, indulged in by a large number of persons today. Others believe the equally erroneous idea that the snake has a posterior stinger like that of a bee.

These have been convictions in the minds, and expressed in the writings, of many people over the centuries. The above quotation from Richard II is only one among many similar allusions in Shakespeare's works. Milton, too, believed and wrote about the snake using a tail-end stinger, as did Chaucer; while in the Bible, both the tongue and tail end of the snake are referred to as having the power to sting.

However, snakes do not sting. They bite with their fangs. The continual darting motion of the tongue has led to the idea that it was used in stinging. Why the reptile uses its tongue in this way is not known, but it is presumed that this organ has a sensory function enabling the snake to feel its way over the ground. The tongue is probably sensitive to smells as well as to vibrations.

It is not true either, that a snake will sting itself when cornered and about to be captured, knowing that it cannot escape.

That Snakes Swallow Their Young

THE BELIEF that snakes swallow their young in times of danger to protect them, and then bring them up again, is pure superstition. Not all snakes lay eggs, and the finding of baby snakes inside the body of the mother may have led to this supposition, since snakes, when born, possess all formations of the full grown snake, including poison fangs.

It is known that large snakes sometimes swallow snakes of another species, for food. The cannibal king snake, for instance, will eat a whole litter of snakelets if he can find it. Young snakes have been known to run into the mouth of their mother in time of danger, but they are not swallowed. If they were, the babies would hardly be recognizable when they came out.

That Snakes Travel in Pairs

THAT SNAKES TRAVEL in pairs is an unfounded superstitious belief. This idea probably arose from the fact that venomous as well as harmless snakes are to be seen in the same vicinity. It is also a fallacy that the mate of a snake that has been slain will eventually get revenge on its slayer.

None of the stories about the mate of a snake having taken revenge has ever been substantiated. However, it is known that the mate may be seen near or at the spot where the dead one lies, because its sense of smell leads it there—but certainly not for sentimental or vengeful reasons.

Mystery and detective stories with an Asiatic background have been one source of these notions. Oriental villains, as a method of murder, sometimes placed deadly snakes where their unsuspecting victim was sure to be bitten. In such cases, two snakes are usually found—a dead one that has been purposely killed and placed there as a decoy, and the other, the killer-snake. This is a murderer's trick to cover up his tracks and befuddle his pursuers. However, there is not a word of truth that the live snake found at the scene of the crime is there on a revenge mission, for a departed mate.

That Snakes Will Not Crawl Over a Hair Rope

IT IS A COMMON superstition out west that rattlesnakes will not cross over a horsehair or cowhair rope. In the pioneer days, the American cowboy, rancher or prospector, often had to sleep on the ground, and so, of course, he was exposed to the approach and bite of the rattlesnake. To protect himself, he placed his rope or lariat around his blanket, feeling safe in the belief that snakes would not cross the circle of hair rope, and do him harm. The probable reason for the one sleeping on the ground not being bitten is that snakes do not generally attack. The magic circle of hair rope may have given the sleeper faith, but nothing else in the way of protection.

To surround oneself with a symbolic circle as a charm and protection against danger is a very ancient superstition. However, the contrary has been proved in experiments using horsehair hoops or ropes. Rattlesnakes as well as other species will crawl in and out of a horsehair rope, instead of going around it. There is no protection against a venomous snake except to be out of reach.

CHAPTER 4

Denizens of the Deep

"Fishing" Superstitions

When the wind is in the East,
Then the fishes bite the least;
When the wind is in the West,
Then the fishes bite the best;
When the wind is in the North,
Then the fishes do come forth;
When the wind is in the South,
It blows the bait in the fish's mouth.

FISHERMEN are a superstitious lot, and this has always been so. Many sportsmen believe it is lucky to throw the first fish they catch back into the water. Expectorating on the bait will bring good luck, because saliva is considered a potent charm. It is unlucky to bait a hook with the left hand. It is unwise to tell anyone how many fish you have caught, while you are fishing, lest you do not catch another fish. It is unlucky to change fishing poles while fishing. There are hundreds more.

In New England there is an odd superstition that if you see a cross-eyed person it is bad luck. The countercharm is to spit in one's hat. Many fishermen insert a coin in the cork floats as an offering to the sea, in order to get a good catch.

"Fisherman's luck" has come to be dependent upon many ancient practices that stem from the primitive method of propitiating unseen spirits who were believed to be in charge of fishing activities. For instance, the Forked River Tuna Club of New Jersey has a fisherman's shrine, and no member dares to neglect to follow the traditional lucky formula of hanging a fish on a tree before starting out on a fishing trip. Every one of the three hundred odd members is confident this means good fishing.

Fishermen of ancient times sacrificed the first fish caught to Poseidon or Neptune, the god of the sea. This first fish was frequently the subject of special treatment, depending on the local tradition. Sometimes, like the Scotch "king of herring," it was thrown back into the water for good luck. Elsewhere, it was talked to with "a sweet mouth," meaning that kind words were said to it, but it was not necessarily returned to the sea.

Those who feel that a fish suffers pain when hooked and then having the hook taken out of its bruised mouth should not worry too much, as the feeling is one of discomfort, and not of pain as humans know pain.

The fact that countless millions of eggs were seen at spawning time made early man think that fish had unusual powers of fertility and many symbols were evolved to interpret them. It was believed that these powers were transferable to man, through the eating of fish.

The fish, because of its extraordinary fecundity, was dedicated to Venus by the Romans. The Christians dedicated it to the Virgin Mary, and decreed that fish was to be eaten on Friday, also known as Virgin Day, or Fish Day.

In ancient Egypt, a fish was a feminine phallic or reproductive symbol. In India, it is one of the eight symbols of Buddha, and indicates freedom, or free motion in all directions, as fish have in the waters. Among the Chinese, fish typified happiness, and two fish were a symbol of marriage. The early Christians used three fish intertwined to symbolize the Trinity, typifying regeneration.

Since the dawn of civilization, peoples who had access to waters devised many ways of catching fish, including how to spear them. Fishing was a daily task, as fish was a basic food. Once upon a time, men watched the birds who ate fish, and through them learned how to find schools of fish where they could do their own fishing. Later on, whales were observed for the same thing.

Today we have submarine detection devices that were developed during the war, for locating the hideouts of the fisherman's prey, but antiquated beliefs continue to combine with the latest inventions.

Is Fish a Brain Food?

SCIENCE AND SUPERSTITION sometimes march hand in hand, but fortunately, not for long. That fish is brain food is a case in point.

It is related in the annals of medicine that Jean Dumas, one of Louis Pasteur's teachers (1822–1895), was the first to establish the fact that fish is particularly rich in phosphorus. About the same time it was proved that the brain, with its four quadrillion nerve cells, contained considerable phosphorus, together with other chemical elements. Whereupon, Friedrich Büchner, the German philosopher of that day, hearing this, originated the famous phrase: "Without phosphorus there is no thought."

Meanwhile, in America, Louis Agassiz, then professor of natural history at Harvard and an authority on fish, not only endorsed both Jean Dumas' discovery and Büchner's philosophic bombshell, but supplemented them by affirming that eating fish, therefore, would be good for the brain, since both contained phosphorus. Furthermore, the fish industry made the most of this suggestion throughout the years, and we have today a very large percentage of people who firmly believe that fish *is* food for the brain!

However, this is no scientific evidence to prove that fish produces gray matter just because the chemical element of phosphorus is contained in both. Fish, like any other wholesome food, helps to provide the vital elements the body requires—no more, no less. And one food is as good as another as far as the brain is concerned. It is worthwhile mentioning that at the time when the brain has its most extraordinary development—from birth to the sixth year—a child is not eating fish!

"Oyster" Superstitions

MANY PEOPLE will not eat oysters during the months in which the letter "R" does not appear, because of the superstitious belief that oysters may make us ill, or actually poison us fatally, during this period. Although this popular fallacy has been exposed time and again, nevertheless it continues to hold the imagination.

There is also a common superstition that eating oysters, as well as lobsters and crabs, at the same meal with ice-cream is deadly. This, too, is a food fallacy, as those brave enough to defy the superstition, have learned.

The oyster is also looked upon as a weather prophet. When oysters are bedding deep, the oysterman believes it is a sign of an early and hard winter. As many old-timers believe that this sign is infallible, there may be some truth in it.

Many old Roman superstitions about oysters eventually reached this continent from Europe, and have been retained to this day. For instance, it was considered lucky to eat oysters the first day they appeared in the market. In keeping with this tradition, oysters are still sent to the White House at the beginning of the season.

Among attributes that have been ascribed to the delicate bivalve is that it is an aphrodisiac. History tells us that it was Casanova's prescription for sex stimulation. An early belief was that foods which in some way suggest or resemble sexual organs produced this effect. Oysters were supposed to remind one of the female organs. In this regard, but in reverse, inexplicable aversions that some people have to certain foods may be explained.

Twenty to thirty centuries ago, Japanese and Chinese were engaged in oyster farming. Among the weirdest of oyster superstitions is that of the Japanese, who hold a most fantastic and sentimental ceremony to "honor" the souls of the oysters they have eaten, among other departed objects such as ships that have been sunk, dolls that have been smashed and needles that have been broken!

On the commercial side, there is the false notion that the size, plumpness and juiciness of an oyster indicate its superior quality. This is not true when size has been induced artificially, by soaking them in fresh water. Because of osmotic pressure, the water enters the cells of the oyster, and the mineral salts—the real food value—pass out!

Oysters, being cold and moist, are widely in use as a poultice to remove a foreign body from an inflamed eye, or to heal a "black" eye.

Strange as it seems, it is a fact and not a superstition that some oysters grow on trees. They are found attached to the roots of mangrove trees which reach into the ocean.

Historically speaking, Colchester, one of England's oldest and quaintest towns, contains the famous oyster bed of the river Colne, which has been thriving ever since the Romans landed there. These oyster beds may have been responsible for the selection of Colchester as the site for the first Roman colony in Britain in 50 A.D. Incidentally, Colchester is reputed to be "Ole King Cole's" capital. In 52 B.C., Sergius Orata, a wealthy Roman, is believed to have introduced artificial oyster beds at Baiae.

Oysters were known as luxury tidbits in ancient Greece, which gave them their name, meaning "shell" or "bone." The Greeks were modern in the sense that they called oysters the "perfect prelude to a meal." The Romans took the Greek term for oysters and modified it with "*ostrea,*" which is now the scientific naming. The Romans, too, deemed oysters, "dainty manna from the sea."

In America, the Indians, long before the white men arrived, were consuming oysters in huge quantities. One "midden," or shell heap, at Damariscotta, Maine, is said to contain seven million bushels of shells. Similarly, so fond were the early Massachusetts settlers of the juicy bivalve, that "by 1775, the natural beds of Cape Cod were exhausted," and laws had to be passed preventing further destruction.

Oyster farming in American waters began when a Chesapeake schooner, loaded with oysters for the Connecticut market, dumped them overboard at New Haven for lack of buyers. These transplanted oysters proved much more luscious than the home grown variety, and thereafter oyster farming began on a grand scale.

To protect the now important industry, most states have introduced marketing and other restrictions which make these mollusks less available on our tables in summer. But this practice is far from modern. In 1375 Edward III of England issued a royal edict prohibiting the collection of full-grown oysters from May to September, thus limiting their use to the eight "R" months. He also forbade anyone to remove young oysters from their beds in any month but May, in order to regulate the planting of oyster beds.

According to the United States Bureau of Fisheries, oysters are edible at all seasons of the year, superstition or no, except in cases of pollution. However, prior to the invention of modern refrigeration, it was not always safe to eat them during the warm months. Therefore, there is no doubt that many of the superstitious fears of oysters originated among those who ate them in warm weather, when they spoil easily, or who became infected with typhoid germs from oysters found in polluted waters.

Although not dangerous to health, there is good reason for not marketing oysters in summer. They are not at their gastronomical best in the months without an "R," because it is the spawning season. A female oyster will spawn as many as one hundred to five hundred million eggs during a summer season. After her work is done, she is said to become a male, as studies have demonstrated that oysters change sex—they are females from June to August.

Pearls in your oysters? Our local species, *ostrea virginica*, sometimes secrete pearls, but they are of little value. (See chapter on "Pearl Superstitions.")

"Gold Fish" Superstitions

SUPERSTITIONS are generally of an evil nature, but in the case of the little gold fish, with few exceptions, it is believed to bring good luck wherever it happens to be. Although these bright little creatures were only introduced to the American public about 1878 by Rear Admiral Daniel

Ammen of the United States Navy, superstitious Americans are generally as one with the Egyptians' idea that the little gold fish are mascots and are particularly fortunate to lovers. A little fish made of gold, silver or mother-of-pearl represents a lucky gift between sweethearts, and gold fish are also believed responsible for the harmony which exists between husband and wife.

The Greeks and Romans also held to the superstition that a gold fish was a mascot which had the power to bring good luck in all affairs connected with courtship and marriage. In early religions, the goddess of Love was closely connected with water, as, for instance, Venus was said to have sprung from the foam of the sea.

Yellow, red and gold are sacred colors in the Orient, symbolic of sun and life. Fish, on the whole, are looked upon as the symbol of fertility because of the prodigious number of eggs they produce. When the fish-mascot happens to be a carp, the gold fish being a member of the carp family, *Carassius Auratus*, it is given the power of bestowing perseverance and good fortune in worldly affairs, as well as of bringing luck to lovers. These Eastern traditional beliefs moved West and reached America.

The extraordinary powers of the carp are founded on an old Egyptian legend that of all the fish, the carp alone had the courage and perseverance to leap the waterfall and so gain the chariot of cloud which carried it to heaven.

It may well be that this belief was the origin of keeping gold fish, which are really golden carps, as pets. Oddly enough, in some parts of England as well as of America, the keeping of gold fish was considered unlucky. This reverse form of the superstition may have come about as a reaction against the old pagan belief in the auspicious attributes of the gold fish.

In the East, the golden carp is one of the emblems of Buddha. It is still venerated in Japan, where until the Second World War, a large gold fish growing industry was thriving. The world market was wide open to the Japanese until the United States and Canada came forth with their own gold fish raising industry. It is, however, in the hands of a very few men in both Canada and the United States.

The gold fish is a native of China, and the product of long years of selected breeding. Centuries ago the Chinese fish culturists interbred light colored specimens and produced beautiful varieties. Fish fanciers further induced and strengthened the golden and silvery colors by regulating the quantity of mineral in the water.

There are about 1,400 species of carp. Albinos seem to be rather common and the Chinese have domesticated these albinos for a long time.

The golden carp, or gold fish, was introduced into Europe about the 12th or 13th Century, and into Japan at the beginning of the 16th.

Gold fish will not thrive in rivers; in large ponds they readily revert to the coloration of the original stock. When a gold fish keeps to the bottom of the jar or bowl, superstitious people of the West, in keeping with those of the East, believe that it indicates rain. The gold fish, however, is not a reliable weather prophet.

"Codfish" Superstitions

ALTHOUGH SUPERSTITIONS about fish, fishing and fishermen are similar in many respects, there are also hundreds of instances where beliefs are related to a specific fish, and the codfish is an excellent example. The codfish, which has universal appeal as a food, and which gives a livelihood to a large number of persons who live on seacoasts in northern and temperate lands, provides superstitions which form a basic pattern wherever codfishing is an industry.

All sea-faring men watch the behavior of the codfish to prophesy a good or bad season of winter weather. For instance, along the New Jersey coast of the United States, whenever codfish are running in October, superstitious fishermen put it down at once as a sign of a hard winter, because codfish are due to run in December, two months later. When a dried fish is hanging up and begins to feel moist, it means rain.

One of the most interesting as well as most persistent beliefs about the codfish is related to the ear stones, called otoliths, which are found in a small sac near the internal ear of nearly every species of fish, but those of the codfish are supposed to have magic powers. The sacs are located under the gill-cover and behind the eyes. In each sac there are two loose, white, irregular stone-like objects. The codfish otoliths are considered especially lucky and no superstitious fisherman, or member of his family, will be found without at least one pair of these stone-charms. They give general protection, but more particularly at sea.

The superstition about these stones grew out of the belief that they keep the fish afloat, and if it works for the fish, it should work for the one who wears them. The stones are usually worn around a person's neck.

As a matter of fact the exact function of the ear-stones has not yet been determined. Some think that the stones are auditory organs which aid in the perception of sound waves. Others think they are connected in some way with the animal's "static sense," by which the fish maintains its equilibrium in water. The stones are composed almost entirely of calcium carbonate and calcium phosphate, and are soluble in weak acetic acid.

Even land-lubbers carry these stones as talismans whether they come from the codfish or not. It is believed that if a stone is placed in a glass of water and taken before a sea trip, it will prevent seasickness as well as act as a protection against sea disaster.

A custom which has stood the test of centuries is to eat salt codfish on Ash Wednesday, as a promoter of good health. As the codfish has been proven a valuable item in anyone's diet, there is more science than superstition in the practice.

Long before the nutritional value of foods had become a subject for scientific investigation, codfish heads were fed to animals to sustain health, and numerous superstitions attached to their health value were observed. The use of cod liver oil to ease rheumatic joints was an ancient remedy. It was also used as a mild form of aphrodisiac as it was supposed to energize the individual.

Today, however, we know that cod liver oil contains Vitamin A which is beneficial to the eyes; and Vitamin D, which is good for the health in general.

Although the use of codfish as a health measure began in superstition, it has now come into the realm of scientific fact. On the other hand, there are still a variety of uses for codfish and cod liver which remain exclusively superstitious practices.

"Whale" Superstitions

THE WHALE is the largest animal in the world on land and sea, and has been surrounded with superstition for ages. The legend of Jonah and the whale has finally been clarified through more accurate knowledge of the Aramaic language. Dr. George M. Lamsa, distinguished Biblical and Aramaic scholar, wrote as follows: "Certain Aramaic words possess the disconcerting faculty of meaning two utterly unrelated things. A dot on one of the letters sometimes indicates the difference.

"In the first chapter of the Book of Jonah (verse 17), we read: 'Now the LORD has prepared a great fish to swallow up Jonah. And Jonah was in the belly of the fish three days and three nights.'

" 'In a great fish' was, and still is, Aramaic slang for being in a per-
plexing dilemma; or, as we would say, 'In a pretty pickle.'

"The Lord had ordered Jonah, a poor illiterate peasant, to go and
preach to the great and wicked city of Nineveh. Jonah was over-
whelmed by the prospect and for three days was 'in a great fish,' or 'in
a stew' over it.

"So Jonah prayed to the Lord who delivered him from his dilemma.
'And the word of the LORD came unto Jonah the second time, saying,

" 'Arise, go unto Nineveh, that great city, and preach unto it the
preaching that I bid thee.'

"So Jonah arose, and went into Nineveh, according to the word of
the LORD." (Book of Jonah, Chapter 3:1, 2, 3.)

To confirm further this linguistic interpretation, we find in St.
Matthew, chapter 12, verse 41: "The men of Nineveh shall rise in judgment with this generation, and shall condemn it; because they repented
at the preaching of Jonah." The only Biblical quotation which refers
to Jesus, Jonah, and the whale, is as follows:

"For as Jonas was three days and three nights in the whale's belly,
so shall the Son of man be three days and three nights in the heart of
the earth."—Matthew 12:40.

Despite popular belief, there is no specific mention in the Bible of
the whale's swallowing Jonah, while the Book of Jonah ends with a
question mark, following a quotation referring to Nineveh.

Whales are not fish but mammals which bring forth their young alive
and suckle them with milk, like domestic animals. Female whales suckle
their young on the surface of the water. Occasionally they give birth
to twins, but a single offspring is the general rule.

A whale does not spout water, as is commonly believed. Cetologists,
the whale experts, explain that a whale rises to the surface for air at
intervals from five to forty-five minutes, depending upon lung capacity.
The first act upon surfacing is to expel the used air from its lungs. The
air is naturally moist and warm, and since this act usually occurs in a
cold climate, the expelled air looks like water. Sometimes the whale
starts to expel air before its nostrils, or blowholes, are clear of the
water, and this action also gives the illusion of spouting water.

Whalebone is not a bone and has none of the properties of bone.
Whalebone, known as baleen, is an elastic substance found in the whale's
mouth.

Ambergris has been a mysterious substance until recent times. Roy
Chapman Andrews, Director of the American Museum of Natural

History, New York City, says: "From time immemorial ambergris has had a fabulous value. Ages before its true source was even remotely suspected it was a component of mediums and love potions. It is even mentioned in some of the tales of the Arabian Nights. Probably not until the middle of the seventeenth century was its real origin suspected. It is found either floating on the sea or in the bodies of sick sperm whales, and is suspected to be a secretion of the liver or intestines." (The *New York Herald Tribune*, December 12, 1937.)

Whales once lived on land, and millions of years elapsed before they changed from land animals to marine animals. Whales and their cousins, porpoises and dolphins, are the only species of mammals that bear and rear their young in the water. It is interesting to note that A. E. Baker discovered a prehistoric whale skull from solid rock on Otter Rock Beach, Oregon, as reported by the United Press, April 27, 1935. The fossil is estimated to be 3,000,000 years old.

Since the whale has been cavorting in the sea for millions of years, the sight of it has been the source of fantastic tales which have been told and retold and transformed in the telling. It is no wonder today that a fabulous account is still a "fish" story, the modern equivalent of a "tall" tale.

Tales About Sea Serpents

EVERY NOW AND THEN, following a time-honored habit, fantastic tales about sea serpents are revived when a fabulous marine monster is reported to have been seen along the coast of America, Europe or other part of the world. These stories become real in the minds of superstitious fishermen and many other persons, and age-old superstitious fears for personal security flare up anew.

While rumors of the appearance of these sea monsters are afoot, investigations are conducted, but eventually the tale dies down, as no true specimen of a sea serpent has ever been captured or photographed. Just about the time when the excitement over the sighting of one of the supposed terrible sea creatures has been forgotten, the appearance of another is reported, again reviving the fears which have thus been kept alive for centuries.

One of the first recorded stories of sea monsters goes back to the Scriptures where the tale of the Leviathan is recorded. Many museums have skeletons of huge water-reptiles of pre-historic times, and it is not altogether impossible that some of the species may still be in existence, as the fathomless ocean has never been completely explored or even navigated. In December 1938, a strange sea animal was landed off the south coast of Africa, closely resembling a pre-historic sea-reptile. This "living fossil" upset the scientific world because it was believed extinct for at least fifty million years. However, it was only a five-foot fish, though very weird, and weighed only 127 pounds, which is a far cry from what superstitious persons describe as a sea serpent.

There are several known marine animals that could very well cause the superstitious minded to shudder at the sight of them. For instance, there is the sulphur-bottom whale, the largest animal in the world today, with a length of ninety feet and a weight of one hundred fifty tons. The great squid of the Mediterranean, with its bulging eyes and body fifty feet long, might easily be identified as a devil of the sea. So would the octopus, that slimy eight-armed creature that lives in deep water, but which may come to the surface occasionally. Some octopi are of great size, and the length of their tentacles adds greatly to their hugeness. There may be a super-octopus somewhere at the bottom of the sea but as yet none has been seen.

There are sea-worms, some of which are over six feet long and proportionately thick. These are fairly abundant, principally along the coast of South Africa. Sea snakes, which correctly might be called sea serpents, are plentiful in tropical waters, and some are enormous, growing to about twelve feet in length.

Porpoises swimming one behind the other, half emerging and then sinking, might give the illusion of some extraordinary monster when seen at a distance as they move with snake-like undulations. Even masses of seaweed have been mistaken for large monsters floating on the surface of the ocean as though they were asleep. There are all kinds of salt water monstrosities which are close reminders of mythological dragons when described by undisciplined imaginative minds.

Sea serpent stories are often the result of subconscious fears in the minds of some who entertain the idea that the floor of the sea is inhabited by monsters that may some day rise in a mass to the surface and make the earth a living nightmare. So far nothing has come to the attention of scientists to account for the hysteria which compels a superstition-ridden individual to describe a monstrous creature gushing thick streams of water from a cavernous mouth containing several rows of teeth, distended nostrils, cavorting and zigzagging at high speed over the water, as though he had actually seen it!

"Shell" Superstitions

SHELLS, including egg shells, snail shells and sea shells, were symbolic of fertility for the most part, and therefore were good omens in their basic nature, unless in the hands of those who would do harm with them.

A spiral or whorled shell, but particularly the cowry shell, was always a lucky piece or charm in early times, looked upon as equivalent to the human ear, and even the navel, both considered invulnerable parts of the human body. In primitive times, many a mother held a small whorled or cowry shell in her hand to help her through the pangs of childbirth. It was thought that this amulet simulated the spiral movement with which the child was ushered into the world. Frequently a red spiral was painted on the door of the home of an expectant mother, to symbolize the solar and lunar symbols as well, so that this heavenly couple would assist her in an easy delivery.

In keeping with the symbolism of the ear, as related to shells, Minerva, the Roman goddess of wisdom, sprang from the head of Jove. This myth was patterned after very early superstitions about birth. The shell was believed to be the giver of life, and any real or fancied likeness to the shell, such as the ear, was related to the process of procreation.

There are many superstitions about egg shells, which were once believed to be the vehicles of fairies, or even witches, in which case there was the suggestion of potential danger. These evil-doers went to sea in empty egg shells and caused shipwrecks. This was an old seafaring superstition.

An empty egg shell left in a cup after its contents has been eaten should be turned upside down or broken to prevent the witches from using it as a ferry-boat, according to ancient superstition.

Another old superstition decrees that egg shells should be burned or else the hens will cease laying.

Conch shells were blown into to scare away malignant spirits. The fact that, when held to the ear, one can hear a murmur in the shell, gave rise to many superstitions, including the poetic fancy that the sound of the waves forever haunted its depths. Then came the idea that shells could guard persons from harm, particularly those at sea, forming a link between the traveler and those he left behind. Shells were used as mascots probably since civilization began.

There is no longer any mystery to the fact that a seashell held to the ear sounds like the surf against the shore. The feeble sound waves which produce this impression upon the ear gain sufficient strength reflection back and forth between the walls of the shell to become audible. This is possible because of the peculiar shape of the shell and the smoothness of its interior. The slightest vibration produces an echo, and numerous such echoes are blended into a rumble, the sound heightened because the shell magnifies the pulses in the head as the sounds are produced near it.

It you have a seashell in front of your door, luck will enter. A seashell indicates by its loud or soft roar whether the sea is rough or smooth, where loved ones may be.

On the other hand, some persons believe that it is bad luck to keep shells in the house, and that they bring discord and strife. They should be kept outdoors for good luck. A spiral shell is believed to guarantee to the possessor a long life. Powdered shells have been used in folk medicine since earliest times, and this remedy was believed especially good for respiratory troubles because of the symbolic connection between shells and the wind.

The study of shells and their uses is called Archeo- and Ethno-Conchology. The subject covers a wide field through the history of mankind, including superstitions, and the other rôles shells have played in man's life.

Many articles in everyday use must have originally been modeled after shells. A few examples are spoons, trumpets, tweezers, bailers for boats, cooking utensils, chisels and axes. Shells are collectors' items, and have become quite a fad in ornamental jewelry. In some parts of the world shells are used as money. The American Indian's "wampum" is known to every school child. In East India cowry shells were used as a medium of exchange.

Shell articles have been found among the ruins of the Incas and the Egyptians. Both these peoples regarded them as phallic symbols, another evidence of the early superstitious implication of the sea shell.

CHAPTER 5

The Animal Kingdom

The Mascot, Bringer of Good Luck

WHETHER REPRESENTED by a human being or an animal, the mascot is everywhere, and never has it been more popular than today. Aware of it or not, by having a mascot represent his team, club, company, airline, university or unit of military or naval service, a man subscribes to a very ancient practice. It is closely related to medieval witchcraft and sorcery in the Western World, and protection against the Evil Eye and other bad influences in the ancient world.

The word, mascot, to signify something or someone that brings good luck, is a relatively modern introduction into our language. Etymologically, the word stems from the Provençal French *masco*, meaning sorceress, and *mascoto*, meaning sorcery and witchcraft. The *masco* or mascot then evolved to mean a bringer of good luck by keeping sorcery or witchcraft away. The rôle of mascot was later extended to include animals; and now it also includes "things," all of which are expected to raise the morale of whatever individual or group adopts them. In fact, at the present time, a mascot has taken on a public and official capacity.

A dog is a particularly popular mascot because he serves the double purpose of being protection for his master as well as good luck. But cats, birds, goats, monkeys and other animals are almost as desirable. Whenever extra good luck is desired, or a change from bad luck to good, mascots in the modern scene express a psychological tie-up with animal totems of primitive times. The godlike animal characters of ancient man were endowed with a supernatural sense, which, in close relationship with man, could guide him in his activities and minimize dangers and evil.

For instance, the ancient Egyptians venerated the serpent as the guardian of the home, and as an infallible conqueror of the Evil Eye. Snakes were believed to counteract disease as well as uphold their owners in battle. In ancient Egyptian paintings we also find cats riding in war chariots with their owners. Statuary dug out of the ruins of Babylon show trained lions and leopards—mascots of the Assyrian kings as they charged into battle. The Greek goddess Athena had her own mascot to help her dispense wisdom, while Zeus had an eagle which was adopted later by the Roman legion. The bulldog of the British symbolizes courage and tenacity, while the bald eagle of the United States plays an equally inspiring rôle wherever it is displayed. There is also the Russian Bear, and the Chinese Dragon, and a host of others.

The reason mascot addicts sometimes lose despite their faith, is something the ancients understood and explained with their usual convenient interpretations. They believed that no mascot would bring good fortune to anyone who was unworthy of it. Failures only meant one must work harder at whatever was expected to bring results or victory, which, in a way, is psychologically sound; mascots notwithstanding.

Today, faith in certain objects or articles has made mascots of them. This also can be traced back into the distant centuries. Nearly everyone has his or her own special mascot, and the variety is endless. Precious stones bear a prominent part in this modern-like belief, but they are not displayed as ostentatiously as other things which are supposed to bring good luck. The modern age has extended the list of mascots so that it now includes talismans, amulets and charms which are also carried to bring good luck. The superstitious faith that some persons have in mascots is very convincing to them, while the adventurous look upon theirs with awe and hope combined.

There are also national mascots, whether they are in the form of pictures, posters, images, papier-mache reproductions or statues of an imaginary character who inspires the citizenry. John Bull of England and Uncle Sam of the United States are notable examples.

"Hunting" Superstitions

HUNTING AND FISHING, indispensable to early man for subsistence, were his first occupations, and were subject to strict tribal laws. Totem or sacred animals could not be killed or eaten except occasionally for sacrificial offerings to appease angry gods or to implore favors when things were not going too well, or for some special ceremony such as a wedding, birth or other ritual.

Ancient man had to rely on his native skill more than on the use of the crude tools and weapons he made from the raw materials about him. He backed his skill with his strong faith in the supernatural. His guides for the weather and to find hunting grounds were the birds and animals as well as the omens and signs from his superstitious beliefs.

Many modern professional hunters and sportsmen who go gunning for the love of it still cling to primitive beliefs and misconceptions that seem never to die out. For example, if a hunter makes a bad start he is beset by a feeling of bad luck. Another unlucky sign is to turn back after once entering the woods. When hunting with a dog, many a hunter thinks he will fill his game bag if the dog fetches it for him as he leaves the house. A gun should never be loaded until the hunting grounds are reached, or bad luck may be expected. A gun should never be carried on the left shoulder.

As might be expected, many hunters carry a rabbit's foot for luck, or a feather or claw from the last fowl killed. Hunters regard some guns as luckier than others, and many would never dream of placing a gun on the shoulder when indoors as it signifies a fruitless hunt, or something worse—danger to their own life.

Primitives may have been short of the proper hunting equipment as we know it today, but they were never short of ingenuity. For instance, the Esquimos of East Greenland pour blubber on the water where swans gather to make it difficult for the birds to take flight while the men approach in kayaks and harpoon them. Another ingenious primitive method is that of the Australian aborigines who have hardly a tool with which to catch ducks. The men swim under water, breathing through a reed, and pull the ducks down by their legs and then wring their necks without further ceremony. The Yurok Indians of California sprinkled berries on the bottom of a shallow river, and stretched a net a few inches below the surface of the water. The unsuspecting ducks, diving in quest of the berries, caught their necks in the meshes and naturally drowned.

"Cat" Superstitions

FAMOUS AMONG cat superstitions is the one about the legendary nine lives of this animal. The Egyptians worshipped the cat and endowed it with nine lives, possibly because of its extraordinary agility in landing on its feet without harm—one among many of the cat's attributes which was a mystery to early peoples. The Egyptians further expressed their appreciation of the cat by associating it with the Trinity, their sacred symbol of Mother, Father, and Son. A multiplication of three times three, or nine, was the highest expression of honor which could be granted the cat.

Egyptologists find reference to the cat as a domesticated animal as early as 2,400 B.C. Other scholars suggest the possibility of its having been known in Africa at an even earlier date. The cat is said to be mentioned in Sanskrit writings of some 3,000 years ago. Fossil remains in many parts of the world point to a very early origin. Many extinct forms of the cat species have been found in North America, and some paleontologists believe that the original stock may even have originated in the North American continent. It is quite generally believed that the cat may have been a close associate of civilized man for some 4,000 years.

The cat was believed to be an animal which could see in the dark because its eyes enlarged and contracted with the waxing and waning of the moon. When stroked it gave off sparks which suggested fire out of its hair, a solar attribute which amazed the ancients. Also the cat loved to bask in the sun, and was given to nocturnal habits under the moon and in the darkest of nights. These strange virtues aroused a spirit of wonder and respect. Male and female cats were thought the counterpart of the heavenly couple, the sun and the moon, and were qualified accordingly. The male became a solar animal; the female, a lunar one.

The reason the Egyptians elevated the cat above all other animals is obscure. There is a traditional belief that the cat rid Egypt of a plague of rats at a time when it was the granary of the ancient world. The cat was therefore promoted to the state of goddess, was named Bast or Pasht, usually represented as a human-bodied and cat-headed figure, and endowed with nine lives. Archeological discoveries point to the fact that worship of the goddess Bast was centered for thousands of years in the city of Bubastis. To this city hundreds of thousands of pilgrims journeyed to participate in elaborate ceremonies in honor of the cat. Laws were enacted to protect the animal, and when it died it was mummified and placed beside mummies of royalty or in the Temple of Bast with amulets and with mummified rice, the cat's food in the hereafter.

The fact that a cat generally, though not always, lands on its feet amazed the ancients. There is nothing supernatural about this ability. The cat's spine is very fragile but it is also very flexible and lends itself to jumping and falling without injury. Slow motion pictures show how a cat manages to right itself during a fall, every part of its supple body working in perfect coordination as it lands on its well-protected, shock-absorbing feet. This is quite a natural gesture as far as the cat is concerned, but not being understood in ages past it formed the superstition that a cat has nine lives. Anyone who hurt or killed a cat was expected to have ill fortune for nine years, if indeed he were spared his life!

Sadistic children not yet fully aware of the meaning of pain may put the "nine lives" theory to the test, and torture a cat unmercifully.

Seafaring people ward off death and disaster by having a cat aboard ship; black or otherwise.

The superstition that the cat has nine lives was further nurtured in Norse mythology when Frigga rode in a car drawn by a pair of cats. The great god Odin gave Frigga power over the ninth world, known as Hel, the abode of the dead. However, when the Norse and Teuton were converted to Christianity, Frigga was consigned to the mountain fastnesses as a witch. Her name-day, Friday, became a day which her wicked cohorts chose for their strange weekly assemblies. The cats that once drew the chariot became the steeds on which the witches flew through the night. Black they were, and demoniacal in nature. It was believed that the cat changed its form into a witch or Satan after seven years of service. Therefore, a black cat crossing one's path nowadays still means that it may be a witch or the Devil in disguise, out for no good. Hence the superstition that it is bad luck to have a black cat, the symbol of darkness and danger cross one's path. Many people change their course to prevent this misfortune.

From that time on, the cat was looked upon with mixed feelings, lucky at times but mostly suggesting bad luck. For those who follow the Egyptian beliefs the cat is an animal of great wisdom and fortunate to have around. But for others the black cat symbolizes the witch and the Devil.

The belief that a cat can see in total darkness probably arose because of the fact that a cat's eyes gleam in the dark, as do those of most of the cat tribe which are nocturnal animals. The glow of the eyes is typical of certain animals whose eyes can pick up faint light rays, as from starlight, and reflect them. But contrary to this belief, cats' eyes are not luminous in the dark. No animal possesses light-giving eyes. A structure called *tapetum lucicum* in the caudal area around the optic nerve is part of the membranous layer between the retina and the outer covering of the pupils. It is brilliant green or blue in color and has a metallic luster. When artificial light is thrown on it, the light enters and reflects back the cat's eyes as though it were a mirror. The eyes of all cats including lions, tigers, leopards, pumas, jaguars, and cheetahs, have this quality.

There is another superstition that cutting the whiskers of a cat impairs its vision. Each whisker has a bulb of nerve substance at its end and connects with the nerves of the lip, thus being an organ of touch. By this means the cat can sense things near its body whether it be day-light or dark. Experiments with cats without whiskers repeatedly demonstrated that judgment of distances was impaired, the cat missing its prey when springing for it. It would seem that the cat's whiskers are an aid in fixing his eyes for a successful jump at his prey. The eyes themselves, however, are not directly affected.

One of the most destructive superstitions about cats is the old but ever recurrent myth that a cat can, and sometimes does, perch itself on the breasts of sleeping babies, old people and invalids, and suffocate them by sucking their breath; and that a cat should never be left alone in a house where there are young sleeping children. The belief probably arose from the fact that cats like to snuggle up to the warmth of human beings, and because, given a chance, cats love to inspect the human face very closely. To conclude that they suck the breath of helpless human beings is, of course, erroneous. This superstition is a hangover from witchcraft days when the cat was associated with the evil spirit of Satan, who could invest his character in the cat and harm the young or the old and feeble while in their sleep. It is closely related to the vampire myth which contends that the vampire drains the blood of its victims while they sleep. Many anemic, pale people during the Middle Ages used to be thought the victims of these dangerous nightly visitors.

The breath-sucking story is simply an old wives' tale. However, there is the danger that a cat in its desire for a warm spot might curl up too close to a baby's face and possibly suffocate the child with its fur. But if the cat has a neat basket with a cushion all its own, the chances are that it will lie in its own bed. More babies are killed by parents rolling on their babies than by cats.

Wherever Manx cats are scarce there is the superstitious conclusion that a tailless cat was fathered by a rabbit. A cross between a cat and a rabbit is biologically impossible. A cat born with only a mere tuft of fur for a tail is a throwback to some tailless ancestor, possibly a Manx cat. There are many breeds of cats with short, gnarled or twisted tails or with no tails at all, particularly in the Orient. Manx cats have found their way as pets nearly everywhere in the world today.

Seafaring people variously interpret the strange behavior of cats during atmospheric changes. If a cat tears at cushions or carpets, or is generally uneasy, it is said to be raising a wind. This belief is popular everywhere at sea, and is widely believed in sea coast towns on Cape Cod and elsewhere. It is perhaps another half superstition, since the truth of the matter is that with its superior nervous organism the cat is conscious of the approach of the wind before man is, by the condition of its fur.

Cats are supposed to wash their fur and rub their ears because of the electricity in the air just before a bad spell of weather sets in. If a cat washes its foot and passes it over the left ear, it means the advent of a stranger. If it licks its tail, it foretells rain. If you are the first person a cat looks at after she has licked herself, and if single, it indicates an early marriage. To throw a cat overboard raises a storm at sea. If a cat washes herself in the usual manner, the weather will be fair, but it will be bad if she licks herself above the ears or sits with her tail toward the fire. If a cat runs across a stage during the action of a play, misfortune is sure to follow. Bad luck will come to those who kick cats, and it causes good luck for the family cat to be present at weddings. These and many hundreds of other cat superstitions are widely believed in today. Some are half-truths, but none are to be relied upon too seriously.

That cats generally hate water is a fallacy. Cats dislike getting wet needlessly because it involves a lot of work drying and cleaning themselves with their tongues. However, many cats are intrigued by water, and they often plunge into water not only to fish but for the sheer joy of swimming around.

To be "nervous as a cat" is a common saying, yet the cat almost never suffers from diseases of the nerves. As a matter of fact, hers is a superior nervous system, tremendously alert and sensitive and therefore easily annoyed if tormented. But cats are seldom nervous in the sick sense of the word.

Although there are millions of people who love cats, there are large numbers who have a morbid fear or hatred for them. This malady is called *aelurophobia* and manifests itself in nausea, fainting spells, and sometimes convulsions. The mere thought of a cat is revolting to such people.

No one is born with a cat-phobia. It is a fear acquired when either too young to recall pulling the cat's tail and being scratched in return, or in some other way which arouses a subconscious association of danger at the sight or thought of a cat.

Many of these superstitions have been explained and denuded of their supernaturalism, yet superstitious people still cherish an unbelievably large number of false beliefs about cats today.

"Dog" Superstitions

THE MOST prevalent superstition about dogs is that when this animal throws back its head and howls, it is a sign of death or disaster.

In ancient myths the howling dog was symbolic of the tempest, or wind-god, who was believed to summon the spirit of death. According to Aryan mythology, the spirits of the dead were supposed to be carried away by the howling night wind, and a dog or a wolf represented this deity, which may explain how the superstition began.

Many think, even today, that the howling of the dog is provoked by the apparition of Death itself, invisible to man, but seen or sensed by animals, especially the dog. It is also believed that a wraith or specter in the exact likeness of a living person appears just before death comes, and can be seen by the dog, causing it to bellow forth these sinister sounds.

The scientific explanation of a dog's night howls, however, is that they are merely the out-cropping of instincts. Our four-legged friend may obey a primitive impulse, which he is said to inherit from the distant time when all dogs' ancestors hunted in packs; the howl being the rallying call. There are two schools of thought, however. One, that the wolves hunt in packs, and the other, that the lone wolf does well by itself; no one denies that in pack or alone the wolf howls, and so does the dog, occasionally.

Psychic powers were attributed to dogs in Greek mythology also. There is the story of Medes, a potent sorceress, who presided over the altar of Hecate, divinity of darkness and terror. She was the goddess of witchcraft, and wandered on earth by night. She could only be seen by dogs, whose howling or barking signified her approach, and warned the unwary.

These ancient legends in which the dog, in some supernatural way, foresaw danger, and protected man, is another illustration of early man's inability to give a rational explanation for many of the phenomena around him. The dog displayed so many uncanny instincts for detecting the approach of an enemy, or for locating prey, that he was credited with the power to sense the approach of invisible evils, such as death and demons, as well.

Today, the dog is called man's best friend, but it was also his first friend from the animal world. It is said to have been domesticated about sixty thousand years ago by savage cavemen. These early dogs, half-wild wolves and jackals, through cross-breeding and domestication, rapidly developed their economic usefulness because they were natural hunters. However, through the thousands of years the dog has walked with man, he has retained the primitive gifts of his wolf-ancestors. Wild dogs never barked nor wagged their tails—but howl they could.

The devotion attributed to dogs for their masters is not always quite as ardent as superstitious dog-lovers would have us believe. An unusually large number of dogs bite their masters, even, and others leave them, never to return. The majority of dogs are faithful, however, and not in the habit of biting the hand that feeds them. Among many legends, there is the famous one about the patience and fidelity of Argos, Ulysses' dog, who waited some twenty odd years for the return of his master; even though disguised, Ulysses was recognized by Argos who, though feeble with old age, greeted him with a happy wag of its tail, and died of joy!

It was because of his keen senses that the dog, at an early stage of civilization, became man's companion, running ahead of his master, to prepare the way, so to speak. Although dogs are color-blind, tests show that their hearing covers sixteen times the range of that of man. Certain sounds, no doubt, such as the moaning of the night wind, or high-pitched musical notes, irritate a dog's highly sensitive ears, and make him show it by howling. A dog's sense of smell is also very keen. He can follow the scent left by a person hours after he has passed. However, it is another superstition that a dog's sense of smell is one hundred per cent accurate.

Because he remained close to man during the process of civilization, the dog became as invaluable to the shepherd as he had been to the hunter. Recently a great humanitarian movement has again made use of this animal, making the most of its natural qualities to obey, guide and protect the blind. This extraordinary achievement has been accomplished by the Seeing Eye organization, which trains the animals for this purpose and then supplies them to the blind, to become truly their best friends.

"Wolf" Superstitions

EVER SINCE the world became acquainted with the tale of the legendary founders of Rome, Romulus and Remus, who were suckled by a she-wolf, superstitions have been woven around the wolf, and the wolf in relation to man, or wolfism. The Roman story was spectacularly brought back to mind a few years ago with the discovery of the Wolf Children of India, Kamala and Amala, who were reported to have been nurtured and raised by she-wolves in the jungle. Of course we all know that Kipling used the same theme in his "Jungle Books," which have become classics.

A very recent colloquialism in America is to call a man a "wolf" if he is suspected of wolfish desires toward women which he shows by ravenous glances and caveman antics. There are men who use the technique of a "wolf in sheep's clothing," when they are all the more dangerous.

The application of the term "wolf" to men of this type is undoubtedly related to an ancient Roman religious celebration which was held on February 15 and known as the Lupercalia. Because of the belief that a she-wolf was the foster-mother of all Romans, the animal was held sacred and was symbolic of fertility. It was reversed also in its basic nature of being ravenous and untrustworthy when in a bloodthirsty mood. Therefore, it had to be approached with great caution.

To meet the situation of a sacred animal that was at the same time a vicious one, the Romans, like the Egyptians and Grecians, elevated the wolf to godhood. Such animal gods, in their dual rôle, had power to revert at will and without warning to their natural characteristics. Aware of the danger of this, and with no control over it, they appointed other gods to watch over their unmanageable deities. Thus Faunus, a rural deity, and similar to the Greek god Pan, was created by the Romans. Faunus and the fauni had legs, feet and ears like a goat, but otherwise had human shape.

The priests of Faunus, called Luperci, had special duties to perform, in their worship of Faunus. Each Lupercus had a wife, called Luperca, who was regarded as the deified form of the she-wolf, or woman symbol of the suckling of Romulus and Remus. At the Lupercalia, the festival in their honor, the priests, clad in goatskins, made a circuit of the Palatine Hill, striking all women they encountered with goatskin thongs to insure fertility and easy delivery.

Instead of the whistling sounds made by the whip-cracking of the goatskin thongs at the Lupercalia, the modern equivalent is the wolf-whistles performed by men when they see a pretty girl.

In America, Indian folklore and pioneer traditions are rich in references to the wolf. According to experts, the North American wolf is not a man-eater; nevertheless, early settlers have left a trail of hair-raising tales describing how native wolves ate human beings. So far, however, no authenticated case has been found.

Whether wolves hunt in packs or not seems to be an open question. It is a very unwelcome belief of those who think they do, but there are as many less fearful ones who think they do not. The expression "lone wolf" is correctly applied to this animal, however, since a wolf usually mates for life. Upon the death of its companion, an older male or female seldom mates a second time, and does not even join the family group or take part in forays.

The coyote or prairie wolf of western North America though not a savage animal like the timber wolf, is the bane of the farmer and ranchman's existence. Its numbers are increasing whereas the timber wolf is becoming extinct. Both Americans and Indians have many superstitions about the coyote, among which is the idea that it is a stupid animal and will eat poisoned bait. Naturalists, however, declare it is very astute. These objectionable animals will eat carrion as well as fresh meat.

There is a superstition that even a starving person should not eat the flesh of a coyote lest he become a coward. Another superstition is that if a coyote crosses one's path, it is a sign of bad luck. Mexicans believe that the coyote possesses the "Evil Eye."

A Navajo legend holds that a coyote must never be killed as it is an evil spirit turned back from the land of the dead to wreak harm upon the Indians. If a coyote is killed, the slayer stands to lose his wits. This may be remedied by chanting the "coyote chant," or performing the devil-chasing ceremonial, and either of these methods will drive away the dead coyote's evil magic.

Wolves are regarded differently in different countries. Russian traditions honored the wolf, while those of Spain and Mexico disparaged it. In Portugal it is unlucky to see a wolf. In Norway, it is generally a sign of good luck to see one.

People in Normandy believe that there is a phantom wolf that wanders about the graveyards at night. It is said to be jet black, and very large. When it approaches anyone, it stands on its hind legs and then disappears howling. The Norman tradition is that this monster is the ghost of the first Duke of Normandy, who was supposed to be the son of a fiend, and his ghost will not be allowed to rest till the Day of Judgment.

Many superstitions pertaining to the wolf as a sinister animal, and especially as an animal that was interchangeable with man, were widespread during the Middle Ages, and gave rise to Lycanthropy or "werewolfism." Werewolves were believed to be persons who could be metamorphosed into blood-thirsty wolves at night and who reverted to meek, kindly-disposed human beings by day. During the Second World War, Allied Intelligence discovered that this belief was being revived in Germany by leaders of the German underground to terrorize into obedience their simple-minded followers.

In medieval times, when the witches really took over, all kinds of witchcraft was carried on by night and by day. Anyone who came under their spell might fall a victim to "wolf-fever," and develop wolf-like habits as well as the appearance of the creature. Among other bestialities, werewolves were supposed to practice cannibalism.

"Hog" Superstitions

IT IS AN interesting fact that the ancestor of the lowly farm hog, the boar, is represented in ancient little bronzes that show the high rank it once occupied among sacred animals. The boar was represented anciently with the mystic three horns and was a companion of the gods, especially when anthropomorphism prevailed in Gaul. When the boar lost its sacred or human attributes, the gods continued to wear its horns and skin, which identified their close relationship. A huntress goddess, similar to Diana, is depicted astride a boar, expressing swiftness and determination, also attesting to the popularity of this animal in the early days.

When or where the wild boar or wild hog was subjugated can only be guessed, since it is known to have been domesticated four or five thousand years ago. Most of man's first concepts and activities were suggested by the animals about him, which he observed very closely for guidance. He endowed them with uncanny wisdom so that many fallacious notions about animals, including the hog, have been handed down to us in the form of superstitions. These go through changes to keep pace with the times.

To kill a pig when the moon is waning means bad luck with the bacon, as it is certain to shrink in the pan. Some say if the pig is slaughtered at this time it will not take salt, and therefore cannot be cured. If a man dreams he is surrounded by pigs, someone will ask him for money. If a pig runs away, there will be sickness in the family. When young pigs are taken from the sow, they must be drawn away backwards or the sow will be fallow. Many persons believe children can be prevented from getting the mumps by rubbing them against a pig trough. When pigs squeal loudly, storms are approaching, for pigs are said to "see wind." To pull a pig's tail breaks a spell of bad luck, or prevents one.

Many farmers believe that when pigs run with straws in their mouths, it is a sure sign of rain. When straws are available, pigs usually stack them up and lie down on them. It often happens that they do this before it rains, because they are sensitive to the dampness in the air, and they like to prepare a dry place for themselves. However, they will do the same thing when there is no dampness in the air, so the weather prophecy is just another superstition.

The belief that the pig brings good luck may have had an economic origin, as implied by the Irish saying which describes the pig as "the gentleman who pays the rent." Nevertheless, the pig has been a popular mascot. The Chinese make little pigs out of gold, or of silk, for good luck in business. In Ireland, however, they tell you the figure of a pig is lucky only if it is somewhat broken. Thus, in that country pig mascots are bought with only one ear.

The pig was probably a sacred animal in very early Egyptian history, and may have been regarded as the embodiment of the corn-god Osiris. The pig was sanctified and endowed with supernatural powers. Whether its unclean habits entered into their considerations is not certain, although primitive feelings of religious awe often blended with those of abhorrence, an attitude that is an old story and well understood today. A sacred animal was taboo and could not be eaten except in sacrifice to a special god.

Plutarch writes that the Greeks could not decide whether the Jews worshipped swine or hated them. On the one hand, they were forbidden to eat the meat of the pig, but on the other hand, they were not allowed to kill the animals. If the rule against eating the pigs indicated that the animals were unclean, then the law against killing them speaks just as strongly for the sanctity of the animals. From this fact it may be concluded that the pig was revered rather than abhorred by the Israelites. The attitude of the Jews toward the pig was as ambiguous as that of the heathen Syrians toward the same animal.

Many persons believed that the dread of trichinosis and leprosy had caused the Hebrews to forbid the eating of pork. This is generally denied because the Bible does not mention a single instance of an epidemic of a malady that could be attributed to the eating of unclean meats. Furthermore, knowledge of hygiene awoke much later than Biblical times. Illness was looked upon as due to supernatural agents, such as the wrath of evil spirits. The possible explanation for the taboo among the Jews against eating pork is that five or six thousand years before our era the wild boar was the totem of the Jews, and as such, it was *not* to be eaten.

There are many misconceptions about the pig, such as that it is a naturally dirty animal, which is untrue. "It is true that in a state of nature the hog loves to go into pools and wallow in the mire, just as stags, buffaloes, and many other beasts do, especially in the dog days," says William H. Hudson, in "The Book of a Naturalist." Hogs have no sweat glands and therefore wallow in the mud to cool off. Experts say that by nature pigs are cleaner than horses and cows.

The superstitious belief that a sow must be watched so it will not eat its young is explained scientifically as due to a protein deficiency in the sow's diet which causes it to do this. Feeding the sows tankage and soybean meal prevents this porker infanticide.

"To eat like a pig" is said to be unfair to the hog, which, according to experts, is an animal with a diet sense. The animal does not overeat, and cannot be tempted to do so even when given an over-supply of food.

Snakes Sucking Cows' Milk

It is popularly believed among country people that snakes, particularly black snakes and milk or house snakes, sometimes suck the teats of cows.

In order to get to the source of this idea, we must go back to Roman times and look into Pliny the Elder's *Natural History of the World* (23-79). He was responsible for the greatest inaccuracies imaginable, and they are at the root of many superstitious beliefs indulged in to the present day! Then, *Boa* was the name applied to a species of watersnakes, now used to designate the non-poisonous snakes that kill their victims by constriction. Boa snakes were not to be found in Italy. But these huge serpents were imported in cages for show presentations, and Pliny reported that, included in their diet was cow's milk. Pliny managed to mix things somewhat, for he left a question in his readers' minds as to whether he meant that snakes milked cows or that boa and *bos* (Latin, for ox or cow) was used only in allusion to its huge size, a question which has remained unsolved through the centuries.

However it may be, we have inherited the erroneous idea that the boa lived on cows' milk and helped itself at times. We have transferred the false notion to snakes which are seen about a farmer's barn, only to catch the mice that eat grain, really. So-called milk-snakes prefer water, and only milk when suffering from an acute thirst; taking only about two teaspoonfuls at that!

Science says that a snake milking a cow is a feat which would be impossible owing to the shape of the snake's mouth; the two rows of sharp and curved teeth in a snake's jaw would make it quite unlikely that even the most docile of cows could stand for it. Also the suction required to draw the milk is much greater than could be exerted by any snake. Actually, the chances are that the cow would do a little kicking and there would be little left of the snake if it ever tried the stunt!

"Cow" Superstitions

Two of the most modern controversies in regard to cows are still unsettled to the satisfaction of all, including scientists. One is whether a cow responds to music, "baby talk" or polite affection in order to yield more milk; and the other is how does the animal rate in intelligence, as animals go.

After years of inquiry, which brought no practical proof of the oft-repeated theory that cows preferred music with a melody to the "high-brow" classical and "low-brow" jazz types of sound, the United States Department of Agriculture furnished us with the following information:

"From time to time newspapers in various parts of the country have published stories concerning individual dairymen who have installed radios in the dairy barn for the purpose of increasing milk flow by having music available at milking time. At one time we wrote all of the dairymen who had received such publicity and asked that they gave us information concerning the effect of music on the milk flow of their cows. We have never received a reply that indicated that music had any positive effect upon milk yield.

We came to the conclusion that radios were installed for the benefit of the workers around the barn rather than because of any increased yield that might be obtained from the cows. We have never been able to obtain any worthwhile data to indicate that cows were influenced in any manner by music." (April 19, 1945.)

As to the other controversy, the fact is that some praise the cow's intellect while others ridicule it. A report in THIS WEEK, of April 4, 1937, is as follows:

"If you have ever been accused of 'having the brains of a cow' or possessing no 'horse sense,' accept it as a compliment. Popular conceptions of the brains of domestic animals have been upset by animal IQ experiments and ratings recently conducted by Cornell University. Cows were found to be actually smarter than horses, and, if smaller, would make ideal house pets."

No wonder cows were held sacred in Egypt and India!

It is claimed that a cow's taste guides her to the proper selection of food. However, a rather distressing admission has come from farmers, cattle ranchers and dairymen in the Western United States who have to be on the lookout for cows—and other cattle—that eat loco weed which causes loco disease. Veterinarians describe this affliction as a serious cattle disease characterized by a slow measured gait, high step, glassy eyes with defective vision, delirium, gradual emaciation, and finally death.

Yearly reports show that several thousand cows die every year from swallowing nails and other pieces of metal which are carried into their stomachs—they have four of them—in hay or other foods. In one year, not long ago, 616,481 calves were condemned and sacrificed because of liver abscesses produced by penetration of bits of metal.

About ten years ago, a cow in Ashland, Wisconsin, was reported suffering from a dreadful hangover—hiccoughs and all—after having guzzled a bucket of radiator alcohol. It was said that during her spree, Daisy the cow bellowed vociferously, experimented with a dance routine, and threatened the rest of the barnyard.

Hundreds of superstitious notions about the cow, calf and ox are importations from the Old World, just as the cattle themselves are said to have been brought here in the 15th century from Spain. A cow licking the forehead of another is said to indicate the death of their owner. If you feed a cow a bunch of her own hairs, she will forget her old home. If cows, when let out in the morning, immediately lie down, it will storm before night. If you cut a piece of a cow's tail, it will never run away. If a cow does not bawl when her calf is sold, there will be a death in the family. If a bull faces a person and bellows, it means good luck to the person. It is a good sign if the cattle lie down on Christmas day. Cattle born or weaned in the waning of the moon will never be good breeders. When an ox sticks up his tail, it is a sign of change of weather. To prevent a cow from bawling when weaning her calf, draw the calf backwards.

Whether a cow perspires or not is still a question. Dr. Richardson of the University of California, who has tested the common American cow rather thoroughly, is convinced that it does not "sweat." But it may perspire through the nose.

There are many superstitious methods to restore the cow's loss of its cud. The United States Department of Agriculture, however, claims that an artificial cud or food of any kind is not the thing to use when ruminating is halted, because the indication is that the cow is already in need of the attention of a veterinarian.

Bulls Do Not See Red

THAT A RED CLOTH excites and infuriates a bull is a very popular superstition. Some years ago, however, experiments were carried out to find out if this were so, and thirty bulls were employed in the test. The bullfighters used red and white cloths alternately. The net result turned out to be that when the bullfighter used a white cloth, he got the same violent reaction as when he used red. And what is more, all the bulls performed exactly alike.

From such experiments it became obvious that it is the waving of the cloth—a strange and unfamiliar moving object—in front of the bull, and not a particular color, that made him charge.

Another evidence of this fact is the story of the farmer who was driving a herd of cattle down a lane. A bull spied a red bandana poking from his pocket and waving in the breeze, and charged. As the farmer turned heel and ran, his hat blew off. And then the bull chased the hat which was *not* red!

So far no one has come forth with specific evidence to prove that red really irritates the bull more than any other bright color. Bullfighters dress in the most glaring colors and wave pieces of gaudy-colored cloth in the arena, as much to attract the attention of the spectators as to infuriate the bull. Red is naturally a favorite color, for it is brilliant, the color of blood, and what is more important, it reacts most quickly on the *human* optic nerve.

Possibly the bright costumes of the bullfighters may have something to do with the superstition that a bull goes wild when he sees red. However, if red is the color which enrages the bull, no matador would dare to wear a suit of brilliant red silk, as he often does. In the arena the bull gets excited only when the matador waves the cape or cloth in front of it. Neither the masses, nor even the aristocrats, in the olden days, understood what made the bull angry. The psychology of color and motion was not yet popular knowledge.

Through an association of ideas, many persons think that bulls are irritated by red because it is the color of blood. There is no foundation for this theory, as tests seem to prove that bulls are color-blind. Incidentally, it is claimed that of all mammals only man and monkeys can distinguish color. All that other animals are said to see are shades of gray.

Although the nervous system of human beings is affected in various ways by different colors, so that "He sees red!" has a definite meaning, it has no application to bulls, this popular superstition to the contrary notwithstanding.

Bullfighting is a very ancient sport. As a matter of record, combats with bulls were common in ancient Thessaly, as well as in the amphitheatres of imperial Rome. The Moors of Africa probably introduced bull-fighting into Andalusia when they conquered that province. The first Spanish bull-fighter lived about 1040. After the Moors were driven from Spain by Ferdinand II, bullfighting continued, and became a national institution lasting to the present day.

That Horsehairs Turn into Snakes

A POPULAR superstition among young people is that a horsehair, when put into water, turns into a snake. Because of this belief, it is also said that snakes can often be found by a pool where horses drink.

The superstitious notion that eels or water snakes grow from horsehairs in water is very silly, and shows a complete lack of knowledge of natural history. For instance, there are several species of worms, known as hairworms, that resemble the long hairs in a horse's tail. These worms are found in ponds, streams and watering troughs.

It is not well known either, that horsehairs decay in about the same length of time that it takes for the eggs of hairworms to mature in the water. It is no wonder, then, that these round worms that are about the same size as horsehairs—from five to ten inches long and as thick as a pin,—are mistaken for miniature eels or water snakes.

Of course, a hair cannot turn into a worm or snake. However, an illusion is created when a strand of hair is placed in water. It will gradually turn, twist and curve, due to the effect of moisture. This fact, no doubt, made many conclude that the horsehair came to life in the form of an eel or snake.

"Horseshoe" Superstitions

ALTHOUGH THE horseshoe is sometimes hung with its prongs up, and at other times with them down, it is nevertheless always a good luck symbol.

There are a great many superstitions about the horseshoe. To find an old horseshoe is lucky, but to find one with the open hoof space toward you means that all your troubles are over—it is so lucky. The number of nails in the horseshoe you find indicates the years of good luck. To dream of a horseshoe is a sign you will receive unexpected money. A horseshoe in a bedroom is a protection against nightmares. To bend a horseshoe nail into a ring and wear it will avert rheumatism. A horseshoe kept in the fire will keep the hawks away from chickens, and so on.

The many traditions behind horseshoe superstitions all point to related symbols which deal with the solar circle, the half-circle or crescent, and the crotch of the human body. This U-symbol, half-circle or crescent, composed of a pair of horns, was variously used as a symbol of fertility to attract good fortune, and to repel evil. Sometimes the points were up to represent the seat of masculine powers, and sometimes down to represent the seat of feminine powers. However, the symbol was always a potent and protective symbol.

One method of attaining protection against the Evil Eye or evil spirits was to suspend an emblem of motherhood above one's doorway. The Arabs of northern Africa used to hang real parts of a cow or other female animal over their holy places.

In ancient Yucatan and Peru there were temples with arched doorways, and at the top of the arches were engravings of the female creator. A very ancient protective sign was to make an oval with the thumb and index finger, the female symbol. There are hundreds of such instances among peoples everywhere in ancient, medieval and modern times—even up to the present day.

The Greeks are said to have originated the horseshoe in the 4th Century to protect the feet of their horses. This animal has at times been considered a sacred one. Until comparatively recently, the horseshoe was made with seven holes for nails,—three on the outside and four on the inside. The lucky number seven, combined with a crescent symbol, added to the potency of the talisman. Greeks and Romans nailed horseshoes against their walls to protect against the plague.

The Druids believed in the charm of the semi-circular form of the horseshoe design, as their religious grounds, such as at Stonehenge, England, clearly show. In Rajputana, India, temples are constructed on the plan of a horseshoe wherein the *yoni*, or female phallic symbol, is worshipped. Windows and doors designed in the horseshoe or arch-style of architecture also represent the phallic symbol.

The Moors have fashioned their mosques and temples with arch formations because they so thoroughly believed in the protective powers of the crescent-shaped, or U-shaped symbol of good luck. In New York City, there is the famous Diamond Horseshoe of the Metropolitan Opera House.

Horseshoe floral designs, door-knockers, and other uses of this idea are expressions that wish good fortune to others or to the owners themselves.

There is an ancient Saxon superstition that witches cannot practice their wiles upon persons in the open air, and in order to harm someone they must enter the home of their intended victim. Because of this superstition, it would appear that horseshoes were placed at the outer entrance of a home rather than on the inside.

Today, when we see a horseshoe nailed over a doorway, with prongs either up or down, we know it is standing guard to protect the occupants of the building, whether man or beast.

Horse Chestnut or "Buckeye" Facts and Superstitions

MOST COUNTRIES have superstitions about the horse chestnut that closely resemble each other.

There are persons who still carry a horse chestnut in their pockets to prevent, lessen or cure the pain and discomfort of rheumatism. Carrying a horse chestnut or "buckeye," as it is sometimes called, is also believed to prevent headache. Another superstition is that when the muscles of the leg contract and become knotted, "buckeye" tea will bring relief.

This tea, made from the pretty blossoms of the horse chestnut tree, is drunk by superstitious addicts to cure a multitude of other ailments, not the least of which is hemorrhoids. Likewise, there are many persons who eat the bitter fruit to guard against infectious diseases.

Although the origin of the name "horse chestnut" is lost in antiquity, it is generally attributed to the fact that the nuts were fed as food and medicine to horses from earliest times, long before the tree was introduced into Europe and the British Isles from Constantinople in the 16th Century.

The fact that this tree is a native of Tibet may explain why the folklore and superstitions connected with it have their roots in Asiatic antiquity. That this tree is unusually long-lived did not escape the observing minds of primitives. In Mongolia, China and other Far Eastern countries, where homeopathic ideas were practiced, horse chestnuts were fed to animals in the belief that "like brings like." And in the Near East as well as the Orient, they were given to cure or ward off cough, short breath and similar disabilities of horses.

Folklore in China has it that the chestnut and horse chestnut trees are not only symbols of longevity and fertility, but have been given these characteristics for man's benefit—so that soon, grandson, and even great-grandson, will be assured of a livelihood from the harvest. The Chinese chestnut tree commands the respect of every hard-working native, both because it is long-lived and therefore a good provider, and because it matures in a very few years.

An interesting story from the long, long ago is that native horses of the Mongolian desert—horses which are today the only remaining species of the true wild horse—had "chestnuts" or warty patches on all four of their legs. These horses were given nuts from the chestnut tree in imitative magic, to relate the horse more closely to the tree. No doubt, it had not escaped the observation of these early people either, that a horseshoe-shaped scar is left on the twig of this tree when the leaves fall,—to their minds, another link between horse and tree.

What must also have touched their imagination in this respect is that the terminal and auxiliary buds of the horse chestnut tree resemble a horse's foot; and that a horse chestnut, cut obliquely, presents a miniature picture of a horse's hock and foot, shoe and nails.

In time, the curative powers of the horse chestnut were believed equally effective on humans. Hence the superstitions.

Here in America, it was thought that the partly opened pods of the horse chestnut resembled the eyes of a deer, which gave the tree the later name of "buckeye" tree. Ohio, where many of these trees are found, is known as the "Buckeye State."

"Rabbit" and "Hare" Superstitions

"Nor did we meet, with nimble feet,
With little fear lepus (hare)
That certain sign, as some divine,
Of fortune bad to keep us."

THE GAMBLER, even today, is rarely without a rabbit foot charm, even though it may be only the small front paw. Incidentally, the small front paw holds no magic significance in folklore, but the gambler, and others for that matter, are seldom aware of this, and have implicit faith in its good luck. Hundreds of thousands, perhaps millions, of such small paws are sold yearly with the buyer none the wiser. With a rabbit foot in his left pocket, the gambler, win or lose, feels lucky holding on to the strange psychology that without his rabbit foot his losses would have been much greater!

To be an infallible talisman, the rabbit's foot must be the left hind foot of an animal killed at the full of the moon by a cross-eyed person. There are hundreds of other rabbit superstitions. If an old hare runs across the path of a pregnant woman, her child will have a harelip, unless she can quickly catch up one of her undergarments and tear a slit in it. Another version of this superstition tells that it is unlucky in general for an expectant mother to see a hare sitting, but if she sees the little white tuft on the end of its tail, her child will be born with a harelip. The countermagic is to unravel a small portion of the seam of her petticoat.

If the hare crosses your path you may look for disappointment. If it runs past your house, there will be a fire. Some believe that a safe journey awaits those whose path is crossed at the outset by a hare, while others believe the opposite.

Superstitious colored people generally believe that if a baby's gums are rubbed with the brains of a rabbit, it will teethe without pain. The skin of a rabbit's stomach tied around a baby's neck helps it cut teeth.

To carry a rabbit's foot in one's pocket will cure rheumatism. Many persons will use wet rabbit skins for swellings or sprains. If the skin is carried as an amulet, it has other prophylactic and curative powers. Superstitious country people often address a few sweet words of greeting to a rabbit when it runs across their path to remove the bad luck that might be in store for them.

The hare or rabbit is considered a weather prophet by woodsmen who base their predictions for the coming winter on signs in nature. If the animal's fur is thick, it will be a hard winter; if thin, a mild one. This form of prophecy is not necessarily accurate. Fur is generally better when an animal has had plenty of good food, and not because of any instinct it has to sense winter temperatures and prepare for them.

Theatrical people, a very superstitious lot, are very good customers for rabbit's feet. They may be bought in most drug stores in America, and are used by the "profession" both as luck-bringers and for make-up purposes. A rabbit foot in the make-up kit is generally kissed for luck, or rubbed on the hands and face before an entrance on opening night to bring success, dispel stage fright, and help remember lines.

In days when hares and rabbits were related to the witch cult, many of the superstitions implied that a witch could hide in an animal and do harm to humans by that means. A witch who had turned into a hare could only be hit and injured by a crooked sixpence or a silver bullet. Silver was the symbol or metal of the moon, while the hare, a lunar animal, was vulnerable to the silver and reverted to its former animal self, and the witch was believed killed.

There was an ancient belief that both the hare and the moon had the power to change sex. The new moon was masculine, the waning moon, feminine. At the same time, it was believed that hares changed their sex every year—the males becoming females and vice versa. In America there is the superstition that jack rabbits are males and cotton-tails are females, although the fact is they belong to two separate groups with males and females of each.

It is very curious that most Americans fail to distinguish between a hare and a rabbit. Animals that belong to the same genus as old world hares are called rabbits. One explanation may be that candy makers at Easter time made hares and sold them as rabbits. However, the Belgian hare is not a hare,—it is a rabbit.

Perhaps one reason for the confusion about these two animals and the superstitions pertaining to them is lack of understanding of the characteristics of each. A rabbit is smaller than a hare and has shorter ears and legs. A hare has powerful hind legs and the tips of its long ears are black. The rabbit lives in burrows which it digs under the ground, building separate tunnels in which to raise its young. The hare lives in the open and has no home, depending upon speed for safety. Both animals differ from other rodents in having four incisor teeth in the upper jaw instead of two. The rabbit is the more easily tamed, but the hare is much quicker in its movement. The fur of certain northern hares is white in winter and brown in summer.

The main distinction between these two animals, which, to the ancients, made one evil and the other good, has to do with their eyes. The young of the hare are born with hair and with eyes wide open, whereas the young of the rabbit are born hairless and blind.

The Egyptian word for hare was "un," which also means "to open" or "the opener." As opener of the new year at Easter time, the hare became associated in the popular mind with the egg, symbol of resurrection from the remotest of ages. The connection between the hare and the moon is due to the fact that the hare is a nocturnal animal and comes out at night to feed. This is a very old association, and is also attributed to the mysterious effect the moon has upon the hare, which early peoples could not fail to observe. On clear moonlight nights hares used to gather in bands, and indulge in weird play, silent and bizarre, as if under the influence of some subtle and transforming elixir of life. Another symbolic tie between the hare and the moon is that the female carries her young about for a month, thus representing the cycle of the moon.

Because of the ancient legendary idea that the white rabbit, found in northern countries of the western world, played in the white Easter moon, the animal came to mean prosperity. A white rabbit was given to children in the hope that they would grow up to be prolific and prosperous, and the gift is still a popular one. The Germans made the hare sacred to the Goddess Eastre, and said that on Easter Eve it would lay eggs for good children.

There are many other characteristics of the hare which made this timid animal both venerated and feared by the ancients. There was a theory that the hare, like the serpent, noted for the magic of its eye, had a counbercharm for its own Evil Eye. With the hare it was its hind foot.

The mystic potency of the foot has always been used symbolically in relation to sex, and the hind foot of an animal as prolific as the hare or rabbit added to the potency of the amulet. The phallic worship of the foot is said to antedate the Evil Eye superstitions.

Another outstanding characteristic of the hare is that it is one of only three animals whose rear feet hit the ground in front of the fore-feet when running rapidly. The others are the greyhound and the cheetah. To observing primitives, this peculiarity implied that the hind foot came first. For this reason, too, American Indians, particu-larly the Cherokee braves, would not eat hare meat for fear it would confuse them in running although they were excellent runners. They believed this so thoroughly that when at war they sprinkled rabbit or hare soil along the path to hinder and confuse their enemies.

Hares thump with their hind legs, which some describe as "speak-ing" with their hind legs. The footprints of hares and rabbits were puzzling to say the least, to people who did not understand the reason, but it contributed toward the magic that was supposed to lodge in the hind leg or paw.

Many persons think that hares never blink their eyes, but this is not so. After watching a hare for several minutes, anyone can see that it finally opens and closes its eyes very slowly and deliberately several times, with long or short periods in between.

Rabbits and hares are the fastest multiplying animals among mam-mals. Therefore, it is not surprising that the rabbit or hare foot is not only a phallic symbol, but also one of unusual fertility, which was held in the greatest reverence in ancient times. Fertility to early man was equivalent to prosperity, for it not only applied to offspring, but to an abundance of other things that made life easier.

The wild rabbit is a native of Europe but has been exported and domesticated for centuries. It may be found in nearly every country of the world, together with superstitions, which for the most part belong to the hare. This confusing of the two was especially true during the Middle Ages, which has made for an intricate mesh of legends and sayings around these creatures.

The hare, a perfectly harmless animal, was the object of supersti-tious fear on all the continents. The ancient Irish killed all the hares they found among the cattle on May Day; believing them to be witches in disguise that would harm their animals. Caesar gives an account of the horror in which the hare was held by the Britons. The Hebrews would not eat hare flesh, as it was believed unlucky, and no hares could be found in Palestine. Hare is never eaten in Spain, because of the superstition that in the night the animals go into graveyards, dig up the graves, and eat dead bodies. However, in Mexico, divine honors were paid to this same animal, while in France, it is almost a national dish.

The ancient Aztecs so thoroughly believed that the hare's eyes had magical powers that they believed that drowsiness and insomnia could both be alleviated with formulas which included throwing the hare's hair on burning embers, and sniffling the odor while someone blew the smoke of the burning hair into the ears of the patient. Next, an eviscerated hare, or the contents of its eyeball, was burnt to charcoal, and then the ash was placed in a new earthen pot, and mixed with water, as a further "eye-opener."

The moon with a hare in it pounding the drug of immortality is frequently represented in Chinese art. This is one of the twelve Chinese symbols of power. The Druids used the hare for purposes of divination. When Boadicea, who lived at the times of the Roman emperor Nero, went into battle against the Romans, she carried a hare in her breast as a luck-bringer. She was victorious for a while, and it is possible that her final defeat may have been the reason the hare acquired so many evil characteristics from then on. The rabbit's foot nevertheless retains its universal popularity as a charm of good luck.

"Goat" Superstitions

GOATS HAVE found their way into the folklore of all nations, and references to this odd animal have become everyday expressions.

Goats are kept in horse stables because of the ancient belief that these animals preserved horses from diseases. A goat on a farm is said to bring good fortune to an otherwise unlucky farmer. The bile of a black goat, when mixed in a salve, is believed to have curative powers. If one meets a goat when embarking on a new business venture, it insures success. A goat's horns under the pillow is a cure for insomnia.

Goats do not eat tin cans and straw hats for the superstitious reason that they will eat anything. This animal got its reputation as a tin can eater from the act of gnawing at the label in order to get at the sweet glue used on the containers it found in rubbish heaps or underbrush. As for the hats, most straw hats are made of straw obtained from dried stems or stalks of cereals, such as wheat, oats, barley and rye. The ever-hungry goats find a questionable bill of fare, but to them it is food.

All breeds of goats like to eat brushwood and weeds, and in some places they are kept especially for their ability to clear brushland.

Ancient Greeks paid much honor to animals. In poetry, art and divination, certain animals were associated with certain gods, such as the eagle to Jupiter, the raven to Apollo, the bull to Bacchus and the goat to Pan. The Greeks believed that the horn of the goat Amalthea, broken off by Jupiter, had the power to be filled with whatever the one who possessed it wished. Hence, the allegorical meaning of the "horn of plenty" or cornucopia.

Because of the great propensity of the billy goat to destroy the vine as it capered about, it was sacrificed to Bacchus, god of the Vine. The expression "cutting capers," referring to an alcoholic spree or other inordinate gaiety, derives from the fact that the Latin word for goat was "caper." To be capricious or goat-like is an adjective 3,000 years old. It signified that a bewhiskered goat would leap hither and yon in a farmer's field, dancing on its hind legs without rhyme or reason. The modern appellation, "a billy-goat" reminds us of the same thing.

On the seventh of July—the Nones of the Goat—or the day on which Romulus was believed to have been caught up in Heaven at the Swamp of the Goat, in the Plain of Mars, women, both bond and free, sacrificed the milky juice of the fig to Juno of the Goat, and feasted beneath the sacred wild fig tree. Originally the tree itself was worshipped, its fruit regarded as a phallic symbol. Today the sign in the form of "fico"—thumb between index and middle fingers—is used as a counatercharm to repel evil influences. It is known as the "fig."

The superstition that the goat can and will eat everything and anything is very ancient, as this animal was the sin-eater of biblical times. The release of a scapegoat, or escape goat, was part of the solemn ritual prescribed by the Mosaic Law for the Day of Atonement observed by ancient Israelites each year on the tenth day of their seventh month. It is related that the Lord, through Moses, commanded Aaron as high priest "to take of the congregation of Israel two kids of the goats for a sin offering."

It was believed in Bible times that the sins of a whole nation could be put on the head of a goat, and that the goat "should bear upon him all their iniquities unto a land not inhabited," or a wilderness. The scapegoat was led into the desert and left there; and it was supposed that peace and innocence remained behind with the people. Later, however, when it became impossible for the sin-laden animal to be sent to a place so far away that it could not return to inhabited parts, the goat was thrown down a precipice. This interesting superstition is described in Leviticus XVI:10. It explains our very common saying, "He's the goat," when someone bears a burden not his own; or "He gets my goat," for personal annoyance of some sort. Symbolically goats are the recipients of all that is not wanted, either from man or animals.

The ancient Israelites were not the only ones who performed the ceremonies of sin-offerings. Similar customs are found among the ancient Athenians, whose scapegoat was a young man. The Arabs used a camel, while many others, such as certain Orientals, used a material object in the form of a native ship which was sent floating down the river, loaded with the year's misfortunes, crimes and all things to be gotten rid of—a primitive form of confessional unloading of their woes onto the sea gods.

"Sheep" Superstitions

MOST OF today's superstitious beliefs about sheep go back to the time when the ancient "looker," or shepherd, in his honest simplicity interpreted as best he could the happenings to his flock. The ancestors of domestic sheep were creatures of the mountains and hills, so the responsibility of close watching rested on the shoulders of the shepherd, for these animals represented food as well as clothing to the tribe. Whatever took place during daylight, moonlight, or even on pitch-black nights made up the shepherd's small universe. With the passing of the seasons, he peopled it with all sorts of supernatural beings, both good and evil, to account in some measure for what was beyond his comprehension. These facts and fancies are related to the large number of superstitions observed to the present time.

The lamb, from time immemorial, has symbolized innocence and self-sacrifice, and figures in the legends of all peoples. This animal was sacred to Juno, the goddess who symbolized the spirit of woman's energy; and lambs were under her protection. The lamb's call, "baa," has been likened nearest to that of a child. Hence, with the passing of human sacrifice, in an effort to save human lives, it became an ideal animal to substitute as a special offering to the gods, and *special* favors were expected in return. The expression "meek as a lamb" implies a self-sacrificing person.

Among a multitude of superstitions about sheep are: a bumper spring lamb yield is viewed with apprehension as a sign of possible great need through a catastrophe of some kind, such as a war; the pomade from a lamb's caul and May dew is still used to restore lost beauty by many country women; shearing sheep on the increase of the moon will produce better and stronger wool; it is a sign of good luck to meet a flock of sheep; to pass through a flock of sheep brings bad luck.

It is also a superstition that sheep always go to a barbed wire fence when a storm is coming and that is why so many are killed during a storm. When sheep turn their backs to the wind, look for a cold spell. Rubbing the gums with sheep's brains will help a baby cut its teeth. It is a sign that one will suffer great pain if one dreams of sheep. Keep a piece of lamb's wool on a corn and after a time the corn can be removed easily. It is very good luck for the couple if a bridal party meets a lamb when they are on their way to church.

A black ewe or ram foretells good or bad luck depending on the traditional background of superstitious people. If a ewe, however, produces two black lambs, it is believed to bring disaster to the flock. To prevent calamity, the superstitious farmer cuts the throats of the twins before they say "baa." Three black sheep are generally considered bad luck. The common saying that a man who does not turn out well is the "black sheep" of the family goes back to the days when a black sheep was considered to be the devil in disguise, or that it was the mark of the devil upon the animal and therefore the animal was undesirable and a trouble-maker.

The ram plays many parts in folklore. It is an animal that brings good fortune and drives away evil spirits; and it is a symbol of the principle of fertility. The ram caught by Abraham and sacrificed instead of Isaac attests to the antiquity of its use in sacrifice. According to Mohammedan legend, the ram is among ten preferred animals that may enter Paradise. The Hindus believe that if the sound of the skylark, the peacock, the mongoose, the king-fisher and the ram be heard, or if the names of these creatures be mentioned, or if they be seen it signifies a gain in wealth.

Today, in Sicily, a man with a ram's head goes from house to house to drive away evil spirits, for a fee. One of the most universal good luck "fetishes" is the ram's horn. In Italy there are ram's horns swinging from the axles of those picturesque one-horse carts which are used to transport wine from Alban Hill towns into Rome. They are carried as protection against bad luck. The habit of attaching these fetishes to workmen's carts dates so far back into antiquity that no one thinks about their origin or the basis of their efficacy.

However, ram's horns are by no means restricted to drivers of wine carts. They are seen in miniature as watch charms on persons with college degrees. There is scarcely a jeweler's shop that does not handle these tokens, which is an indication that they are in demand.

The American custom of having animals for mascots includes the Fordham ram for that university, the Army mule, the Navy goat and the Yale bulldog. Animal mascots go back to that long ago century when animals were present at all important ceremonies.

"Porcupine" Superstitions

PORCUPINES NEVER seem to live down the bad reputation acquired through a traditional fallacy that they roll themselves up when the hunters set their dogs at them and shoot quills or spines with great fury, wounding both men and dogs. This belief goes back at least to the early part of the 14th century and was reported by Marco Polo from his observations of the interior of Asia. This report succeeded in making the porcupine an animal to be feared, except by naturalists, who investigated and found the evidence lacking. Meanwhile, however, misinformation found its way into the literature of superstition and was ingrained in people's minds. The fallacy is still believed in America today.

The truth is that the porcupine cannot throw its quills, and they are not deadly arrows of defense. They are, however, loosely attached. When frightened, the increase of adrenalin causes tiny involuntary muscles to contract and makes the quills point skyward at a defensive angle. It fights by thrashing the tail. The quills readily detach themselves and often may be found on the ground, giving the impression of having been thrown.

One of the reasons the superstition persists is that the porcupine rolls into a ball when in a defensive position. It generally hides its head under a log or puts its nose between its forepaws—the nose is very vulnerable—arches its back, erects its quills, and hugs the ground with its feet close together. Then it charges backwards, flipping its tail from side to side until the enemy retreats, which is usually shortly after the attack has begun. By these means the little porcupine looks twice its size and very formidable, indeed.

"Fox" Superstitions

THE FOX is proverbially a wise animal and for ages has been known for its cunning traits. Traditionally it has been the central character in fables from the remotest times, as in the Aesop fable of the "Fox and the Grapes." Incidentally, Aesop was right: foxes really eat grapes. Aesop was a Greek slave who dramatized his ideas in fables in the 6th century B.C. He endowed animals not only with reasoning powers but with speech as well. Then there were the famous 12th century epic tales of "Reynard the Fox," anonymously written, in which the lion as judge summons Reynard before the animal court to answer for his misdeeds. There is also La Fontaine's "The Raven and the Fox" and many others down to "Uncle Remus."

The fact that the fox almost always displayed infallible strategic ability to keep out of trouble, or out of the path of his pursuer, endowed him with supernatural attributes which have come down to us practically in an unbroken chain. Popular belief in the wisdom of the fox is deeply rooted in fiction and supported by the press. *Time* magazine recently informed its readers that a fox near Bristol, England, had "led twelve hounds to a cliff's edge (and) ducked safely into a hole as the hounds plunged over the brink." Observers less steeped in nursery stories, however, have failed to perceive any particular cunning in the fox. William Barents and his men found, to their delight, that foxes were very easy to catch. Stefansson found arctic foxes "stupid; or trustful, if you prefer that point of view." *Life* magazine had a series of interesting photographs that illustrated the limited intelligence of foxes. But, after all, wisdom is a comparative matter, and we must remember that our chief knowledge of the fox comes from foxhunters.

Like other furred animals, when foxes' fur is unusually thick, it is believed a sign of a long, cold winter. The fox has something in common with the dog in the belief that when the fox howls or cries, he is thought to be wailing at the spectre of death which he sees approaching, and warns human beings that doom for someone is near at hand. Others feel that when the fox begins its nocturnal howling, spring is not far away, and that mating calls are the signals that Winter is gone.

Because the fox is such an excellent runner, a large number of country folk still believe that eating fox lungs will cure respiratory troubles such as asthma.

Contrary to popular belief, the flying fox is not a fox, but a fruit-eating species of bats with a fox-like face. These animals sometimes have a wingspread exceeding four feet. They live in the steaming swamps and tropical jungles of Australia, and are considered a delicacy by the natives.

Another false notion is that the silver fox belongs to a separate species. Actually it is simply a variety of the red fox, as the black and platinum foxes are also. Contrary to popular belief, there is no fox in the fox terrier. Hunters at one time used terriers to drive foxes from their holes; hence the name "fox terrier."

In mythology there were many animal gods, and in many of the sacrifices made to a special god, a primitive type of communion took place in the eating of the animal itself. In the pre-Christian Mysteries there were ceremonies concerned with the red or fiery fox which survived in Rome even after the beginning of the Christian Dispensation. This ceremonial was observed each year at the time of the Spring Equinox, as the Sun enters the sign of Aries. It celebrated with great rejoicing the new red fire of life which was then becoming active again in all nature. According to an old maxim, "It is divine fox-fire that burns up corn." The fox was also used by early astrologers as one of the symbols of the lower or evil nature of Mars.

There is a story to the effect that when a fox steals a goose, he goes off carrying it slung over his shoulder. That is purely imaginary, of course. The truth is that the fox is a fine actor. He lies on the ground feigning death while a flock of unsuspecting geese approach him. As soon as they come within striking distance, however, he is suddenly "re-incarnated" and the feathers begin to fly.

When a woman is called a vixen, the female fox, she should consider herself complimented rather than slandered, for the vixen is distinguished among animals for being a true and faithful mate. She abides by her mate for a lifetime through thick and thin. Rarely are there any family quarrels among foxes, and rather than see her young suffer or have them exposed to danger, she eats them.

"Groundhog" Superstitions

If Candlemas day be fair and bright,
Winter will have another flight.
But if Candlemas days bring clouds and rain,
Winter is gone and won't come back again.

IN EUROPE, the hedgehog is generally responsible for the weather from Candlemas Day, February 2nd, on. Colonists arriving in America could find no hedgehog, so they transferred the superstition to a native animal, the groundhog. This animal is also known colloquially as the wood-chuck, rock chuck and marmot.

It is said that on February 2 the groundhog comes out of its burrow to inspect the weather. If it sees its shadow, there will be six weeks more of bad weather, or winter; and so it goes back into the ground to hibernate longer. However, if the day is cloudy, it is expected to remain outside, because it signifies that spring is already on its way.

As far as the Weather Bureau is concerned, the groundhog is a very unreliable weather prophet. Perhaps that is because February 2 is much too early in north temperature climates for the groundhog to come out in the open, so that if it does appear, it invariably goes back to its burrow until warmer weather comes; shadow or no shadow.

Every February 2, however, sixty-five members of the Slumbering Lodge, founded almost fifty years ago in Quarryville, Pennsylvania, sally forth to ascertain whether the groundhog will see its shadow. At 8 A.M., the members, middle-aged bankers, merchants, lawyers, doctors and farmers, assemble wearing ancient top hats or sombreros, and carrying shepherds' crooks or fishing poles with white flags tied to them for signaling. Forming in squads, they march out over the fields and hills. As each squad finds a hole, they settle down to watchful waiting. The first man to sight a groundhog emerging lets out a blood-curdling yell. Then all get together to hear the formal report of the Hibernating Governor. The rest of the day is spent in celebration by the whole town, for Groundhog Day is to Quarryville what the Mardi Gras is to New Orleans. Other Groundhog Lodge groups have formed in other parts of Pennsylvania.

Like many other harmless animals, the groundhog has been improperly named. It does live in a burrow in the ground, but it is not a hog. It is more nearly related to the rabbit. Under its alias of "wood-chuck," it is the mythical manipulator of problematical quantities of timber. "How much wood would a woodchuck chuck if a woodchuck could chuck wood?" It has never been demonstrated that a woodchuck could chuck wood, but if patiently trained, it can be made into a nice house pet. And it does not eat the furniture!

Groundhog superstitions are perfect examples of how myths can travel. Naturalists report that the groundhog is one of several February 2 weather prophets. In Europe, the bear, the badger and the hedge-hog are the favorites.

The tradition concerning groundhogs as weather prophets on

February 2 stems from the ancient observance of the Roman Catholic festival known as Candlemas, which occurs also on February 2. This holy day celebrates the Purification of the Virgin, and the Presentation of Christ at the Temple. On Candlemas Day, candles are blessed for the year.

The Candlemas custom of the early Christians, however, was based on an earlier Roman purification rite, when women carried candles in honor of the goddess Venus, on February 2, which was the time of the return of Venus to its place as a morning star. This ritual was symbolic of birth and life, the promise of spring, the sun, crops, and all that the season implied in the life of man for his survival.

Fire, as is well known, is a symbol of the sun, and an element which purifies as it destroys evil influences or spirits that are around, especially at the time of childbirth. Therefore it was desirable to burn candles by the side of a mother and her new-born child, a custom still observed in Greece, Germany, and even America, as a symbol of spiritual protection.

Candlemas, and candle bearing on the second of February, was therefore a day set aside for women, especially after childbirth. It was a day of purification, and blessings, by the use of enough candles to round out the year. The candles were used in temples and homes as vigil lamps, just as the custom is observed today.

There is another superstitious association in the observance of Groundhog Day because of its prediction of six weeks of good or bad weather. From time immemorial, animals symbolized the number six, a number greatly revered by early Egyptians and other peoples.

Referring to the number 6, we read in the Apocalypse: "Here is wisdom. Let him that hath understanding count the number of the beast; for it is the number of man; and his six hundred, three score and six,"—or 666, three sixes.

Three sixes inscribed in a circle portray the geometrical construction of the six. As man is said to be an animal, or at least to have an animal or passionate element embodied in his makeup, we can see plainly what this Bible passage refers to in its enigmatical passage.

Folklore attaches a great deal of mystic importance to six, sixty and other combinations of six. A vast amount of prophecy has been based on the number of the Beast in Revelation or six hundred and three-score and six.

And so it is that Groundhog Day with its many associations is observed at the time of the year when the sun was supposed to return with a promise to man that it would shine again on crops and bring all the blessings of warmth and plenty.

"Squirrel" Superstitions

AMERICAN INDIANS have many legends about the squirrel. One of them tells why the small red squirrel bursts into sputtering, scolding, and snapping, and stamps its feet and furiously twitches its tail when it sees a man. It is because, once upon a time, an old Indian brave, with divine permission, reduced him from an enormous animal to his present diminutive size.

In all countries where squirrels are found many myths and superstitions, and even proverbs, have been made up about this little creature's activities. One old proverb says, "When squirrels are scarce in autumn, the winter will be severe." To which scientists reply, "When squirrels are scarce in autumn the hunters have been busy."

As in the case of many animals, the squirrel's behavior is supposed to foretell weather. If a squirrel stores a great quantity of food, it means a hard winter. If he puts away only a normal supply, a mild winter can be expected. Checking these beliefs has failed to substantiate them in any way. The truth probably is that a sensible squirrel gathers all the nuts and other food he can find. The more that is available, the more he stores. The squirrel is a provident little animal, but also a glutton. Sometimes he forgets where he buries his acorns and chestnuts. Nature then evens things up by growing new trees from these buried seeds, adding to our forests and also to this greedy and forgetful little beast's food supply.

Just as the squirrel's food storage has no bearing on the kind of weather to expect, neither has the length of its fur coat or tail any prophetic message. In fact, naturalists find very little difference in the animal's tail or coat from year to year.

In folklore, the squirrel is known chiefly as a "fire animal," that is, it is associated with stories telling how fire was brought to earth by the squirrel for the benefit of man. That this animal was associated with fire is due, no doubt to the orange-reddish color of certain species. The fire-color is just a step removed from the sun color, revered in the sun-worship of ancient times.

In Europe, in the not very distant past, squirrels were burned in the Easter bonfire, and while flames were consuming the animals, as a sacrifice to fire, shepherds would force their flocks to leap over the flames, which they thought would make them immune to disease and witchcraft. At the same time, they hoped this rite would give their animals the same agility as the squirrel.

Because it was the superstition of the time that the squirrel would be a protection against the ravages of fire, it was often captured and imprisoned in a cage. In the cage was a mobile wheel—symbol of sun and fire—on which the poor thing frequently shortened its life; spinning it away on this contraption.

Imaginative artists have done their share in spreading countless myths and legends through their illustrations and other pictures. A typical example, often seen in children's story books, is a drawing showing squirrels crossing a stream, embarked on chips of wood, and using their tails for sails. Squirrels, of course, cross water the same as other animals, by swimming.

There is a superstition that a separate species of white and of black squirrel exists. All white squirrels, however, are mutations or deviations of either the common gray squirrel or the fox squirrel. Whole families of albino squirrels are not unusual. The same explanation applies to black squirrels, which likewise are found in numbers in one locality.

There is a little animal closely related to the ground squirrel that is incorrectly called the prairie dog. Many think it is a species of canine. The prairie dog is not a dog at all. It is a burrowing rodent allied to the marmot or groundhog. The burrows of the prairie dog—called "prairie-dog towns"—are elaborate and extensive. One famous colony of them in western Texas is about 250 miles long and 100 miles wide.

Facts and Superstitions About the Beaver

NATURE HAS endowed the beaver with so many extraordinary features that this animal has been the source of much superstitious belief wherever it is found. For instance, it is believed that when the beaver is hunted, it will bite off the glands which it knows the hunter is after. This particular tall-tale was famous many centuries ago. It was said, "When the beaver is hunted, it bites off the part which the hunters seek, and then, standing upright, shows it to the hunters, so that it is useless to continue the pursuit." Aesop, the Greek writer of fables, and others of his day relate a similar story of a civet-cat which is also hunted for its musk glands.

It is true that the glands of both male and female beaver secrete a substance known as *castoreum*, which is used in medicine as a stimulant and anti-spasmodic. It is also used in the making of perfumes. The superstitious, however, use the medicine to bring on abortion, to cure toothache, and as a quack remedy for a variety of other ills. *Castoreum*, a bitter, orange-brown, peculiar substance is found in two sacs between the anus and the external genitals.

Beavers are believed to take defensive measures, such as slapping their tails in the water as signals, and posting sentinels to warn of the approach of an enemy. This is pure fiction, of course. When beavers dive, they always slap the water with their tails; and also slap their tails when on top of their houses inspecting them; or when they are about their work of building their homes and storing food.

This use of the beaver's tail has given rise to another fallacy which is that it uses it as a trowel when building a dam. As a matter of fact, the beaver carries mud under its chin and puts it in place with its forepaws. The beaver's tail does serve as a rudder while its webbed feet propel it through the water, and serves as a prop when it stands on its hind feet.

Beavers are not always busy, either, and "Busy as a beaver" as the saying goes, is not founded on fact.

A beaver's sense of direction is *not* faultless when it comes to tree felling, for very often the tree the beaver is working on falls on it. The mistaken idea that a beaver knows how to lay a tree where it wants it comes from the fact that around most ponds or creeks, trees lean toward the water and fall naturally into it when cut.

Many persons believe that beavers are weather prophets, but this industrious animal does not always live up to its reputation. Nevertheless, each autumn, the superstitious hunter investigates in order to ascertain whether or not the beavers have laid up an abundance of food for the winter. If he finds a beaver house with piles of food logs— short lengths of birch or aspen with the bark still on—safely anchored nearby, he believes the winter will be one of thick and lingering ice.

However, there appears to be no relation between the food storage and the nature of the coming winter. A large supply of accumulated food indicates simply that there was plenty available.

A weather prediction based on the thickness of the beaver's coat likewise is not borne out. Naturalists have not been able to find much difference in the fur from year to year, no matter what the winter turns out to be.

According to an old Indian legend, the Creator, after separating the land from the water, employed gigantic beavers to smooth down the earth's surface and prepare it for the abode of man. This superstition is due, of course, to the fact that the beaver is an animal of unusual accomplishments. It is a skillful engineer and carpenter. It not only devised the mill dam, but dug the first canal ever used for water transportation. The beaver cuts a canal on low level ground toward the nearest standing trees, which it fells and then floats the trees down the canal for dam building or other uses. This animal is a fast worker. It can bite through a four-inch tree in some twenty minutes or less!

One of the first attempts to direct the beaver's work to man's benefit was undertaken a few years ago. Instead of being trapped and destroyed for their fur and other products, some of them are to be used to prevent soil erosion by constructing dams in small streams, which will increase the water facilities in various parts of the country. The beaver can build a small dam better and cheaper than man.

It is well that the beaver now has an important place in the conservation program in America, as otherwise this useful citizen of the animal world would soon disappear from the land. Although early in American history countless numbers of the species inhabited wide areas in the United States and Canada, they were becoming very scarce due to the irresponsible slaughter for the sake of the furs. In one respect they are a menace as they deplete forests of small trees. This, however, can be controlled.

Beavers have puzzled observers for centuries. One of their ways that seemed unnatural was put to the test by scientists. It has been noted that beavers, though lung animals, can stay an unusually long time under water. A beaver was watched as it was held under water. At first the animal relaxed completely, and laid its head on the bottom of the pond. Then it seemed to stop breathing while the heartbeat all but stopped. After five minutes, the beaver struggled to come to the surface, when, it was observed, the heartbeats became almost twice as rapid as they had been before the ducking. Its breathing rate, however, showed very little increase. The heartbeat indicated that the oxygen deficiency was beginning to tell.

Although the beaver spends most of its time in water, it does not eat fish, but is a vegetarian. It is nocturnal in its habits. Beavers live in colonies and their homes are for the most part submerged. The beaver mates for life, like many wild animals. The young are born in May, as a rule; and the family remains together for two years, after which time the young ones leave to seek mates and start colonies of their own. A fascinating sight is to see baby beavers ride on the broad tails of their parents.

Superstitions and Facts About Muskrats

SUPERSTITIONS persist that muskrats are weather prophets. Many believe that muskrats predict a severe winter when they build the walls of their houses unusually thick and high and deep into the ground; and that if they dig shallow or flimsy burrows, it will be a mild one. Also that muskrats foretell the approach of a hard winter by cutting corn stalks and carrying them underground. Another belief is that when the muskrat builds his home higher than usual, it is a sign of a wet spring, with high water in the ponds and streams, and possibly floods.

There is also this muskrat superstition, not directly connected with weather, however, that placing the furry side of a muskrat pelt over the lungs will bring relief to a sufferer from asthmatic trouble.

Weather predictions based on the behavior of muskrats and other animals are, for the most part, coincidences, rather than accurate conclusions. That unusual activities on the part of muskrats are reliable signs assumes that the animal world offers clues by which man can expect certain weather conditions. This theory has been carefully tested by conscientious naturalists who kept records for a number of years. None of their findings give positive evidence of any relationship between how the mutkrat prepares his home and the coming weather.

Incidentally, the muskrat is not a rat at all, but resembles the beaver. It has an amazing instinct to act as its own surgeon when one of its limbs has been badly injured. It performs the amputation itself, with heroic animal sense; then covers the wound with hemlock gum, thus keeping out dirt and germs.

This little fellow is most profitable to man for his fur, musk, and recently for his meat. Muskrat fur is sold as "Hudson seal," marsh rabbit and other commercially beneficial names. "Hudson seal" is the most common trade name for dressed muskrat and clothes millions of Americans.

The powerful musk that this animal secrets is widely used in the manufacture of perfumes. As a matter of fact, the fur itself is never without a faint, sweet odor.

Muskrat meat grows in popularity every day. However, it has been consumed in some states for a long time, under the more attractive name of "marsh rabbit," removing the disgusting word "rat" in connection with food.

In the fabulous marshlands of Louisiana, a trapper's paradise, some twenty thousand Louisianans camp in winter and trap muskrats. In one area alone, about six million pelts a year are obtained—more than in all the rest of the states combined, and even more than from Canada and Alaska. The seventy day season usually opens December 10.

Fortunately for the fur trade, muskrats multiply rapidly. They breed all year except during August and September, and the females produce a litter of from three to seven three times a year. Were it not for the trappers, the muskrats would soon exhaust their food supply, which is the sweet root of grasses.

The muskrat, a web-footed animal, is native from the barrens of northern Canada to the Gulf of Mexico.

"Mole" Superstitions

"Pray you, tread softly, that the blind mole may not hear a foot fall."
—Shakespeare's *Tempest*

NEARLY EVERYONE THINKS that the mole is blind, but this assumption is erroneous. Although it is doubtful if a mole can recognize objects, it can distinguish light and darkness, which is all it needs for the kind of life it leads. It is generally believed that the mole is blind because its eyes are set so deep in the fur that they are almost invisible. Studies show, however, that the eyes are nearly perfect in young moles. In adults the external eyes seem to have degenerated until they are no longer useful for vision, and the eyeballs then are no larger than pinheads.

The fact that this small animal lives a secluded life underground, and is a very, very timid creature, has wrapped mystery around it for ages.

Because the mole is essentially a burrowing animal and a very active one, parts of its body have been superstitiously used to ease or cure ills specifically related to the movements of the human body. For instance, the paw of the mole is believed a very good remedy to relieve cramps, rheumatism or similar pains, if it is applied close to that part of the body, such as the limbs, where the trouble lies.

It was "reasoned," according to the principle in magic that "like affects like," that since the moles' two hand-like paws serve as such excellent tools to dig its subterranean passages, this power could be transferred to man.

Among many other mole superstitions there is one about a "mole toe-bag," which is used for a variety of purposes. For example, when a woman wants to rid herself of the attention of a man she no longer cares for, she wears the "mole toe-bag" on her leg. The explanation here is that moles are bashful creatures and disappear underground quickly, so the bag is there to make the man disappear also. The same sort of imitative magic is supposed to work when burnt mole powder is thrown in the path of an undesirable individual.

Another superstition is to catch a mole, cut off one of its paws and hang it up to dry. If this dried paw is suspended from a baby's neck the child will not be bothered when teething. The right paw is believed very effective, and two paws still better. The right paw will also cure cholera infantum, and furthermore, will protect a child from any disease during the first year of its life. Believe it or not, such superstitions are still alive!

"Chameleon" Superstitions

ONE OF THE most popular beliefs pertaining to the chameleon is that this little reptile takes on the color of the object on which it rests. This is a fallacy. The chameleon's rapid and striking color changes occur in response to its emotions—fear, anger or other excitement. Speedy and pronounced changes in hue are affected also by marked changes in the temperature about it.

The chameleon's color change can take place in about three seconds without its moving a muscle. This quick transformation usually gives the creature a chance to escape by blending with its background, but it is sheer superstition to believe that it does this on purpose to disguise itself in order to avoid being seen.

We know today that the chameleon changes color by the natural means of color cells containing yellow, green, red and black coloring matter. These cells lie just below its transparent skin. This color-changing mechanism acts somewhat like the quick flush or act of blushing on human cheeks.

Many superstitions have grown around the chameleon's ability to change color, which oddity in ancient times was believed to be a super-natural power with which it was endowed to enable it to escape from an enemy. Ancient superstitions that are still popular include the notion that to wear or own one of these little animals will ward off evil influences; also, that if it is worn as a charm, it will protect the wearer against disease; and that it lives on air.

Because of these superstitions, a tremendous market has been developed for these reptiles, especially among the tourist trade of Florida, and other places where they are found. Women think that when a chameleon is worn on a chain around the neck it will change color to match the color of a gown. This superstition is one, like many others, that has been turned into a profitable 20th-century industry.

The chameleon is an extraordinary little fellow, endowed by nature with many intriguing features. For instance, when caught by the tail it can separate from its tail. The tail of a chameleon, when obtained on a Sunday, is believed a powerful love charm. What is stranger than losing its tail, however, is the fact that it can grow a new one although the new tail will not be able to change from green to brown for a little while. This is why at times a green chameleon may be seen running around with a brown tail.

Other unusual characteristics of the chameleon are that it can shed its skin several times in one spring, and that it has the ability to "blow up" and extend its body as well as its lungs. This distention is made possible because the lungs are very large and extend far down into the body cavity.

Chameleons can swell up to amazing proportions when they hiss and fight, but when they want to escape discovery, they make themselves as thin as possible by compressing the chest and belly by means of their elongated ribs. The body is then put in such a position that only the narrow side is presented to the enemy.

Primitive and later peoples were filled with awe at the sight of the seven inch chameleon "shooting" flies some twelve inches away by means of its lightning-fast tongue, which rarely missed the prey. African hunters take a chameleon along on their hunting trips because of the superstition that they can "borrow" the animal's capacity to shoot with accuracy.

However, there is nothing magical about the chameleon's skill to "shoot" its prey. Scientists have finally explained the feat. The chameleon's tongue is coiled in its mouth like a spring, telescope-fashion, and it shoots out its tongue just as we would shoot a wet melon seed with our two fingers. Ring-shaped muscles contract suddenly on a slippery spike-like bone, and the tongue leaps forward like a whip. The prey is caught with the sticky tip of the tongue.

For thousands of years this fabulous little lizard has been kept as a protection from the Evil Eye. This may be due to another extraordinary peculiarity, that of being able to move each of its bulging eyes separately, and in all directions, as though mounted on a swivel. The animal's eyes can move up and down, forward and backward, literally in all directions, producing the most terrifying effects. Furthermore, while one of the eyes watches for insects, the other one watches for enemies. No wonder superstitious peoples thought it could keep the Evil Eye at a distance!

"Turtle" and "Tortoise" Superstitions

TURTLE AND TORTOISE superstitions are generally related to health and longevity, probably because these hard-shelled creatures are long-lived. They are also looked upon as weather prophets. If, on land, the shell is moist, it prophesies rain. During a fog, if a turtle is taken out of the water and placed on the ground face down, the fog will disappear.

Amulets made of different metals and ornamented with precious or semi-precious stones are worn by women to preserve health in general, but particularly to help them through the discomforts of pregnancy and to minimize the pains of childbirth.

In ancient times, the tortoise was used in some way in at least sixty remedies, as Pliny tells us. Many of these formulas must have been taken to other parts of the world as they are found in almost identical form in many countries, including America. The Chinese also believed in the curative power of the turtle or tortoise, and some of their ideas also reached America.

In primitive medicine, a bouillon made of turtle was used to promote strength—turtle soup is as old as that! A patient's body was rubbed with tortoise or turtle oil to reduce fever, provided the animal was killed when the moon waned, to correspond with the desired result, the waning of the fever.

Turtle oil has no therapeutic value for aches or pains, sore joints or lame back; nevertheless there is a jar of it in many a rural home today for superstitious persons to use in emergency.

To distinguish between a turtle, tortoise and terrapin: turtles are a semi-aquatic marine species; tortoises are strictly terrestrial; and terrapins are a hard-shelled, fresh water species that are edible and have a recognized market value.

The turtle is very healthy and it has never been known to die from a disease, which is probably why it lives so long. Many persons believe it is a good food for bone-building and brain-building. It is considered bad luck to own a turtle and give it away. Today the market is filled with small turtles, decorated and plain, to match any decorative scheme in a room. Buyers, superstitious or otherwise, buy these ostensibly to add a note to the setting, but turtles are also desirable as bringers of good luck and good health. Turtles are supposed to be antidotes for evil influences of all kinds.

There are many other superstitions about the turtle. Like the snake, it is not supposed to die before sundown. Many believe that a biting turtle will not let go till it thunders. If you carve your initials on a turtle's shell, it will never leave your garden. It is unlucky to kill a turtle unless you intend to eat it. Turtle bones carried in your pocket will bring good luck wherever you go. If a pregnant woman is frightened by a turtle, the child will be born with some of the features of the animal. Rheumatism can be cured by rubbing some of the ailing parts with the "gold meat"—yellow meat—of a turtle. A turtle's wishbone placed in a man's pocket will make him cling to you.

According to an old saying, a turtle is composed of seven different kinds of meat. This is untrue. It may be explained, however, by the fact that the flesh is very palatable and has been compared to various meats such as chicken, beef, pork, venison, mutton and the like.

The fact that a turtle can go without food for almost a year, and that the animal has remained the same for the last couple of million years, has endowed it with seemingly supernatural powers which are very ancient but which are still with us among the superstitious.

"Rat" Superstitions

SEAFARING PEOPLE have long believed that rats never board a ship that will have an ill-fated voyage. And it is a universal superstition that rats always desert a sinking ship as though the rats had a prophetic sense of disaster. On the whole, sailors feel that a rat is always bad luck.

The main reason why rats leave ships, and this applies to ancient and modern ships—wooden ones—is because they themselves gnawed holes in the wood, and rushed away when the water began to pour in, so as not to be drowned in the bottom.

In early days men tried to prevent a foredoomed shipwreck by killing all the rats before they swam ashore from a boat. If the rats reached shore alive, it meant that the ship was doomed. When seamen saw them scramble on land, it terrified them, and many refused to sail on the voyage for fear of disaster.

Rats go aboard ships while at anchor, usually by climbing ropes or cables which are stretched from decks to piers. Now there are methods of preventing this by using metal or wooden shields on cables that rats cannot pass over.

In ancient times, rats were also good omens. There was the belief that no house would catch on fire as long as rats lived in it. They were never molested. This is quite different from the modern notion that rats often started fires, many of which became great and fatal conflagrations. Recent experiments, however, have shown that both rats and mice will starve to death before touching the inflammable part of a match, and so rats are no longer looked upon as pyromaniacs.

The rat was honored in several ways in olden days. The Phoenicians made golden images of it. The Romans pictured it on coins. Greek, Roman and Etruscan works of art show the rat engaged in various occupations, such as gnawing the ropes of ships, or feeding on mussel beds. Ancient bronze and terra cotta works from Palestine and Italy indicate that the rat was important there, too. Ancient Hebrews believed that if a rat left one house for another, it was bad luck for the first home, and good luck for the other.

The Hindus considered the rat a sacred animal because they thought he had the uncanny power of becoming invisible. Ganesa, the Hindu deity, remover of obstacles, is always represented with an elephant head, and attended by a rat. Among the Egyptians and Phrygians, the white rat was a sacred animal, deified, and dedicated to Ra, the sun god. Both rats and mice were mascots in Egypt and appear on many monuments.

Roman and other soothsayers of the day interpreted good and evil omens through the squeaking and other behavior of rats and mice. Although as a rule the rat symbolized destruction, it was also believed to be endowed with wisdom, as it was noticed that these pests always chose the best bread when stealing food.

The original habitat of black rats was the Orient, and from its crowded shores these rodents emigrated to every corner of the earth on ships and by land. Originally they lived in trees, but learned to find their way into homes to get food. This is probably why the black species of rat does not like water but it can and will swim, if necessary.

The rodent scourge in Europe in 1030 appears to be the first on record, and followed the arrival of a fleet of Asiatic vessels, which visited several French ports. History points to the fact that these boats carried the first black rat stowaways from India. A very great invasion of black rats, however, took place during the Crusades, beginning with the First Crusade in 1096, when rats boarded the boats of the Crusaders at Palestine, and were carried to Europe in large numbers. They multiplied so rapidly that within a few centuries they infested the whole of Europe.

During the thirteenth century, however, a brown variety made its appearance, crossing from the Orient to Russia, and from there to Europe proper. The newcomers were much larger and more vicious than their black cousins, whom they proceeded to destroy.

From Europe the brown travelers invaded the New World via the wooden ships of the early explorers and colonists. The rats usually settled in the bottom of these wooden sailing boats, and therefore were the first to know when a vessel was beginning to draw water. They had sense enough to swim away, and the old superstition of the East was now transferred to the West.

The white rat or mouse is an albino animal. In ancient times, all white animals were rare and therefore were associated with mysterious power over the destiny of man, and were believed to bring good fortune. White rats and mice are bred successfully nowadays, as pets, and for use in medical research. They have been of great assistance in clinical tests to further the understanding of human ailments and for applying new treatments.

"Frog" and "Toad" Superstitions

For AGES THE FROG has symbolized inspiration. Tiny frog ornaments are sold today and are very much like the amulets with the figure of a frog which were used by the ancient Egyptians, Greeks, Turks, Italians, and others. They have not lost their "charm," and may be found everywhere as "lucky" pieces in the guise of modern costume jewelry.

The relatively modern buttons and buttonholes, called "frogs" evolved from the amulet idea into an exclusive decorative pattern which some astute designer made practical. Since frogs and toads abounded in the mudland of Paris, France, three frogs or toads formed the heraldic device or coat-of-arms of the kings of France, beginning with Clovis. Eventually they became the fleur-de-lis, suggested by the three-frog design. Probably because of food shortage, the practical housewives in the early history of France took to serving frogs' legs in the guise of chicken or squab. The French people are often called "Frog-Eaters" even today.

From frog-eating to frog-medicine is but a step. Old wives' cures of soup made of nine frogs for whooping cough and other ailments were practiced until a comparatively short time ago. Now and then, even in America, one still hears occasionally reports of this remedy.

To meet a frog on the road means good luck for a dice-player, and indicates that he will win money in the next game. If a wish is made upon seeing the first frog in the spring, and if kept secret, it will come true. To cure gout, find a frog when neither sun nor moon is shining, cut off its hind legs and wrap them in deerskin, then apply the right leg of the frog to the right foot, and the left leg to the left foot. Without doubt it will be healed. The frog is used even for the cure of cancer and tuberculosis.

The importance of the frog in ancient Egypt is shown by the fact that it was embalmed and honored with sculpture in the Temple of Thebes. The sages of that far-distant time marveled at the life history of the frog. They had watched the floating masses of jelly-like substance which are the eggs of frogs, and they had seen the tiny specks within the clearness wake to life and hatch out as tadpoles—legless, gill-breathing creatures that are fish to all intents and purposes. Then came the withering of the gills, the development of lungs, the growth of legs; until the whole of that most marvelous metamorphosis was complete and the frog breathed and walked on land. Is it any wonder that early peoples were amazed?

No doubt the enormous number of eggs laid by a single frog impressed the watchers too. They came to regard the creature as the symbol of abundance and of fertility. In its development they saw the growth of strength out of weakness. The remarkable length of life frogs attained was noted as was their power to remain dormant for long periods, frequently buried away from light and air, and to awake apparently none the worse for their experience. These strange powers strengthened the belief in eternal life and in rising from the tomb. Seeing how the frog began as a speck in floating jelly, and by many changes attained its full growth, they saw in the frog the symbol of the Creation, of the growth of life on the world—a teaching curiously at one with that of our most advanced thinkers. The frog was sacred to Ptah, the most ancient of their gods, the Beginning, the Creator of everything.

In Rome the belief in the frog mascot survived, but because of its fertility, was dedicated to Venus. Pliny tells us that the wearing of a frog charm has power to keep love and to attract friends, which brings us right up to date with the twentieth century.

The toad or frog brings good luck to a house if it enters it. Woe to the person who kills it, however, because of the ancient superstition that it is possessed of the soul of a dead child. Incidentally, a frog when tortured will yell with a cry that is almost human. This cry has probably given rise to the belief that in the transformation of souls the frog is the second embodiment of a child. Because of the blood-spilling taboo against sacred animals, there is a popular superstition in America that the killing of a frog will make cow's milk bloody. In India, if a girl kills a frog, it is lucky for her and implies marriage.

Toads and frogs are direct miniature descendants of prehistoric animals. One of the main differences between a frog and toad is that a frog has teeth and a toad has not. Another important difference is that a frog can breathe through its skin while a toad can only breathe through its mouth. Also frogs have longer legs than toads and lay their eggs in clumps instead of strings. Many superstitious beliefs about toads are closely related to those about frogs.

A toad in the cellar brings bad luck, and it must be ejected with care. Gypsies believe that a tame toad brings good luck. It is a widespread belief that the toad is very venomous and that contact with it will make a limb swell, especially if the toad has first been made angry. Many toads on the ground is a sign of great harvests and increased riches. Shakespeare and Milton, and other writers, have generally made the toad a loathsome creature; part of magic brews and dangerous in love affairs. Saliva was the antidote which negated the venom it was supposed to have in its head. Even to look upon a toad was considered risky.

There may be some truth in the saying that the croaking of frogs brings rain. Mythology treats the frog as the "god of rain," and American Indians imprisoned frogs when a drought came so they could induce the frogs to bring rain. They gave the frogs gentle beatings so they would go to work, and if rain did not come as expected, they punished them more severely. Frogs were thought to be weather prophets because they are usually near water and appear in large numbers after a rain. They feel humidity and are more susceptible to atmospheric changes. Their behavior therefore has often been the equivalent of a modern barometer to early peoples.

"Elephant" Superstitions

THE SUPERSTITIONS attached to elephants are a survival of zoolatry, an expression of admiration and marvel at the uncanny instinct of the elephant, one of the wisest, if not the wisest, of all animals. This huge and sacred animal of the East has kept his divinity throughout the ages.

Superstitious beliefs related to the elephant have been disseminated everywhere, including America to which they were brought by traveling circuses. Replicas of elephants with tusks up or down are found all over the world, not only as ornaments, but as lucky charms. Many figures of elephants are seen facing the entrances of houses so that no one with the Evil Eye or with evil intentions passes the threshold. The trunk upward holds the luck, and the trunk hanging down pours its blessings wherever it is placed.

Since elephants come from the East, most superstitions originated there. For instance, to secure success in any new venture, many Hindus wear mascots or lucky charms in the form of an elephant, or Ganesa, the Elephant-Headed god, who was the son of Siva. By so doing they believe they will gain wisdom and foresight, as well as be able to remove all obstacles from their path, as suggested, naturally, by the extraordinary strength of their idol.

According to Hindu mythology, the elephant supports the world. Owing to the belief in the doctrine of *metempsychosis*, or transmigration of souls, it is easily understood why the Hindus believed that the elephant's faculties and functions were similar to those of human beings, and that they could develop at any moment. It was assumed in animal worship that a divine soul might dwell in animals as well as men. In Vishnu's incarnation, a mythical elephant, which was afterwards appropriated by the god, Indra, was revered by the Hindus.

It is strange that so many false notions about the elephant are prevalent in this country, at the same time in its habitat, where it is beloved and worshipped, its ways are well understood. The elephant's trunk is not its nose, but more properly it is its upper lip. The elephant does not use its trunk in combat as its chief mode of attacking is to kick. The elephant does not smell through its trunk, but through the mouth where the olfactory nerve is. The elephant does not drink water through its trunk but draws it into its trunk and then squirts it into its mouth, thereby giving itself an occasional "shower." The tusks of an elephant are actually elongated and specialized upper incisor teeth, growing downward from a point in front of the eye sockets.

Although an elephant's hide is about one-half to one inch thick, it is not rough and tough. A pin-point will actually bring blood to the surface; and it is not bullet-proof. Although the tusks of the majority of elephants are "ivory" colored, thousands of these animals roaming the forests and plains of Africa have brown, rose, and even black tusks.

Elephants are not necessarily docile as they appear when they have been trained properly. The main reason circuses have only females in their herds is because the males become wild and fail to recognize their keepers during the rutting season. However, circus people insist on calling all females "bulls," but the only males are the pigmy elephants. Elephants often live to a ripe old age, but the fabled centenarians are rare.

That the "elephant never forgets" is a persistent superstition with some basis in fact. Elephants, as a whole, have substantially good memories, and sometimes form strong dislikes toward certain persons. However, the oft-repeated story that an elephant will remember the man who fed him tobacco, and when the occasion presents itself, will take revenge on him, is a tall tale. Singularly enough, many elephants actually like chewing tobacco in small portions because of the licorice and sugar that it contains. Once or twice it has been recorded that a person who had abused an elephant was in turn abused by the animal. But this is not enough evidence upon which to pin a habit-pattern. Elephants, when put to the test, have often failed to recognize their own keepers, and no elephant inflicts punishment on anyone as a form of revenge for a grudge held over the years.

As for the proverbial fear of mice, elephants really don't mind them. They sniff at them, and then go back to their eating or resting, generally fanning themselves with their ears—which act as a cooling system—quite unconcerned about the mice around them. It would be quite natural for them to fear mice, however, and that is probably why elephants sleep with the end of their trunks down to keep out an exploring rodent. But there is no truth in the story that an elephant will go mad at the sight of a mouse, fearing the creature will run up the inside of his trunk.

A superstition, believed everywhere, is that there is an elephant graveyard in the Orient. Elephants do not bury their dead, nor do they all go to the same place to die. Elephants, like humans, lie down and die wherever death happens to take place. It is curious, however, that no one ever has found the dead body of an elephant, at least one that had died from natural causes. This has given rise, among natives, to the belief that elephants have secret places to which they retire when they feel death approaching.

There is really no mystery as to what becomes of dead elephants. One of the reasons one of these big beasts seldom dies of old age is because soon or later they fall prey to their only enemy, man. Bones of dead elephants are seldom found and there is a reason for this. Wild animals commonly attempt to hide when they feel dangerously ill, even as does the domestic dog. The elephant generally dies alone and far away from any settlement; in many cases, the animal will seek relief in the rivers which carry the body into the sea.

Climatic conditions are generally the cause for the rapid decay of carcasses; while carnivorous animals, carrion birds and swarms of insects make quick fare of the flesh. Rodents participate in the rapid disposal of the bones. This is why an elephant that dies in the jungle disappears in no time. Whatever may be left of the skull and large bones are soon covered with mosses while the rich vegetation of the jungle does the rest to hide the remains from view.

Among minor elephant superstitions is the belief that anyone who can obtain a hair from an elephant's tail will have success in his undertakings. Hence the popularity of rings made from elephants' hairs, which are found on the market in most countries. It is also a superstition that when an elephant is in a rage only the speech of a black man can pacify it and make it docile again.

From time immemorial, a white elephant or a light gray one has been held sacred. White horses, white mice—albino animals of all kinds —especially in Oriental countries, have been held in reverence, and became the subject for many superstitions. We have a suggestion of this as applied to humans, in the popular term "a fair-haired" or "white-haired boy."

An albino elephant when captured automatically belongs to the king in certain eastern countries. The white elephant was sacred in Burma, where at one time, part of its daily diet was human milk from twenty-four Burmese women. And there is an old story that the King of Siam, now Thailand, used to present a white elephant to courtiers whom he wished to ruin. As the white elephant was sacred, it could not be disposed of and the expense of keeping it usually proved disastrous. Hence our modern expression "white elephant" became synonymous with an unprofitable possession.

The cult of the white elephant is familiar to all students of religion. In Siam it is still believed by many that the white elephant contains the soul of a dead person. The soul, or spirit, or ghost, is always supposed to be white, and therefore the animal might harbor that of an ancient god. When a white elephant is captured, the capturer is rewarded, and the animal is baptized, feted and worshipped. At its death it is mourned·like a human being. The cult of the white elephant is found also in Cambodia, Indo-China, Sumatra, Southern Abyssinia and elsewhere.

When King Thibo of Siam sold a white elephant to P. T. Barnum, he stipulated in the contract, "The rich man who has bought the elephant agrees to love and cherish it, to make its life pleasant and to keep it safe from all pain and injury."

The elephant as a Republican symbol, and the Democratic mule, assumed their present significance by a slow and meandering process of evolution. The elephant is the easiest to trace. We owe him definitely to the genius of Thomas Nast. We can even trace the process in Nast's mind which produced him. In the summer of 1874 a sensational newspaper in New York City invented a hoax to the effect that animals in the Central Park Zoo had escaped and were terrifying the children and nursemaids of that day. The hoax created a sensation which was not forgotten when November rolled around and there was no doubt that this imaginary episode was in the back of Nast's thoughts when he drew a cartoon with the inscription, "An ass, having put on the lion's skin, roamed about the forest and amused himself by frightening all the forest animals he met in his wanderings." Below this, with reference to the Democratic nightmare of a third term for General Grant he wrote, "Third-Term-Panic." In this cartoon appeared an elephant, entitled "The Republican Vote," and this elephant was clearly the great-grandfather of every elephant which has since carried the initials G.O.P. He did not at once become exclusively Republican, for two years later Nast drew a two-headed elephant, with one head pointing toward "The Republican Road," and the other toward "The Democratic Road."

"Worm" Superstitions

OF ALL SUPERSTITIONS about worms, and there are almost as many as there are species of worms, perhaps the greatest misconception is connected with the tapeworm, commonly found in the human body. It is untrue that an enormous appetite, especially in children, is a sign of the presence of this parasite, in that it requires all this extra food.

In the first place, the tapeworm has no mouth and the tapeworm's food is actually absorbed through the surface of its body and never causes an excessive appetite. Other parasites in the human intestinal tract similarly have no mouths. These migrate to other parts of the body and vary in size from less than half an inch to more than twenty feet.

There is another superstitious belief which is that when worm medicine is taken and no worms are expelled, it indicates that they have been "cut" by the drug. The reason this is impossible is that any drug that could act so drastically would affect the lining of the intestines in the same way. Neither is it true that to eat ground or powdered glass will cut the worm to pieces and that it can be gotten rid of by this means.

Among a variety of worm superstitions are: To step on a worm will bring bad luck all day; if worms come out of the earth in the daytime, it is a sign of wet weather; if you kill a worm, you kill good luck; if a measuring worm crawls over you, it is taking your measure for some new clothes. To see earthworms in the autumn directly after rain, or to notice that they stay close to the surface of the ground, foretells a mild winter. If a small green worm crawls on your clothes, it is a very good sign, and it is called a "lucky worm." To cure a ringworm, rub it nine times a day for nine days with your mother's wedding ring; or, rub a copper penny moistened with saliva on it. It is believed that angleworm juice rubbed on the affected parts will remove the pains of rheumatism.

A common superstition is that earthworms turn into lightning bugs or butterflies. The lightning bug, however, is a species of beetle which passes through a larva stage in which it is also luminous, like the glowworm. This resemblance is probably responsible for the fallacy, but no luminous creatures are related to the earthworm.

Another belief is that if an earthworm is cut in two, each half will become a new worm and they will live as two separate creatures. This is incorrect. The end with the "head" will generally grow a new tail and survive, but the "tail" end will probably perish shortly afterwards.

CHAPTER 6
The Human Animal

"Blonde," "Brunette," Red-Haired," and General "Hair" Superstitions

THE ATTEMPT TO READ character by the color of a person's hair has been going on for thousands of years. Scientists, who literally split hairs to arrive at accurate conclusions, have studied the chemistry of hair coloring and do not endorse a character analysis based alone on the color of an individual's head of hair.

The three most popular fallacies regarding hair coloring are that blondes are false, brunettes are sincere and redheads have tempers and are emotionally unstable. These are beliefs which have come down to us practically unchanged although they are unfair; much too generalized and therefore unscientific.

Poets have sung of the fickleness of golden-haired, azure-eyed maidens, and much popular fiction is based on the idea that "gentlemen prefer blondes." This is equalled by another paradoxical and far-fetched superstition that regardless of this preference, men marry brunettes. This would seem to make the stronger sex a fickle lot, which is also a superstition.

The superstitious dread that women who happen to have darker pigment in the color of their tresses feel in regard to the wiles and morals of blondes is as old as the hills. This "blonde-phobia" attacks sweethearts, wives and mothers alike who mistrust and resent a light-haired woman who happens to come into their orbit.

In 310 B.C., which is over two thousand years ago, Meander, the Greek rhetorician and commentator, said: "A chaste woman ought not to dye her hair yellow!" This shows that natural or artificial blondes were none too popular in that day, or perhaps too much so. In order to curb their attraction and distraction, blondes were tabooed by the inference that they were not of good morals, which probably made them more popular since forbidden women, like the proverbial forbidden fruit, became just that much more sought after—a psychological factor which works at all times, superstition or no superstition.

There is a long list of superstitions about the color of hair, both man and woman's. It is good luck to rub the hand on the head of a person with red hair. A red-head is always a spitfire. If the "first-footer" that crosses the threshold after midnight on New Year's Eve is anything but dark-haired, it means bad luck for the year. Bees sting a redhead more readily than one whose hair is any other color. Redheads are supposed to be good conversationalists. Black curly hair indicates the quality of neatness whereas straight black hair denotes extravagance. Thick black hair is a sign of good health. Brunettes have a better chance in the struggle for existence than blondes except in contagious diseases. Men with dark hair are deceitful, but men with hair neither too dark nor too light combine the best characteristics of both. When the hair is very thin and delicate, it indicates a weak constitution, especially in men.

The superstitious belief that persons with fine hair are more sensitive than those with coarse hair is unfounded. Hair has nothing to do with character and emotions as such, except insofar as it expresses meticulousness in an individual by the way it is groomed. There are fickle brunettes, faithful blondes and phlegmatic redheads, which should do away with all superstition to the contrary. Undoubtedly, everyone knows this from experience. The task of anthropologists, dermatologists, endocrinologists and others in related fields has been to establish the relative values of pigmentation which account for different coloring in the hair. They report, for instance, that red hair contains more sulphur, which has no effect on the individual's character traits.

There is an ancient superstition, still believed, that white hair on a very young head is a sign of genius. Likewise, some believe that prematurely white hair indicates that the possessor will live to be very old. On the other hand, the exact opposite superstition obtains among those who expect such individuals always to be ailing and die young. Some think that if a woman's hair turns gray on one side only, she will soon be a widow, or meet with other serious trouble. A man with a single lock of white hair, mixed with the rest of his hair, is unlucky for others but lucky for himself.

There are almost two hundred shades between black and blonde hair, which makes any generalizations about the color of hair in respect to traits of character impossible. Coincidence and association of ideas have given rise to many superstitions and the case of hair is no exception. Queen Elizabeth was said to have had red hair, and this was supposed to account for her red temper. Red is associated with fire, and because of its reddish color, the ancients made the planet Mars the god of War. In some countries both yellow and red hair were considered ominous and unlucky. Cain and Judas are represented in ancient pictures and tapestries with yellow beards. Judas Iscariot, the traitor, is generally identified as having had red hair.

Red hair was unpopular among the ancient Egyptians, Greeks and Romans, although in other parts of the world it was looked upon as lucky. At one time, the early Egyptians regarded red hair as so unlucky that they had a ceremony in which they burned a red-haired maiden alive so as to exterminate this brilliantly colored hair from the country. In New Zealand red hair is highly regarded and there is a superstitious saying in that country that a red-haired woman has a clear road to Heaven. In the Middle Ages, red hair was a sign of witchery, and any woman with hair this color who was discovered in a dubious activity and suspected of witchcraft was persecuted and often burned at the stake.

At the fall of the Roman Empire, most of Europe's ruling classes were of the blonde type. These aristocrats were more financially able to hire artists to paint their portraits, in which they posed in the rôle of fair and virtuous individuals. The artist, more interested in pleasing his customers and collecting his fee than in other considerations, usually painted a sinister or evil character as a brunette, so that the blonde heroes and heroines looked so much purer by contrast.

Hair superstitions have alternated with the centuries, so that blondes and brunettes took turns for favor, with the redhead somewhere in the middle, but usually in disfavor. Today, however, the redheaded woman seems to take first place.

That Hair, Beard, Finger and Toenails Grow After Death

THE SUPERSTITION that hair, beard, fingernails and toenails grow after death is very ancient. It was even reported in the writings of Pliny and others. This myth is still believed by millions.

It is quite understandable how such a false belief could have spread, since after death there is the illusion that these human appendages have kept on growing. The simple explanation is, however, that as the tissues of the skin and muscles dry and contract after death, hair and nails seem to have grown, because more of them are now exposed. Hair and nails do not disintegrate as quickly as other bodily tissues.

Hair, especially, in contrast with the sunken features and tightening of the skull covering, due to evaporation of fluid content after death, gives the appearance of "standing up," which adds further to the illusion that it has been growing.

Frequently men's whiskers seem to grow for several days after death has set in, and it is not uncommon for undertakers to shave men two or three times before the funeral, so that they will look well-groomed. The whiskers probably have not grown at all, but as the skin shrank, the stubble came through more noticeably. It's the old beard—not a new one.

Nevertheless, there are two schools of thought on the subject of whether hair and beard grow after death. The majority hold that they do *not* grow. The minority claim that there are authentic, but rare, cases where hair and beard actually grew after death. They admit, however, that the growth could have been only during a very short period.

There is a possible explanation to uphold the minority view. When breathing and circulation stop, after the oxygen cycle has come to an end, the separate hair cells might continue an independent existence, but only for a very limited time. Even if it were so, however, the growth would be so slight that it could hardly be noticed, and could not possibly account for the fantastic tales which have come down to us.

Among these legends are those in which a man's beard or a woman's hair had grown in the coffin, so as to cover the entire body as a garment. Writers have fertile imaginations, and offer thrills to their readers; some of whom are taken in, and keep alive some very gruesome superstitions.

Hairiness Strength and Hair Superstitions

IT IS A UNIVERSAL SUPERSTITION that an excessive amount of hair, or a hairy body, is a sign of great strength. This false idea probably came about through the assumption that man is descended from the powerful gorilla, and that this simian's chest is hairy—the sign of his strength. As a matter of fact, the gorilla is covered with hair everywhere except on his chest. The biblical story of Samson and the loss of his strength when Delilah had his hair cut off, also helped keep this superstition alive.

If hairiness were really the sign of physical strength, the smallest hairy animal would be as strong as a man, if not stronger. However, the strongest creature in proportion to its size is the beetle, and it certainly is not hairy. If a man were as strong as this bug, in proportion to his size, he could lift a weight of seventy tons.

Another superstition that a girl's long hair saps her strength during an illness, has no foundation in fact, even though the belief in this has made many a young woman lose a beautiful head of hair while she was sick. The only sensible reason for cutting long hair when a girl is confined to bed is that long hair snarls easily, and short hair is more comfortable and easier to take care of, with all the other sick-room duties. With so much bobbed hair among women today there is little reason for the superstition to persist, yet it does.

There is also the superstition that hair on a woman's face means that she thinks like a man and has other masculine traits. Any physician can explain why hair sometimes grows on a woman's face, but hearsay usually has it all over science. The knowledge that glands and hormones are the cause of this condition ought to remove the stigma and implications attached to a woman with a fuzzy face.

Because of the old tale that the Queen of Sheba had legs as hairy as an ape, there are those who believe that a girl with much hair on her arms and legs will be lucky and marry a rich man.

Some babies are born covered with a coat of heavy down. Parents who do not understand this condition are terror-stricken when they see their new infant with this strange covering. However, there is nothing abnormal about this, and a few days after birth it falls off. Hair starts to appear on a baby six months before birth. Four months before birth, it is covered with this downy coat, known as *lanugo*, which generally disappears before delivery.

Can Human Hair Turn White Overnight?

"My hair is gray, but not with years,
Nor grew it white
In a single night,
As men's have grown with sudden fears."
—*Prisoner of Chillon*, Lord Byron

IT IS STILL BELIEVED by many that hair may turn white or gray from sudden fright, or other emotional shock. This is believed by many authorities to be a complete fallacy.

A head of hair may become gray from prolonged worry or from mental and physical disturbances of many kinds. However, the change is gradual—never sudden. Old hairs fall out and new gray or white ones grow in their place. The hair that is already grown keeps its natural color till it falls out.

Hair is not a living tissue, and something has to destroy the pigment at the root of the hair to make it grow out colorless, or minus the coloring that formerly was produced in the root.

We often hear the warning, "Pull out one gray hair, and ten will grow in its place." This too is impossible, because only one strand of hair can grow from each hair bulb—never ten.

A prominent gray or white streak of hair in the head present from birth is not due to too much brain work, or to emotional strain. This peculiarity is hereditary, and runs in families. It has nothing to do with bad heredity either as is sometimes hinted, nor does it make its owner lucky or unlucky, as the superstitious would like us to believe.

There is no magic formula to prevent hair from turning gray, nor will iodine salts help. However, a diet well-balanced in vitamins and rich in minerals goes a long way to retard the process. A faulty diet and disturbances of the glands that secretes hormones are both implicated in the causes that turn the hair gray, or *achromotrichia*. No "new drug" nor vitamin has yet been found to make hair grow again with its original color.

It has been demonstrated, by experiments on rats, that vitamin deficiency is a factor in graying hair. Minute bits of copper added to the diet of these animals prevented their hairs from losing pigment at the roots. But more research is needed to arrive at a perfect formula that will work for both human beings and animals. The substances known as pentothenic acid and paraminobenzoic acid—sometimes called PARA —which were tried with relative success on rats and mice under certain conditions have poor results when tested on men and women. There was an attempt to exploit this product commercially as a cure for graying hair, but the authorities interfered.

Baby's First Lock of Hair

A BABY'S RINGLET or lock of hair has always been kept as a talisman, along with its first pair of shoes, becoming heirlooms of the family for generations. The original reason for preserving a lock of the baby's hair, however, was not a sentimental one, as it is today. The custom sprang from the supertsitious belief that as long as the first bit of hair, clipped from the baby's head, was hidden in a safe place by the parent, especially the mother, all through its life, the child would not suffer any serious harm, and would live to a ripe old age.

In the early days of sun-worship, sacrificial offerings were made to the rays of the sun, believed then to be the solar hair. The crackling of hair and the sparks which sometimes show in the dark—due to electricity, we know now—were believed to show that hair was related to the sun's activities. The sun, like other fire, was thought capable of doing harm as well as good, and so must be appeased. Men, young and old, often offered their hair in sacrificial token to the sun or to fire; that is, hair was placed in the fire to be consumed. Even today, men and women of certain religious orders sacrifice or cut off their hair, as a sign of humility and personal sacrifice. Some priests affect the tonsure, symbolic of the sun's disc.

The belief that to cut the hair of children would affect their eyesight was also related to the sun, in its form of sunlight. This superstition accounted for the long hair of boys as well as girls, although boys' hair began to be cut at an early age. Formerly, the boy's first haircut was quite a ceremony, beginning with the parent cutting a ringlet and carefully putting it away for safe-keeping and good-luck.

For a long time, hair cuttings were burned to prevent anyone with evil intent from getting hold of them and working evil magic against the one on whose head they once belonged.

At one time, there was a belief that to cut the hair of children when they were too young would diminish their strength. The idea may have been handed down from the dramatic story of Samson and Delilah, which is most familiar. However, the superstition may also be traced to the notion that when the warm sun rays, or its hair, are present, as in summer, the sun has great strength. But when it is shorn of its rays, in winter, it is weak.

A current superstition in rural communities, believed by white and colored folks alike, is that combings and fallen hairs should be burned, or else a bird will weave these hairs into its nest, and the person from whose head they came will go insane.

Still another superstition relating to hair is that a lock of hair, curled around to form a circle, is enclosed in a locket and exchanged between lovers to signify union, devotion and romantic desire. Here too, ancient symbols are combined with sentiment.

The Widow's Peak

AN ANCIENT SUPERSTITION holds that a woman born with a V-shaped hair-line will be a young widow, if she marries and will also remarry soon after. This belief persisted because the hair-line makes her outstandingly attractive to the opposite sex in contrast to the less fortunate woman born with ordinary hair-lines.

Objection to the "widow's peak" comes most often not from the women possessing it, but from the man in quest of a wife, who feels that marriage with such a woman will be short-lived.

It is interesting to note that this superstition originated centuries back with a change of style in mourning. The wearing of black for mourning is a conventional custom of Western peoples, which originated in ancient Rome. Then, the women generally wore dresses called *lugubria* to express their sorrow at the loss of a loved one. However, widows' and other black garments were discarded under the emperors, when white was worn instead. White was and still is the customary color of mourning with the Chinese people.

Centuries later in 1498, when Anne of Brittany wore black for mourning at the death of her husband, Charles VIII, it was the first use of black for mourning since Roman times. Queen Anne was so attractive in her black mourning costume that Louis XII of France could not resist her and, in time, she became his wife and Queen of France for the second time.

Capitalizing on the instant success of black mourning costumes, designers of the day created a modified V-shaped black and white bonnet to frame the face with a flattering line. And thus, today, when a woman's hair-line grows naturally in a V-shaped fashion it is called a "widow's peak" because of the old style for semi-mourning when white was added at the end of a year's grieving, as was prevalent in the 16th century.

"Phrenology" and "Head" Superstitions

EVERY MAN's fate is recorded in the sutures of the skull, according to an old Hindu saying. Phrenology is based on the ancient theory that the faculties of the mind are shown on the surface of the human skull. It was and still is believed that the skull points out the relationship between the development of the brain and the manifestations of the mind, discovering each from an observation of the other. Phrenology was first defined to the western world in the middle of the 18th century, and it has remained just about the same, except for a few minor changes, to this day. It is still a thriving business.

After years of extensive research on phrenology, it seems that only phrenologists agree on the merits of phrenology. Other competent persons are unable to differentiate between a criminal and an honest man by the formation of the head alone. Phrenologists claim that heads indicate genius, potential criminals, morons, and maniacs. The characteristics of the face, the profile, size and shape of forehead, hair, ears, eyes, and other structures indicate personality. In 1935 a psychograph, an electrical machine designed to make phrenology easy, was invented. This machine is supposed to register weaknesses and strength of character.

We can offer no better authority than that of the late and great anthropologist, Dr. Alex Hrdlicka, curator of anthropology of the Smithsonian Institution, who says in the *Journal of Criminal Psychopathology* (1939): "Trying to figure out the new neighbor by the shape of his head is dangerous and a waste of time." Dr. Hrdlicka told of extensive surveys, one involving 1,000 children in an institution, which produced no evidence to support the contention of some prison wardens and police officials that the criminal bears a physical stamp which betrays him. "Physical measurements of the criminal," he said, "can show only that he tends to be abnormal, but there is no possibility of connecting such abnormality with criminality."

The intelligence of a person and the size of his head have no direct relationship. Some of the largest brains known to science have belonged to idiots.

Dr. Sigmund Freud, founder of psychoanalysis, as a medical student devised an original phrenological chart which received much attention. At that time, phrenology was a popular study in medical circles.

Eyebrow Superstitions

*"If your eyebrows meet across the nose,
You'll never wear your wedding clothes."*

—Traditional

THE FASHION of plucking eyebrows to make them look neater, or to change the shape to give them a special slant, or to give the face a special expression, stems from many old superstitions as well as from beauty aids followed in various countries in ancient times.

Meeting eyebrows, which may have started the practice of plucking them, has been a subject of interest at all times and places. There are many traditional sayings, in a variety of versions, often contradicting each other, pertaining to persons whose eyebrows meet. As an example, besides the one quoted above, there is the oft-quoted, "When a girl's eyebrows meet, she'll marry someone near home."

Both the English and Chinese agree that men whose eyebrows meet are fortunate and trouble will never come near them. Elsewhere, this characteristic is believed to endow its possessor with great spiritual and occult power. Scandinavian legends are responsible for a sinister attitude toward meeting eyebrows, and a large number of Anglo-Saxons have kept up this superstition. It is not unusual to hear said, even in the 20th Century, in Denmark, Germany and Iceland, that a man or woman whose eyebrows meet should be avoided, if not actually suspected of being a witch, wizard or werewolf. The werewolf and vampire belief attached to these persons is also believed in the Balkans, and especially in Greece, where they are feared and avoided, and believed endowed with the power to return and do harm even after death.

Nearer to home, there are those who believe that meeting eyebrows signify a dishonest or deceitful person, and one possessed of a fiendish disposition. The superstition predicts that women with such eyebrows will make very bad wives; as for men with them, it is said that many of them go to beauty parlors to have the extra brows removed, because many women feel it indicates a violently jealous nature.

The psychological attitude of resentment toward meeting eyebrows is due, no doubt, to the fact that a straight line over the bridge of the nose gives a fierce or disagreeable expression to an otherwise good-natured person.

In connection with eyebrows playing an important part in a woman's beauty, it is interesting to note that Egyptian women in pre-dynastic times used an eyebrow pencil to fashion the eyebrows and emphasize the shape of the eyes. On the other hand, Japanese women used to be compelled to pluck their eyebrows at the time of marriage, presumably to make them look unattractive and therefore undesirable to other men.

Dropped Eyelash and a Wish

THE EYELASH superstition belongs to the exuvial group of false beliefs, exuvial meaning anything that comes off the body of man or animal, such as skin, shell, nails, hair and the rest. From ancient times it was believed that if an evil doer is in possession of another person's eyelash—or any other item of exuvial nature—he can work magic against the owner. Therefore, the eyelash should be destroyed or burned, or some counter-magic formula enforced to negate any possible unfortunate eventuality. The eyelash or "eye-winker," as it is generally known in America, must be one which has fallen accidentally, not pulled.

On the other hand, it was believed that the dropped eyelash may bring good luck as, in certain circumstances, it has the power to make a wish come true. Here is how it works. The eyelash is placed on the back of the left hand and a wish is made, preferably with the eyes closed. This is followed with a rapid blow on the left palm with the back of the right hand. There are only three chances. If by the third try the eyelash is still on the left hand, it means the wish will not take place. Then the eyelash should be burnt or thrown where it cannot be found by anyone else. But, if the eyelash has disappeared with either the first, second or third gesture, strike or blow, it is believed that the eyelash has gone to bring the wish.

This conclusion is obviously infantile, but it is firmly believed by credulous and superstitious people!

"Eye" Superstitions

AT ONE TIME the fear of the Evil Eye was universal, and many superstitious gestures and formulas were devised to combat its evil glances. This dread of the Evil Eye is still with us as expressed in common everyday phrases, such as, "He looked daggers at me," "withering glances," "dirty looks," "if looks could kill," "He put the jinx on me," or "the Indian sign"—its equivalent—and others. There are cases of crime and murder reported in the American press from time to time in which modern witches are blamed for casting the spell of the Evil Eye on someone, which allegedly ended in death.

The Evil Eye was a fearful thing and at one time it was believed that the victim could save himself only if he could out-stare the one who was trying to cast a spell. Amulets and lucky pieces were devised to deflect evil glances. Saliva, also a transformer, was the supreme antidote for contamination by the Evil Eye. As a matter of fact, saliva was used on general principles, to be on the safe side.

In ancient Rome there were professional witches who claimed to have an Evil Eye, in order to be hired to bewitch one's enemies. The superstition spread all over Europe. Gypsies brought similar tales from India, and they themselves were thought to have the Evil Eye. Medieval people grew so fearful of this power that anyone with a peculiar cast in his eye was liable to be burned at the stake as a witch.

Tales of prehistoric monsters, handed down from father to son, led ancient peoples to imagine that terrible dragons still lived on earth. These mythical animals were said to have eyes of emerald that possessed the baleful power of charming a victim so that he could not move. It was not long before men attributed this same power to ordinary reptiles, and blamed their fear-paralysis on the creatures' evil eye. When hypnotism was discovered, the first hypnotists were thought to have some connection with reptiles and that they derived their power to fascinate with the eye from serpents. Hypnotism has been an intriguing theme in fiction and folklore, the tale of "Trilby" and her hypnotist master, Svengali of the Evil Eye, being a notable example.

What we call the "pupil" of the eye is derived from the Latin word *pupilla,* meaning "little doll." No doubt early peoples found it strange to see their own image in miniature in the cornea of the eyes of other tribesmen, and readily believed themselves to be in personal danger if their own likeness should lodge permanently in an Evil Eye. There is the modern belief, with no truth in it, that the eye of a dead person retains the image of his murderer.

The egg, which is still the symbol of resurrection at Easter time, was a mysterious source of life to primitive man. The yolk was believed a yellow eye which transformed inanimate matter into living matter. In time, the human eye was allotted the same power, because of its likeness, however remote, to the egg. The main Egg-Eye, however, was the Sun, which was always believed to be the original source of all forms of life. Human eyes, then, were regarded as having a measure of this power, but rather for destruction than for good.

The using of mascara today had its origin in the darkening of the eyelids to protect against the glances of fascination of the Evil Eye. It was applied in a circle or oval. Kohl, or mascara, was a cosmetic used by both men and women from earliest of times in the East. Medicine men, or soothsayers, prepared the ingredients for the men, while the women prepared theirs with antimony, which was a special base metal, reputed to have magic powers, combining it with other substances listed in their secret formulas.

Eye superstitions appear all through the history of civilization. It is still believed unlucky to meet a cross-eyed person, but the harm may be averted by expectorating or crossing one's fingers. For a young man to be smiled at by a cross-eyed girl is believed to be certain and immediate good fortune by some, and just the opposite by others. However, if you out-stare cross-eyed individuals, they will do you no harm. Some believe that if you play cards with a cross-eyed partner, you can never win, as he will frighten away good luck. If a fisherman meets a cross-eyed person, he can only expect bad luck unless he expectorates in his hat as a countercharm. A rabbit's foot, in order to bring good luck, must be taken from a rabbit killed at midnight in a cemetery or churchyard at full moon, by a cross-eyed man. Many a superstitious man would not have a cross-eyed waiter serve him a meal lest it cause indigestion.

Some persons believe that to wear rings in the ears will cure bloodshot or inflamed eyes. Sailors wear one or two earrings for good luck because of the old superstition that if the ears were bored and a ring put through the hole, it would make for stronger eyesight, which men at sea need. Many persons still prefer to wear earrings instead of glasses because of the belief that earrings will help the eyesight and prevent blindness. Some think that wearing eyeglasses weakens the eyes, and others tell their children that their eyes will become stronger when they get old enough to grow a mustache.

To squirt milk from a mother's breast into a baby's eyes if they are sore, is still a popular superstition. Another superstition is that the ashes of the burnt shells of hazel nuts applied to the back of an infant's head will insure the color of the iris in the baby's eyes from turning gray, but will make them dark instead.

A person with prominent eyes is supposed to be gifted with eloquence. If the eyelid twitches, it is bad luck. If the right eye itches, you will receive a letter, but an itching left eye means bad luck. If the eyes are set too close together, it is supposed to indicate selfishness or dishonesty, while if they are set too far apart, it is a sign of stupidity, and nothing can be done to improve the mentality of the possessor.

To touch a blind man's garment, or come in contact while brushing past him is unlucky. It is a superstitious belief as well, that a blind person has a "sixth" sense. These unfortunates develop a sense we all have, an "obstacle sensation," which enables them to "feel" their way so as not to collide with objects. Persons with vision do not need this ability.

Devices for removing foreign bodies in the eyes run into dozens, and they are largely superstitions. The most persistent of these, perhaps, is that rubbing the good eye will get the cinder or speck out of the one in which it is lodged. Flaxseed as a remedy is supposed to float around and chase out the offender. Another plan is to pull down the upper lid and blow the nose violently, or apply a poultice made with an oyster. Some of these do work sometimes.

Sties are tiny abscesses near the roots of the lashes. Modern treatments include removing the pus by the application of heat and gentle massage. However, many old wives' cures still survive such as rubbing the sty with the tip of a black cat's tail nine times; or using the moisture of one's breath that has been blown on a glass or window pane; or rubbing a gold wedding ring, or a stone from a running stream on the sty.

Because of the association of blue with the heavens, blue eyes were looked upon, in the western world during medieval times, as a divine attribute and a sign of high intellect and intelligence, a superstition still widely believed, especially by persons with racial prejudices. Many persons think that all great men of history were blue-eyed, but of course the color of the eyes has nothing to do with greatness. There is also the belief that blue-eyed people are more sincere than others; gray-eyed more calculating; green-eyed, creative; and brown, flirtatious before marriage, but loyal after. The color of a person's eyes has nothing to do with his character or emotions.

That you can tell an honest person by his ability to look you straight in the eye is another fallacy. Many criminals do so with ease, while honest individuals may be nervous and shifty-eyed. Laboratory tests have disproved this theory time and time again, although, occasionally, some tests are inclined to support to a degree this superstition. On the majority of tests, however, both guilty and innocent persons were questioned as suspects. Then they were quizzed before an ophthalmograph, an instrument which makes a photographic record of eye movements. Upon checking, it was found that deceitful persons kept their eyes more nearly steady than the others; and what is more, they showed less variation in their movements during the questioning.

There is a common superstition that old people are often blessed with "second sight." This assumption is due to the fact that certain elderly persons wear glasses until they are about seventy or eighty, and then discover they can read as well, or even better, without them. What really happens is that the lens of the eye gets harder with age, and along with hardening, its index of refraction so increases that it becomes a stronger magnifying lens, and this is able to replace, either partially or wholly, the glass lens used for reading. The vision becomes better for near objects, but less distinct for distant ones, so that sight does seem to improve in old age. This same hardening process of the lens of the eye is the reason reading glasses have to be worn by persons after they pass the age of forty-five. Their distance vision remains normal, but it has become difficult for the eyes to focus on near objects, especially fine print.

Authorities are of the opinion that looking at the sun is not beneficial, as many uninformed claim. Actually, nature does everything possible to protect us against bright illumination. The lids close mechanically and the pupils contract, so as to reduce the quantity of light that will penetrate the retina. Another popular fallacy is that blinking is not good for the eyes, and that to open and shut the lids frequently is not beneficial.

The idea that the way to treat a "black" eye is with raw meat has been disproved by doctors. A piece of raw meat pressed against a bruised eye will reduce the swelling because the meat is likely to be cool and moist. Anything else that is cool and moist will do just as well, while cold compresses are still better.

As for the old superstitious belief that savages have better sight than civilized peoples, the truth is that they see more than we do because their sense of observation has been trained from early childhood. Their safety depends on high visual skill with which to observe the behavior of prowling animals, birds, reptiles, and to detect the presence of enemies from faint footprints, broken twigs and other signs that would escape our untrained notice. The developed powers of observation of the American Indian gave rise to the erroneous belief that they see better than we do.

"Ear" Superstitions

PEOPLES OF ALL ages have tried to define the ear in their own way, mixing facts, fancies and fables, which made for a general confusion of distorted beliefs and superstitions which have left their heritage on the modern scene. Superstitions about the ear, earache, ear-piercing and ear character-reading, therefore, are universal and comprise a long list, only a few of which are suggested.

If a person's ear is pulled, especially a child's when he is told to do something, he will not forget it. Ear-ringing means either good or bad news. Ringing or burning in the ear generally signifies that the person is being talked about. There are several ways of finding out who is doing the talking. For example, the one whose ear burns or rings should repeat the names of persons he knows and the name at which the sensation stops is the one. If the ringing is in the left ear, the person is being well spoken of or thought of. If the ringing occurs in the right ear, it means evil is being spoken. However, some interpret this superstition the other way around. If both ears ring at the same time, it is a very bad sign. Saliva applied to an ear that burns outwits the one who is gossiping. Or, to make a cross with saliva and then touch the ear is an equally good formula for the same result.

If the right ear itches or burns, the person affected will shortly cry. An itching left ear means laughter instead. Another version of what itching ears signify goes: "Left or right, good at night." And still another: "Left for might, right for spite."

Superstitions concerning what to do for earache and deafness are many. One remedy is to breathe into the ear that aches. Nibbling caraway seeds improves hearing. To cure deafness, rub a gold ring around the ear continually while repeating a traditional formula, which differs among people according to the local superstitious beliefs. Cure earache by keeping the painful ear filled with goose grease. Filling it with hot milk is another way to get results. Lard and ground black pepper rubbed on a piece of cotton and put into the ear will stop an earache. Fat of the skunk, weasel, or rabbit taken from an animal of the same sex as the sufferer and rubbed in the ear is good for earache. Wool from a black sheep constantly worn in the ear will prevent the user from ever having an earache. A method for curing earache followed by many country people today is to have a healthy old man blow tobacco through a pipe stem into the affected ear. Frequently running ears are uncared for because of the superstition that it is healthy to have poison leave the system by this means of exit. This discharge is also known as "the mischief" running out. There are scores of these old wives' cures.

Character-reading by the shape of the ear is still popular. Large ears indicate generosity, but to some they are a sign of coarseness. Small ears show a stingy disposition, and very small ones are a sign of refinement. Some call very small ears "poet's ears," while others say persons who have them are very self-seeking and close-fisted. A broad, well-shaped ear means a long life and long hanging ears indicate the same thing. Full protruding ears are said to belong to persons with a talent for music. Hair growing in the ears is supposed to signify an ill-natured, treacherous and savage-like individual. Long thin ears denote a person who is bold, proud, scornful, and slow to acquire learning. To be able to see the sunshine through the skin of a man's ears means he is a rascal.

The custom of ear-piercing, and the belief that goes with it, namely, that this operation will correct impaired vision, harks back to medieval and even earlier times. Needless to say, it is utterly untrue that piercing the ears and wearing or not wearing earrings has any effect upon the eyes.

There is no doubt, however, that originally the earring was an amulet, and that it was worn, back in earliest times, to ward off evil spirits and bring good fortune. Among primitives living in remote places today, the piercing of a young man's ears is quite a ceremony just as it was ages ago. At one period, one or two earrings were worn by royalty, poets and others, including men of the sea. Sailors wearing earrings may be seen even in the most modern cities of today. A gold ring was believed to be a cure-all for ear trouble, although other metals, jewels and all sorts of materials did as well among primitives and among seafaring men later.

The ear was believed to be the seat of intelligence by the Greeks, Hebrews and other ancients, and so when death was mentioned, it was a practice to touch the ears, which symbolically was supposed to render the ghost or evil spirit that might be around temporarily deaf. This was to prevent the evil being from hearing what was being said and claiming another victim. Evil spirits were believed to be responsible for death, and a recent death meant that a ghost that had recently been released might be lonely and on the lookout for company.

Ears of human beings who were casualties of war or victims of sacrifice, as well as the ears of birds and other animals, were used in homeopathic rituals or sympathetic magic for ages.

Astrologers of old associated the right ear with the planet Saturn, and the left ear with Mars. Anything which happened to the ear such as a tingling or ringing in it had a special meaning. The ringing of the ear was known as "dumb bell," possibly because only one person heard it, and it denoted then, as it does today, startling news, either good or bad. The "ear-finger," the little finger, was used to stop the ringing. Of course, long ago it was not understood that this sensation was due to poor circulation or some foreign body in the ear, or to the presence of ear wax. This ear-ringing was believed to be an objective phenomenon, akin to what is known today as mental telepathy. The sensation was often considered as a message of some kind and prophetic in nature. The Romans believed that to wet the finger with saliva and place it behind the ear would allay any disquietude of mind that might follow a ringing in the ear.

The modern superstition that deafness can be cured by taking a nose-dive in an airplane is erroneous. Corrections of modern superstitions include: sea weeds and seeds will not grow in the ears of bathers; left-handed persons do not have sharper hearing in the left ear; hearing is not more acute in the morning than during the rest of the day; ears do not have to be washed to remain healthy; deaf persons do not hear any better when we shout. These and other ear fallacies go the rounds and are repeated by intelligent persons who do not take the trouble to check the facts.

"Dimple" Superstitions

A dimple in your cheek,
Many hearts you will seek
A dimple in your chin,
Many hearts you will win.

DIMPLES ARE considered a sign of beauty, a bewitching feature, particularly if there is a deep one in a woman's chin. In a man's chin, it is an indication of a passionate and lovable nature. These are the usual superstitions about chins, but there are also some contradictory ones. A girl with a dimple on her chin is not to be trusted as she is a flirt. On the other hand some say that men or women with a dimple on the chin have been touched by Cupid, or that an angel put his finger on them.

"Dimple on the chin, the devil within" means a spirit of fun or mischief in the individual, while to others this same characteristic is a sign of benevolence.

Dimples in babies denote a short tongue so that they will lisp. Dimples at the outer corner of the mouth are another sign of liveliness, and dimples in the center of a girl's cheek mean she has a very sweet disposition. If a man has dimples in his cheek it is a sign he will have handsome children. There is no scientific basis on which to delineate the character of a human being from the presence of dimples, the great collection of superstitions notwithstanding.

It has been said that a man with a dimple in his chin will never commit murder, which led criminologists to make a study of facial characteristics in criminals. Police Commissioner Max Tisza, of Miskoic, Hungary, even wrote a book on the subject a few years ago. He labored the fact that no man or woman with a charming dimple in the cheek or chin has ever been known to commit a crime.

Although Max Tisza's theories have become popular, there is still no foolproof evidence to show that there is any real difference in men; with or without dimples.

On the strength of superstitious beliefs in favor of dimples, and the flattering implications that go with them, out of the swindler's kit came the "Magic Dimpler," a gadget which guaranteed to produce irresistible dimples over night,—for a nominal sum. This contraption is a length of rubber, covered with wire. The ends fasten over the ears like spectacles. The loop slides under the chin, and halfway down the cheeks there are adjustable soft rubber points like pencil erasers. The instructions say to wear it and smile before a mirror three or four times a day; or go to bed with it on, and behold!—next day the dimples will be there. However, the New York Academy of Medicine reported that the Magic Dimpler is more apt to bring on skin trouble than dimples.

Nature's dimple is a slight depression or dent in the surface of the human body, caused by adherence of the skin to the deeper tissues. Dimples appear most frequently on the cheek or chin, and most fiction writers endow their heroines with them.

"Chin" Superstitions

THE CHIN and jaw have given rise to a number of superstitions, one of which is that a receding or "streamline" chin is a sign of weak will or character. Another is that a protruding chin denotes a strong will or strength of character. Others are that a flat chin signifies viciousness; a small chin, cowardice; a pointed chin, craftiness; a soft round chin, fondness for food; a square strong chin, self-restraint and will power. There are many others, but all are fallacies.

Many of these superstitions are obviously the result of false analysis, and an incorrect conclusion drawn from an apparent relation between one thing and another. For instance, the idea that a double chin denotes a glutton mistakes the effect for the cause, as the heavy chin comes from eating too much food. On the other hand, it is wrong to assume that an emaciated chin is a sign of a deep thinker, as it is in fact just a sign that a person preferred his studies or reading to eating.

It is true that prizefighters, wrestlers and battlers of all types are often marked by a protruding chin or jaw. This has led to the belief that this feature indicated physical strength, but men and women with receding jaws are known to have great courage and pugnacity as well.

Character and physiognomy do not necessarily go together, and it is wrong to think that a person's character can be read accurately by his facial expression. In ancient times, long before books were written, and before there was any inkling of the sciences of physiology and psychology, clues to character were sought in man's body, to be used for divinatory purposes. These same obsolete signs are employed by some today, to ascertain a man's character and to prophesy his actions.

It is related that one of his critics said to Socrates, "You have the face of a murderer." To which the great Grecian philosopher replied, "That may be, but I have controlled any such tendency by will power and education."

It is an interesting fact that man is the only animal who has a chin. This has added more to the artistic lines of his face and head than any other feature. One of the reasons that monkeys and gorillas are so ugly is because they have no chins. Of course there are ugly human chins, which are due to bad posture, poor dentition in childhood, or a congenitally badly formed chin. These facts, however, are unrelated to the character development of the individual.

"Mouth"—"Lips"—"Tongue"—Superstitions

THE HEAD was looked upon by early peoples as the medium through which the spirit of life, or the soul, entered and left the body; and the mouth, lips and tongue were considered the sacred trinity of that area. This attitude was suggested by the breath, the symbolic circle of the mouth, the red color of the lips and tongue, as well as by the shape of the tongue itself. The moisture of the saliva was reminiscent of the waters of childbirth, the beginning of new life. All these significances and many more led to various superstitious beliefs and customs, including the reading of the character and emotions of an individual, a practice still very popular.

Superstitions pertaining to the lips include: a protruding lower lip indicates sensuality; a very thick upper lip, extending prominently above the lower lip and having a sharp curve upward, indicates a stubborn disposition and hot temper; a short upper lip denotes sensitiveness; thin lips are a sign of cruelty, meanness and viciousness, as well as irritability; thin, tightly drawn lips suggest stinginess; women who have hair on their lips will be rich; thin lips on a woman suggest cajolery and flippancy, or in other words, flirtatiousness and fickleness; angles at the corners of the mouth that point upward are a sign of light-heartedness and gaiety, and if they point downward, it implies seriousness and pessimism.

Other lip superstitions are: a person with red lips will live to be very old; bloodless lips denote an immoral and treacherous person; a cleft or hare-lip once meant that the possessor was bewitched and harbored an evil spirit; a cold sore or chapped lips have a variety of meanings, none of them flattering; and itching lips predict they will soon kiss or be kissed.

Some mouth superstitions are: a large mouth denotes generosity, whereas a small one indicates selfishness; a large mouth also denotes a good conversationalist, and one apt to judge another without sufficient proof of guilt or innocence; a mouth that displays the teeth when smiling denotes love of approbation and attention; large mouths in general denote a sensuous nature; if the corners of the mouth droop, the person is jealous by nature and not to be trusted; a large number of wrinkles around the mouth signifies a tendency not to tell the truth; a small mouth with small nose and nostrils means indecision and cowardice; a mouth twice the size of the eye goes with dullness of intellect. Some of these superstitions have been interpreted with the opposite meaning by persons who judge from personal experience and racial traits.

A list of tongue superstitions follow: to bite the tongue when the ear rings will make the one talking about the other bite his own tongue; or to bite the little finger under the same circumstance will make the slanderer bite his tongue till it bleeds; biting the tongue while one is speaking means that the next remark will not be true; if a baby sticks out its tongue repeatedly, it means it wants something the mother wanted during pregnancy but could not get; to lick a wart with the tongue on arising will remove it; to get rid of hiccoughs, the blade of a knife should be placed on the tongue by another person, and the tongue should be kept extended with the knife on it; if a baby talks before it walks its tongue will ruin it; dimples in a baby denote a short tongue which means it will lisp; and a blister on the tip of the tongue of a person shows that he told at least one lie.

Ancient Egyptian ladies painted their mouths or lips red for magical purposes. It was believed in that day that by emphasizing the natural red circle of the mouth, they were well protected, as the good spirit of life was safe within them and could not escape from the body. At the same time, the bright red circle kept evil spirits from slipping in to cause troubles, the least of which were soreness, dryness of the tongue, pimples and chapped lips. Red was the color of magic and was the "stop" signal, or danger sign, to any garrison of invaders that would cause fevers and plagues; a condition much dreaded in early times.

"Hand" Symbols and Superstitions

WHEN FOUR persons meet and shake hands crosswise, it is believed to be a sign that one of the group will be married within the year. If, however, they are all married, it then means that any one of them making a wish will have it come true without fail.

This superstition, implying a marriage, union, or contract of some kind, has a long history, going way back to the ancient usage and symbolism of the hand. In the history of man's social evolution, there is an inexhaustible store of facts, legends and beliefs pertaining to manual ceremonies and covenants.

The hand has figured prominently in the expression of man's words and deeds, symbolizing personal integrity in the fulfillment of a promise, contract or partnership. It is still a common practice to shake hands on the completion of a deal, or a bet.

It is often said that the hand is an extension of mind or will, and from time immemorial it has been a symbol of authority. The hand itself was first used for a seal, and this is represented in the familiar phrase in legal covenants to this day: "In witness whereof, I have hereunto set my hand and seal."

The hand was used as a seal after it had been dipped in blood, and very likely the impression of the red or bloody hand was the forerunner of the great red seals so prominently displayed on official documents and state papers today.

There are hundreds of customs and expressions that illustrate the early significance of the hand in man's actions. For instance, we have all heard the expression, although it is rapidly becoming obsolete, "asking for her hand." The hand always played an important part in courtship and marriage customs. Some couples pledged their faith by drinking out of each other's hands, which, at one time among primitives, was the only marriage ceremony. Another ceremony was for the couple merely to cross hands and the bride's right hand placed in the groom's right hand, after which the left hands were joined under the right to form a cross. This simple, but irrevocably binding, gesture for the marriage union is still practiced among natives living in the distant hills of India.

The American Indian had a delightful and sentimental ceremony of crossing hands to form a cross, over a stream, as a betrothal pledge that sealed the union of two loving hearts.

A children's game, known to all nations, is one in which they cross hands slowly, and then increasingly faster, while, at the same time each player makes a wish. The first one who misses his turn, loses the score and the wish in this primitive game of hands.

"I'll put my hand in the fire and it will *not* burn!" is an expression to emphasize the fact that the absolute truth is being stated. This is not very far removed from raising the right hand when taking an oath— another reminder that the hand symbolized truth and integrity.

Palmistry and Kindred Subjects

PALMISTRY and other forms of telling fortunes have not lost one iota of their primitive meanings and classical glamor. The business of looking into the right hand and the left hand to prophecy human activities and events is a highly remunerative occupation which reaps millions of dollars from millions of people.

Palmistry is an ancient art. The Hindus are reputedly the first people to have practiced it, but the Chinese used chirology, the study of the hands, and chirognomy, the study of the mounts of the hands, some 5,000 years before the Christian era. Ancient Greek philosophers wrote at length about palmistry, and the literature of their day is replete with the subject.

Palmistry was very popular during the Middle Ages, although the Church distrusted its pagan origin and frowned upon fortune-telling through hand-reading. Gradually the practice fell into the hands of gypsies and adventurers. In some of the United States it is against the law to predict the future by palmistry. The legislation is based on the contention that it is impossible to predict the future in this way. Palmistry, or the art of divination, has no status in modern science.

There were those, however, who convinced a credulous public that the art of obtaining information about the future from the palm of the hand was of divine origin. They quoted the words of Job, XXXVII, 7: "He sealeth up the hand of every man, that all men may know his work." These words were accepted literally.

Many of the older palmists attached special importance to the shape and form of the hands, of which some 70 varieties were enumerated. All agree that the thumb is the most important part of the hand, and say that the first phalange symbolizes will-power, whereas the second, logic. The ball of the thumb is called the "Mount of Venus." The line around the base of the thumb is the line of life. Every phalange of the four fingers symbolizes some quality, physical or mental. The "Mount of Jupiter" is at the base of the first finger and symbolizes arrogance, haughtiness, and pride. The "Mount of Saturn" is at the base of the middle finger, the *digitus infamis* of the Romans, and symbolized fate or destiny. The "Mount of Apollo" is at the base of the third and symbolizes art, music, easy circumstances, and the like. The "Mount of Mercury" is at the base of the fourth finger and symbolizes learning. The "Mount of Mars" and the "Mount of the Moon" are at the heel of the hand and symbolize violence and light-heartedness, respectively. The line of the heel joins in the line of life under the first finger. Parallel to it is the line of the heart. The line of fate runs up the center of the hand, and parallel to it on the heel side of the hand, is the line of fortune. The curved line from below the fourth finger to the base of the first is called the "girdle of Venus."

The left hand is usually chosen for examination by palmists, but neither the left nor right hands are identical as far as their lines and mounts are concerned. Expert palmists attach great importance to the little crosses and triangles and markings which appear in many hands, and to the lines which are found on the phalanges of the four fingers. Very few agree about the qualities which they think they indicate. Many think that the lines and ridges on the back of the hand are important witnesses to character and disposition. Some deduce information from the lines of the wrist.

Needless to add, the above description speaks for itself, the symbols indicating this or that through lines and mounts, triangles, crosses, and the like, which are related to astrology and mythology of ancient times.

Dactylography is the scientific study of fingerprints. It is an ancient study and comes from the Orient. The thumbprint of a Chinese ruler was his sign and the symbol of his reign. Fingerprints were used on legal documents to prevent one person from posing as another; names can be forged, but fingerprints defy forgery. Now and then attempts were made to foretell the future of an individual from the lines of his fingerprints, but in the main fingerprinting was a practical system of identification. It is interesting to note, however, that it has its roots in superstition.

From the study of finger-figure symbols evolved the highly important device of the finger-alphabet which is used so successfully today by deaf-mutes.

There is no doubt that the majority of palmists are sincere and believe implicitly in their predictions, but in the judgment of highly reputable and competent men and women well grounded in their respective fields, palmistry does not stand scientific test and sanction. For those who are lonely and sad, to have someone hold their hand, even a palmist, is highly satisfying. The added attraction of having someone talk about the most fascinating of subjects, oneself, seldom fails. But to depend on the mystical meaning of a line, curve, or mount of the hand, is a very dangerous superstition.

"Left-Hand" Superstitions

ONE OF THE most common superstitions about left-handed persons is that if they are forced to use the right hand they will become stutterers. Studies at the National Hospital for Speech Disorders indicate that there is no direct connection between the two. Of 1,200 stutterers investigated at the clinic, only seven per cent were left-handed. There is very nearly this same proportion of left-handed persons in the general population. However, forcibly changing a *nervous* child from left to right-handedness could produce stuttering, the survey warned.

The age-old superstition that left-hand users are clumsy was disproved some years ago by Dave Fleisher of the Fleisher Studios in Miami, Florida, who reported that 52 per cent of the seven hundred artists he employed in his film cartoons were left-handed. Considering the small percentage of left-handed persons in the United States, he concluded: "I naturally deduce from my studio survey that southpaws inherently must be artists." An outstanding example of a work of genius executed by the left hand is "The Mona Lisa," by Leonardo da Vinci.

Other surveys have proved that "born" left-handers have the edge on "born" right-handers, mainly because they often become doubly skillful of necessity by living in a right-handed world. With few exceptions, commonplace mechanical appliances are made for operation with the right hand. Hence the ambidexterity of those who use the left hand is more apt to develop.

Up to a few years ago, an enemy was cursed with the wish that his son would turn out to be a left-handed baseball pitcher. "Southpaws," however, are not inferior, by any means, but they do make it difficult for a right-handed batter.

Early peoples took exception to anything that deviated from what they thought was normal. Because left-handed persons were in such a small minority, they were probably looked upon as a group apart, and not to be trusted, since the use of their left hands was confusing to the right-handed.

However, in primitive times, the left hand was the one always used for magic. The heart-side was the left side, and the ancients knew it was an area that had to be watched carefully since life depended on the heartbeat. In other words, the left side was a dangerous side, called the "sinister" side, by the Romans. In nearly all languages, the words meaning left-handed are synonymous with indirection, insincerity and even treachery.

Because the left side of the body was associated with sinister or evil action, it led to many superstitious beliefs and gestures that are still present in the life and culture of people everywhere. One of these beliefs is that a left-handed person is not quite up to the same standard of development as a right-handed one. This idea originated at the time when a left-handed person was thought to possess the Evil Eye which was responsible for his doing things "in reverse."

The traditional attitude toward the left hand makes us still apologize for offering it, with the excuse "It's nearer my heart." According to Plutarch, Roman boys were permitted to use only the left hand for holding bread. Among Orientals, particularly the Brahmins, the left hand is used exclusively for performing acts of the bodily toilet, while the Arabs always use their left hand to pet their dogs, and never the right. To all Moslems, a dog is an unclean animal, and they reserve their left hand for touching anything that is not clean.

To be left-handed is not in itself an organic imperfection as many superstitious persons believe. Left-handedness seems "odd" at times because we are in a world the culture of which is right-handed. This accounts for whatever personal peculiarities the left-hand user seems to display.

Thumbs Up or Down

"THUMBS UP"—symbol of courage and stick-to-it-iveness is not a gesture of recent origin, Churchillian or otherwise, but it goes back to ancient times. The rule of the thumb in ancient Rome and the provinces was a very old custom, originally borrowed from Etruria. The Etruscans indulged in gladiatorial games which the Romans made famous and which in Julius Caesar's day were nothing short of human butchery. If the spectators were in favor of mercy to a fallen gladiator they waved their handkerchiefs. But if they desired the death of the loser—they turned their thumbs downward.

A reverse account says that those who wished the death of the conquered gladiator, turned thumbs toward their breasts as a signal to stab him; those who wished him to be spared turned their thumbs downward as a signal for dropping the sword. The fact remains, however, that the thumb was used—whichever signal it indicated—for a decision. With this single exception all other historical information reveals that thumbs down meant to give the *coup de grâce* to end the man's life.

In keeping with the Roman ideas of thumb-up, the familiar little Billiken figure—drawn from Bes, the Egyptian mascot—seen in modern shops, is modeled with clenched hand and upward thumb to indicate hope and faith in ultimate good and victory.

Apparently the ancients had noticed that before being moved after the last breath, a dead person generally has the thumbs turned into the palm of the hands. Thus it would seem that the Romans were aware that thumbs down meant death, as every evidence points to the fact that the thumb relaxes downward once life has run out.

There are hundreds of superstitions attached to the thumb itself. Among them are: Thumbs which turn back mean that you cannot save money. If ordinarily your left thumb folds over the right when you clasp hands you are submissive and take orders. If the right folds over the left you are domineering. If you fold thumbs inside fists it indicates cowardice or guilt.

Long thumbs indicate a stubborn disposition. Wide thumbs will spin gold, meaning acquisition of wealth. The itching of the thumb indicates a visitor, sometimes an unwelcome intruder. The ancient Romans believed that the pricking of one's thumb was a portent of evil, and Shakespeare has the second witch in "Macbeth" say, just before Macbeth enters:

> "By the pricking of my thumbs,
>   Something wicked this way comes."

A child generally comes into the world with its thumbs folded or relatively down within its hands. Each day, as the child's brain unfolds, as it were, and reacts to life's impressions, so the fingers of each hand release the thumbs. Equally remarkable also is the fact that, as life departs, thumbs generally resume the "down" position as at birth.

Hence, "Thumbs Up" appears to be the sign of life.

"Thumb-Sucking" Superstitions

MANY SUPERSTITIOUS mothers are confused and worried about the baby's habit of sucking its thumb. They believe this habit will push back its teeth, and probably ruin the shape of its mouth, so that when it grows up its looks will be spoiled. This is partly true. Such a condition will take place if the thumb-sucking habit is allowed for too long a period; therefore it should be discouraged.

There is also the belief that thumb-sucking will permanently damage the shape of the thumb or of any other fingers the baby keeps in its mouth. Some mothers think this habit produces dental cavities in the permanent teeth, and that both the first and second sets of teeth will fall out prematurely. Mothers also fear that thumb-sucking leads to digestive disturbances in adult life.

Another superstition in this regard is that a bottle-fed baby takes to sucking its thumb, and at the same time others think it is the breast-fed that do.

As a matter of fact, as far as a baby is concerned, sucking is a natural or instinctive function. He is given the instinct in order to get his food. A baby's feeding, if watched carefully, will generally give the clue to the mother or nurse as to why the infant sucks its thumb between meals. The easiest correction lies in providing substitute diversions.

It is true that excessive thumb-sucking can become a mouth problem unless checked at an early age; orthodontists' reports show an average of some 30 per cent of all malocclusion have a history of a thumb-sucking habit. Infants can force their soft teeth out of shape and into permanent disfigurement. Properly supervised, however, the mouth exercise that goes with sucking, with a substitute pacifier, may, in some instances, be an aid to build up the face muscles, and thus discourage the thumb-sucking and pressure habit. Superstitious parents need not be unnecessarily alarmed but they must be very alert to the child's instinctive need, which is usually expressed by the mouth in infancy.

Babies who have given up the habit of sucking the thumb may have a temporary recurrence during the teething period, but there is no reason for the superstitious fear that this is a sign of a mind that is developing more slowly than normal, or that the habit may lead to infantilism, or any other form of mental or physical retardation. Nor does thumb-sucking necessarily mean that an infant is hungry for food, or starved for affection, as many wrongly believe.

There are many superstitious methods for the punishment of the little offender, as well as "cures" for the habit. One is to coat the child's thumb with a bitter substance. Another is to imprison the hand in a guard so that the little one cannot get it to its mouth. These devices only make matters worse by arousing an instinct of rebellion at such an early age.

Keep Your Fingers Crossed

How OFTEN have we crossed our fingers when making a wish in the superstitious belief that the gesture would aid the wish in coming true? And done so without realizing that the crossed finger gesture supposedly has a dual function; the power to bring good and avert evil!

Hardly an adult can account for using the gesture or explain why he places a superstitious faith in the cross-finger symbol or verbal usage of the phrase "keep your fingers crossed." Yet many of us still use the symbol.

The popular gesture grew out of the belief that the cross was the symbolic sign of perfect unity; that is, when two straight lines cross and meet in the center of the two lines, the wish was held there, as it were; so that it would not slip away before it was realized.

The index finger of a well-wisher was placed on the index finger of the person wishing, forming a cross. While one wished the other mentally supported the wish, so that it might come true. As time elapsed, this custom was altered and was performed singly, with the remark "I'll keep my fingers crossed"; using the index and the powerful middle finger to form St. Andrew's cross-charm, an X offered as a charm-formula to assist in the realization of the wish.

When children tell white lies, as they often do, they cross their fingers, lest they be punished. A white lie is not supposed to count or do any harm if it is made with crossed fingers.

"Fingernail" Superstitions

Specks on the fingers, fortune lingers;
Specks on the thumbs, fortune surely comes.

A SPECIAL DAY for cutting or manicuring fingernails, as well as a system for interpreting character through fingernail analysis are superstitious beliefs which had their origins ages ago when people sought answers to puzzling character questions through special markings on the human body. In the light of present day knowledge, this method of determining characteristics is generally fallacious.

Fingernails have been the source of innumerable superstitions, which young people, especially girls, are well acquainted with. For instance, many persons will not clean their nails after dark. If a person bites his nails, he will not grow tall. If fingernails have pronounced half-moons, it indicates good blood and lineage. If the nails are short-ridged, and there is hardly a sign of the half-moon, it denotes a short life. Persons with short or stubby fingernails are believed to be tale-bearers, while those with long tapering fingernails are believed artistic and due for a long life.

Many manicurists have their own approach to fingernail character analysis: Don't trust a woman with a triangle-shaped fingernail as she cannot keep a secret. Don't expect a man with long, slim fingernails to be a good provider. Don't marry a fingernail chewer. Little round nails show honesty with hot temper. A person with strong half-moons will rise in the world. Ridges on the nails show a nervous temperament. And so on.

When counting the white or "lucky spots" on the nails, superstitious persons make a wish. This is an old formula.

There is a medieval method of fortune-telling by the white spots on nails that is still popular. A white spot on the thumb promises a present; on the index finger, it denotes a friend; on the long or middle finger, an enemy; on the third,—now known as the fourth—finger, a letter or sweetheart; and on the little finger, a journey. Youngsters, especially boys, say that the white spots on the nails indicate the number of lies one has told from one moon to the next.

Another medieval fortune-telling formula for cutting the nails, is often heard today.

> Cut them on Monday, you cut them for news,
> Cut them on Tuesday, a new pair of shoes.
> Cut them on Wednesday, you cut them for health.
> Cut them on Thursday, you cut them for wealth.
> Cut them on Friday, a sweetheart you'll know.
> Cut them on Saturday, a-journey you'll go.
> Cut them on Sunday, you cut them for evil,
> For all the next week, you'll be ruled by the devil.

There was a special system of Finger Divination in ancient times called Onychomancy, which was performed by the fingernails of an unpolluted or morally pure boy. His fingernails were covered with soot and oil, and when turned to the sun they reflected an image which was supposed to be a clue to the answer sought to a specific question. Each spot on the nails had a meaning that supplied the answer whether to do or not to do certain things. These spots were likewise supposed to reveal the character of a person.

The cause for "white spots" on fingernails, popularly called "good luck spots" in ancient times, was unknown in that period. We know today, however, that they are simply imperfections in the nail. Fingernails are formed by the gradual fossilization of living cells into the non-living tissue called keratin. Actually white specks result when some of the cells near the root of the nail are blemished, and as the nails grow, these blemishes are pushed forward. They may be natural imperfections, or produced by a slight injury near the line where the flesh nail is being formed. Today, they are not infrequently due to poor manicuring.

Because of the half-moons which are generally present on the fingernails, ancient peoples identified the nails as having a relation to the crescent of the moon. They related these markings on the nail to waxing and waning fortunes in human affairs.

Long fingernails were looked upon in the Orient, especially in China, as a sign of wisdom, and they were also a high mark of distinction and wealth. There cutting the fingernails was a function not to be trifled with, even by those in the lower social scale. Among the Chinese, white spots generally denoted evil.

There were world-wide superstitions around the disposal of nail cuttings. Nail parings were usually buried or burned, lest a sorcerer make maleficent use of them. Cutting the fingernails at sea was believed to cause a storm.

Pliny said that magicians recommended that the parings of fingernails should be thrown at the entrance of ant-hills, and the first ant caught bearing a piece would bring the best of health and luck to the one who caught it. Walking on fingernail parings was thought to injure the man to whom they once belonged.

Once upon a time the American Indian interpreted the European custom of using a knife and fork to eat with as meaning that his fingernails distilled deadly poison, and therefore he did not pick up his food with his fingers.

Fingernails do not grow after death. Biting the nails does not cause stubby fingers. When nails are bitten it tends to make the fingers look stubby, but when the biting habit stops, and the nails grow normally, the fingers will appear in their proper shapes.

Crossing Little Fingers of Right Hand

IF TWO PERSONS by chance say the same thing at the same time, the superstition is that each must bite the little finger of the right hand while making a wish, and then quickly reach for the other one's little finger and pull hard. This makes a hooked cross which holds a wish. Now, usually after biting the little finger, and giving it a hard pull across another person's little finger, it will hurt. If neither makes a sound to show pain, their wishes will come true. If there is an outcry, the wish will not come true. This is one of the many variations of the same superstition.

In another version, the same procedure takes place without first biting the little finger. Each one then calls out the other's first name. This also makes the wishes come true.

Other addicts of the superstition believe that instead of calling each other's first name, another name or word, such as "Shakespeare" should be called. Immediately the other one who is wishing must reply with an associated word, such as "Hamlet." This calls for quick thinking on the part of the one who must respond, as it must be instantaneous, or otherwise the charm of the cross will not work—the delay causing the wish to escape. This same form of the superstition is illustrated in the jingle,

"I say, chimney, you say, smoke,
Then our wish will not be broke."

To give the wish every chance to come true, the little fingers of the *right* hand had to be crossed, the cross being the symbol of harmony and unity, and the right side, that of wisdom. The three parts of the superstition, first the simultaneous words, then the cross-gesture and, after this the names or last words, rounded up the charm symbol expressing the magic number, three, or the Trinity symbol. The wish was then the result of the "Never two without three" expression, still commonly used and believed in. That things work in threes is one of the oldest superstitions and never seems to die out.

Flat and Deep Chest Superstitions

THERE IS NOT one grain of truth in the superstitious belief that persons with flat chests are physically inferior to those with deep chests. Scientists have conducted research experiments in the past few years among both children and adults, and their conclusions favor the flat chest. They found a distinct correlation between depth of chest and certain lung ailments. All deep chests are not necessarily weaker, but they seem more apt to invite diseases.

This fact should dispel a common superstitious fear, and reassure flat-chested persons.

By way of explaining how such ideas have found their way into the public mind, and traveled from one nation to another, it is possible that one of Martin Luther's dogmatic quotations may have started the fallacy. This great religious leader of the fifteenth century expounded his theory in the following terms: "Men have broad and large chests and small narrow hips and more understanding than women who have but small and narrow chests and broad hips, to the end that they should remain at home, sit still, keep house and bear and bring up children."

An amusing American superstition is that most successful career women have flat chests!

That the Heart Is on the Left Side

MANY SUPERSTITIOUS PERSONS think that the heart is on the left side of the body, and that if they lie on that side, it is dangerous and may cause heart trouble or crush the organ, or even that they will suffocate in their sleep.

Others believe that raising the left arm too high above the head might interfere with the position of the heart and pull it out of place. There are many other such false notions.

The heart, of course, is not on the left side, and even if it were, there would be no danger in using that side of the body as much as the right side, since the heart is protected by ribs and muscles which act as a strong protective wall.

The mistaken idea about the position of the heart is probably due to the fact that the heart beat is felt on the left side. Unfortunately, very few persons know much about the heart, although it is one of the most perfect pieces of mechanism in all of nature.

The human heart is pear-shaped or conical. It is suspended obliquely or slantwise in the chest, between the two lungs. One-third of the broad end of the heart is directed upward, backward, and toward the right. Two-thirds, or the apex is downward, forward and to the left side.

The heart is a hollow four-chambered bag. The compartments are separated from each other by membranous valves which open with each contraction of the heart, and close again when the heart relaxes. The sound, or beat, that is heard is the contracting action of the heart as it hits the chest wall.

The human heart is approximately the size of a closed fist and weighs from eight to twelve ounces. The heart increases in size until the age of fifty years is reached, and the increase is greater in the male than in the female.

Contrary to what many think, the heart never skips a beat. What really happens is that when a faulty beat takes place a trifle too soon, the prolonged interval until the next regular beat gives the feeling or sensation of the organ having skipped a beat.

"Foot" and "Shoe" Superstitions

"Augustus having b'oversight
Out of his left shoe before the right,
Had like to have been slain that day,
By soldiers mutining for their pay."
                                    —*Hudibras*

SUPERSTITIONS CONCERNING FEET and shoes are very old and very numerous, and many of them are still with us. For instance, to start the day "on the right foot," symbolically and factually, one must cover the right foot first and the left one last. To present a pair of shoes or slippers to anyone is a sign that they will walk away from you on the wearer's feet. Another version of this is that such a present will prolong the giver's life and shorten the receiver's.

If a girl places her shoes beside her bed with the heel of one against the middle of the other she will have happy dreams and good luck in love. This arrangement of the shoes obviously makes the tau-cross, a very potent symbol.

If shoes squeak, it is a sign they have not been paid for, but if an actor's shoes squeak on making his entrance on opening night, it is a sign that he will be well received by the audience. Most actors, and many other persons as well will not place shoes on a shelf, because, if raised from the floor, the owner's feet may then be off the floor too, as in a fall, or even as in death.

To place shoes on a table signifies a disappointment or a quarrel, but to expectorate in the right shoe before putting it on, wards off all evil influences for the day.

The majority of shoe superstitions are specifically related to the foot itself, which, for centuries back, was regarded as a phallic or sex symbol. This has led to many theories concerning the real significance behind foot superstitions. One theory is based on the old belief that the crotch of the human body, with its two limbs and feet was an extension from the life-giving semi-circle, known as the repository of life. This concept commanded profound respect among primitives who had no knowledge whatever about the process of birth, which, by the way, remained a mystery for a long time. Foot taboos, and other strange customs, beliefs and fetishisms, running into the hundreds, evolved from that impression.

In connection with foot symbolism, it is to be noted that the phrase, "covering the feet," which appears frequently in ancient writings, does not necessarily mean what the words say, but may refer to another part of the body. This is one of innumerable examples of vague and veiled language found all through religious and other ancient literature, when words which have one meaning are used to mean another. Ancient sages loved to employ the art of parables.

The foot was also a sex symbol among the Chinese, and this attitude accounts to a great extent for the form of modesty observed by young Chinese women of olden days which made them conceal their feet.

The long history of the evolution of foot coverings takes us back to the Egyptians who were among the first to make shoes. Their warriors wore a sort of elaborate sandal, turned up around the foot, and bound around the legs with thongs. These were probably the first crude shoes, and were worn about 4,000 years ago.

Sandals are referred to in the Bible and in other early historical records. The shoes of ancient Jews were made of wood-rush, linen and leather. Among laws governing the daily life of the observant Jew were ordinances regulating which foot to cover first.

The Romans, however, were the first to set the example of costly shoes, and introduced various decorative ornaments such as ivory and precious stones. They were extremely superstitious about their feet and shoes. An old Roman countercharm was to expectorate into a shoe before putting it on, especially before going where there might be danger. They, too, thought it an ill omen to put the left shoe on before the right, as they were mindful of how they used the left—or sinister— side of the body. To them the right foot symbolized the first duty in reverence to the gods who they believed resided in the right side of man. Romans also believed one must enter a house right foot first, lest calamity follow in his footsteps and catch up with him.

Contrary to popular superstitions, the early Romans, like peoples of other nations of their time or before, could not possibly have meant *right* or *left* shoe, since this development in foot covering had not yet been introduced. It was the foot itself that was the immediate concern of the superstitious ancients.

It was not until the beginning of the 19th Century that shoes were made into distinct right and left ones. This is reputed to have occurred in England. As a matter of fact, in America as late as 1880 both shoes were still identical, just as socks and stockings are today.

Folklore contains an interesting story about a shoemaker of the third or fourth century who went as a missionary of the Christian faith, from his own country, presumably Rome, into France. He is said to have maintained himself wholly by making and mending shoes. Tradition further relates that he was beheaded and became the tutelary saint of the shoemakers. Legendary character or not, we still have Shoemaker's Day, which falls on October 25, dedicated to St. Crispin.

Best Foot Foremost

WHEN WE WANT to insure the success of any venture, whether it be a sea voyage or matrimony, we say "let's get off on the right foot." Many a superstitious bride, even in these supposedly enlightened times, jumps out of bed on her wedding morning with both feet at once to make doubly sure that she will not start her married life on the wrong foot.

And seafaring people of old, always stepped onto a new ship on its maiden voyage, with the right foot. This procedure is adhered to faithfully and woe to the one who does not comply, for seamen are still among the most superstitious of people.

Anciently, the right side in general was believed invulnerable, free from disturbing emotions, fears and dangers. Such notions were endorsed because the heart or left side gave expression to feelings and sensations which needed the protection of the right side where no emotions could be located. Feet in general, but the right in particular, were looked upon as a symbol of the male generative power; a charm which protected against evil and failure, and by the same token, invited good and success.

The Romans, among many peoples, exercised this superstitious custom of using the right foot first by having a special guard at the entrance of important places to make certain the people entered with the right foot foremost.

They believed that a kindly disposed spirit kept to the right of an individual and accompanied that person when entering with the right foot. But if the left foot came in first, the good spirit was left behind and an evil one whose place was on the left side came in instead.

Tripping or Stumbling, Bad Luck!

STUMBLING OVER ANYTHING, as one starts the day, has always been interpreted as an evil omen. For example, long ago to trip on the threshold when entering a house was supposed to reveal, by accident, as it were, that the visitor practiced witchcraft and therefore was not to be trusted.

All sorts of counter-magic measures were devised to neutralize the bad luck, and many of these are superstitions to this day. For instance, there is the traditional formula: "I turn myself around three times about, and thus I put bad luck to rout." Turning around three times makes a triple magic circle, which is symbolic of completion, and that makes one free to start anew. Three is known as a powerful mystic symbol, and the use of this number triples the chances of removing the taboo completely.

Another way to undo the evil, when tripping over something, is to go back and pass it again without stumbling, and from then on all is expected to go well. Some superstitious people snap their fingers to frighten away whatever evil spirit was responsible for the mishap.

There are other superstitious interpretations of the dangers involved in stumbling or falling. An interesting one is that the soul or life-spirit in man is a fragile thing, which may leave him because of the shock. Magic formulas, therefore, must be carried out to bring back his soul!

The ancients thought that to stumble *out* of one's house was a warning to watch one's step for the rest of the day. On the other hand, to trip forward, or *into* one's house, presaged good news for the next day. "He fell into it," our common expression for success, is related in origin to this superstition.

General "Blood" Superstitions

IT WOULD SEEM from the long and varied list of prevailing superstitions about blood, that knowledge of this vital fluid has not yet caught up with the march of knowledge in other fields. Frequently we not only altered old beliefs, but we have added our own brand of misconceptions to those we inherited from primitives and the ancients.

That "Negro blood" is different from white man's blood is one of the most deeply-rooted of superstitious prejudices. Blood of all races is almost identical, and can be safely transferred from one race to another provided the blood passes cross-matching tests. A Negro blood transfusion—or blood from any other race—does not transfer hereditary characteristics, personality or mentality, as a great many persons like to believe.

Another false and dangerous belief is to the effect that "bad blood" produces criminals. There is no such thing as "criminal-blood," a phrase which stems from ancient times. Criminals are persons with dangerous habits and the blood of such individuals has nothing to do with the "bad blood" of their parents. The blood of every human being is an individual matter. The socially undesirable belong to all classes and they may be offspring of the healthiest and most moral parents as well as of the sickliest and most immoral.

There is another application of the terms "good" and "bad" blood which is a survival of the notion that the veins of aristocrats were of a deeper blue than those of inferior persons. "Blue blood" was the sign of nobility. Biologists inform us, however, that the only creatures that are really blue-blooded are snails, oysters and lobsters.

A cruel superstition that causes humiliation to the unfortunate victims is the idea that boils and pimples are caused by "bad" blood. Boils are due to disease germs and not necessarily to impure blood. Pimples are caused by microscopic organisms which get into the skin and are not the result of weak or poor blood.

Many persons still believe that certain sicknesses are caused by too much blood. This was a medieval fallacy and in most instances was treated by blood-letting or the use of leeches. The truth is that the average person does not have too much blood. There is also a belief that the normal blood pressure should be one hundred plus the age of the individual. As a matter of fact, there is no normal fixed blood pressure any more than there is a normal fixed temperature.

The superstition that babies derive their blood from the mother is believed by most parents today. However, a baby's blood is entirely separated from that of the mother. Blood forms from the infant's own spleen and bone marrow and not one single drop of it comes directly from the mother. A baby manufactures its own blood, starting about eight months before birth.

A horror of blood has given rise to several phobias, particularly the fear of bleeding to death. Likewise, with some persons the sight of blood or any reference to it produces all kinds of distressing emotions. Venescence, or the slight operation of opening a vein to draw blood for blood tests or blood chemistry, evokes gruesome mental images in the minds of persons with blood phobias because of the fear that an arterial hemorrhage will follow. Many would prefer to die from a neglected disease rather than submit to modern methods.

A superstitious regard for blood pervaded all the early ideas and institutions of mankind. Drinking blood was the equivalent of a blood transfusion at one time with the primitive conviction that the blood was the same as the life. The heart was thought to be the blood-fountain and the core of each personality. Hence this form of transfusion was regarded as soul transference.

The ancient Hebrews were forbidden to eat the blood of an animal because they associated it with the life. Cannibalism, as a tribal rite, was based on the idea that the blood of another was his life and soul. Cannibalism originated in the practice of drinking the blood of the bravest foes to acquire their courage, cunning and other distinctive traits, and thereby increase the fighting force and courage of the tribesmen who partook of the blood.

Brotherhood was created artificially and ceremonially by mingling a few drops of the blood of two persons in a cup of wine and drinking it. Heroes of old German sagas are represented in Wagner's opera "Götterdämmerung," with Gunther and Siegfried swearing inviolable friendship in this manner.

Initiations conducted by college fraternities and other secret societies are in imitation of mythical blood covenants, and many of the ceremonies are in keeping with those of old. They are performed with traditional indignities, some of which are just horse-play and silly cruelty, but others are reminiscent of old rituals of life, death and rebirth; in which the drinking of blood and wine, the life-quickening agents, is a practice.

In olden times, when a secret society was formed, those who were to join opened a vein and let some of their blood drop into a cup. Each member took a sip, swearing an oath of allegiance and fraternity which was considered binding unto death. Sometimes two persons formed a blood covenant by drinking each other's blood. These same rites prevail today in many countries, both civilized and uncivilized. The antiquity of this ceremony may be traced back to the ancient Egyptians and there are several allusions to it in the Bible.

The belief in the potency of blood was the motive behind the sacrifice of animals to the gods. In one form of sacrifice, drops of blood were put into wine or other beverage and the mixture drunk. Later, the wine was drunk without the actual presence of the blood. Today we use wine in pledges of friendship and marriage and on similar occasions. Among the Jews, wine is used symbolically in circumcision, and among Christians it is used in sacraments.

Noah's Curse and Racial Superstitions

ONE SOURCE of the very common superstition that causes prejudice of white races against black may be traced to Noah's curse, Genesis 9:25. "And he said, cursed be Canaan, a servant of servants shall he be unto his brethren."

This curse has been interpreted to mean what was believed in the early days—that Negroes are descended from Canaan, son of Ham and grandson of Noah. Persons who favored the practice of slavery at a later date used Noah's curse as a divine justification for their views. This Biblical reference is also believed to have encouraged the enslavement of human beings when Biblical scholars first began their research on the Old Testament.

Anthropologists claim there is no pure or superior race. Genealogies can go so far and no farther. Practically every member of the human family is a mongrel and there is no way of tracing a direct line that will cover thousands of years.

It is also a fact that intermixture through the ages has been the rule rather than the exception. At the present time, modern inventions and modern wars provide new opportunities for interracial relationships and marriage, so that the racial myth becomes weaker as the years go by. Nevertheless, racial superstitions and prejudices will probably continue to exist.

"Genius" Superstitions

THE FACTS DO NOT substantiate the superstitious belief that one must be unbalanced to be a genius. Many persons believe that if a man or woman is unusually gifted in a specific talent or ability, such as music, art, poetry, mathematics, or other branches of the arts or learning, it means that the individual must be backward or feeble-minded in other directions, if not actually demented. It is also assumed that these brilliant persons are more likely to go completely insane than average human beings.

Psychiatrists often find an unmistakable spark of genius in an insane person, but insanity is emotional unbalance that can strike any type of intellect.

History tells us that many geniuses have died insane, which may be a source of the superstition, which is a superstition, nevertheless.

Another superstitious notion is that precocious children do not turn out well; that is, their mental development is often arrested after a certain age, or else they become criminals, go insane or die young. Authorities who have made a special study of this type of child declare that children given to precocity and genius-like characteristics are generally the healthiest, longest-lived individuals on earth. There are exceptions, of course.

Frustrations, however, are believed to produce both geniuses and criminals. Frustration will drive some persons to work very hard, which ties in with one so-called definition of genius: "An infinite capacity for work." Emotional instability often creates aggressiveness, and that characteristic may be destructive if handled unwisely by one with an otherwise genius-like mind.

Genius is desirable, but balanced emotions are absolutely essential for sanity in both the ordinary person and the genius.

It is commonly thought that a good environment can produce a genius. Unfortunately, being a genius depends on a great many factors and next to nothing is known as to what they are. Some persons think that genius is a matter of proper parentage. As matters stand, very ordinary parents have produced geniuses, and brilliant parents have produced morons. Geniuses do not produce geniuses.

Some of the factors that enter into the making of a genius undoubtedly are the chemistry of the brain, heritage, environment and probably dozens of other contributing causes. Psychiatrists and other men of science seem to be well on the way to solving the riddle, however.

Geniuses are often queer because they are actually above the average thinker in so many ways. This does not mean, as the superstitious believe, that they are erratic or neurotic necessarily. Many a genius goes through life unknown and unhonored, because of his serenity and peace of mind. Sometimes, if they are lucky, the world finds them out.

It is not true that an otherwise bright child who does not like school is a potential genius. However, a child who is a prodigy resents school sometimes, because he is so far above the mentality of his classmates. Doctors warn, however, not to be too concerned about the creative genius in a child because only one in a million has an IQ of 180 or higher, which designates the potential genius.

The subject of genius has puzzled people for ages. The Romans believed that everyone had a personal "genius"—a sort of beneficent guardian spirit that protected each human being from the cradle to the grave. The ancient Romans were so convinced that such a spirit was constantly with them that newly married couples, when furnishing their home, always provided an extra bed for their "genii," presumably a male and a female, to sleep in.

CHAPTER 7

Thy Name Is Woman

That Woman Is the Weaker Sex

When greater perils men environ,
The women show a front of iron;
And gentle in their manner they
Do bold things in a quiet way.
—Thomas Dunn English

MEDICAL RESEARCH, through a series of statistical records, flatly contradicts the popular superstition that women belong to the weaker sex. The records prove that women have a higher disease resistance, and that there are two women for every man who reaches the age of one hundred.

Despite the superstitious attitude toward "the little woman," a female child has more chance of being alive than a male; for every one hundred miscarriages of the female embryo there are one hundred sixty of the male. For every still-born girl baby there are one hundred thirty still-born boy babies. Although men in general are almost twice as strong, muscularly, as women, science says, and proves, that the male is biologically weaker.

To further dissolve the superstition about the ladies, the fact is that the average life expectancy of the American woman is four years longer than that of the Stronger Sex.

Students who were vaccinated or injected with serums were checked, and the result showed that forty-five per cent more young men than women fainted during these administrations. Fifty-five per cent of all pneumonia patients are male, and more men are operated on for appendicitis than women. More men than women suffer from hardening of the arteries. Ninety per cent of the nation's color blind are males. Seventy per cent of the swimmers in distress have been men. Although only one per cent of the people of the United States stutter, seventy-five per cent of the stutterers are male.

The so-called "feminine weaknesses," described by men as timidity, irresponsibility and the craving for someone to lean on, have been exploded as superstitions. Dr. Samuel Johnson observed two hundred years ago, "Nature has given women so much power that the law very wisely gives her very little." Men will admit, however, that the strength given women is mainly in the realm of psychological power, and that it is not all on the surface, like a pair of bulging biceps. These powers admittedly force men to a retreating position on many occasions.

There is another myth, believed for thousands of years, which has now come to an end. It is that women who cry easily are weak individuals. As a matter of scientific fact, that habit of shedding tears easily is really one that makes them emotionally sounder than men, as crying is both a psychological and physiological release.

The truth that women are emotionally sounder than men is evidenced by the fact that four times as many men as women have stomach ulcers, largely a nervous disease. More males than females with dementia praecox are admitted to mental institutions, and they are admitted, on the average, four years earlier in life. The general average of inmates in mental institutions is ten per cent more men than women, while the male death rate due to diseases of the nervous system is thirty per cent greater than that of women. There are more widows than widowers!

Almost any man will admit that a woman's mind can sway a man's. It is happening all the time. The myth of the superiority of men is just as fallacious as the myth of the mental inferiority of women. A woman's mind is not inferior to a man's. It is just "different" and woman's intellect has a different range.

That a Woman Cannot Keep a Secret

BECAUSE WOMEN in primitive times, and in later periods as well, were excluded from the secret societies of men, they have been regarded as tale-bearers, detrimental to men's welfare and unable to keep a secret. All adages to the contrary, a woman *can* keep a secret when she sets her mind and conscience to the task.

One of the reasons, and perhaps the most important, for keeping women out of men's social and tribal affairs for centuries on end is said to have been due to the men themselves. Women were a disturbing element to them, emotionally speaking. Therefore the psychological excuse was conveniently evolved that she talked too much, and that when she talked she was apt to reveal tribal or other important secrets which might endanger the safety of a people. And so it was thought best to keep her out of men's affairs entirely.

Comparing men and women without prejudice, and in the light of 20th Century moral and cultural standards, it is agreed there is no noticeable difference between a man or woman's ability to keep a secret, provided the one to whom the secret is entrusted is selected with care, which just about divides the honors between the sexes.

To those who still believe the antiquated superstition that a woman cannot be trusted, it must seem strange then that highly paid women, as personal secretaries, hold positions which entrust them with the greatest and most delicate confidences which they keep for years and take to the grave with them.

Women physicians and psychiatrists keep the secrets of their patients extremely well. Nevertheless, there are those who retain their prejudices against women in the professions and keep them out of the ministry on the contention that they cannot keep secrets.

Both superstitious men *and* women keep up the antiquated slogan that women cannot keep a secret. At this stage of our civilization it is a superstitious form of slander which accuses all women of being guilty of the same fault.

It is undeniable that women talk too much, but this bad trait applies to both men and women. Keeping a secret requires effort, because telling it is a strong temptation as it inflates the ego. It is probably easier to some persons than others to keep mum with certain information, but at best it is a strain on the individual's will power, whether man or woman.

In primitive times, persons had less control over their emotions than we have today, and had no idea of the meaning of discretion as we know it now. Furthermore, we live in an age of greater personal safety than in olden times, so that many of the original purposes of secrecy in men's affairs have long ceased. It is the informer's inflated ego in the present era that makes men and women break the ethical code of society, and as women on the whole have less of this ego than the other sex, the temptation with them is perhaps stronger. Nevertheless, the superstition which condemns all women is fallacious.

That Beauty and Brains Do Not Go Together

THERE ARE MANY superstitions about beauty, but the one heard most often is that brains and beauty seldom go together. "Beautiful but dumb" is undeservedly applied to most very attractive women. Referring to Helen of Troy, an old quotation goes:

> "It was a face that launched a thousand ships,
> and not philosophy."

Experts in the field of psychology are now in a position to tell us the truth on this subject and they will testify that both men and women who possess charm and good looks, by a large percentage, are more apt to be brainy than their less fortunate brothers and sisters. School teachers have found the same thing to be true.

Because women are the smaller sex, and therefore have smaller heads, it was assumed that they had undersized brains in general. Also, the fact that many spoiled, beautiful women do not bother to develop intellectually, relying on their physical charms for success in life, has led the world to believe that such women are stupid. Regarding the size of the brain, many large brains have belonged to morons, and very small ones to geniuses. Relative to her size, however, a woman's brain is larger than a man's.

It is only recently that a woman's worth in industry has been properly appreciated. During the recent war it was found that except where physical strength was required, women equalled and often excelled men in mechanical and technical jobs. Her position in the professions is also rising fast—and all "career women" are not homely!

The phrase, "Strong back and weak mind," is just another superstition for which there is little basis. The usual argument that most prize fighters and wrestlers are pretty dull company does not prove that a strong and handsome physique necessarily belongs to a man with relatively little gray matter. Strong, good-looking men with brains seldom choose a career in athletics or the sports world. There is plenty of brawn combined with beauty to be found on all university campuses.

Another superstition, that bright children are puny, is not necessarily so. Sometimes too much study weakens health, but the superstition is aimed at children who are congenitally weak, but brilliant. Many geniuses are strong, normal and long-lived despite the belief that they are frail, neurotic and die young. There are both kinds of geniuses.

Undoubtedly the element of envy and jealousy has influenced opinions down through the centuries, and tradition has perpetuated the fallacies through channels of hearsay. Ancient superstitions held that a woman had no soul, and that a beautiful face was the envy of evil spirits. These old beliefs remain with us in new forms.

While brains and beauty do not always go together, there is ample evidence that, in both men and women, this happy combination may be found. History is filled with examples.

CHAPTER 8

The Constant Flame

"Love at First Sight" or "Other Half"

"WHEN BOTH DELIBERATE, the love is slight! Whoever loved, that loved not at first sight!" Christopher Marlowe, 16th century English dramatist, was probably inspired by the old Greek myth which solved the much debated question of "love at first sight" in a most romantic way. The Greeks and many others before them devised a sentimental explanation which assumed that originally every man and woman were ONE. A creative power divided this ONE element into two beings, who, as separated halves, sought ever after to be reunited in human harmony.

Legends relate that the only way to be aware of one's preordained relationship is by the mutual shock experienced when a man and a woman meet for the first time. Psychologists generally agree, too, that there can be a similarity in physical and mental make-up between two persons of opposite sex which establishes an immediate affinity, but that is rarely a conscious emotion, or shock. What probably happens is that mutual ideas and associations are awakened that set off an explosive emotion which may or may not be love—and only marriage determines the answer.

Certain scientists advance the theory of blood chemistry, which is believed to account for these affinities and "love at first sight." Others even venture to explain that the "shock" that comes with love at first sight is an electric one; that when two hearts are at a certain point of beat, the vital spark or force for romantic impulse has been kindled. However as yet there seems to be no known formula to unravel the secret of "love at first sight." All we can be sure of is that it happens.

Superstitious Lovers Never Make a Vow on the Moon

Juliet:
> O swear not by the moon, the inconstant moon,
> That monthly changes in her circled orb
> Lest that thy love prove likewise variable.
> —Romeo and Juliet, Act 2 Scene 2

IN THE ABOVE QUOTATION Shakespeare avails himself of an age-old superstition, which even today keeps many a modern Romeo from swearing "on the moon."

To the ancients the moon's unexplained changes of countenance, and particularly eclipses, were terrifying, and indicative of the dead planet's complete unreliability. Eclipses have always had a most frightening effect upon the minds of superstitious persons; fears based on this astronomical event have been passed on from parent to child for generations on end. Some people have even gone so far as to believe that an eclipse signified the end of the world, and committed suicide. Others have been known to have gone out of their minds, either temporarily or permanently.

Oddly enough, modern scientists, knowing what underlies the moon's seeming inconstancy, do swear by her. Its future motions and phases are recorded with mathematical precision, years ahead, and the moon never fails to behave exactly as predicted. In other words, moon-tables tell us when eclipses are due. Of course, primitive and unenlightened peoples still continue to meet this phenomenon with dread.

The "Lover's Knot"

IN KEEPING with the ancient superstition that a wish is held or retained in a knot, a bride's bouquet is usually decorated with ribbons in which many knots have been tied, to hold the good wishes for her future happiness.

The custom of throwing a bouquet at weddings means not only that the girl who catches it will be the next bride, but also that she can make the wish for this good fortune—and it will come true—as she unties one of the knots.

Incidentally, in France, instead of the bride's bouquet, her garter was thrown to the anxiously waiting group of young women, and whoever caught it would be a bride within the year.

Among Anglo-Saxons, bridesmaids carry their own bouquets with ribbon knots, to add to the picturesque effect of the bridal procession; the superstition applying only to the bride's flowers.

The "lover's knot" has been an emblem in marriage from remotest times. It is symbolic of love and duty, and represents an indissoluble union. The tying of knots, in various ways, is still a practice among some peoples to symbolize love, loyalty, friendship and duty.

The custom of tying a knot at marriage is an old Danish custom which spread to Holland and England.

In some parts of India, before the wedding ceremony took place, the bride and groom had to loosen every knot on their person, or unfasten their garments. This act was believed to let out the evil influences that might have been bound in the articles by hands with sinister motives. Then the actual tying of the lover's knot took place as part of the marriage ceremony.

Emotion Never "Broke" a Heart

"A MERRY HEART doeth good like a medicine; but a broken heart drieth the bones," is a familiar Biblical quotation which has been taken too literally by many. As a matter of fact, coronary thrombosis may rupture a heart muscle, but emotion as such never broke a heart.

However, in view of the fact that in song and literature from earliest times to the latest book, poem or song lyric, the heart is coupled with love, as well as with hate, passion and all other deeper feelings, there must be a reason for the origin of the superstition. The most logical would seem to be the common experience that when the emotions are over-stimulated a physical reaction takes place in the form of accelerated action, particularly rapid beating of the heart. This organ exhibits the fastest and most manifest reaction to the cause.

The conclusion of the ancients was logical. It certainly was a most convenient way of describing the actual resulting state of body and mind after great emotional stress as a "broken heart." This description, however fallacious, is universally accepted and used. If a palpitating heart follows a human experience where the deeper feelings of an individual have been aroused by external causes, it is natural to consider the heart the seat of the emotions.

The real fact is that the heart automatically pumps blood and does nothing else, regardless of the romantic rôle it is supposed to play in the expression of emotions. The chief seat of emotions is in the *thalamus*, a small area at the base of the brain.

When that emotional region is subjected to undue strain and fatigue through fear, anger, sadness or other disturbing causes, the entire body reacts to the impact of the shock, and inevitably will develop general weakness if such condition continues. The stomach and functional organs will be affected as well as the heart, so that one's general health will, in time, be broken.

Only in this limited sense can it be said that the "heart is broken." All else is superstition based on ignorance of what actually takes place in body and mind.

CHAPTER 9

With This Ring

Bachelor's-Buttons' Superstitious Origin

ACCORDING to an old Oriental custom which came, by devious paths, to the peasants of Europe, the flower known today as the bachelor-button was believed to exert a magical influence over love-sick bachelors. Young men in love put these flowers in their pockets to forecast their future happiness in love and marriage.

The formula was to pick the flower early in the morning with the dew still upon it. It was not to be looked at for twenty-four hours, at which time, if the flower was found to be still bright and fresh—still "true blue"—it meant wedded bliss. On the other hand, if the flower had withered, the union would be a long, sad life of matrimonial troubles, with a wife who was without love for her spouse.

As flowers fade quickly, especially in a man's pocket without light, air or water, the blue blossoms generally informed the anxious lover that the outlook was bad. Rather than take the chance of an unhappy marriage, often the young man who found his flower shriveled refrained from matrimony. In time the blossom became known as the bachelor's button, to indicate a man who was not married or would not marry.

Before this superstition grew up, celibacy was frowned upon, and a man who did not marry was suspected of being incapacitated either by accident or by nature. So young bachelors of olden days anticipated matrimony as symbolic of manhood, regardless of emotional feelings. As the centuries went by, however, the romantic spirit made itself felt, and love and the desire for happiness then began to play an important part in the desire to wed.

The Orientals believe that blue flowers express wisdom, piety, respect and fidelity. To say that a person is "true blue" is a complimentary expression of the highest order, even among people of the West today.

Dowry, Trousseau or "Hope Chest" Customs and Superstitions

TODAY, as in olden days, many a girl believes that to insure "finding the right man" and a life of wedded bliss, she has to begin at an early age to fill her "hope chest" with the personal garments and household linens she expects to use later as a married woman. None of the articles, once they are finished, must be tried on or used until the day of the wedding. Otherwise she will be doomed to horrible spinsterhood.

The custom of preparing a trousseau in anticipation of marriage was originally a form of dowry, as it was one way of repaying the future bridegroom for the money or goods he gave the girl's father in return for his daughter. At one period, the suitor was even allowed to inspect the "hope chest" before he committed himself, and if it was not to his liking, he could refuse to go through with the marriage.

Gradually, marriage by purchase—when a man was expected to make a contribution to the family in order to get himself a wife—declined in popularity. Nevertheless, girls continued to lay away pretty things in a "hope chest," in order to encourage and tempt suitors.

There was an old Greek custom which decreed that the sons of a family had to remain single until all the daughters were married. Therefore often the brothers provided the trousseau in order to hurry their sisters into matrimony.

June Weddings, Lucky—May Weddings, Unpropitious!

"PROSPERITY to the man and happiness to the maid when married in June" was a proverb in ancient Rome. The belief that a June marriage is especially lucky is a relic of Roman mythology. The goddess Juno was the devoted wife of Jupiter and proprietress of womanhood from birth to death. When marriages took place in June, the month said to be named in her honor, Juno saw to it that such unions were blessed with joy.

Also in Roman mythology, the ancient goddess Maia, or Majesta—consort of Vulcan, god of the fiery elements—had under her special protection the month of May, said to have been named after her. Therefore May was, and is even now, considered a most unpropitious month in which to take the marital vows.

Although there may be some doubt whether the months of May and June were named after these two goddesses, we do know with certainty that Maia was the patroness of old people and Juno of youth. Perhaps this distinction indicated that it was all right for old people to marry in May, but June was the proper time for young lovers. However, regardless of what the original implications may have been, there are more weddings in June than in any other month, and many couples will not have the knot tied in May.

Superstitious beliefs notwithstanding, statistics demonstrate that despite the fact that a June wedding should bring good luck and happiness, just as many marriages of this month end in divorce, proportionately, as those of any other month.

Wedding Gown Superstitions

IT IS AN OLD SUPERSTITION that the bridegroom should never see the wedding gown before he sees the bride wearing it at the altar. Otherwise misfortune of one kind or another will come to the marriage.

There are many other superstitions about the wedding gown, such as:

> Married in white, you have chosen aright;
> Married in red, you'd better be dead;
> Married in yellow, ashamed of the fellow;
> Married in blue, your lover is true;
> Married in green, ashamed to be seen;
> Married in black, you'll ride in a hack;
> Married in pearl, you'll live in a whirl;
> Married in pink, your spirits will sink;
> Married in brown, you'll live out of town.

White, however, is still the preference of modern brides for formal weddings; but when the ceremony is private, she is apt to wear the color most becoming, regardless of the rhyme. White has been the traditional color of the bridal gown for centuries, as in most folklore, it is the emblem of the bride's purity, simplicity, candor and innocence.

The wearing of white was observed by the early Greeks, who believed that white was also the symbol of joy. White flowers and flowing white garments were the Greeks' attire on all feast days. They even painted their bodies white on the evening of the wedding ceremonies. This custom was also observed by the wild tribes of the ancient Patagonians in South America on their festive occasions.

The white wedding gown, despite its long tradition, is not universal, as there are many countries where other colors have become the national choice.

"Something Old, Something New,
Something Borrowed, Something Blue"

ALTHOUGH LITTLE BY LITTLE, in the western world at least, the age-old rule that the bride must wear no color has been modified; nearly every bride, however modern in ideas and tastes, insists upon "something old, something new, something borrowed, something blue." A line added and observed in England is, "And a sixpence in her shoe."

There are other slight variations of the old rhyme in different parts of the world, but on the whole the symbols and meanings remain the same. The "something old" and the "something new" seem to have come from England. The sentimental idea was to wear, if possible, a used article, such as an old garter, which belonged to a happily married old woman—never a widow. The old article was symbolic of the older woman's happy married lot, and the bride wished to follow in her footsteps. That is, the bride would thereby transfer some of her friend's good fortune to herself. This superstition comes from the primitive belief in "sympathetic" magic, which somehow still intrudes itself into our actions. A new handkerchief was generally selected to carry out the second line of the rhyme.

As to something "borrowed," in ancient times it was usually "golden." It had to be made of gold (as a rule it was a relative's jewel), to symbolize the sun, source of life, and complement of the moon, the protector of the bride and all womanhood. This gesture signified the union between the two, the bride and the sun.

Orange Blossoms as Bridal Wreaths

ORANGE BLOSSOMS have been associated with brides and weddings from time immemorial because the orange tree is an evergreen, believed to symbolize the couple's everlasting love for each other.

Wearing a wreath of orange blossoms as a crown over the bridal veil was a custom of the Saracens which was introduced into Europe by returning Crusaders. At first, orange blossoms, which are delicate and costly, were worn only by the wealthy. The superstitious bride of the poorer class, having been forced to wear artificial blossoms at her wedding, pretended that, like true flowers, they would wither, and so must be discarded before a month elapsed; otherwise it would be unlucky and her married life an unhappy one.

Another substitute for natural orange blossoms were wreaths of corn or wheat—the emblem of fertility among Anglo-Saxons, Greeks, and Romans. It was furnished by the churches and temporarily loaned to the bride for the ceremony.

Because the orange tree bears blossoms and fruit at the same time, the ancient Chinese believed the flowers not only lucky, but symbolic of the purity, chastity and innocence of the bride. Also because this evergreen's fruit is mingled, in every stage of its growth, with its blossoms and foliage, it was identified with the potential fruitfulness of the bride. The blossoms, symbolic of fertility, were worn, therefore, to insure her against barrenness.

In the delightful legend of the Golden Fruit of Hesperides, in Greek mythology, golden apples, believed to have been oranges, were presented to Hera on the night she was married to Zeus. She then became the goddess of celestial phenomena, the genius of womanhood and the guardian of the female sex.

The Bridal Veil

IT IS STRANGE INDEED, that in the modern Western world, far removed from Oriental restrictions on women, the custom of wearing a wedding veil is still such a popularly accepted convention. One of the superstitions related to it is that many brides, in the hope that bliss is contagious, wear, if possible, the bridal veil that was used by a woman friend or relative whose marriage has turned out happily.

The bridal veil is evidently of Eastern origin and is a relic of the bridal canopy held over the heads of bride and bridegroom. Some folklorists are of the opinion that the custom of wearing a veil at her wedding was a sign of the bride's submission, while others think it was the emblem of freedom. There is also the theory that it is a survival of the Purdah custom, which forbade a man ever to look upon the face of a woman until she was married. An unmarried girl was secluded and covered from head to foot until her wedding day. After the ceremony, it was the privilege of the bridegroom to "lift the veil," and proclaim loudly his enthusiasm over her beauty.

In a later period, the Evil Eye superstition seems to have become the more general reason for hiding a bride's face under a veil. Her beauty and delicacy had to be protected against evil and ill-omened glances. In China today, an umbrella is held over the bride for the same reason.

Grecian brides used to offer their veils to Hera, the goddess of marriage, to assure themselves of easy childbirth. A modern superstition is found among French peasant brides who put their veils away to be used again only when they are buried.

The canopy, forerunner of the wedding veil, is still in use. The square cloth used by the ancient Hebrews takes the form today of a canopy held over the couple during the marriage ceremony. And a canopy is also used today when weddings take place in the Catholic Churches of some countries. Long ago, among Anglo-Saxons, it was customary to have a "care-cloth" held over the bride and groom by four men when the knot was tied. Later it was held over the bride's head alone. The change is interesting.

Bridesmaids and Groomsmen

THE CUSTOM of having the bridesmaid dressed in a costume similar to that worn by the bride has been observed by many nations. In the early days it was done in order to confuse the evil spirits that were eager to harm the young couple, since unseen wicked beings were reputedly very jealous of two happy persons about to be married.

It was thought that if friends of the bride resembled her somewhat in appearance, the spirits would not know which was which, and so would not be able to carry out their designs. For the same reason, the young escorts of the groom, or groomsmen, had to be attired like him.

In modern times, a bridegroom usually presents the bridesmaids with gifts, undoubtedly a survival of a pre-nuptial custom in ancient Asia, after marriage by capture no longer prevailed. The maiden companions of the future bride would stand on the threshold of her house and refuse to let the groom-to-be and his friends enter. They showered the men with balls of boiled rice, and would let them into the house only when the men gave them presents.

It is generally agreed that the institution of having bridesmaids and groomsmen in attendance at wedding ceremonies evolved from the old Roman custom requiring ten witnesses to be present at a marriage. These witnesses then became the means of outwitting the jealous demons.

"Thrice a Bridesmaid, Never a Bride"

THE AGE-OLD SAYING, "Thrice a bridesmaid, never a bride," is related to the superstitious idea of "Never two, without three," which had both good and evil applications. In other words, two good things would not happen without the third following. Or, on the negative side, as in the case of the bridesmaid, to be a bridesmaid twice, followed by the inevitable third time, meant complete failure to find a husband.

"Three" was regarded as the mystic number which expressed the continuation of life or good fortune, but it could also, at times, mean the reverse, or tragedy.

To offset the bad omen, many a would-be bride believes that if she is a bridesmaid seven times the jinx will be broken, and then she, too, will become a happy bride.

The number seven is closely associated with the cycle of the moon which changes every seven days. In the case of the seven-times bridesmaid, the *change* is very favorable to the superstitious girl.

Kissing the Bride

KISSING THE BRIDE is a very old custom which began in the Western world, but has now reached the four corners of the earth.

At most weddings today, a sort of free-for-all osculation takes place immediately after the ceremony. However, from time to time, there have been interesting variations of bride-kissing. For instance, in Scotland, the pastor had to be the first to kiss the bride as her happiness was said to depend on it. In some places, the bride had to kiss all the men present. There was another custom that when the groom kissed the bride she had to cry, because if she did not, her married life would be full of tears.

Today, however, the groom's kiss seems to be part of the ceremony —a symbolic gesture to seal the matrimonial vows and sacred pledges just exchanged.

The act of kissing for sentiment originated with people of the white race. Its origin is unknown, except that it probably began in Asia Minor, as ancient records first mention it there. Men showed obedience to a ruler by kissing his hand, or kissing the ground in front of him. Women kissed their children as a way of fondling them. But the kiss to show affection between two persons seems to have been unknown then.

The kiss between husband and wife is believed to have started in ancient Rome, for a strange reason. A suspicious Roman husband pressed his lips on his wife's to learn if she had been drinking wine! This in time led to the betrothal kiss—to show good faith between lovers!

Among primitive peoples of the world today, the kiss is generally unknown as a gesture of love, or of affectionate greeting. In some countries in the East, the kiss is still associated with sacred rites, and is looked upon as a mark of homage to gods and men of high rank.

Breaking Hollow Article, Ancient Wedding Ritual

MOST PEOPLE believe that the custom of breaking a glass is restricted to the Jewish wedding ceremony, and that it is a symbol of the destruction of the Temple of Jerusalem by the Romans in 70 A.D. The Jews, it is well-known, have been taught throughout the centuries never to forget this great tragedy even in moments of deepest joy. However, this custom of crushing a breakable object with the foot is also practiced today in the marriage ceremony of a Hindu couple.

In the study of folklore, many symbolic explanations are suggested for shattering hollow objects when a couple is being married. For instance, among most, if not all, primitive peoples, this action is supposed to scare away evil spirits—the noise being very offensive to them. Like the Jews, the Hindus shout "Good luck!" after the wedding is over, for they believe the noise of the shouting and the words themselves will frighten away the jealous devils who are supposed to be present at all weddings, bent on disrupting harmony between the newlyweds. Similarly at a Jewish wedding today, all present yell "Mozol Tov," which means "good luck."

Another explanation of the superstition is that the breaking of a glass under the bridegroom's foot indicates the consummation of the marriage itself—the foot representing the man's virility, and the glass representing the receptacle or generative part of the bride's body. The ancient symbolism is probably implied in both the Jewish and Hindu marriage ceremony. That is, that it is the hymeneal rite, symbolic of the physical act of union. The Hebrew equivalent to "May you have many offspring," a phrase commonly used at Jewish weddings in days gone by, is pronounced in its Hindu wording at some weddings in the East even today.

Wedding-Cake Customs and Superstitions

A POPULAR SUPERSTITION in America, England and France promises a girl that if she passes a small piece of wedding cake through a wedding ring, then places it in her left stocking, and finally puts it under her pillow and sleeps on it, her future husband will appear to her in her dreams that night.

Nowadays pieces of wedding cake are usually packed in little boxes for the guests to take home with them. This simplifies the superstition for the romantic miss, who puts box and all under her pillow in the hope that the happy vision will appear.

Another wedding-cake custom of today requires that the bride be the first to cut the cake if she wishes to be happily married. If anyone else does it her happiness and prosperity will be jeopardized. The bridegroom is supposed to place his hand over the bride's as she cuts the cake—a sign that he expects to share her good fortune. Frequently they kiss at this point to add emphasis to their mutual hope of enjoying the good things of life together. After this sentimental byplay, each of the bridesmaids helps herself to a piece of the cake.

For bride and groom to sit down to a repast after the marriage ceremony seems to be as old as marriage itself. In primitive times the eating of special foods was part of the marriage formalities. In Rome, *conferreatio*, meaning "eating together," was strictly observed at weddings, and it may have been here, that the wedding-cake itself originated. A peculiar cake, made from flour, salt and water, was broken over the head of the bride as symbol of fruitfulness and prosperity. The guests took home a piece of this "cake" to have a little bit of that good luck themselves.

Rice-Throwing at Weddings

A WEDDING TODAY without rice-throwing would be a comparatively sad affair. Rice-throwing is a very old custom, believed to be a survival of the ancient religious rites of the Hindus and Chinese. Among most Orientals, rice is the symbol of fruitfulness and prosperity; rice-throwing symbolizes the bestowal of fertility on the bridal pair. Although the origin of the use of rice as a part of the marriage ceremony is lost in antiquity, the throwing and eating of rice or other grains symbolized that health, wealth and happiness would attend the newlyweds.

The ancient Romans threw nuts and all kinds of sweets at the bride. This custom eventually changed to confetti-throwing and has spread throughout Europe and America. In Saxon times wheat and barley were scattered in churches for brides to walk upon so that the use of rice may not be so much an innovation from the East as an adaptation from the Saxons.

However it may be, because rice has been the emblem of fecundity, and, as a fact, a food which promotes health, the general use of rice at weddings was to insure the couple against sterility and want. Among the Polynesians, Melanesians, Dyaks of Borneo and many others, the eating of rice constitutes marriage.

From time immemorial, rice has been the main dish of most Oriental people. No doubt they are aware of its nutritive values but do they know (very few people anywhere know except, perhaps, chemists and food experts), that a single grain of rice contains the following items: iron, potash, cellulose, phosphoric acid, magnesia, sodium, silicic acid, sulphuric acid, lime, chlorine, and nitrogen? Beneath the superstitious gesture of throwing rice, there lies deep in the nature of man an unconscious knowledge of what is good for him; a symbol is merely a convenient substitute for the real thing.

Rice was also thrown because of the very ancient supertsitious belief that at weddings evil spirits hovered near; the throwing of rice was supposed to be food for them, thus keeping them away from the bridegroom, of whom they were extremely jealous.

As a matter of fact, in Italy and elsewhere in Europe, during the Middle Ages, it was actually believed that there were male and female demons who were available respectively as husbands and wives of human beings. One method of dealing with these jealous supernatural beings at weddings was the distribution of rice thrown in the air as a sop to the injured feelings of the spirits!

Carrying the Bride Over the Threshold

NEARLY EVERY prospective bride dreams of being carried over the entrance of her new home in the arms of her beloved bridegroom. Today this sentimental and agreeable act is performed to bring good luck to the pair, but the custom actually is descended from the time of primitive man's marriage by capture.

It was the Romans, however, who attached a superstitious meaning to the custom. A Roman bridegroom carried his new wife into their dwelling for more than one reason. In the first place, it was to prevent her from tripping—a very bad omen indeed. This was based on the belief that supernatural beings, both good and bad, kept competitive vigil at the threshold. The evil spirit, intensely jealous of human happiness, hoped to trip the bride as she entered, thereby ruining her happiness. The good spirit, on the other hand, was there to prevent this from happening.

The other superstition was that walking into the house with the left foot foremost meant that the spirit of evil accompanied the pair. They would be "on their heels," so to speak. On the other hand, the right foot foremost implied that the kindly disposed spirit accompanied them, leaving the hateful one outside. Therefore, the only safe way for the groom, knowing that a woman in a highly emotional state is very apt to be careless, took no chances, and picked her up in his arms and carried her into the house.

In some far-away places, even today, a sheep is sacrificed on the threshold of the home as a tribute to its spirit-guardian—a form of inauguration. The couple step over both the sheep and threshold, without touching either, to insure a long and happy life together.

Shivaree, a Noisy Custom

THE SHIVAREE, a rural American custom, consists of the boisterous serenading of a newly married couple. Usually a playful but kindly crowd of young people beat on pans and kettles outside the home of the newlyweds, sometimes continuing the din until the bridegroom tosses them a handful of coins.

Shivaree is a corruption of the French word *Charivari,* a custom introduced into North America by the French by way of Canada and Louisiana. The custom is Latin in origin, and has been practiced in rural France from remotest times. It is a survival of a superstitious ceremony, observed among many primitive peoples, in which making noise by beating drums, or breaking or beating on other objects to make a loud racket, was done to keep evil spirits away from the newlyweds. These spirits were very jealous, and if they were allowed to enter the new abode, were bent on harm to the happy pair. Noise, however, frightened them away.

The modern version of this primitive custom frequently sounds like a jitterbug serenade played on out-of-tune instruments, or even on kitchen utensils, if nothing else is available. Whether the participants know it or not, they are supposed to be driving away evil spirits, but there is no doubt that the newlyweds who are annoyed and tormented by the racket think the "evil spirits" are present in full force!

Charivari was once a universal custom in French provinces, but it degenerated into coarse horseplay to plague the new bride and groom who had neglected certain conventions, or in some way failed to conform to the rigid proprieties expected of them.

Origin of the "Honeymoon" and "Best Man"

THE WORD "honeymoon" originated with the ancient Teutons, among whom there was the practice of having a newly married couple drink metheglin or mead, a kind of wine made with honey, for a period of about thirty days or one month after the marriage. This custom is said to have put the word "moon" in honeymoon.

The honeymoon—going away from friends and relatives immediately after the ceremony—goes back to the days when a bridegroom captured his bride by force, and then had to hide away with his prize until her outraged father and kinsmen grew tired of searching for her.

It is believed that the custom of having a "best man" stems from this same circumstance, as it was necessary in those days for a friend of the groom at the "ceremony" to fight off and delay the relatives while the young couple made its getaway. When they returned home, the couple generally brought back gifts to subdue the father's wrath.

In North America, a favorite and reputedly lucky destination for a wedding trip or "honeymoon" is Niagara Falls. This custom is believed to have been made popular by Napoleon Bonaparte's young brother, Jerome, who took his American bride, Miss Elizabeth Patterson of Baltimore, Maryland, to this great scenic wonder on their bridal trip.

Superstitious couples who do go to Niagara Falls on their honeymoon believe that if they toss pennies into the Bridal Veil Falls, which is on the American side—Horseshoe Falls being on the Canadian side—and make a wish as they do so, they will reap much good fortune during their entire married life. Local authorities report that the custom of throwing pennies is so popular that they collect in heaps below and behind the flowing veil of waters.

Casting pennies or other things into waters while making a wish has been observed from time immemorial at betrothal time as well as following the marriage ceremony. This superstitious gesture is in keeping with the ancient belief that paying a tribute to the gods of the sea or other water-gods brings good luck.

In olden times, and this goes on even today, "wishing-wells" were commonly used to look into the future. For example, a girl desiring to marry would throw a coin into a well, making a wish with the hope of seeing her future husband's face at the bottom of the well. This was generally done in the full of the moon as it was believed that the moon assisted greatly in matters of the heart.

The custom of casting a coin into a well is so old that it was a forerunner of the practice popular in Greece and other countries of that period of paying a tribute to the gods and spirits of the water so they would not let the wells run dry.

"Widowhood" Superstitions

"He who married a widow will often have a dead man's head in his dish."
                                                                    Proverb

THIS CYNICAL PROVERB could well be applied to widowers, too, on occasion, as being a second wife to a widower is not always, unfortunately, a bed of roses.

A late husband's spirit is *still* feared; that is, the remarried widow may feel that he will return to haunt her as well as her second husband. Some second husbands are also susceptible to that sort of traditional suggestion! When such a state of affairs exists, it is frequently the underlying factor which brings about quarrels, sometimes separation, and often is a cause for divorce, even in these modern times.

This mental attitude is a sort of atavistic hangover from the days when it was not the correct conduct for anyone, once widowed, to remarry. One was expected to mourn the rest of one's days for the deceased husband or wife, or else be accused of not having loved the departed enough during life.

When a widow or widower remarried, the disagreeable gossip of the day wished the ghost or spirit of the one gone to the Great Beyond to come back and haunt the new couple, because they had trespassed the narrow, conventional path of bigoted tradition. And, as we all know, to wish for a thing to happen, especially if it is of an evil nature, often may bring it to pass. Therefore, for centuries, the spirit of a later husband or wife has been believed by many to return to make life intolerable. "Blithe Spirit," the successful comedy by Noel Coward, is based on this idea.

Because of the ancient prejudice against a second marriage, persons who have taken part in the wedding ceremony twice have been known to develop a feeling of guilt later on. This erroneous attitude happens oftener than is realized, tragically enough! On the other hand, frequently it is a convenient excuse to find fault with the marriage on the ground that there is a ghost between the new husband and wife.

"Mother-in-Law" Superstitions

WHAT WOULD the modern jokester or professional humorist do today without the "mother-in-law"? Though forms of marriage have undergone transitions through the ages, a mother-in-law's unpopular status has never changed.

Among the taboos with which primitive man surrounds marriage, none is stranger than the mother-in-law taboo. It varies with different peoples, as do the penalties for breaking it—but in general, the mother-in-law is scrupulously shunned.

The Navajo and Apache Indians, for instance, never looked directly at their mothers-in-law for fear of becoming blind. Other American Indians adopted a quaint method of avoiding the mother-in-law taboo: the groom went through the marriage ceremony with the bride's mother prior to marrying the real bride.

Nearly all of the primitive Australians, Melanesians, Polynesians, as well as Negro races of Africa, have created rules for the subjection of the mother-in-law. For example, the Zulu-Kaffirs require a man wishing to address his mother-in-law to stand at a distance. He may not address her by name, for such familiarity might imply she still has authority over her daughter. Often he prefers to communicate with her by means of a third person. Furthermore, he is not allowed to look at her, for he must conform with the Zulu proverb that "man should not look upon the breast that has nursed his wife." If, by chance, they meet, they pretend not to know one another.

In the region of the Nile, a Negro of the Basogas tribe will converse with his mother-in-law only when a wall separates them, or through a third person.

Other tribes forbid any intercourse between husband and mother-in-law whatever. When a man of the Celebes Islands meets his wife's mother, by chance, he expectorates in order to rid himself of the evil influences which may result from seeing her.

In group marriage or *exogomy*, a system of taboos seems to have been nurtured by primitive clans to prevent any sexual relations with mothers-in-law. The horror of incest among both primitives and moderns seems to be related to the fear of such contacts.

Among certain primitive tribes, ostracism prevented the groom, who belonged to an alien tribe, from ever becoming a member of the bride's clan. In such an instance, the mother-in-law would refuse to recognize her daughter's husband as her son-in-law. Many authorities believe, however, that this taboo is a survival of the marriage-by-capture era during which the bride's mother never forgave the man who carried her daughter away by force.

It should be interesting to modern feminists that apparently no taboos were evoked against the bride's mother-in-law.

Should Cousins or Close Relatives Marry?

THERE IS AN OLD TABOO, prevalent even today, against the the marriage of first cousins for fear it will lead to sterility, or that the children of such a union will be feeble-minded or diseased. In some cases the taboo is justified, in others it is not.

The marriage of cousins who know their antecedents well, and find only good traits among them, will produce offspring bearing the best of the traits themselves. However, if the stock is tainted with hereditary defects, the children of cousins are liable to inherit these defects more readily than in other marriages.

In other words, exception to the marriage of cousins must be taken when both the man and the woman suffer from the same hereditary disease or weakness. For instance, children of diabetic cousins are very apt to inherit their parents' illness. But the same thing applies to offspring of parents who are in no way related. In fact, any marked hereditary tendency present in both father and mother may be transmitted to the next generation, which proves that it is not the close blood tie that accounts for the results.

To better understand how the marriage of cousins, or, for that matter, of any two persons, will produce good or bad offspring, it is necessary to know that each human being inherits *dominant* and *recessive* traits, as explained in genetics, the branch of biology which deals with heredity and variation.

For instance, under normal circumstances, the *dominant* trait does not skip a generation, whereas a *recessive* trait does not show itself unless both parents inherit the same *recessive* trait. A *recessive* trait explains itself. It recedes from sight; that is, if the same defect, such as feeble-mindedness, has not occurred in either family for three generations, then it is safe for the cousins to marry.

On the other hand, the *dominant* trait always exhibits itself in the offspring, even if only one parent possesses it. If both carry a similar *dominant* trait, however, it makes itself doubly strong in the progeny. If the qualities and characteristics of the family are of superior stock on both sides, the healthiest and most intelligent offspring may be expected.

In the light of this knowledge, it becomes apparent that keeping track of the "family tree" is essential for the sake of future generations. Furthermore, if we apply present-day knowledge of hereditary laws, there is no reason why society should interfere with cousin marriages when the two persons are healthy and have a sound ancestry.

Close interbreeding of full brothers who have married full sisters, not to say marriages of cousins, and uncle and niece, have not shown defective children, as records covering long periods of time have proved. The outstanding case is the history of the Ptolemies, who gave sixteen rulers, including Cleopatra, to ancient Egypt from 323 to 30 B.C. Intermarriages have continued in Egypt through the centuries with no apparent sign of degeneracy, either physical or mental.

On the other hand, records of inbreeding of unsatisfactory families show disastrous results by producing human beings who are a social menace.

The uncertain biological consequences of consanguineous unions have long been recognized by the Church, which forbids such unions on the ground that they will seriously interfere with the moral foundations of the family. Only after the fourth degree of kinship are such marriages approved. Dispensations to this rule are granted, but not frequently, and are not looked upon favorably. Taboos concerning marriages between blood relatives were devised by primitive peoples and others to prevent the possibility of the much-dreaded incest relationship. Nearly all primitives expressed a horror of incest.

Seventh and Eighth Month Baby Superstitions

CONTRARY to the traditional belief that a baby born after only eight months of pregnancy cannot survive, medical authorities report that such a child has an excellent chance to live and grow up. This baby is almost completely formed at the time of birth, which is greatly in its favor.

Side by side with this superstition is the one that a "seventh month" baby always lives, which is not necessarily true. It is another fallacy that a seventh month baby may be born without hair, fingernails, eyelashes and toenails—and thrive.

With many primitive and ancient peoples, natural phenomena relating to women were connected with the lunar cycle, or seven phases of the moon. Seven was considered a lucky number for women, and therefore a seventh month baby would live.

The ancients, however, despite their ingrained beliefs, could not help noticing that eighth month babies frequently managed to stay alive too. So, to explain this seeming contradiction of their fixed notions, the wise ones declared there were two-prenatal periods for "creation"—one a seven months period and another a nine months period. When the baby was born in the eighth month, it was then said to be a seventh month birth, but delayed due to a freakish "mistake." Any answer or rationalization coming from the exalted ones of the tribe sufficed. And the fact remains that for centuries many weird superstitions clung to the premature eighth month birth.

We know today, of course, that a newborn infant's chances of survival depend more on its physical condition and development than on whether the pre-natal period is seven, eight or nine months.

CHAPTER 10

Everybody Loves a Baby

"Pregnancy" Superstitions

HUNDREDS of old wives' tales, ages old, pertaining to pregnancy have become part and parcel of women's fears and formulas when they find themselves in this condition.

One of these superstitions concerns prolonged nursing, a control method believed to prevent pregnancy, wherein many credulous women believe that while they continue to breast-feed the baby they are immune to conception. Only a few years ago studies were conducted to check on this ancient theory. The net results were that there may be a short period following delivery when conception is less likely to take place, but it cannot be relied upon. Statistics showed that about fifty per cent of the women became fertile after childbirth and could conceive during the nursing period.

Another of these ageless superstitions is that a mother must expect to lose a tooth for each child she brings into the world. With modern methods of pre-natal examinations, it is now possible to check the dental condition of the mother-to-be. An adequate diet before, during and after pregnancy can generally prevent the loss of one or more teeth. A pregnant woman's system does suffer, and her teeth are often affected, so there is some truth in the belief. It should not be classed as a superstition because of the scientific operation of cause and effect in this case.

The popular superstition that a pregnant woman must eat for two is another delusion associating "like with like." It is the quality of the food that is of primary importance and not the quantity. The adherence to this superstition may lead to overweight on the part of the mother, and also to toxemia which can disturb the entire system. It is not true either that liquid foods such as broths are more easily digested at such times.

The "strange craving" for certain foods by a pregnant woman does not indicate a deep physical need, which, if not satisfied, will affect the child. Most of the "odd" desires for a specific food can wait, since they are mostly hysterical whims and the denial hurts the unborn child in no way. The best medical advice for a pregnant woman is a balanced diet in moderation. A mother's diet during pregnancy does not necessarily control her baby's weight at the time of birth. Other factors are involved, such as heredity, for example.

A craving for sweets, if indulged in, is believed to influence the unborn babe to become a female. The sex question, however, is settled irrevocably at the moment man's spermatozoon unites with the woman's egg through the vaginal channel. The millions of spermatozoa in one emission are composed of both male and female cells, and whichever one reaches the ovum first is fertilized. The determination of sex is mostly a matter of chance, though vaginal alkalinity favors the incubation of a male cell. Science has frequently checked on vaginal acidity or alkalinity, which threw light on many elusive theories of the past, but these two conditions are not to be relied upon to fix the sex of a child.

Countless superstitious customs, beliefs and formulas were devised to remove the stigma of barrenness which was always placed upon the woman. Statistics reveal, however, that at least one third of cases brought to the attention of doctors show the man to be sterile. Science finally discovered that the man may be at fault, but failure to conceive is oftener the woman's fault. The deception which subsisted through the ages was probably due to the mistaken idea that man's virility proved him to be fertile, but scientific evidence of today proves there is no relationship between the two. About half the cases of sterility are now curable and much progress has been made along these lines in recent years.

Other pregnancy superstitions may be mentioned, such as that babies born to parents of mature years are more likely to have brilliant minds. This is false because maturity comes after birth and depends upon advantages given youngsters which affect equally their mental and physical health. Superstitious brides fear that the first baby is more likely to be born prematurely than the second or third. This fear is unfounded, although, not to seem facetious, many first-born do come prematurely, but they are fully developed!

Women over 25 used to fear that the birth of their first child would be very difficult if not actually dangerous to their lives. Figures, however, demonstrate that childbirth dangers are less likely between the ages of 20 to 35 and over, and that the infant and maternal mortality is higher with mothers under 20. The belief that in the last six months of pregnancy the fetal heart beats can be determined remains in the realm of speculation.

Women who fear childbirth and believe abortion relatively safer are courting a dangerous superstition. The death rate from illegal abortions is ten times as high as that from normal childbirth. Another false belief is that the prolonged use of contraceptives contributes largely to a woman's failure to conceive, or brings about sterility in a man. If otherwise normal, a woman can only bring about sterility by using injurious mechanical contrivances or harsh chemical contraceptives which can damage her tissues and effect a state of barrenness.

Wives have blamed husbands who were heavy drinkers for the birth of idiots or subnormal children. Conclusive experiments with alcohol on the germ plasm show that nature is kind to the germ, which is said to be well protected against the possible damage which alcohol could cause. However, the mental deficiency which is greater among offspring of alcoholics than among the rest of the population occurs because alcoholics frequently come from families in which there is hereditary moronism, a fact generally overlooked by the layman. Hence the superstition about alcoholism as related to progeny. During pregnancy alcohol may or may not have an effect on the unborn child, but drinking alcohol while nursing a baby is definitely known to be harmful to the child's health.

"Sterility" Superstitions

DESPITE INFORMATION which is constantly being made public in the last few years, a very ancient superstition persists in coupling a man's virility with fertility. The two are not necessarily related, for they are two separate functions. Fertility is primarily a biological function, whereas virility is a physiological one. Hence a virile man may be sterile.

The traditional notion of blaming the woman rather than the man for a barren marriage is false. This time-worn accusation which has prevailed for thousands of years has finally been corrected by increased knowledge and research. Statistics recently available place the total of male disability at about 33 per cent.

Because of the fear of barrenness, thousands of superstitions and formulas to make women fertile have evolved. Young girls followed certain superstitious measures calling upon supernatural beings to grant them the privilege not only of finding husbands, but once married to be able to bear children and thus retain the love and respect of their husbands. A woman's barrenness made for a very unhappy life, since a childless marriage was often equal to disgrace. Primitive custom gave the husband the advantage of repudiating or divorcing a sterile woman and of replacing her with another.

Some years ago, hundreds of sterile women visited the famous Canadian quintuplets and took home one of the "magic pebbles" in the hope of bearing a child. Dr. Allan Roy Dafoe reported at the time that a large number of these women returned to Callander a year or so later with their babies. Oddly enough, many of these women had been childless for as long as fourteen years. No one seems to know when this belief in the "magic pebbles" of Callander started. Dr. Dafoe said that there was a constant demand for them, even by mail. Money was often sent along with requests, but was always returned to the sender.

The belief in the magic properties of pebbles and stones, large or small, is of the greatest antiquity and probably a survival of the Stone Age. It is known that stones were worshipped for a variety of purposes by the Greeks and Galicians of pre-Christian times. In Roman times it was believed that a stone which had been used purposely to kill certain powerful animals, sometimes a sturdy man, had the power to make childbirth easy and painless. This odd superstition was carried out by casting the magic stone over the roof of the house where a woman lay expecting her child's birth. Metaphorically, stones denote hardness and insensibility, firmness and strength.

Superstitions About Ovaries

VARIOUS THEORIES for the determination of sex before birth have been advanced by superstitious persons for many centuries. But none persists more than the belief that only males will be born to a woman after the removal of the left ovary, and only females after the right ovary has been taken out. Sometimes this superstition is the other way around, depending upon what part of the country one lives in.

Ancient folklore always assigned the masculine, or solar, influences to the right side, and feminine, or lunar, attributes to the left side. That is why countless superstitions were invented to give a special significance to each side of the human body.

Science, however, has long ago disposed of these superstitions, and there is no ground whatever for the theory that the sex of a baby is determined by the ovary involved. Girls have been born to mothers without a left ovary and boys to those minus the right one.

Because of this and other foolish notions about ovaries, many women will suffer for years from a diseased ovary. They delay or put off indefinitely the operation that will relieve their suffering, in spite of the fact that modern surgery regards this operation as comparatively simple and quite safe.

Time of Conception and Birth Facts and Superstitions

ONE SUPERSTITION out of many connected with conception and birth is that more geniuses are born in the month of February than in any other month. In America, the two greatest men, Washington and Lincoln, were February babies; Franklin D. Roosevelt missed February by two days.

Eugenists, after careful study and tabulation, are now offering evidence that certain months of the year are more propitious for having babies than are others. February, March and April seem to produce babies with better health, a longer life span, and greater chances of becoming geniuses—on the average, of course,—than the other nine months. Other fairly accurate records show that, in the Western world, persons born in March live longer, on the average, than those whose birthday is in July.

Recent experiments (1946) reported in the *Journal of Social Psychology* indicated that prisoners who had been born in the darker, colder months of the year showed a higher intelligence rating, with the month of January in first place. However, the same test showed that the reverse is true in the case of Negroes. The experimenters acknowledged that the number of birthdays checked was not sufficiently large to draw definite conclusions.

It might be plausible that babies of the North Temperate Zone born during summer and autumn have to struggle for their first lease on life through months that have the least sunlight, coldest temperatures and food with less nutritive value, than infants who come into the world during a chillier season. But what about babies in tropical and semi-tropical climates, or those of the South Temperate Zone where the seasons are reversed?

One answer to the riddle may be based on the theory that the reason our cavemen ancestors survived other types of pre-historic men was because they may have adhered to the rhythms of early spring births as it occurs in the animal world. Early human beings, like children of today, imitated what was in the world about them. Eugenists may have proof, some day, that planning the date of birth of babies, so that they arrive at the best of all possible times, will raise the average quality of the human species.

"Caesarean Operation" Superstitions

WOMEN WHO have had one Caesarean operation are fearful of a second pregnancy, because of the old saying that "a woman always dies with the second Caesarean operation." This superstitious attitude can have a very dangerous effect on the morale of the expectant mother, and there is no scientific basis for the belief. The truth is that there are scores of cases on record where a woman had four, and even five, such operations without any abnormal consequences.

As a matter of historical fact—distorted with time—in 715 B.C., the king, Numa Pompilius, codified the Roman laws, including a law to permit an operation to be performed on a woman in advanced pregnancy, but only after her death. This was a religious measure so that mother and child might be buried separately; or so that, as in some rare cases, the child might be delivered alive. Later, under the rule of the emperors, the original laws became known as the Caesarean Laws, and the law pertaining to the childbirth operation became known as the Caesarean operation or section.

It is commonly believed that the term, Caesarean operation, or the word, Caesarean, alone took its meaning from the fact that Julius Caesar was born by this method of delivery. But this is not so, as his mother, Julia, lived for a long time after her illustrious son was born, as is attested by his letters to her of which there is record.

The true explanation of the fear attached to a Caesarean section is that in the Middle Ages operations were performed on living women, when delivery could not be normal, without proper hygienic or surgical knowledge, and a high mortality resulted.

Today, due to the great advance in surgery, Caesareans are not unusual and are uniformly successful. One advantage in this operation is the elimination of any possible brain or nerve injury to the child. This may account for the fact that a higher I.Q., on the average, has been noted in Caesarean babies.

Spacing Births or Birth Control Superstition

BIRTH CONTROL, or planned parenthood, has been decreed a sin by some religious laws, and as a result, many superstitious taboos sprang up against it. As sociologists point out, controlling the morals of society, and of women in particular, has been the self-imposed task of well-meaning reformers for centuries. The sin-suggestion in birth control became, therefore, a powerful weapon over the heads of women, and an opportunity to impose moral and ethical laws on large groups of society.

Spacing of births, or regulating the size of one's family, on the other hand, was understood and practiced long before it became a "sin" with dire consequences. Knowledge of it existed as far back as the days of ancient Egypt.

Fear of Premature Birth

THERE IS a world-wide superstitious fear that a baby born prematurely will suffer injury to its head, and the nerve tissues of the brain will be greatly endangered, if not permanently hurt. However, obstetricians generally agree that, as far as these injuries are concerned, there is little to fear.

The truth is that all other factors being favorable, during labor there will be less pressure exerted on the bones of the baby's head, and so less chance of squeezing its brain tissue, because a premature baby's head is smaller. This condition likewise makes confinement easier for the mother.

Birthmark and Prenatal Superstitions

MANY AN expectant mother lives in the constant fear that she will "mark" her unborn child, through prenatal mental impressions, shocks, fears, and ungratified desires. This is one of the oldest and most unfortunate of human superstitions.

Probably the earliest record of belief that "marking" can be induced is found in the Book of Genesis, Chapter 30 and 31, where Jacob's troubles with Laban, his double father-in-law, are detailed. Cattle were "marked" because the female animals had had before their eyes the spotted wands Jacob had arranged, and were influenced by maternal impressions that "marked" their offspring.

The cause of birthmarks is unknown. What doctors do know is that there is no connection between the nervous systems of the mother and the unborn child at any stage; the two nervous systems are entirely independent. Therefore, ideas and impressions cannot travel that way.

Actually women have passed through shocking experiences during pregnancy and have given birth to perfectly normal children. A further illustration is that if an unborn child were subjected to whims, outside influence and ungratified desires of the mother, nearly every child would be born a monster!

Birthmarks are not hereditary either; they are present at birth probably because of injuries, or lesions of the tissues, physiological malformations in the developing embryo and the nutritive maternal structure known as the placenta. The vital connection between the mother and her unborn child is through the blood stream.

Fears of marking a baby would quickly disappear if it were generally known that the child's body is completely formed between the sixth and eighth week, sometimes before the mother knows she is pregnant.

Today, radium and X-ray treatments are generally successful for removing birthmarks.

Born with a Caul, Believed Lucky

> *"But still the jolly mariner*
> *Took in no reef at all,*
> *For in his pouch confidently*
> *He wore a baby's caul."*
> (—Hood, *The Sea-Spell*)

WIDESPREAD is the ancient superstitious belief that a child born with a red caul is endowed with prophetic powers and double sight, and even more important, that the lucky babe will never die by drowning or encounter fatal shipwrecks. By the same token, he would protect others at sea with him. There is the exception, however: if the caul is blackish in color at birth, it means ill fortune, and a short life.

The caul superstition, because of its application to the sea, is particularly prevalent among ship-masters and other seafaring men. They believe that being in possession of a caul—anyone's caul—is a talisman which protects against drowning and evil in general. Midwives used to carry on quite a trade, selling cauls to sailors or travelers about to undertake a long voyage. These cauls were taken at the birth of infants, without the parents being the wiser. During the seventeenth century, advertisements offering cauls for sale were quite common in the newspapers. Even in America today, a caul is occasionally offered for sale.

Lawyers and politicians of other days believed that the ownership of a caul endowed them with the gift of persuasive eloquence. In Scotland, the caul was called "the Virgin's Vest," and was an object of great veneration. If thrown away, sickness or death would overtake the child born with it, and the mother would be spirited away by the fairies. The only way for the husband to prevent this from happening was for him to watch for the "yearly riding" of the fairies and throw his wife's wedding gown in their path!

Another superstitious notion is that the caul shows the exact state of health of the person who was born with it, no matter how distant that person may be. If the caul is crisp and firm, the person is alive and well. But if it becomes soft and limp, the owner is either sick or dead.

As a matter of physiological information, the caul is the amniotic or water sac, which is like a toy balloon filled with amniotic fluid. Sometimes a child is born with this sac, or caul, intact, which is not rare; and it is a sign of good fortune in general. But when the caul covers only the face, it is believed to have saved the child from drowning before birth—a relic of the age-old superstitious beilef which associates "like with like," or water with water, in this case. Not understanding the function of the caul, the ancients interpreted this covering of the face to mean immunity from drowning and water perils of all kinds, not only to the one born with it but also to those in his presence.

It is interesting to note here that the process during the first stage of childbirth labor is hydraulic in character; the sac or caul usually rupturing spontaneously at this time. The pressure the water exerts is essential to make way for the child to be born. "The water breaks" is an old and familiar phrase to denote that birth is about to take place.

Lucky First Born

THAT THE first born in a family is the lucky one is not a false belief in the true sense of the word, although an accurate explanation of why this is so is still forthcoming. According to extensive biographical records in America, the eldest child fares better in life than the younger or youngest. This, however, applies only to smaller families, as the statistics break down for families of more than five or six children.

What knowledge we have of the subject seems to indicate that the first born's advantage is dependent on the health and vitality of the mother. On the other hand, many first born do not grow up healthy and wise, even when their mothers were known to have been young and in the pink of condition at the time of birth. The paradoxical problem is still unsolved.

Boys More Welcome Than Girls

To THIS DAY, the majority of prospective parents prefer boy babies to girl babies. To want the newcomer to be a boy rather than a girl was also a very ancient desire.

This superstitious preference was perpetuated by word of mouth from generation to generation, and writers of old strengthened the belief that it was better to have male than female offspring. For instance, there is a Talmudic saying that when a boy is born he is welcomed into the world; but when a girl arrives the walls weep. This was long before the days of primogeniture or property considerations.

What the reason was that the earliest peoples looked with such favor on the male of the species has never been explained satisfactorily. There is evidence, however, that ancient documents contain a number of statements which, in time, have been tampered with to suit the character and intention of later writers who quoted them.

The most plausible reason for wishing male progeny instead of female in the early days is, of course, that they were needed as prospective warriors among peoples constantly fighting one another.

"Twin" and "Multiple Birth" Superstitions

AMONG PRIMITIVE peoples the incident of twin births was not always looked upon favorably, especially if the pair consisted of a girl and a boy. In this case, the girl was often sacrificed. On the other hand, with some tribes the occasion of the birth of twins was one of rejoicing and regarded as a sign of manly powers.

To early man, multiple births were of special importance, calling for superstitious tribal formulas. In that day the advent of birth was mysterious and was accompanied with procedures to forestall the doings of supernatural beings, who might not be disposed in favor of the parents, and thereby endanger the existence of the whole tribe. Therefore, the strange visitation of twins required more than ordinary measures to cope with the situation.

Ignorant of biological facts, multiple births also suggested to primitives infidelity on the part of the wife, or a shameful accomplishment at best. Where this idea prevailed, the life of the twins was spared, but the mother was not only punished severely, but driven from the village for a period of isolation and not allowed to speak to anyone, except from a distance.

In some parts of Africa, where dual births are still frowned upon, the worst insult to a woman is to hold up two fingers to her as a reminder of the fact that she once brought twins into the world.

Since, in some places, the birth of twins was believed to be under the command of the gods, and a sign of their anger, the infants were put to death, and the father mildly punished. On the other hand, with other tribes, magical powers were attributed to the twins themselves. They were given the position of rain-makers, and were expected to produce weather to order. "Calm down, breath of the twins," is still the prayer of many African peoples as an appeal to the gods of wind and rain.

Because of the extra trouble they caused, the women of the Lower Congo do not take kindly to twins. Hence it is the general practice to starve one of them. When a twin is thus starved, or dies a natural death, a piece of roughly carved wood, representing the dead child, is carried with the live one so that it will not feel lonely. However, should the second baby die, the image of the other twin is buried with it. In the ceremony, the corpse of the second twin is placed on leaves and covered with a white cloth, and buried at the crossroads like a suicide or a man killed by lightning. Among the Yorubas of West Africa, when one of her twins dies, the mother has a wooden figure made, representing the same sex as the dead child. She too, carries this with the living child so that the spirit of the dead child will be happy and not disturb the living one.

The phenomena of birth and death among primitive tribes were covered by thousands of superstitious proceedings which varied according to the customs and beliefs of each tribe. Many of these have come down to us more or less changed, but nevertheless discernible in the modern mind.

For instance, when a husband is careless enough to tip the container and spill the pepper, he must throw a dash of it over his right shoulder so that his wife will not have twins. If twins are to be married on the same day, they should be married in separate churches if they wish a happy married life. A superstition of Roman origin, and believed by many Italians, is that the first born of twins is the child of love, and the second the child of lightning. The second born is said to be favored by fate with good fortune ever at his heels.

The confusion which sometimes existed as to which twin was the elder, the first one delivered or the second, gave rise to curious solutions. In ancient Hebrew law, the child delivered first was legally the first born. In Latin law, however, the one brought into the world second was considered the elder, on the logic that it was farther back in the womb and therefore must have been the first conceived. Modern law, however, gives seniority to the first born twin.

There is also a widely spread superstition that twins cannot grow as strong and as intelligent as a single child because the mother's energy in producing them has been divided. This is not so. A very dangerous superstition with no basis in fact is that one twin out of every pair is sterile.

Another superstition is that if there is a red streak down the middle of a woman's stomach it is a sign she will give birth to twins.

Twins are thought, even today, to have only one soul between them. Since there is no way of knowing what a soul is, it is impossible to prove or disprove this notion. To the primitive mind, when one twin became sick, the other was suspected of having violated a family taboo in order to get for himself all the powers which were supposed to be divided between them.

The most modern of all beliefs pertaining to twins is that they have a psychic or telepathic bond between them. Scientists persistently deny this as the principle back of telepathy is still an unknown quality; and what appears to be telepathic communication should not be mistaken for the long arm of coincidence. Although telepathy, as such, is a relatively modern term, the idea that twins have something intimately in common is anything but a new idea.

Among certain poor white and colored people in America's southern states, the unlucky two-dollar bill is associated with the economic disaster of an addition of twins to the family. Should a two-dollar bill enter the house, one of its corners is immediately torn off to work magic against so unwelcome a possibility as twins.

Since the recording of births is relatively modern, very little authentic data as to twins, triplets or quadruplets is available. However, Pliny, the Elder, who recorded the customs and superstitions of the Romans, mentions that the birth of twins or triplets was favorably looked upon. Parents were greatly alarmed, however, when quadruplets were born, because, in line with many primitive notions, it portended ill fortune for all within the family circle. Incantations were used as counter charms against the impending fate expected to strike parents and babies alike. The scientific study and attention being accorded to the development and careers of the famous Dionne quintuplets may throw a great deal of light on the physical and psychological aspects of multiple birth.

The original Siamese twins have left their name to describe the congenital malformation of twins. This famous pair were born in Siam of Chinese parents in 1811. When they were about 13 years old, the King of Siam heard about them and ordered them put to death because he believed they were "a portent of evil to the country of their birth." They were rescued by a British merchant, and after a successful career in a circus sideshow, settled down as farmers in North Carolina where they died in 1874. A similar type of twins are said to have been born in England in 1100.

There are many famous twins in mythology, among them, the ancient Egyptian twin-gods, Heru and Sut, better known as Horus and Set. All children were under their protection. Another pair of legendary twins were Romulus and Remus, founders of Rome. Two stars in the western sky were called Castor and Pollux by the Romans, in honor of twin mythical heroes by that name. When the Romans wanted to take an oath, they commonly swore by the stars of Gemini. The use of the term was so widespread that it has survived in our own civilization in the form of "by jiminy," to express surprise and consternation.

That Babies Are All Born with Blue Eyes

THERE IS a very popular superstition that all new-born infants have blue eyes. There is no truth whatever in this traditional belief, which goes back to the days when a faulty observation was made by a pseudo-scientist on what is the perfectly normal appearance of a baby's eyes at birth.

Babies that have just come into the world have all shades of eyes. But the cloudiness of the eyes at birth hides their true color. This murky look of the baby's eyes is best described as dark blue or gray, giving rise to the superstition. As the infant's eyes settle and clear, their true color becomes visible, but it was always there.

Kissing New Born Baby for Good Luck

THE CUSTOM of kissing a new baby for good luck is a western superstition of comparatively recent origin.

Kissing a child directly on the mouth was substituted for an earlier custom of "blowing a kiss," such as is done today when saying good-bye. Originally a kiss was "blown" as an expression of reverence, or as a well-wishing salute. This gesture is still the custom among millions of Orientals.

The history of kissing on the mouth goes back to the symbolism of the mouth itself—the door of the body through which the breath of life entered and departed. The natural red circle of the lips expressed two superstitious beliefs. The color red, in folklore the color of magic, represented magic power; and the circle formed by the lips symbolized life everlasting, without beginning and without end.

We find a relic of this ancient belief in the common act of kissing a child's sore finger or other slight injury, or blowing the breath on it, or pretending to release saliva on the hurt. The original idea was to confer healing powers on the injured part through the mouth.

Naturally this form of medication, as well as kissing a helpless new infant, is frowned upon by doctors who are always aware of the presence of germs in almost every mouth.

Fear of Rocking a Baby to Sleep, Unfounded

THE RARITY of cradles and rocking chairs today is due to a superstitious notion evolved some years ago by pseudo-specialists that a child rocked in infancy would acquire an irresistible desire to be rocked all its life. This conclusion implied that as the child grew into adulthood the habit of being embraced and fussed over could not be given up. In other words, babies should be trained to go to sleep without rocking or else grow up with psychological or neurotic disturbances.

According to many experienced pediatrists, no such thing happens; except, of course, in cases where a person, from lack of affection in adolescence or later, develops a state of mind that craves attention and love to the point of wanting to be cuddled and petted like a child. This is rare and not due to a cradle or rocking chair in infancy.

Most sensible people believe that rocking a baby is good for both mother and baby. Babies need love and must know they are loved.

And as for the mother, she gains by the sense of joy she feels when holding her child in her arms and rocking it to sleep.

An accurate answer to the baby-rocking question, it must be admitted, will not be known for a long time. It will take careful observation and checking over several generations to arrive at a conclusion which would benefit human beings one way or the other.

One thing is certain. Our ancestors managed pretty well with cradles, crude or otherwise. Judging from history, cradle-babies, as all were in the past, grew up to be sturdy men and women who aided in the march of civilization.

The rocking chair evolved from the cradle, and the question whether Benjamin Franklin invented it or not has never been settled.

Black Baby to White Parents, a Fallacy

ALTHOUGH scientists and physicians have explained at length and with diagrams and charts that the superstitious fear of a black baby being born to pure white parents is impossible, nevertheless, this unfounded belief still persists in the minds of white women and white couples today.

This superstitious fear is due to a foolish notion that has been spread about that if there is one drop of Negro blood in one or both of the prospective parents, a black-skinned baby could be born to them.

The fact that over two million United States Negroes have crossed the color line has not helped to allay the fear in the minds of some. Likewise, the fact that many light-skinned members of the Negro race pass as pure white has added to the feeling of uncertainty.

Meanwhile there are certain facts which should clarify the situation. In the first place, if one of the parents is pure white, it is impossible for the child to be darker than its dark parent. The chances are that the child will be lighter.

Secondly, if both parents have Negro blood, whether they are aware of it or not, there may be some accentuation of Negro characteristics in the offspring. This is not an infallible rule, and in most cases, the child will have only slight Negro traits. If both parents have been able to pass for white, there is every reason to believe that the child can also.

Thirdly, if both parents are mulattoes, quadroons or octoroons, the child may be darker than either, but not necessarily very dark.

Actually, the only chance that negroid offspring could be produced by white parents is when the couple, apparently white, carry in their blood stream Negro characteristics which tend to be recessive, until combined. The laws of heredity, however, are such, that it is impossible for truly white persons to become the parents of a black child. Legends notwithstanding, there is not a single case on record to justify fears that are based only on superstitious hearsay where no dubious family history is involved.

CHAPTER 11

Give Us This Day

General "Food" Superstitions

THAT LARGE quantities of meat will make a person stronger, improve mental and physical vigor, and make for virility or belligerence is pure superstition. The more food, the more energy, yes; but not necessarily meat. Mental and physical stamina depends on the health of mind and body; an affectionate or pugnacious nature depends on character, habits, environment and other intangibles, but not on the kind of food one eats.

Many superstitions revolve around the notion that raw food is best for man, but raw food is *not* the best diet for man. Many products digest properly only if cooked, because cooking bursts the starch cells, coagulates the proteins and softens the cellulose, thereby making assimilation more effective. Many sensitive systems are thrown out of kilter by the intake of too much raw, coarse-fibered foods.

Roughage food fads do more harm than good to some persons. The superstitious attitude that vegetables are best eaten raw is erroneous because they are not only more appetizing when cooked, but what is more important, the effects of heat permit the digestive juices to get at the starch cells better.

The words of the wise man, "For everything there is a reason, and there is a time for everything" may well be applied to foods. The diet should contain a moderate amount of roughage, as well as of concentrated foods, but on the other hand, the abuse of this principle may lead to difficulties.

That instinct or individual appetite is a guide to the proper selection and quantity of food is another fallacy. This superstition is obviously incorrect because everyone would then know when he has had enough food to satisfy his need without discomfort; or, in cases where persons do not eat enough, they would know enough to eat more.

In the matter of taste as a safe guide to the proper selection of eatables, there are two schools of thought. On the one hand some claim that men and animals know by instinct what to choose for food. There is little evidence for this view. On the other hand, it is claimed they have no discretion. For instance, fat persons themselves frequently create their condition of overweight through extravagant indulgence in food, which leads to fatigue, disease and a shorter life expectancy as the mortality tables of life insurance companies prove.

If instinct really played its rôle correctly, all the problems of over-weight, underweight, and nutritional diseases in general could be eliminated. As for animals having an infallible instinct for choosing their food, farmers and hunters have disproved this faulty notion. On the whole, animals fare well, but millions of ducks die of botulism or ptomaine poisoning, other animals eat poisoned bait, and cows eat loco weed, to cite a few examples.

Superstitions and false notions create food aversions and fears. How often we hear, "I just naturally hate" such and such a food. This is a fallacy of opinion because most loves and hates in regard to foods are due to environment, such as childhood menus in the home, and not to instinctive or natural reactions. Other food aversions are due to customs or conditioning. An individual's likes and dislikes in dishes are therefore more generally due to a form of imagination. Aversions can be overcome by re-educating oneself and by getting a fresh mental approach to the once disliked article of food. That food dislikes are deep-seated and beyond one's control has no scientific basis.

There are hundreds of other common food superstitions. To eat lobster or crab at the same meal with ice cream will make one deathly sick. To eat fish and drink freshly pasteurized milk with it is very dangerous. Refrigeration, not freezing, kills germs of dysentery in water or food. Lettuce and cucumbers are "cooling" foods. Lettuce and onions induce sound sleep. Meat is bad for the kidneys and causes high blood pressure. Mushrooms are poisonous if a silver spoon boiled in the water with them turns black. It is dangerous to eat acid foods, like strawberries, with milk or ice cream, because acids curdle milk or cream. To chew hard foods strengthens the enamel of the teeth. Eating irregularly causes stomach trouble. Rye bread is more healthful than white. Too much sugar causes diabetes. Every single one of these is a superstition!

"Eating" Superstitions

Early man, not knowing any better, conveniently blamed all his stomach troubles on supernatural agencies. Modern man also has fears and phobias about eating. Parents have a hundred and one ways to encourage or discourage the youngsters' choice of foods, and so succeed in passing on superstitions from one generation to the next.

Here are some everyday eating superstitions: for seven people to eat together brings luck to all, but if thirteen eat together, one of the number will die before the year is out. If you take the last portion on a dish at the invitation of someone, you will have a handsome husband or wife, or if married, anything else you might want badly. Eating before retiring is thought to hinder sleep. Eating at irregular times causes stomach trouble. Singing while eating is unlucky. Foods you eat which you don't like will not digest. These and many others are common beliefs today.

Because of the lucky number "three," the traditional "three square meals a day," no more, no less, was and is still believed to make for a long and healthy life. However, it appears that there is a difference in the type of eating various persons require; some may get along on small meals at frequent intervals, while others seem to thrive on the usual three-a-day schedule.

The common saying that a person has a "bird-like" appetite because he or she eats but little is quite an erroneous idea. Birds may eat little at a time, but they are always hungry and must eat often if not continually. Their bodily functions are geared to a much higher level of activity than that of other animals, including man.

Until the Roman era people ate with their fingers, licking them clean during and after a meal, which was eaten from the floor or ground. In fact, more than one-third of the entire population of the world still eats sitting on the floor or ground. Among many people, men and women still eat separately. We can thank King Francis I (1515–1547) for starting our civilized custom of seating women and men next to each other at dinner.

Superstitions and Facts About the Knife, Fork and Spoon

THE SUPERSTITIONS attached to knives, forks and spoons are numerous and vary greatly in their interpretations. To drop a knife accidentally brings good luck or company, that is, if the blade sticks into the ground. The direction towards which the knife leans is that from which the company or good fortune will arrive. If the knife does not stick in the ground, it is interpreted to mean that a disappointment or quarrel will follow, or that a stranger who is not welcome will call.

Whoever picks up the knife, however, will have good luck, but it must not be the one who dropped it or worse luck will happen to him.

The general belief in America is that if a fork falls to the ground during a meal it means that a feminine acquaintance will call. If a knife drops, it will be a boy or man. On the other hand, in some parts of the world, a knife indicates the visit of a member of the female sex, and a fork, one of the male.

That company is coming to eat—when an eating implement drops to the floor—is an obvious association of ideas in the minds of those who believe in superstitious signs.

Crossing a knife and fork, cutting implements, pointed tools or other sharp instruments of any kind, is believed unlucky unless the crossed articles are uncrossed from right to left, or counter-sunwise. Superstitious parents warn their children against crossing sharp objects, not knowing why this act should be avoided.

Back in the days when crucifixion was a common form of capital punishment, all crosses formed unnecessarily were avoided because they suggested the horror of this penalty. In later history, following the death of Christ on the cross, the accidental crossing of objects served to emphasize the fear of a misfortune or tragic end. That fear of crossing dangerous objects has remained an instinct in the minds of persons to this day. However, just as with most superstitions, there was countermagic to avert the evil action. The traditional formula was to spin backwards each of the articles which formed the cross, to let out the wicked forces that might have operated.

Before man learned to reason clearly, implements made of flint, iron or other metals were supposed to retain the magical properties attributed to them in their original form. As implements, they could therefore signal the nearness of good or evil by their behavior. Early man recognized no difference between inanimate and animate matter. To him everything was filled with mystery.

History reveals that a sharp instrument was man's first eating aid, but for a very long time it was not employed in the manner we use it today. Both the spoon and the knife have been in use for thousands of years, while the fork is a comparatively modern invention. The first fork was fashioned, no doubt, after the forked stick, which primitives used for many purposes. They held it in reverence because of its usefulness, as it was a natural implement. It was also a reminder of the human crotch, particularly that of a woman's body, from which new life issued. This was in the days when such a happening was beyond man's comprehension.

The pitchfork was made originally with only two prongs. Later, as man created his gods in his own image, the trident—the sea-god's staff—came into being. From a two-pronged fork, feminine symbol, evolved the three-pronged fork, masculine symbol. Therein lies the confusion in the superstition, that in some parts of the world the dropping of a fork refers to a man; whereas in other places, where the change never took place, it still refers to a woman, and remains the feminine symbol.

The table fork has been in use in Italy since the 11th Century. The wife of the Venetian Doge, Dominico Silvio, was so dainty that she would not eat with her fingers, as was the common custom, and so a tiny golden fork was fashioned for her in the form of the large meat fork then in use. As a matter of record, it was not until the middle of the 17th Century that the Duke of Montausier introduced the large table fork and the large spoon into France.

The spoon has also a symbolic ancestry, starting with the use of a scooping implement in man's dim past. The hand was a natural spoon— a handful. Then two hands coupled together probably suggested the original cup. "Cupping the hands" or palms is a familiar gesture, and a common descriptive phrase. In time, crude spoon-like implements were devised.

A spoon holds things, and so we have our word "spooning" meaning loved ones holding each other in close embrace.

"Digestion" and "Indigestion" Superstitions

FOOD FADDISTS as well as those who are given to food prejudices have an idea that greasy foods, or foods containing oil or fat, are hard to digest. A person in questionable health, or one who has an allergy or food idiosyncrasy, may have cause to feel that oil and fat are not easily digested when they "repeat" or cause a rash of some kind. However, people in normal health can easily tolerate oil or fat, and any other belief is a superstition.

There is also another widespread superstition that fried foods are hard on the stomach, making digestion difficult. Careful study and tests so far have given no evidence for this assumption. Fried food is as easily digested as boiled food. It is true, however, that fat remains in the stomach longer than do other foods, but that does not mean that it is indigestible.

Other superstitious causes attributed to indigestion are numerous. To eat proteins in the same meal as carbohydrates, or starches, is one of them. Mixtures of starches and proteins are believed to "explode" in the stomach. This is based on the false idea that certain foods are good by themselves but harmful in combination. As a matter of fact, many of our best foods are combinations of these same two compounds.

Men and women in early stages of certain diseases seek relief in diet fads, thinking that certain foods will upset the digestion, or not digest at all; and so they avoid these items, especially the combination of proteins and starches. The popular notion that these foods should not go together when a person is not in the best of health has been flatly disproved. Tests taken with sick persons suffering from stomach troubles, gall bladder disease, nervous disorders and other ailments, proved that it took only about three minutes longer to digest the beef and potatoes together than the meat alone—and with no ill results.

Another unfounded food taboo is that tomato juice and milk must not be eaten in the same meal. The cause of indigestion, however, in a great many cases has a psychological basis.

Blood is needed in digestion, but when superstitious fears, worry, anger, or some other emotional disturbance are experienced at mealtime, the circulation is necessarily affected. The blood needed for digestion rushes to the head instead of the stomach, and without this blood the digestive juices do not act properly.

In connection with the digestibility of food, in days of old "fools" and jesters were employed at court, or by the top European nobility, to keep those at the table in good humor during the meal, so that they would not have indigestion from the quantities of food they were served. Soft music does the same thing today, provided, of course, that the one who is eating is a normal individual, and not the victim of superstitious fears and food fixations.

"Diet" and "Sex" Superstitions

PRIMITIVE peoples the world over have associated "like with like"; so that the belief in foods as sex-stimulants stems mostly from superstitious notions that there is some resemblance, either real or vague, between certain foods and the phallic or sex generative organs of man and woman. Among those which in some way suggest the sexual organs are asparagus and celery as the male organs, and clams and oysters as the female.

For similar reasons, such resemblances are often responsible for otherwise inexplicable aversions some persons have to certain foods. Other foods which are believed stimulating to sexual appetite and potency are onions, eggs and caviar.

The neurotic ascetic person, usually a woman, who has superstitious notions concerning the potency of certain foods, and who does not think she ought to have any sexual feelings, avoids these foods with the firm conviction that her feelings should not be unduly aroused, or ever aroused for that matter.

When potatoes and tomatoes were introduced into Europe, both these foods were considered aphrodisiacs, or sex stimulants. This belief lasted until comparatively recently. In fact, tomatoes are still referred to as "love apples," in this country and abroad.

There are, however, sex stimulants which are entirely psychological. Alcohol, when taken in moderate quantities, usually appears to stimulate sexual feelings. In reality what happens is not a direct stimulation, but rather a paralysis of the inhibitions.

Many persons think that their sexual desires are slight or absent, while actually it is their superstitious fears and prejudices that keep their natural desires so repressed that they never reach their consciousness, or reach it only to a minimum degree.

The sexual instinct is an integral part of every healthy individual. It needs no stimulating. If something seems to be wrong the remedy does not lie in eating special foods, or taking aphrodisiacs for stimulation. These are only superstitions, based on symbolic association with the male and female organs. The only remedies are improving the general health or in treating the deficiency as a psychological problem to which psychiatric methods should be applied.

Aphrodisiacs of the cantharides or "Spanish fly" type, opium and other derivatives, taken in small quantities, will have a stimulating effect, but this is probably produced in the same way as alcohol. However, any notion that food which resembles human organs or aphrodisiacs serve as sex stimulation is utterly false.

"Canned Food" Superstitions

THE FEAR of ptomaine poisoning, or botulism, is a persistent superstition to the effect that eating food that has remained in an open can, for no matter how long a time, can be fatal. Repeated information on this subject in the press and elsewhere has shown the absolute fallacy of such an attitude. Food will spoil no faster nor slower in the open can than in any other container. There is no truth, either, in the superstitious belief that after a number of years frozen canned food is no longer safe to eat.

Chemists and food experts have exploded the myth that food should be removed from metal cans as soon as opened. With certain foods, however, from the standpoint of quality, it is desirable to remove the contents of the can as soon as it is opened. Such foods, usually those of an acidic nature, may act slowly on the can after the air is admitted, and a small amount of tin and iron may be absorbed. Traces of such metals, however, are usually harmless, even though they impart a slight taste to the food. But there is no danger of ptomaine poisoning, as the uninformed believe.

There was a time, and not too long ago, when there was cause to be afraid of eating canned goods, but the canning industry has so improved its methods that there is little likelihood of botulism from commercial cannery products.

The superstitious fear of ptomaine poisoning from canned foods is firmly rooted in the popular imagination, because when someone has eaten something that made him ill, he immediately attributes it to the canned food recently eaten. For instance, some individuals are allergic to certain foods, which produce a reaction such as the rash that appears after eating strawberries. If a canned food has been eaten at the same meal, the canned article is apt to be blamed. "One man's meat is another man's poison" has some truth in it, but this does not apply to whether the food comes out of a can or not.

Another common food superstition is the fear that decayed food is poisonous. This need not be so even if the food is actually in a state of putrefaction. It is a fact, however, that food which contains ptomaine poison is always decayed.

Home canning and preserving are now of great interest to the housewife. Home canning and food poisoning often do go together, because the germ that causes botulism can withstand ordinary boiling. The food should be processed under steam pressure to make destruction of the germ certain. To be absolutely sure that home canned foods are safe, boil 15 minutes after opening the can.

Many of the superstitions relating to food poisoning go back to the times when pork, particularly in sausage meat, was believed to be the cause of many diseases. Originally botulism was actually caused by sausage poisoning, Botulus means sausage in Latin.

"Death in the Pot," as related to pork or ham sausages has been replaced by the unwarranted superstitious fear of "Death in the Can." Ptomaine poisoning is a much dreaded phrase, applied indiscriminately by superstitious persons to any stomach disturbance. Actually, however, cases of true ptomaine poisoning are very rare. An open can, when it is kept cool and covered in the refrigerator, is quite safe for saving food until it is to be used again.

There is no need to fear to eat the contents of a can, even if it has been frozen for a long time. Canned food that was 93 years old was found in a cache on Dealey Island in the Arctic regions a few years ago. Laboratory tests showed that some of the food was still in good condition. This is startling evidence against the superstitious belief that frozen canned foods cannot be kept over the years.

"Salt" Superstitions

ACCIDENTAL spilling of salt and then throwing a pinch of it over the left shoulder to nullify the bad luck to come is a fairly universal superstition. Salt has been used for positive and negative magic in everyday life throughout the evolution of man's customs. No subject, around which superstitions have grown, stands out so conspicuously.

Saltiness is easily associated with tears, which are saline, and this fact has produced many superstitions. According to popular Norwegian belief, as many tears will be shed as are needed to dissolve the salt spilled. In certain parts of Yorkshire, it is also held that every grain spilled means a tear to be shed. In New England the particles of the spilled salt are thrown on the stove so as to dry up in advance the tears to be shed.

A belief existed that a witch or evil spirit must first count the grains of salt used as a countercharm, but since they are such busybodies, they never find time enough to do it, so they leave the premises. In order to keep witches away from the milk, this same logic was supposed to work if one put salt on the lid of the churn.

In many places the old saying, "Help me to salt, help me to sorrow," is still heard. In some districts of Scotland, it was the usual thing to carry salt around with a new-born child, to keep away any evil spirits that might take advantage of its weak condition.

Language is filled with expressions of ancient origin in which salt is linked to good and bad characteristics of things and persons. "I'll take that with a grain of salt," or "He's not worth his salt," or "He's the salt of the earth," are a few examples.

Salt is often associated with friendship because of its lasting quality. It "preserves" things, and so it was usually presented to guests before any other food, or was the first thing placed on the table, to signify the abiding nature of friendship.

So valuable was salt in ancient Greece that a stranger would be welcomed by an offering of a pinch of salt in the right hand, the salt being a guarantee that the stranger would be safe under his roof. Spilling salt, however, was always a great misfortune everywhere, and regarded as an outrage to hospitality.

The ancient Egyptians believed that salt excited the passions. In Italy, in the early days, it was considered an insult for a man to offer salt to the wife of a friend. It was equivalent to a suggestion of friendship of a doubtful character. The use of individual salt containers was in keeping with this old notion that we should not help anyone to salt, lest it appear that we were forcing our attention on a person of the opposite sex.

Salt figured conspicuously in the rules of etiquette during the Middle Ages. An enormous salt-cellar divided the table of a nobleman. Those seated above the salt were always the guests of a higher rank than those who were placed below the salt-cellar.

Because sea water was salty, which was believed to be its secret of purification, a goddess of salt was designated at the time when unseen spirits were taking form in the minds of more advanced peoples. For instance, the Greeks called their goddess of Health, Hygeia, and its Roman equivalent was Salus, goddess of Salt. This goddess was supposed to be present at the birth of a child, and an offering of salt was placed on the child's tongue in her name. This symbolized long life, good health, and future protection. The same ceremony is performed today by some peoples. The salt made the baby cry, and so the salty tears were blended with the goddess' salt to create immunity. If the child did not cry, it was a sign that it would not live long.

Prehistoric Romans generally led their criminals to an altar to be sacrificed, in punishment for their crimes. The officiating Augur placed a bit of salt on each guilty one's head so that he might have better luck in the Hereafter. If any of them spilled the salt, it was a bad omen not only for the condemned, but for all those present. To counteract this emergency, the Augur had a verbal formula which he used: "May the gods avert evil."

Because salt was incorruptible, it was associated with immortality, and a goddess to represent this fact appears in the legends of peoples in many widely scattered parts of the world. The Mexican Indians called their goddess of Salt, Huixtocihuatl and certain days of the year were set aside to conduct festivities in her honor.

The sacredness of salt in those days is also illustrated by the fact that the Hebrews, Greeks and Romans used salt in their sacrificial cakes, and flung it on altar fires.

Owing to the scarcity of salt in ancient times, soldiers, officials and working people in Greece and Rome were paid with a portion of salt. This pay was called "salarium," from which our word salary is derived.

The earliest mention in the Bible of salt appears in the story of the destruction of Sodom and Gemorrah. It is stated that King Abimelech sowed salt where the cities had been, which showed them to be in complete ruin.

The spilling of salt by Judas, portrayed by the great artist, Leonardo da Vinci, in "The Last Supper," suggests the great tragedy that is about to follow. The ill-omened number of thirteen at the table, and the act of spilling salt, were superstitions of long standing, and da Vinci used both to heighten the tragic portent of his composition.

In Eastern countries salt is invariably placed before strangers as a pledge of good will. In Hungary, it was long the custom to sprinkle the threshold of a new house with salt, so that no new witch or evil thing would ever enter it after the family moved in. Salt is still the first thing brought into a new house or apartment by many superstitious persons.

Salt is of special significance among wandering Arab tribes, and in many places in the East, contracts of importance are ratified and confirmed with it. Gypsies also used bread and salt to confirm an oath. Among the Jews, the Covenant of Salt is one of their most sacred. In Denmark, in the 16th Century, oaths were taken on salt.

Although we have no way of knowing when or how man discovered salt, or what was his first use of it, there is no doubt that its properties have puzzled and fascinated peoples for ages. However, legends, myths and superstitions of various peoples give valuable clues as to what salt meant to man in primitive, ancient and medieval times.

Since primitive man took particular notice of what happened in nature around him, it is probable that animals flocking to salt-licks, aroused his curiosity. He probably imitated them, liked the salt, and soon recognized it as a necessity of life.

Certain properties of salt may have led them to believe that it possessed a supernatural quality, which could protect them from evil and destructive influences. The taboo against spilling salt in early times was as much a matter of strict economy as of supernatural implications, as salt was a precious item and scarce in some regions.

At the time when early man believed that all good spirits congregated on the right side of the body and evil ones on the left, it was conceived that the bad unseen beings might be bribed with salt, so a pinch of it was thrown to the left side. Others thought that these demons could be blinded if the salt were thrown in their eyes. Whether the bad spirits of the left side were bribed or subdued, the superstition survives that the countermagic when spilling salt is to throw a bit of it over the left shoulder.

Another early and ancient belief was that salt could prophesy weather, and it was looked upon as a barometer. When salt became moist, a humid or rainy day was to be expected. When it was dry and smooth, the weather would be dry and clear. This same system of forecasting the weather is well known to all of us today. We also know the fact that salt thaws the snow and freezes ice-cream.

Another evidence of the belief in the magical properties of salt is found in the old saying that it is easy to catch a bird if we put salt on its tail. In conjunction with this superstition is a strange story recorded by Strabo, ancient Greek geographer, who wrote, "If birds touch the surface of Lake Tatta, they immediately fall down because of the weight of the salt on their feathers, and are caught." Similar instances have been reported at the Great Salt Lake in Utah in recent years, when birds flew close enough to be wetted by the salty water, and became so weighted down with it that they could not fly, and were therefore easily caught.

Spinach, the Health Fetish

LEGENDS pertaining to the nutritive and even quasi-miraculous qualities of spinach prevail in almost every country, and have appeared in all ages. In America the humble green leaves became almost a fetish. Many parents who had been forcing their children to eat spinach were amazed when food chemists announced that the nutritive value of spinach had been considerably over-rated. Some nutritionists even asserted that eating this vegetable does more harm than good.

There was a popular saying: "Eat spinach and be calm." It was claimed that persons who ate spinach were less irritable than those who did not. Some pseudo-nutritionists went so far as to proclaim that spinach was directly responsible for the romantic feeling that bubbles up in the spring in the hearts of men and women. Is it any wonder that spinach became a fetish?

The history of this green is long and varied. The plant was introduced into Europe from Persia about the 15th century. However, this curly "grass" is mentioned in many records of the ancients. It was eaten by Nebuchadnezzar, King of Babylon, 605 B.C. The Chinese discuss the cultivation of spinach in their chronicles of the seventh and eighth centuries, while in Spain in the twelfth century it was called, "the prince of vegetables." In the thirteenth century, European monks ate spinach on fast days, believing it to be a life-saving vegetable which would sustain them on an otherwise lean diet.

A recipe for "spinoches" was included in a cook book for Richard II of England in the fourteenth century. And in the eighteenth century, Boswell's biography of Samuel Johnson makes known the fact that "we had a very good soup, a boiled leg of mutton and spinage."

All through English history spinach figures in various records, while in France it has been known for centuries as "the broom of the stomach" which sweeps out impurities and is essential to good health and strong bones. Not very long ago a famous race horse was called "Épinard," the French word for spinach.

At the beginning of this century American comics, motion pictures and advertisements of all sorts featured spinach: and nutritionists of that day backed them up. Spinach then became a *must* for youngsters, most of whom hated it.

Then in 1930 we witnessed the birth of Popeye the Sailor, created by Elzie Crisler Segar, who made spinach the source of his strength. This brought spinach into the limelight and the fad was in full swing! To crown this hysteria, in Crystal City, Texas, the spinach capital of the United States, a statue was erected displaying Popeye the Sailor in its central square.

Despite its unusual historical background, spinach has now been debunked. We know now that this food, which is supposed to be eaten for its calcium, among other elements, also contains oxalic acid which forms an insoluble compound with calcium. It is claimed that the oxalic acid in certain types of spinach robs the body of its own calcium. Furthermore, contrary to popular belief, spinach is a relatively poor source of iron. Only twenty per cent of its iron content is nutritionally available. In other words, whatever important mineral elements the spinach contains are not readily assimilated in the human body. Nevertheless, spinach undoubtedly will continue to be in demand as a vegetable dish, which when properly prepared is very palatable.

"Bread" Superstitions

ALTHOUGH the ancient Egyptians are generally given credit for the invention of bread some 6,000 years ago, it is also known that the Swiss lake dwellers of the New Stone Age, a few thousand years previously, ground barley and wheat on flat stone and baked the flour into cakes. Bread folklore has traveled throughout many lands since then.

One of the outstanding modern superstitions about bread is that it is fattening. This notion came about in America some years ago when the slim waistline became fashionable. Bread became practically taboo in a woman's diet, although dietitians agree that bread judiciously used is not any more fattening than any other carbohydrate of equal caloric value.

Among the many bread superstitions are the following: it is bad luck to cut bread at both ends of the loaf; it is bad luck to break bread in anyone's hand; never leave a knife stuck in a loaf of bread; to drop bread on the floor is a good sign and a wish made when it is picked up will come true; to dream of bread portends a happy event; two persons reaching for bread at the same time means someone is coming to the house soon; to drop bread butter side down means bad luck; to take the last piece of bread is bad luck, and if unmarried, means a life doomed to spinsterhood; if you take another piece of bread when you have one, you will feed someone hungry in the near future; scouring a breadknife on Sunday is unlucky.

Passing the bread at table is merely a polite gesture nowadays, but in ancient times it expressed a wish for longevity and good health. Because it was eaten at the Last Supper, bread came to have great religious significance. In early Christian times all forms of bread were considered sacred. Economically, of course, bread has always been important, and is often called "the staff of life." In early cultures it typified life's four essentials: water, the stream of life; grain, the field; sustenance, the earth; and goodness, the sun.

Various interesting omens have been ascribed to certain uses of bread. The medieval housewife would reserve the heel of her home-made loaf for someone in the family, for if she gave it to a stranger she gave away her luck.

A loaf of bread upside down on the table means a death in the family. To seafaring people it means a ship in distress. This belief can be traced back to Sir Walter Menteith, when some centuries ago he gave the English signal to attack the ambushed Scots. He did so by turning a loaf of bread upside down. Needless to say, the Scots have been superstitious about that position of bread ever since.

Eating with friends at table is an old social custom. We all know of the Eastern belief that once a man has "broken bread" with another, they are friends. In early times bread was broken, not cut, as is the fashion nowadays.

"Corn" Superstitions

INDIAN CORN or maize is a native plant of the New World, raised long before the white man came to American shores. The large number of superstitions about corn are typically American or Indian, although now much of Old World grain-lore forms a number of false beliefs and notions widely believed.

Corn originated somewhere in South or Middle America. Ears of corn have been found in Peru that are known to be 2,000 years old. All authorities agree that it must have been cultivated sometime between 3,000 and 4,000 B.C., but whether in Peru or Mexico is still unsettled. However, it may be that the Indians grew all kinds of corn which they ground into corn meal. Some tribes raised red, blue, and purple corn, as well as white and yellow.

Most Indians imagined that maize was created by the Great Spirit during a famine, and that whoever wasted it would be doomed to wander hungry and alone, and eventually die. Other Indians believed that the origin of corn came about when a beautiful girl was pursued by a river god. While hiding among the weeds, she was changed into corn. In general, the Indians held in horror any action or person who would waste corn. If anyone saw it on the ground and did not pick it up, he would be punished.

The "Red Maize," a sub-clan of the Omaha Indians, believed that if they ate red maize they would have running sores about the mouth. There is an odd similarity between the Egyptian "corn spirit" and that of the Omaha Indians. At one time the Egyptian god, Osiris, was called upon for good harvests and offered sacrifices of red-haired puppies or dogs to invite good crops. Red-haired men and oxen, believed to represent the corn-spirit, were also sacrificed. Their ashes were scattered over the land to make the grain turn red or golden. The Omaha Indians did not eat red corn probably because they believed it to contain the corn-spirit, a fiery element which would harm them.

The European idea of corn includes any of the cereal grasses, wheat, rye, oats, and others. The Corn Laws of the English settlers at first applied only to these grains, but later were applied to the Indian maize as well.

Longfellow tells of a superstition regarding the husking of maize: "In the golden weather the maize is husked, and the maidens blushed at each blood-red ear, for that betokened a lover; but at the crooked ear of corn, laughed, and called it a thief in the cornfield." In time a red ear of corn was looked upon as a good luck symbol, particularly in love and health.

Among the legion of superstitions about corn are the following: corn planted in the dark of the moon will have large ears low on the stalk; if the seeds are planted in the light of the moon, the ears of corn will grow near the top of the stalk; if the first ear of corn that you see has white silk, you will be ill or will go to a funeral; if it is red, you will attend a wedding; if you find a red ear of corn and you are single, you will be married within a year; never finish cutting corn before sunset; hang up a corn-stalk over the looking-glass for good luck; if the husk on the corn is thin, it will be a mild winter, or if heavy, a cold one; green corn is used for all kinds of magic formulas, especially to spite a rival.

The Hopi Indians of Arizona still observe a traditional colorful corn ceremonial in February each year, during which they make offerings to the sun-god and expect good crops in return. The modern Maya Indians believe that the human soul is fragile and needs support, especially at the birth of a child. An ear of corn is placed beside the infant as a protective guardian and symbol of strength, and also to prevent evil spirits from snatching the newborn's soul.

There are many planting superstitions. Native Indians of Guatemala and Yucatan planted four kernels to a hill, a superstitious custom honoring the cardinal points. This custom was adopted by North American Indians and by most of the first white colonists, and still is practiced today. The Pilgrim Fathers planted five grains of corn plus a herring, for fertilizer, in every hill, accompanied with the following doggerel:

One for the blackbird,
One for the crow,
One for the cutworm,
And two to let it grow.

"Onion" and "Garlic" Superstitions

THE ANCIENT EGYPTIANS frequently took their sacred oaths with their right hand on an onion—one of their many symbols of eternity because of its formation of one sphere within another. The onion was believed to be a powerful agent not only to keep evil spirits away but to ward off plague.

In keeping with the old Egyptian idea, many persons still believe that to leave a piece of onion on a shelf will absorb the germs of disease in a house, so that the occupants will remain healthy. This superstition is also widely observed in malarial districts. The cut onion in sleeping quarters is also supposed to absorb the poisonous odors which the sleeper might not detect and which might prove injurious if not fatal.

The superstitious belief that the onion is a special vegetable which protects human beings and animals alike against infection was taken so seriously in the Middle Ages that even the hands were anointed with onion juice to prevent contagion from spreading, and also to protect those who were exposed to infection.

Many medieval superstitions have been kept to the present time. For example, a piece of onion over a wasp sting or other insect bite will stop the pain and prevent swelling and infection. If a piece of onion is placed on the back of the neck it will stop nose-bleed. Epileptics are advised to carry a piece of onion in their pockets to prevent fits. Onions sowed in the new moon are not expected to amount to much. To ward off a cold, cut an onion in two, hang it on a string, and knock it when you pass. If you burn the skin of onions you will receive money.

At one time onion juice was recommended for sore eyes, an old Greek remedy.

Because of the characteristic growth and development of the onion, a large number of farmers, gardeners and housewives believe that if the coverings of the onion are especially heavy, the winter will be cold. If, on the other hand, the skins are thin, the winter will be mild. Sometimes this belief works, sometimes not, as the onion cannot be relied upon to predict an entire season's weather.

The following doggerel, however, is quoted by nearly everyone who has anything to do with onions:

> "Onion's skin very thin,
> Mild winter coming in.
> Onion's skin thick and tough,
> Coming winter cold and rough."

A cut onion is believed to extract venom from a snakebite. And some people believe that eating onions at night causes insomnia.

Modern science has made important discoveries in regard to the onion, proving it not only a highly nutritious vegetable, but one containing chemical compounds, which, when isolated, are said to possess the means to combat germs in human beings. This fact would make it seem that the ancients sensed a valuable property in the onion when they associated it with warding off disease.

Garlic, a near relative of the onion, was also used in folk medicine from earliest times. The Egyptians took oaths on it as they did on the onion. It has been ascertained recently that garlic has wonderful nutritional value, and that the vapor from crushed garlic will kill bacteria.

Oddly enough, however, the bacterial agent is not one of the substances that gives it its characteristic odor. The strong odor comes from the oils it contains which have no effect on bacteria. In early times, however, it was the garlic's pungency that was believed especially potent against all kinds of contagious diseases. Eating garlic was also supposed to protect one against the dangers of the Evil Eye and Vampirism.

The original reason for stringing garlic bulbs together was make a necklace to hang around the neck before going to sleep to repel the most hazardous of vampires. Wild garlic gathered in May was considered the most effective for the purpose; and if one ate it as well, it afforded personal protection for a year.

Many old superstitions about garlic are prevalent in America at the present time. To hang a bunch or place a bunch of garlic on the mantel brings good luck. Sprinkle garlic and sulphur at the entrance to a mole's run, and the animal will come out of the hole. If you rub a horse's teeth with garlic, it will soon recover its appetite. Keep a piece of garlic in your clothes, take a bite of it now and then, and you never catch a disease. If there is a disease in the house just hang a few garlic bulbs and they will draw the disease. To stop a child from wetting the bed, feed him garlic. A good remedy for worms is finely chopped garlic. Eating garlic will cure bronchitis, colds, rheumatism, and lung trouble. Insert a piece of garlic in the cavity to stop a toothache. It would seem garlic is truly a wonderful vegetable.

In classical times, garlic was attributed magical potency and was believed strong enough to destroy the magnetic powers of the lodestone. It was placed at crossroads as a supper for the goddess Hecate, one of the Titans of Greek mythology. The garlic was to protect travelers and to prevent Hecate from exercising her deadly powers. Among her supernatural duties was to teach witchcraft and sorcery and act as goddess of the Dead. Other offerings to this sinister deity were honey, dogs and black lambs. The animals were sacrificed at the crossroads, her domain.

In the temple of Pelusium in ancient Egypt, the fragrant bulbs of garlic were worshipped as deities.

Not only was garlic considered effective as an amulet against many diseases in ancient times, but demons and evil fascinators were supposed to be allergic to its odor. In fact, the very mention of the name was supposed to break their spell. In Greece no midwife went about her business without a plentiful supply of this magic vegetable. Garlic was served regularly to Roman soldiers in the belief that it excited courage in battle.

Wherever garlic is cultivated, it is still a custom to hang a wreath of it over the door to keep evil away from the home. The origin of rubbing garlic on cooking utensils was for the same reason. Aristotle recommended garlic as a specific against hydrophobia, and to purify the blood each spring.

"Egg" Superstitions

As THE SYMBOL of the source of life and of fertility, and also as the emblem of resurrection, the egg has been employed actually and symbolically in all kinds of magical practices everywhere and by all primitive and ancient peoples. Eggs were the symbol of Creation, and many mythological tales were woven around this idea. There is hardly any doubt that eggs were one of the chief features of diet of primeval man, who probably ate them raw.

Farmers and those living in rural communities are naturally more given to egg superstitions than urbanites. Some of these superstitions are: if you see a great many broken eggs, you will have to go through a lawsuit in the near future to get your rights; to find a snake's egg in a hen's nest betokens enemies who are supposed to be friends; it is a sign of ill luck to bring birds' eggs into the house; it is unlucky to bring in or take out eggs after sunset; if you find a hen has laid a soft-shelled egg, do not keep it, throw it over the house and thus throw away your bad luck. If two different persons beat the whites of eggs they will not remain firm. An even number of eggs under a hen for hatching is unlucky. An egg marked with a black cross and placed under a hen will keep weasels away. Eggs should be eaten on Easter for good luck until the next Easter comes around. Dream of eggs and you will quarrel with friends. Eggs laid on Friday will cure stomach-ache.

Although brown and white eggs are identical in food value, a superstitious preference is expressed, with brown the favorite in certain parts of America, and whites in other sections. Those who favor brown eggs think they are "richer" and more nutritious. In large cities some young housewives even think white eggs are fresher! On the other hand some associate white eggs with something pale and anemic and think they have a lower nutritive value. As a matter of fact, all eggs are designed by nature for the development of chicks, and whether they are brown or white, they contain a great deal of nourishment in a limited space for the potential fowl.

There is a superstition that two yolks in one egg is usually lucky for the one who gets it, and that a wish made when it is eaten will come true. This superstition is based on the notion that the supernatural reproductive powers which the egg symbolized, and which always meant good luck, were doubled in this case.

Anciently the yolk of an egg was believed capable of unbewitching a person who had come under the spell of the Evil Eye. For example, the Mayas often imagined that some enemy had placed his evil eye on a child. The medicine man was then summoned. He passed an egg in front of the child's face many times, broke it, and looked at the yolk as though it were the Evil Eye itself. He hurriedly buried the yolk in a secret place and from then on the child was believed saved.

The Egyptians, Gauls and Romans figured that the solar year started in the spring because that was the time when the sleeping seeds came to life, and birds built their nests and laid their eggs. Everything in nature seemed to take a fresh start.

According to archeologists, a race of egg-worshippers, now vanished, lived on Easter Island, two thousand miles west of Chili. The people chose their rulers by holding an egg-gathering contest in which the winner became the King. The inhabitants of this strange island are said to have lived in egg-shaped huts.

Greek philosophers thought the egg represented the Universe, the shell signified earth and air, the white of the egg, water, and the yolk, fire. The yolk symbolized the solar eye among all sun-worshippers and those who placed their faith in the sun and fire as primary sources of energies. The life of the Indian and Egyptian gods was in the egg, and the hieroglyphic of the sun-god Ra was a point in a circle, patterned after the egg.

The ancient Romans held egg games at their New Year in honor of Castor and Pollux, the deified twins who were supposed to have been hatched from an egg, and who ended their existence as twin stars in the sky.

"Tomato" Superstitions

THE TOMATO under the misnomer "love apple," was strictly taboo as a food in the 1820's and for years after. Within the century, however, it has made such progress that it enjoys the distinction of being the most highly consumed vegetable on earth! What was once deemed poison, is now—paradoxically enough—on its way to becoming a panacea for all ills.

Nevertheless, there are still many superstitions for and against this rosy vegetable. Examples on the negative side include: tomato seeds will cause appendicitis; if the skin is not removed, it will stick to the lining of the intestines and cause cancer; so, too, will the combination of unskinned stewed tomatoes and mashed potatoes; tomato juice will aggravate a high blood pressure condition; drinking tomato juice at the same meal with milk is very indigestible; ripe, sun-warmed tomatoes picked off the vine and eaten right away will cause brain fever. There are a host of others.

But there is a brighter superstitious side to the tomato. In Italy and among Italians in the United States, it is believed that tomato sauce brings health and wealth. Some Italians put a large red tomato on the mantel to bring prosperity to the house. When placed on the windowsill, or in any opening, it wards off evil spirits, and protects the occupants of the house. All in all, the tomato signifies good fortune to these believers.

The red tomato pincushion is a survival of this belief, and it is seen in many homes, although the original superstition may be unknown to the owner of the cloth tomato.

Another good luck superstition advises a girl who wishes to find a husband to wear a sachet of dried tomato seeds hung around her neck. If it doesn't invite courtship and marriage as it is supposed to, it will at least make her popular with the boys.

Another belief about tomatoes and the brain is that eating this vegetable makes for clearer thinking. This is not true, of course.

Tomato superstitions are all modern, since this food is one of the more recent to find universal favor. They are all products of the imagination, spread by hearsay, and not one of the superstitions has any scientific basis.

In days gone by, the tomato was believed to be an aphrodisiac, or sex stimulant. In the 17th Century, gallant young men delivered tomato plants to their wives or sweethearts as tokens of love. Today, however, it is considered a perfect alkalizer, which has led to a fetishistic attitude with some who feel cheated if they do not have their tomato juice daily.

Taken in moderation, the tomato has its place in the diet of human beings, but while it causes none of the evils some would have us believe, neither is it a substitute for the fountain of youth.

"Apple" Superstitions

Ate an apfel avore gwain to bed
Makes the doctor beg his bread.
           —Devonshire rhyme

AN APPLE a day is said to keep the doctor away, but of course we know that apples have no magic power to prevent or cure disease. However, the potassium the apple contains is a highly essential mineral in the human body. In the light of scientific discoveries, the old saying may have more than a grain of truth in it.

There are many other popular apple superstitions. If you can break an apple in two after someone has named it, the one named loves you. Put some apple seeds on the stove or in a hot plate, get a friend to name each, and the one that pops first is the one you love best. "He loves me, he loves me not" is an innocent little game played with apple pips today. Besides this game, there are others played with apple pips and apples for fortune telling, especially in regard to love and marriage.

Of a different sort is the superstition that green apples cause a stomachache. Opinions are divided on this question. However, predominating is the report that on the whole, there is nothing in green apples to cause such physical discomfort. An unripe apple is hard, coarse and unpalatable, and in order to avoid a stomachache, it must be eaten slowly and with proper mastication, thoroughly mixing the apple with saliva. Then the proper digestion of the green apple is assured. It is the insufficient chewing and not the greenness, it is claimed, that causes the stomachache.

Apples play a great role in Christmas as well as Hallowe'en festivities. If the sun shines through the limbs of the apple trees on Christmas day, it is a sign there will be a good crop of the fruit the next year. Ducking for apples is still fun for young people on Hallowe'en and Thanksgiving. Most customs like these go back to pagan times and pagan ceremonies performed in honor of Pomona, a Roman goddess who presided over fruit trees.

The apple has been used in magic of all kinds since remotest times, especially for prophesying special events, to assist in finding a husband, or to help those in love.

The esteem in which the fruit was held anciently is attested by the story of Adam's temptation when Eve offered him an apple. Because the apple tree was represented by the ancients as the Tree of Life and Knowledge, it has given rise to countless myths, fables and legends, and it figures prominently in the folklore and superstitious beliefs of peoples and races the world over.

The list of legendary references to apples, besides the story of the forbidden fruit in the Garden of Eden, is notable. It was the wedding gift of Zeus to his daughter, Hebe. It was born in the hand of Aphrodite, and watched by dragons in the Garden of the Hesperides. The apple figured in one of the twelve labors of Hercules. It was the prize for beauty awarded by Paris, and also known as the Apple of Dicord, leading to the Homeric Trojan War. Iduna, wife of Bragi, son of Odin, kept, in her magic basket, the apples of which the gods must eat to obtain eloquence, knowledge and perpetual youth.

The apple was grasped at in vain by Tantalus in hell. In Atalanta's Race, three apples saved Hippomenes, who married her. They comforted the love-sick maiden in the Song of Solomon. Apple trees formed the groves of the blessed Isle of Avalon, known as the "Isle of Apples." Walt Disney revived the fairy tale of Snow White in which the apple contains the sleeping potion, and this animated picture story has been enjoyed by millions.

The apples of the Garden of Hesperides are generally believed to have been pomegranates or oranges, but the fact remains that they are called "golden apples" to this day, and there is no one who can prove that they were not apples. It was the fruit of the gods!

"Tea" Superstitions

TEA, in America, is not only a beverage at mealtime and at social gatherings, but has a superstitious value in the practice of tea leaf readings for which every year millions of pounds are sold, and millions of dollars spent—mostly by women. With some women this addiction begins harmlessly in a tête-à-tête with the "oracle" just for fun, or with tongue in cheek. However, many sooner or later join the ranks of regular devotees who take their teacup divination very seriously and direct their lives accordingly.

Instead of the Oriental custom of serving tea with fortune-rice-cakes in which are mystic or philosophic messages, or bits of common sense advice in the form of proverbs and sayings, we developed a modernized version of European gypsy fortune-telling with tea leaves which has become a profitable business on a nation-wide scale. Distraught and wishful-thinking women who seek "inside" information about their affairs find solace of a kind in symbols which are thousands of years old.

Books are written, and sold by the millions, to tell how to read tea leaves at home; the symbols forming a subject of intense study for an ever-growing number of believers.

In addition to the superstitious practice of tea leaf reading, there are many general superstitions about tea. To stir a teapot is to stir trouble, and is a sign of a quarrel between friends. A tea stem floating in the teapot foreshadows the coming of a stranger. Old people say you must butter his head—the tea stem—and throw him under the table. Love is crossed when cream or milk is put into the tea before the sugar. A singing tea kettle foretells pleasant news before long. It is considered unlucky to drain a tea kettle dry. If you break a teapot, it is a sign of trouble. To pour tea back into the teapot is bad luck. If a young girl drinks tea out of the spout of a teapot, her children will have strange mouths. If the lid of a teapot is left open by chance, it foretells the visit of a stranger.

The origin of the tea itself is shrouded in mystery, in true Oriental style. However, various legends account for it. The dates are obscure, and the stories are couched in colorful symbolism and peopled with mythical as well as real characters, who were believed to be the discoverers of the magic evergreen herb.

Among these legends, one of the oldest attributes the discoveries of the virtues of tea to the Chinese Emperor Chin-Nung, in about 2737 B.C. when he accidentally dropped some tea leaves into boiling water. Incidentally, tradition traces all agricultural and medical knowledge to this venerable monarch. To Chin-Nung, celebrated scholar and philosopher, are credited the lines: "Tea is better than wine, for it leadeth not to intoxication; neither does it cause a man to say foolish things and repent thereof in his sober moments. It is better than water, for it doth not carry disease; neither does it act as poison as doth water when wells contain foul and rotten matter."

Tea was used as a medicine long before it was indulged in as a social beverage. If we are to believe the sages, tea was first used during a cholera epidemic in China which almost depopulated the Flowery Kingdom. It was learned somehow that cholera germs were carried in drinking water and on green vegetables which were frequently eaten raw because of lack of fuel. The ruling king, the great Chin-Nung, ordered the inhabitants to boil the drinking water under penalty of death for those who ignored the decree. Thus the boiling of the water killed the cholera germs and the epidemic ended. Tea was added to the boiling water and became the favorite drink of the Chinese. I⁺ was supposed to be endowed with supernatural properties and was recommended as a cure-all, not only in China, but wherever the plant was found. In this way tea was brought to the attention of the world.

Social teas are an offshoot of tea rituals and ceremonies that were first observed in China, then Japan, to be followed later in other countries. The idea originated with Buddhist monks who are said to have introduced the custom into China centuries ago. Pilgrims of wealth going to shrines often gave tea parties to those who composed their trains. The largest known of these parties provided tea bowls for some eight thousand worshippers.

Oriental traditional bowls, which, by the way, are still in use, were round objects without handles, symbolic of the solar disc. They were held with both hands to form the double solar circle, while the drinking of the "liquid jade," as the Chinese once called tea, completed the trinity of circles, a most potent symbol to enhance the chances of health of mind and body which worshippers sought in their pilgrimages. Western cups with handles evolved from these early bowls.

There is another charming legend to account for the origin of the use of tea. It is said that the first tea plant was given by Heaven to Bodhidharma, or Darma, a Hindu ascetic and pilgrim who vowed to contemplate the virtues of Buddha through nine successive sleepless years. In the eighth year—some say less—worn out by toil and prayer, he broke his vow. As he woke up, in humiliation, he cut off his eyelids and flung them to the ground. And from their blood as it sank into the ground grew the herb whose infusion should forever be a specific against sleeplessness. Gratefully this Buddhist monk taught the value of the prayer-assisting herb which he carried with him on a mission to China. As Buddha, founder of Buddhism, lived in the fifth century B.C., this story is old.

Tea came first to Europe as a medicine, and later became a food and an international drink. No reference to tea has been found in European literature prior to 1588. Mention of it was made by Marco Polo, and knowledge of the plant appears not to have reached Europe until after establishment of intercourse between Portugal and China in 1557. But is was some time after the middle of that century that the English began to use tea. In 1776 it precipitated the American Revolution, which completely changed the course of modern history.

With the introduction of tea into America, a variety of Eastern superstitions pertaining to it were also imported, and we added generously to the list. A modern superstition is the fear that tea-drinking will stunt the growth of children, and also cause barrenness and sterility. Recent experiment, however, have proved that if humans react like white rats, these fears are completely unwarranted.

A superstition existed in tea-growing countries that only tea picked by delicate feminine hands retains its sweet flavor, and so only women were employed at this task. Tea leaves were never thrown away. Sometimes they were ground to a pulp and used for various purposes, including in a drink. Tea leaves were also placed on burns, a remedy which science picked up and recommended as a help in small burns because of the tannin content of tea. Confucius (551–471 B.C.) also advised drinking tea leaves with boiling water as a way of solving the problem of diseases from polluted water.

Poets and other writers have written at length about the glorious beverage that is tea, but none as eloquently as a Chinese mystic of the Tang dynasty, 618–905, who said: "The first cup of tea moistens my lips and throat, the second shatters my loneliness, the third causes the wrongs of life to fade gently from my recollection, and the fourth purifies my soul, while the fifth lifts me to the realm of the unwinking gods!"

"Alcohol" Superstitions

THE MOST vicious superstition about alcohol is the one which looks upon a chronic alcoholic as a sinner, and moral weakling. He may be an inferior citizen but he is certainly not a scoundrel. Dr. Anton J. Carlton, professor emeritus of physiology, says: "Alcohol addicts come from all classes of society, rich and poor, educated and ignorant." He urges that they be given hospital care, not just for "sobering up," but for real treatment. An alcoholic fiend may be a very sick person in need of both psychological and social therapy. Alcoholic psychosis, a form of "insanity" in which there is some deterioration of brain cells, usually requires hospitalization.

Another dreadful superstition is that a child is born with a hereditary predilection for alcohol because the parent was intoxicated at the time of the child's conception, or that alcoholism runs in the family. Dr. Anna Roe of Yale's Section on Alcohol Studies reported in the *Quarterly Journal of Studies on Alcohol*, December, 1944, that "Children of alcoholic fathers or mothers do not inherit their parents' weakness for strong drink."

Another false notion about alcoholism is the popular belief that if an addict can be made to take a hypnotic "cure," he will be rid of the habit forever. While some results of hypnotism seem miraculous, it does not work with the same effectiveness in all cases. Hypnotic suggestion will make almost anyone stop drinking temporarily, but since compulsive drinking is usually a symptom of some deep-lying disturbance, the condition is not materially altered and may even get worse.

There are many popular superstitions about alcohol, such as: Give the juice of two lemons to sober up a drunken person; blow the foam of your glass of beer for good luck; an intoxicated person always tells the truth; it is unlucky to put liquor back into the flask or bottle; a floating cherry in a cocktail means reverses in business or love unless you quickly reverse something on your person, such as a hat, wrist-watch, etc.; alcoholism is incurable.

The records of old Babylon declare that beer was a common beverage as long ago as 5,000 B.C. The fermented brew played an even greater part in the ancient civilization of Egypt. The invention of ale or beer is ascribed to Isis, and was fermented from barley. The ancient Greeks were heavy wine drinkers and considered themselves superior to the Egyptians, who drank beer. The Romans looked upon beer as fit only for barbarians.

Mythology contains many references to gods of the grain or vine; Dionysus, the son of Zeus and Semele, was originally the god of vegetation, but later became god of the grape and its wine. He was worshipped with orgiastic rites and considered the leader of a wild rout of satyrs, maenads, and sileni. Among the Romans he was called Bacchus, and in the Eleusinian mysteries was hailed as Iacchus. Bromios was his poetic title, while Liknites and Dithyrambos referred to him as a child. Dionysus was also regarded as the bull god of Zagreus; the tree god, Dendrites; and as the wild Thracian deity, Sabazios. As the Cretan Lenaeus, he was the inventor of wine culture. Our comparatively modern equivalent is John Barleycorn.

Spilling Wine—Wine Superstitions

IN ANCIENT times it was believed that the juice of the grape was blood and contained a spirit. This conclusion was reached through the fact that wine was intoxicating and the soul or the spirit of the vine could be felt actually at work in the person who drank the wine. Thus, to spill wine was a superstitious warning, by the spirit, of an impending danger, therefore an unlucky gesture; the counter-magic gesture was to rub some of the spilled wine behind the ears, with the middle finger of the right hand. Since the area behind the ears, which was considered invulnerable—the belief is famous in folklore—and the right middle finger were used, the gesture is readily understood; the middle or phallic finger is the proper digit with which to undo evil influences.

But the superstition of spilling champagne—dreaded by gamblers and theatrical performers—originated in France in the 17th century. The best French wines came from the province of Champagne but were not sparkling wines as we know champagne today. The accidental discovery of this wine by a monk gave rise to a new superstition. This monk used stoppers of cork instead of the customary leaky flax wad, and the carbonic acid generated in the sealed bottles produced the sparkle. But superstitious people attributed this sparkle to the devil and the manufacture of the new wine was forbidden. It was made surreptitiously, however, and eventually came into royal favor and was known as the wine of kings and the king of wines. Among the ignorant, however, the superstition persisted. Even the gamblers and actors who used the wine, especially to celebrate a great event, were not too sure about the "sparkle," and to be on the safe side, whenever any was spilled they made the gesture of touching the ear with the wine. And so today, among these same people, and others too, when champagne is spilled, the ear is touched with it and a wish is made, which is expected to come true.

That Whiskey Is Good for Snake Bite

ALMOST the world over, it is a superstitious belief that whiskey is an antidote for a venomous snake bite. Though misguided persons still place great faith in this treatment, authorities agree that all the whiskey does for the victim is to effect a temporary state of well-being and quiet his nerves.

Early American colonizers of the west, where snakes abounded, brought along Old World superstitions and old wives' cures with which to preserve life and health in the absence of medical aid. They administered whiskey to both human beings and animals for snake bite. Some victims survived, but most of them died.

Alcohol is actually dangerous as a remedy in that it speeds up the circulation of the blood, which hastens the spread of the venom through the body; for this reason whiskey should never be used.

The reason some persons recover from snake bite after drinking alcohol is because the bite was not from a poisonous reptile in the first place. In such cases, the whiskey or other hard liquor alleviates the nervous shock, and it is then assumed that it also cured the bite.

"Smoke" and "Tobacco" Superstitions

WHEN a smoke-ring is wafted, it is generally an occasion for ring-snatching by the smoker. Frequently, too, a non-smoker reaches out to put his finger through it before it loses its shape and dissipates into thin air. A wish is made at such a time or a smile or air of serenity reflects the pleasant mental attitude of the participants. Little does modern man realize that this is a superstitious gesture which is as old as smoke. In the main the gesture is a phallic symbol and implies fertility.

Early and ancient peoples everywhere employed smoke and smoking for superstitious reasons. When a human or animal sacrifice was offered to the gods, either to seek favors or to give thanks for them, the smoke from the burning victim had to rise upward. This was an unmistakable sign that the gods were pleased and accepted their wishes graciously.

From the smoke of human and animal sacrifice to smoking the native cigar or pipe, there is but a step. When the peace-breathing calumet was born, it was fringed with eagle's quills, that powerful solar bird which defies the elements and builds its nest on the highest peak. There is also a war calumet, but it is made differently.

When the Incas smoked, they puffed first to the sky and next to each corner of the earth, for good luck. The Sioux Indians present the stem to the north, south, east, and west, and then to the sun above their heads, meanwhile pronouncing "How-how-how!", and drawing a whiff or two. After the pipe is charged and lighted, it is considered an evil omen for anyone to speak until the chief has drawn the smoke through it. Should anyone break the silence, the pipe is immediately dropped. Their superstition is such that they would not dare to use it again.

Indians always pass everything to the left. The principal chief in the ring faces east to the sunrise and hands the pipe to the man at his left, thus going "sunwise." If anyone refused to smoke the pipe when it came his turn, it was considered worse than an insult, for disaster would be visited upon the whole tribe.

The pipe was often used to cast lots, or select a man for a special or dangerous mission. It was passed from one hand to another with regularity, and the man in whose hands it went out was the person indicated by the medicine-man for the task.

There are all kinds of superstitions about tobacco and smoking. Some of them are: it is unlucky to be offered a broken cigar; it is a sign of trouble if in smoking the cigar burns unevenly down one side; it is unlucky to light your cigar from another; if you are smoking a cigarette and it keeps going out, it is a sign that you are in love, and not in vain; it is said by old tobacco chewers that it is unlucky to refuse a cud to anyone asking for it; lighting a pipe from the fireplace is considered unlucky; if the smoker sends forth a ring of smoke, catches it, puts it in his pocket, he will have money inside of a day; chewing tobacco is believed to act as a disinfectant and to prevent disease; a tobacco leaf is thought to be a cure for carbuncle; to relight your cigar three times is a bad omen; tobacco burned as incense is believed to keep evil influences away. Little bags of fine tobacco are sometimes worn about the neck to ward off infections and headaches, toothaches, and so forth.

Tobacco was used in medicine in various ways. The leaves were chewed by medicine men until they were soft and pliable, then formed into a poultice and bound firmly to the affected area. The medical lore of the American Indians is still a part of the folkways today. During the plague, 1664-1665, tobacco chewing became a part of the English social life. The passing of the plague did not end the fad, for men, women and children kept chewing it for a long time.

Probably no article has produced so much literature as tobacco. 4,000 volumes in twenty languages, all on the lore of tobacco, were recently the gift of George Arents, Jr., to the New York Public Library. The history of tobacco is traced from the time of the crude pipe of the Maya Indians to the cellophane-wrapped cigarettes. What is there in tobacco to write so much about? Because it concerns spiritual things, and expresses feelings in a spiritual way. Tobacco-smoking is quite obviously an offshoot of early man's smoke superstitions, and later incense burning. The variant shapes and hues of smoke and its odor send away or call forth supernatural forces to free man of his fears or to sustain him in his faith.

Sir Walter Raleigh is said to have brought smoking to the white man, but he in no sense invented it. Nor were the Indians the first people to discover the reactions of smoking upon the human brain. Snuff was a tobacco powder to be inhaled through the nose. It was believed to expel the evil which might have run into the head.

Many famous women were users of tobacco in one of its varied forms. The Dowager Empress of Russia, the Queen of Rumania, the Queen Regent of Spain, the Queen of Italy, and the Queen of Portugal, as well as two wives of United States Presidents, Zachary Taylor and Andrew Jackson—all were habitual smokers of the pipe and joined in with their husbands for an after-dinner smoke.

Among civilized races smoking of one kind or another is thousands of years older than tobacco. It is known that the Greeks inhaled the fumes of coltsfoot to relieve asthma. It seems fairly certain that tobacco was known in Spain several years before it was known in England. Its first carrier was probably Francesco Hernandez, a physician, who brought its plants to show them to Philip the Second. About the same time, Jean Nicot is said to have bought some tobacco seed in Lisbon and to have sent it to the Grand Prior of France, after whom it was named "*Herbe du Grand Prieur*." Nicot's own name became nicotiana and nicotine.

It is curious that "tobacco" was not originally the herb, but the pipe. The nomenclature of smoking is somewhat confused. "Cigar" is probably derived from the Spanish verb cigarar, to roll; if so, it was again the medium, not the substance, which determined the name. In Cuba, cigars are still called *tabacos*.

Many smokers confuse the smoke stain with nicotine, whereas it is mostly tar. Approximately nine-tenths of the nicotine is burned up in smoking, but it is the other one-tenth, absorbed into the blood from the lungs, which interests doctors. Studies are still being seriously conducted to remove the false notions and beliefs about tobacco going the rounds daily.

"Funeral Feast" and "Funeral" Superstitions

THE FEAR OF DEATH developed strange customs and beliefs in ancient and medieval times. Hundreds of these same superstitious notions are still indulged in by modern people everywhere. Many young people are told by parents and others that they should never point at carriages or automobiles of a funeral procession, unless they turn their backs to it. Many other such morbid warnings serve only to continue superstitious fears of death.

Funeral feasts, or "wakes," are ancient practices and are by no means restricted to Irish people, as some suppose. The generous imbibing of liquor which goes on at most wakes was once believed essential. Each drop of the spirit of the wine or other alcoholic beverage was supposed to assist the deceased in making his way to the spirit world, and to wash away his sins. Watching the corpse is a custom which also goes back to the primitive notion that evil spirits or some such agents of the invisible world might snatch away the body the moment it was left alone and unprotected. There are many ways and means to forestall all manner of evil, among them singing, toasting loudly, swapping jokes and laughing heartily. These jollities were traditional activities to give the corpse the proper send-off into the Great Beyond. Frequently the body of the deceased was propped up to play silent host at his last party.

Other foolish notions include the following: a pregnant woman should not attend a funeral lest the life of her unborn child be endangered; never carry a baby in a funeral procession or attend a funeral service with it before it is a year old, else it will die; a bride or bridegroom will be unlucky in marriage if anything that suggests death, such as a funeral procession, is met on the way to church; to dream of marriage indicates that you will attend a funeral; if a strange black dog is seen by those attending a funeral, another member of the family will die; to keep the gloves which have been worn by a pall-bearer will bring bad luck.

The Greeks and Romans thought that a house wherein a death had occurred was impure and dangerous, so they placed a bough at the door to warn the passers-by. The black and white crepe on the door of the deceased is a survival of this custom. The formality of leading the horse of a dead warrior to the grave is the result of an old superstition that the soul of the warrior rides into the other world on the back of his horse. Originally the horse was buried with him.

CHAPTER 12

Fashion by Folklore

"Sewing" Superstitions

SEWING SUPERSTITIONS come to us from the days when clothes were made at home, and every girl had to learn how to sew in order to have something to wear. In fact, at one time women had to spin the cloth as well as do the sewing.

Perhaps the leading superstition in regard to making a garment is never to begin one on Friday or there will be bad luck for the wearer. As with most superstitions, there is a way to get around this, which is that if the article of clothing is started on Friday, and completed the same day, no hard luck will befall. This superstitious belief does not affect the industrial or commercial "garment centers" as the taboo applies only to the home-made variety of clothes. Neither does it apply to other seamstresses or dressmakers who make their living by sewing.

However, everyone that sews, whether to make her own clothes, or as a trade, observes many superstitions connected with pins, needles, scissors, buttons and other items used in sewing.

Among these superstitions are: to sew anything new on an old garment brings bad luck; when the thread knots while sewing it is a sign of a quarrel; to burn a hole in a dress being made is bad luck for the sewer and wearer; if one is forced to begin a dress on Friday, and does not finish it before the next day begins, it will never be done on time for whatever occasion it is made; if, however, it should be ready on time, the dress will be an unlucky one for the wearer; sewing on Sunday is generally taboo, and to some, Saturday is also an unpropitious day; it is unlucky to lose a thimble; to drop a needle is a sign of good luck unless it sticks into the floor, when the opposite may be expected; it is unlucky to break a needle; some think the garment in which the needle has been broken will never be worn by the person for whom it is being made, since it means death; on the other hand, there is a more cheerful notion in regard to a broken needle which decrees that the wearer of the dress in which the needle broke will be kissed in it;

to drop a pair of scissors is unlucky but if one places the foot on them before picking them up, the evil can be averted; two pairs of scissors should never be crossed, but if they are, they must be uncrossed counter-clockwise; a single pair of scissors should not rest open, that is, with the blades apart forming a cross, as this signifies crosses or ill luck for the wearer.

> "If you mend your clothes on your back,
>   You will live much money to lack."

This bit of doggerel was heard in ancient households and is almost as popular today. The notion here is that if one sews or mends a garment one is wearing, or has another do it for her, it sews up the brains, and will drive the wearer mad, unless a piece of thread is held between the teeth. The symbolism here is that the process of sewing will not reach the top of the head. Many persons have seen seamstresses and dressmakers fitting or altering garments with a bit of thread in their mouths, but never knew why. This superstition is almost universal, each nation or race having an individual reason for it. Of course, many professional dressmakers and tailors do not abide by this ancient belief, but the majority bite on a string, rather than take a chance of bad luck for themselves or the customer.

Milliners' Superstitions

IF THE FIRST customer of the day tries on a hat and goes away without buying it, it is often a matter of great concern to the superstitious milliner or saleswoman, because to her it means that it will be a bad day for business. This superstitious attitude goes back to the idea of "sympathetic magic" or "like with like," which, in this case, means that having lost the sale of a hat to the first customer, the rest of the day will be poor in sales, unless some form of countercharm is used.

And so to remove the chance of bad luck, or the curse left behind by the first customer, the countermagic formula is to expectorate into the hat. The implication of this is that the customer who failed to buy the hat possessed the Evil Eye; or, since evil doers are believed to reside in hair, she may have transferred them from her head into the hat, so the saliva acts as a cleanser of this evil.

Even in large modern cities today, many men and women blow a gentle spray of saliva into their new hats for good luck. This is in line with the milliner's countercharm to dispose of the evil ones who might have lodged themselves in a hat at some time or other.

There is an old superstition that if a woman, playfully or otherwise, puts a man's hat on her head, the man has the right to kiss her. According to an old formula, this is a peace offering, so that any evil doers in the man's hat will not move into the woman's hair. The kiss negates the evil doings of supernatural beings whose favorite haunts are heads of hair, and who use hats as a means of transportation.

That a Garment Worn Wrong Side Out Brings Good Luck

A COMMON superstition everywhere is that to put on a garment wrong side out accidentally, and to wear it that way, means good luck for the whole day.

This belief comes down to us through various traditional paths, and most of them start from mourning customs of widely distributed peoples, both primitive and civilized. Death, with many peoples, was believed caused not only by tribal or personal negligence, but was also attributed to the work of unseen evil spirits. Death itself was believed contagious.

Early man knew nothing of what caused diseases nor what brought about death, and so he invented all sorts of countermagic gestures and formulas to forestall these calamities. Primitive man's method of averting death was often by means of the native device of affecting a disguise to confuse the evil spirits who were held responsible for the loss of a friend or relative. It was feared that these spirits were in quest of more victims until the body of the deceased was disposed of. And so man thought that in a strange garb he would not be recognized by the demons, and thereby escape the same fate.

Originally, however, the garment was not only worn purposely wrong side out, but put on backwards as well. Weird designs were smeared or painted on the body itself for the purpose of scaring the evil doers until the funeral ceremonies were over.

These primitive customs of affecting a disguise led to mourning customs the world over. Various types and colors are worn by different peoples for long or short periods to hide or disguise the mourner. The modern mourning veil is a form of hiding device of early times, although the wearer little knows the original intention for wearing it.

Any mourning apparel is symbolically a reminder that one has been near a dead body. It was formally the signal to others to keep at a distance for measures of personal safety. Many mourning customs prevented the closest relatives of the departed from appearing in public, except for strict necessities. Mourners were expected to refrain from wearing ornaments or jewels of any kind, and were not supposed to participate in any activities, particularly gay functions. All these restrictions are related to the ancient idea that to be close to persons during the mourning period endangered others through contagion.

As the centuries wore on, the accidental wearing of a garment wrong side out was believed a warning from a protective spirit, guardian or angel, supposed to reside on the right side of each individual. The article of clothing on the wrong side is a suggestion that an impending evil might have befallen the person, but the protective disguise will bring good luck instead. This good fortune may be helped by making a wish which is expected to come true, because the air has been cleared of all evil doers by means of the disguise which has removed all interference.

Linked with the primitive thought of contagion, there is the current superstition that to try on anyone's mourning clothes is a sign of death. This is believed by colored and white people alike, and is prevalent among African natives and others. The giving away of mourning clothes when they are no longer needed is next to impossible, because of the primitive contagion taboo, which still means death or other misfortune to come.

Modern Triangular Kerchief, Old Superstitious Custom

STRANGE AS IT may seem, the quite recent fashion in the Western world of wearing a triangular kerchief over the head is a very ancient style which was originally designed as a protective head covering, using the symbolic triangle. There was the idea, among many peoples, that a decent woman should never be seen in public, especially outdoors, without a protective covering for her hair, because her crowning glory was a source of envy to evil beings who tried to get into her hair and harm her.

Although it never occurs to the wearer of a triangular kerchief today, there was a definite reason for this three-cornered pattern. However, just as it often is today, the kerchief was really a square cloth, folded diagonally to make a triangle. The square cloth in itself was highly protective as a basic pattern, representing the earthly four, or square-symbol. When folded in two crosswise, it formed a triangle, a mystic, powerful symbol and talisman that protected the wearer's hair.

The square-symbol was used by men to stand on during certain legal and other formalities, but for women, it appeared on their heads.

Likewise, the common everyday hair net or snood also started from the notion that a woman's hair was the nesting place for evil doers. Kerchiefs and snoods were used as protections mostly outdoors, but many women wore head coverings indoors, especially on festive occasions, when these same supernatural naughty beings, envious of the joys of humans, would be up to mischief. The net-like skull cap worn by an ancient aristocratic lady was in reality a trap to catch the mischievous imps, so that they could not go any farther and settle in my lady's hair.

The Arab believed in supernatural beings which he called Jinn—and still does, for that matter. These Jinn were supposed to be eager to get into women's long hair, their favorite haunt. From time immemorial, women of the East, when outdoors and immediately after sunset, wore some kind of head covering to protect their hair, because of the old superstitious belief that the invisible Jinn goes seeking a woman's hair in the dark. The modern expression, "He gets in my hair" applies to a person who is annoying, or who disturbs one unnecessarily, the original implication of which is rooted in Arabian folklore.

In old Russia, only a shameless woman would dare appear in public with her hair uncovered. Peasant women, young and old, wore the *babooshka platok*—grandmother's kerchief—which gypsies have popularized all over the world.

The fact that hair crackled was interpreted also as a sign that evil entities inhabited a woman's tresses, and manifested themselves that way. Knowing nothing of electricity, ancient peoples believed these crackling noises were signs of the anger of the evil ones, providing another reason for head coverings of various kinds.

Bad Luck to Place Hat on Bed

THE OFT-USED PHRASE "He gets in my hair" is just one version of the hat superstition. The ancients believed the hair often harbored evil spirits who manifested their presence, on occasion, by making a crackling noise; while in darkness both a fiery star and a crackling noise gave evidence of their dangerous selves!

Because certain evil spirits or demons were believed mischievously inclined to play tricks only at night and outdoors, by hiding in women's long tresses, we had the custom of wearing something over the hair, often in the form of a net skull cap, so as to catch the evil pranksters and get them all tangled up. Thus, the saying "he gets in my hair" which implies an individual who is annoying and disturbing, in keeping with the wicked attributes of evil-doers of other days.

Many people will never place a hat on a bed. This belief stems from the Orient and Near East where a turban or headgear of any kind is never supposed to be placed where another person's head may rest lest the owner of the hat might have the Evil Eye, always a great danger. By the same token the hat may cast a spell through the transference of its evil inhabitants, apt to change domicile at the least provocation.

Another superstitious belief is that placing a hat on a bed is followed by an altercation which may end the friendship between two persons, and perhaps involve their entire families. This belief is indulged in because evil spirits, like evil beings in general, are thought to have wicked tongues and may, if the mood moves them, tell all the secrets of their former host. Moreover, if the owner were a thief or a murderer, his characteristics may be inherited together with the new evil tenants.

The superstitious conclusions of the ancients were in reality based on a misinterpretation of a reasonably known fact. Scientifically speaking, here is what really happens. There is static electricity in the hair and when combed a crackling noise results as a spark jumps the gap between the hair and the comb—which has nothing to do with spirits or headgear itself.

Sanitarily speaking, the basic reason for the hat or headgear taboo was to keep vermin where they belonged—if such pests belong anywhere!

Turning One's Cap Front to Back for Good Luck

TURNING THINGS around, such as a woman's apron, a man's cap, or pulling a pocket inside out, is done very often by superstitious persons of today to bring about a change of luck, or to avoid an unpleasant situation that seems almost certain to take place.

To turn a cap or hat from front to back is a symbolic gesture to bring about a reverse action, or change the order of things, especially for warding off bad luck and making it good instead. For instance, to see a black cat is considered a bad omen by many, but turning one's hat around, even for a few moments, will prevent any misfortune from happening. Aprons and pockets will serve as well.

Doing something in reverse to counteract another action, is after all, not very far removed from the law of physics that opposites create attraction. This law, of course, was not known to the ancients, but they must have sensed that there was a dual law of nature that ordained that action and reaction are equal and opposite.

They showed this instinctive knowledge in their strong impulse of self-guidance, which was universal in scope. This same instinct of trying to equalize the positive and negative is found among all peoples, regardless of their ever having been in contact with one another.

The instinctive concept of a hidden potential power everywhere and in everything was expressed in symbols, or crude replicas of objects and beings, and was employed to reverse or counteract potential evil. Turning something around, such as a hat or cap, is the modern form of countermagic which is directly descended from similar measures used since the beginning of history. However, primitive minds did not discriminate between animate and inanimate objects, and believed both had innate good or evil powers.

"Glove" Superstitions

AMONG MANY glove superstitions, the outstanding one today is that when a glove is dropped accidentally, it should be picked up by another person, which will mean a pleasant surprise for the one who dropped it. If it is picked up by the one who drops it, however, it invites a disappointment or something else of an unpleasant nature. The glove, therefore, should be left just where it falls, if no one is around to pick it up, to prevent anything disagreeable from taking place.

There is also the superstition that when a person drops a glove and it is picked up by another individual, the dropper may make a wish and expect it to come true. Picking up the glove by someone familiar with the superstition, makes it work better. In this case, the one who picks up the glove will know enough to say, "I hope you have that pleasant surprise," or "I hope you get your wish." These measures further remove the possibility of a disappointment or a quarrel which the act of dropping a glove might cause.

This type of superstition implies that an inanimate object has its own reason for falling. In early times, the unexpected fall of anything was always witnessed with foreboding, so that the feeling of some trouble about to befall when a glove is accidentally dropped is one that has been carried over from those days when it was believed that everything and anything possessed a "spirit" of its own with which to do good or evil.

Symbolically, gloves, like flowers and jewels, speak a language of legends and imagery which keep pace with advancing social conditions of each country. There is no doubt that, originally, the glove was worn for protection from cold. It also served to protect the fingers when handling hot food, before the advent of knives and forks. It is a matter of archeological record that gloves, (that is, a very crude form of covering for the hands), were worn by cave dwellers in Southern France thousands of years ago.

Leather gloves were used at a very early period in war and hunting, but women did not wear them until 1300 A.D. when the glove-making industry begin.

Since Biblical days, gloves have been given as a pledge, and the practice survives in the Orient. Made of pure linen, the glove was a token of the stainless purity of the early Bishops, at a time when no layman dared clothe his hands when in the presence of the clergy. Kings and chieftains also had the privilege of wearing gloves as a badge of state, while they were denied to underlings.

There are a great many symbolic expressions attached to the glove. For instance, one "throws down the glove," or flips it, as a challenge. To "bite one's glove" is a sign of hostility. "An iron hand in a velvet glove" indicates hidden strength or cruelty. To "handle with kid gloves" means to use tact. There are hundreds of others.

We find that gloves were symbols of death when worn on the hands of a victorious army. They were symbols of rank and authority on the hands of kings, who *bequeathed* their gloves to the heir of the throne.

A very ancient custom that has survived is to give gloves as a forfeit, or "glove money." Originally the connection between gloves and forfeits was for stolen kisses. If a girl saw a man whom she liked sleeping, and kissed him before he woke up, he had to give her a pair of gloves.

In grandmother's day, a young lady was taught that the only gifts she might accept from a man were gloves and flowers. Today, as in olden times, when a woman makes a bet with a man, the wager is generally a pair of gloves. Gloves were the customary gifts between lovers and friends. To give a glove represented offering the hand in friendship, and therefore a glove became a mascot. Gloves still retain, in the best sense, associations of good fortune and pleasant thoughts.

The path of centuries has been strewn with a trail of romantic episodes in which women have made coquettish use of the glove to attract attention to themselves, or to get a closer view of some handsome charmer. By dropping a glove in his presence, it served as an introduction, from which milady could go on with her flirtatious designs.

In days when a young lady had to be under the watchful eye of a chaperone, especially if she were being courted, many a couple made use of the language of the glove which was devised to carry on a surreptitious conversation, either in the presence of the chaperone, or, if she were too wise, when she turned her back.

With numerous variations, the language of the glove was somewhat as follows:

"I love you," dropping both gloves.

"Indifference," drawing glove half way on the left hand.

"I wish to be rid of you," biting the tips.

"No," clenching glove, rolled up in right hand.

"Yes," clenching, rolled up in left hand.

"I wish acquaintance," holding tips downward.

"Do you love me?" left glove on with thumb uncovered.

"Kiss me," right glove on with thumb exposed.

"I am shocked," striking glove over the hand.

"Follow me," striking glove over the shoulder.

"I love another," striking chin with glove.

"I am engaged," tossing glove up gently.

"I hate you," turning glove inside out.

"I am vexed," putting gloves away.

"We are watched," twirling them around the fingers.

"Umbrella" Superstitions

FEW REALIZE the innocent origin of one of our commonest superstitions, that to open an umbrella in the house will bring bad luck and disappointment. It came from the Old World, where umbrellas were made to open by means of a stiff clumsy spring, which was dangerous if handled carelessly by grown-ups and youngsters alike. When this umbrella was opened suddenly, too close to a person or object indoors it would invariably hurt somebody or break something. Frequently following such a mishap, there was not only damage, but the accident provoked unpleasant words and even a serious quarrel,—bad luck indeed.

That carrying an umbrella will ward off rain is another superstitious attitude which only works, of course, when the weather is fine. This belief is a hangover from the days when it was believed that the reverse of what was expected to happen would take place, such as in the interpretation of dreams, to cite a good example.

There are dozens of superstitions pertaining to the umbrella, indoors and outdoors. Many of these have come down to us from the "Language of the Umbrella (or Parasol)" which was evolved in the days when a lady was obliged to have an attendant or chaperone when she appeared in public. There was also a "Language of the Fan" and "of the Glove," and all of these sign languages were used to carry on a love affair or flirtation behind the chaperone's back.

The word "umbrella" is a western word, taken from the Italian, *ombrella*, meaning "little shade." The word parasol is derived from the Italian, *parare*, meaning to ward off or to parry, and *sole*, sun. Though sunshades and parasols were known in antiquity, it was not until the end of the 18th century that this device was adapted to waterproofing, as a protection against rain.

Umbrella-like objects of all sorts were used as early as the 11th century, B.C., in China, Babylon, Egypt and elsewhere. They were carried in ancient Greek ceremonial and sacred processions. The Jews, in observing the Feast of Tabernacles, employed a similar overhead covering.

In the East, the umbrella has been part of the insignia of state and power since early times. It was evolved from the "canopy of state" and both canopy and umbrella are used in ceremonials. The umbrella is a Hindu mascot of great power, believed to bring universal good fortune, and venerated as one of the Eight Glorious Emblems of India —similar to the western Eight Beatitudes. The warlike Mahratra princes of old used to be styled, "Lords of the Umbrella."

Umbrellas used to be made with the lines of the double-cross, or eight ribs, symbolic of the sun's travels over the four points of the compass,—but the cross was doubled for good measure. Incidentally, "double-cross" which in those days implied the blessings of good fortune, has degenerated to mean the opposite in America today.

The umbrella was supposed to protect royal heads and chiefs, not so much from the hot sun or the rain as from the forces that might be let loose by evil spirits, who were jealous and envious of great personages, and would do them harm. It is easy to understand that in regions where the sun's heat is very intense, its cruel rays should be regarded as possessing hateful spirits; anything that shaded these rays was considered "good luck," that brought immunity from harm to those under the umbrella.

After being an exclusive privilege of monarchs and members of religious orders, the umbrella was finally permitted to "commoners." It was first used by women, and later by horsemen, who fastened the handle to one of their thighs.

A modern evolution of the umbrella or parasol is the parachute.

Shoe-Throwing Superstitions

IN THE THROWING of an old shoe after the happy couple as they leave on their honeymoon, traditions of an astonishing antiquity are renewed. Old shoes are always to be seen, found, encountered or have thrown after one. As an old charm rhyme puts it:

> For this thou shalt from all things seek
> Marrow of mirth and laughter;
> And whereso'er thou move, Good Luck
> Shall throw her old shoe after.

From very early times, shoes have been linked with fertility. In China, for instance, a childless woman goes to the shrine of the Mother Goddess and borrows one of her votive shoes, promising that, once the goddess has granted her petition, she will return another shoe to the shrine.

Ages ago the placing of a shoe on a tract of land was a symbol of ownership. To close a contract for a land purchase, the ancient Assyrians and Hebrews handed a sandal to the buyer.

From these ancient traditions and practices evolved the custom of throwing an old shoe after the bride, symbolizing the forfeiture of all right over their daughter by the parents. Among the Anglo-Saxons, the father gave the bride's shoe to the future husband, who touched her on the head or nape of the neck with it to show his authority. A bridegroom used to hang a slipper in a conspicuous place in the house for the same reason.

In many countries it is believed that leather will keep evil spirits away. In India, an old shoe turned upside down on the roof of a new house assures the married couple prosperity and wards off evil influences. In Scotland and in Ireland, old shoes were thrown not only at bride and groom, but at anyone who started on a new venture by way of wishing him success.

Authorities differ as to the origin of the throwing of shoes at weddings, but they agree that the real significance of the custom has always been associated with power, ownership and good luck. It is also generally accepted that the shoe, representing the foot, is a phallic symbol and as such is potentially a lucky charm, especially for a new venture in matrimony.

That Rubber Shoes or Soles Indoors Are Dangerous to Health

MANY PERSONS in America believe that if rubbers are worn indoors it will cause eye trouble. Another idea is that any kind of rubber on the feet—rubber heels, soles or overshoes—while in the house, will cause disease and fever, and ruin the eyesight generally. Only a few years ago a survey showed that nearly one-third of the high school seniors and college freshmen, plus thirteen per cent of the adults interviewed, believed this superstition.

No doubt the fear of wearing rubbers in the house is due to the fact that when they are kept on for a long time, the feet perspire. Undue perspiration is generally feared because of its association with the possibility of chills; chills are usually followed by fever which is sometimes the first stage of a more serious ailment. It is well known, too, that a predisposition to eye trouble is apt to become a fact after a severe siege of fever or disease.

For this reason, when parents forbade their children to wear rubbers indoors with the admonition that it would make them ill, it no doubt contributed greatly to building up the superstition. Of course there is no truth in the belief. It is just another instance of a popular misconception,—one that keeps persons from wearing types of shoes with rubber soles and heels indoors that they would find both economical and comfortable.

It is interesting to note that the rubber taboo is a comparatively modern superstition. Rubber was first introduced in America, in the form of rubberized clothing, at the beginning of the 19th century, but with little success then. The discovery of vulcanizing was made by Charles Goodyear, an American inventor, in 1839, who perfected the processing of natural rubber. The first rubber heels were made in Lowell, Massachusetts, by Humphrey O'Sullivan, who obtained a patent for the invention on January 24, 1899.

"Comb" Superstitions

COMBS, as objects of magic, have figured in primitive customs, beliefs and superstitions. They were supposed to comb out evil influences, and were considered so important that they were used as offerings to pagan gods. In the march of history, combs were worn as symbols of royalty and romance, and have played other important rôles in the evolution of man's culture.

We are greatly indebted to the efforts of archeologists of many lands whose findings have enriched museums with rare collections of combs belonging to various peoples at various times. They bridge many gaps in our knowledge of the progress of civilization. For example, in the British Museum in London, there is one of the finest collections of combs in the world. Among them are combs made of yew wood, dating back to the Stone Age. There is a carved bone comb of Egyptian origin, an ancient Hellenic comb of bronze, and an iron comb from County West Meath, Eire.

These combs show the variety of material that has been employed in making them, in addition to ivory which was used for thousands of years. In America the combs of Stone Age Indians were made from the horns of animals.

The diversity of shapes, materials and uses of the comb—aside from its utilitarian use—have made it a rich subject for superstitions, and many of these are regarded with great seriousness even at the present time. For instance, dropping a comb is considered very unlucky; and when professional persons, such as singers and actors, let one fall accidentally, they walk around it three times, making a sunwise circle, before picking it up. If the comb is dropped in a dressing-room before a performance or on opening night, it is considered especially bad luck. Another countercharm measure to offset the harm is to step on the comb with the right foot, and make a wish. A small spray of saliva is also considered efficacious.

To the superstitious, dropping a comb means various misfortunes, such as a disappointment, a quarrel, or losses. To some, however, it signifies that company is coming. To use a dead man's comb will make one bald. If a comb falls behind one, there will be a death in the family.

A modern superstition is that a girl must never let a man carry her comb in his pocket if she wants him to be interested in her. It is bad luck for a woman to go to bed with a comb in her hair. Anyone who counts the teeth in a comb will lose his own teeth, or will attract as many disappointments. One should never burn a comb. One should never pick up a comb he has dropped. He should either let it lie, or have someone else pick it up and then the one who dropped it must make a wish.

In ancient Rome, a bride's hair, like that of a high-caste Hindu woman about to give birth to a child, was ceremonially parted. The hair was believed to be a favorite haunt of jealous spirits who might cause trouble, particularly on such occasions. To part the bride's hair for the wedding, the Romans used a blunt spearhead, called the "bachelor's spear." This custom may have originated in the remote past when an old disused spear was the handiest tool available for arranging the hair. This strange comb is another example of the ancient belief in the magical property of iron to combat evil spirits during a dangerous time.

A similar superstition is to be found in Italy today, where the bride and bridegroom, if superstitious, will not allow themselves to come in contact with certain articles such as combs and scissors, when they are exchanging gifts, as they are believed to be the hide-out of witches and therefore taboo at such times.

In comb-lore there is often a water spirit, or mermaid, who makes use of the comb in her hair when she wants to produce a flood, or in some other way show her anger toward human beings. On the other hand, combs have a favored place in other stories, such as when the worshippers of Venus, wishing to win her approval and secure her blessings, brought combs to her shrine.

Among the Arabs and other Orientals, the comb was an amulet which guarded against the Evil Eye. They believed that the hair was a place where evil spirits took refuge, and whose presence was indicated by the crackling noise which was their way of showing resentment when the teeth of the comb came in contact with them to oust them.

The late eminent American anthropologist, Franz Boas, has this to say about combs: "It is not only language that was carried by migrations all over the world; it is easy to show that inventions and ideas were carried from one area to another, partly by migration, partly by cultural contact. One of the most striking examples is found in the distribution of folk tales. The European folk tale of the couple that escaped a pursuing monster by throwing backwards a number of objects which were transformed into obstacles, is well known all over Europe. A comb thrown down becomes an impenetrable thicket, a whetstone an insurmountable mountain, a small amount of oil an extensive lake; all of which detain the pursuer. This complicated story containing all the elements mentioned is found not only all over Europe, but all over the Asiatic continent and also in north-western America reaching as far as California, and eastward even in Greenland and Nova Scotia. In more recent times we find that the most isolated tribes of South America tell tales which were carried by Negro slaves to the coast of Brazil."

"Mourning" Superstitions

IN EARLY TIMES it was believed that death was caused by personal neglect of some kind, that evil spirits wedged themselves into the body and caused the fatality, and even that death was contagious. Therefore, anyone who had been close to the corpse, such as the immediate members of the deceased's family, were to be marked in some obvious way so that they might not pass the danger on to others by too close contact. Early identification marks were scars, disorderly appearance, uncombed hair, or a particular color of clothes. This latter mark is the origin of mourning clothes popular today.

The custom of wearing black clothes, formerly known as widow's weeds, is practically a thing of the past, at least in America. However, a modified form of mourning is still in effect with many superstitions attached to it, depending upon the traditional background of race, creed, and nationality.

Some of the most familiar mourning superstitions are: when going into mourning it is lucky to give away your colored clothes; do not wear mourning beyond the second year or you invite another tragedy in your life; it is bad luck to wear gold ornaments with mourning; never accept as a gift an article of mourning, for if you do, fate will quickly arrange for you to be present at another funeral of someone dear to you; it is unlucky to keep black-edged writing paper in the house after the period of mourning; mourning gloves must be made of cotton or else one death will follow another until your home is empty; if you wear something blue after taking off mourning you will stay out of mourning for several years, but if you put on red, you will be in mourning again soon; if you kiss a friend through a mourning veil you will soon see him or her in mourning.

White is the color of mourning in China and Japan; the Egyptians and the Burmese wear yellow. In parts of South Africa, the mourning color is red; in Ethiopia, light brown; Syria and Armenia, violet; in Iran, sky blue. To the Iranians, blue signifies that their late beloved has gone to the beautiful places beyond the sky.

Arabian women sometimes still stain their hands and feet with indigo for eight days. During that time they refuse to drink milk because its hue does not harmonize with their state of mental gloom. Indians of North and South America painted their faces and bodies as a sign of mourning and some tribes made incisions on their arms and legs in the belief that grief is internal. The only way to be rid of it was to provide an outlet through which it could escape.

In many European countries including France, a widow is dressed in solid black for the remainder of her life. Even the small children in the family wear black.

Thirty years ago or so in America, full mourning was worn for a year, and black-and-white for six months. The fashion was in general practice but has waned steadily since then. Today, with black a constant style item, mourning wear can readily be assembled for a funeral. Thereafter, a reasonable period of conservative dress is observed during which dark blue and brown are worn.

CHAPTER 13

Eye of the Gods

The Opal, Lucky and Unlucky Jewel

THE COMPARATIVELY modern superstition that the opal brings misfortune to its owner is probably due to a careless reading of Sir Walter Scott's novel (1829) "Anne of Geierstein," which featured the opal as an enchanted gem, the soul of which was bound up with that of Lady Hermione, the heroine of an old legend. It is generally assumed that Scott did not intend to convey the idea that the opal was unlucky. The plot is a story within a story, derived from an old legendary tale in which an old German baron, a returned Crusader from the East, bartered his soul for a most magnificent opal. At first it works magic for him, but after a while, he suffers a tragic death.

The opal is said to be a lucky gem for those born in October. But there is a condition attached, as only those who are pure of heart and of good intentions can expect an opal's traditional protection.

Formerly, the opal was thought to possess great virtues as a talisman, a belief that still exists among Orientals and others, today. In keeping with the superstitious idea of the East, the opal was supposed to be alive, and endowed with a soul which was attuned to that of its wearer. It expressed gaiety by sparkling, or anger by shooting out red gleams.

As far back as the fourteenth century, the opal was unfavorably associated with the Black Death, particularly in Venice, Italy. Then it was believed that the opal marked its owner's death from the plague by emitting fiery hues for a few seconds. It grew dull the moment its owner passed away.

There is also the superstition that the opal was dangerous to the eyesight, based on a legend that seems to have had its origin in Scandinavian mythology. A Norse god fashioned gems, believed to be opals, from the eyes of children. The superstitious notion that opals dimmed the eyes, or made one blind, persisted for centuries. Others believed that opals bestowed the gift of invisibility, and for a time, only thieves were said to own them.

In the Middle Ages, the brilliant tongue of fire that burns in the true opal was regarded as ocular evidence of demoniac occupancy.

In reality, the opal is literally cracked. Minute cavities produce the refraction of light in the gem and make it radiant, as well as extremely delicate and breakable. Because the opal contains an unevenly distributed amount of water, it may break into pieces with a change of temperature. Lapidaries agree, however, that it would take a hundred years, normally, for an opal to disintegrate.

Lucky or unlucky, the opal has been endowed by the imaginative with magic and supernatural attributes that run into the hundreds.

Age-Old Coral Superstitions

THAT A GOITRE can be cured by wearing a necklace of coral beads is one of a great many superstitions attached to this ornamental marine product, and popularly observed in America today. The belief in the healing and other magic powers of coral came to America mostly by way of Italy. Italian women continue the ancient custom of wearing little pieces of branched red coral, no matter where they are, in Italy or other parts of the world, or else they keep a piece of this substance in the house, or carry it in their pockets.

The belief in the protective powers of coral is strong among all Latins around the Mediterranean, where it is the special mascot of children and prospective mothers. Corals are even used in rosary beads to keep all that is evil at a safe distance. A typical gift to religious parents who have a new born baby is a red coral horn, to protect the health and growth of the infant.

Other magic powers attributed to coral include the belief that it will turn pale if the wearer is about to become ill, and that it returns to its former color once the patient recovers. Coral is still worn by those who suffer from epilepsy, formerly known as "falling sickness." Even today, English country folk believe it will prevent or cure sore throat. Hung on fruit trees, it is supposed to multiply the amount of fruit produced.

An old belief promises that a coral necklace around a baby's neck will ensure easy teething, prevent fits, falls and whooping cough. Of course, there is one sensible reason for a baby to have a coral necklace or plaything, as it is very good to bite on during teething, by providing a hard substance on which to rub the feverish gums, and thin the flesh to help the tooth push through. Almost any other hard substance will do as well.

Coral was believed to cure or prevent fever because it kept the body cool. There is some scientific basis for this, because of the minute cellular structure of coral, which could be the means to carry heat away from the body—but only a few coral beads are hardly enough.

Looking back into ancient history we find that great importance was attached to coral. Coral was sacred to Isis, Egyptian goddess of fertility, centuries before Rome was ever heard of. In Roman times, however, in line with the Egyptian idea, coral was dedicated to Venus, goddess of Love.

The Egyptians believed so thoroughly in the potency of powdered coral to shield their crops from destructive storms, fungus diseases or locusts and to provide a rich harvest, that they scattered this powder on their fields immediately after they were tilled.

Whether the ancients knew it or not, we know today why coral powder in large quantities may have helped the crops. Corals are petrified skeletons of polyps, tiny forms of marine life. The coral, during the formation of its cellular structure, entraps minute quantities of other chemicals besides the all-important calcium or lime. All these minerals are vitally necessary for the healthy growth of plants. Today farmers pay for the same thing when they buy lime for acid soil.

Powdered coral, swallowed with water, was also taken medicinally to prevent intense internal pains, especially those of childbirth. Burnt coral, crushed into a powder and mixed with grease, was said to be an infallible cure for ulcers and sores, a formula that cannot be taken seriously today.

According to Hindu belief, the ocean is the final home of the sainted dead. Hence, pieces of coral, coming from the sea, are considered powerful amulets. The ashes of burnt coral still form an important part of the native medicines.

There is a Norse legend that coral is fashioned beneath the waves by one of their gods, and those who wear it, and the ships that carry a piece, are under his protection. Corals used to be inserted into toy bells for babies, to frighten away evil spirits by their jingling.

The word "coral" is derived from two Greek words, signifying "daughter of the sea."

"Diamond" Superstitions

MANY A BRIDE-TO-BE would feel unhappy as well as unlucky if she did not wear a ring, set with a diamond however small, for her engagement ring. It was a very ancient belief that in order to exercise its full power, a diamond had to be worn on the left side of the body, the so-called heart-side, and the jewel had to be so set that it touched the skin. Hence the custom of wearing a diamond engagement ring, with a "clear setting" on the left hand.

Once upon a time it was believed that a diamond in an engagement or wedding ring would surely bring bad luck to the wearer and her husband, because the interruption of the circle,—magic symbol of continuity—destroyed the harmony and love which would otherwise have been eternal. In time, the fear passed, and the diamond became the favorite stone for an engagement ring, in the belief that its sparkle was the fire of love that not even an interrupted circle could cool off.

Diamonds have played a very important rôle in the history of romance. The sparkle of the diamond was supposed to have originated in the fires of love, and to wear this gem inspired love and constancy to a remarkable degree. History tells us that Cleopatra used a brilliant diamond to win the love and loyal devotion of Mark Antony. On the other hand, in the Middle Ages, in the Near and Far East, an attractive woman wore diamonds about her face to divert the Evil Eye's admiration—with wicked intent—from her beauty.

Since diamonds were first known in the East, most of the countless superstitious attributes with which these carbon-crystals have been endowed began among Orientals. Beliefs in their supernatural powers in time circled the earth, as diamond superstitions are now found everywhere in the world.

A typical Eastern superstition is that the possession of extremely large diamonds always brings misfortune. A long history of blood, theft, intrigue, loss of empire, loss of life and other disasters belongs to each of the most celebrated diamonds, and for the most part, the stories are historically true. This fact only strengthens the belief in the minds of the superstitious that large diamonds are the cause of the misfortune of their owners, and the shattering of the lives of many of them.

Somewhat in line with this superstition, is a very ancient conviction that the diamond has powers beyond man's control, so that good fortune may be expected when the owner is pure in soul and mind. If, however, the diamond has been acquired by theft, or is owned by one whose thoughts and motives are low, the diamond will have power to bring all sorts of misfortune upon the individual.

Oddly enough, during the Middle Ages, and even before and after, many believed that diamonds could propagate, and so it became the custom to set two of these stones in one ring, with the belief that at certain seasons they would produce others.

Many modern folk, like the ancients, think that a diamond can never wear out; yet diamonds used in fine glass engravings are worn out in six to eight weeks. It is the truth, and not a superstition, that "only a diamond will cut a diamond."

Crystal Gazing

It is not given to everyone to see scenes, shapes and faces in a crystal. In fact it is estimated that the percentage of crystal-gazers or scryers is about one in twenty, while some investigators are inclined to consider the margin much too generous.

Crystal-gazing or crystalomancy has been practiced all over the world for ages, in different ways and with different objects. Some of these objects are a disc of polished metal, a bowl of water, a clear spring or well, a pot of ink or wine, a mirror, a sphere of glass, a glass bead, a natural crystal, a golden ball, or even a polished fingernail. In fact almost anything with a reflecting surface will serve for staring and lend itself to close concentration.

A most natural example of unconscious scrying is suggested by the holder of a glass of wine, who stares into it before drinking the contents while he salutes someone present. By looking at the wine, or whatever liquor may be in the glass, the one making the toast projects his good wishes to the recipient as though they could go through the glass into the other's mind as a mental vision.

There is nothing supernatural in the results gained occasionally by a crystal gazer or scryer. The privileged few are said to be endowed with keen visualizing powers, so that scenes long forgotten are revived and go through the process of traveling from the unconscious to the conscious mind. This is not divination of past or future events, however. Only that which is already known to the scryer comes before his vision, if he has the gift to release these impressions for his own edification.

To see anything in a crystal is not an optical illusion, it is not hallucination, it is not hypnotism, but it is suggestion. Whether the gazer sees what he is told to see, or whether it is the result of that which emerges from the confines of his mind—or mental antics—whatever reflects itself in the crystal springs from the gazer's own storehouse of experience. These experiences, whether known to the scryer or not, may be recent or very old; that is, they may have started from the day of birth, and, according to some authorities, may even go back to impressions in the mother's womb.

It is not even necessary for certain persons to have a crystal or similar object in which to look in order to see people or things. Visualizers have only to close their eyes to conjure the vision of old friends, or old scenes, calling upon the memory's treasures to recreate dream patterns at will.

The success of crystal-gazing experiments is not dependent on bright or simple minds. The power of "seeing" is wholly related to individual characteristics and mental attitudes that are necessary for conjuring through concentration. This concentration has to be combined with a feeling of confidence, solitude, and preferably a dimly lit atmosphere. There must also be a strong soul-desire to see something in answer to a wish.

A physiological condition takes place when the mind's images begin to project themselves onto the crystal as though it were a screen, on which the mind, acting as camera, throws its wealth of scenes and experiences from the time the mind first received these impressions. This is why persons who have no conscious recollection of certain happenings are startled at the things they see, not realizing that they are actually looking within themselves, as if in a dream, but of course they are fully awake.

Just as the "Rorschach Test," using ink blots, is now a standard testing method for certain phases of one's mental makeup, so the "Witch's Mirror," as the crystal was called in the Dark Ages, may now be coming into its own. Experiments have already shown that crystal-gazing can assist in finding hidden fears, and can reveal the deeper feelings and emotions of a suffering human being. Thus it may be possible to find clues and cures for mentally confused or even deranged individuals. This, of course, is far of the mark of what superstitious crystal-gazers, and those who consult them, expect to find when they look for predictions of the future in order to have their wishful thinking realized.

"Pearl" Superstitions

The liquid drops of tears that you have shed
Shall come again transform'd to orient pearl.
Shakespeare, *Richard III*, iv, 4.

WITH SOME PERSONS, pearls mean tears, while with others they are gems that pour the blessings of the gods upon their owners. These opposite superstitions are an illustration of the varied beliefs connected with this unique sea jewel. The mythologies of Eastern and Northern lands have widely separated tales to explain the origin of the pearl.

A Scandinavian legend tells that when Baldur, god of the Sun, was slain with an arrow of mistletoe, the tears of the goddess Frigga brought him back to life. These tears congealed and became pearls on the mistletoe.

In the Orient, however, pearls are related to the fullness of the moon, which overflowed with heavenly dew, drawing oysters to the surface of the sea. They opened their shells and received the dew-drops, which hardened into mysterious all-perfect pearls.

Because the pearl was a product of the sea, it was closely associated with seagods and was thought to share their attributes. Likewise, the pearl and the moon were believed closely related,—in some languages the moon is the "pearl of heaven." Pearls were supposed to shine at night, and they were expected to watch over the "tides in the affairs of men," as they, too, waxed and waned. The pearl by its quality of losing luster and its brittleness was supposed to give warning of danger, sickness or even death.

Experts say body warmth will enhance the beauty of a pearl, but in the unenlightened past, this was mistaken for a magical property inherent in the pearl, and was given a special interpretation. Although pearls will shine brighter in contact with the human body, it is also true that they are harmed by perspiration. Under certain conditions, if pearls are in contact with distilled water, some of the calcium carbonate of the jewel dissolves. This makes it lose its luster and quality, and turn white. Anciently, when anything happened to a pearl, it was blamed on the devil within the wearer.

Besides perspiration, other skin exudations due to injuries or diseases, very common in the Orient, will affect pearls and make them deteriorate. Exposure to sulphurous smoke, or even to very bright sunshine, will also have a bad effect on them. All these peculiarities of the pearl made it a magic jewel in days before science was born. Pearls were only worn at night because that was the time when they shone at their best.

Pliny wrote that if a pearl diver is fortunate enough to catch the leader of a bed of oysters first, then the rest of the pearl oysters would readily follow it and allow themselves to be caught in the nets,—which is a myth, of course. In Europe and elsewhere, as late as the 17th Century, it was believed that pearls and other gems could reproduce themselves. This was a curious old Oriental superstition that had reached Europe, somehow—probably through the Crusades. Pearl divers used to take the ninth pearls of the catch, whether the jewel was large or small, place it in a bottle and cork the bottle. These pearls were known as seed pearls, and were expected to multiply.

All pearl-bearing shells, such as the oyster, came to be regarded as life-giving, since it was believed that the pearls had received vital powers from the parent shell, which became a symbol of fertility and growth.

Superstitions, old and new, concerning pearls, are numerous. If a string of pearls broke, it was once believed that the remaining pearls signified the number of tears to be shed. Never sing before putting on pearls, or you will shed bitter tears. Pearls are said to be lucky for those born in June. They are a protection against fire, because, according to the ancients, pearls were a product of the moon and water, and the magic water could extinguish a fire. Burnt powdered pearl, mixed with water, was believed to be a cure for insanity, hemorrhages, jaundice and other ailments.

The truth about the pearl is not as romantic as its superstitions and legends. When the tiny tropical parasitic worm, the trematode, gets into the body of an oyster, it causes trouble. To protect itself, the oyster secretes nacre, or mother-of-pearl, and coats the intruder with it, which produces the pearl. In other words, a genuine pearl is the work of a sick or irritated oyster!

The pearl is the softest of all gems, composed chiefly of a substance called aragonite. The story of Cleopatra dissolving the valuable pearl and drinking it may or may not be true. However, pearls, like all carbonates, will dissolve slowly in acid wine or vinegar, or other weak acids. It takes some time for a pearl to dissolve because of its great hardness. Pulverized pearl will not only dissolve readily in strong vinegar, but it will effervesce mildly.

Adventure stories are often built around a plot in which pearls are found in oysters that are not pearl oysters. This is impossible. Only pearl oysters and certain fresh-water mollusks have sufficient iridescence and translucence to produce valuable pearls!

Origin of Birthstones Linked to Ancient Beliefs in Magic

ALTHOUGH the modern custom of wearing or owning precious or semi-precious stones may be, for the most part, a matter of ornamentation or sentiment, originally such gems were acquired in the belief that they had magical virtues. They were believed to give protection to the wearer against poison, disease or other calamity. It was the superstitious belief that there were inherent qualities in each jewel which could automatically be transferred to the owner.

Based on the findings of historians, it is generally accepted that the custom of selecting birthstones, that is, according to the month in which a person is born, had its origin six thousand years ago. Egyptian hieroglyphics furnish the clue which links the use of birthstones to ancient beliefs in magic.

Birthstone history is definitely traced back to the high priest of Memphis, Egypt, about 4000 B.C., who wore a breastplate made of twelve small objects representing Egyptian amuletic hieroglyphic symbols, which were expected to safeguard him against all kinds of evil.

Another link is found in the custom that was later adopted by the ancient Hebrews who had been prisoners in Egypt. Aaron, the high priest of the Hebrews, also wore a breastplate. It was similar to that of the Egyptians and was composed of twelve large gems, but instead of hieroglyphics, each stone represented one of the twelve tribes of Israel.

Following this, the meaning of the twelve gems evolved as follows: the twelve angels of Paradise; the twelve foundations of the Apostles; and finally, the twelve months of the year.

From the twelve months of the year as symbolized by gems, the birthstone idea, as we know it today, has come to us. New gems have been added, and supposedly talismanic powers have been combined with decorative designs and settings. The details of gems, flowers and symbols vary slightly in different parts of the world, but principally they are:

January:	Garnet—Snowdrop	Constancy
February:	Amethyst—Primrose	Sincerity
March:	Bloodstone—Violet	Courage

April: Diamond—Daisy ....Purity
May: Emerald—Hawthorn ....Hope
June: Moonstone or Agate—
                Wild Rose or Honeysuckle..Health
July: Ruby—Lily ....Passion
August: Sardonyx—Poppy ....Conjugal Happiness
Sept.:   Sapphire—Convolvulus ....Repentance
Oct.:   Opal or Amber— ....Lovableness
Nov.:   Topaz—Chrysanthemum ......Cheerfulness
Dec.:   Turquoise—Holly ....Unselfishness

Wedding Ring and Other Ring Customs, Beliefs and Superstitions

MANY WOMEN to this day never take their wedding ring off once it has been placed on the fourth left finger by the groom. When and where the ring was introduced as part of the wedding ritual is a long lost secret.

Customs pertaining to the use of rings have a rich historical and legendary background. The original use of a circle, or ring, is lost in antiquity, but we know that it was regarded as a potent and powerful symbol for thousands of years. The Egyptians were probably the first to fashion a ring to be worn on the finger. In their hieroglyphics, a circle represents eternity, therefore an idealistic symbol for union between man and woman.

We know, too, that the Egyptians were the first to have the idea that there was a vein—love's vein, so-called—which was supposed to extend from the heart to the fourth finger of the left hand. This fallacy was mentioned in the writing of Appianus, the Egyptian, who wrote in the second century A.D. of this belief, which, judging from his writings must have been very old, even then.

Then Macrobius, Roman grammarian and scholar (395–423 A.D.), appropriated this ancient and false notion, and enlarged upon it in such a manner that it found its way into the hearts of the sentimentally inclined of that day. He said the wedding ring should be placed on the fourth finger of the left hand to prevent the sentiments of the heart from escaping from the organ, then regarded as the seat of love, as well as other emotions. Furthermore, when so placed, it became a binding token of a woman's eternal love for the man who placed the ring there, and under no circumstances was she to remove it lest her love go with it.

The ancient Hebrews formally introduced a ring as part of the marriage ritual, but before the service actually took place, as a symbol of the pledge or contract. They deviated from the custom of the Egyptians, Greeks and Romans, by placing the ring on the index finger of the right hand. It is done the same way among orthodox Jews of today.

A wedding ring was used by Christians as early as 860 A.D. Among early Christians, the thumb and first two fingers symbolized the Trinity —the ring being placed on the bride's fourth finger of the left hand, in the threefold Holy Name.

Among Anglo-Saxons, the groom gave a pledge or "wed" to the bride at betrothal. This pledge was a ring placed on the right hand, and worn there till the wedding, when it was changed to the left hand.

There are other superstitious origins for preferring the left hand for the wedding ring besides the "love-vein." One is that the right hand was considered the hand of power and authority; the left, the hand of subordination. Therefore, the ring on the left hand of the bride meant she became her husband's servant henceforth.

No doubt, the more practical reason why the ring was put on the fourth finger of the left hand was that this finger is the least active, and the ring less exposed to wear and tear.

Rings had other applications besides being the sign of wedlock. In the days when even nobles could not write, rings were inscribed with the family coat of arms and were used as seals. Rings bore other seals of authority for use on documents and other important papers.

As the ancient Egyptians used gold rings as coinage, the gold wedding ring was regarded among them as a token entrusting the bride with the care of her husband's property. In many marriage ceremonies today, when the groom says to the bride at the altar, "With all my worldly goods I thee endow," he is probably unaware that an Egyptian bridegroom went through the same formality thousands of years ago.

All sorts of ring fads come and go. Up to about a century ago, it was the custom in Europe for single men and women to indicate their eligibility for marriage by wearing a ring on the first finger of the left hand. When they wished to avoid a proposal, however, they wore a ring on the little finger of the same hand. If a man wanted it to be known that he was a bachelor and never intended to marry, he wore a plain band on the little finger. Widowers, on the other hand, displayed their status by wearing a wedding ring on the middle digit of the right hand. To add more confusion, a ring on the second or middle finger of the left hand indicated that the wearer was engaged. This was in the days before the engagement ring, now conventionally worn on the same finger as the wedding ring, had been popularized.

At present, men are wearing wedding rings almost as much as women, but a man reserves the right to wear it on either hand.

CHAPTER 14

Perchance To Dream

"Relaxation" and "Sleep" Superstitions

A GREAT MANY persons believe that a brisk walk in the open air, or physical exercise of any kind, will act as an aid to sleep. This is not so, as neither the fear of not being able to fall asleep, nor a state of wakefulness, will be removed by this means.

The fact is, that when one is tired, bodily activity, even though it induces physical and muscular tenseness, is much more apt to keep one awake than to put one to sleep. It is better to start the day with exercise, than to end it.

Both children and adults react in the same way to physical exertion. The child who runs, jumps and goes through all sorts of gymnastics in a bedtime romp may be having a good time, and entertaining his elders, but he is not preparing for rest and sleep. Before the child's muscles calm down, just as in the case of the adult who walks or takes exercises at night, much valuable sleeping time is lost.

Any form of mental excitement also delays relaxation and the ability to fall asleep. Psychologists and doctors alike recommend old-time lullabies or pleasant fairy tales, instead of hair-raising thrillers, to put a child into a state of drowsiness in which it will quickly fall asleep. Soft music before bedtime is good for both young and old.

Another superstition connected with walking is that the reason a brisk walk outdoors is invigorating, is because there is more oxygen in the open air. However, it is the exercise of walking rather than the extra oxygen that is stimulating to the body.

"Insomnia" and "Sleep" Superstitions

"COUNTING SHEEP," mentioned in the ancient shepherds' legend famous in folklore, is not the solution to wakefulness. Nor is eating sweets, reading, or listening to music a cure for insomnia. Many doctors assert that those who cannot fall asleep normally are lacking in self-discipline, and no one should need artificial aids.

The mind can never be tricked by mental gymnastics into the kind of relaxation necessary for sleep. These devices, including counting sheep, require concentration, however unconscious it may be, which would make one more wide awake.

Neurologists claim that insomnia is a person's own fault, and that emotional over-stimulation is the principal cause. Remorse, fear, love, anger, sorrow, and even joy, will keep one awake. However, it is also true that the majority of persons who make much ado about poor sleep, do not sleep as poorly as they claim. They are either looking for sympathy, or boasting about being able to get along with fewer hours of rest than ordinary folks.

The phenomenon of sleep and its counterpart, insomnia, are still puzzling to scientists. However, we know slumber can only be achieved when the muscles are relaxed, and when the will can prevent mental action. Thoughts which flow into the field of mental vision must not be allowed to hold the attention—the mind must be indifferent and relaxed. In this same way, worries and other unpleasant ideas which keep one awake will not have a chance to take hold.

Closing the eyes, and relaxing the neck and face, should put one to sleep quickly. In other words, one must "let go."

Somnambulism or Sleepwalking Fallacies

FOR ONE THING, most sleepwalking episodes are transitory, and there is no need for worry unless the practice persists, in which case medical attention should be given. Primitive peoples, however, attach a more mysterious significance to the act as they believe a man's spirit or soul may wander away from him while he is asleep, as evidenced by his dreams. And so they conclude that if a sleepwalker awakens suddenly, his soul might not have time to return. Hence he would fall ill and perhaps die.

A similar superstitious belief persists among many civilized persons to the effect that to awaken a sleepwalker will do him harm and cause irreparable damage to the nervous system. As a matter of fact, except for the temporary confusion and embarrassment to the sleeper, there is not the slightest danger in doing so; a person can be awakened gently and kindly, and led back to bed.

It is not true that a person allowed to go undisturbed while in a somnambulistic state is safe from all dangers. The truth is that the sleepwalker may meet with real trouble if left to wander at random, although most sleepwalkers are uncanny in their skill at avoiding obstacles.

Scolding sleepwalkers, especially youngsters in their teens, shocks them much more than their being brought back to a state of consciousness. Sleepwalking is comparatively rare with young children, possibly because the fundamental causes for somnambulism such as childhood fears and unhappy experiences which affect adults, have not yet disturbed their subconscious.

Fortunately there are several devices available which can be placed at the side of the bed so that when the feet touch them the individual awakens sufficiently to go back to bed and sleep. Such repeated awakenings often effect a permanent cure.

Contrary to popular belief, sleepwalking is not a sign of an overactive mind, nor does it indicate insanity or mental aberrations of any kind. Sleep irregularities, such as nightmares, and to some degree talking in one's sleep, and others, are all signs of emotional disturbances, which, if they persist, should be diagnosed by a competent specialist.

The reason a sleepwalker is apt to act strangely is simply because he has most of his faculties about him except the one of consciousness. A sleepwalker may go through amusing or ridiculous pantomimic activities which seem complex to the observer, but these are in keeping with the sleeper's subconscious occupations.

That Sleep Is More Beneficial Before Midnight

THE SAYING "Early to bed and early to rise, makes a man healthy, wealthy, and wise," which has been attributed to Benjamin Franklin, American statesman and all-around genius, has greatly strengthened the superstitious belief that sleep is more restful before midnight. About the same time, Henry Fielding, English novelist of the 18th century, made famous the expression that "An hour of sleep before midnight is worth two hours thereafter." Another famous Englishman, King Alfred the Great, of the tenth century, had this to say about sleep: "Eight hours for work, eight hours for play, and eight hours for sleep."

That it is better to go to bed before midnight has not been verified by science. Sleep, on the whole, differs according to individual idiosyncrasies and needs. For instance, persons who live in cool climates need less sleep than those in warmer regions.

There is an old superstition that claims that sleep before midnight is favorably influenced by the moon and stars. This fallacy was probably based on ancient astrological notions.

There are reasons to believe that the first two hours of sleep are probably the soundest, no matter what the time of night; and that the last hour, just before waking, is the most restful. The only advantage in going to bed before midnight is that one is apt to get more hours of rest by so doing. But it is not always the time spent in bed that means the greatest rest. It is better to have six hours of "high quality" sleep, than eight hours of restless tossing. Regularity of hours contributes to a feeling of wellbeing when awake; the body, like most things in nature, responding to rhythm.

And, by the way, no one "sleeps like a log," a log being motionless. Studies show that the sleeping position changes from twenty to sixty-five times each night. "Sleeping like a top" is senseless. The expression comes from the French, *"Dormir comme une taupe"* meaning, to sleep like a mole. *Taupe* means mole, but somehow or other it was translated, "top." The mole was believed to have no eyes, which suggested that it slept all the time.

Sleep, Head Lying Due North

THE DISCOVERY that the earth was round led to a very curious superstition, still taken seriously today, when fact and fancy have been scientifically separated. This belief is that the head of the bed should point due north so that the sleeper will be lulled to sleep by the magnetic waves which are supposed to flow between the North and South Poles. Some persons, when traveling, carry compasses so as to be certain of the position of due north. Others put glass block under the feet of the bed, as insulators, to prevent electrical earth currents from delaying sleep by interfering with the magnetic impulses from the poles.

It is maintained erroneously, scientists say, that it is actually dangerous to sleep crosswise to the magnetic pull and push, that is, east and west, because this position disturbs the nervous system. Complete relaxation is believed to come only when the head is north and the feet south.

One theory for this custom was that the iron in the body responded to the magnetic attraction of the poles. However, present day scientists deny this as there is not enough iron in the human body to be affected in the slightest degree by polar magnetism. Furthermore, what iron there is, is in liquid form.

Many other theories have been advanced to try to prove a relationship between the sleeping position and the magnetic poles, but all are without proof. We do know, however, that both mind and body will respond to a preconceived idea, right or wrong. For this reason, those who believe they will sleep better if the bed is placed from north to south, probably do!

That Child or Adult Should Sleep Alone in a Bed

It is not true that anyone, young or old, who sleeps in the same bed with a stronger person acquires strength and vitality from the other. Nor is it true that the stronger one thereby loses some of his own energies. People who are obliged to sleep two abed, usually those who live in humble quarters, are apt to require longer hours of rest to make up for the poorer quality they are getting from not sleeping alone. It is not because of the superstition that strength leaves one and revitalizes the other.

It is highly dangerous for a baby to sleep with its mother or with anyone else, because of the risk of crushing or suffocating the infant. Cases of such accidental deaths are frequently reported in the papers and most doctors have had experience with them.

A very important reason for a child or adult to sleep alone is that the rest is more complete, and therefore of greater value. No one sleeps completely still and motionless, and the movements of one disturb the other.

A less serious aspect of the question is the advisability of twin beds for married couples. Recent matrimonial statistics reveal that only thirteen per cent of married people in the United States occupy twin beds. Therefore it would be difficult to determine whether twin beds are one of the major causes of divorces as has been asserted so often.

Twin beds, incidentally, are not a new idea. This innovation is attributed to Thomas Sheraton, the English designer of furniture, who lived between 1751 and 1806. He was known for many extravagant creations, but it took many years for his revolutionary idea of twin beds to find favor with the general public.

Despite deep-rooted convention and old-fashioned prejudice, there is not the slightest doubt that more rest is enjoyed by sleeping alone than by sharing a bed with another, whether child or adult.

Plants and Flowers in Sleeping Quarters, Harmless

THAT PLANTS and flowers are unheathful in a bedroom at night because they use up oxygen is a popular superstition. Many people also believe that these sympathetic tokens from friends and family when one is sick, give off mysterious and noxious emanations which are harmful to human beings, both well and ailing. Therefore, it has been the customary thing to remove plants and flowers from a sick room at night.

One explanation may be that plants have been in magic for ages. Their flavors and odors have been part and parcel of early man's and old wives' cures, long before carbon dioxide was discovered as such. The unconsciously inherited fear that some harmful gas may be released from a plant or blossom is undoubtedly responsible for the present superstition.

It is true that plants give off carbon dioxide, but not in the manner or amount to be harmful. According to some authorities, plants may actually be beneficial in sleeping rooms, provided, of course, that they are of the non-poisonous varieties. Any other fear should be discarded since there is no scientific basis for it.

However, plants and flowers are usually removed from patients' rooms in hospitals at the end of the day. When it was not known why this is done, it served to strengthen the superstition in the minds of some. The intelligent reason, of course, is to change the water to keep them fresh, and to remove them from the sight of the patient until next morning, when their return will restimulate the patient's pleasure in their beauty and cheerful effect—a psychological factor.

Occasionally, a certain type of plant or flower may have to be removed from the vicinity of a patient to prevent possible irritation from the pollen of the species to which the patient may be allergic. Likewise, cut flowers are apt to wither fast and may produce an unpleasant odor in the process, just as the water in the vase may, if it is allowed to remain unchanged for several days. These are normal happenings and there is no superstitious taboo involved.

Getting Out of Bed on the Right Side

IT IS GENERALLY said of persons who are grouchy, especially in the early morning, that they got out of the wrong side of the bed. This remark has at least two superstitious implications. The first is, that if one gets out of bed on the left, or sinister side, bad luck is ahead for the whole day. The second is that one should get out of bed on the same side that one got into it, otherwise, the interrupted "circle" also suggests symbolically a bad or unpleasant day. The bad mood one starts the day with is a sure sign that the first action that morning was incorrectly performed, whether one is aware of it or not. This, of course, is according to the superstitious notions of some.

Many versions of bed superstitions were invented to predict an inauspicious day. It is bad luck to go to bed over the footboard, to climb over anyone in bed, or to get into bed on the side that is not the accustomed one, right or left.

Modern architects, aware of the traditional left-side taboo, often plan hotel bedrooms so that a bed will be placed with its left side to the wall. This permits superstitious guests to get out of bed on the right side.

The ancients who feared the left or sinister side of anything had many suggestions and superstitious antidotes for the violation of the rule against using the left side. One of them was to reverse the action by walking backward into bed, and then to start all over again in the correct way. This was supposed to neutralize the mistake.

Cold Water Thrown in the Face of a Sleeping Person, Old Custom

THE CUSTOM of throwing cold water in the face to awaken a sleeping person is very ancient. It goes back to the days when people believed that night was the only time in which to sleep. Daytime slumber was thought to invite illness, and more particularly to induce fever, especially in summer. Tibetans still observe this custom by sprinkling water even in the face of an invalid, so that person may not sleep except at night.

This superstition originated because it was assumed that anyone who was sleepy or slept during the day had a fever, or was otherwise ill, and that the shock of cold water would change the body temperature and effect a recovery. Needless to emphasize, this method was not always a cure for a very sick individual.

Primitives attribute everything beyond their control to supernatural forces or beings—the cold water would drive out the devils, and it worked sometimes. Failures did not count.

There is another side to this superstition. In some uncivilized tribes, a person is not awakened suddenly lest his "spirit," which may be wandering abroad, should not return in time to reenter his body.

In our modern age, pranksters who think that throwing cold water in one's face is a good way to awaken a sound sleeper, should realize that this uncouth act has come down from savagery and ignorance.

Dream Book to Find Out What Dreams Mean

"DREAM BOOKS" that presume to explain the meaning of dreams of all descriptions, are in great demand today, just as they have been since the art of writing, even in its most primitive form, was devised. As dreaming is a universal function of the brain, human beings have always attached great importance and curiosity to what goes on in the mind during sleep.

In the modern dream book every subject that could appear in one's dream is given a specal significance, which the superstitious swallow hook, line and sinker. One universal belief is that "dreams go by contraries," an old, old claim that goes back to a primitive concept that things happen in "pairs," or in contrast to each other to create attraction or balance. This early observation may have been the forerunner of the positive and negative rhythms or attributes which are now recognized in many laws of nature, including those of psychology.

Another dream superstition is that an individual who dreams he is falling will never reach bottom, for if he does, it will kill him. Some dreamers do hit bottom, however, and have lived to tell the tale.

There have been countless cases of prophetic and psychic dreams. Many dreams have come true, and instances where a person dreams of a tragedy or other startling event while it is actually taking place are legion. So far, however, there is no way to prove that there is such a thing as "supernatural" sight or power in the human make-up.

Shakespeare said, "We are such stuff as dreams are made on." Perhaps modern psychologists and psychoanalysts are beginning to find out what this "stuff" is. They have put a new meaning on dreams, and have made it a diagnostic technique by which to treat and cure nervous disorders and social maladjustments. However, in this new field of mental hygiene, even the experts are not in agreement. The late Sigmund Freud's ideas, that practically all dreams are the result of repressed desires of a sexual nature, are challenged by many competent psychiatrists. Scientifically speaking, there is yet much to be learned about the interpretation and cause of dreams.

There is general belief that the sub-conscious mind does not reason, but the opinion seems to be gaining weight that it does, but not as clearly as does the mind when awake and conscious.

An interesting slant on how the mind works in dreams is observed in the dream-life of the congenitally deaf and dumb. The memory images stored in their consciousness are devoid of sound and speech, and are likewise missing in their dreams.

Experiments have shown that dreams can be induced artificially by drugs and hypnotism. Careful analysis of these shows that, as in the case of natural dreaming, dreams represent the ideas which are symbolic of the natural content of our minds.

In the long long ago, powerful rulers employed professional interpreters to discover the significance of their dreams, which they regarded as divine messages. How strongly the mystery and riddle of dreams has appealed to man's imagination is strikingly evidenced by its dramatic use in all types of literature, in ancient chrónicles and in the Bible.

Good or Bad Dreams Not the Result of the Food We Eat

EVERY DAY millions of persons blame the food they have eaten for the bad dreams or nightmares they experienced the night after. This superstitious idea, not to say phobia, is expressed not only by hypochondriacs, but also by emotionally stable individuals.

The truth is that food does not determine the content of dreams, pleasant or unpleasant. However, in some cases there are foods which may not be suited to an individual's diet, and the indigestion that results often interferes with sound sleep. When this happens, following a light sleep, a person is more apt to remember what he has just dreamed.

Dreaming is a perfectly normal function of the mind, and one may dream a great deal without cause for anxiety. On the other hand, dreams of the nightmare type are usually due to some emotional disturbance, which calls for the advice of a competent specialist to determine what lies behind the emotional dream-manifestation.

Sleep on Either Side of the Body

A GREAT many persons still believe that it is better to sleep on the right side of the body than on the left side. This superstitious notion has come to us from the ancient fallacy that the heart was entirely on the left side of the torso. For ever so long, children and adults alike were warned that if they slept on the left side, the weight of the other internal organs, pressing on the heart, would in time not only bring on serious heart trouble, but even premature death. Furthermore, by sleeping on the wrong side they would expose themselves to suffocation, nightmares and even sudden death from a crushed heart.

Scientific observers have long established the fact that a sleeping person changes his position many times during the night, but the old fear is still tormenting thousands of sleepers. We are well aware also that the heart is approximately in the center of the body, and cannot be affected by an extra weight coming from either side of it. One may rest or sleep comfortably and safely on either side because ribs and muscles act as a wall of protection to the organ. Even when the left side of the heart is enlarged as in certain forms of heart disease, there is no danger in lying on that side.

Difficulty in falling asleep may be due to lying on the wrong side, meaning, of course, that an individual has his own particular preference, due to habit. This side may be either the right or the left—one is as good as the other. The body, if left alone, will decide for each person which is the most comfortable and proper.

That Dreaming of Fish Means Having a Baby

THE OLD superstitious saying that a woman who dreams of fish will have a baby is a traditional interpretation derived from the ancient association of fish with sex-worship.

Because fish express the most prolific of all forms of animal life, they have been a symbol of fertility from remotest times. It was a sacred symbol of Isis, the Egyptian goddess of Motherhood, the Assyrian Mylitta, the Japanese Kwannon, the Roman Venus, as well as to the Christian Virgin Mary.

The oval that surrounds the Virgin represents the almond, an emblem of virginity and self-reproduction. The oval once was formed by two fishes wtih noses and tails brought together to form an elliptical figure signifying the Hindu *yoni* or feminine principle.

The fish as a symbol of fecundity is one of the oldest known to man and was displayed in ancient temples for purposes of veneration. It also denoted knowledge, wisdom, intellect, and water. In the first incarnation of Vishnu, she returned as a fish, and so the fish was also associated with life and transformation.

The fish was especially sacred to the Assyrian goddess Mylitta, and it was eaten as a feast on the day of the Virgin, known as Mylitta Day, or Freya Day, or Friday—the Virgin Day of present times.

A sterile woman was not well looked upon in ancient times. At least once during her married life, she was permitted to eat fish from the sacred ponds, and to remain in Mylitta's temple overnight, in the hope that with the aid of the goddess and the eating of the consecrated fish, she would become a mother. If she dreamed of fish, then she was sure she would have a baby.

Even though thousands of years have elapsed since this took place, the "fish" and the "baby" have not lost their old related meaning, although few, if any women, who believe the dream superstition know its origin. Dreambooks, however, also help to popularize the superstition and keep it going.

Fear of the Dark

FEAR OF THE DARK in children and adults is traceable to primitive man—who had every reason to fear the dark. Often at night he had to wander alone and unprotected through forests haunted by huge beasts of prey. The instinct which prompted him to fear and flee was his greatest protection.

Anciently the fear of darkness was such an obsession that various means of protection were resorted to. Among the Romans, for instance, the seeds of the peony were worn around the neck as a charm against the powers of darkness, a superstitious belief imported from the Orient and particularly China, whence peonies came to Europe and America.

Pluto was named after the Greek god of darkness because the planet is almost four billion miles from the sun and receives very little light. This god has always been associated with the powers of darkness and the underworld.

Among savages and semi-civilized peoples, the traditional fear of darkness made them believe also that the night air was harmful. Although ignorant, early man approached this problem quite intelligently by sleeping it off—retiring as night approached and rising at dawn!

Moderns have no cause to fear the dark any more; that is, not in a primitive sense, unless, of course, they are in a jungle or where real danger exists. However, we still retain the instinct of self-protection which is not real fear. In this case, it is an emotional excitement, set up by an inherent instinct, the use of which we seldom need nowadays.

The wrong use of this protective instinct causes real fear and frustration.

The fear many moderns experience, however, is more like a phobia and termed *nichiphobia* or fear of the dark, and is especially prevalent among children. Youngsters generally take their cues from the behavior of their parents, friends and others, who unconsciously transfer their fears to the young ones. And so children often grow up with the dread of the dark.

It has been found extremely helpful to paste little paper stars, coated with luminous material which glows when the light is turned off, on the ceiling of the child's room. This will divert attention and relieve the mental and physical tension.

The Fear of Drafts

THE FEAR of being in a draft, of either hot or cold air, is very ancient. This superstition belongs not only to Orientals, Europeans, and Africans, but also to Americans.

Southern Negroes, for instance, believe that a layer of air, warmer than the surrounding atmosphere—usually noticed on a summer evening—indicates the presence of an evil "spirit." This devil or other fiend is supposed to come from the lower regions, where the fires of hell are assumed to be, so that superstitious Negroes, and even some white folk, rush from the warm air current, fearing it to be of ominous portent.

The protective antidote for this fear is for these persons to cross themselves, and without speaking, at the same time holding their breath, to walk through the draft of air to a safer spot where the malicious designs of his Satanic Majesty cannot touch them.

For a historical parallel, we are told by Marco Polo, the Venetian adventurer, (1254–1323), that the emperor, Kublai Khan, founder of the Mongol Dynasty of China, believed implicitly that there were intelligent demons who controlled the weather. Marco Polo further relates that every year Kublai Khan entertained certain crafty astrologers and enchanters in his palace, who were adepts in necromancy and diabolic arts. He kept them always within his shadow, as they were supposed to be on good terms with the air devils and would protect him. These aerial spirits were believed to cause disturbances in the air, where they were reputed to have their living quarters. When they were in a bad temper, they would strike men they did not like.

How the soothsayers pacified these air demons when they were bent on hurting someone, however, is not explained. Anyhow, the dispensers of magic tricks were credited with preventing any cloud, storm or sudden gust of wind—or dangerous drafts—from passing over the spot on which the emperor's palace stood.

When drafts of air cause sneezing, followed by the much dreaded cold, it is an individual matter. There are some who are immune to drafts and can stay in them as long as they please. Others, through low resistance, or susceptibility to a changeable atmosphere, or through physical fear—which at times is nothing short of phobia—always sneeze in a draft. If they take cold or become ill, they attribute it, of course, to the draft. The fear is always real, even if no danger exists.

Cold air on an over-heated body may produce a cold, but that is a true cause and effect and not a superstition.

Belief That Night Air Is Evil Air

> ". . . What, is Brutus sick,—
> And will he steal out of his wholesome bed
> To dare the vile contagion of the night,
> And tempt the rheumy and unpurged air
> To add unto his sickness?"
>
> —Shakespeare, *Julius Caesar* (Act II, scene I.)

THE BELIEF that night air is "evil air" is endorsed by millions of persons, especially elderly ones, the world over. In order to let in as little night air as posible, they keep their windows almost tight shut. This, however, actually produces "evil air" indoors, through lack of good ventilation, which deprives the lungs of the fresh air so necessary to health.

It was an ancient superstition that noxious and infectious particles, rising from the ground, particularly in marshy or damp regions, floated in the air at night. This belief, of course, was false, and has been scientifically debunked again and again. Nevertheless, the fear of night air till haunts and plagues the minds of many.

The evil effects of night air have been described from generation to generation, so that the ancient notion persists even in large modern cities where there are no swamps or marshes around. Night air will hurt neither young nor old, and there is little difference between air in the daytime and air at night. There is less humidity at night and less stirring of dust, which is an advantage. This, however, is offset by the fact that during the day the air receives the highly beneficial refracted rays of sunlight.

Many of our customs, beliefs and superstitions in the western world are inherited from the Romans. A striking instance of this is that we have accepted as a fact, a Roman legend that air blown off the soil of the fields around the Eternal City was responsible for malaria (mal—aria,—evil air), the disease which once prevailed in Italy and devastated it for so long.

In 1880, Charles Louis-Alphonse Laveran (1846–1922), a French army physician in Algeria, made good use of the common observation that mosquitoes and malaria appeared together and he contributed the first valuable link toward solving the enigma.

After several years of research based on Laveran's theories, Italian pathologists in 1898 proved conclusively that the mosquitoes that infested Italy were responsible for malaria, and not the air one breathed at night. The city of Rome and other malarial districts were cleared of the insects by proper drainage.

Though the discovery was made that the disease was caused by a microscopic parasite in the blood, introduced there by the bite of an infected mosquito, and not by night or "evil air," the name, malaria, has never been changed. As this species of mosquito, *anopheles*, rarely bites by day unless in dark places, exposure at night was avoided, if not forbidden. To ignorant persons, this warning meant that night air was dangerous in general.

CHAPTER 15

That Flesh is Heir To

That Children Cannot Avoid Youngsters' Diseases

SUPERSTITIOUS PARENTS believe that children cannot avoid diseases of childhood, such as measles, whooping cough, chicken pox and scarlet fever. It is generally thought that sooner or later a child *must* contract these ailments. This is a wholly fallacious, not to say dangerous, attitude, for it often means leaving children unduly exposed to contagious diseases. The longer and more carefully a youngster is guarded against contracting these diseases, the less the chance to "catch" them.

It is also erroneous to believe that once a child has had one of these sicknesses, it is immune from further attack. However, with the exception of measles, susceptibility lessens with age. On the other hand, there are numerous cases where children do have absolute immunity to the diseases that commonly afflict others.

The greatest tragedy of these childhood contagious diseases is that many of them may result in heart ailments, or impairment or even total loss of sight and hearing. An outstanding case in our modern world is that of the beloved American woman, Helen Adams Keller, who worked miracles with her sense of touch when she lost her sight, hearing and sense of smell as the result of an attack of scarlet fever at the age of nineteen months.

Therefore, it is vitally necessary to safeguard children for normal adult life by giving them the maximum of protection against contagion. Immunity *can* be achieved through watchfulness, proper care, and the best health and hygienic conditions possible in the home and school.

"Sneezing" Superstitions

ONCE UPON A TIME man believed that the basic essence of life—spirit or soul—resided in the head in the form of air or breath, which could be accidentally expelled, for a short time, or forever, by a sneeze. Therefore to forestall calamity all kinds of superstitions were devised from which survive our "God bless you!"; or if you are German, "Gesundheit"; or if you are Italian, "Felicita"; or if you are French, "Que Dieu vous bénisse," and so on.

For centuries the simple reflex of sneezing remained a mystery. However, as civilization slowly marched on, each nation or people came to look upon sneezing as a nasal salute which was sometimes a good omen and at other times a bad one.

For instance, when the soul was believed temporarily expelled, a person became ill; and when it returned, the person got well. When the soul was dislodged permanently, death followed. Other superstitions took on a more cheerful attitude, but sneezing was always responded to with a typical greeting formula.

Some people even believed that sneezing indicated an intrusion into the body of foreign objects or beings, such as evil spirits in various guises as ghosts, fairies, gnomes or demons which jumped out when the act of sneezing took place. Hence there was danger to others when someone sneezed in their presence, because the evil occupants expelled might become tenants of the body of another individual. Spirits were supposed to travel from person to person.

The ancient Greeks expressed superstitions on sneezing in various ways. For instance, a sneeze to the left was deemed unlucky, but to the right was a sign of immediate prosperity or future good fortune.

Both the Greeks and Romans looked upon sneezing as the most manifest and most sensible operation of the head. But during a plague, the Romans regarded it as so dire a symptom that a short prayer was offered to one of the gods when it occurred. Expressions they used included, "Long may you live," "May you enjoy good health," "Jupiter preserve you!" or "Jupiter, help me!" These exclamations were supposed to protect those present, and to expel the evil within the one who sneezed.

The custom of uttering words of blessing or self-protection when someone sneezed spread over Europe. The seriousness of the attitude is illustrated in the expression, still commonly heard, "Not to be sneezed at!" In Greece when a person sneezes, his companions generally bow low, in memory of an epidemic of sneezing which tradition relates once depopulated Athens.

Aristotle explained sneezing as an emotion of the brain, which suddenly expelled, through the nostrils, whatever foreign and offensive substance may have crept in. A sneeze could not but afford some evidence of the brain's vigor, he believed, so those that heard it, honored it as a sacred thing and a sign of sanity. Even today the ancient superstition prevails that an idiot cannot sneeze.

Prior to Aristotle, Hippocrates, the Greek father of medicine, gave his views as to sneezing, which were that a sneeze was a sure cure for hiccoughs, and was profitable to women in lethargies, apoplexies and catalepsies; but it was bad in pernicious diseases of the chest, in incipient catarrh and similar conditions.

The ancient Hebrew rabbis declared that God made a general decree that every living man should sneeze but once, and that at the instant of his sneezing, his soul should depart. Jacob did not like this unprepared way of passing out of the world, wishing to settle his family affairs and those of his conscience in advance, so he prostrated himself before the Lord and earnestly entreated the favor of being excepted from this decree. His prayer was granted and he sneezed without dying. The news spread far and wide until the princes of the known world learned of the fact and ordered that henceforth sneezing should be accompanied with thanksgiving for the preservation of life and good wishes for its prolongation.

The custom of saying "God bless you!" was adopted by the Christian world, however, from pagan practice. But in the History of Italy, written by Carolus Sigonius, we are told that it started during a pestilence in the days of Gregory the Great (590-604 A.D.), that proved fatal to those who sneezed. In the time of the Pontificate, the air was filled with such deleterious influences that those who sneezed expired immediately. Thereupon the Pontiff ordered a special form of prayer, or wish, to be addressed to persons who sneezed, to divert their attention from the fatal effects that were about to follow.

About three hundred years ago, orders were issued to discharge from hospitals every patient who sneezed three times, because of the superstition that he would get well and did not require further hospitalization.

The rules of "civility" in the book of etiquette for the year 1685 instructed the plain people how to behave when a person of title sneezed: "If his lordship happens to SNEEZE, you should not cry out, 'God bless you, sir,' but doffing your hat, you should bow to him handsomely and make the observation to yourself." The same custom prevails today, as we bow to the person who sneezes, after he has excused himself for doing so.

The practice of dipping snuff and breathing it into the nose to provoke sneezing was an artificial way of securing the blessing of friends and at the same time expelling whatever foreign matter might have lodged itself in the nostrils.

The Hindus, who connect sneezing with an evil spirit trying to escape, use the formula "Live," when anyone sneezes. This is responded to with "God bless you!" or "God be praised," at the same time snapping the thumb and middle finger vigorously to scare away the evil being so that it will not jump down someone else's throat.

Among the Mohammedans, it is customary to wash out the nose at night with water so as to prevent evil spirits from entering the nostrils, and at the same time prevent sneezing.

In Egypt, when a man sneezes, he says, "Praise be to God!", and those around reply, "God have mercy upon you!" to which the sneezer then says, "God guide us and keep you!" The Arabs believe that the universe was created by a sneeze of Allah!

Among the superstitious Hebrews, sneezing is an impediment to good work. When a workingman, starting on the job, hears another one sneeze, he quits at once and resumes work later, because he thinks sneezing is unlucky.

To sneeze on the threshold of a home is believed by many to be a bad sign, while another superstition, in common with the beliefs of the Zulus, is that it is a good omen. They think that the household gods are on the side of the sneezer, who returns thanks. If a child sneezes, the people say "Grow," for it is regarded as a sign of health.

In China, if your friend is about to sneeze, you clasp your hands and bow solemnly until the spasm is over. Then you quietly express the hope that the bones of his illustrious ancestor have not been rattled or been disturbed by the sneeze-provoking demon.

In the Sadda, a sacred book of the Persians, all people are required to pray when a person sneezes, because Satan is hovering overhead and may descend. A sneeze is supposed to be the draft from the motion of his evil wings.

North American Indians regarded the sneeze as an omen. If a person sneezed once, anyone present called his name, whereupon the one who sneezed exclaimed, "My son" or "My mother" or whatever relationship was represented. This was a form of grateful ritual to remain alive.

Because sneezing is always spontaneous and unexpected except during colds and hay fever, when it is induced by germs, virus, or pollen, it was believed to have the power to forecast future happenings. Today, however, medical science recognizes the sneeze as one of the most dangerous ways that respiratory infections can be spread. So the ancients were not too far off when they called evil spirits what we call germs. The virus of the common cold and the germs of pneumonia, for instance, are spread from person to person on the minute water particles that are expelled when sneezing. Instead of a verbal formula, or counthercharm, doctors advise holding a handkerchief before the nose so the germs will not actually jump down another's throat!

In a scientific sense, sneezing is recognized as one of the primitive reflexes of the human body—an instinctive and unconscious act to guard the body against harm. A slight irritation in the nose that may not be consciously noticed is often sufficient to produce a sneeze. Some medical authorities think there are sneezing patterns, that is, in the number of times we sneeze and in the particular way we do it. This may be hereditary and vary in different families.

There are many superstitious cures and sayings connected with sneezing, besides those mentioned. It is good to sneeze while reading. It is lucky to sneeze when beginning an argument. It is lucky to sneeze when going to bed. If anyone looks at you when you want to sneeze, you cannot do it. Trying to sneeze, and not being able to do it, is a sign of loss.

To cure sneezing, pull out wild hairs growing in the nose. Shoot off revolvers or anything that will produce sudden fright. Press the upper lip hard and recite the alphabet backwards, or squeeze the bridge of the nose at the point where spectacles would fit.

The nose is the proper channel for the air we live by, and our brain is so constructed that when anything interferes with this channel, we breathe it out violently through the nose and that is a sneeze. Sometimes a sneeze can be stopped, when we feel it coming, by pressing on the nose, half way down, just where the bone ends. There is a little nerve there which acts as a signal to the brain to go no further, but no one really knows why.

The following superstitious lines are still widely believed.

> "Sneeze on Monday, sneeze for danger.
> Sneeze on Tuesday, kiss a stranger.
> Sneeze on Wednesday, receive a letter.
> Sneeze on Thursday, something better.
> Sneeze on Friday, sneeze for sorrow.
> Sneeze on Saturday, see your lover tomorrow.
> Sneeze on Sunday, your safety seek
> Or the Devil will have you for the rest of the week."

"Feed a Cold and Starve a Fever"

"FEED A COLD AND STARVE A FEVER," is a saying which belongs to the long list of old wives' home cures. It is a word-to-mouth formula handed down from ancient times and is commonly followed today. There is another version, which directly contradicts the other: "He who is fool enough to feed a cold will have to starve a fever." Neither piece of advice has found medical sanction, despite continued research to reach the right answer to the problem.

No doctor ever advises, "stuffing a cold," or "starving a fever." In fact, many physicians treat colds by cutting down on food, and, in cases of protracted fever, they may advise forced feeding.

In "Gastroenterology," Dr. J. I. Goodman and Dr. R. O. Garvin report an interesting experiment. Seventy-eight patients out of a larger number who were acutely ill were fed a high-calory diet. On the other hand, liquid or semi-liquid food, large in volume and low in calories, was the normal feeding of the other patients in the group. The patients under the heavy-feeding program made excellent progress, and at the termination of their illness, did not have to go through a long period of convalescence, having gained weight and recovered their sense of well-being during the regular course of medical treatment. Those, however, who were kept on the less nourishing diet, manifested symptoms of malnutrition for some time, and convalescence lasted much longer.

There seem to be almost as many old wives' methods of treating a cold as there are families in the world. Many of these superstitious and obsolete "cures" are harmless much of the time. But it is also true that a large number of them will make the patient worse rather than better. As a matter of fact, colds are still a puzzle to medical authorities —one of the most elusive problems in medicine. So far, there is no known specific drug or mixture of substances with which to prevent or cure a cold, although effective means have been found of alleviating the pains and discomforts that go with the ailment. It is believed that a diet deficient in vitamin A does lower resistance to certain diseases, particularly those of the respiratory tract, such as colds, influenza and pneumonia.

Another fallacy in regard to the common cold is that climate has a lot to do with it. The most recent theory about colds is that they are caused by viruses—and that climate is not necessarily a factor.

Woolen Sock Around the Neck for Throat Ailments or Cold Cure!

IN MANY RURAL PARTS of North America, as well as in large cities, towns and villages, there are people who still believe that throat ailments or a cold are cured by placing a soiled sock or stocking around the neck!

A man's sock is a more potent cure for a woman's throat, and a woman's woolen stocking for a man's throat. Besides, the sock or stocking should belong to a strong, healthy person. The sock or stocking (turned, without fail, wrong-side out), is wrapped around the neck, the foot-covering being placed immediately upon the sore spot, generally under the chin proper, where it has to remain all night.

Now, *why* a soiled sock or stocking? And *why* should these objects, by preference, belong to healthy members of the opposite sex? And *why* should the foot-covering part be placed on the sore spot itself? All these directions have symbolic significance which was believed long before socks and stockings, as such, were known.

We have in these gestures several superstitious notions combined. The soiled article implies that the moisture absorbed into the fabric is a curative agent; the fluid from the strong and healthy person to whom it belongs is believed transferable to the patient. That the sock or stocking should be one which has been worn by a person who is the complement of the other is important in that it expresses unity: male and female represent the continuation of life, and life should mean health.

But the strongest point of all, perhaps, is the fact that it is the foot-covering part of the sock or stocking which *must* be applied to the affected areas, regardless of the ailment, because it is the foot part which is believed to play the main rôle in healing! The believer's attitude of mind is linked to a very old, symbolic and superstitious notion: namely, the association of the foot with sex and regeneration. The foot was considered an extension of sex—a symbol to be used as a phallic expression, capable of effecting wonders when man felt depleted of health and energies!

Sex symbols were used by early man and the ancients, who, with their uninhibited imagination, believed their employment promoted good and defeated evil. They believed that sex was creative—spiritually as well—not destructive nor ignominious.

The Far and Near East peoples originated and practiced customs which made use of sex or phallic symbols as powerful weapons or talismans. Havelock Ellis, writing of these Oriental beliefs, said that the foot was at one time "the focus of sexual attraction"; and there are thousands of instances throughout history to substantiate this assertion. Anything relating to foot-symbolism today is a relic of foot-fetishism of ancient times, whether we realize it or not.

Scientifically, the throat glands are related to sex glands, as witnessed in the change of voice of those who reach maturity, particularly boys. The voice, except in glandular disturbances and other ailments, denotes the sex of the speaker, and also differences between youth and old age.

However, despite the symbolic power of the foot-covering, a sock or stocking remains just that, and nothing more. Wrapped around the neck, the woolen article undoubtedly keeps the throat warm, but this result might be obtained in other ways too. The best that can be said about this procedure, as far as cure is concerned, is that perhaps the warmth thus induced sends more blood to the affected areas, and this, together with the patient's faith, relieves his anxiety so that some comforting rest or sleep may be obtained. The treatment has in itself no magic power to cure anything!

"Yawning" Superstitions

TODAY TO COVER THE MOUTH when yawning is considered an essential of good manners. The origin of this custom, however, stems from the fear of early superstitious peoples that when they yawned they would literally lose their breath and possibly die; or else they were afraid to risk letting an evil spirit enter who would cause illness, pain and even death because these afflictions were blamed on the entrance of evil beings into the body. In consequence, trepanning—making a hole in the head—was devised in order to let the demon out!

Traces of many ancient superstitions appear in connection with our behavior when yawning. For instance, in the presence of others we turn our head away to yawn, and apologize. It was once believed that a yawn was infectious and therefore exposed persons to danger, even though it was an action quite out of man's control. It is true that sometimes when one person yawns, others in the room will do so also, but what the ancients believed was that there was danger of some kind involved, and a yawn was feared to be a warning, even for the one who "caught" it.

Most Hindus consider yawning an omen of impending danger. To prevent it, they snap their fingers three times, and audibly call on a divinity for protection. Snapping the fingers three times triples the chances for the countercharm to work.

In the Middle Ages, it was a common belief that yawning was brought about by the devil, who watched his chance to enter the body through the mouth and take possession of a man or woman. The countercharm was to make the sign of the cross over the mouth so Satan could not enter, for he could not pass that sign. Many persons still cross the mouth when yawning, especially when outdoors. It is done as inconspicuously as possible, to evade the attention of others, by the thumb being manoeuvered quickly to make the cross.

Many believe that to yawn when one is not sleepy is a sign of disappointment. Others feel that if two persons yawn simultaneously one of them will soon be ill, unless each makes a wish and repeats the other's name. To some, yawning indicates that the person nearest to them is disliked. Yawning during an illness is generally regarded as a bad omen.

It was not known in times gone by that yawning may come from a variety of causes, such as nervous tension, lack of oxygen, or just seeing someone else do it. According to science, the reason for yawning, or pandiculation, is that some unconscious signal seems to go from the sight center of the brain to the yawn center, which promptly responds with a similar performance of its own. Hence yawning is infectious.

Early peoples were ignorant and evolved superstitious methods of protection, usually for the wrong reasons, but they observed very closely what went on about them. For instance, when they noticed that one of the first things a baby does when he comes into the world is to yawn, it was very significant to them, and regarded as closely related to life itself. They did not realize, of course, that the phenomenon of yawning is a wise provision of nature—a demonstration of the effects of insufficient breathing, sluggish blood, that it is bedtime and that copying another's yawn is a form of safety valve. All they knew was that it had something to do with the breath, which had a great deal to do with life!

"Hiccough" Superstitions

ORIGINALLY, primitive, semi-civilized and even civilized peoples, baffled by the commonplace physical discomfort of hiccoughs, believed that they were caused by the Evil Eye, that favorite explanation for everything unpleasant. This affliction even found its way into the classics.

Plato relates in his Symposium that the physician, Eryximachus, recommended to Aristophanes, who had hiccoughs, either to hold his breath or to gargle with a little water; but if it still continued, to tickle his nose with something and sneeze. Sneezing once or twice was supposed to cure the most violent hiccoughing.

Medieval and weird "cures" ran into the hundreds and are still advised and practiced by millions of people today.

In all fairness to old wives' tales, it should be mentioned that occasionally an old remedy works. One of these odd cures for hiccoughs is to drink nine swallows of water without taking a breath. Another method to stop the nuisance is to press a special spot at the base of the neck. These two remedies have been used by Orientals since time immemorial. Oddly enough, both these remedies have a scientific basis, as they produce pressure on the phrenic nerve, which in turn relieves the impulse.

Then there is the famous device of blowing into an ordinary paper bag, held close to the mouth, and breathing in and out of it. What happens here is also scientific. The oxygen in the bag is used up and an accumulation of carbon dioxide results. The increased carbon dioxide in the lungs stimulates normal breathing reflexes, and stops the hiccoughs. Modern science has improved on this old-fashioned paper bag method, by putting some dry ice, which is actually carbon dioxide, into the bag.

Many of the formulas which have not found medical sanction work at times, merely by the power of suggestion. As hiccoughing is often of a psychic nature, being caused by worry, excitement or fear, almost anything that snaps the tension will relieve the hiccoughs. Irritating foods and liquids, especially alcohol, bring on this embarrassing activity, but as a rule in such cases the hiccoughs are apt to disappear as suddenly as they came.

It is not commonly known that babies hiccough before they are born. This may take place about three months before birth, at intermittent periods. It is now known that this is due to certain foods that the mother eats, and to which the unborn baby is allergic. The hiccoughs can even be automatically induced when the allergic foods are given to the mother during tests.

"Stuttering" Superstitions

IN PRIMITIVE SOCIETIES, children do not stutter. But early civilizations were well acquainted with this speech disorder and prescribed many unscientific and quack cures for it, including eating snake eggs—a popular Suwannee superstition, and a *sure* cure; and keeping the mouth full of pebbles while trying to talk. Demosthenes, a victim of stuttering, is said to have cured himself of this disability by rehearsing his orations with his mouth full of small stones before an audience of restless Mediterranean waves!

Many absurd causes were attributed to stammering; such as, that if a child is tickled, it will become a stutterer; or tickling a baby on the feet before it is a year old will produce this same result. The philosopher, Francis Bacon, thought that stuttering was caused by a "cold" tongue, and he prescribed heavy doses of strong wines. His theory was somewhat like that of the American Indians who believed that "fire water" gave them the gift of a fluent tongue.

The popular superstition that there is a connection between left-handedness and stuttering has no scientific basis. There are, of course, left-handed individuals who stutter, but one has nothing to do with the other. Forcing a congenitally left-handed child to use its right hand may bring on stammering; that is, if the child has a nervous temperament.

Stuttering is probably not hereditary, but the predisposition may be due to pathological conditions before or at the time of birth, such as natal injuries, and difficulty in starting to breathe. A baby's slowness or backwardness in learning to sit up, talk and walk may also be a cause for later stuttering.

However, no one knows exactly what causes stuttering. Authorities agree that it is not caused by malformation of the speech organs. It is believed that this affliction is generally due to psychological conditions such as a feeling of inadequacy and other fears. Persons stammer and hesitate in many more ways than in speech, but it is only when we apply it to the voice that it is identified as stuttering.

It is an odd fact that stuttering is many times more prevalent among males than females. Psychologists are of the opinion that this is because girls learn to speak earlier, and due to their more emotional nature, have larger vocabularies with which to express this characteristic of their sex.

A stutterer is not mentally inferior, as it is often believed. Intellectually and physically he may be up to par, emotionally he is victimized by instability, often caused by lack of an outlet for surplus feelings.

Speech is the finest of our motor functions, and it is the one most easily disturbed, especially in the formative period of childhood. It is, therefore, also a superstitious fallacy to assume that a falsetto voice indicates lack of masculinity, when in reality it is a defect contracted at the time of change of voice.

Very little progress in correcting speech defects was made until the beginning of the 20th century. As late as the 1880's French physicians believed that stuttering and stammering could be relieved by surgery, cauterization and other painful procedures, which usually did more harm than good, even removing speech altogether.

"Teeth" and "Toothache" Superstitions

WE ARE TOLD THAT the daily task of caring for the teeth has been observed in China for more than four thousand years, and it is said that the practice is even more ancient with the Egyptians. Despite modern medicine and dentistry, there are almost as many superstitions and old wives' aids in regard to teeth and toothaches as there are years since attention to the teeth began.

Millions of persons in America have a fear of going to the dentist that amounts to a phobia. About two years ago, a shocking but authoritative statement was made publicly that Americans over three years of age needed about 238,500,000 tooth extractions, and about 632,000,-000 fillings. Most of these persons stood little chance of receiving the attention of dentists, not necessarily for economic reasons, but because of their dread of the dentist's chair.

Perhaps lack of acquaintance with the dentist accounts for the almost endless string of superstitions about the teeth. Only a few can be mentioned. For example, baby teeth or "milk teeth" need not be attended to. A clean tooth never decays. Chewing hard food strengthens and hardens the enamel of the teeth. If wisdom teeth cut through before the age of twenty, it means a short life. Chewed tobacco used as a poultice will cure a toothache. Other poultices to cure a painful tooth are made of garlic or hops. Good teeth are a sign of sexual weakness, and bad teeth means the opposite. The bite of a Negro with bluish gums is poisonous. Teeth wide apart mean the owner will be lucky, wealthy and travel far. It is bad luck to count the teeth of an infant. Two persons with false teeth should not marry as it will be an unlucky union. Drinking milk prevents tooth decay. If a baby is born with teeth it is a sign of future greatness. A safeguard against toothache is to wear a spider enclosed in a nutshell around the neck; a mole's paw will do as well.

Incredible as it may seem, nearly everyone has his own charm or magic formula to cure a toothache. Furthermore, an unbelievably large number of persons wear amulets, lucky pieces and talismans of all sorts as toothache remedies. A badger's tooth has taken the place of the wolf's tooth that was once carried for preventing toothache.

There is character-reading by the teeth, just as by other facial characteristics.

Do not trust persons with pointed teeth.

Persons with protruding upper teeth are short-lived.

If a person's teeth are ridgy, he will die of fever.

When teeth are well separated, it signifies a fine voice.

Teeth far apart means one will live far from parents; close together he will live near the folks.

Or, teeth far apart warn that the possessor must seek his fortune far from his native place.

Breaking a tooth is a sure sign that a friend will die.

There are also lucky and unlucky days to have teeth extracted or filled, but they are matters of individual beliefs and superstitions.

"Cancer" Superstitions

IN SPITE OF MEDICAL FACILITIES and scientific knowledge, a tremendous number of supertsitious persons still try to cure cancer by magic.

The long list of medieval old wives' cures found in rural communities, and in densely populated areas as well, is amazing. For example, to cure an external cancer, use a poultice of ripe cranberries or sweet violet leaves. For internal cancer, make a tea of violet leaves and drink it. A fantastic cure is a paste or ointment made from the ashes of burnt toads. A live toad placed on the cancer is expected to draw the cancer to itself, and when the toad dies, it should be replaced by another live one. The second one is supposed to effect the cure, which is for an external cancer. Amber taken from a pipe stem, or oil from a turtle's back, are among other remedies, or "cures."

A very dangerous type of superstition, more prevalent than cancer itself, is the widespread dread of the disease, called in extreme cases, cancerphobia. This fear is often based on false associations of events, such as when a blood relative dies from cancer.

So far, science has not proved that cancer is inherited. It is true that this affliction recurs in some families, which may mean a hereditary tendency, which is not the same thing as inheritance. No one should fear that he will have cancer because another member of the family had it; experiments show that, in general, this malady is not passed from one generation to another.

There is a superstition that birthmarks are dangerous, because they are likely to develop into skin cancers. This is unfounded. Birthmarks may be ugly, but they are not precursors of skin cancer.

Cancer is not contagious nor infectious. One cannot "catch" cancer merely by taking care of cancer patients, or even by sleeping with them. There is no truth either in the belief that eating foods cooked in pots made of certain metals will produce cancer.

The superstitious fear that the use of contraceptives will cause sufficient irritation to result in cancer is not true. Properly fitted by a physician, contraceptives will not cause cancer.

Many believe that the skin of tomatoes clings to the lining of the intestines, and tears the lining from both the stomach and intestines, causing cancer. This silly idea probably originated in the days when tomatoes were considered poisonous. No food or food preparation has ever been found to give a specific clue for the causation, prevention or cure of any form of cancer.

There are no "best" medicines for cancer. The only three treatments known to medical science which can effect a cure or arrest development are X-rays, radium and surgery. These are sometimes used in combination. Many of the reported "miraculous" cures attributed to home remedies, were prescribed for cases that were not cancer in the first place.

Studies show that millions of persons cherish misconceptions about cancer. Gallup's poll, reported in the *New York Times* of October 21, 1945, when analyzed showed that "one fifth of the adult population still believes that cancer is catching." Fewer than half the population acknowledged that they knew any of its signs. Among the weirdest guesses about the cause of cancer were: eating too much salt; eating raw pork; bad mental attitude; horse bites; fungus growths; cooking in porcelain pots; eating small peas from cans; elements in the air; and—"badness coming out of you"!

"Wart" Superstitions

ONE OF THE MOST tenacious superstititions attributes warts on the hands to contact with frogs and toads. Perhaps the idea originated because of the wart-like appearance of the toad's skin, and since this superstition is very ancient, it may have been based on the primitive theory that "like produces like." The remarkable thing is that nothing is ever mentioned about persons who have warts who have never touched a toad or frog, or who have not been within miles of one.

The "charming" away of warts has quite a literature of its own. The superstitious faith in "charms" grew out of the observation that warts often disappear as mysteriously as they come.

An early American cure for warts was to pour vinegar on the hinge of a door after seeing a shooting star. The warts would then drop off, like the star. Another way, also observed in America long ago, was to steal someone's dishrag and bury it. Still another method to eliminate warts was to rub a piece of stolen meat, or a bean, on each wart, and then bury whatever had been used for the purpose. As the meat or bean rotted, and was gradually absorbed by the earth, so the warts were expected to disappear back into the skin from where they came. Or, one could tie a knot in a red string for each wart, in the belief that a wart was symbolically tied in the string, and therefore would fall off. To make this charm more effective, the string was buried at a crossroads at midnight.

All of these superstitious cures for warts that involved burying something, or the recital of "charms," are relics of the days when man believed in imitative magic, or "like brings like."

Warts have been "given" or "sold" to parents or friends, or to strangers, symbolically of course, and the presentation was not minded because adults seldom have warts. A penny was the price for a sale.

A modern formula for getting rid of these unsightly lumps is to rub a grain of barley on each wart, and then give the barley to birds or fowl to eat. Not so very long ago, youngsters advised that a freshly-killed frog or cat, rubbed on warts while in a graveyard at midnight, was a sure cure.

It is possible that one origin of the superstition associating toads and warts may have come about because in rural districts, parents fabricated all sorts of stories to keep their children out of trouble. Children were probably admonished to keep away from swampy places or ponds where frogs and toads habitate, so that they would not get too wet and become ill. As most of the parents themselves were raised on the belief that warts came from toads, they passed it on to the next generation in all seriousness, at the same time keeping the children out of mischief.

Many superstitious persons have a morbid fear that warts on hands and fingers may develop into cancers in later life. There is no evidence, however, that common warts are ever cancerous, nor that the presence of them indicates a predisposition to cancer.

The cause of warts is yet to be discovered, but many doctors think they are produced by filterable viruses. The modern scientific method of getting rid of them is by destroying their blood supply with the electric needle, which makes them fall off. They may also be removed by X-ray treatment or the application of strong acids which burn away the tissue.

The superstition that warts could be removed by "charms" was given a boost when it was demonstrated that these ugly little growths often actually disappeared through suggestion, hypnotism, or simply sterile distilled water injections! And so the "powwow" doctor, who claimed to make warts disappear with the wave of his hand and a few gibberish words, came into his own. In fact, about twenty years ago, when psychotherapy was introduced, he was labeled authentic.

And so it would seem that psychotherapy has something in common with the folklore theory that certain persons can cause a type of wart to disappear by touching it. Also, it may be possible that the one who has the warts can get rid of them by touching them with a finger tip at the same time every day for a month, as has been claimed.

We know that the toad's parotid gland secretes a substance that is highly irritating when in contact with an open sore. Since warts are sometimes due to a skin irritation, the superstition that warts and toads are related may have had a factual origin. Handling toads, however, does not necessarily cause warts.

"Mole" or "Birthmark" Superstitions

SOME PEOPLE BELIEVE that a mole is a focal point from which cancer will develop. This erroneous notion haunts superstitious persons all their lives, but actually there is no more danger that a mole, if left alone, will develop into cancer than there is for any other part of the body.

The small mole is a protuberance generally more or less flat; a birthmark which is either congenital or acquired. Sometimes it is quite dark and may be hairy as well. Moles are actually changes in the pigment of the skin and are not caused by infection as most people believe. They are seldom dangerous unless constantly irritated. It is never safe, however, to touch the hair of a mole or wart unless it is done by a physician. It may be clipped off from time to time, but nothing else should be done. The real danger exists when unscientific methods are applied by the layman.

The Greeks considered moles lucky signs. Centuries ago, "The Language of the Mole" was developed. It has many versions, but here are a few interpretations:

Right Eye (above)	—Wealth and a happy marriage;
Left Eye (above)	—You have great liking for the opposite sex, and will thereby gain much happiness;
Temple	—Happiness in love;
Nose	—You will succeed in business;
Cheek	—You will be happy but not blessed with fame and fortune;
Chin	—Fortunate in your choice of friends;
Ear (either)	—A contented nature;
Arms	—A happy nature, but with something of the "don't care" attitude;
Shoulders	—Will face difficulties with fortitude;
Hands	—A practical nature, able to take care of yourself;
Legs	—Strong willed;
Neck	—You have a great deal of patience.

Like the Valentine custom, the "Language of the Mole" began as a love token and then was used also as a means of ridicule and caricature. A whole book called "Molesophy" was written some years ago by a man who had faith in moles as a sign of the character of an individual. Depending upon the color, nature, and situation of the mole there was a theory, associated with the planets, by which character and personality were told.

A woman wasn't considered beautiful unless she had a mole on her face. It may have been that the sages of old, beginning with Greece, knew their psychology, and with the creation of a happy symbol language of the mole, elevated the mole from a blot to a sign of beauty. The beauty patch in various forms such as round black dots, half moons, stars, etc., became popular and no coquette worthy of the name would be seen without one. The place and location of the beauty patch was a language all its own. The prim and proper young lady who wanted to be left alone wore hers high on the left cheek.

Surgical diathermy or a desiccating current is the best method of removing moles, but many old-fashioned superstitions and formulas are still practiced. Rubbing on the milk of cottonweed thrice daily for three days at a time; tying a silk thread around the mole; making a circle around it with the monthly fluid—these are a few of the remedies.

For those who consider moles lucky, there is the gesture of throwing black pepper on an expectant mother so that her child will have moles.

"Shingles" Superstitions

VICTIMS OF THE SHINGLES, from ancient times to this day—if they are superstitious—have feared that a complete encirclement of their bodies by the rash would mean certain death. Although this more violent form of the disease is extremely rare, it is not fatal. Records point to the fact that Pliny, the ancient naturalist (23–79 B.C.), started this superstitious dread of shingles by writing: "It kills if it encircles."

Old wives' tales for the cure of shingles are legion, and include a poultice of cranberries, and a salve made of sulphur, lard and ten drops of camphor. A primitive treatment, still followed in this country, is to rub warm, fresh blood from a black cat or hen over the affected areas. It is said, however, that this formula only succeeds when the shingles have not gotten out of hand. Equally gruesome applications are believed by some to be efficacious for this eruption.

Shingles or *herpes zoster* is a very ancient disease. The Greeks called it *zona* because it occurs in definite zones of the body. The Romans called it *cigulum* which means "girdle."

Shingles is a virus disease, and the infection attacks beneath the skin, not the skin itself. It is a most disagreeable ailment, producing pain and itching, and a mass of tiny blisters along a certain nerve line. Relief from the discomforts of the disease is obtained by injections of a local anaesthetic, which also make the blisters heal rapidly.

"Tuberculosis" Superstitions

THERE IS AN OLD SAYING that if you have tuberculosis, March will search you, April will try you, and May will tell you whether you will live the year out.

A most dreadful superstition, prevalent today, is the belief that tuberculosis is inherited. Tuberculosis is not inherited, and once the disease is cured, there is no danger of transmitting it.

Many superstitious expectant mothers are fearful lest they pass tuberculosis, or what they call the "tendency" to it, on to the unborn child. The truth is, that even if a pregnant mother is tubercular, there is not a single instance on record where the tubercle bacillus from an infected mother has passed through the placenta into the foetus. Babies are not born with tuberculosis.

The principal reason why tuberculosis afflicts more than one member of a family is because babies and others in the home acquire the infection from contact. It is not the "tendency" to the disease that brings it to the babies—it is ignorance and lack of hygiene.

For years and years a curious superstitious attitude prevailed which prevented anyone from talking about tuberculosis, a subject that was taboo until a comparatively short time ago. To mention the disease in connection with a member of one's own family was merely inviting social ostracism. Due to this taboo, a tubercular patient secretly harboring this disease planted the "evil" germ in others, and spread this dread malady around, often through kissing on the mouth, which is a regular greeting custom in America.

However, there are still many persons who talk about tuberculosis only in a hush-hush tone. Fortunately the superstitious taint is disappearing with the advance of scientific knowledge, which has clarified the treatment, and the necessity for the isolation of cases. Nevertheless, millions of persons still turn to old wives' formulas for cures, instead of going to a doctor or to a sanatorium.

Even if the fried heart of a rattlesnake is no longer taken internally as a cure for tuberculosis, a wrist band made of rattlesnake leather, or a belt, or some other token made from the snake and worn close to the body, is still believed to cure tuberculosis in backward parts of America.

Incredible as it may seem, live snails and small frogs are swallowed whole today as a cure for tuberculosis. And many persons believe that if you have ever had smallpox, you will never have tuberculosis, no matter how much you may be exposed to it.

From earliest times, cow's milk fresh from the udder was believed to contain magical properties. This false theory was applied for the cure of consumption or phthisis, as it was formerly called, or tuberculosis. The chances are that drinking fresh milk from the udder caused an increase in the number of tuberculosis cases, since this disease can be transferred from the cow to the human being.

Anciently, it was thought that tuberculosis was an illness due to witchcraft. A person suffering from the disease was often fed butter made from the milk of cows that pastured in churchyards, churchyards and graveyards being one and the same in those days. This, of course, increased cases, rather than cured them.

As a hangover from the time of the butter cure from cows in churchyards, a belief persists that raw milk, not pasteurized, is still the best food for babies. This may be so only if the cow is not infected with bovine tuberculosis, a most serious disease to which children are especially susceptible.

"Hunchback" Superstitions

THE SUPERSTITION of the "lucky hunchback" is universal in scope. It is one of the most ancient talismans to protect against all manner of evil, particularly the Evil Eye.

Egyptian Pharoahs always had a hunchback charm in sight. Phoenicians—Aramean Semites—placed the image of their hunchback god Bes (a deity borrowed from the Egyptians), in their trading galleys and elsewhere, to protect them in their manifold enterprises. The ancient Romans carried a miniature hunchback with them. And it is still regarded as a powerful luck-bringer among Italians today.

Ancient peoples believed the hunchback's powers were dual in nature. Its likeness was nearly always made to emphasize the deformity, with eccentric and grotesque gestures, the sight of which was expected either to scare away evil spirits, or to drive them into such fits of laughter as to make them forget their evil intentions.

In former times kings often had a hunchbacked court jester, not only to amuse the court, but to bring good fortune to all who gazed upon him. To touch a hunchback's hump was a gesture to change one's luck from bad to good, and this superstition is still very popular.

In contrast, we find the belief that a deformed body was marked by nature as evil; that it was intended to be mischievous, have the Evil Eye and be of bad temper. Constant allusions to this are met with, such as the Jewish dictum, "The blind and the lame shall not come into the house," or "Look out for those marked" (German proverb), and Bacon's definition, "Deformed persons are commonly evil by nature, for as nature hath done ill by them, so they by nature are beings devoid of natural affection." All these expressions are outgrowths of primitive ideas and beliefs that a deformed person harbored an evil spirit.

Primitive and ancient peoples had no way of knowing that most hunchbacks were congenital defectives and not human beings possessed of the Evil Eye, on which they blamed their misfortunes, or endowed with supernatural powers to combat evil.

During recent years, public health measures, such as the inspection of cattle and the pasteurization of milk, have increased the control of tuberculosis of the spine, often responsible for the hunchback's deformity.

"Rheumatism" Superstitions

IT IS SAID THAT the most prevalent of chronic diseases is rheumatism. Science does not claim to have a specific way as yet to cure it; consequently it is subject to countless superstitions and remedies as incredible as they are varied. Rheumatism, or arthritis, known as the "Great Crippler," has plagued mankind and animals as far back as the prehistoric dinosaurs.

The United States Public Health Service has estimated that one out of every four persons afflicted with rheumatic diseases, between six and eight million, is deluded and robbed annually by the use of fake appliances, which include "electric belts," magnetic soles, and other high-sounding devices.

Some of the ancient remedies such as bee venom and gold injections are being given special attention in scientific experiments, but so far nothing has been achieved which could be said to be a real cure.

A few of the many false notions about rheumatism are the following: wearing the buckeye, or horse-chestnut, and the Irish potato, one on the right side and the other on the left side of the body, to ward off rheumatism; wrapping the skin of a rattlesnake or blacksnake around the affected part, or wearing the rattle in a hatband; holding a buzzard feather behind the ear; wearing a horseshoe nail bent into a ring on the little finger; rubbing the ailing parts with the "gold," or yellow, meat of a turtle; rubbing angleworm or "red worm" juice on the aching joints. Camphor, nutmeg, red flannel and many other such substances are also used.

It is interesting to note how cures by analogy are suggested to the superstitious-minded. For example, the fact that a lodestone will draw particles of iron led to the belief that it would draw rheumatism out of the body. When the principle of magnetism was relatively unknown, mystic powers were ascribed to it. Our ancestors carried around small magnets to avert or cure disease. This reasoning accounts in part for the success which quack doctors enjoy with their fraudulent, and often medieval, devices.

Paracelsus, a Swiss chemist and physician (1493–1541), used an organic gold compound, which he administered orally and claimed was effective. The wearing of a gold or copper ring to prevent rheumatism may have come from this prescription.

When rheumatic victims announce a turn in the weather by the way they feel, a half-truth is being voiced, for low barometric pressure causes greater dehydration of the body which, in turn, induces pain. Rheumatic twinge and aching joints, however, do not predict a storm; only a change in the amount of moisture in the air is indicated.

"Epilepsy" Superstitions

BECAUSE OF ANCIENT FEARS and superstitions which have filtered through the ages, epilepsy still suffers from a social stigma like that once attached to tuberculosis.

Ignorance and fears in regard to epilepsy have been so great that only a few years ago the *Layman's League against Epilepsy* was organized for the specific purpose of fighting the superstitions and misconceptions by disseminating facts about the disease. They sought to guide distraught and confused victims into the best channels for modern treatment, and to do away with hundreds of old wives' formulas and cures which were retarding the possible recovery of millions of cases in America today.

As a means of easing the modern mind as much as possible, so that deeply-rooted fears, prejudices and the hopelessness attached to the word "epilepsy" may disappear, this term is now on its way out to be replaced by the technical term, "Cerebral dysrythmia." It is hoped that the attitude of defeat attached to the old connotation will be disposed of.

There are several types of epileptics, but most, if not all, the victims can be helped with the modern approach. For thousands of years there was no treatment for the disease, and the symptoms were regarded as manifestations of a demon within the individual. To this day, superstitious persons are ridden with ancient fears and hide themselves; or their families keep them out of hospitals and clinics where they could be helped, because epilepsy is looked upon as a disgrace to the family.

Although the light of knowledge has been thrown on other afflictions, once regarded in almost the same way, epilepsy still remains a skeleton in the dark closet of public prejudice and ignorance. Fifty years ago cancer and tuberculosis were a family disgrace, and twenty years ago public discussion of syphilis was taboo. For twenty centuries, a mass of superstitions, half-truths and inhuman attitudes accumulated around the dread leprosy. The same intelligent methods of treatment and control that have been applied to these diseases may be expected to change the lot of epileptics.

At least 500,000 persons in the United States are said to be subject to seizures. Approximately 10,000,000 carry a predisposition to epilepsy, and about 5,000,000 are subject to the socially acceptable, but genetically related, sick headaches of migraine. All these persons can be helped immeasurably, if not cured, when superstitious notions are eliminated from the consciousness of the great mass of the public, and the intelligent approach becomes universal.

There are superstitious believers in the theory that only the physically strong are victims of epilepsy. There is no truth in this. The disease can occur in any type.

The fear of inheriting the disease is almost as bad as the disease itself. Of course, eugenics play a part, but only to the extent that the family history of each patient is a deciding factor when predisposition is to be determined. However, there is an element of heredity in most cases of epilepsy, as evidenced by knowledge that it has run in the family of kings, artists, and other well-known characters. The science of eugenics is not far enough advanced for us to know the exact way in which epilepsy is transmitted. It is known, however, that it is not directly inherited—it is classified as a recessive trait—which means a predisposition to it may be transmitted.

The most harmful misconception concerning epilepsy is that it denotes insanity. Study shows epileptics to be no different in mental efficiency than persons afflicted with some other disorder.

In the matter of employment and marriage, where epileptics are concerned, the law makes it difficult for such unfortunates. For instance, marriage is forbidden in many states, although doctors now approve of the idea of epileptics having children. More than seventy per cent of epileptics are employable, but they are discriminated against and so must become dependents. Such statutes are outmoded bugaboos that survive because this disease is still cloaked in hush-hush stigma and superstition.

Epilepsy was called the "Sacred Disease" by magicians, wizards and charlatans of ancient times, who declared that it was induced by visiting spirits who took over the bodies of selected victims. The spirits occupied them so as not to be disturbed, or for the purpose of acting as oracles or for other supernatural intention. Few disorders of the human body have been so clouded with mysticism and weird beliefs as epilepsy. As recently as two hundred years ago, Europe's leading doctors thought it was the work of witches.

"Diabetes" Superstitions

THE PERSISTENT BELIEF that diabetes is due to an over-consumption of sugar is denied by physicians, who claim that the disease is due to a disordered endocrine gland system. So far, there is no known way of preventing this malady.

Country people in various parts of America believe that alfalfa tea or sauerkraut juice will cure diabetes. Another superstitious remedy to relieve diabetic attacks is to give the patient some meat that has been fried in paper—particularly brown wrapping paper—and served well done, or well browned. Such old wives' cures are harmful superstitions because there is no cure for diabetes, but the symptoms can be greatly alleviated by injections of insulin. All odd superstitious formulas for the treatment of diabetes, however, long antedate the discovery of insulin.

Although it is true that diabetes takes its heaviest toll among heavy-weight persons of all ages, bathing in salt water is no cure, as some think, nor will it reduce the sugar in the blood, an oversupply of which is a symptom of the disease.

Many superstitious persons have a dread of having sugar in their blood, but the presence of sugar there does not mean one is diabetic. Some sugar in the blood stream is essential to life, but when there is an oversupply, the condition of diabetes is indicated.

Diabetes is said to be hereditary. Medical research shows that children of two diabetic persons are almost certain to have diabetes. The dangers in pregnancy of a diabetic woman have been greatly reduced since most women respond well to daily injections of insulin. Many specialists agree that they see no reason why potential diabetic victims cannot marry whom they please, since the disease may not appear till middle life, at which time it can be controlled.

Many men as well as women who are potentially diabetic have a superstitious fear that they may be sterile. Many women who are completely free of the disease are afraid that if they marry a man who is diabetic, or who may be disposed to the ailment through heredity, he will be sterile and that there cannot be offspring from such a union. Diabetes does not render an individual sterile. It may cause a person to be low in energy, as a result of the failure of the system to utilize its sugar, but with proper diet and insulin treatment, a diabetic can be otherwise perfectly normal.

It is another fallacy that diabetics suffer excruciating pain when they die.

It is very interesting to note that the ancients sacrificed goats to their gods thinking that the gods would be flattered if the worshippers ate the raw pancreas of the animals. This would seem a very gruesome practice and superstition, and yet, today, sufferers from diabetes, under the doctor's order, take insulin which is derived from the pancreas. The ancients often erred, but some of their pagan ideas finally landed in the lap of science.

Superstitions About Appendicitis

AN ERRONEOUS NOTION, fortunately now disappearing, is that swallowing fruit pits, grape seeds, tomato and peanut skins and the like, may cause appendicitis. Of course, this malady is not caused by eating such indigestible particles, for the reason that these things are not likely to settle in the appendix.

During a lifetime, nearly everyone swallows some indigestible morsels, yet very few who do suffer from a diseased or inflamed appendix. In exceptional cases, when the surgeon does find a seed or other unassimilated matter in the sac, there is no positive proof to substantiate the superstitious fixation of the patient, that the seed was responsible for the inflammation and presence of pus germs.

Another unfounded notion is that a laxative or cathartic takes care of the abdominal pains. If there is actually an inflamed appendix, this treatment may be dangerous. In fact, warnings against indiscriminate use of this remedy are now printed on labels of most laxative containers.

The likewise superstitious idea that the use of an ice bag will "freeze" the appendix is also erroneous, as chilling the affected area may court gangrene trouble.

Following an appendectomy, many patients hold to the superstitious fear of resultant adhesions. Unless checked in time, these fears can develop into a psychopathic complex where the patient actually develops the symptoms and pains without any physical cause.

It is interesting that superstitions about appendicitis are quite modern, as the first operation to remove the appendix is said to have been performed in England in 1848, and in the United States in 1886. What once was known as "inflammation of the bowels" was finally diagnosed as appendicitis. Scores of superstitious beliefs and home remedies that had formerly been applied to the old complaint were transferred to the later discovery.

There are at least twenty different conditions that may be mistaken for appendicitis, which may explain why there are those who blame all their abdominal ills on "chronic appendicitis," a disease that, in reality, is one of the rarest. Fear of an operation of some kind is usually the reason for this self-diagnosis of a "chronic" condition.

The appendix is an obsolete formation in our bodies—a vestigial and useless part of the intestinal tract. It is a heritage from the days when we were less developed mammals. From the point of view of evolution, it is highly significant that anthropoid apes have appendices, and other monkeys do not!

"Menstruation" Superstitions

THE SUPERSTITIOUS ANTIPATHY men feel toward any contact with menstrual blood is thousands of years old. As in early times, men fear that copulating with a menstruating woman will infect them with all sort of diseases such as syphilis, or cause them to become insane. Millions of women, as well as men, regard menstrual blood as poisonous, as though it were bad blood leaving the body. They are ignorant of the important and dramatic rôle the menses play in a woman's life. It is not "the curse" it is frequently called.

There are many other superstitions about menstruation, and it is remarkable that so much ignorance on the subject persists among even educated persons in an age in which truth on the subject is available to almost everyone. For instance, it is believed that taking a bath during the period will not only stop the flow but will cause tuberculosis. Drinking milk is supposed to produce cramps. A common belief is that a mustard foot bath will bring on delayed menses. Many women think that their hair will not take a permanent wave while they are menstruating. It is also believed that preserves will not turn out right, cakes will not rise, cream will not thicken when whipped and other culinary undertakings will spoil if attempted during the menstrual time.

Other superstitions are: to burn menstruation cloths will dry up the blood, stop the period permanently and lead to lung trouble; mistletoe tea will renew the flow that has been stopped by a cold; a young fruit tree will die if touched by a menstruating woman; and if three women sitting in the same room are menstruating, one of them will be pregnant before the year is out.

Blood meant life itself to primitive man who considered it as a potent factor in accomplishing either good or evil effects, depending upon whose blood it was and where it came from. This same belief holds with primitives in the world today. Early man observed that blood played a part in ushering a new life into the world, and also that a person could bleed to death. With his strong instinct for the preservation of the race and his concern for his own survival, he looked upon blood as a deep mystery that confused him at every turn. He was further amazed by the fact that a woman had periodic losses of blood which signified in his mind that life's fluid was being wasted and irrevocably lost. Therefore his superstitious nature made him dread contact with a woman during menses lest his own life be endangered according to the primitive rule of sympathetic magic that "like produced like."

In order to prevent this contact, tribal laws compelled menstruating women to seclude themselves and remain out of sight. This was not only to protect the men, but also their food or anything else that would be in danger of contamination. Punishments were inflicted upon women who were careless about observing the law. If, by chance, a man encountered a menstruating woman and he became ill she was punished. For it was believed that "if a man looks upon a menstruating woman his bones will soften, he will lose his manhood and will even die, while his weapons and implements will become useless, his net will no longer catch fish, his arrows will not kill deer." Each tribe had its own taboos, which, for the most part, have come down to modern civilization.

"Menopause" or "Change of Life" Superstitions

ALTHOUGH MODERN SCIENCE has lifted the veil of mystery which for ages surrounded a woman's *climacterium*, or change of life, superstitious fears have not disappeared and this whole period—before, during and after menopause—is still laden with forebodings.

Old wives' tales and other hearsay fallacies picked up by women in their forties are a serious threat to their happiness. Some false notions are highly dangerous and women who pay attention to them can make life miserable for their husbands and children. There is a long list of the fears and phobias that continue to plague uninformed women. For example, there is no scientific basis for the phobia that the menopause is a common cause of insanity. However, if a woman is disposed that way by heredity, or her mental health has not always been the best, she may go through a period of serious mental disturbance. Doctors report, however, that only an occasional psycho-neurosis manifests itself during the menopause. At the same time, they call attention to the fact that middle age is the time of life when insanity is most likely to affect both men and women; but the condition is not necessarily related to the change of life.

Another fear that persists is that pregnancy at such a time of life is not only dangerous to the mother but may produce a child that would be old-looking, deformed or feeble-minded. This false belief has caused many hysterical fixations and climacteric psychoses.

It is also a superstition that an otherwise childless or seemingly barren woman may be impregnated at about the end of the menopause. Only a very few cases of childless women having conceived at this time are on record, and they are looked upon more as rare occurrences than as the general rule, as many women believe.

There are some women who believe that pregnancy is possible long after the change of life has taken place. This fixation is a hangover from Sunday school recollections of the tale of Abraham and Sarah. Sarah, though grown old, received a divine message that she would give birth to a son. The story goes that Sarah laughed within herself as she knew that her internal organs could no longer conceive. Nevertheless, a child was born to Sarah at the age of ninety. This miracle has been taken literally for centuries by susceptible women who are familiar with the story.

The superstitious dread of frigidity may be so overpowering to a woman during the menopause as to create a condition which can destroy, at least temporarily, otherwise normal emotions. Cessation of ovarian functions does not mean the end of sex life. This is one of the greatest fallacies associated with change of life. Many men endorse this superstition which unfortunately swells the divorce records. Contrary to the belief, authoritative sources report that many women who have completed menopause have their first normal sex reaction. One explanation offered is that they no longer fear the possibility of pregnancy.

Fear of losing their physical attractiveness obsesses many women during the menopause, particularly if they have had to control a tendency to put on weight. Dietary measures, regular exercise, and if necessary, glandular treatment under a doctor's direction, can offset obesity. In other respects, if a woman keeps her mind active, and acquires the wisdom and serenity of middle life, she can be more attractive than before.

Another dread that fills the mind of many women is that of developing masculine features when menstruation has ceased. Only a very small percentage of women grow hair on their faces, or have their voices drop to a lower register.

Cancer is in no way related to the menopause, although this malady does occur in middle age and therefore could be coincident with the change of life. Excessive bleeding is not a true symptom of the menopause. It may indicate some other condition such as a tumor, or even a cancer, so that bleeding in middle life demands a doctor's attention.

Most men today are aware that they, too, go through the change of life period at middle age and many of them are victims of unwarranted fears and superstitious rubbish pertaining to their virility, fertility and general condition of well-being. But their fears do not compare with the worry and distress that most women experience when they have to face the fact of losing their youth; the story of Faust notwithstanding!

"Syphilis" Superstitions

BECAUSE IT IS CONTAGIOUS, syphilis may be contracted innocently as the disease is acquired mainly because of lack of education in sex hygiene, and because of superstition. Thousands of syphilitic superstitious victims harbor such a fear of being found out that they by-pass available, modern clinical facilities until the ravages of this dread disease are beyond medical control.

Primitive ideas lie at the root of this superstitious attitude which regarded all diseases as the work of unseen supernatural beings who inflicted punishment upon humans; in the main, exorcism was the only formula to rid the body of its evil tenants.

As civilization slowly progressed, new superstitions were added, among them the general public opinion which considered immoral or sordid any reference to a disease transmitted by sexual relations. This is in keeping with the attitude of the ancients who asserted that sexual or vice diseases, or "sins," of the father would be visited upon the children even unto the third and fourth generation, and that there was nothing that could be done about it.

Up to the 15th Century there was no record of the existence of the disease known as syphilis in Europe and Asia Minor. Shortly following the return of Christopher Columbus from America, the disease was recognized and recorded. There are those, however, who adhere to the belief that syphilis existed in pre-Columbus Europe, and point to the existence of remains which have been exhumed, the skull formation of which indicated ravages similar to those resulting from syphilis.

Spaniards called syphilis the Haitian disease, the Italians called it the Spanish disease, the French called it the Italian disease, Mohammedans called it the Christian disease, and so on around the world.

Whether Columbus brought syphilis to Europe or not it must be admitted that through his companions he brought a new strain of pallid spirochete.

In 1838, Ricord finally distinguished syphilis from other venereal diseases, and Hutchinson and Fournier later added fresh information. But the disease remained a "shameful" malady, and superstitious fears, moral or otherwise, kept people from mentioning the fact that they had it, so that, as it had for centuries, syphilis continued to plague humanity.

Paracelsus used arsenic in treating syphilis back in the 16th Century, and mercury was another remedy that was tried when this sinister disease first swept across Europe. However, it was not until 1910 that Ehrlich's effective treatments were introduced for the earlier stages of the disease. Then a vigorous campaign began in America to bring syphilis into the open, but with minor success, mainly because no one could mention the word syphilis outside of a doctor's office without being frowned upon. It was not until comparatively recently that the word was even allowed to be mentioned on the radio because of the taboo on anything relating to sex going over the air.

But the primitive school of thought had not died out completely, and many believed that to interfere with the punishment of the gods was more dangerous than the disease. And so epileptics, lepers and others, including syphilitics, were allowed to contaminate others and die without ever being treated. People have not yet divorced themselves from this superstitious ignorance and false modesty, even in this age of advanced science, hence syphilis is still rampant.

Sexual or social diseases such as syphilis were looked upon not only as repulsive, but as the well-deserved punishment for a mortal's sin of infidelity and indiscriminate contacts,—known as "sins of the flesh."

Many superstitious victims believed that infection communicated to another left the infector free. And for centuries there was the belief that a virgin could cure a man of syphilis and not get it herself. A dreadful superstition, prevalent today, is that menstrual blood is apt to give a man a syphilitic infection. Some persons suffer from syphilophobia, the fear of syphilis, and even though they never had the disease, or had it and were cured, the superstitious dread that it is still with them haunts them. More often than not it may be a guilt complex.

Superstitious persons often refrain from marrying when a premarital test for syphilis is required, because they cannot face the fact that the report may not be negative. There is also a persistent superstition that a pregnant woman who has syphilis will have a diseased child, which is a fallacy. Medical care can protect the child and cure the mother as well.

The popular idea in America that most Negroes are syphilitic is not founded on fact. This dangerous misconception is described as a "growing belief" that close proximity to Negroes or even casual contact exposes one to danger of infection. It is reported that this superstitious notion works against the Negro in industry, where it is said that working near Negroes or handling tools after them exposes white workers to the disease.

Another superstitious attitude toward Negroes is that their greater sexual promiscuity accounts for the greater prevalence of syphilis among them. The fact remains, however, that syphilis was unknown in Africa, and that it was first called the "white man's disease." Promiscuity occurs among the black race just as it does among the white race, in groups and communities everywhere, including America. Wherever ignorance prevails there are hotbeds of superstition.

A String as a "Cure" or Aid to Memory!

TYING A STRING on one's finger, to remember something, is related to the belief of the ancients in the magic value of constriction or binding as an aid to solving a problem. Today, although superstitious persons are not aware of it, the implication of tying the string was, as it still is, to hold the thought or the wish to do something that otherwise might easily be forgotten.

Nowadays, as in olden times, a mother ties as many strings on a child's finger as there are errands or duties to be remembered. It does not matter which hand or which fingers; nevertheless, the result is that a child often grows up with the idea, now subconscious, that this is the only sure way not to forget certain things that must be done.

Long ago, a string, usually red, was tied on the left hand, by preference, because the left side was the heart side, or seat of intelligence, and of knowledge gained through memory. The common phrase "learning by heart," goes back to the days of this idea in regard to the heart.

A red string was believed more effective, because that was the color of magic in folklore, and was supposed to be more potent as an aid to memory or to carrying out a wish. Very probably, red was also selected because it is quickly seen, although it is doubtful if early peoples were as sensitive to color vibrations as we are today.

The string-tying habit is a hangover from the days when bracelets, anklets, garters, collars, belts, pieces of cloth and so on were placed on the affected parts of the body to limit pain or infection to one area, and to keep the inflammation from reaching other parts of the body. It was a very important belief in the lives of early peoples, that the spirit of life, or the soul, could be confined to one affected area, so that this spirit, or supernatural being, would stop the pain or cure the diseased part.

Many pains and diseases are still treated by the string method, applied in various ways. All except the tourniquet are superstitions and have no medical value. Among the useless remedies is the one that advises a person, when the right nostril bleeds, to tie a cord around a left hand finger, and for a bleeding left nostril, to tie it around a right hand finger,—the old superstition of opposites or contrasts being included in the formula.

The following are other string usages: The child who wears a black silk cord around its neck will never have diphtheria nor other throat troubles. Any string around the neck keeps away a cold. Wearing a piece of red wool yarn around the neck prevents nose-bleed, a tarred string around the neck keeps one from catching any contagious disease.

Despite the spread of medical knowledge by radio, magazines, newspapers and other media, farmhands, and other persons, too, wear a red string around their otherwise bare necks to keep off rheumatism.

A comparatively modern extension of the primitive and ancient custom of wearing a string as a curative aid is the scapular, consisting of two small square pieces of cloth, connected by cords, worn over the shoulders and under the garments, so as to be out of sight. Although the scapular is worn as a devotional observance, many wearers believe it protects them against many ills, and also against drowning.

"Memory" Superstitions

Two PROVERBIAL SUPERSTITIONS in relation to memory are, first, that an individual needs to have exceptional mental powers to develop a capacity for memorizing; and, second, that he may be too old to learn to recall or retain anything new. Memory experts and psychologists are as one in rejecting these beliefs, and suggest that what is most needed is a system, either one's own or someone else's, plus the desire to adapt oneself consciously and assiduously. It does not require a mental giant nor a youth to develop a retentive memory!

There is nothing supernatural about so-called memory gifts. Young and old people alike cannot possibly remember what has not been adequately impressed upon the mind. Memory experts say that if names are quickly forgotten, the memory is not necessarily at fault but the system, whether the teacher's or one's own, is. There are freak minds which can recall chance associations, but on the whole people can always remember names, places, and things which have a definite interest for them.

The superstitious notion that when people get old their memory is bound to be lacking in "spots" is a fallacy. These lapses of memory are sometimes due not so much to age as to the "gaps" created by what they do not hear or see, when these senses are weakened and not reenforced by eyeglasses or hearing aids. There are those persons whose brain cells have been damaged by alcohol or disease, or by too many electric shock treatments.

There is a very popular superstitious saying to the effect that professors are consistently absent-minded individuals. Some are and some are not. Professors, like other human beings, are sometimes unable to concentrate on two vital thought processes at once, and their untrained memories may fail to recall to do a certain thing at a certain time.

This false belief about absent-minded professors goes back at least to the sixth century B.C. when Thales, the Greek professor, absently fell into a well while taking a walk! Ever since then all professors have been called absent-minded. A definition to end all superstitious doubt about professors' quality of mind has been expressed by the inimitable Professor Irwin Edman of Columbia University. Professor Edman makes it clear that "absent-minded" professors have done well for humanity in discoveries of all kinds in chemistry, physics, mathematics, engineering, psychology, etc., and have rewarded the less absent-minded with the fruits of their prolific minds.

There are many superstitious notions to the effect that only intelligent people have good memories. Literacy and memory do not always go together. We need only to recall some of the prodigious feats of memory commonplace in primitive peoples who were totally illiterate! Entire national literatures, codes, and sacred books have been handed down from generation to generation by word of mouth.

That "concentrating" helps to remember is a false idea, as can be readily disproved when someone forgets something. Even the best trained minds occasionally experience lapses of memory if tense, fatigued, or disturbed. At such moments concentration may only heighten the tension and continue the blocking, but the moment the mind reverts to thinking of something else, it relaxes and clears the way for the forgotten item to be recalled.

Superstitions about memory are legion. Tying a knot in a handkerchief as an aid to memory. Rubbing the hand over a bald-headed man is believed by students to aid in remembering the answers in examinations. This superstition considers the head the seat of memory. The older the man, the more knowledge and wisdom.

To know something by heart, you must put it under your pillow at night. Possibly this gesture gives one confidence and the mind being properly relaxed the next day aids memory. Memorization is easier before breakfast than after.

The wearing of the stone *iris*, which is crystalline in structure, is said to improve the memory of those who wear it. Some believe that to read the epitaphs in a cemetery will be punished with a loss of memory.

There is quite a modern superstition which dictates that hypnotism can wipe out painful memories. Psychiatrists and psychologists report that hypnotism may assist in recalling painful material from the subconscious with a consequent improvement in the condition of the patient. But such improvement is apt to be of a temporary nature, and the condition (usually hysteria) recurs. It is not the memory schemata for particular events or experiences which are harmful, but the emotional charge accompanying such schemata. William James has expressed the idea that the art of living is a healthy-mindedness made up of remembering the good and forgetting the bad, a habit which makes for a balanced personality. There is no magic road to memory, except that of good health and good habits of adjustment to life.

"Camphor" Superstitions

A DANGEROUS SUPERSTITION is the practice of carrying blocks of camphor around the neck or on one's person, not as a disinfectant, but as a specific with which to ward off contagious or infectious diseases. Whenever there is a rumor of an epidemic, actual or imaginary, such as of infantile paralysis, the sale of camphor increases tremendously— a superstitious yardstick that indicates that old wives' formulas and remedies are going the rounds again.

In the large assortment of superstitious notions about camphor, as a preventive or cure, some are simple, while others are quite gruesome. These are observed almost everywhere,—in rural communities, suburbs and cities. For instance, if camphor is placed near or even in the bed, it will prevent the chills which lead to dangerous fevers such as typhoid and pneumonia, but principally, it will prevent catching "cold in the head." Another antiquated method to boycott germs of all kinds is to wear bags containing camphor, sulphur and assafoetida around the neck. This is supposed to be good for young and old alike. If a mother does not care to nurse her baby, she rubs her breasts with camphor for some time before the baby is expected, believing the milk that is already there will recede, or go back to where it came from.

Up to about a decade ago, Japan had the monopoly on natural camphor, processed from the wood of camphor trees, most of which came from the Island of Formosa. Now, however, the United States gets a large portion of its supply from southern pine trees.

The camphor hunters, members of the indigenous tribes of Borneo, Penang, Sarawak and elsewhere, are very superstitious about camphor. Among their beliefs is one that if a wife commits adultery in the hunter's absence, the camphor in the jungle will evaporate. While on their hunting trips, Malay natives in search of camphor eat their food dry and use only coarse salt, careful not to refine or pulverize it. The reason is that they hope to find large grains of camphor in the cracks of the trunk of the camphor tree. Were they to pound their salt fine, camphor grains would be fine too, and perhaps dissolve and disappear from the crevices of the trees.

Coming back to civilization, all doctors agree that camphor is not an effective germ killer, and that it does not ward off infection. This notion belongs to the era in medical practice of hundreds of years ago when demons of disease were supposed to be frightened by the bad odors of camphor, garlic, assafoetida and other strong-smelling substances.

Applied externally, camphor acts as a counter-irritant, and to some degree, as a local anesthetic. It is a definite antiseptic. Although it is a popular remedy for a "cold in the head" it is not to be relied upon as a prophylactic against ordinary cold, or influenza infections.

"Weight" Superstitions

ONE OF THE most common and dangerous superstitions pertaining to weight is that water changes to fat in the body. Consequently, people who dread overweight may injure their health by drinking too little water. Water may temporarily increase weight, but it never turns to fat.

There is another false belief which dictates that indulging in sugar helps to burn excess fat and thus reduces weight. This notion is a convenient excuse for addicts of sweets with a strong desire and a weak will. Sugar, however, does not reduce weight. On the contrary, excess sugar is turned to fat and stored in the body.

Many people believe that in dieting honey is better than sugar because it is lower in calories. Honey contains more water than sugar, but it does not lessen appreciably the chances of reducing unless used sparingly.

Fat people are not necessarily well-fed. Psychologists frequently have patients whose overweight is not due to food, either quantity or quality, but to an emotional state which affects the body metabolism and digestive processes. When the emotional disturbance is alleviated, the problem of overweight or underweight, as the case may be, takes care of itself.

Vinegar may reduce weight but only at the cost of damage to the digestion and appetite. It is diluted acetic acid, an item not recommended by competent physicians and dietitians. The belief that lemon juice, which is citric acid, will prevent excess food from turning into fat is equally erroneous and ill-advised.

Bath salts are thought to reduce weight. However, it is the profuse perspiration accompanying a hot bath rather than the salts which causes the reduction of weight.

Cathartics are sometimes used to reduce weight. The principal ingredient of a cathartic is usually salts, the excessive use of which may produce inflammation of the large bowel (colitis) and digestive disorders. This treatment does not effect a normal reduction of weight nor a permanent one, and illness may result.

Thyroid extract is very effective in reducing weight in certain cases but it is also very dangerous and should never be self-administered. Doctors themselves use it only with extreme caution to protect their patients against harm.

One of the latest chemicals used as a weight reduction agent is dinithrophenol, frequently the active ingredient in patent-medicine for obesity cures. The dangers courted with this medicine include blindness from cataract-formation. A number of deaths have been reported as the direct result of self-administration of this drug.

Dieting can be dangerous and even fatal. Severe dietary measures should never be undertaken without the counsel and guidance of a physician, regardless of superstitious convictions and hearsay!

Are Fat People Lazy and Thin People Quick of Action?

THAT FAT PEOPLE are lazy and thin people energetic is pure superstition. Laziness is now regarded as a mental illness, affecting the fat and the thin alike, and usually due to physical causes.

One of the main reasons fat persons appear lazy at times is that due to the greater weight they carry, their motions and movements are of necessity slowed up. Therefore, persons of large size are placed in the awkward position of seeming to perform fewer activities and accomplishing less work, in proportion to the time utilized, than leaner individuals.

Of course, slower action does not indicate that victims of avoirdupois are slower in thinking, as is often assumed. Contrary to popular notion, many thin persons are also slow of motion. Their lessened energies, however, are not due to the physiological causes which retard the activities of their stouter brothers and sisters. Unknowingly, thin persons are underweight and listless from psychological causes such as emotional instability, confusion, and all sorts of fears and frustrations. Fat people who are neurotic and do not lose weight, are as a rule victims of a glandular condition which produces excess fat on the body. In these cases, the mental condition is the result of the physical.

Thousands of seemingly lazy persons, both fat and thin, are cured of their inertia and become active, alert and energetic when they are fitted with the necessary and proper eye-glasses, which in this instance, proves that their sight was at fault, and not their minds or bodies. Others are found to be suffering from a chemical deficiency, which, when remedied, causes them to shed their laziness.

To the thin, energetic and active person, the lackadaisical movements of the fat person are sometimes irritating. This is simply a clash of temperament—not an indication that one is cleverer than the other.

Fat People, Gay—Thin People, Morbid

"LAUGH AND GROW FAT" is an old superstitious saying which has led many to believe that fat people are always happy. Modern science and recent statistics, however, have thrown an entirely new light on this subject. Instead, it is now known that the majority of overweight persons are not happy. Far from it.

This undeserved reputation for good nature and happiness attributed to fat persons, both young and old, is probably due to the fact that expressions of strain or displeasure are less apparent on their faces. Needless to say, the extra fatty tissue under the skin causes the muscles to be less flexible so that a frown or drawn lines are less evident on the faces of obese individuals than on thin-faced persons.

Another fallacy is that there are more fat boys than girls, as they are about numerically equal. Youngsters and adults alike do not know why they over-indulge in food. Often it is their subconscious that makes them keep on eating when they are no longer hungry. Psychologists claim it acts as a form of compensation for unsatisfied emotional needs and cravings. Biting fingernails is the same kind of reaction to inward unhappiness or self-uncertainty.

As a classic example of this there is the Shakespearian character—the feast-loving, unhappy, overweight Falstaff. The great English dramatist, (no mean psychologist himself), understood how outward behavior is affected by inward emotional starvation. Falstaff ate mainly to hide his disappointment over his wasted life—just as many persons do today.

"Falling" Superstitions

GRAVITATION, beneficial to man in ever so many ways, is also the source of one of his greatest fears—that of falling. And where there are fears, we know there will be superstitions.

Ordinarily, however, most falling fears are the result of traditional beliefs expressed in various ways. For instance, many superstitious persons believe that to fall over a stone, a chair or other object, means bad luck which can be negated by a countercharm which is to go back and touch the stone or whatever has caused the fall. Kicking a chair or table is equally good countermagic.

Paradoxically, it is a sign of good luck to fall uphill, which is symbolic of going up, of course. For centuries, a stumble or a fall of any kind has been associated with an impending catastrophe in the sense of a bigger fall about to come, unless prompt countermagic is used.

A common superstition nowadays is that if a picture falls from the wall, someone in the house will die before the end of the year. In this case, the countercharm is for the owner not to be the one to pick it up.

The superstitious fear of falling objects has its roots in earliest times, when man, keen as any animal in the jungle, could sense the slightest rustle near his cave, or the faintest approach of beast or man jumping out of trees to attack. Primitive man had every reason to be on the alert as he was beset by enemies all about him.

As man slowly developed, he lost much of his keenness, but he never lost entirely his fear of unexplained sounds, such as rustling and falling things. Today, when a window shade falls suddenly, or a picture, or anything else that causes a sudden sharp noise, even the bravest person becomes tense and alert for a moment, whereas a superstitious person is struck with terror by the same incident.

For thousands of years, man knew little of the phenomena of nature, whether in relation to animate or inanimate creations. In his simple way he attributed a soul or spirit to inanimate objects and believed them capable of actions similar to his, even including such powers as man himself had no control over. In keeping with primitive man's fears and beliefs, sudden noises and falls still instinctively arouse in many of us today the same premonitions that something uncanny or unpleasant, or even fatal, is about to happen.

An example of misinformation for which persons who themselves fear high places are responsible, is the belief that, despite definite knowledge to the contrary, a person who falls from a great height becomes unconscious or dies before landing. Fortunately parachute jumpers have provided the information which should allay such fears. It has been demonstrated that persons can drop from more than ten thousand feet, and still be conscious enough to release the parachute at three thousand feet from the earth and land in a state of perfect consciousness.

There are several types of falling fears, each with its own technical description. The fear of falling objects is known as *batophobia*, while the fear of falling downstairs is known as *climacophobia*, which is a companion phobia to the fear of height or *acrophobia*. *Acrophobia* is the fear which creates the feeling of vertigo when looking down from a high place, such as a building, tower, or any steep elevation.

The feeling of insecurity one feels at a dizzy height is quite natural, and an attitude that is innate in man. It is only when it becomes a phobia that it is a serious matter. When the symptoms are extreme, such as dizziness, or swimimng of the head, or the illusion that stationary objects are moving in all directions, this then becomes a case for a physician. Such a condition results from a change in the blood supply to the brain and may precede a dangerous affliction.

"Jinx" Accidents

MANY PERSONS are seriously hurt or die every year as a result of preventable accidents, because they think they are "jinxed." Recent surveys have shown that approximately 23% of workers had repeatedly met with accidents on their jobs, for the reason that they had a fatalistic attitude that they were unlucky and could not avoid something happening to them.

This accident-producing attitude varies among different types of workers of different nationalities. In Ireland and other countries, there are people who are still convinced that fairies are real beings who sometimes develop personal grudges, or get out of mood, and so contrive plots and pranks which cause accidents. Some go so far as to wear socks with white toes to prevent them from being tripped by the "Little People." In fact, this is how this type of sock came to be designed.

By wearing the protective white-toed sock, the fearful one gains faith in himself and hopes for a good turn of mind in the unseen supernatural being that might harm him. With his fears allayed, there is now little chance of an accident.

The up-to-date equivalents for the white-toed socks include all sorts of lucky charms that are sold to millions of superstitious-minded persons. These supposed accident preventives include the rabbit's foot, four-leaf clovers, bracelets, anklets, and others,—all worn or carried to keep evil spirits from tripping the wearer.

The fatalistic attitude toward accidents has been explained, psychologically, as an unconscious or conscious longing to be pampered and nursed after an accident, or a desire for revenge, or as a substitute for suicide. Repetition of unavoidable accidents is extremely rare. Fear, or other emotional upset, is responsible for a large percentage of the casualties and hour losses of labor. When a worker loses confidence in himself, or is beset by strong feelings of resentment or dissatisfaction, a lack of coordination is invariably the result, a most dangerous condition in the handling of tools or machinery, and sure to invite accidents.

"Hexing" Superstitions

In AMERICA, voodoo and witchcraft are still practiced in a number of states. An incredibly large public believes in the power of the modern witch or hexer to put others under the "spell," or that they themselves have come under it.

Those who harbor the fear that they are being hexed by a witch or character with an evil eye, seek the advice of hex-healers who are believed experts in the art of de-hexing or removing the curse on the supposedly bewitched one.

There are any number of powerful countermagic formulas of every imaginable description to unbewitch the bewitched. Whenever a whole household is under the impression that it has been hexed, the powwow doctor's favorite method for catching the witch is to place a broom across the doorway. It is believed that the spell will be lifted when the broom is picked up by the "witch," who will not be able to resist it, as this article has long been thought to be an indispensable article for working out her wicked deeds.

Another method is to start bonfires in front of the house suspected of harboring a witch to make her undo the harm she had been working on others in the home. Fire is a potent countermagic element as witches dislike it very much.

Mumbling a meaningless mumbo-jumbo is a common formula that it "breathed" on a child or adult who is believed seriously or dangerously hexed, especially when the hexing has taken the form of a wasting illness which may lead to death. It is believed that the voodoo curse of a witch will take effect unless the victim is convinced that he is being un-hexed and thereby can recover.

Pow-wow doctors recommend odd adjurations which many take seriously. For instance, a good remedy against slander is to take off your shirt, or another garment will do if it is close to the body, turn it wrong-side out, and then run your two thumbs along the body against the ribs, starting at the pit of the heart and going down to the thighs.

Another formula to prevent injuries is to carry the right eye of a wolf attached to the inside of the right hand glove. The one who does this will be free of harm, no matter who tries to hex him.

For those who wish to win in a game they are about to take part in, the heart of a bat, tied with a red silken string and attached to the right arm of the player will make him lucky, especially in a game of cards.

On the romantic side, to swallow a four-leaf clover is a charm that will help win a husband, providing a witch has prepared it in a special way before the unmarried girl swallows it. Placing onions under the bed will attract a sweetheart to the house, because it keeps away the evil ones who are jealous of anyone's happiness, by its strong odor. Before the onion is used, it must first have a charm put on it by a witch.

These are all harmless practices, but they still mean something to a very large number in America today.

From time immemorial, hex marks have been placed on all sorts of implements, and even furniture, by owners to prevent them from being stolen by sorcerers, or from having spells cast on them which would cause injury to someone.

Everything and anything can be hexed to do harm, according to those who believe in hexing. A "hex doll,"—(similar to an effigy)— or photograph, or other likeness of a person, may be pierced with pins and needles to drive the original mad, or even to bring about his death. When the superstitious victim learns what is happening to his image, his fears and fright are likely to fall in line with the evil designs, with tragic results. A man and woman may be hexed away from each other, causing sorrow and unhappiness.

"Being hexed" is an expression first used in Germany and imported into America by German immigrants who had not shed their beliefs in witchcraft. The German word "hexe" was not applied originally to human beings, but to child-devouring demons, corresponding to the Roman "lamia," a word used in that sense until about the 14th Century. In its present meaning, it appeared some time in the 13th Century. The modern interpretation is that a woman, believing herself a witch, has made a friendly pact with an evil spirit, which enables her to perform strange deeds by means of a variety of objects, words or formulas.

Persons susceptible to superstitious beliefs, usually those suffering from some type of mental disturbance, such as hallucinations or delusions, place faith in the power of such women to do good or evil,—whenever, of course, she is paid a fee or reward which she expects in return for handing out magic.

One modern approach to the hexing problem is to use hypnotism on the bewildered victim, to remove the fears of the "spell." This method does not guarantee to dislodge permanently the deep-rooted superstition.

Phobias

SUPERSTITIONS are closely related to phobias, as fear is the basis of all superstitions. It is the commonest of all human emotions and, except for the basic protective fear of insecurity, that of falling and of loud noises,—the last two present at birth,—nearly all other fears are acquired early in life. This is the consensus among psychiatrists and psychologists. Often, however, an adult acquires a fear or phobia which expresses an unfilled desire, although the desire may have no relation to the phobia except in a symbolic way.

Modern man, with a background of over five thousand years of recorded history, still lives amid constant though diverse fears, scientifically known as phobias. There are almost as many fears as there are objects and situations—an endless list.

Most fears have been named and among those that are better known to the layman are, claustrophobia, a morbid fear of enclosed places; agoraphobia, a morbid fear of wide open spaces; hydrophobia, a morbid fear of water; acrophobia, a morbid fear of high places which sometimes causes vertigo and a sense of unbalance; astraphobia, a morbid fear of thunder and lightning; hematophobia, a morbid fear of blood; aelurophobia, a morbid fear of cats; heliophobia, a morbid fear of the sun, due perhaps to suffering from severe sunburn; and others.

It is claimed that almost everyone possesses one or more phobias. A phobia is defined as any persistent exaggerated or senseless dread of something or someone. Phobias are purely mental, and very often can be traced to some early experience in life. They are curable, with the advice and treatment of a psychiatrist.

Nichiphobia is a morbid fear of darkness which can be traced back to mothers who have punished their children by placing them in dark closets or leaving them alone. In fact unintelligent mothers are to blame for many fears that reach the phobia stage. In some cases, too much attention to a child's timidity causes the fear to become a phobia. Accidents or personal injuries frequently cause a fear in the victim that the same thing will happen again and again. Hence the phobia.

Hematophobia, the fear of blood phobia, makes the victim useless if not hysterical at the sight of blood. The panic which occurs may be caused by an unconscious dread of pain or death. In certain instances, even the color red, not the blood itself, causes a mental and physical shock.

The subconscious mind, which has no reasing power, only remembers the fear which brings on the panic. The aggravating thing, from the victim's standpoint, is that he does not know why he has the fear or phobia. However, specialists in the field of psychology are well aware of the clues which reveal the type of phobia from which a person suffers. Their task, which is difficult, is to obtain a retrospective mental survey of the patient, to get at the roots of the trouble. When these are recalled and brought into the open, a cure may be effected in time.

CHAPTER 16

Sounds in the Night

"Sound" and "Word" Superstitions

THERE ARE "SOUND AND WORD" fans in modern America who are more superstitious than enthusiastic, although they do not realize it; and who display their fetishistic desires in a variety of ways. A good illustration is the use of the term, "The Voice" whether it applies to a worshipped singer or speaker. Then follows a peculiar type of fickleness, which may be an unconscious form of hysteria, when the public, sometimes overnight, shifts its adoration of a radio favorite, or other sound appeal, to new "rages."

Strange as it may seem, these countless radio "fans" are not far removed from those who came under the influence of oracles of ancient times. There are millions of cultists who crave modern incantations in one form or another, and who are victimized by the "word" or "sound" of the modern man or woman who happens to be the "oracle" of the day.

Radio, the ultra-modern system of word and sound communication, is rapidly becoming the magic channel through which primitive and medieval superstitions are revived in the minds of listeners who are given to fetishistic impulses and emotions.

Words and phrases, for evil purposes as well as good, were uttered long before any form of writing was possible, and probably since the dawn of speech. This particular type of superstition is generally included in the category of fetishes. It is universal, and is expressed under various guises by peoples of all colors, creeds and nationalities.

Sounds and word-formulas to exorcise evil are present not only in the modern scene, but words themselves are still believed to have supernatural power with which to cure the sick, or make the "end" easier. Formerly, when a sick person refused to take medicine, fearing it to be poison—sometimes with good reason—the doctor recited several Latin phrases, to give the patient confidence, just like the rôle of the "medicine man" in early times. The Latin words, incomprehensible to the sick person, were believed to have magical properties, and so the medicine was swallowed without further ado.

A similar rôle is performed today by the religious attendant at a bedside, who, both here and abroad, recites a prayer in Latin on one side, while the doctor gives the medicine or treatment on the other side of the bed. Superstitious fear is in this way doubly soothed—by the one representing the patient's faith, once the soothsayer's rôle, and by the man of science, who has replaced the witch doctor of other days.

The written word, which may be described as "imprisoned" sound, is psychologically soothing when reading prayers, but it is not a magic cure for all ills. However, some 250,000 Mohammedans today believe the sick can be cured by quotations from the Koran. Furthermore, the boundless faith and reverence of the Moslems reaches its climax when words from their sacred book are written on narrow bands of paper, rolled into pills, and given to the patient to swallow. If the patient recovers, it is due to his faith in Allah, his god. If he dies, he lacked proper faith.

Another interesting instance of word fetishism is found among the Polar Esquimos, the Iglulik group, who have certain word-formulas which are inherited as personal property. Each immediate family group in the tribe owns its own formula.

The Chinese, the Tibetans and a great number of other peoples all over the world use word-formulas or word-charms, for a variety of purposes, such as casting spells, or exorcising evil spirits, like the "hexing" of modern days.

"Kibitzing" or Looking Over One's Shoulder Superstitions

THE WORD "KIBITZER," a mildly opprobrious term, stems from the colloquial German word "kiebitz" which eventually found its way into the Yiddish language. It is the name of a bird variously known in English as peewit or laughing gull, green plover and lapwing. It is said that the "kiebitz," or bird in question was one which was frequently seen around in the fields undisturbed even when farmers were at work. True or not, the belief was that at the approach of hunters, its shrill cry gave warning to the game that the enemy was at hand.

In time, the word "kiebitz" was used to designate annoying and meddlesome spectators. But it was in the sixteenth century that German card-players called a person who looked over one's shoulder and by fair means or foul became an informer, a *kibitzer*.

The relation between a "kiebitz" bird and a *kibitzer* is obvious, in the sense that the bird's call found its equivalent in the informer or intruder.

Kibitzers, or their equivalent, however, have a long history. It is interesting to note that the ancient Egyptians actually sought the advice of official kibitzers; this function was based on an old superstitious belief that everyone is a second best and true guesser by nature!

There are in existence Egyptian tombs which show in paintings on them the Pharaoh playing the favorite and ancient game of dice, while official kibitzers are asked for their advice. This gesture is depicted by the Pharaoh who has turned toward the kibitzer directly in back of him, obviously by their mutual expressions of face and hands seeking and getting suggestions.

The kibitzer of today, however, is often called a "jinx" personage, rarely tolerated and more often than not asked to go. For that matter, kibitzers were even forbidden in the Old Testament.

On the darker side of the kibitzer picture, primitive tradition also suggests that he is a very undesirable character, especially if his shadow rests upon a person. It is well known that among primitive peoples, a person coming from behind was automatically considered dangerous. In the light of the real dangers which surrounded early man's crude way of life, he was justified in being afraid of beast and man who might catch him offguard. It is quite natural, therefore, that looking over another's shoulder, in primitive society, was a gesture which was made taboo!

Although it may be called etiquette in modern society, when we apologize for looking over a person's shoulder to read a newspaper or to see his playing cards, we are actually giving expression to the age-old fear of danger which a savage felt when he had no chance to defend himself if approached from the rear.

"Falsehood" Superstitions

PRIMITIVE PEOPLES living today, just as tribes long ago, are superstitious about telling the truth, and purposely avoid revealing facts about themselves. This is the opinion of anthropologists. The reason for this attitude is the belief that once the laws, customs and other information about a tribe are known, it would get the natives into trouble, not only with other tribes, but with unseen evil beings whom they suspect of always being on the lookout to learn how to cause the misfortunes that can be accounted for in no other way. Lying, therefore, is resorted to as a tribal as well as personal means of security. Hence, misstatements of explorers and travellers who have visited far away lands, and who have repeated what they have heard, have earned many of them the reputation of being liars.

This primitive type of prevarication, or the "gentle art of lying," has survived in the civilized world, and perhaps on a much larger scale. It is found in all walks of life with the excuse that some lies are a matter of self-protection.

There are a variety of popular falsehood superstitions. People with short fingernails are supposed to be tellers of tall tales. Many wrinkles around the mouth also indicate that the person is given to lying. If a woman burns a hole in her dress, someone is going to tell a lie about her. A person who is about to speak and forgets what he was going to say was prepared to tell a lie. Each speck on the fingernails discloses a lie that has been told. Anyone who clips his fingernails on Sunday will have evil stories told about him during the week.

The superstitious belief that blushing is a sign of lying is very unfair. Although the blood pressure is altered during deliberate falsification, it seldom produces a blush. There is about only one person in a hundred who blushes and it may be a truthful person.

That a person cannot look one straight in the eye while telling a falsehood is a superstitious notion denied by tests that show that at least three-quarters of the number of persons who lie can look straight into another's eye and tell a cold-blooded falsehood. As a matter of fact, it is claimed that the general tendency among those who lie is to look squarely at the one to whom the lie is being told.

The almost universal belief that hypnotism will make persons tell the truth is discredited by many authorities, and it has proved quite a failure so far at trapping liars. This superstition about hypnotism has been used as a fact repeatedly in literature, such as in imaginary court scenes and other settings when villains were supposed to be hypnotized into telling the truth.

Persons who are slow of speech are said to be liars, but that is not necessarily so. Handwriting cannot reveal the distinction between a liar and an honest person. As for the "lie detector," it is an instrument of the "third degree," and not a means of scientific crime detection. The chief usefulness of the gadget is as an aid to the police in scaring an ignorant or superstitious person into making a confession. An empty black box would serve the same purpose,—and has been used.

"Singing" Superstitions

NEARLY ALL SUPERSTITIONS that pertain to singing at certain times began as admonitions to children, but with time, they turned into superstitious beliefs which were taken over by adults.

One of the most popular superstitions about singing is that if you sing before breakfast, you will cry before the day is over. There are many versions of this, such as:

> "If you sing before you dress,
> You'll have trouble before you undress;
> If you sing before seven,
> You'll cry before eleven;
> If you sing before you eat,
> You'll cry before you sleep."

A few of the superstitions exclusively for children include: go to bed singing and you'll wake up crying; sing in bed and you'll get a whipping the next day; sing at the table and you may expect a whipping soon after.

The child who sings early in the day may be a happy child with a wonderful disposition, but in early days, parents thought it necessary to discipline this type of child. This is a form of psychological superstition that may have had its origin in ancient Greece where it was believed that it was presumptuous to show gaiety as the day began when nothing had been done to account for it. A child so careless as to sing too early in the day was tempting fate and was apt to bring about an unhappy mood by getting a whipping.

This superstition also demonstrates the idea that things often work in reverse, so that it was a form of warning mothers gave their children that their time might better be occupied with more serious things at the beginning of the day.

Among adult superstitions are: it is unlucky to sing in bed; if you sing before breakfast or at the table, expect a disappointment in love or business; if you unconsciously begin to sing in the bathtub, you will have good luck; if two persons begin to sing the same song at the same time, spontaneously, both of them will be lucky; anyone who sings while playing cards will lose the game.

A curious, and relatively modern, superstition surrounds the song, "I Dreamt I Dwelt in Marble Halls," from the opera, "The Bohemian Girl" by the Irish composer Michael Balfe. To sing, whistle, or even hear it played is a sign of bad luck to come. This is believed especially by theatrical folk and soldiers. During the World War, regimental bands often played this tune, and soldiers noticed that casualties were particularly heavy after it had been rendered. From this observation, the song became taboo and is seldom played by military bands either in America or abroad.

To Whistle or Not to Whistle

A whistling girl and a crowing hen,
Always come to no good end.
—Proverb

THE GREAT VARIETY of implications attached to whistling contains a mixture of both positive and negative magic. In modern times, for example, whistling occasionally—but not all the time—expresses self-satisfaction, such as in one's work. It also takes the place of a verbal exclamation to indicate a pleasant surprise, or a pleasant sight. Or, again, as John Dryden, the English poet, said, in *Cymon and Iphigenia*: "He trudged along, unknowing what he sought, and whistled as he went for want of thought!" On the negative side we have the school-boy, with his school-bag in hand, whistling aloud on his way to school, to keep up his courage, a familiar picture to this day.

Yet, ancient taboo placed on whistling survives to the present time, reminding us that it is still a sign of potential bad luck. For instance, in the theatrical world, whistling in dressing rooms is strongly objected to, to put it mildly, because it means the show will close or that some calamity will fall on one or all of the cast. Even actors who do not believe this superstition—a very few—will purposely refrain from violating the rule against whistling because of those who believe it an ill omen.

Today, in many parts of the world including America, children—boys especially—are told that to whistle in the house invites the devil to come in. From time immemorial, it has been considered unlucky for a woman to whistle, the implication being that she talked with the devil. At one time, a woman's mouth was said to remain impure for at least fifty days after she whistled. Little girls were told that if they whistled they would grow a beard.

Among grown-ups, especially when visiting or entertaining guests, to whistle in the presence of others was an unforgivable breach of manners, and if one whistled, accidentally, it had to be followed by an apology. This custom prevails today among the more conservative groups of society.

The phrase "You can whistle for it" is used every day as a taunt following a request for something, and means that the chances are the object asked for will never be given. A prescribed formula when passing or entering a cemetery at night is to whistle, to give the impression of nonchalance, when the whistler actually feels quite scared. It serves as a psychological antidote or countercharm in this case. In many localities, whistling in the dark is believed to keep away witches and ghosts. At least it produces a sound to offset the instinctive terror one feels in dead silence.

Whistling is frowned upon aboard the United States and English naval vessels, not so much as a breach of decorum, but because many sailors and seamen are superstitious and believe it will raise a storm. Sailors often say that whistling is mocking the devil, and it is sometimes called "devil's music." Another reason that whistling is forbidden aboard a naval ship is because it might lead to confusion since the pipe of the boatswain's mate—petty officer in the United States navy,—to call attention before issuing orders resembles a shrill human whistle.

Reporters are still called down for whistling in editorial rooms. Miners and others working underground believe that if anyone whistles, it means bad luck. More than once a group of laborers have had to quit work until the next shift because someone whistled, perhaps unintentionally, and disturbed the emotional balance of the men.

The Arabians believe that Satan touching a man's body causes him to produce a whistling sound. In Iceland, the natives warn the would-be-whistler with this phrase: "Who knows what is in the air?" France is probably the only country in the world where a law was enacted, 1690, forbidding whistling in a theatre.

To trace the origins of the taboo against whistling, it must be stated that primitive man interpreted, as best he could, what happened to him and around him. Often he used similarity as a basis. Certain sounds puzzled early man which made him condemn similar sounds. There was the snake's hiss when it was angry, the sound of arrows with their hissing messages of danger and death, and the weird and ominous noises of the wind, to mention a few. The sources of these sinister sounds could not be seen, but they were there, because they could be heard. Therefore a whistling or hissing sound of any kind was regarded as a sign of danger, a belief that became a deep-rooted taboo, and is still identified in our daily habits the world over.

The belief that if there were unheard sounds there must also be unseen beings was a natural primitive conclusion. Therefore, it came to be accepted that evil spirits were ever about, ready to perform mischievous and even fatal acts. As further evidence of this to the primitive mind, it was noticed that a dog would not only cock its head and howl at certain sounds, but would act strangely, at a time when a man could not see a thing about. When some early man first found he could whistle, he probably thought he had discovered a way of signalling. From this observation he then presumed that evil spirits might respond to the call or whistle, and so it was forbidden to all for that reason.

In time, as man advanced in intelligence, he would whistle for his dog, provided the whistling were accompanied by the snapping of his fingers, as countermagic. Even today, many snap their fingers when whistling for a dog.

The discovery of the act of whistling by using the mouth and breath in a certain way goes back to very early history. It is well known that in that way, whatever was associated with the mouth—saliva, breath, teeth and so on, had special superstitious meanings. Whistling came to be tied up with the casting of spells, and was forbidden at certain times and in certain places.

CHAPTER 17

Holidays and Holy Days

"New Year" Superstitions

NEW YEAR'S is man's oldest holiday, although celebrated at different times of the year by different peoples and races with highly diversified customs, beliefs and superstitions.

Astronomically, the year is based on the earth's circuit around the sun, which has no beginning and no end, but the approximate 365 days that the revolution takes have brought forth many calendars through the centuries, including Chinese, Hebrew, Mohammedan, Russian, Siamese, Egyptian, Ethiopian, Iranian and our own Gregorian.

All nations that use the Gregorian or reformed Julian calendar celebrate New Year's on January 1. The first day of the year is naturally of importance to superstitious persons as its events may have a tendency to affect all the days that are to follow during the year. Tradition dictates that what you do on New Year's Day you will do all the year through.

New Year's resolutions started with the Romans who by sacrifices and good conduct during January, hoped to please the god Janus and make the year a lucky one. They gave gifts to their relatives, and later by law, to the Emperor as a kind of tax. This is why, in Latin countries, gifts and visits are still exchanged on New Year's Day. This custom was also popular at one time in Anglo-Saxon nations, but has lapsed in recent years.

The ancient Anglo-Saxons celebrated the New Year by drinking Wassail, which means "to be well," and so we still drink toasts to one another's health at the year's opening.

Noise on New Year's Eve at the stroke of twelve, with bells and horns to send out the evils of the old year and to clear the air to give the New Year a good start, is a superstitious gesture whether we like to admit it or not.

Many persons are still conscious about the "first-footer" to cross the threshold after the New Year started, as he brings with him much or little luck according to who he is. For much luck, he should be a dark man, and for the best of luck, he should bring a gift of food to the house, for that signifies prosperity to the home for the rest of the year. If a blond, no luck at all.

At one time a good "first-footer" was so important that the "right" man was hired to appear at the exact time so as not to trust Fate to bring misfortune for a whole year. A widower always meant bad luck, and a redheaded person the worst luck of all.

England, America and the Scandinavian countries were the last to accept the changes in the old calendar. These countries, from their Druid heritages have retained many of the New Year superstitions of these peoples.

The American Indians celebrate their New Year's Day, the great winter solstice, with sun-dances.

"Valentine" Superstitions

"A magic spell will bind me fast
And make me love you to the last.
Let Cupid then your Heart incline
To take me for your Valentine."

THE LEGENDARY personage, St. Valentine, whose name has been taken as the sponsor of courtship, has given rise to superstitious beliefs, love charms, and customs which are just as popular today as they were centuries ago. The persistence of certain symbols throughout the centuries demonstrates the hold that folklore and tradition have upon people.

An ancient tradition in the folklore of many peoples is that at about the 14th of February, birds choose their mates for the coming year. The idea that man should imitate the winged and feathered creatures which could sing, fly, appear and disappear in the heavens, was suggested, and so a "mating" day was born.

In ancient Rome, the middle of February was the time of the Feast of Lupercalia, a festival in honor of Pan and Juno. At this time amid due rites and ceremonies, each young man drew by lot the name of a maiden who shared the festivities with him. In the newly Christianized Rome, Pan and Juno along with all the other gods and goddesses were discarded, but the feasts and celebrations continued in honor of St. Valentine, one of the first martyrs and saints of those days.

A common legend has it that on February 14th, 269 A.D., there was a priest or bishop in pagan Rome who was imprisoned for helping persecuted Christians. While confined he is said to have restored the sight of the jailer's blind daughter, who fell in love with him. Later he was clubbed to death. Another legend patterned on the same idea has it that it was a handsome Roman youth sentenced to die on the Appian Way. While awaiting execution he fell in love with the blind daughter of his jailer. His farewell message to her was received by his lady love at the tragic moment of the execution and was signed, "From your Valentine," presumably the young man's name.

Valentine was the name of several saints and martyrs of the Christian Church. According to the Acta Sanctorum, February 14 is observed as the day of seven of them. These martyrs had lived in various parts of the world. The two most prominent ones were a priest at Rome and a bishop in Umbria, both of whom lived in the third century.

Classic historians generally agree, however, that the holiday dates back to the early Roman festival of the Lupercalia, a lovers' festival patterned after nature and the return of Spring. In old Rome the 15th of February was the festival of Juno Februata—June the Fructifier—and the Roman Church is said to have substituted St. Valentine for the heathen goddess. At the festival of the Lupercalia, it was customary among other ceremonies to put the names of young women in a box, from which they were drawn by the men as chance directed. The Christian clergy of the day, finding it difficult or impossible to extirpate the pagan practices, substituted the names of particular saints for those of the women. The saints whose names were drawn were proposed as examples to be imitated by those who drew them. In many religious houses where this custom still prevails, each member preserves his billet during the year as an incitement to imitate the virtues and invoke the special intercession of his holy Valentine. The substitution of names of saints for lovers could not please the young people forever, and although the clergy repeatedly forbade the custom of Valentines and ordered the use of cards with Saints' names, the old pagan customs could not be entirely abolished.

Valentines appear to have taken root in England and to have survived there through all the mist and darkness of the Middle Ages. Heart-shaped epistles of greeting were in common use by the beginning of the 14th Century. Many of the great bards of England devoted a part of their talents to the writing of valentine verses, and it is a profitable business in the United States today.

The old English custom of drawing lots on St. Valentine's Day was that the person being drawn became the valentine and was given a gift of some kind, particularly a pair of gloves. If the young man had serious intentions of marriage, this custom in some way was a symbolic expression of asking for the young lady's hand.

Many still look upon the bird seen on the day of St. Valentine as a prophet. Among these beliefs are:

A blackbird: she will marry a man of the clergy.

A redbreast: a sailor.

A bunting: also a sailor.

A goldfinch: a millionaire.

A yellowbird: a reasonably rich man.

A sparrow: love in a cottage.

A bluebird: poverty.

A crossbill: a quarrelsome husband.

A wryneck: she will never marry.

A flock of doves: good luck in marriage in every way.

Red is the luckiest Valentine color, symbolic of the color of the heart. Above all it expresses fervor and devotion. Valentine is believed by some authorities to be a corruption of the word *galantin*, meaning lover or dangler, a French expression. St. Valentine was chosen as the patron saint of lovers.

"April Fool" Superstitions

". . . One fool expos'd makes pastime for the rest."
—Poor Robin's Calendar for 1728

WOMEN, in America and England, who are told that their slips are showing or that there is a run in their stocking grin as graciously as they can when they hear the derisive cry of "April Fool!" However, few, if any, realize how ancient this saying is, and that it deals with superstitious beliefs which interpreted symbolically the mysteries of nature.

Ancient peoples invented superstitious beliefs and customs around events such as their New Year, a spring holiday, when mythical beings played hide and seek, in imitation of nature, with the emotions of these men.

No one knows exactly the origin of this superstitious saying. Many traces in the folklore of races and nations couple it with the mythology of the Hindu, the Romans and other ancients, when fears were associated with the imaginary doings of gods and goddesses in charge of the New Year, which varied somewhat in different countries. Among the Romans it was about March 25, and the festivities ended about April 1.

In Roman mythology there is a legend that indicates that "April Fool's Day" may be a relic of the festival of Cerealia, held at the beginning of April. The tale comes from the Greek and relates that Prosperina or Persephone was sporting in the Elysian meadows, and had just filled her lap with daffodils, when Pluto carried her off to the lower world, where he made her his wife. Her mother, Demeter, searched for her disconsolately through long wanderings. In her anger and despair, she made the earth barren until it was arranged that Persephone should spend two-thirds of the year with her. Ceres was the Roman name for Demeter, and it is poetically said that Ceres heard the echo of her daughter's screams and went in search of the voice, but her search was a fool's errand, since all she found was the "echo of a scream."

In India, a festival corresponding to the Roman festival of Cerealia, and known as the Huli Festival, occurs on March 31. It has been an immemorial custom to celebrate this occasion by playing tricks on others, and on the last day of the festivities, which are dedicated to the vernal equinox, people for generations have amused themselves by sending their friends on foolish and fruitless errands.

Someone's imagination has connected April Fool's Day with Noah's mistake in sending out the first dove before the waters had abated. According to Hebrew legend, this occurred on the first day of the old Hebrew month that corresponds to our April. There are some persons who explain April Fool as related to the uncertainty of the weather in April. Another explanation is related to the mockery trial of Christ, the Redeemer, when he was sent hither and thither, or as they say, from Annas to Caiaphas, from Caiaphas to Pilate, and from Pilate to Herod, and from Herod back to Pilate; the crucifixion having taken place about April 1.

"Easter" Superstitions

THE GOOD LUCK superstitions that go with the Easter holidays are related to ancient sun-worship. The word Easter comes from Eastre or Ostâra, a mythical Norse deity, goddess of life and spring. A festival was held in her honor every time spring came around, and the month it was held was known to the Anglo-Saxons as "Eastre moneth." Easter is also known as "Pasch," a Greek word, which is similar to the Hebrew word for the spring holiday of the Passover of the Jewish people.

Easter is spring, and there was spring rejoicing in pagan times as there is today. Being sun-worshippers, ancient men were far more conscious of their dependence upon the warmth of the sun than we are. Its return toward the earth and the renewal of its life-giving qualities caused joy and worship.

The egg was symbolical of resurrection centuries ago, signifying the return of life. The hare represented abundant life and the fertility of the earth. Such symbolism is ancient beyond the records of history.

A modern descendant of the ancient ritual feasts to celebrate the spring holiday is the elaborate Easter breakfast which is especially popular in rural communities. In America the favorite dish is ham and eggs, symbolic of plenty. The variety of dishes served on Easter, however, goes back to early agriculture and stock-raising, which have left their mark on our menus. For instance, in India, the hen was of great importance. In ancient Egypt and China, pigs and hogs were highly regarded. Other dishes and customs have come from Scandinavia. Easter or spring festivals have circled the world with symbolism and superstitious beliefs and customs most of which have left traces in our own ways and observances.

In ancient Greece, the rites of Adonis were held on the vernal equinox, the original New Year. An ancient Celtic superstition said that the sun danced on this day, so that in parts of Ireland people still arise on Easter mornings to watch the sun "dance" in a shimmering bowl of water.

The return of spring at Easter meant the return of life so that the egg, symbol of life, came to be used in Easter celebrations. Easter eggs were highly colored to represent the flowers that would soon bloom. In old England, hard-boiled eggs were given to children, who sang in the streets and rolled them down a hill. The last egg to break brought good luck to the one who rolled it. This egg-rolling was practiced on the White House lawn in Washington, D. C., until very recently.

Because hares were born with eyes open, they were sacred to the "open-eyed" moon in Egypt, and thus connected with Easter, as the date is set by the moon's orbit to this day. The Germans made the hare sacred to the goddess Eastre, and said that on Easter Eve it would lay eggs for good children. In America the hare became a rabbit, or

Easter Bunny, an error for which candy-makers were probably responsible.

To imitate Nature's emergence in her own gorgeous new attire of delicate green, in ancient times, when Easter was New Year's Day, people cast off their old clothes to start the new year right. Therefore the custom of wearing a new outfit on Easter is a hold-over from this time. The custom of wearing new clothes prevailed also in northern Europe as it was considered discourteous and therefore bad luck to greet the Scandinavian goddess of Spring, or Eastre, in anything but a fresh garb, since the goddess was bestowing one on the earth. Needless to say, the Easter Parade on Fifth Avenue, New York, is the most famous survival of this old custom.

There is an old superstition that wearing three new things on Easter assures good luck throughout the year. It is interesting also, that in early times, the Easter "bonnet" was a wreath of flowers or leaves. The circle or crown expressed the round sun and its course in the heavens which brought the return of spring. From this crude crown of leaves or flowers evolved the hat or cap worn by all today.

The Easter lily, among many other Easter emblems, is the white symbol of purity, its V-shaped cup signifying the cup of life.

There is a quaint old Easter superstition by which the head of a household divides a gaily colored egg so that each member of the family gets a piece. Later on in life, if any member of the family should get lost, thinking of those with whom he shared the egg will make the others think of him, and their thoughts will help him to come home.

The determination of the date on which Easter will fall has an interesting background. The date is fixed by the first Sunday after the full moon which appears on or next to March 21. If the full moon is on that Sunday, Easter is one week later.

The reason why the Feast of Easter is not a set date on our Gregorian calendar is because it is determined by the ancient paschal or Jewish lunar month. This paschal moon itself is not an actual moon, but a sort of arbitrary moon governed by European longitudes. If local longitudes were considered, Easter would appear on a different date in America. The Church itself decreed the present method of determining the date at the Council of Nice in 325 A.D. Under this system of reckoning the date of the observance of the Resurrection of Christ may vary as much as 34 days on our calendar, for it can fall anywhere between March 22 and April 25.

The two celebrations, the Christian Easter and the Hebrew Passover, come approximately at the same time. With the Hebrews, however, it commemorates their flight from Egypt and is called the Passover because the angel of death "passed over" and spared their homes on the eve of the Exodus.

In the United States Easter is primarily symbolic of the return of spring for everybody; Christians and Jews alike observing their respective holidays at about the same time.

"St. Christopher" Superstitions

IT IS NO EXAGGERATION to say that millions of superstitious persons would not drive a car, take a sea trip, ride in a plane, or undertake a trip of any kind without carrying the traditional good luck safety token of St. Christopher. This little medal or image of the patron saint of travellers is sold wherever the superstition prevails, which is practically all over the world.

In peace and in war, those who have the St. Christopher medal on their persons believe they will live a charmed life. For instance in the Second World War, servicemen had these silver charms hammered into the soles of their shoes.

The custom of attaching an image of St. Christopher to an automobile is so universal that a great many cars come from the factories with this image worked into the body design. And yet ultra moderns claim this is *not* a superstition!

And who was St. Christopher? He is a legendary martyr of the third century, supposedly a native of Palestine and Syria, and a giant in stature and strength. He was of a boastful nature, always in quest of one stronger than himself. Finally he enlisted in the service of the Devil. Christopher was a non-believer and carried travellers across a river or stream on his shoulders as his trade. One night while carrying a child, its weight steadily increased until the giant's strength gave out and he was forced beneath the water and thus baptized. The child was revealed as the Christ, carrying the world in his hands!

Then, the legend further relates, finding out that Christ was stronger than the Devil, St. Christopher left the services of the Fallen Angel. He became a wonder-worker, suffering himself to be beheaded so that his blood might heal his enemy.

Thus it happened that St. Christopher became one of the most popular saints of Europe and Asia. He was frequently the subject of early Christian art, and the Churches honored him as a patron of ferrymen. That is why today, the superstitious believe that he who sees St. Christopher, or his image, on land or sea or in the air, will not be hurt that day.

Another legend reveals that St. Christopher was believed to have inherited some of the attributes of Hercules, who achieved the twelve great labors of mythological lore.

The feast of St. Christopher is officially July 25, on which day his images and medals are sprinkled and blessed with holy water. In Europe in earlier times, St. Christopher is said to have had attributed to him some of the characteristics of Thor, the powerful Norse god. In some places the peasants believe in St. Christopher as the protector of their crops and the one who safeguards them against tempests and destructive pests.

"Hallowe'en" Superstitions

HALLOWE'EN is now a day of merry-making instead of the gloomy festival it once was. The holiday is celebrated by the younger generation everywhere, in the pattern suggested in days gone by, dressing up as spooks and trying their hand at foretelling the future by various means, as well as indulging in other traditional customs.

Although the direct ancestor of Hallowe'en is the Druid "All Souls' Day," many of the practices observed in the celebration are far older. For instance, the bonfires which are built outdoors or in hearths on October 31, stem mostly from the worship of Baal, the Syrian sun-god, whose worshippers built fires in his honor about the same time of the year as Hallowe'en. The building of the bonfire is related to the worship of the sun and solar activities symbolized in fire itself.

As western civilization is heir mostly to Roman customs, we find another indirect ancestor of Hallowe'en in the Feast to Pomona, goddess of fruits, which was held on November 1, the day stores of fruits and nuts were put aside for the winter. These customs were combined with the Druid Thanksgiving for harvests which occurred on October 31. The Druid Thanksgiving was the feast of Saman, lord of Death, who called together at that time the souls of all the wicked ones that had been condemned to inhabit the bodies of animals during the year. The good souls were believed to take human form. As it was impossible to tell the real human beings from the ones inhabited by ghosts a great deal of caution had to be exercised. Furthermore, during the feast, the witches were free and in the mood to tell things, so that predictions in various forms took place.

Because of their old superstitious belief that once a year the dead came to life, the festival came to be called All Hallow Even or All Souls' Eve. Pope Gregory IV in 837 set aside November 1 as All Saints' Day for honoring the saints instead.

Although at first the day was observed only in the church, lower classes took an interest in the festival. They circulated weird tales about ghosts and goblins being abroad on the eve of All Saints' Day, and built great bonfires to keep them away. Fears were calmed by groups getting together and feasting on nuts and apples from the summer harvest. This lasted all night as they were afraid to go to bed lest a ghost or spook would be there.

Ghosts were believed to be entertaining in their former homes, sitting around the fire with their living relatives serving them refreshments. It was also believed that any harm that might be inflicted by a wicked soul could be lightened by gifts. A good soul was believed to enter the body of another human being for the occasion, but the wicked ghosts, bewildered, had to roam about in search of some form of abode.

During and following the Roman occupation of England, many of the customs of the Roman Feast of Pomona were absorbed into the custom of the Druid celebration. Among them were roasting nuts in large bonfires. Apples were used in divination of one kind or another, especially in marriage prophecies. It was also the Roman custom of honoring their goddess of Fruit Pomona, that led to the superstitious belief that eating apples would drive away evil spirits. Another superstition developed, that if a girl ate an apple before a mirror on Hallowe'en, the mirror would have the power of showing her the face of her future husband.

Since ghosts or spooks are invisible, and figments of the imagination, mischievous children on All Saints' Eve undertook to play the part of ghosts and witches, disguising themselves in the garments of adults. The fears and gloom of former observances of Hallowe'en were turned into mockery by lively youngsters who now played pranks of all kinds, much as they do today; ringing door-bells, stealing gates and posts, carrying pumpkins with lighted faces, chalking coats and windows, and so on.

The black cat figured in Hallowe'en because Satan, especially during the Middle Ages, was believed to take the form of a black cat while consorting with the witches. To be lucky, a rabbit's foot—not a hare's foot—had to come from a white rabbit shot at midnight in a cemetery on Hallowe'en. Evil spirits were supposed to leave their animal bodies on this night. Medieval people believed cats and rabbits were inhabited by these wicked souls, and when these animals were seen on the ground where the dead were supposed to rest forever, the animals found were taken for ghosts in disguise.

The American custom of carving grotesque faces on pumpkins was also a form of thanksgiving celebration in olden days. The pumpkin was a symbol of the harvest, and making pumpkins into jack-'o'-lanterns is reminiscent of the sun and the warmth which brought them out of the earth.

Chalking backs came from the English custom of drawing a white circle on one's back to show that the rule of the sun, or summer, was over. The fortune-telling phase of Hallowe'en has many origins, combining Druid paganism and medieval superstition.

The Celtic New Year was the time for marriage prophecies as well as auguries of death. Winter was the mating season—in colder regions—and boys and girls wished to know their future partners. Fortune-telling on Hallowe'en continued through the Middle Ages and is a lively feature at the modern Hallowe'en party.

Hallowe'en walnuts were each named and thrown into the fire by the maidens, and the nut that burned the longest represented her future husband. The same is done with chestnuts today. "Call-cannon," a vegetable dish, was cooked with a gold ring in the center, which foretold marriage for the one who found it. Nowadays all sorts of tiny objects are baked in a cake, each one a message of the future to the one who finds one. For instance, a thimble signifies an old maid; a coin, wealth; and so on.

Many of the games and superstitions of the Middle Ages survive in Ireland, Scotland, Wales and Brittany. In eighteenth-century England, each family carried lighted torches into fields and marched about sunwise—right to left—for good crops. In Brittany, pebbles with chalk crosses or circles are placed in smouldering ashes of the Hallowe'en bonfire and left overnight. Next day everyone looks to see if the pebbles have been moved or changed in any way. If so, the one who marked that pebble is doomed to die.

The delightful legend of Theseus and the Minotaur probably suggested to a Medieval maiden that she could lead her future husband to her if she threw a ball of yarn from her window. The story tells that Ariadne, the daughter of Minos, king of Crete, fell in love with Theseus, who, by the clue of a thread she gave him, was able to escape from the Labyrinth after he slew the Minotaur, a celebrated monster, half man and half bull. Ariadne fled with Theseus, who abandoned her on the Isle of Naxos, where Dionysus found her and made her his wife. The peel of a whole apple, unbroken, if thrown out of the window, is believed to take the shape of the initial of the future husband if the peel is found in one piece the next day.

"Thanksgiving" Superstitions

THANKSGIVING is one of the world's oldest holidays, beginning in prehistoric times, when all tribes and peoples who tilled the soil set aside a time each year to give thanks to their gods for the harvest.

The first Thanksgiving Day in the United States was celebrated at Plymouth, Massachusetts, in appreciation of their first harvest, by the colonists who came over from England to find religious freedom. The exact day of the solemn occasion is not known but some historians believe it was February 22. On October 3, 1864, President Lincoln in the first national Thanksgiving Day proclamation set aside the last Thursday in November for a country-wide observance of thanksgiving. Thanksgiving has been nick-named "Turkey Day."

Thanksgiving and the eating of turkey on that day is older than the Plymouth colony, however, as it has been traced to the Mayans. When football fans turn out for a Thanksgiving game, unknowingly they are conforming to a typical old American custom. As a matter of fact, Thanksgiving football games were instituted in America about 2000 B.C. The ancient Mayans dined on turkey and had a day set aside on which they offered up the first fruits of the harvest season, feasted, played, or watched a ball game in a stone-walled enclosure.

Some years ago the department of Middle American Research at Tulane University discovered that the Mayan games were like the present American games in many respects. Just as fans travel miles to see Thanksgiving games, so did the Mayans journey across the land, on foot or on animal back, to Chichen-Itza, holy city of these people, to view the holiday spectacle.

These ancients even added to the excitement of the game by providing band music for the spectators. Gourd-headed trumpets and wooden drums took the place of modern instruments, and in their weird way, they were no less harmonious and thrilling than the Army and Navy bands of the United States today.

In his description of the Mayan game, Maurice Reis then on the Staff of the Department of Middle American Research at Tulane, says:

"As it began when Rome ruled the waves and Frenchmen wore bearskins as their Sunday best, football wasn't just football. That is, the ball wasn't kicked with the foot, and the scores were produced by persuading the ball to pass through a perpendicular ring high in the stone wall."

When the thousands of pilgrims who came each year arrived at Chichen-Itza, they offered sacrifices to the earth gods in an impressive thanksgiving ceremony led by their ruler. Superstitious beliefs and custom of all kinds were a part of the many formalities.

"The earth gods," says Alfredo Barera Vasquez of the staffs of the Mexican National Museum and the National University of Mexico, who is of Mayan descent, "are called the four Bacabs and are represented as supporting the four corners of the earth. Each god has an appropriate color: red for the East where the sun rises, black for the West where it sinks into darkness, yellow for the warm South and white for the cold North. Yum K'ax, Lord of the Forest, resides at the center of the universe and is characterized by the colors blue and green.

"The thanksgiving ceremonies still take place in some parts of Mexico today although most of the old customs are dominated by the Catholic influence.

"The name of the principal god of the harvest is lost. However, we have many representations of him on ancient monuments. He is always depicted as being young and handsome, symbol of life and growth. From his head grows maize instead of hair."

A picture of this nameless god stands out from that of other gods, for he is one of the few whose features are not distorted in some grotesque way. His maize-leaf covered head reminds one of the young Greek god, Dionysus, with the grapevine in his hair. One of the Mayan's hands is extended in a gesture of giving.

Football players are very superstitious, even today. Among many superstitions is the famous gesture of the midshipmen at the United States Naval Academy, at Annapolis, Maryland, who are said, for instance, never to go to a football game without first giving a left-hand salute to the wooden figure of Tecumseh—an Indian Shawnee Chief, popularly called "the Prophet,"—as well as throwing pennies to it before playing games or passing examinations. An outstanding instance of the survival of the fear of shedding blood is evidenced in the warning given to most, if not all, of the football teams, which cautions them that the team that sheds blood first will lose.

Since prehistoric times festivals have been held everywhere to express gratitude to the respective gods and goddesses with offerings of the first fruits of the season, for the blessings of the harvest. The ancient Greeks, for example had an annual nine-day holiday in honor of Demeter, goddess of Grain Fields and Harvest. The Israelites observed Thanksgiving in a grand manner. It was observed not only for the bounties of the land, but more particularly because of their escape from Egypt. It is called their Feast of Tabernacles and lasts seven days.

The Thanksgiving customs and superstitions of the Romans and Druids were combined in their harvest festival on October 31, Hallowe'en Day. The pumpkin pie eaten at the end of the turkey dinner in the United States is a hangover from the days when the pumpkin was a solar and harvest symbol.

There are many superstitions connected with the fowls eaten on Thanksgiving, particularly in the colder regions where weather is a vital factor. If the breastbones are light in color, there will be a great deal of snow; if dark—reminder of the earth—little snow may be expected. And of course, there is the usual wishbone superstition.

Canada also has a Thanksgiving Day, but the date is not uniform as it is fixed each year by the Governor General's Thanksgiving Day proclamation. The second Monday of October seems to be the date usually settled upon for this holiday. It would seem then, that the Canadian Thanksgiving date keeps closer to that of the ancient Roman, Druid and English holiday of a similar nature.

The tradition of thanksgiving goes on everywhere, with its tribute to the sun, source of plentiful crops and all fruit of the earth. Even the golden football, dancing in the air on Thanksgiving Day, may be regarded as a solar symbol, expressing man's gratitude to the sun.

"Christmas" Superstitions

CHRISTMAS was originally a solar holiday, celebrated when the Winter Solstice marked the start of the sun's course to the north. The ancient Scandinavians celebrated the return of the sun by kindling special log fires to symbolize the sun's heat, light, and life-giving virtues. In the feast of Jul a great fire was kindled in honor of Thor. The Goths and Saxons called the festival Jul, and thus we get the words "Yule," "Yuletide," and "Yule Log."

There are many superstitions about the Yule Log. In olden times it was burned in a hearth, and whenever possible took a year to consume itself. Each year the ashes of the log were carefully collected and strewn over the fields in the belief that the crops would be benefited. The customary procedure was to bring a large log to the hearth with much ceremony, and to light it with a brand saved from the Yule Log of the previous Christmas.

In feudal times the cutting of the Yule Log from a huge root was accompanied by much singing and merriment. In the baronial hall of the well-to-do, the bringing in and the lighting of the Yule Log became the most joyous of the Christmas celebrations. Today the Yule Log is lighted in rural communities and its name given to the Yuletide Season. Chocolate Yule Logs or cakes are made in America today, in keeping with the beliefs which symbolized the sun, fire, warmth, fertility, and life in general.

The sky was early man's calendar, and many festivals such as Christmas and Easter owe their origin to astronomy. The rebirth of the sun was also believed influential on human beings for the birth of a son or child, since the sun in its better aspects symbolized the seed of life and offspring.

Modern customs and beliefs stem from ages past and are closely inter-related. Solar festivities mainly symbolize the Sun, or Fire and express appreciation to the Heavenly Eye. The most important rôle of Agni, one of the Vedic gods of India, was primarily the god of the altar fire. Agni was also represented as the trinity of life. It was believed that this fire-god was the mediator between the gods and men among whom he lived. He was represented as red, and with two faces. Janus, the January or fire-god, is also represented with two faces, round as the sun, to see the old year go out and the new one come in.

From the Vedic hymns one gathers that Agni was the supreme deputy of the deity in each home, guarding, rewarding, and punishing the occupants when they so deserved. This has been the rôle of the hearth or fire-god for thousands of years among many people, especially the Chinese. The custom that a home must be swept, scoured and cleaned for the reception of the hearth spirit is very old. The modern approach has added that Santa Claus will reward only worthy children.

In China this regard for the hearth spirit is not only for the little ones, but for the elders as well. Some adults are often so fearful of what this spirit, Tsao Wang, will tell about them in heaven that they smear the lips of his picture with syrup to seal them. It has been the duty of this fire god, who is represented to housewives and children as wearing a pointed red cap and jacket, to make a trip to the heavens each year to report to the gods. He returns in time for the feast to distribute appropriate favors, in line with modern customs at Christmas time and the rôle played by Santa Claus.

It is not altogether clear why the modern Santa Claus descends by way of the chimney, except as patterned after the god of fire, Agni, and other similar solar gods, for whom the fireplace would be the natural entrance and exit. It is interesting to note that in China and Germany, a little red Santa Claus dressed with a red cap and jacket is kept in niches near the fireplace the year round. Women still whisper their secrets and worries into the chimney or oven so that this ancient friend of the house will intercede for them when the yearly journey to heaven occurs again.

In the pagan religion of the Romans, the solar festival was given in honor of the god Saturn, the god of seed-sowing. This festival, the Saturnalia, began on December 17, on which day the official rites of the sun were celebrated. Unofficially, it was a sort of carnival, in which masters served slaves and a king was chosen to preside over the feast. Today this is performed with a few differences at the Feast of the Epiphany, also known as Twelfth Day—the 6th of January in the present calendar—at which time a bean or pea cake custom takes place, and festivities are held to name a king or queen.

The modern evergreen and red trimmings help make the indoor scene like that of the forest sanctuaries of olden days. The custom of decorating Christmas trees is said to come from Germany. At one time trees were decorated outdoors with voluntary offerings to the god of fire, or solar god.

Evergreen twigs are still used for trimmings and decoration because of the old superstition that forest elves and fairies came into the house with the evergreen and freed the inhabitants from harm. Evergreen sheltered these spiritual beings outdoors during inclement weather. Food was generally left, as a form of supper offerings, for the Christmas spirits.

Santa Claus is none other than Saint Nicholas, a Bishop who lived at Myra, in Asia Minor during the fourth century. Bishop Nicholas distributed gifts to the poor and sweets to the children. The modern equivalent is good cheer, good-will, and the joy of children who ask him to fill their Christmas stockings with gifts.

The relatively modern word Xmas is thus spelled as an abbreviation for Christmas, having its origin in the fact that the Greek letter *chi* was written X. Many people identify the X as representing the cross, and associate it with the death of Christ on the cross.

Christmas was not always celebrated on December 25th. Prior to the third century it was celebrated at various times, sometimes in the spring. In 1650 the Puritans in Massachusetts banned Christmas, believing that the frivolity and feasting were associated with pagan rituals.

"May" Superstitions

THE RETURN of the spring sun has always been a signal for celebrations and festivals, which began thousands of years ago, when customs were born in superstition. Many of these ancient practices are still observed in May Day activities, such as the Maypole dances, sun dances and the May Day Parade.

The dances around the Maypole were of great importance to the Druids, Romans and Phoenicians, because it was their way of entreating Mother Earth to be fruitful and to give them a prosperous season. The ceremonies were held also to drive away the evil spirits who were responsible for cold, darkness, illness and barrenness. The Maypole was the symbol of life and fertility.

In ancient Rome the celebration was called "Floralia," or the feast of Flora, and lasted five days. In ancient Briton, the Druids, who were sun-worshippers, lighted fires on the first day of May as a mark of honor to the sun. This practice was called "Beltun," meaning "Bel's Fire," or the Celtic name for May Day. Lighting the bonfires became known as "Beltane fires."

In order to demonstrate more forcibly the dual principle of life and fertility—male and female—it was customary to light two fires close together; and between these, both men and cattle were driven, in the belief that health was thereby promoted and diseases warded off. The ceremony also has a suggestion of fertility for them.

It is only within the last century that the annual celebration with the Maypole ceremony has been changed to its present form in the United States where it has become a gala occasion for children. To dance about the Maypole stems from the pagan worship of the mighty tree, wherein kindly disposed supernatural beings were believed to reside. The spirit of growth and renewal of life was demonstrated in its spring budding or in its evergreen qualities.

The eve of the first of May was believed a dread night by the early Britons, and certain rites were performed. Sinister powers were supposed to ride through the air. To banish them, fires were built around villages. The next day, the young folks brought new green boughs and flowers to their cottages to be used in the ceremonies.

At dawn a wreath was left at each cottage door by the troop of joyous carolers who wakened the staid community to greet the morning of May Day. Good fairies blessed the house which had something green upon the door and those who believed in fairies put out bowls of milk for the refreshment of their tiny visitors, and soon the milk was gone!

Another ceremony, that of blessing the water, also took place early in the morning of May first. Girls believed that if they washed their faces in the dew of May mornings they would gain perfect complexions and lose their freckles. May Day was also an occasion for divination of all kinds, especially of looking into the future for a husband-to-be.

The Maypole decked with bowers and garlands used to be brought into the village in a cart drawn by oxen. It was set up in the village green, and nearby the Queen of the May was enthroned. The prettiest girl in the village was chosen. Her subjects sang and danced before her. The winding of the Maypole developed later. Bells formed a significant part of the old May Day festivities, and were rung as a kind of alarm clock to awaken the soil to activity, and to make the seeds and roots flourish.

With the coming of the Romans, the Druids as a group were destroyed, but their customs and superstitions which had spread over England and Wales and across the Irish Sea became traditional. They have reached American shores, where their symbolic significances are still part of the American scene.

One of these inherited May Day customs was very popular in New England at one time. Dainty baskets covered with crepe paper, filled with fresh flowers, decorated with bows and containing confections were hung on doors. After ringing the bell, the donor ran away and hid. A merry search followed, often unsuccessful.

The American Indian celebrated the May or spring festival with sun dances around a pole fastened by thongs to represent the rays of the sun. The multicolored ribbons streaming from the modern Maypole began as symbols of the sun's rays also. In all parts of the ancient world it was a good omen to circle with the sun, and merry Maypole dancers skip in the same direction as of old.

Children's nursery jingles suggest songs that were sung on May Day in ancient Rome and Greece. Examples are: "Come out, dear sun," or "Rain, rain, go to Spain."

The Merry month of Mary, or May, was also a time of gay processions. However, the May Day Parades of today have been taken over by labor unions and now have political significance sometimes pitched a little too emotionally for a patriotic demonstration.

May Day Parades, however, have a precedent that goes back to the Middle Ages, when contestants in games during the May Day celebrations became over-enthusiastic and the occasion sometimes ended in violence.

It was customary for whole villages to be in the forest on May Day to witness the symbolic Nordic games which had been introduced by the Danes into England. The contests represented the driving away of winter by spring. The fight between the seasons sometimes became too realistic and turned into hard conflicts; spring, of course, being determined to win out.

On the eve before the celebration, the villagers spent the night outdoors, romping and gathering greenery in anticipation of the next day's events.

"Friday" Superstitions

FRIDAY is a proverbially unlucky day, especially when it falls on the thirteenth of the month. Superstitions connected with Friday, however, vary and to some it is a day of good luck.

There are those who believe that Friday is a bad day to start a journey to move from one house to another or to begin new work of any kind unless finished on the same day. In general new undertakings are best left alone on Friday, lest misfortune follow.

Many versions have been given for the origin of Friday superstitions. One of the best known is the tale that Eve tempted Adam with the apple on Friday, and because he partook of the forbidden fruit, they both forfeited their right to remain in the Garden of Eden. Due to their disobedience and their expulsion from Paradise, Friday became a fast day on which fish was eaten. In folklore the apple symbolized woman, and fish was the feminine symbol of fertility, the two being traditional reminders that the pair broke God's command to remain pure.

Tradition also has it that the Flood in the Bible, and the confusion in the tower of Babel, also took place on Friday. Another traditional belief is that Jesus died on the cross to redeem humanity on this ill-omened day, which has become a day of fast and penance observed by humble and grateful people.

Still another superstition, but much more ancient, goes back to savage and primitive tribes who are said to have set aside a "no-work" day which was to be given over to primitive religious devotions in which the gods were implored with sacrificial offerings to provide good crops, health and happiness. Those who worked on this day instead of worshipping could not expect the "good luck" to come as favors from their gods. This explains the taboo against starting or doing anything important on Friday, observed in large cities even today.

In Europe, the custom of executing criminals on Friday dates back to the Middle Ages. It used to be known as "hangman's day." The custom is still observed in this country.

In ancient times, Friday was the Sabbath with many peoples. The word, Friday, comes to us from the combination of three Norse gods, —Frey, Lord of the solar disc and god of fertility, Freya, his sister and goddess of love, and Frigga, the wife of Woden or Odin, the one-eyed god. Originally these three deities were one and there is disagreement in the versions regarding these Norse deities and the naming of Friday.

All these mythological gods and goddesses were related to much more ancient deities who symbolized the Sun, and who were believed endowed with all the attributes of the Solar Eye. Freya's signature was represented as the prehistoric solar cross, now known as the cross pattée, consisting of four conventionalized triangles with curved sides, arranged with points meeting in one center. Most of the early myths, legends and superstitions give the same attributes of the ancient Egyptian god, Ra, the Lord of all creation, to the sun gods.

In honor of Frigga, the Norse goddess of love and marriage, the early Scandinavian peoples regarded Friday as their luckiest marriage day. Many Hindus regard it the same way, and today most Scotch people expect the best fortune to follow if they marry on Friday.

Friday used to be the seventh day of the week, according to the old Jewish lunar calendar, and a day on which fish was and still is eaten. Later Saturday became their Sabbath.

In ancient Assyria, Friday was sacred to the goddess Mylitta, similar to the Roman goddess, Venus, and Friday was consecrated to marriage and other festivals which commemorated the union of the sexes. Fish was eaten to invite fertility and help propagate the race. Such pagan Friday ceremonies fell into disrepute when Christianity took over, and the day that had once been one of licentiousness became one of fasting and humility instead.

A fish is an ancient Syrian totem. Among Syrian tribes, which included Jews, some persons abstained from certain fish. Others kept sacred fish in ponds and ate them on Fridays to sanctify themselves. This practice was adopted by the early Christians. Tertullian, Latin Father of the Church (160–240), says: "We are little fishes born in the waters of baptism." A Christian inscription of 180 A.D. speaks of Jesus as "the great fish."

The eating of the sacred fish was a primitive form of the Eucharistic meal, as this ritual was earlier than the birth of Christ. Eating fish on Friday is a custom which persists under various forms among the Jews and Christians alike, and stems from the greatest antiquity and for the same reasons, although distinct traditional interpretations are given for eating fish on Friday by different groups. Friday is the Sabbath among Mohammedans, another instance of the importance of this day anciently.

Saturday, or Saturn's Day, was shifted from its first place in the week, and Sunday replaced it. The many changes in the calendar have created much confusion, especially as Friday customs and beliefs as a day of rituals and meditation were transferred to other days which represent the Sabbath to other peoples. Today, the Sabbath falls on each day of the week according to the customs and beliefs of each people.

Our words "hell" and "Friday" both come from goddesses intimately associated with cats. Hel was the daughter of Loki, and goddess of the dead and the underworld. The Norse mythology, in common with that of the Egyptians, made the cat a figure of worship. Freya, the Venus of the North, goddess of beauty and fruitful love, rode in a car drawn by a pair of cats. A cat, if not the most affectionate of animals, is one of the most fecund, which emphasized symbolically the functions to which this deity was dedicated.

In time, in Southern Germany, Freya came to be known as Hell, and though still kindly and beautiful, she now represented only the winter season, and became known not only as the goddess of life, but also of death. When the Norse and Teutons were converted to Christianity Freya was consigned to the mountain fastnesses as a witch, and her name-day, Friday, became the day chosen by witches for their strange meetings.

These witches met on their Sabbath, generally in cemeteries, in the dark of the moon and in a group of twelve. Freya is said to have given the witches one of her cats, making it the thirteenth to them, one source of the origin of unlucky thirteen.

Friday superstitions, which number hundreds, have their roots in the mythological soil of the ages, probably too deeply ever to die.

CHAPTER 18

Of Work And Play

"Business" Superstitions

WHETHER IT IS connected with buying or selling, success in business is expected to be aided by observing certain superstitions, which began in the trading of ages ago and to which new beliefs and taboos are being constantly added.

The ancients believed that the use of mascots, such as a bee, cricket, bull, deer's tooth, elephant, or jewel, either real or imitation, brought good luck in business provided all transactions were honorable. Otherwise, the gods and goddesses, under whose protection the animals and objects were, would disapprove, and show it by punishment with losses, accidents and other business misfortunes. Early traders, however, who lived up to the expectations of their supernatural sponsors felt insured against the evil practices of their competitors who were less fearful of the gods and more daring in their undertakings. Times have not changed in this respect very much!

Many superstitions are related to opening a business such as the best day of the week, the phase of the moon as well as the season of the year, depending on whether the traditional beliefs are English, French, Italian, Hebrew, Greek, Hungarian or of other nationality or race.

There are those who believe that dowry money, or what a woman receives when she marries lends prosperity if used in a husband's business. Others believe that it is good luck to begin a new business venture at the time of the new moon, symbol of growth. In America the proverbially lucky horseshoe of flowers is presented on the day a business opens.

Omens of all kinds are used to make a business prosper, such as carrying a "lucky piece"—usually a coin—a rabbit's foot, a four-leaf clover, a "lucky" ring, or a luck-stone with a hole in it. A special necktie, associated with a successful transaction, particularly on the stock exchange, is worn to a shred in the hope of more such deals. All these charm-like objects inspire confidence in the wearer and confidence is an important business asset.

In many retail stores today, if a sale, however small, is made before 9 o'clock on Monday morning, it is a sign of good business for the whole week. Many superstitious persons make it a point to wipe the money given out in change on the first sale of the week lest their good luck go away with it. Other shop-keepers expectorate on the first piece of silver received, to remove any evil influences that may be left on it. It is also a popular superstition that the first customer of the week must make a purchase, however small, or else business will be bad all week. This superstition applies from day to day.

As far as superstitious business people are concerned, it is unlucky to keep moving from year to year as this factor would keep them from "making money." Hence, long-term leases were evolved. Leases were generally for an odd number of years, because in material things, even numbers were believed to be under evil influences. Therefore, we have a ninety-nine year lease instead of one hundred years.

The number nine was favored for its symbolic expression of three, or three times three. Three is a mystic number which represented the renewal of life and nine, or thrice three, assured that much life to the business, which was long enough to guarantee success. There were special days and months for signing long term leases, such as the first three days of the first three months of the year, or the third day of the waxing moon. The superstitions that pertain to the days and months for closing an agreement stem for the most part from Sumerian and Babylonian days when astrology was an integral part of life to chart the daily activities of individuals. This is not unlike the practice of millions of persons today who follow the same routine with astrological charts.

The shaking of hands, following the completion of a business deal, or to bind a bargain, is a very ancient custom. Shaking hands symbolized the unity of purpose and mutual good fortune, the two hands forming a cross, which in its good aspect is a potent solar symbol of life.

The proverbial "drink" that often follows a successful transaction likewise has an ancient background. Wine was under the special patronage of Bacchus, god of the Vine, and was believed to add further life to the deal.

Many superstitious business men will not sign a contract on Friday,

Friday the thirteenth, or on the thirteenth of any month. Nor will they start a business trip on any of these days.

At one time women were kept out of the business world altogether because of the ancient superstition that they were a disturbing element to have around, and therefore evil. There are still many taboos placed upon women to keep them out of certain positions. An elderly woman is believed to bring bad luck if she is the first customer on Monday morning. This superstition must indeed be a very old one as prejudices against women in the business world, even against "old" women, are fast disappearing.

"Cornerstone" and "Building" Superstitions

ALTHOUGH the familiar laying of a cornerstone or foundation is a harmless ceremony today the custom originated with our primitive ancestors, who believed that a human sacrifice was the price of appeasement for invading the earth-god's territory. The construction of most of our important buildings, including churches and temples, is begun officially with the cornerstone celebration, but instead of a human victim a scroll or other substitute is placed in the cornerstone.

One of the current superstitions in connection with laying a cornerstone is that it is bad luck for an unmarried woman to attend the ceremony. If she inadvertently witnesses it, it means that her marriage will be delayed at least a year. The origin of this quaint idea comes from the ancient superstition that a maiden was the preferred human offering to the gods, and many of them were fed to the earth-god.

Today, a dignitary is honored with the task of laying a cornerstone, whereas in the past, the act of propitiating the supernatural spirits was done by a medicine-man, or a magician, who alone was expected to know how to make the sacrificial offerings.

Following the custom of human sacrifices, rams, sheep and bullocks were offered, and later, the first fruits of the harvest. In some places today, the shadow of a man or animal is measured and imprinted in the walls of a building to insure its safety and that of its occupants.

Once upon a time, nearly every man who owned a house literally had a skeleton in his closet, or somewhere in the house. Many skeletons have been found over the centuries, imbedded in the stone and mortar of a variety of types of buildings. Several authentic accounts exist of human victims who were sacrificed, and whose remains were found in the walls or at the base of pillars where they were placed so that these structures would not fall.

This superstitious custom existed among the Celts, Slavs, Teutons and Northmen, to mention only a few. Incidentally the Druids, who were sun-worshippers, also indulged in human sacrifices, and like other peoples offered human victims yearly to the Earth Goddess to insure good crops.

The belief in haunted houses that is widespread in England today dates back centuries, and is due mainly to stories passed from one generation to the next, that there was a skeleton or the ghost of someone in the house that pestered anyone who tried to occupy the house, once the owner had departed. Superstitious persons have a way of twisting incidents and turning them into legends and ghost stories which haunt the minds of their gullible listeners. And so the weird stories have been passed around and with them the fears of haunted houses.

Although today the ceremony of laying a cornerstone takes place only for important buildings, in primitive times, every habitation had to go through a ritual of offerings to unseen beings, before anyone could safely enter and live in it. The threshold was considered the vulnerable spot as it still is.

Until comparatively recently, superstitious and conscientious builders drew a circle and placed a knife in it which was then imbedded in the wall of a house, to protect the future occupants from evil influences. In those days builders were concerned with the happiness and good fortune of their customers. "He has a lucky hand" was a coveted compliment, and taken literally.

"Moving Day" Superstitions

IN ALL PROBABILITIES "moving day" has always been an eventful occasion in people's lives everywhere, beginning when every change of locale for nomad and wandering tribes involved potential new dangers. No doubt the experiences, superstitious fears and hopes of the race or tribe, recorded mentally, were passed on by word of mouth from one generation to the next, since many of them are still with us.

In America, millions of families move each year either on May 1st or October 1st, while in other countries, where the "gypsy tendency" is not quite as prevalent, the national days for moving vary. On the whole, no matter in what part of the world, each family has its traditional or pet superstitious beliefs which have not changed much since nomad days, in the sense that the fear of the "unknown" compels people to do or not do certain things to insure happiness and good fortune in the new abode. Most superstitions connected with moving, such as the luckiest day, what to carry into the new home first, and what should not be brought in are symbolic in nature.

There is a long list of taboos and lucky things to do on moving day. Always take the old salt-box along, and never empty it until you have begun using the new one. Many people will not move downstairs in the same apartment or building in the belief that it is unlucky. The move must always be "upward." Many will not move on a Saturday because that may mean a short stay. On the other hand it may mean a long stay which is not always desired either. Never move back into a house where you once lived, or you will have bad luck. Do not sweep the old house clean after everything has been removed, or you will have bad luck in the new place. However, if you leave something behind after the final sweeping, that offsets the bad luck. If you sweep away "dirt's luck" says an old Scotch proverb, the new tenants will be unhappy or will not remain long in the house. Some think that taking an old broom into new quarters is bad luck; but before moving in, if one sends a new broom and a loaf of bread, that will bring good luck.

Each day of the week is an unlucky day to someone for moving. Moving van companies report that they come in contact with many moving-day jinxes. For instance, if it rains, some persons will not move, as it means bad luck in the new home. The custom of a "house-warming" soon after moving into a new residence, with each guest bringing a good-wish gift, is supposed to insure good luck to all the occupants. It is a very common occurrence in the United States.

"Traveling" Superstitions

MODERN TRAVELLING superstitions, such as not wanting to leave the ground, not sleeping in an upper berth, sitting backwards on a train, are in essence not materially far removed from the inexplicable forebodings which assailed early and ancient man when faced with a journey of some kind. These strange premonitions and abstract sense of insecurity, when no apparent danger exists, are for the most part feelings which are deeply rooted in fear and fear is the basis of superstition.

Early man watched the heavens and the elements, the birds and animals, and even people's behavior, for propitious signs. He would never start out on a trip without the proper auspices. Modern man carries a St. Christopher medal, a rabbit's foot a four-leaf clover, a caul, a special ring and gem, or other good-luck charms. He knocks on wood if he as much as mentions his destination lest evil listeners make his journey unsuccessful.

To prevent train sickness there are all kinds of lucky tokens included in luggage or pocketbook; a black cat crossing your path is bad luck; starting a trip on Friday or Friday the 13th is unlucky; chambermaids are often instructed to pull down shades on moonlight nights so that the travelling guests will not be "moonstruck" and carry on their business in the wrong way; most hotels have no 13th floor, numbering it 12A or 14 so that patrons will not blame the hotel if their trip is unsuccessful or tragic; to turn back in an automobile to get something which has been forgotten is unlucky.

There is a dangerous modern superstition that a pregnant woman who travels is courting serious mishap or miscarriage. This belief not only restricts her activities but fills her with unnecessary fears in the event that abortion takes place following the shortest of journeys. A guilt complex plagues her, and she believes she is responsible for the death of her child. Recent surveys have been made and show that three times as many miscarriages took place with those who stayed at home as with those who traveled where they pleased.

To wave goodbye to people and watch them out of sight is not only bad luck, but it is believed that in so doing one may never see them again. And so the superstitious-minded turn their backs as soon as the train leaves or depart before the "all-aboard" signal is given, so as not to yield to the temptation of taking a last glance at their friends.

"Walking" Superstitions

WHILE WALKING with a companion, grown-ups and children alike are generally superstitious when an object, animal or person comes between them. When this happens, they repeat certain verbal formulas, or make counter-magic gestures, to avoid the bad luck that is supposed to follow. This routine for warding off the jinx is practiced by millions of modern-minded individuals in cities as well as in the country.

One method to avert trouble when a person, a dog, cat, tree, lamppost, or whatever, separates two people is to retrace one's steps to where the separation started and continue to walk from there. This means a magic circle has been effected which will prevent the friendship from being broken. Sweethearts, especially, should do this, and the safest way to do it is to hold hands at the time, because if they should be separated again, they will not marry each other.

A jealous person must be prevented from "cutting in" on two sweethearts while they are walking. If he cannot "cut in," the bad luck he wishes the couple will be his. If, however, a third person accidentally passes between the two, it means bad luck to them, usually in the form of a serious quarrel.

If three persons are walking in a row, and one of them wishes to change places with another, the formula used to require that he or she make a cross on the sidewalk with the foot to keep away bad luck. Nowadays, to save time, and more probably to avoid ridicule, the superstitious ones cross their fingers.

Perhaps the most popular formula among both children and adults, when two of them are separated while walking, is to say, "Bread and butter" aloud, or under the breath, at the same time crossing the fingers. Then no disappointment or other form of ill luck will come to them.

The simple explanation of all the counter-magic devices in this superstition—the circle gesture by retracing one's steps, the making of the cross with the fingers, and the verbal formulas—is that they form a symbolic union and repair the "break through" of the third person or object. The interpretation of the phrase "bread and butter" is that these two ideas belong together, forming a unity or unit, a method used in other superstitions to neutralize an evil omen.

"Exercise" Superstitions

WHETHER EXERCISE is injurious or not to the heart and to health in general is still controversial, with many superstitious notions involved. As regards the heart, strenuous exercise will not injure it, unless the heart is weak to begin with—either slightly off normal, or actually damaged.

In order to throw light on the subject, hundreds of autopsy records were studied, and the conclusion reached is that exercise never damaged a healthy heart. Those, however, with slight or even serious heart ailments do not have to forego all forms of exercise, as, under medical guidance, certain exercises are permissible. Without a doctor's direction, too much activity in these cases may be dangerous—which would give the old superstition another lift.

The opposite assumption, that regular exercise is a panacea for all ills, including most disease germs, is as fallacious as the previously described superstition.

Athletics do not make for a long or short life, although we are all familiar with the expression: "He has an athletic heart." There is no such thing as an "athletic" heart, or "athlete's" heart. These terms are usually employed to describe the premature death of someone in the sports world, who was not aware of or neglected, a heart condition that proved fatal when strenuous exercise was not abandoned at the first symptoms.

Experience has shown that good posture, sleep, vacations and hobbies have successfully replaced exercise for maintaining good health and a long life expectancy. On the other hand, a fair amount of nonviolent exercise, such as walking, for muscles that have not been used much, will greatly benefit those of sedentary habits.

It has been noted that animals such as the elephant, tortoise, parrot and swan take practically no exercise, and yet live to be very old. On the other hand, such animals as the dog, squirrel and the hare, which are very active, have a life expectancy of only ten to fifteen years. In the human family, however, statistics give the same life expectancy to those who take strenuous exercise as to those who do not. One man's meat is another man's poison.

"Dice" Superstitions

ALL GAMBLERS are superstitious. Gambling authorities say that dice is the most popular game in the United States, and millions of players, while billions of dollars are changing hands, are constantly begging Lady Luck to smile on them, using charms, "lucky dice," "sweet" talk, and hundreds of superstitious gestures and words in order to win.

Dice has been a gambling game with nearly all peoples since time immemorial, and superstitions connected with it are found in nearly all languages even including that of the American Indian.

The word "crap" has an interesting background. Early in the history of France, young boys who wanted to "shoot" dice surreptitiously, because their parents objected to the game would stoop, like toads in doorways or other inconspicuous places, to carry on their fun. And so dice-playing was given the name, "crapeau," the French word for toad, which in this country has been shortened to *crap*.

There is another version of the origin of the word. Sylvan Hoffman reports in his volume *News of the Nation*, "It is said that Bernard Xavier Philippe de Marigny de Mandeville who had seen the French versions known as 'Hazards', introduced 'craps' into New Orleans. The game 'craps' after the Creole, nicknamed 'Johnny Crapeau.'" No doubt this nickname tied in with the Paris gamins' pet name for what is variously known in America as "bones," "ivories," "galloping dominoes," "African golf" and other affectionate appellations.

New terms, exclusively American, have been added to Old World superstitions. "Come seven, come eleven," is a favorite cry of crap shooters as they snap their fingers to keep away evil influences. As in ancient times, there are automatic charm gestures to avoid rolling "snake-eyes," the lowest and losing number. Crap shooting has likewise acquired a vocabulary that defies its source and all the terms are of superstitious nature. For example: "Gypsy Curse"; "Voodoo dice"; "Sweet little clickers"; "Sting him, twelve dollar bee!"; "Rabbit dice, multiply"; "Snake-eyes bit you"; "Come naturals", (invitation to the lucky seven).

Many ancient superstitions are still believed in relation to dice for fortune-telling purposes. Rub the dice on a red-headed person and it will bring good luck. Carry dice in your pocketbook and you will always have money. If you find a die, or cube, with one spot up, you will receive a letter or document of great importance. If the die has two spots up, you will take a long journey that will be of great benefit. Three spots up, a big surprise is in store for you, and also, you will sleep on a strange bed. Four spots up is a bad omen,—the finder will soon meet with ingratitude from a source least expected. Five spots up, —change in domestic and family affairs, and inconstancy in love. Six spots up,—a very good omen. You will shortly receive unexpected money, and peace and prosperity are in store for you.

Dice are marked so that each pair of sides adds up to seven, the lucky number, which is the symbol of the moon or feminine symbol. When gamblers lose for a long stretch of time, they say they are followed by a jinx, or hoodoo. Dice used to be rolled out of a dice-box, but today most players use their hands.

Various countries claim the honor of having originated the game of dice. In India, the use of dice is said to go back six thousand years, and Hindus claim not only the invention of dice, but the earliest use of "loaded dice," found in the story of Doorjoodhen, who challenged Judishter and won his wealth, kingdom and banishment with false dice. The custom of fortune-telling with dice is universal throughout

India, where it is regarded as a science under the name of *ramala*. This so-called art is practiced as a means of livelihood by a large number of natives who are called *ramali*.

Greece is another country where dice may have first been invented. Tradition says that this type of game was a pastime of Greek soldiers during the Trojan Wars. Dice, made three thousand years ago, were found in Thebes and they differ in no way from the six-sided cubes of today with dots on each side, from one to six.

Another legend has it that the ancient Lydians, under pressure of famine, invented dice to divert the people's minds from hunger. There is also the story that Ts'ah Chin, Chinese priest and philosopher, invented the game, *sugoroku*, around 200 B.C.

Regardless of who invented them, dice figured in the gambling games of the early Teutons, and "on the throw of the dice" they would not only lose their fortunes, but their liberty as well, becoming slaves to those who won. Henry VIII bet such sums on the "turn of the dice" that he became the prey of unscrupulous sharpers, who posed as friends, but who, upon being discovered, were dismissed from court.

Because the mystic number seven was an important factor in dice, the cabbalists attached a super-fortunate significance to this number, adding a further lure to the gambling instinct.

To be "on the square" is an ancient superstitious phrase, meaning to be honest or having the reputation for honesty. With the early Egyptian, to be "on the square" meant literally just that. Oddly enough, the cube or die, opened out, makes a cross, and the cross was man's own symbol. In primitive times a pair of dice represented a human couple. The four sides of each die were equivalent to the four cardinal points; and the top and bottom, represented the two poles. For ages, the expression "the four corners of the earth" meant that the earth was square.

The combined sides on two dice equals 12, or the year cycle of 12 months. Besides these symbols, the die or cube represented the triad or trinity, as only three faces of the die are visible at a time, the opposite three being hidden from view to symbolize the unknown and the law of opposites, a law which early peoples devised to show that everything and everyone was endowed with an opposite.

The little die or cube may have begun its existence as a basic symbol in early magic and pagan belief, but in its present association it represents the most democratic of all games,—with players ranging from bootblacks to bank presidents!

"Baseball" Superstitions

ALTHOUGH, as games go, baseball is a comparatively new sport, players have already accumulated an unusually large number and assortment of superstitions.

A mascot of some kind is generally indispensable to a baseball team, and the person who handles the bats is frequently the mascot.

When bad luck persists, a batter—or other player—feels someone put the "Indian sign" on him.

If a bat is rubbed with a bone, it will have more power.

Never cross baseball bats when laying them down.

If a player breaks a bat, it means a batting slump.

Never change a bat after the second strike.

Never stand on the plate with the large end of the bat down. It brings bad luck.

Never stop on the foul lines.

There are only a certain number of hits in each bat. When they are used up, the bat is no longer any good.

Most players refuse to sign autographs before a game. Others will not be photographed before a game.

The most common gesture of all is to expectorate in the hands before taking over the bat. Though players may not be aware of it, saliva is not only an ancient countercharm, but it is also an aid for a better hold on the bat, since moistened hands create friction which prevents the polished handle of the bat from slipping.

Superstitious baseball players interpret dreams in reverse. If a team meets a funeral on the way to a game, it means they will win. Some teams think that it is a sign of bad luck if, on the day they are to play, one of the team gets a shave. This may or may not be a hangover from the days when famous "whiskers" adorned the faces of baseball players at the inception of the game around 1839. Incidentally, baseball is said to have evolved from a similar game known in England as "Rounders."

Baseball players often pull the little finger for luck. Some teams will not permit all members to sit together. Many baseball players consider it bad luck if a dog crosses the "diamond" before the first ball is pitched.

A very common superstition is that if a baseball team meets a load of empty barrels on the way to play, it means sure defeat. However, the significance of this superstition was in reverse for a player named Mike Donlin in the old days of the New York Giants.

As the story goes, one summer when the Giants were fighting for the lead, Donlin saw a team of horses pulling a truck load of empty barrels past the entrance to the Polo Grounds in New York City. Donlin, at the time, was trailing Wagner, the greatest short-stop of the Pittsburgh Pirates. Donlin went to bat that day and smashed out four hits, two of them for extra bases. Yet every hit was of the "lucky" type, either luckily placed, or just out of reach of a player of the opposing team.

"What struck you today, Mike?" asked John McGraw, as the players took their showers after winning the game.

"It must have been that load of empty barrels," said Donlin. "Lord, Mac, it gave luck to the whole team."

The next day Donlin did not see the barrels and his luck fell away— Hans Wagner passed him in the batting race again. "If I could only see a wagon of empty barrels," moaned Mike, "that would give us back the luck."

McGraw overheard the remark, but said nothing. The next day and for ten days thereafter, until the team started west, Mike saw the same truckload of empty barrels. Again base hits rattled from his stick and the Giants plowed through to victory. They took ten games in a row.

"Are you superstitious?" a baseball writer asked Mike Donlin, after the Giants had won the pennant.

"I wouldn't call it that," said Mike, "but it sure was good luck seeing those empty barrels." He told the story to the sports writers. McGraw was listening, a faint smile on his face. After Donlin left, the sports writers asked McGraw:

"How much did it cost you to hire that truck to drive by the Polo Grounds? And how did you find the man?" McGraw grinned. "It cost me plenty of dough and some time and trouble, but it was worth it," he said.

And so today, a player always tips his hat to a truckload of barrels, but they must be empty barrels. He also tips his hat to a load of hay.

Other baseball superstitions are that nearly all players have a horror of having a hat placed on a bed; players dislike to start on a Friday, so the schedule makers avoid this as much as possible. A player who has a hitting streak will wear his sweat shirt until it mildews, if his luck lasts that long. There are numerous superstitions connected with gloves, bats and other paraphernalia of the game.

"Southpaws" or left-handers were unfavorably looked upon in days gone by, but this feeling is abating. A left-handed baseball pitcher is called a "southpaw" because baseball diamonds usually are laid out so that the pitcher's left hand, as he stands facing the batter, is toward the south. It is claimed that the reason there are no left-handed short-stops is because any speedy ball thrown by a left-hander has a curve in it which makes it harder for the first baseman to catch. Therefore "southpaws" are rarely if ever used as shortstops, second basemen or thirdbasemen.

As for the seventh inning when baseball fans stand up, this custom is said to have originated in the old days of pine boards without backs which served for seats in ball parks. To rise and stretch at about the seventh inning was the natural result of a desire to relieve cramped muscles. Then came the superstitious notion that it brought good luck to the home team to stretch in the seventh inning. Seven, of course, has been a lucky number since the remotest times. The custom grew until now, resting in the seventh inning is a universal practice wherever the game is played.

Playing Card Superstitions

CARD PLAYING superstitions are very ancient, and run into the hundreds. The best known may be mentioned.

Unlucky at cards, lucky in love.

Wear a soiled garment of some kind, and it will keep evil influences away, and make you win, especially in a game of poker.

To bring better luck, twist your chair three times on its forelegs. It is even better luck to follow the sun's course, east to west by south.

Change your seat to change your luck, or walk around the table three times, clockwise.

Blow on cards for good luck. Pretending to expectorate on the deck is supposed to help, too.

Expectorate on your hands before beginning to play and you will draw good luck.

You can break your bad luck by sitting on a handkerchief, as sitting on a square is an old device for good fortune of any kind.

To change your luck in the game, turn the back of your chair to the table and sit astride it.

Never allow a person to stand over you and look at your cards, unless that person never plays cards. In that case a kibitzer becomes a mascot, or lucky person.

It is unlucky to gamble in a room where there is a woman unless she is gambling too, not matter what game is being played. Many serious poker players, however, claim that a woman is generally unlucky, which may explain the origin of stag parties. In all primitive societies, and among later peoples too, women were excluded from the social activities of the men, and the custom is still observed today. This taboo undoubtedly reflects the fact that a member of the opposite sex generally distracts the men. Women, on the other hand, seldom resent the presence of men. For some reason or other, for centuries, whether in primitive or civilized society, men have objected to women being present at their games or meetings.

A famous bridge superstition observed by many players in North America requires that the pack of cards that gave the highest card when cut to the dealer, must be the same one used in the game that follows. In other words, the one who cuts a high card wants to use the same deck in the game that brought him luck in the deal, and thereby insure winning the game. Since there are two decks used in every game of bridge, this is a highly important superstition to the dealer.

The Puritans called playing cards the "Devil's picture books," and they did everything they could to discourage their use. Here and abroad, countless superstitions have been attached to card games, and as many countercharms involved, to undo the evil that might result in games which were not approved of by the general public.

Unlucky in Love, Lucky at Games of Chance

"Lucky at cards, unlucky in love," is an oft-quoted adage. Nevertheless, this is more apt to be taken seriously when winning at cards happens to coincide with a waning love affair.

This superstitious association of cards and love is due to the fact that most people believe that success depends upon an element of luck which cannot work two ways at once. The love urge, of course, has never been satisfactorily explained; likewise, theories of winning and losing in games of chance are just as confused. Therefore, success or failure, in love or in games, is persistently attributed to an incomprehensible something called "luck."

We know that the path of love between two persons is quite as unpredictable as the cards that will be dealt in a game of chance. However, in the romantic game of love, the human element provides greater uncertainties in the outcome than there are in card games, where the little known, but scientific, "law of probabilities" can determine the chances of winning or losing, to some extent.

It must be granted that an element of luck, good or bad, seems to work at times in all things. And it must be granted also, that with many persons, believing a thing makes it so. Therefore, despite facts and logic, the belief in good or bad luck has a tremendous influence on the thoughts and actions of all people.

And there is always the age-old superstition, which lurks in the back of most people's minds, that things generally work in reverse!

CHAPTER 19

Water, Water, Everywhere

"Water" Superstitions

MAKING A WISH at a wishing-well is a very ancient superstition and is still very popular today all over the world. There are various ways of making this gesture, among which are the dropping of a penny or pebble while making the wish, and waiting until a girl sees her face reflected in the water. Students, young people in love, engaged couples, and those just about to be married make a wish at a wishing-well with the supreme confidence of the ages in their hearts that the wish will be granted.

Water has long been looked upon as a symbol of fertility. The rôle which it played in the production of life and procreation has found expression among all peoples in one form or another. The ancient Egyptians used a vessel of water to express womanhood, the matrix in which the seed of life grew. Water was also believed to be a purifying agent, and symbolized a new life or rebirth. Special lustration rites were performed to wash away by magic some taboo which prevented conception, or to wash away sins.

Perhaps the reason for the belief in the magical and life-giving qualities of water arose from the fact that the moon controlled the tides and woman was believed to be under the influence of the cycle of the moon. Hence women and water were closely related to the moon itself, a mysterious relationship which endowed women with the virtues of fecundity, so highly appreciated in early times.

However that may be, large numbers of "holy" wells and springs were held in high repute, especially for curing children's diseases. Water cures, or hydromancy, are closely connected with the worship of wells and sacred springs. Water was also believed to be a cleansing agent, preparatory to a long and healthy life. The ritual of baptism is simply a sequel to the primitive method of dipping a newborn baby in the waters of a lake, river, or pond, at birth—a custom which was observed for ages by peoples of the earliest of civilizations.

From local wells evolved local shrines to which flocked sick people from near and far in quest of cures. Many modern health resorts follow these primitive beliefs in water cures. Denuded of their various superstitious guises, we are now acquainted with their specific therapeutic values for certain types of diseases.

Springs which appeared overnight, so to speak, were looked upon with awe and were endowed with supernatural healing powers. Sick people drank or washed themselves with such waters, not being aware that the spring was a natural phenomenon. Various ills were believed washed away in running water. Dish-water is still believed to be a therapeutic agent for many ills today.

One of the most important things for a bride-to-be was the ritual bath, a prelude to the marriage ceremony. Water from a particular well or river was selected to cleanse the body and to keep evil influences away. The magic charm of the water was supposed to remove the possibility of the much dreaded condition of barrenness, and to confer fertility.

Many young modern girls believe that a wish made as they cross a short bridge will come true if they hold their breath while wishing. In ancient times it was thought that the evil spirits in the water were opposed to changing the nature of things,—such as having a bridge over them—so the gesture of holding one's breath in order to keep out these evil spirits was prescribed, and the wish made was expected to be granted by the good water spirits who were also present.

Primitive peoples invented countless superstitions about water because they were ignorant of basic values; nevertheless, they came close to the truth at times. They lead the way to modern usage of water in physiotherapy.

"Drinking Water" Superstitions

To DRINK OR NOT TO DRINK water has superstitions on both sides of the question. On the one hand, there is the belief that drinking water with meals distends the stomach, causes digestive disorders, including ulcers, makes persons fat, and brings on other physical troubles. The opposite view is that not to drink enough water will cause the stomach to shrink and dry up, and possibly develop cancer and other terrible things.

The amount of water one should drink depends upon a number of factors, and when one is in doubt, a physician should decide. Self-determination for or against drinking water is apt to be the wrong solution and may do more harm than good. However, it is not bad to drink water with meals, unless too much is used to wash down food that has not been properly chewed or masticated.

Water does not dilute the stomach contents to any extent, but runs out of it quickly, most of it being absorbed by the large intestine. The average rule, when there are no symptoms or feelings of illness, is that when the urine is practically odorless and of a very light straw color, the water intake is normal and the condition is healthy. Deeper color or the suggestion of an odor indicates that more water is required.

For those who are superstitious about drinking water lest it make them fat, the answer is that water may temporarily increase the weight, but it never turns into fat!

As for ice water, the superstition that this is dangerous in hot weather is believed by millions today. Others think that cool water is fine, but icy drinks, particularly while eating, are harmful because they interfere with the digestive tract. As a matter of fact, ice water does slow stomach action, but only briefly while it is being warmed up to body temperature. Large amounts of water, however, either cool or ice cold, if drunk immediately before meals may give the feeling of being "filled up" and temporarily repel the appetite, but that is about all they do.

Some years ago, tests were made, and it was found that ice water (37 to 50 degrees Fahrenheit) is not harmful, as many believe, and there is no evidence that water at this temperature causes injury to the alimentary tract. The more ice water taken with meals, the more it will slow up digestion because of its low temperature, but this is probably of little significance. The reason many persons prefer ice water is because they have the impression that the real thirst is stopped at once; a false belief.

Superstitious persons, that is those who are not scientific-minded, are always at a loss to know how much or how little water they should drink. The answer is that a normal thirst is generally a good indication for drinking sufficient fluids vital to normal health. On the other hand, there are other superstitious ones who believe that large amounts of water are good for them and they often harm themselves by forcing down too much.

A current superstition is that drinking medicinal waters at health springs is in itself a cure for all ailments. The truth is that these waters have nothing but a more or less laxative effect. The benefit derived at health springs comes from simpler diets, change of habits, the avoidance of excesses and proper guidance.

Another superstitious attitude, around a subject little understood, is the morbid fear of water in connection with the disease of hydrophobia. Actually, if such a condition should exist, there might be an intense desire for water, but it would be very difficult to swallow because of the painful spasms of the throat muscles. Modern medicine, however, has a way of dealing with this condition, and the superstitious fear of this phase of the disease,—undoubtedly a most horrible experience—is no longer warranted.

"Dowsing" or "Water-Finding" Superstitions

THE HIT AND MISS system of finding water hidden underground brings to modern times similar functions of diviners with divining rods in antiquity and the Middle Ages. People still look with favor upon "dowsers" or "water-finders" who are kept busy everywhere, including America. Wizards with witch-hazel forked twigs have kept alive the superstitious belief that a supernatural power—or something supernormal—is at work in the hands of "dowsers." Using the divining rod, or the act of *rhabdomancy*, is a time-honored method of locating not only water, but metal, oil and treasure, where they are expected to be and where they are the least expected.

Long before Moses, of biblical lore, brought water out of a rock, water-finding and other uses of the divining rod were already ancient practices. Babylonians employed divining rods; so did the Magi of ancient Media and Persia, as did the Hindus as long ago as when the Vedas were written, 1500–1000 B.C. Even in those early days hidden things were supposed to be discovered by "magic wands." Wands or forked sticks were in common use also among the Greeks, Romans, and Druids as well as among the Maoris of New Zealand, and the Zulus of Africa. In fact they were used everywhere, and even by men who had some pretensions to scientific knowledge.

Of course, there was no way of checking cause and effect in ancient times, as the tools with which to achieve the exactitude of the scientific methods of today were lacking. Therefore it is very interesting to note that almost without interruption, in ancient, medieval and modern times, the superstition that there are individuals who hold within themselves a magic spark with which to locate the so-called unknown, has been so universal.

The Chinese made their wands of peach twigs, while European nations generally had faith in hazel branches, sometimes known as witchhazel twigs. The word *wych*, derived from the wych-elm of the Old World, has caused confusion by being spelled *witch* to describe the witch hazel.

According to the supersition, there are highly gifted individuals whose personal *magnetism* is responsible for their success with divining rods. This magnetism is now identified with the modern term *electricity* in the human body. Dowsers explain their success by the fact that the V-shaped hazel stick they use is "sappy," so that it acts as a conductor, signalling the position of underground water, by automatically pointing in that direction. Dowsers believe it is the electricity in their bodies that does the trick.

Tests were conducted at the Pennsylvania State College in 1937 to learn more about dowsers and it was concluded that "A guess is as good as a divining rod." However, we have today an electric "dowser" and geophysical instruments which, under certain conditions, and in the hands of specially trained operators, are of value in the search for certain kinds of mineral deposits. The simplest of these instruments are the dial compass, the tip needle and the magno-meter; all of them are based on the attraction of a magnetized needle by magnetized substances.

Despite the fact that dowsing has been the subject of numerous scientific investigations which have shown that the claims of diviners can be substantiated in many cases, there is still no real explanation of the phenomenon. The Department of the Interior in Washington has many requests as to where to find the "divining rod." The chances are that fact and folklore are apt to be scrambled for some time to come because opinion is so divided. There are some who absolutely deny any merit whatever to the "dowser"; some who believe implicitly in its efficacy; and others who are open-minded because they have seen water located by this mysterious means.

Divining rods were used by German miners in the 15th Century to locate mineral deposits. Today, however, the rod is used only to find water, although some diviners claim their rods will locate human bodies either lost or drowned. These medieval German methods were renewed in 1935, when Nazi Jew-hunters used a pendulum as a divining rod to determine Jewish blood from Aryan blood, as reported by the Associated Press, September 3. We find the heading: "Can Jewish blood be determined? Experiences with a pendulum!" A few edited extracts from the article follow:

Just as streams of water, the existence of oil or metal, and so forth, can be determined by a divining rod, so hand-writing, finger prints and many other things can be determined by a pendulum. With the aid of a pendulum can also be found whether letters have been written by a male or female hand, whether by persons of pure Aryan, mixed or Jewish blood. All pure Aryan blood belongs to gold and platinum, and Jewish blood to zinc and lead.

Contending that the pendulum constructed had yielded many excellent results, on the "correctness" of their investigations, it was deemed necessary to build a mechanical apparatus to further the blood proofs they were seeking! And so on.

Superstitions About Tides

Time and tide wait for no man.
—Proverb

Death at ebb tide is a very ancient superstition still believed today by people living close to the sea, who continue to spread the belief to those with whom they come in contact. Aristotle is supposed to have said that no one can die until the tide goes out, but the superstition is older than Aristotle, and is traceable to the most primitive people who lived along ocean fronts.

Shakespeare was familiar with this superstition, for he has Falstaff die, "even just before twelve and one, even at the turning o' the tide." (Henry V, Act II, Scene III). Dickens and other famous authors have kept this superstition alive in their works.

Although it is not true that many persons die as the tide goes out, the superstition persists, and is believed by an ever-increasing number, including inhabitants of large inland towns and cities.

The superstition connecting the tides with death is based on the assumption that the ebbing of life has some relation to the flowing out of the tide. This goes back to what is known as sympathetic magic, or "like attracts like."

Tides are caused principally by the gravitational pull of the moon, but the ancients, unaware of this, were mystified by the ebb and flow of the sea on the shores, and in their confused way, saw a similarity between this and the cycle of life and death.

Another superstition believed by many persons is that if a child is born as the tide comes in, it is a sign of good luck for the little one. A fantastic belief was that tides are caused by the breathing of a sea monster, who draws in his breath for six hours, which makes the tide low. Then he lets out his breath for the next six hours and the waters return. Strange as it may seem, this belief is still current in places in Europe, from where it was brought into this country a long time ago. Primitive and semi-civilized peoples of today still believe there are sea monsters in the ocean.

Although well-informed persons are apt to think that only the moon is responsible for the tides, the fact is that the sun also exerts a gravitational attraction on the waters of the earth. However, the effect of the moon on the tides is two and one half times greater than that of the sun, which is so much farther away from us. It is now believed that all heavenly bodies, including stars, planets and satellites, play some part in producing our tides. Tidal forces are at work on all bodies of water, large and small, from pools to oceans; each affected according to its size.

The Sun Does Not Draw Water

THE SUPERSTITIOUS saying that the sun "draws water" is incorrect. The apparent drawing of water by the rays of light coming from the sun to the earth is a common and beautiful phenomenon, but this illusion is produced by dust particles floating in the air and made visible when the sun shines through the clouds. Actually, water is evaporated by nearby heat and in its invisible form becomes part of the surrounding atmosphere.

When the ancients observed the rays extending from the glowing orb of the sun, they called them the sun-god's hair. They represented this spectacle in the form of a double-wheel cross with eight spokes, signifying the rays. The design was either just the simple lines, or outlined from point to point, star-fashion. This double-wheel cross then became a frame for the face of the sun drawn within the solar circle. As time elapsed, artists depicted the real face of an old man appearing out of the clouds, with floating hair and beard—a more humanized impression of Old Man Sol.

An early religious adaptation of the double-wheel cross with eight rays—the sun symbol—was the Eight Beatitudes. They were originally called the Eight Emblems by sun-worshippers in ancient India.

Superstitions About Bubbles

IN PRIMITIVE medicine, bubbles, foam, suds or the like were looked upon as akin to saliva emitted from the mouths of unseen water spirits. Therefore, the swallowing of bubbles, coming as they were supposed to, from the sea gods' very mouths, means that some invisible, but benign, force would enter the body of the swallower. Whether it was dew, foam scum or suds—any form of bubbles—the superstition was that it would bring good fortune, good health and even good weather.

This belief is undoubtedly the ancestor of the coffee superstitions we meet today. For example, bubbles that gather on top of a cup of coffee, or chocolate, indicate, if they cluster in the middle or form an "island," that the drinker will receive money. If, however, the bubbles gather at the side, he will not receive the money.

Another version is that if one gets some bubbles out of the coffee cup with a spoon, and drinks them, he will get money. If they dissolve before the spoon reaches the mouth, and so cannot be swallowed, the money will disappear too.

Bubbles in the morning cup of coffee may also predict the weather. If they rise after the sugar is put in, and stay in the center of the cup, it will be fair. If they move to the rim, it will rain.

Like most superstitions, this bubble nonsense reveals the universal and eternal human longing for peace of mind and freedom from worry —especially as each day begins. The ancients, however, unaware of the laws of physics, could not possibly know, as moderns are supposed to, that bubbles are, for the most part, merely the result of air stirred into a liquid and becoming encapsulated in it.

"Drowning" Superstitions

THERE IS LITTLE evidence to support the popular superstition that a drowning person comes to the surface twice before going down for the third and last time. Despite repeated information given out for years by the press and other mediums, this notion is still widely believed.

A drowning person cannot be relied upon to rise to the surface three times, because very often he sinks at once. On the other hand, if he manages to hold some tidal air on each downward trip, he might be able to appear, not once or twice, but even a half dozen times. The rising is caused by a struggle to reach the surface for air. In this struggle, water may be drawn into the windpipe, but the victim may be able to rise for breath repeatedly until the lungs are filled with water.

How to find a drowned body has given rise to many superstitions. Mark Twain's method, it is said, was to place some quicksilver in a loaf of bread and float it. It is supposed to stop over the body. Likewise, the body of a drowned person is supposed to be discovered by floating a cedar chip which will stop and turn at the exact spot.

An old Indian superstition is to row a boat with a rooster on board around and around, and the rooster will crow over the spot where the body lies. Many fishermen believe that a drowned person's voice will be heard from the water before a squall or severe storm. It is still believed that the body of a drowned person will float on the ninth day. Drowned women are supposed to float face downward and men face upward.

It is another superstition that when a drowned person is touched by a near kinsman, he begins to bleed at the nose. A caul is believed not only to protect persons from drowning, but safeguard them against shipwreck.

A man whose hat blows overboard is marked for drowning; and any man who kills one of "Mother Carey's chickens" (any of several species of small petrels), is inviting all kinds of bad luck on his head, even drowning. An umbrella on board ship is still looked upon as a foreboding object that might endanger the whole crew. Many believe that to be born with blue veins on the side of the nose means death will come by drowning.

There are many persons who have a superstitious reluctance to rescue someone from drowning, because of the primitive belief that to save a drowning person robs the water spirits of their lawful prey and so offends them. Primitive fishermen and early sea-faring peoples had a superstition that fishing was good in the water where a human being had been drowned.

According to Chinese law, the rescuer of a drowning person is responsible for the upkeep of that individual. Even today, the Chinese throw salt into the water where a person drowned to appease the sea gods. An ancient and very morbid superstition prevails that sooner or later the person saved will do his savior an injury.

> "Save a stranger from the sea
> And he'll turn your enemy."

Breaking a Mirror, Seven Years of Bad Luck

THE AGE-OLD superstition that breaking a mirror is an omen of seven years of bad luck is believed by millions of persons today. That it means a death in the family within a year is believed by almost as many persons.

There are innumerable other mirror superstitions. For instance, some parents will not allow a child under one year of age to see itself in a looking-glass, lest its growth be stunted by having its reflection caught and held in the mirror. Others believe that if a baby is allowed to look into a mirror it may die before its first birthday. Young people, particularly girls, are warned that if they look into a mirror too often, some day the devil will appear.

Then there is the custom among many, even today, of covering mirrors after a death in the family. This is explained by the fear that the soul of the departed will enter the mirror, and its journey to the land of happy spirits will be delayed. In the same vein, many persons in this day and age hang a cloth over the bedroom mirror when they retire at night for fear their wandering soul or shade will be caught in it while they are asleep, which would mean death.

However, regarding a broken mirror, it is believed that the bad luck for seven years can be averted by pounding the broken pieces so fine that no mortal can ever see in it again.

Breakable mirrors were first made in Venice in the fourteenth century, but it was not until 1673 that glass mirrors began to be made in England.

For thousands of years, long before breakable mirrors were invented, a shiny surface was considered an implement of divinity. No doubt early man was puzzled and bewildered at seeing his reflection on the still waters of ponds and lakes—nature's own mirrors. Having no scientific knowledge whatever, least of all, perhaps, of optics, he naively analyzed this phenomenon as the shade, soul or dual part of himself. This dual, or "other" self was familiar to him, as he recognized it in his dreams. Therefore, he believed that this elusive being which was his reflection was readily exposed to injury, if disturbed in any way.

Ancient peoples, such as the Egyptians, the Hebrews, the Greeks and the Romans, used mirrors made of polished metals including brass, bronze, silver, gold and various alloys. In ancient Greece, divination practiced with crystals and mirrors was given the specific name of *catoptromancy.*

At a later date in the march of civilization, as a result of seeing one's own image, false vanity came into the picture, and parents had to discourage this trait by suggesting that the devil would some day appear in the mirror if one spent too much time admiring oneself. The mythological story of Narcissus appeared to further illustrate the warning.

Narcissus was a young hunter who caught sight of his own reflection in a stream, and fell in love with his own image. He languished and died, and out of his blood bloomed forth the flower we call narcissus. Echo, his beloved, is still calling for him. Today a person in love with himself is said to have a "narcissus complex."

The Etruscans, inhabitants of an ancient district of Italy, are supposed to have transferred the belief in the magic powers of a reflector to the Romans. About the first century A.D., the Romans added the superstition that breaking a mirror would bring seven years of misfortune.

At that time, it was believed in Rome that life renewed itself every seven years—which has no basis in fact, according to medical authorities. Inasmuch as a mirror contained an individual's likeness, when the mirror was broken, the health of the person who was responsible for the breaking—he or she who last looked into it—was likewise "broken," and would not get well for seven years.

Another reason that the Romans may have chosen the number seven is because the phases of the moon suggest this number. The moon was held responsible not only for the tides of the ocean but also for the "tides" or ages of man.

A somewhat different early superstition was that when a mirror was broken, it was an effort on the part of the gods to prevent the one who broke it from seeing some tragic happening about to take place in his life. This is probably the origin of the belief that breaking a mirror presages a death in the family. Also, to see one's reflection in the water in a dream was a sign of approaching death.

There was probably a sensible reason, even in days long ago, for handling a mirror carefully. They were very expensive, and only the wealthy could afford them. Servants who cleaned these treasures or otherwise touched them had to be terrified into handling them with care. Similarly, if a mirror was owned by a poor family, it might take about seven years to replace. Seven years of bad luck as the price of awkwardness or carelessness was a most effective deterrent.

The phenomenon of being able to see oneself has had strange applications all over the world. The Chinese hang brass reflectors over idols in their homes, because it is thought that evil spirits, when entering and seeing their own reflection, would be frightened away. Also in China, a concave metal mirror, placed on the door, brings good luck. A superstitious Chinese lady thinks it is bad luck to look in a mirror when in a strange place.

The Aztecs kept sorcerers away from the house by leaving a vessel of water with a knife in it behind the entrance door. When this evil fellow entered, he became so alarmed at seeing his ugly reflection, transfixed with a knife, in the water, that he turned and fled.

Strange to say, this custom of the pail of water with a knife in it is in use in America to this day—especially to protect cattle in barns.

"Saliva" Superstitions

SPITTING AS A countercharm is a folklore practice of universal distribution. Today, a favorite remedy for cuts and minor bruises is to moisten with saliva the middle finger of the right hand—most potent digit and capable of working wonders at times—and rub it on the injured place. It is also believed that saliva will lessen the pain of a blow, even remove it completely. Mothers use their saliva on their young ones when they are hurt, and the psychological reaction is truly magical at times.

The gambler today spits into his hands to bring good luck, just as the ancient Greeks did for the same reason.

Classical literature contains scores of examples of spitting to avert evil. It was a charm against enchantment among the ancient Greeks and Romans, and also a protection against a contagion from a maniac or an epileptic, both of whom were believed to be under the spell of the Evil Eye.

Human saliva was considered a cure for blindness; spitting on a serpent killed it. The formula to unbewitch the bewitched was to spit in the right shoe of the unfortunate person. The Chinese expectorate over their shoulders to frighten away the possessors of the Evil Eye. Among the Masai, the fiercest tribe of Africa, spitting on a visitor is a sign of reverence. Everyone who sees a newborn baby must spit on it for luck.

The origin of the many superstitions about saliva is not definitely known. But it is safe to assume that when man discovered that saliva is an agent in the process of fermentation, and was used in primitive brewing, he believed it must have other magical powers.

Possibly because it was observed that saliva had power to transform matter, as human saliva is an enzyme, virtues useful and effective against demonic powers were attributed to it, as well as healing powers.

Early man was a great observer and analyst in his own way. From the dawn of the domestication of animals he noticed their practice of licking their wounds, which apparently were healed with the moisture of their tongues, and regarded it as nature's cure. And so, of all fluids and excretions of the human body, saliva was selected as the magical fluid, par excellence. It was the one most used in ancient and medieval medicine, when it was looked upon as a "conveyor" of vital energy.

The practice of spitting on the hands to insure a secure grip has an interesting scientific explanation. It has been proved that the cold perspiration that appears on the skin when one is afraid was a psychological protective mechanism necessary to our cavemen ancestors, since the moisture on the body made them slippery in a tussle.

Sweaty or moistened hands and feet helped the barefoot caveman climb a tree in a hurry, without slipping, when someone or something was after him. So, today, a little spit on hands assures a better hold or grip on something,—and that is no superstition!

"Boat" and "Ship" Superstitions

FISHERMEN ARE perhaps the most superstitious of all sea-faring people, with sailors a close second. What happens to a boat on its maiden voyage is of primary importance, and founded on a tradition of the sea which began with the first crude type of boat. No fisherman will launch a fishing boat on Friday, least of all Friday the 13th. Nor, when starting on a trip, will a fisherman ever turn a boat against the sun, as this also means bad luck. Horseshoes are nailed to the masts of fishing boats to bring good luck. In addition to superstitions pertaining specifically to the fishing industry, most fishermen subscribe to all other taboos and superstitious beliefs of the sea, which are legion.

It is good luck to be rowing and see a fish rise to the top of the water as though looking at you. Any hand who comes aboard a ship with a black bag is bringing bad luck. To store a canoe or boat which can pass through the entrance of a home is bad luck and means the boat will not go into the water again, or if it does, someone will be drowned. If one points at a boat, while at sea, the hand must be used and not the finger. When sharks persistently follow a vessel it is a sign that someone on board is going to die. It is very bad luck to tear or lose the ship's colors.

Many men who sail the ocean still believe there are ghost or phantom ships that drift aimlessly over the seven seas. Some sailors believe the crews of these ships are corpses under the direction of the devil as captain. When a phantom ship crosses the path of another vessel, it is believed that shipwreck is sure to follow. The death-ship is supposed to put a spell on vessels, and the only way to get the spell out of the ship's timbers is to have a minister of the gospel come on board, and call all hands to prayer. This will purify the ship and drive the devil away.

The most famous phantom ship is the Flying Dutchman, seen in stormy weather off the Cape of Good Hope. To see it forbodes ill luck. There are many versions to explain this ghost ship. One of them is that it was a vessel laden with precious metal, and that a horrible murder took place on board. Plague broke out among the crew and no port would allow the ship to enter, so it was doomed to float like a ghost, and never be able to come to rest. This phantom ship is still a source of apprehension for those who must sail around the Cape of Good Hope.

Attaching good or bad luck to a ship is such a strong conviction with seafaring men that ship-owners will rarely buy a vessel that has met with repeated disaster. Bad luck is supposed to pursue certain ships and they acquire the reputation of being jinxed ships.

An old superstition of the sea is that when sailors are troubled about the fate of their ship, there is someone who watches over them, whom they choose to call "Cherub that sits up aloft." Superstitious sailors believe that when some other boat at sea sinks in a gale, unseen bells ring in the midst of the storm to inform them that a ship has succumbed to the pounding of the sea and that another crew has been added to Davy Jones' Locker.

Sailors like mascots, and a cat is the favorite. A cat's actions are supposed to keep sailors posted ahead of time as to the weather, so that they can prepare for it. When in port, if the cat leaves the ship and fails to show up before it sails, many sailors believe it spells doom to the ship. Perhaps this is why sailors refuse to have a cat aboard a ship—but there is also the reason that some think a cat carries a storm in its tail, being the devil in disguise.

When lightning strikes the mast of a ship, a bright flash lights it up for a second or two. Those who have faith in St. Elmo believe that this means he is bestowing his blessings on the ship, while others believe the exact opposite. Three persons who are taboo on a cargo ship are a woman, a lawyer and a preacher. These are all considered a sign of bad luck for the voyage. For some reason or other the words *hare* and *pig* are unmentionable on shipboard.

Carrying dead bodies in ships has always been a dreadful experience for sailors, who regard this as an omen of disaster. In times of war, however, the tradition is dispensed with, and does not signify death for a member of the crew as on other occasions.

The Chinese believe that a ship is blind, and no Chinese sailor will board a junk that does not have an eye painted on either side of the prow. In September, 1940, when the 17,000-ton freighter *Mormacsun* took to the water at Oakland, California, eyes had been painted on the prow as a good luck gesture, bringing an Oriental custom to the western world.

"Ship Launching" Superstitions

LAUNCHING A SHIP ceremonially is only one among many nautical superstitions which stem from the days when human sacrifice provided the blood which dampened the ship, an offering to the sea gods, before the vessel touched the water. As time wore on this cruel custom was replaced by the slaughtering of a lamb or an ox. The blood of an animal was believed to add life to the ship, together with the "blood" tribute to the sea spirits, as some of it reddened the water near the prow.

Originally the reason for offering the blood was to spare the blood and lives of those who would man the ship, who were in danger if the sea gods had not been given their due share first.

The Vikings launched their galleys on rollers down an inclined way to the water's edge. They bound captive slaves between the rollers to be ground to pulp by the ship's fast moving weight, and the blood of these helpless victims was the vessel's libation of human blood to the sea gods, without which the otherwise hardy and fearless Vikings would not feel safe in their undertakings.

It was only in the 15th Century that launchings became less sanguine and more religious in character. French fishermen, particularly in Brittany, launched their boats with very elaborate and colorful celebrations of the full Sacrament, a custom that continues to this day.

Although, at present, launching ceremonies take place simultaneously with the floating of the ship as it slips down the ways, in England for a while the launching ceremony was held immediately after the ship floated. This was for the reason that as ships become larger and heavier, the launching became correspondingly more difficult. When modern techniques were achieved, launching ceremonies reverted to a dry vessel.

Although nowadays women perform the ceremony of launching and naming a ship, it was a masculine prerogative until the 19th Century, when the Prince of Wales broke the precedent and began to have women of the court act as sponsors. Champagne is a relatively modern innovation.

In primitive times the medicine-man or witch-doctor launched water craft of all kinds. Later on, those endowed with sacerdotal orders —monks and priests—were entrusted with the privilege of launching and naming sea-faring vessels, with a libation of red wine—symbolic of blood—to propitiate the water deities, insuring the safety of men and boat alike.

It was the Greeks and Romans, however, who were the first to spatter their war craft and triremes with libations of red wine to win the protecting favor of the gods. Libations were offered in the name of Bacchus, god of wine, and to Neptune, god of the sea. Although Neptune was the god of the sea, a goddess' head came to adorn the prow of a ship, and the libations were then offered to her. Therefore a ship is still called "She."

Because of the taboo placed on women aboard a ship in ancient times, many sailors refused to sail on a vessel that was named by a woman. The superstition gradually disappeared, although the taboo against launching by married women and widows lasted longer.

If the bottle does not break when it is thrown, it is considered very unlucky, and to prevent this calamity, the bottle is generally suspended from the forecastle on a rope bedecked with ribbons, and a "bottle-catcher" other than the sponsor is on hand in case the lady misses. In many shipyards there is an official "jinx-buster," a kind of "pinch-hitter," in case a woman, through lack of strength or jittery nerves, or a wild swing, drives the bottle wide of the mark or prow. The "jinx-buster" stations himself under the official platform where he can break the bottle of champagne against the ship's bow, so the vessel can safely sail the ocean's bosom without interference from the sea gods.

Years ago, before the champagne era, it was customary, instead of smashing a bottle, to spill wine on the ship and then launch and name it as the goblet was thrown overboard as an offering to Neptune. After a time, a net was strung under the water around the ship to retrieve the offering. Later still, a bottle was used, and thrown at the bow. The bottle often went wild and hit someone, so it was then encased in a mesh-holder and yards and yards of red, white and blue ribbons woven around it to keep the shape of the bottle and at the same time to prevent pieces of glass from flying about and hitting and cutting the sponsor.

A ship launched with water is considered unlucky by superstitious seafaring folk, and that means practically everyone who mans a ship, since these persons are all superstitious and staunch followers of traditional sea customs and beliefs.

"Charms" or lucky pieces are placed in boats, especially schooners, as they are being built. Silver coins under the mast are favorite tokens of good luck even today.

A ship launched on Friday is generally believed to be an unlucky boat, so that day is avoided. Many seamen will not work on a boat launched on Friday, or a ship that has not been formally launched and named, even in this 20th Century. For this reason, most vessels carry a securely placed metal plate stating when, where and by whom the ship was launched.

In the wake of the idea that a ship was under the personal guidance of a famous god or goddess, ships came to be named after famous royal persons, such as Caesar, in line with the ancient superstition of the divinity of kings.

Incidentally, a ship is named and not "christened." It is impossible to christen a ship with champagne or any other thing. The meaning of the word "christen" is to make a person a Christian; only persons can be christened and not ships. The blessings now offered at launchings have replaced the mumbo-jumbo of the medicine man who, in primitive times, appeased the sea gods by addressing them with special tribal verbal formulas.

CHAPTER 20

Apollo's Chariot

Early Sun Mythology

MANY SUPERSTITIOUS customs grew out of the primitive awe of the sun and its great powers over man, beast and all creation in nature. The sun became a symbol of eternity—of the rising again after death. Easter, the spring holiday we celebrate, was originally connected with sun-worship. The early church merely added to its rites those already in vogue, giving Christian significance to pagan customs. This example is only one among many of our customs which stem directly from the sun-worship of our very early ancestors.

The beginnings of sun-worship in Babylonia, Assyria, Persia, Phoenicia and Asia Minor are lost in antiquity. We know, however, that it was adopted as the official religion of Egypt in the Fifth Dynasty, 2,500 years before Christ. The Egyptian hieroglyphic of the sun-god Ra is a point within a circle, which is still used as the astronomical sign of the sun. An axe was another symbol of the sun among the Egyptians. The double-axe was used as the sacred symbol of the sun among the early inhabitants of Crete. Incidentally, marking a track through a forest is still described as "blazing a trail." The Cretan legend of the Minotaur is supposed to be the mythical marriage of the sun and moon. The Druids were also sun-worshippers. As has been mentioned elsewhere, the rays of the sun were regarded as the hair of the sun-god, and carrying out the fancy, the strength of the sun was supposed to be lost when he is shorn of his hair in winter. Hair became sacred to the sun-god, and cutting the hair became a sacrificial offering. The priest's tonsure represents the disk of the sun. Crowns worn by kings and other rulers also symbolized the rays of the sun.

Even in modern times, the Japanese placed the highest deity in the sun, and the living emperor of Japan, up to the time of World War II, claimed direct descent from the sun-goddess.

Sunday, the day generally observed as a day of rest and religious devotion, was named for the "sacred" sun.

Sunwise or Clockwise Movement for Good Luck

SUPERSTITIOUS persons believe that to whip cream counter-clockwise, or counter-sun-wise, will prevent it from thickening or turning into butter. This is called doing it the "wrong way." Some housewives firmly believe that bread and cake dough also must be beaten "with the sun," that is, sun-wise. Card players often get up and walk around their chairs—also from east to west—to bring about a change of luck.

In all parts of the world it is still believed to be a good omen to circle with the sun, and a sure sign of bad luck to go the other way around.

In Ireland and elsewhere, including America, Maypole dancers skip around the pole in the same direction as the sun appears to move. The ribbons extending from the pole are imitations of the rays of the sun, to honor the returning warmth and glory of spring.

These superstitions and ceremonies and many others originated in deference to the sun's course in the heavens at a time when it was believed that solar activities had power to affect human affairs, and therefore must be honored.

Happy the Bride the Sun Shines On

"While that others do divine
Blest is the bride on whom the sun doth shine."
—Robert Herrick (1591-1674), *Hesperides*

THE SUN shining on a bride on her wedding day is believed even today to be a good omen. This is the survival of the primitive belief that the sun's light had extraordinary influence over reproductive capacity and would, therefore, bring about a happy union.

It is still the custom in India for the bride to face the sun as it rises on her wedding day. In Central Asia, many still believe that the bride and bridegroom should look at the sun together to attain future happiness. A Parsi bride would not think of being married before she has looked east at the rising sun on her wedding day.

No doubt a fine day does improve the spirits, but the real reason, in the western world, to wish that the sun would shine on wedding days, was a practical one indeed. All marriages in Old England took place in the open air, generally at the church door, and not inside the building.

The open-air custom was in keeping with an old and much beloved superstition of the East. But in England, where the sun is apt to be wanting and fog or rain more in keeping with the climate of the country, it must have been unfortunate for the bride if it rained.

Therefore, by reversal, it was considered good luck, if the sun shone on her. King Edward VI (1537–1553) is reputed to have altered the custom of outdoor weddings and the marriage rites thereafter were performed under cover.

That Snakes Wait to Die Until Sunset

CONTRARY TO popular superstition, a snake does not necessarily wait until sunset to die, although its tail may be seen wriggling for quite a while after it is actually dead. Persons well acquainted with this peculiarity of snakes know that it is due to reflexes that delay *rigor mortis*. These reflexes have been observed in the heart action of snakes, and there have been cases where the heart has continued to beat for as long as twenty-four hours after its head had been cut off.

Reflexes after death act in other animals besides the snake. The hind legs of a frog, for instance, will move for quite a while, even after they have been severed from the body. Eels have scared many a housewife when their reflexes made them seem alive in the frying pan.

No doubt the superstition that a snake waits until dark to die arose from the fact that after the sun went down its squirms and wriggles, caused by muscular contraction, could not longer be seen.

CHAPTER 21

Moonbeams Shining

Early Moon Mythology

The moon like a flower,
In heaven's high bower
With silent delight
Sits and smiles on the night.
—Blake, *Night*

ONE OF THE most popular superstitions today is wishing on a new moon. It is a very ancient idea and comes down to us in direct line from moon-worship, which is as old as civilization.

Primitive people noticed that the moon appeared to change shape, and then came back to its old shape again. Therefore, it was reasoned, a wish on the moon would come true as soon as the moon returned to the shape during which the wish was made.

Moon-worship is believed by many scholars to be of even greater antiquity than sun-worship. At first the moon was regarded by many peoples as masculine in nature, and the sun, feminine. Later, however, the ancient Egyptians called the moon the "mother of the world," and believed her to have both male and female qualities because, according to their myths, the moon was first impregnated by the sun, and then she herself scattered generative principles on the earth.

The moon was thought to be the source of all moisture. Everything from the sap of plants to the blood of living creatures was supposed to be vitalized by the waters of life which the moon controlled. This probably came from the earliest observation of the relation between the moon and tides. In ancient cults, there is a close connection between moon, earth and water worship, all three representing the female or passive principle in nature.

The moon was early man's first calendar, and to some degree, time-keeper.

Moonlight Superstitions

IT IS COMMONLY believed that a person who sleeps with bright moonlight shining directly upon him is likely to become mentally defective. This notion that the full moon affects the minds of human beings, causing periodic insanity, has persisted for ages. So far, however, no proof has been advanced to substantiate the fears and dangers attributed to moonlight. The fear of moonlight and not the moonlight itself may be harmful—but that is another story.

It seems the primitive mind must have concluded that persons already afflicted mentally were inclined to be more upset by certain phases of the moon, particularly a brilliant full moon. Therefore, in the early days, those who were perfectly normal in mind came to fear the baneful influence of the light of the full moon, and avoided it lest their sanity be endangered.

In time the word lunatic, from *luna*, meaning moon, and *tic* meaning struck, evolved from this primitive idea—that moonlight was responsible for the erratic actions of those who had been exposed to its penetrating rays. It blanched their brains, so to speak. The etymology of the word "lunatic" is one of our sinister legacies from the Dark Ages, and from the still darker ages before that.

There is no denying the fact that there are some individuals who seem affected or disturbed by the full moon. This does not apply to all persons who are "moonstruck," a term usually signifying the romantic effect of the exquisite beauty of full moonlight. Poets, artists, lovers, and just ordinary people, have been inspired and moved by this heavenly wonder ever since the eyes of man first perceived it; a perfectly normal reaction. The abnormal and odd cases on record of persons who feel an urge to start fires in the full of the moon have amazed and baffled specialists in mental hygiene. Bureaus of Fire Investigation are aware of the pyromaniacal tendency in some individuals and are on the alert during the full moon as they expect a few of these dangerous characters to be at work. The brightness of the full moon helps in their capture—which is seldom difficult. Psychiatrists claim that a true pyromaniac is a "throwback" whose destructive nature and love of fire is stirred when the moon pours out its silvery beams.

There is little evidence that a normal individual will become demented or act irrationally because of moonlight, regardless of the superstition.

Oddly enough, in the animal world there is unquestioned proof that sea-creatures, such as the palolo worms, which live in tube-like burrows on the side of coral reefs far under the sea, and grunions, are animals ruled by the full moon. Whether the moon is visible or not, at the exact hour of the full moon, the eggs are sent up to the surface of the water. Even when these moon-influenced creatures are kept in an aquarium, they respond to the moon rhythm just the same, even though they are where there are no tides, which used to be the reason given for this strange reaction to the full moon.

Making a Wish on the New Moon

What is there in thee, Moon! that thou shouldst move
My heart so potently?

—Keats, *Endymion*

WHEN A PERSON sees the new moon for the first time, the superstitious believe that he should bow to it, preferably three times, or three times three, in honor of the ancient Egyptian Trinity, namely, Osiris, Isis and Horus—the Father, the Mother and the Son. And if possible, while looking at the new moon, he should turn or shake silver coins in his pocket or hand, as he makes a wish which he hopes will come true.

Because of the moon's silvery glow, it was anciently believed to be made of silver, and so that metal became one of its symbols. This symbol applies especially to wishes made regarding money matters and success in business. Today, when a man who is trying to reach a decision, is seen shaking or jingling coins in his pocket, unknowingly, of course, he is observing the age-old superstition of calling upon the moon for assistance through the use of silver.

Among the commonest superstitions connected with the new moon are: that to see the thin crescent over the left shoulder is lucky; to see the moon straight before you signifies good luck to the end of the season; and any wish made at first sight of the new moon will come true. Superstitions in regard to the new moon vary according to the traditional or local beliefs of peoples in different countries, so that some say that the new moon should be seen over the right shoulder to be a good omen. There is general agreement, however, that when a man or woman uses silver when making a wish on the new moon, the chances of success are increased.

Women are very apt to wish on the new moon because of the ancient belief that this celestial body was feminine, and therefore responded more readily to the appeals of its earthly counterpart. However, based on the belief that opposites attract, when a male calls upon the moon-female with a wish, he feels symbolically, though not perhaps consciously, that the fullfilment of his wish is assured.

The sickle moon symbolizes something new, and this "newness" is also a quality of the things wished for. So that, as the moon grows into its larger phases, it is hoped wishes will grow from the thought to the reality.

Superstitious persons believe that the time of the new moon is propitious to planting, courtship, the starting of new business ventures or trips, cutting the hair and fingernails to effect a better growth, and so on. However, the idea of growth is purely one of association with the first crescent or "quarter" of the waxing moon.

Sickle Moon and Star, Ancient Lucky Symbols

THE RARE sight of a star above or in the cusp of the new moon is considered a sign of good luck even to this day.

In their earliest known faith, the ancient Egyptians saw in the crescent moon the symbol of Isis, the All-Powerful Celestial Mother. This idolatrous belief spread to many countries, and the crescent, symbol of virginity and chastity,—frequently with a star beside it or over it,—was adopted as a mascot to be worn or carried by mothers, children and young people.

The crescent, or anything similar in appearance, was looked upon as a repository of life, related to the crotch in humans, from which birth and a new life came forth. The five-pointed star, in this same group of superstitions, was symbolic of the whole human being, whose destiny was dependent on the magic growth due to the lunar influence. In other words, great importance was attached to the combination of the crescent and the star.

In ancient Rome, silver symbolized the moon and possessed female powers. For this reason, young married women wore silver crescents on their shoes to insure bearing healthy children. This silver ornament in contact with the foot—symbolic of the masculine generative powers —became a triple passport to protection and to the realization of their wishes.

An interesting historical item in connection with moon-symbolism is that when the Turks took Constantinople in 1453, they found a carved crescent at the base of the statute of Hecate, a moon goddess, who was the ancient guardian of the city. The conquerors saw an auspicious omen in the fact that they should unexpectedly have come upon this symbol, so familiar to them, and adopted it as their emblem. The national flag of Turkey today still has a sickle moon with the five-pointed star of Destiny next to it.

Change of Moon, Change of Weather?

THERE IS A comon belief that a change in the phase of the moon means a change in the weather. This has no foundation because the phases of the moon are the same the world over at precisely the same time; whereas the weather prevailing in differing parts of the globe is as variable as can be.

Long ago, lunar phases were interpreted to mean that the moon actually changed shape seven times, and that in some way this cycle of activity made for corresponding changes in weather. Possibly it may have been observed that sometimes a change in the moon and a change in the weather took place at the same time; this coincidence leading primitive man to a false conclusion, as was usually the case.

The Moon Tipped Up, Sign of Rain, or Other Way Around

IT IS COMMONLY believed that a "wet moon" is a new moon, with one horn or point lower than the other—somewhat resembling a tilted bowl. But in America, and other countries too, there is disagreement that the up-pointed horns mean that the "bowl" is overflowing and rain will fall. On the other side, it is argued that with the points upward, the moon is in such a position that it will catch all the rain in the heavens, and so the weather will be clear.

When the horns or points turn downward, some claim that all the water has run out and the sun will shine. The opponents of this position declare that the "bowl" is now upside down and therefore the water will pour down. If the reader isn't too confused by all this, he may ponder over this profound problem.

As the moon and its behavior have always intrigued man, a great amount of weather lore has been created through the centuries, based on imagination and fantasy. Astronomers, however, now can predict the tilt of the crescent moon hundreds of years ahead, although the weather man is limited to a few days at most.

The Full Moon and a Cloudless Sky

IT IS A COMMON superstition that the full moon drives all the clouds out of the sky. Meteorologists tell us, however, that at the time of full moon skies may be either clear or cloudy. The explanation for the wrong observation is quite obvious. It is very easy to see the full moon on a clear night, but on a dark, cloudy night, even though the same phase of the moon may be in the heavens, it is completely hidden.

Harvest and Hunter Moon Facts and Superstitions

IN NORTH temperate latitudes, the full moons of September and October are popularly called "harvest moons." But to be exact, the harvest moon appears at the time of the autumn equinox, approximately between the 15th and 20th of September. Some country folk, however, think the October full moon is the real harvest moon. After the harvesting was over, the next full moon was generally called the "hunter's" moon, because now, in autumn time, the work being over, farmers could enjoy their leisure by hunting.

This extra supply of moonlight that prolonged the natural twilight of day gave rise to many superstitions in the minds of the ancients. They assumed that kindly-disposed supernatural beings gave them this boon. In these early days, harvesting by moonlight was eagerly looked forward to, because of the good times that followed, rustic dances and festivities. Farmers who had delayed harvesting their crops till the last minute were also grateful. These longer days, as it were, allowed them to store their produce before the frost of winter came upon them.

To the enlightened there is nothing supernatural about the radiance of the harvest moon, although to simple minds the moon's behavior at this season seems amazing. The reason the harvest moon is so bright is a natural phenomenon due to the ecliptic or oblique direction of the moon's path which makes a smaller angle with the horizon at this time than during the rest of the year.

In the southern half of our hemisphere, this extension of moonlight takes place in late March or April.

Farming by the Moon

TODAY, before planting, many farmers carefully consider the phases of the moon. "Planting by the moon," a belief that there are favorable and unfavorable times for laying out crops, goes back to the days when agriculture was still young, and the moon was the only calendar. Periods of time were reckoned by "moon" in those days.

The moon's influence on human affairs is a survival of moon worship that dates back thousands of years. It is strange that moon folklore that assigned certain powers to the waxing and waning of the moon is still a guide to many people in rural communities, despite widely disseminated astronomical knowledge.

Planting in the "light of the moon" means in the time between the new and the full moon, or the waxing moon. Planting in the "dark of the moon" refers to the period between the full and the new moon, or the waning moon. Scientists, however, apply different meanings to these terms. They describe the light phase of the moon as the time it is above the horizon—from dusk to midnight; and the dark phase as the time between midnight and dawn.

As the moon shines on earth because it reflects the solar light, moonlight is technically known as polarized light. Experiments conducted with polarized and sunlight or ordinary light do not show any difference in the growth of seedlings exposed to both types. Therefore, if there is any basis for the superstition of "planting by the moon" some other factor must be involved.

Very recent discoveries have been made that reveal that there are electrical changes in trees, as well as variations in radio receptivity, with the changing phases of the moon. It is a fact that an electrical cycle of about twenty-eight days has been observed in trees, but this newly discovered phenomenon needs more study before definite conclusions can be offered.

Perhaps when we have more knowledge on the subject it may be necessary to alter some of our ideas about the moon. It is highly doubtful, however, that it will be found that the moon phases have noticeable influence on farming.

The Man in the Moon

YOUNG PEOPLE and adults alike still make a wish on the Man in the Moon, even though they know very well how the illusion of the face in the moon is produced. In the southern hemisphere the Man in the Moon appears upside down, of course, because this satellite of the earth presents only one side to us.

Primitive races were always fascinated by the moon, and many legends were inspired to explain what was going on there. The moon and moonlight were endowed with powers of both good and evil. Some peoples believed that the moon was the abode of the dead, the "pale face" of the moon lending credence to the belief. A later notion was that the Man in the Moon was the outline of a continent, but evidence tends to show that there is neither water nor atmosphere on that cold heavenly body.

CHAPTER 22

Twinkle, Twinkle, Little Star

To Point at the Stars Is Unlucky

ORIGINALLY taboos were attached to the gesture of pointing at the stars, moon or to a person. This was long before the days of etiquette and good or bad manners.

Throughout the East and elsewhere, for centuries, the twinkling of the stars was regarded as such a mysterious manifestation that it gave rise to numerous legends and superstitions, many of which are believed even today. One of the old beliefs was that twinkling stars were supernatural beings—later on, angels—whose eyes looked down on earthly humans in a protective manner. To point at them, it was feared, would put out their eyes. And so the gesture was forbidden.

Another version of this superstition is that to point a finger at the stars will make it drop off, but to avert the punishment, one may bite the finger first, to save the star the trouble of doing it.

The taboo against pointing at a star was so widespread, it was even found among the Ojibway Indians of North America. Certain superstitious beliefs are known to have sprung simultaneously in the minds of races so far apart, it was impossible for them to have been aware that they held the same fears.

Even the scholarly Pythagoras, widely traveled Greek philosopher of the sixth century B.C., instructed his disciples never to point a finger at the stars, or punishment would befall them.

In the past, it was also believed that pointing at or to a person, singled him out for attack by evil spirits,—another ancestor of the modern aversion to pointing at things.

Although we know today that the twinkle in the stars is caused by a momentary variation of brightness, due to the reflection of the atmosphere, pointing at a star, or just pointing at anything, remains taboo. "Pardon my pointing" continues as the apology for a breach of etiquette, but bad manners is a very far cry from the original stigma connected with the act.

Do the Stars Affect Our Destiny?

To "hitch your wagon to a star" is a lofty ambition which has a figurative value in that it spurs one on to worthwhile aims in life, but it should not be taken too literally, unless astrologers have a correct theory.

Believers in astrology have the view that stars influence the lives and behavior of human beings. From this belief came the idea that each person was born under his own particular guiding star—a temperamental Star of Destiny—which waxed and waned, lunar fashion, and was responsible for all the events of his life.

If a person came under an evil star, this accounted for his failures, a fatalistic attitude. It was also believed that, when in the ascendant, a man's star was shining in his favor, and only good things would happen to him. If, however, his star was on the descendant, he could expect nothing but hard luck and trouble.

The heavenly light of a star is associated with the legends of Moses, Confucius, Jesus, the Caesars and many others. Many characters in history believed themselves the instrument of destiny, notably Napoleon Bonaparte, who believed that his actions were governed by the occult influence of his guiding star. He even claimed that he saw his personal star shine before him during some of his great victories. One of his recorded remarks is: "It never deserted me (his star of destiny)! I see it on every great occurrence, urging me forward. It is my unfailing omen of success!" Hitler, another great egotist, also believed in his Star of Destiny, as well as in astrology itself.

Millions of persons today, the world over, put stock in astrological guidance, and spend a great deal of money for advice on love, marriage, business and world affairs, and so on. So far, astrologers' predictions have found little favor with the more scientific minded, and there seems, as yet, to be no way of proving whether or not stars have any influence on individual lives. Astronomy, on the other hand, makes accurate predictions regarding the universe as a whole, and has given us knowledge that has greatly advanced civilization.

Astrology was a very popular cult among the early Chinese, Babylonians, Egyptians, Greeks and Romans. Even pioneers in the science of astronomy tried to combine both subjects into one. Astronomy is said to have been first developed by the Moors, who introduced the study into Europe in 1201. The rapid progress of modern astronomical knowledge dates from the time of Copernicus who lived from 1473 to

1543. Books on astronomy, however, were destroyed, as infected with magic and heresy, in England in 1552, under the reign of Edward VI.

"Shooting" or "Falling Star" Superstitions

ALL RACES, creeds and nationalities, the world over, have different interpretations and superstitions for "falling" stars. Shakespeare made several allusions to this phenomenon in the heavens, such as:

> "Whenever a mortal falls in sin,
> Tears fall from angels' eyes.
> And that is why at times there fall
> Bright stars from out the skies."

To some, seeing a "falling" or "shooting" star means death. Others believe that if you want money, repeat the word "money" three times as the star is falling, and you will get your wish. Other superstitions consider shooting stars lucky for lovers, travelers and sick persons, but only if the wish is made before the star is lost to sight. If not made quickly enough, the wish will not come true.

There are some who believe that when a star "falls," it means that someone in the family will soon get married. One of the commonest superstitions, that nearly every child in America hears before it is grown, is that each time a star shoots through the sky, a soul has gone to heaven.

A shooting star to the left indicates that someone was wicked and his soul has just entered the infernal regions. A very pleasant fancy is that a shooting star guides a new soul from heaven to earth, in the same path in which a soul that has just departed from earth finds its way back to heaven. There are many other such beliefs.

"Shooting" or "falling" stars, we know, are wandering meteorites which enter the earth's field of gravity and so fall upon the earth. No one can actually see a "shooting" star because it is composed of very tiny meteoric particles, fragments of celestial bodies that originally were comets. The comets became disintegrated by the action of solar forces. What one does see, and which are incorrectly called "stars," are the trails of light in the sky, caused by the particles in the meteor being heated to incandescence as they strike our atmosphere. This shower of brilliant particles is known as "stardust."

It was not generally believed that meteors fell on our planet until the beginning of the eighteenth century, although such falls have been recorded from earliest times. Before the days of science, meteorites were regarded as miracles, and were worshipped as belonging to the supernatural.

"Dancing Light" or "Foolish Fire"

> *An ignis fatuus, that bewitches*
> *And leads men into pools and ditches.*
>   —Butler, *Hubidras*

THE DANCING LIGHTS which are often seen in the air over marshy places play a very prominent part in superstition and folklore. There are just as many stories to explain the mysterious nature and origin of this phenomenon as there are names for it, and they run into scores.

Some people believe these lights to be elves or fairies who hold their dances at night over swamps and marshes. Others think they are souls that have escaped from purgatory, and who have come back to earth to obtain prayers and masses for their delivery.

Others, again, call them the spittle of the stars, or mucus sneezed from the nostrils of rheumatic planets. To many, dancing lights or "foolish fires" are ominous signs, predicting evil or even death.

Dancing lights are believed to appear to mislead weary wanderers at night. There is also the belief that dancing lights indicate hidden treasure, by hovering over places where it is buried, especially gold. "Foolish fires" are also supposed to be the spirits of unrighteous men, and the best safeguard against them, when they appear, is for a man or boy to turn his cap inside out, and then no harm will come to him.

Many a Negro of Virginia believes that if he does not hurry and change his clothes, the dancing light will strike him a hard blow. English, Irish, Scotch and French, believe exactly the same thing. Sometimes, instead of changing their garments, or turning their caps inside out, or front to back, they stick a knife in the ground to cut out the spell. Some foolish persons think that if they can find the knife the next day, it will have blood on it.

Among the Russian peasants, there are those who think that dancing lights are the ghosts of unbaptized children, who cannot rest in their graves and must hover between heaven and earth. This belief is common in other parts of Europe and even in America.

One of the most popular superstitions connected with dancing lights is that they are the souls of dead men who, during life, fraudulently removed landmarks, and who, for punishment, must flit about after death, hunting for the right boundaries which are now mysteriously hidden from them.

On the other hand, the Basque people believe that a dancing light is a guardian spirit which accompanies a person and warns of danger. The light, it is thought, will float toward a person, and block the path of danger.

In reality, the dancing light or fire seen floating in the air in swampy regions is a flame-like phosphorescence. This natural phenomenon is produced by the spontaneous combustion of highly inflammable gases formed from decaying vegetable matter.

A startling impression is made on those who do not know this, when they see this eerie light in cemeteries, for instance. In such places the soil is particularly rich in the chemicals that create an effect easily mistaken for something supernatural.

Persons familiar with the truth about this natural phenomenon will sometimes playfully set fire with long lighted sticks to the gas bubbles that float over the surface of marshy ground. The bubbles will explode readily, but the puffs of fire quickly disappear in the air.

The reason that dancing lights do not float across a stream, is not because "goblin lights" avoid water, but because the brisk current of air produced by running water keeps back the lighted whiffs of gas, and stops them from crossing the stream.

"Lightning" Superstitions

THAT LIGHTNING NEVER STRIKES TWICE in the same place is a statement heard over and over again. But lightning can and does strike more than once in the same place, because whatever attracts one lightning discharge is quite likely to draw another, and even a third. The Eiffel Tower in France, the Washington Monument, and the Empire State Building in New York City, have each been struck by lightning several times, in fact, more than once during the same storm. There are a series of photographs of lightning that show the little flashes bombarding the same place.

The superstition that a flash of hot lightning will start a fire while one of cold lightning will not is a fallacy. All lightning is a form of electricity and, under proper conditions, will start a fire.

It is not true that lightning always comes from the sky down to earth. The earth contributes its share, and sends up streamers of electricity that meet discharges from the clouds to make the flashes. Earth bombards the heavens just as the heavens bombard the earth.

Some people believe that thunder, even if it is not heard, must follow every bolt of lightning. Actually, however, noiseless lightning is a very common phenomenon.

Another popular superstition is that fire caused by lightning cannot be extinguished with water. Some even think it has to be milk! All fire is fire, and the fire produced by a streak of lightning can be put out in the same way as any other fire.

There are superstitious persons who believe that a fire caused by lightning should be allowed to burn itself out and not be extinguished by human hands. This piece of ignorance is in keeping with an ancient belief that a fire caused by lightning was a punishment or revenge from powerful gods, whose ways with human beings could not be questioned, and whose laws were inexorable. To interfere with the work of the gods, once it had begun, was to invite more fury from these same gods.

There are many more lightning superstitions. It never is supposed to strike a barn where the swallows nest. If you burn the wood of a tree that has been struck, there will be a death in your family. Others will not burn the wood of such a tree for fear that their houses will catch on fire or be struck by lightning. This is an old African superstition that has found its way into America, particularly into the south.

All lightning superstitions started from early fears of this natural spectacle, and total ignorance of the principle of electricity. Not so long ago, our forebears fell flat on their faces when lightning flashed and thunder growled. They thought the demons were loose. Now, however, most peoples understand the fearsome phenomenon of lightning and the best ways to keep themselves and their homes out of its path.

The ancient Persians knew somehow that iron attracted electricity, and they applied a scientific principle without being aware of it. They planted sword-blades with the point upwards to deflect lightning from their houses. In Roman rituals observed in honor of Jupiter, an iron rod was placed on the highest towers of the Dunio castle on the Adriatic, with a soldier constantly on guard, so that when a thunder storm threatened, the soldier would place a javelin close to the rod. If sparks came out, he ran to warn the sailors.

Benjamin Franklin was the first to make scientific experiments with metal conductors and lightning safeguards. Franklin flew a kite during a thunder storm, and brought electricity down a silken string to a key at the bottom of it. This led to the invention of the valuable lightning rod, based on the identification of lightning with electricity.

CHAPTER 23

The Worship of Things

A "Lucky Break"

THE QUESTION OFTEN COMES UP as to how the popular American saying, "a lucky break" originated. One idea is that it grew out of circus slang that referred to the weather—a very important subject to circus people. If it rained, snowed or turned chilly, when the circus came to town, it "broke bad." Another version is that "lucky break" started in the poolrooms of the United States, many years ago. If a player pocketed balls, or even one, on the first break, it was "lucky."

Regardless of where or how the phrase was revived in our day, a "lucky break" was known as far back as primitive times. In those days when a member of a tribe wished to frighten away invisible evil-doers —who always try to interfere in the affairs of man—or to make sure of the success of a coming event, he took a stick and snapped it in the middle to make a loud noise which he firmly believed would do the trick. If things went well, it was, of course, due to the "lucky break."

The instinct to pick up a bit of dry weed, or twig, or, in modern times, even a match, and playfully snap it in two survives from the time when early man made use of this sort of sound to scare away harmful influences. We still snap our fingers and knuckles, making a crackling sound, but hardly anyone today is aware of why this gesture was once used.

Another application of the expression, "lucky break" is used by superstitious actors in the theatre, who always step hard on an empty package of cigarettes, labelled, "LUCKY STRIKES," as an omen of good luck, especially on opening nights.

"Name" Superstitions

THE POWER AND MAGIC OF NAMES is an old story in the field of super-stitions. When names were first given to people, places, animals and anything else, they were chosen with a view to endowing whatever was named with some sort of magic. It was very important to have the "right" name, just as in modern times, especially in America, many persons already named seek a "luckier" appellation.

In early times names were among the words used in divination. The medicine-man or oracle or whatever he was called by his tribe or nation, uttered special names which implied magical messages when calling upon supernatural beings for divinatory purposes. "Curses" and "blessings" originated in this way.

Whenever a person finds he has earned a bad name, he might as well be resigned to his fate, since one seldom lives down a bad name regardless of whether it was acquired by circumstances beyond one's control or not. The well-known saying, "Give a dog a bad name and you might as well hang him," expresses the experience of ages. Some persons who feel they have unlucky names change them because of an unconscious, or conscious, inferiority complex that makes them attribute their troubles partly to a name that has been a hoodoo.

There are thousands of foreign-born Americans who change their names to something more Anglicized, and thousands of native Americans who change theirs for professional or personal reasons. All these changes are made with the superstitious view of effecting a substitution that will bring more happiness and good fortune.

Most psychologists and psychiatrists interpret the act of name-changing as mild or serious cases of split personality. In such cases the new name becomes a psychological crutch which often gives the newly-named more confidence in himself.

Name superstitions run into the hundreds. A girl should not marry a man whose last name has the same initial as her own. A girl whose name is Mary begins with a good start in life. If the initials of your name backwards spell a word, it means good luck. It is lucky to have the letters of either your first or last name composed of seven letters. Men whose names contain thirteen letters should add one to take away the bad luck.

A superstitious notion that stems from patriarchal times and is observed by orthodox Hebrews is not to name a new-born child after a living person as it is believed this signs the death warrant for one or the other. However, there is a modern approach to get around the taboo, which is to call a child Israel I and the next generation Israel II and so on. The naming of a girl is much less complicated.

Although naming a child after a living person was not popular at one time, as centuries passed, the superstitious belief reversed itself and it has become the custom to name a child after its living grand-parent so that the child will enjoy a long life just as his name-sake seems to be headed for.

There is a superstitious fear among some persons of mentioning the name of a dead person. This, in keeping with various primitive beliefs, gave rise to countermagic measures. Primitives believed that a person's name was as much a part of him as his eyes or nose or any other part of the body, so that to mention his name disturbed his spirit or ghost. This peculiar attitude produced many of our superstitious sayings when using a dead person's name. These include, "May he rest in peace," "Bless his soul" and others.

To mention the name of an evil character was considered especially dangerous for fear his malign spirit would respond and cause misfortune to someone.

On the other hand, there were those who specialized in psychomancy or sciomancy, the art of raising or calling up the souls of deceased persons to give intelligence of things to come. This was a primitive form of spiritualism not unlike modern seances. The story of the witch instead of the medium, who conjured up the soul of Samuel to tell Saul of the battle he was about to begin, is a well known Biblical legend. There are many other such stories in sacerd literature that describe the use of the name in divinatory rites.

Modern etiquette which dictates that the most important person be named first in an introduction goes back to oldest times when the chief of the tribe or the king had to be mentioned by name before others, because of the supernatural power his name implied.

Names were very important to the Pythagoreans who taught that the minds, actions and successes of men were dependent upon their fate, genius and names. Plato himself inclined to the same opinion. It was Pythagoras who popularized the superstitious idea that blindness, lameness and similar misfortunes would fall upon a man's right or left side according to the odd or even numbers in his name. An ancient rule in divination by names was that the one in whose name the letters added up to the highest sum would be the happiest and most fortunate. One of the principle rules of Onomancy, or divination by the letters of one's name, was that an even number of vowels in a name signified an imperfection in the left side of a man and an odd number placed it on his right side.

Various countries have individual systems for bestowing names. The Chinese, like the French, often give a *nom de lait*, or milk name, to a child temporarily so that later he may change it to one of his own selection. A similar custom obtains among the San Blas Indians where, after a certain age, individuals may choose their own names. This system has its merits as many adults are dissatisfied with the names their parents have given them, and most of them do not like to go to the trouble of making any change.

Among ancient inhabitants of northern Mexico, a child's name was chosen by its mother, who walked around the house with her eyes closed, and upon opening them, the name of the object she saw first became the child's name. This was supposed to be lucky for the child.

The ancient Hindus gave three names to a child, the *common name*, the *secret name* and the *astrological name*. The common name was frequently an ugly, repellent and inauspicious name such as "Famine," "Filth" or even "War." The fearful nickname was supposed to be a powerful antidote to protect a child whose beauty might excite the envious glances of the Evil Eye of malicious persons.

The selection of names both by parents for their children or by adults for themselves with the aid of astrological charts or numerological formulas is still very popular. On the other hand, there are others who entertain the superstitious fear that if they so much as change a single letter in their name, they will meet with dire disaster.

"Effigy" Superstitions

"KILLING" IN EFFIGY is one of the strangest atavisms of our times. The frequent demonstration of hanging or burning a person in effigy in America to show public hatred or contempt is a hangover from witchcraft practices thousands of years old.

Primitive man believed that the likeness of a person or object was intimately related to the original. Witches and sorcerers modelled wax dolls to represent the ones they wanted to hurt or kill, using sharp instruments on them which were supposed to cause intense pain or even death to the living person.

In America and other places as well, hexers and voodooists still exercise this form of witchcraft in private. Modern witches burn candles and mutter charms to bewitch clay or wax images or photographs; and stab with an ice pick, scissors, nails or pins the heart of an unfaithful lover's likeness so that he will return. Diseases are also supposed to be inflicted in this manner, unless by the hated one's actions the cure is lifted.

In most of our modern cities today, on occasion rag likenesses or other types of effigies are burned or hanged in public squares or paraded in ridicule through the streets. During sympathy strikes, effigies of company officials have been treated this way, and unpopular politicians are subjected to the same form of humiliation.

To burn books, effigies, models of Old Man Winter, nail parings, stray hairs and similar suggestive articles is a superstitious practice in which these things are all related to the same aim: to destroy, symbolically, the things or persons connected with an intense animosity, or to eliminate an undesirable situation.

The Romans practiced the custom of killing in effigy. Medieval witches placed a wax effigy before a fire and watched it melt, believing this would cause the victim's life to melt away. Mohammedan law, however, forbids the use of effigies that represent the human figure. All Mohammedans believe that anyone who makes an effigy or dummy will be called upon to provide a soul—his own—on Judgment Day.

One of the most interesting facts about killing in effigy is that in France, in the old days, if a criminal could not be found, he was executed in effigy, and pronounced legally dead, in spite of the fact that he was still at large.

Among the Yorubas of West Africa, when one of twins dies, a superstitious mother has a small wooden figure made to represent a child of the same sex as the dead twin. She carries this along with the living child, and believes that the spirit of the dead child will not disturb the living one, because it has taken refuge in the wooden effigy and is happy there.

Members of a Negro tribe on the border of Liberia believe that a dead ancestor's spirit or soul may be captured in an effigy; and through this means, natives consult dead chiefs as oracles, or relate their woes and pray to them to help them.

In England, burning in effigy is part of the celebration of Guy Fawkes Day. Guy Fawkes attempted to blow up the Houses of Parliament. Although the effigy burnings were suspended during World War II, they have now been resumed.

In America, Benedict Arnold, the traitor, was often burned in effigy on the Fourth of July. In recent years Hitler and Mussolini have become favorites for this ceremony.

The practice has been widely condemned, but its popularity goes on. Newspapers frequently carry pictures of effigy parades and burnings as they are considered "news." However, a modern psychological view might be that the custom provides a harmless vent for working off indignation.

Photograph of Disliked Person Upside Down or Face to Wall

MANY YOUNG PEOPLE turn the picture of someone they dislike to the wall, or upside down, to punish him, hoping to give him a headache or other form of chastisement. This injury *in absentia* is inflicted in the hope that the guilty one will be sorry and perhaps return to the person who has been spurned or scorned. In other cases, this face-to-wall or upside-down position of the likeness means one desires never to see the original again.

There are even those who feel that placing pins in the region of the head or heart on a photograph will affect, in similar areas, the one whose resemblance it is. Others go so far as to believe that if this treatment is kept up indefinitely, it will eventually kill the hated one.

This type of superstition stems from a very ancient form of magic for doing good or evil, but more particularly evil. It explains why primitives in uncivilized regions refuse to be photographed. They are afraid that the one who will own their likeness may play magic with it and do them harm. Even highly civilized persons everywhere hold a lingering belief that any possession of theirs in the hands of someone who wishes them harm may cause their distrust to become a reality. In fact, many persons still blame their troubles on a jinx that has been placed on some property of theirs. In other words, it is believed that some personal belonging can be used as a prop in "hexing" another.

"To turn him down," a phrase meaning to refuse a proposal of marriage, originated in America in Colonial days. When a bashful suitor wanted to find out, without asking, if the woman he was courting would marry him, he would place a "courting mirror," face upward, on a table in front of his sweetheart, after first looking into it himself, and presumably leaving his own likeness in it. If the young woman cared to accept him, she would pick up the mirror and smile at his likeness, which she was supposed to see there. But if she did not want him, she simply turned the mirror down, and with it his magic face.

This familiar expression "She turned him down," is another application of the old idea that the wish of an individual may be conveyed through the real or imaginary likeness of someone.

Superstition About Forgetting Something and Returning for It

THE MOST POPULAR superstitious "antidote" to nullify the bad luck that is supposed to follow when forgetting something, and going back for it, is to sit down, and then count ten, recite a so-called magic word-formula, or make a wish, before starting out a second time. There are other variations of this procedure, but they all amount to the same thing: that to forget something, and then to turn around and go back for it, is sure bad luck unless a countercharm measure is taken to remove the potential misfortune.

It is generally agreed among psychologists that we never really forget anything, but what happens is that we drop things out of our conscious memory. However, the ancients knew nothing of psychological theories and tests, or of conscious and subconscious memories. All they were concerned with was to abide by the action-pattern of their ancestors, which, in this case, was that to forget something and return for it was a bad omen that had to be overcome by sitting down and saying something to exorcise the evil.

The evil that would follow this forgetfulness was that other things would be forgotten during the day, meaning that the whole day would turn out badly. This conclusion assumed that similar mishaps would follow the first, and something had to be done quickly to avoid trouble ahead.

The superstitious gesture of sitting down after returning for something may be explained by the old familiar meaning, the circle, symbol of the sun's unbroken course. By sitting down, the broken circle, or interrupted journey, is rounded out or completed as it were. Going out a second time represents a new circle or journey. The countercharm of counting, or reciting a phrase, is just thrown in for good measure to create absolute immunity against the inevitable evil to come when a circle was broken.

The wish that some make in the countercharm hokus-pokus is expected to come true because now all the evil influences of the day have been removed by the action of sitting down and closing the old circle. The eyes must be closed when making the wish, because of the ancient custom of facing the sun and making the wish to the sun, which compelled one to lower the lids to keep out the glare.

Here are a few formulas and magic words used in America today to remove any jinx caused by forgetting something:

"If I sit, bad luck will flit."

Take nine steps backward, and expectorate over your left shoulder. Saliva is an enzyme which transforms matter through fermentation, and therefore destroys evil.

Count seven steps backward, and whirl around like a dervish—the circle again!

Count up to ten. This is the most common formula. Ten is twice five, the sacred directional number, or the cardinal points of the earth and of man, according to ancient Oriental occultism, particularly Chinese. Five represents West, East, South, North and Center—Center being symbolic of the solar plexus of the human body. The number ten is the ancient decimal lucky number, related to the ten fingers on the two hands, or five fingers on each. Counting ten, therefore, was a great help in removing the bad luck of forgetting something.

An ancient biblical example of the bad luck that follows turning back, or looking back, is illustrated in the story of the dreadful fate of Lot's wife.

The modern superstition that women are more forgetful than men is impressively expressed by the Batsileos of Madagascar. Here, when a woman's funeral procession is near the grave, the attendants go back to her home for about an hour, to give the dead woman's ghost a last opportunity to gather up anything she might have left behind. These natives believe that no woman, even when dead, ever leaves her home without forgetting something.

Prophecy and Kindred Subjects

> *"And why so stupid to lend an ear*
> *To false alarms of amazing fear?*
> *If evil comes not, then our fears are vain,*
> *And if they do, dread will increase the pain."*
> Sir Thomas More

THE WORLD GOES ON in spite of "prophets" who predict its end. The latest prediction by the Rev. Charles G. Long of Pasadena, California, was scheduled for September 21, 1945, but when it seemed unduly delayed it was re-reported for October 1 of the same year. However, in keeping with other such gloomy prophecies of the past, the earth-planet is still in one piece.

On the border-line of popular superstitions stands the widespread belief that a dying man is endowed with a prophetic gift and is able to foretell the future. The history of folklore gives thousands of examples of prophesying all kinds of things, but the most dangerous is that of setting a date for the world to come to an end.

The past hundred years has been prolific in false prophets who named doomsdays that failed to arrive. Perhaps the most famous in America is the prophecy made by William Miller, founder of the "Millerites," or Second Adventists, who set the date for October 21, 1843. On the appointed day of doom frenzied believers donned their robes, tucked an ultimate lunch in the folds, and took their places on the housetops, facing east. On the 22nd they ate their lunch and climbed down. Miller confessed his disappointment, but insisted "the day of the Lord is at the door."

Another partial destruction which failed to take place was scheduled for 10:20 A.M., September 15, 1910. Again in 1925, Robert Reidt of Freeport, Long Island, became very popular when he prophesied the end of the world on February 16. In 1932, he foresaw the destruction of New York City at 11 o'clock Sunday night, October 9th. Disappointed, he quit making predictions and opened the Mystic Tea Room on North Main Street, Freeport. Many other predictions coming from various parts of the world obviously did not work out.

Modern prophets are more on the spot, as it were, than the ancient ones who gave themselves quite a bit of leeway. The late and beloved Stephen Leacock, a great scholar as well as wit, said: "Look at those prophets of the Old Testament. They were mature men 500 to 600 years old with a bombing range of 3,000 years."

The Bible offers many passages concerning prophecy. Two of the most arresting ones are in the words of Jesus, from Matthew 7:15: "Beware of false prophets which come to you in sheep's clothing, but inwardly they are ravening wolves." From Matthew 24:11: "And many false prophets shall rise, and shall deceive many." A word to the wise is sufficient.

Spiritualism and Kindred Subjects

THE BUSINESS OF COMMUNICATING with spirits, ghosts, or any other form of so-called spiritual or supernatural beings, is anything but new, and is not materially different from what it used to be though it has been known under various forms and names. Webster defines briefly the related trilogy of spiritual activities under *Oracle*, *Necromancy*, and *Spiritualism*.

Let us see what these definitions are. First, *Oracle*: the revelation or utterance supposed to issue from a divinity through a medium, usually a priest or priestess thought to be inspired. The utterances of the ancient oracles were commonly obscure and enigmatical. *Necromancy*: the art of revealing the future by pretended communication with the spirits of the dead. *Spiritualism*: a belief that departed spirits hold intercourse by means of physical phenomena, as by rapping, or during abnormal mental states, as in trances, commonly manifested through a medium.

Belief in ghosts is age-old and stalks through the literature of the last 6,000 years. But the medium business had its beginning in the United States in 1848, and is related to what is known today as Spiritualism. The movement began in a single family, in a plain little farmhouse at Hydesville, Wayne County, New York. Mr. and Mrs. J. D. Fox and their two young daughters, Margaret and Kate, were much disturbed by unexplained knockings. It is the only genuine American-born cult or faith which has prospered abroad.

One phase of spiritualism offers a panacea for those who fear death and ultimate extinction. It is reassuring to believe that spiritual beings can be summoned and materialized by the living, for it indicates to those who seek solace that they, too, may be able to return to earth after they are deceased and see what is going on. Spiritualists and mediums know of this urgent need and fear which grips the minds and emotions of millions of persons, and they capitalize on it.

The doctrines and practices of "spiritualists" have been thoroughly investigated and every form of ghost or spirit materialization has been reproduced. Ghost-writing has been duplicated, and communications with the ether world have been disproved. All the mediumistic paraphernalia is no secret to the magicians who can perform the same feats. Spiritualism is spreading alarmingly; an indication that fear is on the increase rather than decrease.

If there is life after death such as imagined by the spiritualists, there are millions of people, including scientists, who stand open-minded ready to face facts, not ectoplasm or any other impressive spooky manifestations with sound effects. Julian J. Proskauer, past national president of the Society of American Magicians, says, in part, that the magicians feel that magic should be worked for legitimate entertainment, not for the exploitation of customers. He adds that to be an honest magician may be rendering a public service of high order, but that it is an uphill fight, since the customers want to be fooled, and not for fun.

Selling spiritualist accessories by mail to amateurs who wish to become mediums is a tremendously successful business today. Spirit trumpets, talking skulls, and floating tables are among the stock items. The first firm to sell ghosts by mail began in Chicago some 75 years ago, named Ralph E. Sylvestre and Co. Today there are several supply houses which deal exclusively in supernatural appliances and "spook shows." One firm has to issue a 500-page catalogue to list adequately its thousands of items.

Some mediums know that they are out-and-out fakes and make the most of superstitious and fear-ridden people. Others vary in their approach to spiritualism, half-believing and half-doubting. A few believe sincerely that they are gifted practitioners and can hear and see the supernatural. Rich and poor, ignorant and brilliant minds alike are victims of this superstition and patronize seances. However, most clients are listed as women; grief-stricken souls who are generally below average intelligence and are emotionally immature. Such reports come from qualified investigators, psychiatrists and other disinterested persons who are out to help and not hinder the progress of science toward humanitarian ends.

Dr. William S. Sadler writes at length on spiritualism and related subjects in *The Mind At Mischief*. A few passages follow: "That we mentally follow our friends and associates to the other world is shown by the funeral rites and customs of primitive peoples. The Chinese worship their ancestors and seek to live on good terms with them. The savage knows that his compatriots are composed of both good and evil traits of character, . . . and so after the departure of his friend to another world he seeks in devious ways to appease him. . . .

"It cannot be said that modern spirit mediums have done much to refine this primitive concept. They tell us about the clothes that departed spirits wear, and other material things in their environment. . . . The spirit land of today seems just about as material and puerile as the Happy Hunting Ground of the North American Indian. In fact, this spirit land can hardly approach in beauty and imagination the mythological spirit abode of the Greeks. The ancients freely and frankly indulged their most fantastic dreams and then projected them out to constitute the stories of their mythical folk-lore. The ridiculousness of the modern spiritualistic concept is born on the fact that we feel constrained, in these days, to preserve a semblance of scientific thinking, and so we only become the more ridiculous when we seek to combine scientific reasoning with the fantastic imaginings of spirit beliefs."

Fetishism

A UNIVERSAL TENDENCY of the human mind is reflected in fetishism, which is not, as is sometimes supposed, the worship of material objects, but is the friendly intercourse between man and the spirits that are supposed to inhabit these objects. Fetishism falls right in line with modern superstitious beliefs and behaviorism. In modern parlance, "fan" or fanatic hero-worship hysteria is fetishism in nature. Twentieth-century fetishism is evidenced on all sides by millions of persons, young and old, of all classes, who idolize either a "crooner" or "blues" singer, baseball player, football player, prize-fighter, or any kind of "head-line" hero or heroine, and for whom the fan cherishes an inordinate desire, and thereby departs from the so-called "normal" conduct of a human being. This worship gives an individual a sense of emotional security and ecstatic joy, though temporary, which is realized when looking at, listening to or talking to one's idol.

What is a fetish? A fetish is best defined as a material object believed to be the dwelling of a spirit, or to be the representation of a spirit, which may be induced or compelled to help the possessor. Primitive animism, however, evolved into fetishism, and fetishism is the first step toward idol-worship. When we idolize a human being in an extreme sense, as such fanaticism expresses, that hero or heroine becomes part of modern fetish-worship, for which the word "fan" qualifies only when the emotional expression and action do not have all the earmarks of an hysterical outburst.

A typical, but not pleasant, illustration of hysterical fetishism is when vandals—in the guise of souvenir seekers—go to the scene of a disaster, and exhibit their irresistible desire to take things. It is kleptomania with a new twist, but this gesture also falls into the pattern of fetishism or fetishistic mania.

Fads and obsessions, and the greedy desire for inordinate possessions, is also fetishistic. For instance, persons who accumulate dozens of hats, shoes, gloves, and things of that nature, that they will never wear, as well as perfumes, soaps, and the like, are victims of fetishistic impulses, perhaps unconscious, but nevertheless real. Hoarding or an uncontrollable desire to acquire an over-supply of things is a dangerous fetishistic infatuation with inanimate objects. At the same time, persons who *must* have a large number of cats, dogs or other kinds of animals around them fall into the same category, particularly if they live in crowded city rooms or apartments. It expresses cruelty to animals to boot.

A typical fetish tree is the Wishing Tree of Hope, of Harlem in New York City. It was rededicated October 6, 1941. It is but a stump of dead wood, but as everyone in Harlem knows, if you pat, kiss, hug or touch the Tree of Hope, your wish will come true. This is an actual fetishistic superstition in the modern tempo, and yet it is an unbroken link in the chain of beliefs in the "spirit" magic, or animism in inanimate objects.

Tattoo marks are another modern expression of an ancient vintage. They evolved from symbols that were originally fetishistic in that they were potent with the respective spirits which they harbored. The tattooed symbols are expected to protect their possessor, and are designed to comply especially with the individual's faith in them. They are believed to become a permanent part of the person, once they are indelibly patterned into the skin. It is well not to lose sight of the fact that a fetish is primarily a material object.

To the question, "Is fetishism an unusual neurotic pattern?" Lawrence Gould, eminent psychologist, answered: "Yes, in the extreme form of the strange 'perversion' which drives men to cut off locks of women's hair in subways, or steal articles of feminine attire from clothes lines. But it's not uncommon to make an unconscious 'fetish' of some feature in a member of the other sex, which is associated in your mind with your first 'love ideal'—blue eyes of a certain shade, for instance. When you fall in love at first sight with a person you really know nothing about, it is usually an unrealized form of 'fetish worship'". (New York *Journal-American*, February 20, 1947, in syndicated feature: MIRROR OF YOUR MIND).

"Circle" Superstitions

MANY CUSTOMS that stem from early sun-worship are still with us. A few of them are: to walk around a chair—clockwise or sunwise— once or three times for good luck; to have strands of hair, a loved one's or baby's first lock, curled in a locket; or to wear any round object such as a ring, bracelet, or even hat crown. Originally, sun-symbolism of all kinds was invented in imitation of the sun circling the heavens, going down under the earth and back again—representative of life, death, and resurrection, or in other words, life eternal.

The return of the sun at dawn puzzled man for ages, long before the days of astronomy. Despite their ignorance, early peoples were also inspired with the "Sun-Eye" action. The all-seeing eye, with its light, warmth and protective presence, was valued and worshipped, because it was well understood that without it there would be no life.

Our everyday phrase, "the family circle," or the "family cycle" was devised by ancient sun-worshippers in symbolic reference to the sun, which in its circling course signified to man the greatest manifestation of creative energy. The sun was looked upon to "keep the home fires burning" in more ways than one, and it was regarded as the creative essence of the masculine principle.

"He who venerates the sun, venerates his own soul" is an expression that originated in earliest times when men were convinced that the sun was life itself. Fire, as a means of heat and comfort on earth, was worshipped as a secondary principle of solar creation.

In keeping with the circling of the sun, a divination system came into being, called Gyromancy, meaning "rounds" or "circles." The flipping of a round coin, making circles in the air, or spinning it in a circle marked with letters which were key-letters for a "yes" or a "no," was the system for answering important questions and making weighty decisions. This is evidence of the implicit faith man had that the sun would aid him at all times. We still flip a coin to get an answer to something, just as it was done in Caesar's time.

Today, when we put a circle around a figure, we are using an old mark that was originally made with blood. The legal red seal of today grew from this and its many star-like points are in imitation of the sun's rays.

A ring or circle has served as a charm or countercharm for ages and we find it in use up to the present time. The betrothal or wedding ring was originally a sun-symbol to form a matrimonial bond that was expected to last a lifetime, and to produce many children to keep up the family cycle or circle. Housewives still believe that batter must be beaten sun-wise to assure good results in baking, and if the wrong method is used, it is blamed for the failure that might result .

Egyptian ladies of old rouged their lips ceremonially at first. This was long before it became a matter of personal vanity. By emphasizing the red circle formed by the mouth—believed the door to the human body—the spirit or soul within was prevented from escaping too soon. At the same time, it prevented evil spirits from entering the body. As we know, the pyramids were built in Egypt to commemorate the sun's position. Their grandeur and amazing construction will remain forever to attest to the genius of these inspired sun-worshippers.

"Going around in circles," an expression to describe one who is mentally or physically confused for the time being, has been found to have a basis of reality behind it, so that the expression is not exactly a superstition. Experiments with blind-folded subjects demonstrated that there must be some sort of steering mechanism in human beings and animals that makes them turn in spirals in order to get control of a situation. This spiral motion principle even applies to small swimming creatures. The indication seems to be that a spiral or circling movement is a universal law of life. However, life itself is part of a cycle, which binds man intimately to the sphere in which he lives, as well as to the broader cycles of the universe.

"V" for Victory, a Very Ancient and Potent Symbol

THERE ARE TWO FAMILIAR VERSIONS as to how the great inspirational symbol used in World War II, the "V" for "Victory," came into being. Both stories originated in Belgium and are probably related to each other.

One version is that Belgian students at Courtrai, together with their Walloon fellow-students formed a sort of Freedom Movement and planned to escape from Belgium via Lisbon, to join the Belgian army in England. They decided that the first letter of the Flemish word, Vrzheid, which means freedom, would be a sign of identification among them and would be indicated by the index and middle fingers. Any newcomers who wished to take part in this victory campaign could also use the sign. Those who reached England introduced the "V" symbol, which spread like wildfire wherever Allied forces were fighting the cause of freedom.

The other story, perhaps more familiar, credits a Belgian refugee, Victor de Lavelaye, with having started the campaign in England. It was taken up by Col. V. Britton, who popularized the "V" sign in a wide publicity plan presented for the first time on the British Broadcasting network in 1941.

The use of the letter "V" or the "V" sign for spiritual and moral courage has a long and ancient history of which very few are aware. In the mythology of the Egyptians, there is a delightful story of the super-strength of the All-Powerful Horus, god of the ladder and the staircase. Horus was thrust into darkness by Set, or Typhon, the Principle of Evil, but he escaped by means of the ladder which his father, Osiris, the Sun God, let down to save him. In gratitude for his rescue, and to inspire others to have faith and moral courage, Horus used the crotch or fork of his powerful index and middle fingers to save others. It is interesting that, according to the story, the ones who wished to earn the support and protection of Horus showed their reverence toward him by wearing amulets, symbolizing the ladder and the two fingers of this god.

There are several parallel legends concerning Horus, and all exploit his highly moral character. He was looked upon as a great and powerful hero who always managed to escape from the demons of the underworld, symbolic of evil temptations, and to appear at dawn each day in a blaze of glory, symbolic of victory over evil.

Notwithstanding these myths about Horus, amulets in the shape of two fingers—the V symbol—were used in ancient Egypt from earliest times. Christian priests, even today, hold up the same two fingers, though not parted, as a sign of blessing.

The letters "V" and "U" at one time were interchangeable and both symbolic of the crotch of the human body, the source of life. To the ancient Egyptians the two fingers, V-shape, were the symbol of the continuity of life, or immortality—a definite victory.

There are many examples of the early use of the "V" or fork-shape in practical as well as symbolic ways. For example, the earliest plough was V-shaped, and the basic pattern has not changed. The practice of divination employed forked symbols such as the wishbone, the horseshoe and the divining rod.

The question may be asked, what happened to the ancient "V" symbol during all the intervening centuries? Whether the "V" sign as a symbol of ultimate victory in World War II was a sudden flash of patriotic and inspired enthusiasm, we cannot say, but it cannot be denied that this sign was revived in one of the greatest moments in history. It circled the globe and stimulated into action all freedom loving peoples. Its extraordinary fascination was manifested by the instantaneous acceptance—a cosmic response. The symbol traveled like lightning from hand to hand, becoming a sign of mutual identification and heroic purpose.

Since the war everyone has become familiar with the international Morse code for transmitting the letter "V," three dots and a dash. It is strange that this beat or rhythm, forms the opening notes of Beethoven's Fifth Symphony of victory, "fate knocking on the door." Was this great composer prophetic?

Cross Worship and Symbols

THE CROSS, AS A MAGIC DEVICE, stands unparalleled in the maze of symbols and superstitions. Its significances combine the spiritual, physical and intellectual expressions of mankind, and there is no symbol, either in art or religion, which has been as universally employed. It is one of the oldest mystic and esoteric symbols of creative power, and has been used for ages as an anti-demoniac charm or talisman.

The cross antedates the coming of Christianity by thousands of years. Crosses have been found among the ruins and remains of the oldest races that inhabited the earth.

There are several very old Egyptian symbols of the cross, one of which represents the Trinity of Life, the *crux ansata*, or Tau cross. Its familiar design is a T with a loop at the top, symbolizing generation and enduring life. This handled cross is seldom missing from pictorial representations of gods, priests or kings of ancient Egypt.

When the ancient Romans reached the island of Crete, they found that the cross was an object of worship there. In the royal residence of Cnossus, the fabulous palace whose countless passages gave rise to the myth of the Labyrinth, a large equal-armed cross, the Greek cross, was a feature of the Cretan queen's private shrine. It stood in the center of the altar-ledge, close by the faience figure of the Snake Goddess herself, the giver of children.

Crete is the home of a very old civilization, and archeological excavations have revealed that the Cretans had open comunication with the Nile Valley at the time of the earliest Egyptian dynasties.

The Thau of the Jews, and the Tau of the Greeks, from which came the letter T of the alphabet, were regarded not only as letters, but also as sacred symbols because they suggested the cross. The Assyrians, Chinese, Gauls and many other ancient nations venerated the cross. It was also a religious symbol among aborigines of the New World. The Incas, Mayans, and Aztecs gave the cross a prominent place in their religious systems.

When the Spanish conquerors found crosses in the temples of Mexico, they were very much surprised, and believed other Christian contact had preceded their arrival in the land, which, of course, was not true. Most North American Indians also regarded the cross as a mystic symbol, representing the four cardinal points of the compass.

Among the Scandinavians, Thor, the god of thunder, had a hammer as his symbol. This hammer was a cross. In Iceland the cross of Thor is still used as a magical sign in time of storms as protection for the inhabitants against the fury of the elements.

Illustrations of the universality of the cross as a symbol are endless. It is worn by priests on their sacerdotal robes, by distinguished laymen as a sign of great dignity on occasions of state. It is engraved on eucharistic vessels, embroidered on altar clothes, and cut in relief on tombs and ornaments. Some of the greatest churches and cathedrals in Christendom are fashioned in its shape.

In Europe, as well as in Mexico, Canada and the United States, it is a common sight to see crosses erected in public places, at crossroads, and as landmarks. Babies wear the cross on chains around their necks, and adults wear it as an expression of faith, or perhaps just for decoration.

Although gods have fallen, temples have crumbled, and creeds have decayed and disappeared, it must be mentioned that there has never been a moment in history when mankind, somewhere in the world, was not reverencing this great religious symbol—the Cross.

Virginia Fairy Crosses or Lucky Stones

THERE IS A TREMENDOUS DEMAND, year in and year out, for the Virginia Fairy Crosses, or lucky stones, for watch charms or lockets to be worn as amulets against witchcraft, to prevent disease, or to avert misfortune generally.

These crosses are little grayish-brown stones which range in size from one quarter of an inch to one inch. They find favor in the hearts and minds of superstitious persons here and abroad, and are acquired either by purchase through the mail, or in shops that have the supply.

The Fairy Cross was the favorite amulet of Theodore Roosevelt, Woodrow Wilson and Warren Harding, all presidents of the United States. Many other important persons have carried them, as well as thousands of ordinary folk.

These little curiosities have been shaped by nature's own hand, and bear exquisite carvings of some form of the cross. The Greek, Roman and St. Andrew crosses all appear in the formations.

The best specimens are found in the rugged foothills of the Blue Ridge Mountains, in Patrick County, Virginia, a region famous for the fact that the old Indian king, Powhatan, head of the confederacy of Virginia Algonquin tribes, held undisputed possession there. These crosses are also found in Maine, New Hampshire, Massachusetts, North

Carolina, and Georgia. Somewhat similar to the Fairy Crosses are the large twinned crystals with rough surfaces found in Brittany.

The Blue Ridge mountaineers have several legends concerning the origin of these crosses. One of them is that when the red man was supreme in America, the Great Spirit showered down the crosses as a sign of coming salvation to the savage race. Another is a beautiful legend from which the Fairy Crosses got their name.

Hundreds of years before King Powhatan's dynasty came into power, good fairies inhabited this delightful mountain region and had their workshop there and flourished. Once, while the fairies were dancing around a spring of limpid water, playing with the naiads and wood-nymphs, an elfin messenger arrived from a strange city, far, far away in the land of dawn. He brought the sad tidings of Christ's death, and when the fairies heard the terrible story of his crucifixion, they wept. As their tears fell upon the earth they were crystallized into little pebbles, on each of which was formed a beautiful cross as a meorial of their sorrow. When these fairies disappeared from this enchanted spot, the spring and the adjacent valley were strewn with these unique mementoes of the melancholy event.

Due to the very human habit of attaching a mystic meaning to anything unusual in nature, and endowed further with the legend of the cross, these Fairy Crosses became lucky charms. Actually, however, they are twinned crystals of staurolite, a dark silicate of aluminum and iron. The scientific name for this mineral is derived from *staurus*, cross, and *lite*, stone.

Travelers from all over the world know of these Fairy Crosses or "tears," and continue to buy them as lucky pieces to keep away misfortune, especially in times of danger.

Cross-Stitch Embroidery

SYMBOLS AND CHARMS in cross-stitch embroidery are still framed and hung in the home over the front door for good luck. They are also supposed to keep out anyone with the Evil Eye, who might enter and practice witchcraft and black magic upon the family. This word-charm cross-stitched embroidery is a survival of the written mystic offerings of ancient and medieval times.

To be super protected, in some homes one of these framed cross-stitched proverbs or mottoes was placed over every single doorway in the house. Nowadays, however, these embroidered charms are looked upon more as interior decoration than as the household protection they once signified.

Cross My Heart!

"CROSS MY HEART, HOPE TO DIE" is an expression and form of oath, familiarly heard where there are children. Sometimes parents require their young ones to repeat this saying when they suspect a child of lying. The gesture of crossing the heart goes with the words.

Children, however, are not the only ones who use this traditional formula of crossing the heart to emphasize the truth of what they are saying. This gesture is made by sweethearts and devoted friends also.

There is an eloquent symbolic implication in making the cross over the heart. In ancient folklore, the heart was the seat of knowledge. Combined with the cross-symbol, it is supposed to lend sanctity to words that are spoken, and insure their truth.

The Red Cross

A RED CROSS was used in antiquity to mark the spot of an impending danger or the scene of a crime. Often the cross was made with the blood of the victim,—red, in folklore as well as at the present time, being the color of danger and warning.

The only instance in olden days we know of where a red cross was used for another purpose except as a danger signal is in early Greek history. A Greek sovereign or magistrate of the fifth century placed a red cross both before and after his signature on important documents. The cross before his name represented the customary invocation of the name of God, and the other red cross signified his own trustworthiness.

Although probably not connected with the modern implications of the red cross symbol, it is interesting that a cross was used as a symbol in ancient Egypt by a group of men who studied the "mysteries" or art of healing. They were devotees of Thoth, the god dedicated to making the sick well, and one of their ceremonies was to make the sign of the cross on the affected part of the body, or the forehead or even in the air to bring back health to the afflicted. Later this gesture was copied by the Greeks, Romans and others. Today it is still practiced as a form of blessing.

We find another instance of the "healing touch" or "royal touch" among the kings of England. The superstitious idea that the royal head had divine healing powers originated with Edward the Confessor (1042–66). However, not all kings after him believed in the efficacy of their touch, and following Queen Anne's death in 1714, the custom was abolished. The rulers of France also claimed divine healing powers up to the time of the French Revolution in 1789.

The red cross on a white ground is the flag of Switzerland reversed. This design was chosen as the Red Cross emblem in honor of Henri Dunant, a Swiss citizen and member of the International Committee of the Red Cross which met at Geneva in 1864. Dunant drew up the charter for the organization under the auspices of his government.

Another famous health symbol is the double-barred red cross used in the world-wide campaign against tuberculosis. In 1902, at a meeting of the International Conference on Tuberculosis, Dr. Sersiron of Paris proposed the ancient Lorraine cross as the emblem of the crusade against the "White Plague." In 1906 the National Tuberculosis Association adopted this double-barred cross as its emblem and it has been associated with the movement in the United States ever since.

Although in times gone by the red cross was, on the whole, a symbol of death and taboo all over the inhabited world, nevertheless it is now the proud emblem of the organization which has achieved the only successful international treaty since history began. The Red Cross has come to stand for all expressions of human kindness and compassion.

The Windmill's Cross Wheel

THE MAMMOTH wheel-cross of the windmill, with its four limbs outstretched in mid-air, seems to challenge the elements and at the same time beckon the four winds to spin it. Nevertheless its original use was as a diminutive symbol, but with very profound implications.

Windmill wheels are presumably descended from sun-wheels or prayer wheels, especially characteristic of Tibet and Mongolia. At first these sacred wheels were turned by hand, and later made to run by themselves, harnessed to a running brook or stream. This device was then enlarged upon and was gradually developed into the windmill of today.

Among Hindus and Buddhists, the turning of the wheel represents rebirth. It is also used as a substitute for, or aid to, prayer. The spokes in prayer wheels are as a rule multiples of four, and the wheel is generally turned in the direction toward which the sun moves. It is believed that the spokes of the wheel, uniting in a common center, symbolize divine unity. These prayer wheels are inscribed with a magic formula, or else prayers are mumbled as each turn of the wheel is made.

At first, even before prayer wheels were used, the first wheel-cross represented the rays of the sun. When it was encased in a circle, it became the sun-wheel of the ancients. The sun-wheel charm is one of the oldest symbols of the occult power of the sun, and it was assigned to all the sun-gods as a symbol of universal dominion.

The prayer wheel, or sun-wheel with eight spokes or double-cross, is known in India as the Eight Glorious Emblems, or the Wheel of the Law. It has other symbolic names, the best known to the western world being the Eight Beatitudes. In its original use a double-cross was a powerful talisman, and it is too bad that it has an unfortunate connotation in America and other places today. However, the wheel-cross of the windmill remains as a pleasant reminder of its noble background.

The Cross as Signature and Kiss

PERSONS WHO ARE unable to write are required to make a cross in place of signing their names. This practice, while embarrassing to illiterates, has a very dignified origin.

Centuries ago, the use of the cross mark was not confined to un-tutored persons. Kings and nobles used the sign of the cross on official papers whether they could write or not, as it pledged, by their Christian faith, the truth of the matter to which they affixed it. Because of its sacred nature, the cross was the symbol of an oath as well as evidence of a signature.

Among the Saxons, the cross attested the sincerity of the person signing a letter or document, and was required of all, whether they could write or not.

The expression, "God save the mark," which is almost an oath, and also an ejaculation to avert evil, is traceable to this practice. "God save the mark" did not derive from an old saying in archery, as some have claimed. The expression undoubtedly was used by a man who hit the mark, and who did not want anyone else to hit it and disturb his arrow. It had no other meaning.

Another familiar expression, "He made his mark in the world," emphasizes the fact that in the days when the majority of people could not write, a man who had signed documents with a cross, and had become successful, had made his "mark" not only on paper, but in the world.

There was a time when illiteracy was more the rule than the exception. A man who could write, or even read, was assumed to be in holy orders. Clerks and ecclesiastics were the penmen of the day, and the laity did not feel the necessity for reading or writing as in our present time.

Scholars are not agreed as to which type of cross was most generally used in the old days,—the St. Andrew's cross like the letter X, the cross of Calvary with the horizontal bar near the top, which is the Latin cross, or the Greek cross, resembling the plus sign. In America, where, unfortunately, there are still too many illiterates, the X cross seems to be universal.

The use of the cross as a man's signature also explains why small crosses are now used to mean kisses at the end of a letter. During an age when the cross was a religious symbol, it was not only affixed on wills, deeds and other documents which needed the mark, but the signer would often kiss the cross he had just made as a pledge of good faith and as an act of reverence. However, it is safe to say that very few who today make crosses to mean kisses do it with the same seriousness and sincerity that the act once implied.

We Cross Ourselves for Various Reasons

DEVOUT PERSONS will cross themselves in the face of danger, when it is lightning, when hearing of a death, passing a cemetery or funeral, or under similar unpleasant circumstances. The gesture is performed as a countermagic to protect one against a calamity of a similar nature.

Crossing oneself before eating or before other acts of daily routine is not done exclusively by those of the Christian faith. The higher Lamas of Tibet use the same symbolic movement before commencing their devotional exercises.

The cross as a symbol has been regarded for centuries as a means of protection against evil. Among early Christians it was believed to break spells, exorcise the devil, and safeguard the believer from witches, demons and all kinds of evil spirits. Making the sign of the cross with the hands was an outgrowth of this. Nowadays, the wearing of the cross not only denotes the faith to which one belongs, but gives the wearer a feeling of added security.

The motive behind an individual's act determines his thoughts and intentions, so that in the hands of a hypocrite or charlatan, the cross and its representations become powerful instruments with which to carry out evil designs. History and literature abound with such characters.

Crucifixion—The Cross of Sacrifice

THE CROSS was not always a symbol of honor, and punishment by crucifixion was widely practiced in ancient times. This form of execution was known to have taken place in countries as far apart as Assyria, Egypt, Persia, Greece, Carthage, Macedonia, Rome, India and Scandinavia. It is also thought that crucifixion was used by the Jews themselves, based on an allusion to it in the Old Testament (Deut. XXI, 22, 23). The allusion is about hanging on a tree, but trees were used to make crosses also, and the exact method remains more or less of a question.

Crucifixion, or nailing to the cross, was the punishment inflicted on slaves, robbers, assassins and rebels. Jesus suffered this fate because his accusers called him a rebel for proclaiming himself King, or Messiah.

This savage means of ending a life was also performed in some countries as a sacrificial offering to an important god. Baal was the outstanding deity among many ancient Semitic nations, and not only human beings, but the choicest and most valued animals, were nailed to the cross to please him.

On one occasion, when Malcus, a Carthaginian general, wished to secure the favor of Baal, he clothed his best and most beloved son in royal robes and crucified him as a sacrifice. The Phoenicians, also Baal worshippers, used the cross for the same purpose.

The frequent allusions of St. Paul to the humiliation which Christ endured when he was put to death on the cross suggested to the early Christians that they take the cross as the emblem of their faith. The symbol that had degenerated into one of shame and disgrace was then restored to its rightful position of old—symbol of glory for all time.

The Cross Marks Our Dead

> *They are neither man nor woman,*
> *They are neither brute nor human;*
> *They are ghouls.*

—Poe

WE KNOW that the cross expresses a powerful symbol against evil of all kinds. Therefore, it seems logical that the cross would be placed over a grave, both as a protective emblem—figurative representation of man, himself—and also as a warning to those who might rob the dead of jewels or other valuable possessions buried with them.

In Europe in the Middle Ages, and even later, so-called witches were known to be notorious grave thieves. Their dissection of corpses for parts of the body needed in the "witches' brew" is famous in folklore. The witches, however, were themselves fearful of the cross that marked a grave, and they would not desecrate the bodies so protected. They believed that punishment by death would be their fate if they molested a grave bearing the cross.

Originally, crosses were erected only over graves of kings, heroes and other important personages. Later, it became the general custom, in order to insure acceptance into Heaven of those whose spirit had been liberated from earth bonds.

In keeping with their own idea of the Hereafter, primitive and ancient peoples buried, with the corpse, the articles considered necessary to start life anew in the next world, even including food. Archeologists and anthropologists have greatly enriched our cultural heritage by their findings, derived from the contents of ancient tombs and other burial places.

In these early days, just as at all times, measures had to be taken to prevent the looting of graves. In ancient Eastern countries, it was the belief that ghouls,—imaginary evil beings—robbed graves and ate the corpses. Undoubtedly, there were real human beings abroad in those days who despoiled graves and stole what they could find, and then disposed of the bodies. And so the ghouls were blamed.

In spite of the sacredness of the cross, now in universal use on graves, modern cemeteries have not been left untouched by "grave snatchers" either. Not too many years ago, the only way for medical students and medical schools to obtain corpses for dissection and study was to hire grave robbers. Sometimes when students were unable to hire others to do the gruesome job, they were obliged to do it themselves—a serious offense with a severe penalty.

The Swastika or Hooked-Cross

SINCE PREHISTORIC times, the swastika has appeared everywhere, in different forms and for different reasons on all kinds of objects, but always basically as a symbol of the Wheel of Life, or continuation of life. In buried cities of the remote past, archeologists have found the swastika, or hooked-cross, drawn, painted, cut, woven, scratched or otherwise imprinted upon sacred objects as well as upon articles of everyday use. Sometimes the swastika combined several ideas, such as the four points of the compass, the four winds, or symbol of man himself, the equilateral cross. This diversity of symbolism shows that the Wheel of Life was venerated not only as a religious symbol, but was closely associated with ordinary human interests.

The wide distribution all over the globe of ancient fragments and ruins bearing the swastika design proves that it is neither an Aryan nor a non-Aryan symbol, Hitler notwithstanding. The term, Aryan, was introduced by Professor Max Muller of Germany (1823–1900) and incorrectly defined by him, as, properly, it only designates the Indo-Iranian languages—not races. The old assumption that the similarity of languages implied race relationship has been decisively disproved and rejected by scientists.

The swastika was revered in India three thousand years before the Christian era, and it is from India that we have the most convincing evidence that the swastika, with its wings or arms—forming the Wheel of Life, is symbolic of the sun and its solar rays and energy. The Hindus today believe that when the arms of a swastika are on the right of the central cross, they indicate the movement of the sun, from east to west—a beneficent sign. When the arms are on the left, they represent the dark period when the sun is hidden—the sinister side of the cross.

There are "right-angle" and "left-angle" swastikas, which must be explained in order to understand all the implications of this now famous symbol. To begin with, the swastika becomes a right or left one as the point of view changes. Imagine a cross made of two equal lines, one vertical, one horizontal. Now add the arms, beginning at the top of the vertical line. If the first arm is drawn from this point to the right, and the other arms continue in this rotation, the swastika becomes a right-angle one, as you look at it. However, place it upon your forehead, and it becomes a left-angle swastika. Or, draw a left-angle swastika and hold it in front of a mirror, and you now have a right-angle one.

The Hindus attributed to the right-handed swastika the male principle, light, life and glory—all empowered by the sun as it wheels its daily course in the heavens. The left-handed swastika, on the other hand, represented the direct opposite. It was looked upon as the emblem of the goddess Kali, the female principle. It implied darkness, death and destruction. In one of her numerous forms, Kali the Black is an ominous character, and the very mention of her name terrifies the superstitious Hindu to this day.

Simply stated, the two swastikas stand for the sun by day and the moon by night; the right-arm, male; the left-arm, female. In India, Tibet and other Asiatic countries, these two emblems were called the Sun Swastika and the Moon Swastika, and regarded as complements of each other. Frequently the lunar crescent was inscribed in the center of the cross for the moon-swastika, and the solar disc for the sun swastika to further distinguish them. The moon swastika was sometimes called the "winged," possibly to indicate the phases of the moon.

The dual character of the swastika, that is, solar or male, and lunar or female, complementing each other, is in keeping with the Hindu emphasis on rebirth or the perpetuation of life. The degradation in which women were held is disappearing, but there is no doubt that Adolf Hitler's swastika must have been the left-angle one, with all its evil implications.

The Swastika is the Hindu cross—a symbol of blessedness and benediction. Its name comes from the Sanskrit "su," good, and "asti," to be, —like amen or "ammau" of the Hebrew. In India Buddhists and Brahmans alike believe the swastika to be a symbol of good luck.

The swastika is also one of the many symbols connected with Buddha and appears on the headdress of Vishnu, the preserver in the Hindu Trinity. Statues and images of Buddha have the swastika carved either on the soles of his feet, or in the region of the solar plexus, or the region of the heart, or, to symbolize light and knowledge, above the head.

The hooked-cross, or swastika, is a popular sun-symbol in many countries of the Orient besides India. In China it signifies "many years," "long life" and "good fortune."

In northern Europe, where pagan worship has long been abandoned, the left-hooked swastika represented the Hammer of Thor, Scandinavian god of thunder and unrest, and symbol of death. The swastika was also identified with the thunderbolts of Jupiter. To the ancient Arabs, the left-angle swastika signified death just as the lunar emblem did to the Hindus.

Swastikas have been found in North America, carved on shells taken from prehistoric burial mounds in Tennessee. Other specimens of this symbol, in copper, were taken from similar mounds in Ohio, notably

Hopewell Mound near Chillicothe. Today, as in the long ago, to some tribes of American Indians, the swastika represents the highest expression of life in all its phases, reminding us of the Hindu concept.

"Clock" and "Timepiece" Superstitions

"Time is the image of eternity."
                    —*Diogenes Laertus*, Plato

THERE IS A superstitious belief that when a "grandfather's clock" casts the shadow of a coffin, it means that someone in the house will die. This false conclusion is undoubtedly drawn from a morbid fear of death coupled with the association of the coffin shadow. However, when a death actually takes place, as is apt to happen in any home, it substantiates the fears in the minds of many in whose houses there are grandfathers' clocks. Thereafter such a tragedy is looked upon as if it actually cast its shadow beforehand.

Another clock superstition was glamorized into a song, first sung in the rural districts of the United States from which it spread all over the continent, including Canada. The refrain of this strange song embodies the old idea that clocks are in sympathy with their owners:

> "Ninety years without slumbering,
>   Tick! Tock! Tick! Tock!
> But it stopped . . . short,
>   Never to run again
> When the old man died."

The theme of this old song, "Grandfather's Clock," is fiction, of course, but few things are written as fiction that cannot be rivalled in fact. There are countless cases which lend an air of truth to the fact that a clock or watch stopped at the exact time of death of an individual. In the light of science and reason such an event appears to be just coincidence. Many learned persons, including some in the medical profession, however, refuse to accept the happening as mere coincidence. The simultaneous stopping of the human heart beat and the ticking of a clock or watch is an appalling phenomenon, to say the least. This happening, which has been reported frequently, cannot be explained, one way or another. It must, of necessity, remain in the realm of coincidence until further proof comes along.

There is no denying that those under emotional stress are more easily impressed by coincidental happenings, and so contribute to the exaggeration of events, which under other circumstances might pass unnoticed. This is how most fables and legends, which make up the huge bulk of *hearsay* parade in folklore, began.

It is also a superstition that if you should become the owner of an old "grandfather's clock," and decide to sell it, you will never have any luck. One by one, you will have to sell your possessions until you have sold the last. This superstition has actually affected the market, and accounts for the few old "grandfather's clocks" found on sale; except, of course, when the family line has come to an end.

There are various superstitions which, if followed, will prevent dreaded events. One is that it is best to stop the clock at the moment of a person's death, to limit the power of death by introducing a new period of time. The clock must be started again after the funeral, when a new cycle of time is supposed to begin.

Heart-Shaped Charm, Tattoo or Food

HEART-SHAPED ORNAMENTS, Valentine paper hearts, and other heart patterns are designed in modern times to express affection, or deep feelings of love, as coming from the heart, believed to be the seat of the emotions.

In olden times, however, the liver, and not the heart, was considered the seat of love, and the heart was assigned other significances. The traditional belief was that the heart was the seat of courage and intelligence, so that the familiar heart-shaped symbol tattooed on a sailor's body is not necessarily in remembrance of a favorite sweetheart, but probably expresses the age-old meaning.

In early times, the heart was called the "counsellor heart," implying that all wisdom proceeded from it. By displaying the heart symbol, the individual believed he could be endowed with greater knowledge and wisdom, and have better judgment and good fortune generally. "Learning things by heart" is an expression derived from the ancient belief that the heart was also the seat of memory.

Eating the heart of a powerful enemy slain in battle was a common custom because it was assumed that it would give extra courage and strength to the slayer. "It gives one heart," meaning courage, is still a popular phrase. A lion's heart was anciently eaten so as to acquire the animal's strength. Animals' hearts used to be prescribed for those who suffered from heart ailments, in the definite belief that not only would this strengthen the heart, but would cure it completely.

Heart-burial—the heart buried apart from the body—was an ancient practice which lasted well into the 19th Century. It signified a special reverence toward the heart and its association with the soul of man, his courage and his conscience. In medieval Europe, heart-burial was fairly common. The custom was forbidden by Pope Boniface VIII, (1294–1303), but Benedict XI withdrew the prohibition.

Flipping a Coin

IN OLDEN TIMES, superstitious people who could not arrive at a decision of their own, or who would not trust another individual, looked for the answer "yes" or "no" through various forms of divination, among which the thumb played an important part. This is carried over into modern times in the familiar saying "Heads you win, tails you lose," which combines the flip of the thumb with the tossing of a coin, to settle a question or to find out to whom a desired article is to go. Gamblers, especially, like this system of reaching a solution.

Coin-tossing to settle a controversy is a custom which has outlived many older and newer methods used for the same purpose, and no doubt will remain with us for centuries to come. This method implies that both parties to the dispute are "good sports," and evidence proves that it brings about a decision that has caused less trouble than any other means of settlement.

The custom of tossing a coin in the air with a flip of the thumb is especially popular with those who believe in "luck." Many of this superstitious type have their own "lucky" coin, one which they never use in their games, if they are gamblers, for fear it would be lost, and with it, the good luck they attach to it.

Historically, coin-flipping dates back to the time of Julius Caesar, when his head was engraved on one side of every coin. When an argument arose, a coin was flipped, and if the side of Caesar's head showed, whoever chose the head was right,—and this decision was final. Such was the power of Caesar!

It is an interesting fact that King Ptolemy I of Egypt in 306 B.C. was the first living ruler to have his likeness stamped on coins. But coins themselves have been in use since the 10th Century B.C., when they were minted by the Lydians, whose last king, Croesus, was so rich that his name is still synonymous with great wealth.

General "Money" Superstitions

THE ANCIENT PRACTICE of carrying a coin or giving one for good luck has not changed materially today. Bracelets and brooches with one or more coins may be purchased in the most modern shops. When a superstitious person makes a gift of a purse, money is tucked inside so that the owner may never be without it.

Carrying a large, old-fashioned penny for a pocket piece is popular with men and women everywhere. Finding a penny is believed to bring good luck because it means more to follow. Gamblers do not like to lend money while playing because it means they will lose theirs. The itching of your left hand is an indication of receiving money unexpectedly. If someone gives you a penny to wear with a new gown or suit, it will make it a lucky garment. A bride believes that a coin given her by the bridegroom is good luck for a happy marriage, if she wears it in her shoe at the wedding. It is lucky to keep pennies in a jar in the kitchen.

Lydians are said to be the first people to coin money. Their last king, Croesus (B.C. 560–546) was so rich and powerful that his name was proverbial for wealth and has remained so ever since. Sacred inscriptions or mystic symbols were then often represented on coins, some of which were carried as a mascot or lucky piece by the superstitious people of ancient times. A coin which was associated with a happy event or a favorable bargain was carried as a charm or "lucky coin."

There is the superstition that to carry a coin with a hole in it is lucky, particularly if worn on the left side of the body or hanging from the neck. Long before the dawn of coinage, it was believed that a pebble or shell with a hole in it had been worn previously by the god of the sea; hence, the finder wore it to be closer to the water deity. When coins came into use, this old belief was transferred automatically.

Many of the Oriental coins were and still are made round with a square cut in the center, symbolizing the round sky and square earth. There was the "healing coin" specially minted of gold and touched by the King of England, long believed to cure scrofula, a disease known as "The King's Evil." A well known custom intimately connected with the dead was the placing of coins on the eyes or in the mouth of the dead as payment to the ferryman, Charon, for taking the soul across the mythical river Styx.

If you have a piece of silver in your pocket and turn it over upon seeing the new moon or the full moon, your wish will come true. This habit is generally considered a man's gesture, but oddly enough women started the custom.

The origin of the belief that the moon had female powers is lost in antiquity. We do know that gold was a symbol of the sun, and silver the symbol of the moon. When a woman wished to have some special favor granted, she called upon the moon with the use of silver, the lunar metal. So the popular practice, even today, is for a woman to bow to the new moon when she sees it for the first time, and to turn a silver coin and make a wish.

The fear of refusing to give money to a beggar is a hangover from the days when a beggar's curse was something to be heeded. Originally it was necessary to give coins to the first person seen coming out of a temple, especially on the eve of a journey or wedding. The poor people stood by to receive such coins, and in time this practice led to the professional beggar who voiced a curse upon the person who did not give him anything. Many a superstitious person today, therefore, is forced into giving money to a "panhandler" lest he curse under his breath and bring bad luck.

Chain-of-Luck Letter Superstitions

IN MODERN SOCIETY, here and abroad, it is believed by millions that anyone who breaks the chain-of-luck by not sending out the prescribed numbers of letters, after having received one, will meet with disaster. But if everything is carried out according to instructions, he will be the recipient of unexpected good fortune.

There are very few persons who at some time or other have not received a chain-of-luck letter at least once, if not more often. Many non-superstitious persons feel strangely uneasy when they tear up the chain letter, which shows the power of suggestion upon all of us.

The chain-of-luck letter has slight variations, but it always expresses an ominous threat if not mailed exactly as required.

It is said that an American lieutenant in Flanders was responsible for the chain-letter vogue which started in 1920, and during World War II, the chain letter became more popular than ever. The Luck of London chain letter, that started in England during the blitz, is still circulating in Europe as well as in America!

"A Letter of Protection" was printed during the first World War, and sold to thousands of young superstitious recruits in America. Here are some characteristic remarks:

> "Whoever carries this letter with him, he shall not be damaged through the enemy's guns or weapons. God will give him strength that he may not fear robbers and murderers, nor guns, pistols, swords; muskets shall not hurt him. . . . Whoever carries this letter against all danger, and he who does not believe in it may copy it and tie it tight to the neck of a dog and shoot at him and he will see that it is true. Whoever has this letter, he shall not be taken prisoner nor wounded by the enemy," etc.

It is interesting to note that the dime chain-letter of today was really started over two hundred years ago by two men named Howard and Evans, who had their printing shop at 42 Long Lane, West Smithfield, London. The letter sold for a penny or sixpence, and sometimes even for a shilling. It was represented as a copy of a letter written by the Saviour himself, which, of course, was a hoax. The letter, however, was very popular, and a few extracts may be quoted:

> "And he that hath a copy of this my own letter, written with my own hand, and spoken with my own breath, and keepeth it, without publishing it to others, shall not prosper!
>
> "But he that publisheth it to others shall be blessed of me; and though his sins be in number as the stars of the sky, and he believes in this, he shall be pardoned.
>
> "And if he believes not in this writing, and this commandment, I will send my own plagues upon him, and consume both him, and his children, and his cattle.
>
> "And whosoever shall have a copy of this letter, written with my hand, and keep it in their house, nothing shall hurt them, neither lightning, pestilence, nor thunder, shall do them any hurt. And if a woman be with child, and labor, and a copy of this letter be about her, and she firmly puts her trust in me, she shall safely be delivered of her birth.
>
> "Ye shall not have any tiding of me, but by the holy scriptures, until the Day of Judgement.
>
> "And goodness, happiness and prosperity, shall be in the house where a copy of this letter is to be found."

The chain-of-luck letter comes in direct line from one of the earliest known methods to effect a cure, bring good luck or cast a spell, through verbal charm, spoken or sung. This primitive system of magic is as old as speech itself. Certain words had magic power to keep evil spirits away, bring good fortune, or make a wish come true. The chain-letter is a more tangible form of obtaining the same results by using written words on paper.

The bartering, buying and selling of oral phrases supposed to be endowed with magical influence—for better or worse—is a commerce of the greatest antiquity. Magic word-formulas or oral charms are still the stock in trade of sorcerers or of professional dealers in this kind of hokum. In the Orient, especially in China, the written word has been of magical importance for centuries, and is still revered in many places.

Printing and hand-writing have helped to popularize magic word-charms. The chain-of-luck letter of today aims to effect, on a world scale, the magic circle, by reaching every human being, with the purpose of bringing happiness and good fortune to the human race. This, of course, is an impossibility, since a large portion of humanity cannot read or write.

Although there is no law prohibiting the beginning of a campaign of good-luck chain-letters, the Post Office Department tries to discourage it, and advises the public to ignore such mail.

"Pin" Superstitions

See a pin and pick it up,
All the day you'll have good luck.

THERE IS A GREAT variety of superstitions connected with the pin, and many of them are directly contradictory. "Pick up a pin, pick up sorrow" has the opposite meaning of the quotation heading the chapter, which may be said to correspond with "Pass up a pin, pass up a friend." There is also "See a pin, let it lie, all the day you'll have to cry." The superstitious ones have their choice.

Other pin superstitions may be mentioned. Never give a friend a pin, or it will spoil the friendship. To prick oneself with a pin before starting on a trip is a bad omen. It breaks up a romance to present a man with a scarfpin. Black-headed pins should not be used when having a new dress fitted. If a person, especially a man, carries a supply of pins about with him, he will never marry.

If someone hands you a pin or needle, you must smile, but not say "thank you," or else it will hurt the friendship. If you find a safety pin, it is good luck; and if you give it to a friend it is a sign of lasting friendship. A hairpin working itself out of the hair is a sign that your sweetheart is thinking of you.

Superstitious persons feel that pins or sharp objects should be bought and not given or received. However, the bad luck is removed if a coin, or some other small object is given in return for the gift that has a sharp point. The countermagic of giving a slight token when receiving a pin for a gift, dates back to the primitive system of bribing jealous evil spirits when good fortune befell anyone.

Superstitious fears pertaining to sharp pointed objects began, no doubt, at the time of the earliest races, when real danger was always present. Pin superstitions probably evolved as such from the danger attached to the primitive use of pin thorns, fish bones, fowl or animal leg bones or the like in their crude garment-making, tent-making, or other fastening purposes.

Any liquid or shiny surface in folklore was believed to be a means through which magic or divination could be worked. Many of the thorn superstitions of early peoples were transferred to the pin or other sharp object, and the superstitions, in some form or other, survive to this day.

Ancient fears that later turned into superstitions stemmed not only from the danger of being hurt, but also from the fears that through spilled blood, magic might be worked by evil-minded persons against the one to whom the blood belonged. Today, when a person pricks his finger with a pin, inevitably he will put his finger in his mouth, just as primitives did ages ago. In those days it was done, however, so that no one else might get this blood for evil purposes. Accidental bloodshed in primitive days was interpreted as a sign of a coming calamity, and all sorts of counter-magic gestures were performed.

As has been mentioned elsewhere, in the long, long ago, pins were stuck into the wax images of those against whom one had a grudge, in the hope that the live original would feel intense pain. If this absent treatment were kept up long enough, it was expected to kill that person. A later use of pins was to throw them into wells to bring good luck, especially to unmarried women who wanted husbands.

Pins were made as far back as the Bronze Age. It is impossible to say when wire pins were first made, although we know they were manufactured in England in the 15th Century. In 1483 a law was passed forbidding their importation, so pins must have been manufactured elsewhere before this. Pin superstitions were brought into England from the continent, and the American colonies learned them from the English.

There is a superstitious notion that a sliver or splinter should never be removed from the skin with a pin, but with a needle, which is safe. However, scientifically, there is no difference in the effect on the body of a steel needle or a metal pin of any kind, provided it is sterile, just as the needle must be. A superstitious explanation of why the needle, rather than the pin, is the proper implement for removing the sliver is that in its design it combines both masculine and feminine symbols, which are supposed to negate any possible evil.

"Wishbone" Superstitions

A VERY ANCIENT superstition that never seems to lose its popularity is for two persons to make a wish and then pull the ends of a wishbone. The one who breaks off the larger piece will have the wish come true.

In ancient bird-lore, the hen and cock were in great favor, other birds being too inaccessible for divination and other purposes. Since the cock announced the coming of day, and the hen announced the laying of an egg, these fowl came to be looked upon as capable of revealing to men the answers to their problems, as interpreted by the diviners and soothsayers of the day.

As early as 322 B.C., the Etruscans had a "hen oracle," the medium by which a special god was called upon to reveal hidden knowledge and solve important matters. This sacred fowl was killed, and her entrails examined by the appointed diviner. The bird's collar bone was put in the sun to dry and the person seeking the answer from the god made a wish on it, which gave the name "wishbone." Afterwards, two persons snapped the dried wishbone, and whoever held the larger piece got his wish, or a "lucky break."

The reason for choosing the clavicle or "wishbone" was because of its remote association with the crotch of the human body—symbolic of the repository of life—and with this idea in mind, the wishbone was believed to hold the answer to a wish.

The Romans picked up the wishbone ceremony from the Etruscans and carried it to England during their occupation.

The wishbone became known as "merrythought" in derision of the custom of making "merry wishes" as these were called. This was during the 18th Century, and afforded much amusement to gatherings at the dinner table.

Mythologies, legends and fairy tales reveal that the hen was held in high esteem since earliest times. It is mentioned with honor in the older Sanskrit hymns, the Veddas, and it is quite probable that the Hindus were the first to raise hens for their commercial value. An ancient law, however, forbade the use of the flesh as an article of food. Only the eggs could be eaten,—probably an economic measure.

Tradition has it that in Egypt all hens were put to the profitable service of hatching peacock and duck eggs. White and yellow hens were excluded from this task as they were reserved to be sacrificed to the gods in return for favors asked.

In Greece, Pythagoras, (600 B.C.) would not allow his children to eat the flesh of a white hen, because it was sacred to Zeus, the mighty god of the Hellenic people.

The hen and cock became part of another game of divination, called alectryomancy. In order to look into the future, a circle was traced on the ground and divided into twenty-four parts representing the alphabet. Grains of corn were arranged in each section. A cock or hen was then led into the circle, and the first grain of corn he picked, indicated the first letter of the name of a future husband. All sorts of questions were answered in the same manner. Then the fowl was usually sacrificed to a special god, and the wishbone removed. It was then snapped by two wish-makers, just as it is done today.

The wishbone of any fowl is a well-known mascot. A century or so ago, it used to be the fashion in Europe to carry a miniature wishbone made of gold or silver, because of the ancient belief that this was an article of good luck. Bracelets, pins, charms, sugar tongs and other objects with wishbone motifs are still sold every day because of their auspicious implication.

"Ladder" Superstitions

It is still a widespread superstition that it is unlucky to walk under a ladder leaning against a building, a tree or against some other object unless a countercharm is performed, such as stopping long enough to make a wish, or to cross one's fingers. The sign of the "fico" or fig is another powerful antidote. This is effected by closing the fist and allowing the thumb to protrude between the index and middle fingers. This is believed an unfailing phallic masculine symbol which negates the impending bad luck of walking under a ladder.

To dream of going up a ladder is a sign that you will rise in life. To dream of descending a ladder means that you will sink into poverty; but if, in your dream, you climb it again, you will overcome your troubles in a short while. A child that is noisy should be put through a ladder three times, and it will become quiet. There are many other such superstitions.

From the point of view of myths, legends and mythologies, there are contradictory origins for the superstitions attached to the ladder itself as well as to the ladder symbol. They signify both good and evil. For instance, one of the most elaborate and ancient references to the ladder and ladder symbols appears in the story of Osiris, the Sun God of the ancient Egyptians. This legend, oddly enough, applies to other mythological solar gods which identified Osiris with Baal of the Phoenicians, Zeus of the Greeks, Jupiter of the Romans, as well as Thor, the Norse god of Thunder and Lightning. All these gods are related to the same myth of the ladder in some form or other.

Osiris carried on a perpetual warfare with Typhon, the spirit of Darkness, in order that light would come up the ladder of light rays which effected the return of the sun each day. Once, tradition relates, Osiris was unceremoniously defeated, and thrust into the darkness of the grave by the terrible Typhon. However, with the aid of two very powerful and ancient amulets, namely the Ladder, and the Two Fingers in the form of V, Horus, the Hawk-Headed god of the Rising Sun, assisted his father, Osiris, to climb out of darkness up to the Sky to his heavenly rest. From then on Horus became the official god of the Ladder, the Staircase, or general means of communication. Whoever wore his ladder symbol was under his protection on earth as in the hereafter. And so the ladder was the favorite symbol of the ascent of the gods.

Small ladders as amulets were placed in the tombs of Egyptian kings and miniature ladders are still carried as amulets and lucky charms in Egypt as well as in America and elsewhere.

According to some of the paintings of ancient Egypt, there seem to have been two ladders; one on which the soul had to climb out of the darkness of the grave, and another leading upwards to the pinnacle of eternal light.

The Biblical story of Jacob's dream gave a mystical significance to the ladder. The story was probably an offshoot of the Egyptian myth and the belief that one could mount to heaven on a ladder. After dreaming of angels ascending and descending on a ladder that "reached to

Heaven," Jacob promised God that "Of all thou shalt give me I will surely give the tenth unto Thee." (Genesis 28:11–12.)

This dream is reproduced on the cathedral of Bath, England. A giant Jacob's ladder is built on each side of its façade, with angels ascending to heaven on one and descending on the other.

Walking under a ladder was forbidden for various reasons, one of which was that it represented the Sacred Triangle, a venerable symbol of life from the remotest of times. One of the beliefs was that walking under a ladder would cut short the stay of supernatural visitors to earth, and bring punishment upon the offender. In those days, if one was compelled to walk under a ladder, many countercharm gestures could be performed, the same as today.

Another walking-under-ladder taboo was derived from early pictures of the Crucifixion, in which a ladder leaned against the Cross. Beneath the ladder stood Satan, gnashing his teeth, cheated by the fact that Christ died to save humanity, leaving him frustrated and without company. "Under the ladder" became associated with Satan's territory, and crossing one's fingers, symbolic of the cross, became the sign of safety and protection against the devil's revenge upon the trespasser.

Among punishments for criminals in ancient Asiatic countries was one in which a culprit was hanged upon the seventh rung of a ladder propped up against a tree. The seventh rung cleared the ground and at the same time suspended the victim from the lucky number rung or the seventh, so that good fortune would take effect in the hereafter. It was forbidden to walk under such a ladder, even after the body was removed, because a person might contact the ghost of the victim, whose sudden death left it in a quandary as to where to go. So this ghost might be around for some time afterwards.

No one knew, of course, when a ghost was around, since it is an invisible entity; so that to walk under a ladder was strictly avoided. The warning was that contact between a ghost and a living person not only invited death, since death was believed contagious, but if the human being was allowed to survive, all the bad qualities of the late victim would become his—that is, if fright did not kill him on the spot.

In connection with the ladder as synonymous with death and danger, there was an old custom in France which compelled criminals on the day of their execution to walk under the ladder which they were to mount afterwards to the gibbet and their doom. Other criminals walked *around* the ladder. The executioner, called the Groom of the

Ladder, a jocular designation of the day, expectorated between the rungs as he climbed up and down the ladder of the platform, to negate any possible evil that might affect him.

One analysis of the ladder superstition from the most primitive point of view, has been consistently overlooked or purposely avoided, except by a few discriminating anthropologists. This interpretation of the ladder taboo, regardless of mythological, mystical and religious meanings, is possibly the original reason for the superstition, and the danger implied when walking under a ladder. Specifically, it dealt with the blood taboo.

When a woman was under menstrual taboo, she could not be approached by any man. Even her shadow was polluting, so that if she walked abroad she was forbidden to use the ordinary trails. Anything that she touched was immediately destroyed. There was also a very widespread scruple among primitives against passing under overhanging boughs, for fear a woman might have climbed over or sat upon the bough. In many tribes, the men are reluctant to lean against a fence or a house wall, for fear a woman might have leaned there before and contaminated the spot with menstrual blood.

Briffault suggests that a similar idea may underlie our own superstition against walking under a ladder. The usual reason given for the wisdom of observing this taboo is that something may be dropped on you from above. In England it is repeatedly said that a drop of red paint might fall on you. No one ever heard that there is any danger of green paint or white or black. It is always red.

A good luck ladder in courtship is the Lovers' Ladder, frequently alluded to in history and literature. In the Dolomites, in Italy, it is still the custom for a youth to set up a ladder against a girl's window, climb it, and talk to her,—an ancent custom which Shakespeare utilized in "Romeo and Juliet."

The most plausible explanation for not wanting to walk under a ladder nowadays is the possibility of an insecure ladder which might collapse, or that someone on the ladder might accidentally drop a tool or other object that would harm the person below—purely common sense.

"Broom" and "Sweeping" Superstitions

THE BROOM was believed to be the vehicle of the witches in the Old World, and many of the broom superstitions of today are related to the activities of these evil-doers. This household article was believed either to work a magic spell or to prevent one from being executed.

Current broom superstitions are many. Never take a broom along when you move. Never step over a broom lying on the floor. If you do, and are unmarried, there is no hope—you'll be an old maid. When you move into a new home, send in a loaf of bread and a new broom for good luck. It is bad luck to move a broom across water. It is bad luck to lean a broom against a bed. To keep a ghost or witch away, lay a broom against the doorsill. If an expectant mother steps over a broom she will have a hairy child. Never burn a broom. To drop a broom is a sign of company. To give away a used broom is bad luck. There are hundreds of others in which, just as in these, the old connection with witches is apparent.

The little brooms one sees at carnivals or on Hallowe'en are similar to those used formerly to immunize the holder against witchcraft, and to sweep away evil influences. The reason that a miniature broom is not used to brush the crumbs off the table goes back to an old Hebrew superstition that it would bring poverty.

Jockeys are a superstitious lot, and they will not touch a broom as they believe it will bring them bad luck. When sweepers appear near them with brooms, they exit as fast as their legs will carry them. The fact that witches were reputedly broom-riders symbolically suggests them as competitors to the horse-riders of the present.

There is a long list of sweeping superstitions, probably derived from the same sources as the broom superstitions. If you sweep the dust out of the house by the front door, it means that you sweep out the good fortune of your family as well. The dust must be swept inwards. If anyone is sweeping a room in which you are sitting or standing, and the sweeper accidentally passes the broom across your feet, it is called "sweeping your feet," and is a sign that if single, you will not be married that year. If you are married, something unpleasant is at hand. Others believe that the penalty for being touched by a broom when someone else is sweeping means nine days of your luck will be swept away. To sweep a house at night is the greatest insult to the fairies and the spirits of the dead. Never sweep dirt from one room to another. Always take it up. A new broom should sweep something into the house before it sweeps something out, otherwise you sweep out your good luck. Some believe that you must put the sweepings or dust into the fire, to retain the blessings you possess.

These sweeping superstitions, like those of the broom, pertain to the everyday uses, which make them easy to understand by those who are susceptible to superstitious beliefs. No symbolism could be simpler than the act of sweeping good and evil into or out of a house.

The Poltergeist, a Noisy Spirit or Playful Ghost

THE ALLEGED phenomenon known as a poltergeist, is believed to be a manifestation of the supernatural by many persons today. Poltergeist phenomena are reputedly the doings of a ghost or spirit who throws objects, plucks bedclothes, makes noises and does other mischief such as might be expected of unseen supernatural agencies in so-called haunted houses or other spooky places. Poltergeist is a German term from polter, noise; and geist, spirit.

Since 530 A.D. poltergeist phenomena have been recorded and investigated. Until a few decades ago, some 318 cases of these phenomena were on record, of which 22 were undoubtedly fraudulent, and eighteen doubtful, leaving 278 unexplained to the present day. In other words, only one case in eight has been traced to a normal agency. This report naturally precludes the assumption that all such cases were fraudulent.

Some cases of poltergeist activities are doubtless hoaxes, but others have baffled sincere investigators. The chances are, however, that if and when the time comes for us to find the real clues to these mysterious happenings, they may turn out to be very simple phenomena—so simple that they elude our attention just now.

There is the possibility that poltergeist phenomena are due to some unexplained or undiscovered natural agency which may be at work in the majority of cases. A simple example of this would be the case of a person, completely ignorant of the existence of steam heating systems, who, while sleeping alone in a strange house, is suddenly awakened by hammering, whistling or knocking sounds, originating from the steam expanding the pipes. This person could only report incorrect and weird interpretations of the event, whereas to those who are familiar with the noises that sometimes arise with the steam, there is nothing mysterious about them.

Nearly all of us are well-acquainted with phenomena which were not understood by our ancestors, such as the fact that lightning is electrical. These things still petrify primitives all over the world. Ignorance of cause and effect easily sends superstitious persons, as well as backward tribes, into fits of terror, and makes them jump to the conclusion that mysterious happenings are the work of supernatural agencies. Science is gradually dispelling much of the wrong thinking that blamed evil doers for the operation of natural laws.

"Gremlin" Superstitions

ALTHOUGH GREMLINS are imaginary little people whom no one has ever seen, they are nevertheless quite real to English and American aviators who had to put up with their pranks. They are devilish little imps who test the ability of over-confident pilots, clog oil and fuel lines, fog the windows, play merry-go-round on the compass, tamper with controls, drink the tank dry of gasoline, and the like. Gremlins make life anything but pleasant for sky-pilots, who could manage very well without them and their mates, the Fifinellas, not to mention the Widgets, their youngsters, who hang around also at various times.

Gremlins proper are said to operate only at relatively low levels. At high altitudes the strato-gremlins, called Spandules, take over. These are much larger than their relatives and the ones blamed for putting ice on the wings.

Long before the days of aviation, the great-great-grandparents of 20th Century gremlins were active. Having no aviators to pick on, they pestered everybody. For centuries artists have depicted evil spirits more or less similar to Gremlins as we know them. They were responsible for human sufferings, accidents, and all manner of unpleasant and fatal happenings. So in a way, the modern habit of blaming troubles on Gremlins is a throwback to these early days when accidents were blamed on some outside cause rather than on one's own action. The modern Gremlin is an excellent example of bringing superstitious beliefs up-to-date, of streamlining an old motif.

Superstitious airmen generally believe that a passenger pigeon will keep them free from Gremlins, since the pigeon is their arch-enemy. An empty bottle of beer, called a "Gremlin Cradle," is also believed a powerful charm against having them aboard a plane of any kind.

There are many legends about their origin. One relates that they lived in hollow banks beside river pools in England, and later moved to mountain crags. They like altitude so much that they started sneaking rides in airplanes as soon as they were invented. Gremlins are said to have become active in World War I, when aviation was in its infancy. By the time World War II came around the Gremlins took to aviation seriously.

The fear of Gremlins, however, became a serious menace. In order to combat gremlinitis, Walter Frisch, of the United States, originated in 1943 a little figure called Frendlin, a typically American little fellow, boyish in appearance. Sculptured in papier-mâché, and bubbling with good-luck, he was sold as an anti-gremlin mascot.

The air-wise Gremlins had their counterparts in the Valkyrie of the Norse saga, who traveled swiftly on clouds. Later on the witches of medieval Europe were represented as sailing through the heavens on their broomsticks or black cats. Today airplanes are convenient vehicles for all air-minded supernatural beings.

In the language and literature of folklore and superstition, Gremlins are not to be confused with a host of other imaginary beings who often inhabit man's world, for better or worse. For example, the leprechauns, little men who live where treasure is buried; elves, tiny spirits in human form who inhabit bizarre, unfrequented places, but which have no souls; kobolds, gnomes inhabiting deserted mines; Nereids, nymphs who live deep under the sea; trolls, Scandinavian dwarfs who live in caves by the sea; brownies, wee brown men who haunt old farmhouses; dryads, Greek and Roman maidens who live in trees; fairies, banshees, pixies, goblins and many others.

CHAPTER 24

Tell Me Not in Mournful Numbers

The Two-Dollar "Curse"

A LARGE proportion of the American public objects to the two-dollar bill. This is one of the few typically native American superstitions. At race-tracks, however, this bill is generally in favor with the management, as it is easier and faster in making change. But superstitious gamblers and bettors are prejudiced against the two-dollar bill; so, to take the "curse" off, they invariably tear off a corner.

As far as the Treasury is concerned, a little bit off the corner does not constitute mutilation, so that there are huge numbers of two-dollar bills without corners in circulation all over the United States.

But why is a corner torn off each time a two-dollar bill gets into the hands of a superstitious person? It is a countermagic gesture—the corner is a triangle, symbol of three, a mystic and potent number. The fifth time the two-dollar bill passes to a superstitious person,—that is, with all corners gone,—it is usually torn to pieces to remove the "curse" for good. There are even those who tear up the two-dollar bill when they get it the fourth time!

Many versions have been given to explain why the two-dollar bill is considered unlucky, but the origin seems to have been in the vocabulary of gamblers in the early history of the United States, when two was called the "deuce"—the lowest value in cards—a degenerated word derived from "devil" and meaning bad luck. But today those who have an antipathy for the two-dollar bill do not know why they dread getting one.

Among the poor whites and Negroes, the two-dollar bill superstition implies the obvious bad luck of twins in the family. Therefore, to prevent this economic burden falling on them, they, too, tear off a corner of the bill. Some persons, especially cashiers in restaurants, when they receive a two-dollar bill, make a pretense of, or actually kiss the bill. In this case the mouth is the counter-magic charm, although those who do this are not aware of the meaning of their action. Saliva, which keeps the lips moist, was believed to be a powerful transformer of evil into good. (Saliva is an enzyme and was used in primitive brewing.)

Short-change artists make the most of a two-dollar bill, the bad luck of one is the dishonest good luck of the other. The two-dollar bill also became a bill of ill repute in early days when it was supposed to be the price of a vote. After the transaction, the bribed voter got rid of it in a hurry lest it be evidence of his dishonesty.

Nowadays it is customary, when making change, for a cashier to say, as he hands a customer a two-dollar bill, "Do you mind?"

One serious objection to the two-dollar bill has been pointed out by authorities—it is easy for counterfeiters to make a "20" out of the "2." Nevertheless, periodically the Treasury launches a campaign to encourage the greater use of this unpopular greenback. But the American public turns a deaf ear to the pleading, and continues to shun two dollar bills as though they were infected, and tears off the corners with renewed vigor. The Treasury, however, keeps on printing them for two reasons. First, in making up large cash pay rolls, the use of two-dollar bills means less counting and less chance for error. Secondly, and obviously, it costs half as much to print the same amount of money in two-dollar bills as it does in one-dollar bills.

According to Treasury records, in 1946 there were 33,425,340 two-dollar bills in circulation. The Treasury does not recognize the "curse."

"Three" Superstitions

"There is nothing either good or bad but thinking makes it so."

—Shakespeare

THAT "GOOD OR BAD things come in threes" is a superstition believed from time immemoral to the present day. The mystic three, a potent charm for ages, has been considered the perfect number, symbol of the godhead.

Numbers as such began, however, by being symbols or characters of some sort and later developed into serial figures as we know them today. Symbolically, three represents the beginning, the middle and the end—which does not necessarily mean the end in the sense of finality, but that the beginning and the middle are a means to an end, and that life begins all over again.

It was with that attitude in mind that the ancient Egyptians worshipped the Trinity of the FATHER, MOTHER and CHILD. If civilization or life's cycle were to go on, there should never be two without three.

There is no denying the fact that things do happen in threes, as well as in fours, fives, and so on. But the superstitious belief that failures and successes must constitute a series of three is unjustified. In the main, the good or evil side of "Never Two Without Three," is a psychological superstition. Things happen all the time, and events do seem to occur in series, so that the suggestion becomes a superstition or anticipated climax.

As a psychological superstition, isolated happenings interest us through their real content because of their actual importance. However, those that form part of a sequence strike our attention also, and very naturally, by reason of their succession. Therefore, the psychological origin of the saying "Never Two Without Three" is to be found in the kind of expectation evoked by the repetition of an event. It is not difficult to imagine instances in which an emotional state is added to the mere succession of phenomena.

The superstitious belief that one misfortune is immediately followed by a second, and a third, is in keeping with another old superstitious expression that "It Never Rains But It Pours," meaning that certain events come together or follow rapidly on the heels of one another. This implies an unconscious fear of the unknown.

The traditional superstitions regarding the symbol of three and all it stands for have come down to us from many sources, but they all spring from the same basic observations related to the mystery of birth. If lucky, the contact of two persons brought forth life, so that three meant life, or action in everything. Therefore the number two became fixed in the minds of early peoples as depending on a sequence, whether it took place or not. When an evil sequence of three took place, however, superstitious people felt relieved, as they do today, in the belief that it was the end of a cycle.

In folklore and occultism, three is more potent when it is doubled and becomes six; and when trebled, it is a more powerful number still. And so nine—three times three—finally evolved from its superstitious symbology to become a key to mathematical problems and a science in itself, as we all know today.

The Egyptians immortalized their three symbols in a pyramid. The upward point of the triangle was the masculine symbol, and the downward, the female symbol. The Druids held that three was the number of the Unknown God.

A Trinity is by no means confined to the Christian creed. The Brahmins represent their god with three heads. The world was supposed to be under the rule of three gods, according to the Romans,—Jupiter, heaven; Neptune, sea; and Pluto, Hades. Jove is represented with the three-forked lightning; Neptune with a trident, and Pluto with the three-headed dog, Cerberus. The Fates are three; the Graces, three. Man is represented as threefold, body, mind and spirit. The world has earth, sea and air. The kingdom of nature is mineral, vegetable and animal. There are hundreds of other natural groupings of three.

A few "three" superstitions and symbols in Biblical lore, literature and common expressions in our daily life include: Peter's three denials; Jonah's three days in the whale; Daniel's adventures with three lions; Macbeth's three witches; morning, noon and night; faith, hope and charity; fish, flesh and fowl; liberty, equality and fraternity; three strikes and three outs in baseball; life, liberty and the pursuit of happiness.

The simple formula by which, given the relation of two entities or facts, the proportional relationship of a third can be ascertained, is expressed all through man's experience.

Three on a Match

THREE HAS BEEN a mystic number since the world was young; the miracle of birth fascinated the primitive peoples as well as the ancients everywhere. Each two, by contact with humans as well as animals, became three, if lucky. Three therefore meant life; continuance of the line of life.

Among many primitive and semi-civilized peoples, when a chieftain died, all the fires of the tribe, except the chieftain's fire, were extinguished in ceremonial order. And as the godlike ruler lay in state, the medicine man, the witch-doctor or the shaman officiated and relit the tribal fires three at a time with a firebrand from the life-giving flames or spirit of the chieftain's fire. This ritual was definitely a funeral formula exclusively performed in honor of a dead chief but fire was the element of life eternal, associated symbolically with the sun itself; a sun-worship gesture!

As the centuries rolled along, this pagan custom was adopted by the Christian church. In Russia, during the early part of the 10th century, when Vladimir I introduced his people to Christianity, the death rites were performed in a church, and three candles were lit from one glowing taper, the idea being to light the departed spirit into eternity. Candle-lighting was a priestly prerogative which naturally became taboo for lesser mortals, and the taboo spread to the lighting of three lamps, pipes, cigars, and finally cigarettes.

The Russians passed this belief to the British during the Crimean War, and it became firmly entrenched in the British mind during the Boar War, when thousands of Tommies fell victims to the deadly accuracy of Boer marksmen. Three-on-a-match all too frequently spelled death to one of the three, for flashing the light of a match at night made a perfect target for keen-eyed Boers shooting to kill!

Lucky Four-Leaf Clover

One leaf for fame,
One leaf for wealth,
And one leaf for a faithful lover,
And one leaf to bring glorious health,
Are all in a four-leaf clover!

—Traditional Saying

FOUR-LEAF CLOVERS are still highly prized. They are kept by the finders as lucky pieces, or given as "charms" to a friend or sweetheart to express friendship or love, or to bring good fortune in general. No one seems to know just why the four-leaf clover should be luckier than any other bit of green.

One fact may account for the good luck that has been attached to the finding or possessing of a four-leaf clover. It is a freak deviation from the normal three-lobed leaf of the plant and is very rarely found in clover fields. Nowadays, however, "good luck" in the form of four-leaf clovers is available in large quantities. Horticulturists have developed a species of clover that produces leaves exclusively with four lobes. Due to the superstitious demand of millions of Americans, four-leaf clover plant cultivation has developed into a large industry. Anyone can grow this lucky plant on the window-sill, or buy good luck in the form of a single leaf for a nickel, or the whole plant at various prices up to as much as a hundred dollars for one in a de luxe setting.

History and legend are filled with allusions to the benign powers of this tiny leaf. One of the most popular legends is that Eve, upon being ejected from the Garden of Eden, carried a four-leaf clover with her. Therefore, because the original source of this rare species of clover was this famous paradise, its presence in one's own garden was a sign of good luck.

The four-leaf clover was held in high esteem by the Druids, who were sun-worshippers, and it was looked upon as endowed with magical powers. Whoever found a four-leaf clover was believed to have supernatural sight—solar symbol of light—and to be able to see evil beings, including witches, not visible to ordinary persons. Being able to detect evil-doers, and therefore avoid them, was indeed good luck.

In Ireland, the four-leaf clover became venerated together with the shamrock, the plant that supposedly keeps snakes away from that country.

There is another indication in folklore which points to what might have been the origin of the four-leaf clover as a good luck charm. The four parts of this rare growth on the clover plant have a remote association with the cross—not the cross, however, as a religious symbol. The first symbol of the cross was evolved by very early man to represent the four cardinal points—known now as north, east, south and west.

Early peoples learned to tally with a line from east to west, or sunrise to sunset. With another line they tallied from north to south, or from south to north. The crossing of these two lines is known as the prehistoric solar cross, and with the cross thus formed, primitive man established his first crude but basic system of direction.

In time man noticed that his body also formed a cross. From this similarity, he related himself to the sun or its symbol, the cross. Many other cross symbols were evolved along the path of civilization, such as crossing one's hands, crossing oneself, a cross to mark the dead, and so on. All were originally patterned from the sun's course in the heavens and arose through sun-worship.

The old, but still popular saying "He's in clover," meaning "He's in good luck," probably stems from the old four-leaf clover superstition. However, modern science has discovered a beneficial attribute of the common lowly clover plant, to give this expression more backing. It was observed that cows and other bovines who munched spoiled sweet clover became ill with a strange bleeding malady. After careful research and experiment, a drug was derived from the sweet clover which delays the clotting of blood in an operation, and has also been employed with success in the treatment of coronary thrombosis.

The Number "Five" Symbols

IT IS GENERALLY accepted that we have five senses, namely, sight, touch, taste, hearing and smell. This classification of the senses falls into the pattern of the ancient Greeks' idea of divine and cosmic conception, from which we inherited it. The Greek word for "world" was *Gea*, and the number five was a symbol of the "world." Their words, *pente*, (five), and Pan, (the God), meant "all" or "complete."

There are a great many other symbols which attest the antiquity and dignity attributed to the number five. Among these are the five-pointed star, still popular today. The Greeks always used a flower with five petals for symbolic representation. There was also a very ancient Greek idea that divided the vegetable kingdom into five classes; the botanical signs are still formed into a semblance of the number five. An old Jewish religious reference forbids the eating of fruit from a tree until the tree is five years old.

As a matter of scientific knowledge, instead of five senses, there are actually eleven, which are easily identified. The sixth, or muscular sense, pertains to the amount of resistance encountered in moving or lifting a heavy object. The seventh, or temperature sense, tells of the difference between heat and cold. It is quite unlike the sense of touch.

The eighth, or pain sense, needs no explanation. The ninth, or articular sense, is the consciousness we get in moving the joints of our body. The tenth, or distance sense, is a power that is especially cultivated by the blind, but is also possessed by every normal person. It is a sort of uncanny feeling for space—like stepping off a curb without looking. It is an experience in which we all participate, but habit has made us forget that we once had to estimate our distances while we grew from infancy to childhood. However, those without sight, must feel through this sense all the time.

The eleventh, or static sense, is the balance or equilibrium, which makes persons walk straight instead of falling over or weaving to and fro. This sense of orientation of the body in space is located in the semi-circular canals of the inner ear.

These extra six senses are now well known and accepted. They are important senses with which babies and young children must acquaint themselves in order to grow up into balanced adults. However, we still speak and think in terms of the five senses only, because traditional beliefs take a long time to be replaced by the newer and more exact knowledge of the day.

Everyone has heard the expression, "Scared out of my seven senses!" According to ancient teachings, the seven senses represent the soul of man or what was then known as his "inward body." These so-called seven senses were reputed to be a compound of seven properties, which came under the influence of the then known seven planets. The astrologically-minded seers of other days designated these senses as animation, feeling, speech, sight, taste, hearing and smelling. This theory is no longer taken seriously, but the phrase remains a common expression, the original meaning having long been forgotten.

The belief in a "star of destiny," that is, a guiding star for each person, which disappears when the individual dies, is a superstition common to people of all nations. It is also a fact that a star is always represented as having five points, with one or two exceptions. In the flag of Australia, there is a seven-pointed star to symbolize the six states of the nation and its territories.

Many credit Pythagoras in the sixth century, B.C., with having invented the five-pointed star. He is said to have believed it was the expression of perfection in geometric terms, and it was used as the badge of the Pythagorean Society. This Greek scholar had great faith in the magic of the five-pointed star, and his superstitious reverence for the magic symbol of five was handed down through the centuries.

In the Middle Ages it was called the "Wizard's Star," and the magicians of that period made use of it in their strange rites. It was looked upon as a powerful talisman, endowed especially with occult powers. Who has not seen a fairy wand, topped by a five-pointed star, as it is about to transform something or someone into something else?

Many famous men since Pythagoras' day have believed in their "star of destiny," always a five-pointed star. As a symbol of man, or his destiny, it is interesting to note that it represents, somewhat remotely perhaps, a human form in the sense that the top point symbolizes the head; the two side points, the arms; and the two downward points, the legs.

Stars, of course, are not five-pointed, but there is an explanation of why they seem that way. It is an optical illusion, due to the imperfections in the human eye, which cause the point of light to spread out as it reaches the eye. As an example of what the eye may do to deceive us, look at a lighted electric bulb outdoors through a window screen, and you will see the light spread out to form a cross.

"Seven" Superstitions

NUMBERS ORIGINALLY were symbols which interpreted literally rather than numerically. For example, the number three, the triangle, signified the trinity of life as symbolized by the Mother, Father, and Son. The number four was represented by the cross, square, or cube and signified the solar symbol; that is, the sun's course in the heavens, or the four cardinal points of direction.

When the cross is folded it forms a cube, man's symbol hidden from view but always present nevertheless. Hence when the ancient Egyptians took an oath they literally stood on the square by stretching out their arms and forming a human cross, as well as standing on a square-pedestal.

The earth was believed square. Our expressions "a square deal" and "on the square," used to indicate honesty, are of great antiquity.

When the "three" and "four" symbols were combined they symbolized man's complete house: the spirit or mind in the upper part, which was the triangle, and the body or earthly house in the basic square—a combination which equalled seven, and which was represented by the figure ⌂. Thus "seven" became a mystic or sacred symbol, the supreme symbol of the house man lives in. It is a number expressed in a thousand and one superstitions, intermingled with fact and fancy, for good or evil, since time immemorial.

The seven days of creation, the seven seas, the seven heavens, the seven graces, the seven sins, the seven ages in the life of man—these are a few of the ancient expressions used by the Babylonians, the Egyptians, and others.

Only five of the planets were known to the ancients, namely, Mercury, Venus, Mars, Jupiter, and Saturn. To make the total number seven they added the Sun and the Moon. Each was given a god or goddess who was under its individual planetary influence. Apollo was the Sun-god; Diana, the Moon-goddess. There were also seven metals, gold for the Sun, silver for the Moon, quicksilver for Mercury, copper for Venus, iron for Mars, tin for Jupiter, and lead for Saturn. Man himself came under the influence of the stars, and astrology was born.

A man could be scared out of his seven senses, since according to ancient teachings, he was composed of seven substances whose properties were under the influence of the planets. The Greeks kept to the original pattern of five planets and five senses, to which we subscribe today, though some scientists claim that there are eleven senses already accounted for in the human body. However, physiologically the basic sense is feeling. All other senses are reputedly subsidiary.

We need only look in the Bible to check a few of the many references to the number seven, such as the seven churches of Asia, seven candlesticks, seven trumpets, seven plagues, a seven-headed monster, and the lamb with seven eyes.

There were also the seven gifts of the spirits: Wisdom, Understanding, Counsel, Power or Fortitude, Knowledge, Righteousness, and Godly Fear.

Seventh Son of a Seventh Son Superstitions

THE SEVENTH SON of a seventh son, or for that matter, the seventh daughter of a seventh daughter, is still believed by many to be a child with supernatural healing powers through its hand. Such a child, especially a seventh son, is supposedly destined to become great and prosperous.

That the number seven is lucky, especially in connection with the seventh boy to arrive in a family, is almost a universal belief. It dates back to remote times, and ancient Hebrews and Egyptians were known to believe in the efficacy of lucky "seven." Seven was an important number also to the Assyrians and Babylonians, who believed it portended both good and evil.

The seventh son of a seventh son, and a seventh daughter of a seventh daughter, are comparatively rare, but as far as we know, they have the same chances in life as their brothers and sisters.

Thirteen, Lucky or Unlucky

EXCEPT PERHAPS among the ancient Chinese and Egyptians, the number thirteen has had an unsavory reputation ever since that misty eon when man first learned to count.

However, those who believe that thirteen is unlucky have unwittingly been carrying many lucky symbols of this number whenever they had an American dollar,—at least since 1935. The design on the back of this bill bridges ancient Egyptian allegorical motifs to our own times, as symbolic uses of the number thirteen have been arranged around each of the two sides of the Great Seal of the United States.

Among them, for example, is an incomplete or truncated pyramid of thirteen steps. There are thirteen leaves and berries on an olive branch, and in the left talon of the American bald eagle are thirteen arrows. Incidentally, this native American eagle is symbolic of invincibility, whereas the ancient Egyptian golden eagle was the bird of regeneration.

This design was ordered on the dollar bill by Henry Morgenthau, Jr., who was Secretary of the Treasury at the time. As all Americans well know, the many uses of the number thirteen in the design refer to the thirteen original colonies—indeed a lucky number for millions of Americans today.

The ancient Hindus are reputed to have started the superstition that when thirteen persons sat or squatted together, it was unlucky. But it is in Scandinavian legends that we find the story that specifically tells us that thirteen at a table is a sign of ill omen. Loki, the Principle of Evil, though uninvited, joined the twelve demi-gods at a feast. He had instructed Hodur, the Blind One, symbol of darkness and night, to shoot Baldur, the Bright One, symbol of the sun, with an arrow of mistletoe. Henceforth, thirteen at a table became taboo.

There is a countercharm, however. If thirteen persons find themselves seated at one table, the approaching death of one of them, as the superstition predicts, may be averted if all join hands, and arise as one. Then the lives of all are safe, say the superstitious ones.

To the ancient Egyptians, who regarded thirteen as a lucky number, it represented the final step or stage of earthly existence, in which one was merged into permanence or spiritual transformation. Symbolically, there were twelve steps to be climbed during a lifetime up the pyramid or ladder of knowledge, and the thirteenth step or rung was the one which led to everlasting "life." What we call *death* was called *transformation* by the Egyptians. Therefore, transformation, or death, symbolized by the number thirteen, was misinterpreted as it traveled the centuries, particularly when it reached the west and eventually America.

The Egyptians were well acquainted with astronomical phenomena of all sorts and generally patterned their lives, in both the physical and spiritual aspects, on their philosophy of the universe. They noticed that the phases of the moon occurred thirteen times a year. We are well aware today that there are thirteen lunar months in the year, each of which is shorter, naturally, than the twelve calendar months.

Undoubtedly the Egyptians were greatly impressed by the fact that there were thirteen "moons" a year, and gave a name to each, such as Harvest Moon, Fruit Moon, and others. Once in a great while a "blue moon" showed up as the thirteenth moon, which was the occasion for great rejoicing when this rare event combined with the lucky thirteenth month.

A "blue moon" is an astral oddity, which, owing to unusual conditions in the upper atmosphere, gives the moon the appearance of being blue or green. Blue was the favorite color of the Egyptians, which made them feel even more strongly that a thirteenth "blue moon" was a most auspicious manifestation. To the Egyptian moon-gazers of ancient times, the thirteenth moon was generally called a "blue moon" whether or not it was blue; it was simply synonymous with the thirteenth moon, as a manifestation of the year's complete cycle!

The traditionally lucky as well as unlucky character of the number thirteen seems to affect the ignorant and the educated alike—which is not usually the case with superstitions. The "devil's dozen," as it is often called, has happy associations for some, while to others, who connect it with personal misfortunes, it is taboo.

This taboo may be traced back as far back as the days when man first learned to count. Using his ten fingers and his two feet, which he regarded as units, he arrived at the number twelve. Beyond, lay the unknown, the unpredictable—thirteen! He probably began counting on one hand, or as far as the number five. We still measure animals by hands. Then he used two hands—the origin of the decimal system which is very ancient.

Doubtless early man first counted his possessions by using tallies—numbers as such not being known then. He must have wondered at the triangularity of three, and the squareness of four. As he progressed, larger values, such as twelve, became easier to divide in all sorts of ways; while others, such as thirteen, were impossible. In due time, twelve became a noble, generous symbol to him, and the indivisible thirteen, a disreputable outcast! Our universal use of twelve, or the dozen, is evidence of its importance in our modern age.

Like everything else, numbers have had an evolutionary history, the earliest phase being when man first related the number of his fingers to the fact that objects about him could be measured. Man's amazement at fundamental discoveries led him, as we know, to endow inanimate things with potent powers. And so it was with numbers. Both the ancient Hindus and Chinese, as well as Persians and other early Orientals, believed numbers had good and bad attributes. Some believed that ciphers had sex. Odd numbers, beginning with thirteen, according to the Hindus, were feminine; even numbers, masculine. The Chinese believed the other way around, that is, that even numbers were feminine, and odd masculine, as did the Egyptians. Numerology still intrigues many modern minds.

Regardless of other numbers, thirteen remains full of implications for most persons today. From observation and survey, it still leans to the side of a taboo—almost as long-standing as human life itself.

Sudden Silence—It Must be Twenty After . . . !

> *"The inaudible and noiseless foot of Time."*
> —*All's Well That Ends Well*—Shakespeare

SUPERSTITIOUS PERSONS have several ways of interpreting a sudden silence that comes, for no apparent reason, during a conversation. For instance, religious-minded people say that an angel is passing through, which commands a respectful pause that comes about quite naturally.

Others believe that when a sudden silence falls upon a group of persons while talking, it means that one of those present will die within the year. From time immemoral, silence has been associated with death; today we have the custom of observing a few moments of silence in reverence to those who have died, especially under tragic circumstances. Those who interpret a sudden lull in a conversation as the omen of another tragedy sometimes cross themselves as a countercharm, or cross their fingers, in the hope of averting a dire calamity. For certain persons, a sudden stillness is in itself symbolic of a void, or gap—an ominous sign in nature.

The most popular superstition on this subject, however, is the belief that when, for no apparent cause, everyone in a group suddenly seems at a loss for something to say, it must be twenty minutes after the hour. This idea is generally accepted by superstitious Americans, and is purely American in origin, going back to a legend which has grown around Abraham Lincoln's death.

For those who believe that the Great Emancipator died at 8:20 o'clock, a sudden silence is supposed to occur automatically ever since, through some supernatural agency. By the same token, there are those who believe that it is also a special reminder that the moment is of great significance and should never be forgotten. This superstitious belief has grown into a national tradition among all classes of society.

There is also the popular belief that the man who painted the first wooden clocks which were used as signs in front of jewelry stores had just heard of Lincoln's death, and so he painted the hands to perpetuate the fatal hour. According to one version of the story, the hands commemorate the exact time of Lincoln's *death,* and according to another, the exact time of his *assassination.* The truth of the matter is that Lincoln was shot at 10:10 in the evening and died about 7:30 the next evening.

The clock myth in regard to Lincoln's death is even more conclusively disproved by the fact that wooden watches and clocks, with the minute hand pointing to eighteen past the hour, were hanging in front of jewelry stores long before Lincoln was assassinated.

Obviously, the reason for so painting the hands is that it is the most symmetrical arrangement for them; it is more pleasing to the eye, and at the same time, leaves the greatest amount of space for the advertising. For example, Elgin watches use 8:18 as their stationery design; Hamilton watches 10:12; and Waltham watches 7:21. This indicates that the legend is slowly dying out officially, but it is still accepted in the popular mind.

It is an odd fact, however, lending strength to superstition, that when a sudden silence occurs, it is generally twenty minutes to or twenty minutes after the hour; the law of averages notwithstanding.

BIBLIOGRAPHY

Allier, Raoul. *The Mind of the Savage*. G. Bell and Sons, London. 1929.

Budge, E. A. Wallis. *A Short History of the Egyptian People*. J. M. Dent & Sons Limited, London. 1914,

Burriss, Eli Edward. *Taboo, Magic, Spirits*. The Macmillan Company. New York. 1931.

Brewer, Rev. R. Copham. *A Dictionary of Phrase and Fable*. (New edition) J. P. Lippincott Company, Philadelphia.

Brydlova, Bozena. *Io Unveiled*. Macoy Publishing. New York. 1922

Bienfang, Ralph. *The Subtle Sense—Key to the World of Odors*. Norman. University of Oklahoma Press. 1946.

Budge, Sir E. A. Wallis. *The Book of the Dead*. E. P. Dutton & Co. New York. 1938.

Caldwell, Otis W. and Gerhard E. Lunden. *Do You Believe It?* Doubleday, Doran & Company. Garden City, New York. 1934.

Castiglioni, Arturo. *Adventures of the Mind*. Alfred A. Knopf, New York. 1946.

Daniels, Cora Linn, and Stevens, C. M. *Encyclopedia of Superstitions Folk-Lore and Occult Sciences of the World*. J. H. Yewdale and Sons, Company, Chicago. 1903.

Deerforth, Daniel. *Knockwood. Superstition through the Ages*. Brentano's, Publishers, New York. 1928.

Dietz, David. *The Story of Science*. The Home Library, New York. 1942.

Ditmars, Dr. Raymond L. *Strange Animals I Have Known*. Brewer, Warren & Putnam Inc. New York. 1931.

Evans, Bergen. *The Natural History of Nonsense*. Alfred A. Knopf, New York. 1946.

Eichler, Lillian. *The Customs of Mankind*. Doubleday, Page and Company, Garden City, New York. 1924.

Fiske, John. *Myths and Myth-Makers*. Houghton, Mifflin & Co. 1887.

Fielding, William J. *Strange Customs of Courtship and Marriage*. The New Home Library. New York. 1943.

———. *Strange Superstitions and Magical Practices*. The Blakiston Company, New York. 1945.

Fishbein, Morris. *Shattering Health Superstitions*. Liveright, New York. 1930.

Frazer, Sir James George. *The Golden Bough*. The Macmillan Company, St. Martin's Street, London. 1932.

Furnas, C. C. and S. M. Furnas. *The Story of Man and his Food*. The New Home Library, New York. 1942.

Gordon, Benjamin Lee, M.D. *The Romance of Medicine*. F. A. Davis, Company, Philadelphia. 1945.

Graubard, Mark. *Man's Food: Its Rhyme or Reason*. Macmillan Company, New York. 1943.

Goldsmith, E. Elizabeth. *Life Symbols as Related to Sex Symbolism*. G. P. Putnam's Sons, New York & London. 1924.

Hyatt, Harry Middleton. *Folk-Lore from Adams County Illinois*. Memoirs of the Alma Egan Hyatt Foundation, New York. 1935.

Haggard, Howard W. *Devils, Drugs, and Doctors*. Harper and Brothers, New York. 1929.

———. *Mystery, Magic, and Medicine*. Doubleday, Doran and Company. Garden City, New York. 1933.

Halliday, William Reginald. *Greek and Roman Folklore*. Longmans, New York. 1927.

Harding, M. Ester. *Woman's Mysteries Ancient and Modern*. Longmans, Green and Co. 1935.

Igglesden, Sor. Charles. *Those Superstitions*. Jarrolds, London. 1931.

Ingersoll, Ernest. *Birds in Legend Fable and Folklore*. Longmans, Green and Co. New York. 1923.

Jeans, Sir James. *Physics & Philosophy*. The Macmillan Company, New York. 1943.

Krappe, Alexander Haggerty. *The Science of Folklore*. Lincoln Macveagh. The Dial Press. New York. 1930.

Kanner, Leo. *Folklore of the Teeth*. The Macmillan Company. New York. 1933.

Kunz, George Frederick. *The Curious Lore of Precious Stones*. J. P. Lippincott Company, Philadelphia. 1913.

Kaempffert, Waldemar. *Science Today and Tomorrow*. The Viking Press. New York. 1940.

Lewis, Nolan D. C. *A Short History of Psychiatric Achievement*. W. W. Norton & Co. 1941.

Lang, Andrew. *Myth, Ritual and Religion*. London: Longmans, Green, and Co. Vol. 1 and Vol. 2. 1887.

———. *Custom and Myth*. Harper & Brothers. New York. 1885.

Lowie, Robert H. *Are We Civilized?* Harcourt, Brace and Co. New York. 1920.

Müller, F. Max. *Lectures on the Science of Language.* Longmans, Green, and Co., London. Vol. 1 and Vol. 2. 1880.

Menninger, Karl A. *Man Against Himself.* Harcourt, Brace and Company. New York. 1938.

———. *The Human Mind.* Alfred A. Knopf. New York. 1942.

Noble, Ruth Crosby. *The Nature of the Beast.* Doubleday, Doran & Co., Inc. Garden City. New York. 1945.

Olcott, William Tylor. *Sun Lore of All Ages.* G. P. Putnam's Sons. New York. 1914.

———. *Star Lore of all Ages.* G. P. Putnam's Sons. 1911.

Reinach, Solomon. *Orpheus. A History of Religions.* Horace Liveright, Inc. New York. 1930.

Stimpson, George. *A Book About the Bible.* Harpers & Brothers. New York. 1945.

———. *A Book About A Thousand Things.* Harpers & Brothers. New York. 1946.

Sumner, William Graham. *Folkways.* Ginn and Company, New York. 1929.

Sadler, William S. *The Mind at Mischief.* Funk & Wagnalls Company. New York. 1929.

Scheinfeld, Amram. *Women and Men.* Harcourt and Brace & Co. New York. 1943.

———. *You and Heredity.* Garden City Publishing Co., Inc. 1945.

Thompson, Sir. J. Arthur. *Riddles of Science.* Liveright Publishing. New York. 1932.

Thomas, Daniel Lindsey. *Kentucky Superstitions.* Princeton University Press. Princeton, New Jersey. 1920.

Thomen, August A. *Doctors Don't Believe It—Why Should You?* Simon & Schuster. New York. 1941.

Trachtenberg, Joshua. *Jewish Magic and Superstition. A Study of Folk Religion.* Behrman's Jewish Book House. New York. 1939.

Tyack, Rev. George S. *The Cross in Ritual, Architecture, and Art.* William Andres & Co. 1900.

Thomas, Daniel L. and Thomas B. *Kentucky Superstitions.* The Princeton University Press. 1920.

Talman, Charles Fitzhugh. *A Book About the Weather.* Blue Ribbon Books, Inc. New York. 1931.

Vechten, Carl Van. *The Tiger in the House*. Alfred A. Knopf. New York. 1920.

Wiggam, Alberd Edward. *Exploring Your Mind*. Bobbs-Merrill Company. 1928.

———. *Sorry but You're Wrong About It*. The Bobbs-Merrill Company, Indianapolis. 1931.

———. *The New Decalogue of Science*. Bobbs-Merrill Company, Indianapolis. 1923.

Index